TEACHING ENGLISH LANGUAGE AND CONTENT IN MAINSTREAM CLASSES

Second Edition

Teaching English Language and Content in Mainstream Classes

One Class, Many Paths

Linda New Levine
Mary Lou McCloskey

PEARSON

Boston Columbus Indianapolis New York San Francisco Upper Saddle River
Amsterdam Cape Town Dubai London Madrid Milan Munich Paris Montreal Toronto
Delhi Mexico City Sao Paulo Sydney Hong Kong Seoul Singapore Taipei Tokyo

Vice-President, Editor-in-Chief: Aurora Martínez Ramos
Editor: Erin Grelak
Editorial Assistant: Michelle Hochberg
Executive Marketing Manager: Krista Clark
Production Project Manager: Elizabeth Gale Napolitano
Manager Central Design: Jayne Conte
Cover Designer: Suzanne Behnke
Cover Image: © CEFutcher/iStockphoto.com
Full-Service Project Management: Pavithra Jayapaul, Jouve India
Electronic Composition: Jouve India
Printer/Binder: RR Donnelley
Cover Printer: Lehigh-Phoenix Color/Hagerstown
Text Font: Times

Credits and acknowledgments borrowed from other sources and reproduced, with permission, in this textbook appear on the appropriate page within text or on page 334.

Library of Congress Cataloging-in-Publication Data
Levine, Linda New.
  Teaching English language and content in mainstream classes : one class, many paths / Linda New Levine, Mary Lou McCloskey.—2nd ed.
     p. cm.
  Rev. ed. of : Teaching learners of English in mainstream classes (K-8), c2009.
  ISBN-13: 978-0-13-268514-6
  ISBN-10: 0-13-268514-0
  1. English language—Study and teaching (Elementary)—Foreign speakers.   2. English language—Study and teaching (Middle school)—Foreign speakers.   3. Second language acquisition.   I. McCloskey, Mary Lou.
II. McCloskey, Mary Lou., Teaching learners of English in mainstream classes (K-8)   III. Title.

PE1128.A2L39 2012
372.652'1—dc23

2012001389

7 2019

ISBN 10: 0-13-268514-0
ISBN 13: 978-0-13-268514-6

ABOUT THE AUTHORS

Linda New Levine is a consultant for ESL and EFL programs for school-age children. She has assisted in the development of English language programs for successful academic content learning in countries in the Middle East, Africa, and Asia, and for school districts and professional organizations within the United States. In addition, she works with mainstream classroom teachers for differentiation of teaching and learning in the content areas and for the development of literacy for ELLs in English language classrooms K through 12.

Dr. Levine has worked as an ESL teacher and a staff development facilitator in the Bedford, New York, school district, and as an assistant professor at Teachers College, Columbia University.

She has taught EFL in the Philippines with the Peace Corps and in the People's Republic of China as a Fulbright professor. In addition, she has worked with faculties and ministries of education in Egypt to implement English as a Foreign Language programs in elementary schools throughout the country and to improve the skills of school supervisors. As part of a design team for USAID, Dr. Levine evaluated language programs in Egypt and designed a format for future funding in that region. She currently consults for the Center for Applied Linguistics.

Dr. Levine was the Homeroom columnist for TESOL's *Essential Teacher* and the author of the *Teacher's Edition to the Oxford Picture Dictionary for the Content Areas* (2nd Ed.). Her publications include *Helping English Language Learners Succeed in Pre-K-Elementary Schools* (2006) with Jan Lacina and Patience Sowa (TESOL International).

Dr. Levine holds a Masters in TESOL and a Ph.D. in Applied Linguistics from New York University.

Mary Lou McCloskey, former President of Teachers of English to Speakers of Other Languages, is Director of Teacher Education and Curriculum Development for Educo in Atlanta. As a consultant and author in the field of English language education, she has worked with teachers, teacher educators, and departments and ministries of education on five continents and in thirty-six of the United States.

Dr. McCloskey has taught in undergraduate and graduate programs at Emory University, Georgia State University, and the University of Memphis. The author and co-author of many journal articles, chapters, and professional texts for educators including *American Themes*, *Integrating English*, *Teaching English as a Foreign Language in the Primary School*, and *Leadership Skills for English Language Educators*, she has also developed six programs for English learners, including *On Our Way to English*; *Visions: Language, Literature, Content*; *Voices in Literature*; *Teaching Language, Literature and Culture*; and was consulting author and ESOL specialist for the 2008 *McDougal Littell Language Arts, Grades 5–12*. During the summer, Dr. McCloskey works as a teacher educator in the Teaching Tolerance Through English program conducted for middle school teachers and learners from countries throughout Central US Department of State Regional Language Office in Budapest and U.S. Embassies in the region.

Dr. McCloskey, who holds an M.S. degree from Syracuse University and a Ph.D. from Georgia State University, considers her most important qualification her years of experience with English learners from many cultures, at levels from preschool through graduate education.

CONTENTS

Preface xv

Chapter 1 PRINCIPLES OF INTEGRATED LANGUAGE TEACHING AND LEARNING 1

Activity-Based Language Teaching and Learning 2

Principle 1 Active Engagement 2

Principle 2 Cultural Relevance 3

Principle 3 Collaboration 4

Principle 4 Learning Strategies 4

Communicative Teaching and Learning 5

Principle 5 Differentiation 5

Principle 6 Comprehensible Input with Scaffolding 6

Principle 7 Prior Knowledge 7

Principle 8 Content Integration 9

Principle 9 Clear, Appropriate Goals and Feedback 11

Questions for Reflection 15 • Activities for Further Learning 15 • Suggested Reading 15 • References 16

Chapter 2 LANGUAGE ACQUISITION AND LANGUAGE LEARNING IN THE CLASSROOM 18

What Do We Know about First Language Acquisition? 19

Language Acquisition Is Universal 19

Language Acquisition Is Natural 19

First Language Acquisition Does Not Require Formal Instruction 20

What Is the Nature of the First Language Environment? 22

Children Are Immersed in Language 22

Language Is Highly Contextualized 22

Language Is a Tool for Purposeful Use 22

Children Are Physically Active While Learning Languages 22

Acquisition Occurs within a Social Environment 23

Children Choose Those Aspects of Language That They Wish to Acquire 23

Language Acquisition Is Emotionally Embedded 24

Language Acquisition Is an Integrated Learning Experience 24

How Do Acquisition and Learning Differ? 24

The Acquisition-Learning Hypothesis 24

The Natural Order Hypothesis 25

The Input Hypothesis 25

The Affective Filter Hypothesis 25

The Monitor Hypothesis 26

The Interactionist Position 26

What Are Factors Affecting Language Acquisition in the Classroom? 28

Limited Language Input 28

Classroom Organization   28

High Content and Language Load   28

Academic Language and Social Language   29

Negative Bias   29

Cognition, Age, and Social and Cultural Differences   30

Error Correction   31

Culture Shock   31

What Strategies Do ELLs Use to Acquire Languages?   33

What Are the Characteristics of a Culturally and Linguistically Appropriate Response to Intervention (RTI) Model?   33

What Are the Characteristics of an Effective Classroom Environment for ELLs?   34

What Are the Characteristics of Culturally and Linguistically Appropriate Tier 1 Instruction for ELLs?   34

What Are the Characteristics of Culturally and Linguistically Appropriate Tier 2 Instruction for ELLs?   34

RTI Tier 1 Sampler   36

RTI Tier 2 Sampler   36

Questions for Reflection   37   •   Activities for Further Learning   37   •   Suggested Reading   37   •   References   38

Chapter 3   CULTURALLY RESPONSIVE INSTRUCTION: CONNECTING WITH HOME CULTURE   40

Culturally Responsive Instruction   41

What Are the Features of Culturally Responsive Instruction?   41

Communication of High Expectations for Learners   41

Learning within an Affirming Cultural Context   42

Culturally Responsive Instructional Practices   42

Teacher as Cultural Mediator   43

How Do Teachers Connect to The Homes and Families of Their Students?   45

How Can the School Community Support the Education of English Language Learners?   48

How Can the Community Outside the School Support the Education of ELLs?   49

How Does a Culturally Responsive Classroom Connect to Students' Cultures, Languages, and Family in an RTI Model?   52

RTI Tier 1 Sampler   52

RTI Tier 2 Sampler   53

Questions for Reflection   53   •   Activities for Further Learning   53   •   Suggested Reading   54   •   References   54

Chapter 4   ORGANIZING THE CLASSROOM FOR LANGUAGE LEARNING   56

First Things First: Feeling Ready to Learn   57

Provisioning   57

Gathering Information   57

Organizing the Physical Environment to Promote Language Learning   58

Furniture Is Important   58

Public Areas   59

Private Space   61

Organizing the Classroom Social Environment to Promote Language Learning 61

Social Integration 61

Presentation Formats 62

Grouping 62

Matching Learning Styles 63

English Language Instructional Programs 66

Organizing Instruction to Promote Language Learning 67

Differentiated Instruction (DI) 68

Culturally and Linguistically Appropriate Response to Intervention 71

The Cognitive Academic Language Learning Approach (CALLA) 72

Sheltered Instruction 73

Cooperative Learning 75

Problem-Based Learning 79

Project Learning 79

RTI Tier 1 Sampler 81

RTI Tier 2 Sampler 82

Questions for Reflection 82 • Activities for Further Learning 82 • Suggested Reading 83 • References 83

Chapter 5 STRATEGIES FOR ORAL LANGUAGE DEVELOPMENT 86

Conditions for Oral Language Learning 87

Academic Language Learning 87

Culturally Diverse Language Patterns 89

Oral Language Development 90

Stages of Oral Language Development 91

Preproduction 91

Level 1: Starting—Early Production 92

Level 2: Emerging—Speech Emergence 95

Levels 3, 4, & 5: Developing, Expanding, Bridging—Intermediate Fluency 96

Teacher Tools for Oral Language Development 97

Increasing Clarity in Teacher Language 97

Question and Response 100

Scaffolding Oral Language Development 102

Assessing Oral Language Development 108

Response to Intervention 110

RTI Tier 1 Sampler 110

RTI Tier 2 Sampler 111

Questions for Reflection 111 • Activities for Further Learning 111 • Suggested Reading 112 • References 112

Chapter 6 ORAL LANGUAGE DEVELOPMENT IN THE CONTENT CLASSROOM 114

Content Learning and Oral Language Development 115

Language Arts 115

Social Studies 118

Math   122

Science   129

Oral Language Development Every Which Way   132

Songs and Chants/Poetry and Rap   132

Role-Plays, RAFTS, and Simulations   134

WebQuests   136

Listening In While Not Tuning Out   136

Listening for Understanding   137

Assessing Listening and Speaking Skills in the Content Classroom   139

RTI Tier 1 Sampler   140

RTI Tier 2 Sampler   141

Questions for Reflection   142   •   Activities for Further Learning   142   •   Suggested Reading   142   •   References   143

Chapter 7   TEACHING VOCABULARY TO ENGLISH LEARNERS   144

Why Is Learning Vocabulary Important for English Learners?   145

What Do We Mean When We Speak of Vocabulary? How Many Words Do Students Need to Learn?   145

What Words Should We Teach?   146

What Are the Characteristics of Effective Vocabulary Instruction?   149

What Doesn't Work?   149

What Does Work: Characteristics of Effective Vocabulary Instruction   150

How Should We Provide Direct Vocabulary Instruction?   151

Steps for Direct Vocabulary Instruction   151

How Can We Help Learners Develop Their Own Tools to Deal with Unknown Words Independently?   152

What Are Active Interactive Strategies to Support Vocabulary Development?   154

Drawing Pictures   155

Semantic Mapping   156

Word Square   156

Word Sorts   157

WordSplash   158

Word Wall   159

Semantic Feature Analysis   159

Read, Retell, Summarize   160

I Have, Who Has?   160

Conga Line   161

Sentence Machine   162

How Can We Assess Vocabulary Development of English Learners?   162

Conclusion   164

RTI Tier 1 Sampler   165

RTI Tier 2 Sampler   165

*Questions for Reflection   166   •   Activities for Further
Learning   166   •   Suggested Reading   166   •   References   167*

**Chapter 8 DEVELOPING LITERACY WITH ENGLISH LEARNERS:
FOCUS ON READING   169**

What Is Literacy?   171

Top-Down Approaches   171

Bottom-Up Approaches   172

Integrated Approaches   173

ELLs Developing Literacy Require Special Instruction   174

**What Is Unique About English Language Learners
Who Are Developing Literacy?   174**

What ELLs Bring   175

What ELLs Need   175

The Language/Literacy Matrix   179

**What Tools and Strategies Can We Provide to Help ELLs
Develop Literacy?   181**

Strategies to Support ELL Reading Development   182

Issues in Literacy Development with Older English Learners   194

What Are Our Recommendations for Developing Literacy with
These Older Learners?   195

Assessing ELL Literacy Development   199

Standardized Reading Achievement Tests   199

English Language Proficiency Tests   199

Holistic Measures of Reading Development   200

Reading Skills Tests   200

Publisher-Made Reading Assessments   201

Teacher-Made Reading Assessments   201

Student Self-Assessment   201

RTI Tier 1 Sampler   201

RTI Tier 2 Sampler   202

Conclusion   202

*Questions for Reflection   203   •   Activities for Further
Learning   203   •   Suggested Reading   203   •   References   204*

**Chapter 9 DEVELOPING LITERACY WITH ENGLISH LEARNERS:
FOCUS ON WRITING   207**

Why Teach Writing with English Learners?   210

How Does Writing Develop to ELLs?   210

**Connecting Writing to Active, Communicative Language Teaching
and Learning   211**

Challenges of Teaching Writing to English Learners   212

Developing a Writing Environment   212

Getting Started: Interactive Writing   213

Scaffolding Learners Through the Writing Process   216

Steps in the Writing Process   217

The Shared Writing Process   218

Preparing Learners for Different Text Types   221

Issues in Teaching Writing to Students with Interrupted Formal Education (SIFE)   221

Assessing Writing   225

Mini-Lessons and Checklists   225

Determining Goals: Standards for ELL Writing   225

RTI Tier 1 Sampler   228

RTI Tier 2 Sampler   229

Questions for Reflection   230   •   Activities for Further Learning   230   •   Suggested Reading   230   •   References   231

Chapter 10   **STRUCTURING AND PLANNING CONTENT-LANGUAGE INTEGRATED LESSONS   233**

Lesson Characteristics That Support Learning   234

Teacher-Directed Instruction   234

Heterogeneous Grouping   235

Appropriate Content   235

Attention to Language   236

Supported Practice   236

Corrective Feedback   237

A Lesson Format for Integrated Learning   237

Into the Lesson: Defining Objectives, Activating, and Preparing for Learning   239

Defining Content Objectives   239

Defining Language Objectives   240

Defining Learning Strategy Objectives   244

Performance Indicators   245

Activating Prior or Current Knowledge   246

Through the Lesson: Input for Active Understanding, Vocabulary Development, and Practical Purpose   249

Vocabulary Learning   249

Language and Content Input   250

Guided Practice   251

Beyond the Lesson: Providing Reasons for Further Communication   254

Independent Practice   254

Summarizing   256

Assessment   258

Response to Intervention   259

RTI Tier 1 Sampler   259

RTI Tier 2 Sampler   260

Questions for Reflection   261   •   Activities for Further Learning   261   •   Suggested Reading   262   •   References   262

Chapter 11   **ASSESSMENT TOOLS FOR THE INTEGRATED CLASSROOM   265**

What Is Assessment?   266

What Are the Fundamental Principles of Classroom-Based Assessment for ELLs?   267

Conduct a Fair, Reliable, and Valid Assessment   267

Inform Teaching and Improve Learning   270

Use Multiple Sources of Information   270

Use Familiar Instructional Techniques   271

What Are the Critical Factors Affecting the Assessment of ELLs   273

Summative versus Formative Assessment   273

Formative Assessment   275

Cultural Issues in Testing   275

Language versus Content   277

What Are Examples of Authentic, Performance-Based Classroom Assessment?   277

Performance-Based Assessment (PBA)   277

Self-Assessment   280

Visible Criteria   280

Rubrics   281

How Do Standards Affect Classroom Assessment?   285

Assessment for ELLs in an RTI Organizational Model   289

RTI Tier 1 Sampler   290

RTI Tier 2 Sampler   291

Questions for Reflection   292   •   Activities for Further Learning   292   •   Suggested Reading   292   •   References   293

Chapter 12   PUTTING IT ALL TOGETHER THEMATICALLY: DEVELOPING CONTENT-BASED THEMATIC UNITS   295

What Is Thematic Instruction?   296

Criteria for Thematic Instruction   297

Why Teach Thematically?   298

How Are Thematic Units Structured?   300

Concrete to Abstract   300

Low to High Cognitive and Language Levels   301

Simple to Complex Content Structures   303

What About Standards in a Thematic Unit?   304

Organizing Content Curriculum in a Thematic Unit   306

Organizing Language Curriculum in a Thematic Unit   309

How Can Learning Strategies Be Incorporated into Thematic Instruction?   310

A Last Word   311

RTI Tier 1 Sampler   312

RTI Tier 2 Sampler   313

Questions for Reflection   313   •   Activities for Further Learning   314   •   Suggested Reading   314   •   References   315

Glossary   316

Index   325

PREFACE

We have written this text to provide guidance to classroom teachers working in grade-level classrooms with diverse groups of students, including children who are learning English. We understand the challenges you face. We have worked in those classrooms and with those children ourselves. We hope to help you understand critical aspects of language development, the ways in which culture affects learning, and approaches and strategies for teaching English and content-area subjects to your English language learners. At the same time, we will provide you with ideas for classroom management and suggest strategies that will enable you to challenge learners at many levels to grow and develop.

WHAT'S NEW IN THIS EDITION?

This Second Edition includes new resources and an emphasis on a culturally and linguistically appropriate Response to Intervention model. Each chapter describes the way RTI is related to the topic of the chapter. You will find:

- The characteristics of a culturally and linguistically appropriate Response to Intervention model in Chapter 1
- RTI Samplers in Chapters 2–12 listing specific and appropriate interventions for Tier 1 and Tier 2 instruction in grades PreK–12
- A description of an effective classroom environment (Tier 1) for ELLs in Chapter 2
- An expanded description of culturally responsive instruction and practices in Chapter 3
- Descriptions of English instructional program models in Chapter 4
- Descriptions of differentiated instruction and RTI program models in Chapter 4
- References to the use of the Common Core Anchor Standards for English Language Arts and/or the Common Core Standards for Mathematical Practice with ELLs in Chapters 6, 7, 8, 9, 10, and 12
- A new Chapter 7 dedicated to vocabulary teaching and learning that contains many practical strategies
- An expanded section related to reading and writing development of older preliterate learners as well as undereducated learners in Chapter 8

In addition, you will find updated features from the first edition:

- A teaching vignette begins every chapter, showing how the principles and practices for ABC teaching are integrated into daily classroom instruction
- An emphasis on oral language development in two chapters—one of them pertaining to oral language development in science, math, social studies, and English language arts
- Questions for Reflection, Activities for Further Learning, and Suggested Readings accompany each chapter

WHO ARE ENGLISH LANGUAGE LEARNERS?

First, a quick word about terminology. Many terms have been used for students who are learning English. For many years, the legal U.S. government term for students in special programs for language learners was Limited English Proficient (LEP). Other terms that have been used are English as a Second Language (ESL) students (even though English may be the third or fourth language these youngsters are learning), or English Language (EL) students. We have chosen to use the term English Language Learners (ELLs) for the purposes of this book, as we think it is both positive and descriptive. Likewise, classes for ELLs have many terms: ESL classes, English for Speakers of Other Languages (ESOL) classes, and English Language Development (ELD) classes are among them. In our book, we have described programs for ELLs as either English as a Second Language (ESL) programs or English Language Development (ELD) programs.

   ELLs comprise a large and growing population of children in our schools. The growth of the ELL public school student population from the 1998–1999 school years to the 2008–2009 school years was more than 51 percent. At this same time, growth in the total school enrollment was 7.22 percent. ELLs represented 10.8 percent of the total school population in 2008 to 2009, with an enrollment of more than five million students (National Clearinghouse for English Language Acquisition and Language Instruction, 2012).

The ELL school population includes the children of immigrants, although they themselves are not all immigrants. Three-quarters of ELLs were born in the United States. And they are, for the most part, poor. Young children of immigrants (age 0–8) account for 29 percent of poor children and 30 percent of low-income children (Fortuny, Hernandez, & Chaudry, 2010).

Although their numbers are growing, the level of academic achievement among ELLs, measured as a subgroup, remains lower than that of proficient English-speaking learners. Students classified as LEP (Limited English Proficient) do not meet state norms for reading in English according to reports from 41 state education agencies (Kindler, 2002), score below their classmates on standardized tests of math, and are deemed to have lower academic abilities and are placed in lower ability groups than native-English speakers (President's Advisory Commission on Educational Excellence for Hispanic Americans, 2003). The largest ELL group is the Latino population. They represent 22 percent of all K–12 students, but only half of them earn a high school diploma on time (http://www.whitehouse.gov, 2011).

In spite of these commonalities, immigrant ELLs are a diverse group. Some of them come to school as excellent readers and writers in their first languages. Others are illiterate in any language. Some ELLs start school in kindergarten, whereas others walk through our doors in adolescence as first-time students. Middle and high school age ELLs are most likely to have missed years of schooling and thus have significant gaps in their education (Ruiz-de-Velasco & Fix, 2000). Some ELLs come from countries with an alphabet system similar to that of English, such as Spanish and Haitian Creole. Others come with language skills from a widely different reading-writing system, such as Arabic or Chinese.

Many ELLs have been born and raised in the United States but speak a language other than English at home. They may come from highly literate homes or from homes where there are no magazines and newspapers, and family members cannot read at all. ELLs born in the United States are as diverse as those who immigrate here.

In addition to language proficiency, other factors put ELLs at risk for educational failure: economic circumstances, trauma of war or dislocation, race, educational environment, geographic location, immigration status, health, family structure, age, learning disabilities, cultural bias, and many others (Christian, 2006).

All of them have come to us, their teachers, to help them find the promise that education can bring to their young lives.

LANGUAGE AND CULTURAL DIVERSITY IN THE CLASSROOM

The most important items children bring with them to school are their cultures and their languages. We need to learn all we can about the languages and cultures of our students in order to prevent the kinds of miscommunication that can occur when cultures clash. Children coming from countries with very formal schooling will be confused with the informal style of some elementary classrooms. Children who have been taught to be self-reliant at home will not respond well to expectations that they depend on their teachers. Children whose cultures emphasize cooperative work styles will feel isolated working alone at a single desk. Children with holistic learning styles will not respond quickly to linear thinking. Children from countries in which same-sex groupings are common will be embarrassed working in girl-boy partnerships. Effective teachers are aware of children's cultural histories, life experiences, and learning strengths. They use this information to tailor the curriculum and their instructional strategies to the child. In close collaboration with colleagues, teachers create learning environments that promote success for their students.

ELLs can help us to create a positive cultural climate in our classrooms as a result of the interactions they have with us, their teachers, and the experiences we create to help them learn. We need to be the teachers who take the time to listen to students and answer their questions, who take the time to prepare lessons thoughtfully and to ensure student interest. We need to be the teachers who provide a safe classroom environment for students—one where all will feel comfortable participating and where no one is fearful of ridicule. We need to be the teachers who are patient when ELLs are struggling with the burdens of a new language and culture, and feeling lost in a country where friends may be far away. We need to be the teachers who are knowledgeable and comfortable with diverse cultures, and sensitive to the needs of young people.

WHOLE SCHOOL INVOLVEMENT

Teachers within a school community are responsible for all learners within that community. For too long, teachers closed the doors of their classrooms and individually worked with their own students. We need to open our doors and talk to each other about "our" students. We need the collective intelligence of all of our colleagues to teach all of the students in school today. We cannot do it alone any more because the problems are too great and the stakes are too high.

Racism, low student expectations, discrimination, rigid school structures, cultural mismatch, and disrespect for linguistic diversity are some of the issues that cause school communities to be less than optimal for all learners (Nieto, 2003). Because racism and discrimination are deadly to students' self-esteem and ability to achieve at a high level, we need to eradicate all vestiges of them from our schools.

We value schools that search for and maintain a diverse, highly qualified teaching staff. Schools that discourage discrimination often include the study of racism and the study of differences as part of the curriculum. These schools cannot condone an attitude that allows some students to be viewed as "slow" or deficient because of linguistic differences. Teachers working in these schools know that although their ELLs cannot produce a five-page academic essay today, they will in time. They just need to learn how.

There are structural factors in schools that encourage failure for ELLs. Tracking, standardized testing, teaching with rigid and traditional pedagogy, and maintaining isolation from the rest of the school community (Nieto, 2003) are some factors that need to be reconsidered. Schools that promote multicultural learning are those that encourage the integration of all learners through collaborative projects involving teachers planning together to create interdisciplinary learning units with a focus on community problems. Parent and community involvement are encouraged in these schools, flexible grouping procedures are used, classroom-based assessment is given a high priority, and teachers use innovative instructional strategies in an effort to help all children achieve.

We believe culture is a powerful curriculum source for students at all grade levels. We have seen teachers use culture as a stepping stone to student involvement in learning. The sharing of culture is compelling to all students. By integrating culture into the curriculum, we are likely to engage the attention and interest of English-speaking and non-English speaking students alike. In addition, we convey the clear message that we respect the cultures and traditions of our students.

Respect for the language skills of our students is often overlooked in North American classrooms, where English-speaking students are struggling to learn a foreign language while multilingual students are not encouraged to display their language abilities. Respect for the languages of our students begins with respect for their names. Students deserve to have their names used and pronounced correctly. The use of the native language as a tool for learning in the classroom is another area where teachers convey respect for ELLs and their cultures. Learning a little of our students' languages helps us to be aware of how difficult language learning is and creates a comfort level in the classroom when we attempt to make our students feel more accepted by speaking a few words of Chinese, Spanish, or Arabic.

OUR PURPOSE AND BELIEFS

Throughout this book you will discover the underlying belief systems that drive us. We believe, first, that all children can learn to a high level. We believe children in schools are capable of learning more than one language and can use their languages to learn content courses even to the high standards that our schools demand. We believe all children are entitled to a challenging, innovative, and intellectually rigorous curriculum. In the classroom vignettes we have included at the beginning of most chapters, we have provided models of best practices that we have compiled from the many great teachers we have worked with over the years. Unless we have included citations, the names of teachers, students, and schools we have used are pseudonyms.

We believe language acquisition is an innate ability of children everywhere, and this ability is honed through interactions with knowledgeable teachers and peers. We believe the community of learners in a school and within the larger community outside of school is important to the learning process. Most importantly, we believe the teacher is the critical factor in every classroom. What we do and say, and the decisions we make affect the learning environment for our students. We support the notion of the teacher as a critical thinker—one who arranges, changes, and modifies the curriculum in ways that will support the learning and emotional needs of all students.

It has taken us many years to accumulate the beliefs, concepts, and strategies described in this text. Simply reading about them will not help you to grow and develop as an effective teacher of diverse learners. You will need to question them, experiment with them, ask your colleagues about them, and, finally, test them out in your own classrooms. We believe that teachers need to develop a philosophy of education and a system of educational practice that works for them. It is helpful to take courses and attend workshops, but in the final analysis, these ideas and theories must be developed within the confines of our daily classroom practice. When teachers approach education in this way, they continue to grow and develop professionally throughout their careers.

ACKNOWLEDGMENTS

We would like to thank our families for their support. There have been many hours spent away from them as we worked to complete this text. All the while, our children's and our grandchildren's voices have been ringing in our ears as we worked. They are our messengers to the future: David, Martha, Perrin, Jonah, Norah Jane, Tom, Julie, Kevin, Mary, Sean, Lenore, Ciaran, Finn, and Chichi. Thanks to reviewers: Joanne Burnett, University of Southern Mississippi; Leah Fonder-Solano, University of Southern Mississippi; Holly Hansen-Thomas, Texas Woman's University; and Gina Zanolini Morrison, Wilkes University.

REFERENCES

Christian, D. (2006). Introduction. In F. Genesee, K. Lindholm-Leary, W. M. Saunders, & D. Christian (Eds.), *Educating English language learners: A synthesis of research evidence.* New York: Cambridge University Press.

Fortuny, K., Hernandez, D. J., & Chaudry, A. (2010). *Young children of immigrants. The leading edge of America's future.* Brief No. 3. Washington, DC: The Urban Institute.

Kindler, A. L. (2002). *Survey of the states' limited English proficient students and available education programs and services: 2000–2001 summary report.* Washington, DC: National Clearinghouse for English Language Acquisition and Language Instruction Educational Programs.

National Clearinghouse for English Language Acquisition & Language Instruction Educational Programs. (2012). http://www.ncela.gwu.edu/files/uploads/4/GrowingLEP_0506.pdf.

Nieto, S. (2003). *Affirming diversity: The sociopolitical context of multicultural education* (4th ed.). New York: Longman.

President's Advisory Commission on Educational Excellence for Hispanic Americans. (2003). *From risk to opportunity: Fulfilling the educational needs of Hispanic Americans in the 21st century.* Washington, DC. *http://www2.ed.gov/news/pressreleases/2003/04/04092003a.html.*

Ruiz-de-Velasco, J., & Fix, M. (2000). *Overlooked and underserved: Immigrant students in U.S. secondary schools.* Washington, DC: The Urban Institute.

White House Initiative on Educational Excellence for Hispanics. (2011). *Improving educational opportunities and outcomes for Latino students.* http://www.whitehouse.gov.

SUPPLEMENTS FOR INSTRUCTORS AND STUDENTS

CourseSmart eBook and Other eBook Options Available

CourseSmart is an exciting new choice for purchasing this book. As an alternative to purchasing the printed book, you may purchase an electronic version of the same content via CourseSmart for reading on PC, Mac, as well as Android devices, iPad, iPhone, and iPod Touch with

CourseSmart Apps. With a CourseSmart eBook, readers can search the text, make notes online, and bookmark important passages for later review. For more information or to purchase access to the CourseSmart eBook, visit http://www.coursesmart.com. Also look for availability of this book on a number of other eBook devices and platforms.

MyEducationLab™

Proven to **engage students**, provide **trusted content**, and **improve results**, Pearson MyLabs have helped over 8 million registered students reach true understanding in their courses. **MyEducationLab** engages students with real-life teaching situations through dynamic videos, case studies, and student artifacts. Student progress is assessed, and a personalized study plan is created based on the student's unique results. Automatic grading and reporting keeps educators informed to quickly address gaps and improve student performance. All of the activities and exercises in MyEducationLab are built around essential learning outcomes for teachers and are mapped to professional teaching standards.

In *Preparing Teachers for a Changing World*, Linda Darling-Hammond and her colleagues point out that grounding teacher education in real classrooms—among real teachers and students and among actual examples of students' and teachers' work—is an important, and perhaps even an essential, part of training teachers for the complexities of teaching in today's classrooms.

In the MyEducationLab for this course you will find the following features and resources.

STUDY PLAN SPECIFIC TO YOUR TEXT   MyEducationLab gives students the opportunity to test themselves on key concepts and skills, track their own progress through the course, and access personalized Study Plan activities.

The customized Study Plan—with enriching activities—is generated based on students' results of a pretest. Study Plans tag incorrect questions from the pretest to the appropriate textbook learning outcome, helping students focus on the topics they need help with. Personalized Study Plan activities may include eBook reading assignments, and review, practice, and enrichment activities.

After students complete the enrichment activities, they take a posttest to see the concepts they've mastered or the areas where they may need extra help.

MyEducationLab then reports the Study Plan results to the instructor. Based on these reports, the instructor can adapt course material to suit the needs of individual students or the entire class.

CONNECTION TO NATIONAL STANDARDS   Now it is easier than ever to see how coursework is connected to national standards. Each topic, activity and exercise on MyEducationLab lists intended learning outcomes connected to either the Common Core State Standards for Language Arts or the IRA Standards for Reading Professionals.

ASSIGNMENTS AND ACTIVITIES   Designed to enhance your understanding of concepts covered in class, these assignable exercises show concepts in action (through videos, cases, and/or student and teacher artifacts). They help you deepen content knowledge and synthesize and apply concepts and strategies you read about in the book. (Correct answers for these assignments are available to the instructor only.)

BUILDING TEACHING SKILLS AND DISPOSITIONS   These unique learning units help users practice and strengthen skills that are essential to effective teaching. After presenting the steps involved in a core teaching process, you are given an opportunity to practice applying this skill via videos, student and teacher artifacts, and/or case studies of authentic classrooms. Providing multiple opportunities to practice a single teaching concept, each activity encourages a deeper understanding and application of concepts, as well as the use of critical thinking skills. After practice, students take a quiz that is reported to the instructor gradebook.

ONLINE THEMATIC UNITS   Two content-based, multi-disciplinary thematic units—one at the primary level and the other geared to the intermediate grades—are included, so readers can see how to successfully integrate content instruction, language instruction, and learning strategies described in this book.

LESSON PLAN BUILDER   The **Lesson Plan Builder** is an effective and easy-to-use tool that you can use to create, update, and share quality lesson plans. The software also makes it easy to integrate state content standards into any lesson plan.

IRIS CENTER RESOURCES   The IRIS Center at Vanderbilt University (http://iris.peabody. vanderbilt.edu), funded by the U.S. Department of Education's Office of Special Education Programs (OSEP), develops training enhancement materials for preservice and practicing teachers. The Center works with experts from across the country to create challenge-based interactive modules, case study units, and podcasts that provide research-validated information about working with students in inclusive settings. In your MyEducationLab course we have integrated this content where appropriate.

A+RISE ACTIVITIES   A+RISE activities provide practice in targeting instruction. A+RISE®, developed by three-time Teacher of the Year and administrator, Evelyn Arroyo, provides quick, research-based strategies that get to the "how" of targeting instruction and making content accessible for all students, including English language learners.

A+RISE® Standards2Strategy™ is an innovative and interactive online resource that offers new teachers in grades K–12 just-in-time, research-based instructional strategies that:

- Meet the linguistic needs of ELLs as they learn content
- Differentiate instruction for all grades and abilities
- Offer reading and writing techniques, cooperative learning, use of linguistic and nonlinguistic representations, scaffolding, teacher modeling, higher order thinking, and alternative classroom ELL assessment
- Provide support to help teachers be effective through the integration of listening, speaking, reading, and writing along with the content curriculum
- Improve student achievement
- Are aligned to Common Core Elementary Language Arts standards (for the literacy strategies) and to English language proficiency standards in WIDA, Texas, California, and Florida.

COURSE RESOURCES   The Course Resources section of MyEducationLab is designed to help you put together an effective lesson plan, prepare for and begin your career, navigate your first year of teaching, and understand key educational standards, policies, and laws.

It includes the following:

The **Preparing a Portfolio** module provides guidelines for creating a high-quality teaching portfolio.

Beginning Your Career offers tips, advice, and other valuable information on:
- *Resume Writing and Interviewing:*   Includes expert advice on how to write impressive resumes and prepare for job interviews.
- *Your First Year of Teaching:*   Provides practical tips to set up a first classroom, manage student behavior, and more easily organize for instruction and assessment.
- *Law and Public Policies:*   Details specific directives and requirements you need to understand under the No Child Left Behind Act and the Individuals with Disabilities Education Improvement Act of 2004.

The **Certification and Licensure** section is designed to help you pass your licensure exam by giving you access to state test requirements, overviews of what tests cover, and sample test items.

The Certification and Licensure section includes the following:

- *State Certification Test Requirements:* Here, you can click on a state and will then be taken to a list of state certification tests.
- *You can click on the Licensure Exams* you need to take to find:
  - Basic information about each test
  - Descriptions of what is covered in each test
  - Sample test questions with explanations of correct answers

- *National Evaluation Series*™ by Pearson: Here, students can see the tests in the NES, learn what is covered in each exam, and access sample test items with descriptions and rationales of correct answers. You can also purchase interactive online tutorials developed by Pearson Evaluation Systems and the Pearson Teacher Education and Development group.
- *ETS Online Praxis Tutorials:* Here you can purchase interactive online tutorials developed by ETS and by the Pearson Teacher Education and Development group. Tutorials are available for the Praxis I exams and for select Praxis II exams.

Visit www.myeducationlab.com for a demonstration of this exciting new online teaching resource.

Teaching English Language and Content in Mainstream Classes

CHAPTER 1

Principles of Integrated Language Teaching and Learning

Ms. Varma, first-grade teacher, has taken advantage of a beautiful autumn day to take her class, which includes seven English learners, on an English scavenger hunt. Working in pairs, the class walks around the school, the school grounds, and nearby streets looking for words in English. They carefully observe and take turns writing down all the words they find. They will use these words to study phonics and the alphabet as well as to create and share sentences, stories, and maps when they return to class. The list grows and grows: *Grade 1, Ms. Varma, Boys, Girls, School, Library, quiet, Garden Hills, Georgia, Fulton County, Delmont, Lookout, Drive, Street, Park, Bus, Bakery, Police.* . . . Desta, a new arrival from Ethiopia, looks at the long accumulated list in amazement. "Ms. Varma," he cries, "There's English everywhere!"

Ms. Varma has designed a lesson that offers opportunities to learners at all levels and illustrates the usefulness of spoken and written English. She has structured a lesson that promotes conversation and connects to themes the class is studying in reading, science, social studies, and math. She has brought a new learner to delight in the language around him that he is beginning to learn, and she will use this experience as a starting place to take the child beyond delight to competence in using his new language. But on what does she base her choices and practices as a teacher of culturally and linguistically diverse learners?

Though we still have far to go toward a thorough understanding of language development, language teaching, and language learning, the teaching profession has a rich body of research upon which to base our instructional decisions. Teachers need to understand and be able to articulate the principles that underlie their teaching, and these principles should be based on sound research about how language is learned and what works best in supporting language development in the classroom. The principles that teachers hold not only make a difference regarding how and how well they teach but they also make teachers more able to learn from observation of their learners and from reflection on their own teaching.

What are the principles of integrated language teaching and learning?

- What principles can we draw from research about language learning and teaching?
- What are strategies and practices that exemplify research-based principles?

In this chapter, we outline nine principles that apply our best understandings of research on both effective teaching and learning for school-age learners and specific knowledge about how language is most efficiently acquired and best taught. We have named our model the **activity-based communicative teaching and learning model** (or the **ABC model**). The nine principles are organized along two dimensions: (1) activity-based teaching and learning and (2) communicative teaching and learning.

Language is best developed when it is used in ways that are active, convey meaning, and have a communicative purpose

Activity-based teaching and learning focuses on what learners bring to the classroom and the active role that learners play in the language acquisition process. Research on learning and memory (Sprenger, 1999), on language acquisition and language learning (Cameron, 2001), and on the functions of the brain (Genesee, 2000) shows us that English language learners in elementary and middle school are *not* passive recipients of learning. Rather, they are actively constructing **schema** (organizational structures of language and content) and meaning. Thus, all teaching—even direct teaching—must be planned so that learners play active roles as they learn. Four of the ABC principles describe how classroom instruction can be planned and conducted to promote active student roles in learning.

Communicative teaching and learning focuses on the importance of authentic, comprehensible communication in the learning of language. For teaching and learning to be effective and efficient, language must be used in ways that clearly convey meaning and have communicative purpose. Five of the ABC Principles fall along this dimension and outline how our instruction must include communicative elements.

These two dimensions and nine principles are designed as guidelines for organizing and planning instruction for classrooms in which language develops as quickly and smoothly as possible. Although there is necessarily some overlap among the nine activity-based and communicative principles, we have found each to provide unique guidelines and organization for planning and evaluating the instruction of English language learners, and we apply them in the aspects of instruction detailed throughout the book. In the following paragraphs, we introduce each principle, provide a brief theoretical/research foundation for it, and give an example. These examples offer snapshots of the principles in action in the classroom in various content areas at various grade levels. Although we work to cover the range of school-age learners, we encourage readers, as they study the principles, to transform these examples by thinking about how each might be adapted and revised to best depict their own current or potential teaching situations.

ACTIVITY-BASED LANGUAGE TEACHING AND LEARNING

Principle 1 Active Engagement

Learners play enjoyable, engaging, active roles in the learning experience. Language and literacy development are facilitated by a comfortable atmosphere—not only one that values, encourages, and celebrates efforts but also one that provides the appropriate level of challenge to motivate and

Active Engagement in Practice

To help his multicultural, multilingual third-grade students "use" language authentically in studying the food pyramid, Ted Burch had his students keep a written and/or pictorial food diary and then use word source tools (such as a picture dictionary, bilingual dictionary, or Internet search) to list in English the foods they ate. Next the third-graders made word cards of the foods and taught their classmates and teacher names of unfamiliar foods from the various cultures represented in the class. As a final step, students classified all the foods they had eaten two ways: by locating them on a map of the world showing where the foods were grown and by placing word and picture cards next to the appropriate category on a large food pyramid.

engage learners (Cummins, 2007; Guthrie et al., 2004; Jensen, 1998; Sprenger, 1999; Krashen, 2003). When **active engagement** is practiced, language is learned while doing something with it, not just learning it. Language is best viewed as a verb (language as something to use and do) than as a noun (language as a content to be learned). School-age learners develop language and literacy best first by using language as a tool for creating and sharing meanings (Vygotsky, 1986); and later, as they are developmentally ready, by studying language structures and features as they are needed and used in authentic contexts (Lightbown & Spada, 2006).

Principle 2 Cultural Relevance

Classrooms respect and incorporate the cultures of learners in those classes while helping them to understand the new culture of the community, the school, and the classroom. Teachers play the most important role in determining the quality and quantity of participation of ELs in their classrooms. When teachers develop a climate of trust, understand children's social and cultural needs, and model for the rest of the class how they, too, can include English learners in classroom conversations and activities as important members of the classroom learning communities, ELs' active involvement in the classroom and their learning show improvement (Yoon, 2007).

Research has also led to a wide consensus concerning the value of parental involvement in students' school achievement and social development (Cummins, 1986; Delpit, 1995), and in literacy development in particular (Bronfenbrenner, 1975; Tizard, Schofield, & Hewison, 1982; Heath, 1983; Snow, Burns, & Griffin, 1998; Reese, Garnier, Gallimore, & Goldenberg, 2000). Creating a culturally responsive and **culturally relevant** classroom goes beyond "parental involvement" and requires thoughtfulness and effort on the part of teachers to learn about students' cultures from students themselves, families, community members, and library and Internet resources; to value and include what learners bring to the classroom from their cultures; and to take into account the different world views represented in the classroom. Creating such a classroom requires an understanding of culture that is deeper than viewing the "exotic" differences between cultures, or focusing on holidays, foods, and customs. Instead, it integrates a multicultural perspective on the daily life of the classroom (Derman-Sparks & Edwards, 2010).

Cultural Relevance in Practice

Lydia Achebe knows that her first-graders want to see themselves in the books that they read, and recognizes how they appreciate it when they and others view their home cultures in a positive light. She works closely with the school library media specialist, who tries to acquire texts from and about the cultures of children in the school. When a new student arrived who was from the Ndebele region of South Africa, the teacher and media specialist found the delightful book, *My Painted House, My Friendly Chicken, and Me* with text by Maya Angelou and photographs by Margaret Courtney-Clarke (1994). All the class enjoyed looking at a globe and discussing the path the new student took to come to the United States from Southern Africa. They shared the book as a read-aloud several times, compared and contrasted schools and homes in different places where they had lived, and then painted their own pictures using elements of the bright designs of the Ndebele.

Principle 3 Collaboration

Learners develop and practice language in collaboration with one another and with teachers. As language is a tool for meaning-making, and communication and thinking are developed through using language to accomplish things (Vygotsky, 1986), and as learning cooperatively has been shown to be effective at improving learning (Kessler, 1991; Slavin, 1995), so instruction should be organized to facilitate interaction and collaboration. Learning should provide two-way experiences through which learners solve problems, negotiate meaning, and demonstrate what they have learned.

Collaboration in Practice

When Kamal Gebril's fifth-grade class studied ancient Egypt, collaboration among peers included a simple "elbow buddy" or "pair-share" activity, in which partners restate to one another something they have learned about burial practices in the time of the pharaohs. Collaboration between teacher and learners included a shared writing activity in which students, after studying pictures in David Macaulay's classic book, *Pyramid* (1975), described and illustrated the process of building a pyramid. Kamal was careful to include discussion of contemporary Egypt as well, describing such family customs as visiting ancient monuments and traveling outside the city on special holidays to visit graves of their forebears and having a family picnic. The assignment was extended to collaboration between school and home when children took home pictures they had drawn and stories they had written about customs of ancient and modern Egypt. First they read the story in English to family members and then they retold the story in the home language. A final collaboration at the end of the unit was a "numbered heads" review of what they'd learned. In this strategy, children, in groups of about four, are each given a number. Kamal asks a question and the groups put their "heads together" to find the answer. Then a number is chosen randomly and the child with that number gives the group's response. Even newcomers are able to participate meaningfully and actively in the review as a result of the coaching and support of their peers to prepare them to answer the questions.

Principle 4 Learning Strategies

Learners use a variety of language and learning strategies to expand learning beyond the classroom and to become independent, lifelong learners. **Learning strategies** (also called *learner strategies*) (Chamot & O'Malley, 1996; Nunan, 1996; Oxford, 1996; Lessard-Clouston, 1997) are steps taken by learners to enhance their learning and develop their language competence. These strategies can be observable behaviors, steps, or techniques, such as **SQ3R (survey, question, read, recite, review)** (Robinson, 1970), a reading strategy, or nonobservable thoughts or mental practices, such as visualization or positive thinking. Although learners do use strategies unconsciously, the focus in teaching learning strategies is to bring them to the learners' attention and make them consciously part of the learners' repertoire. Learning strategies allow learners to control and direct their own learning. These strategies also expand the role of language teachers beyond teaching language to that of helping learners develop their own strategies. They are generally oriented toward solving problems and can involve many aspects of language to be learned beyond the cognitive.

Learning Strategies in Practice

To help her eighth-graders become more independent in learning new vocabulary, Lenore Duink first used modeling, supported practice, and independent practice to develop learners' ability to ask questions when they don't understand—teaching them polite phrases for asking a teacher, peer, or other person appropriately for repetition, clarification, or explanation of vocabulary. Then she taught her students various ways to support their vocabulary learning, including making **word squares** (see Table 1.1 for an example), sorting terms into categories, visualizing meanings, practicing with a peer, drawing pictures, composing and singing songs with new terms, highlighting verb endings, listening for words on the radio and TV, using mnemonic devices, and finding ways to put new terms to use in conversations both in the classroom and beyond.

TABLE 1.1 Word Square Graphic Organizer

Mammal	
Definition a type of vertebrate **Translation** in my language (Spanish) mamífero	**Characteristics** • Are warm blooded • Produce milk • Give birth to young alive • Have hair • Are vertebrates • Have lungs to breathe air
Examples • Human • Monkey	**Nonexamples** • Rooster • Fish

COMMUNICATIVE TEACHING AND LEARNING

Principle 5 Differentiation

Learning activities accommodate different language, literacy, and cognitive levels and incorporate many dimensions of learning: different learning styles, intelligences, and preferences. All learners are not the same: they have different native intelligence, learned intelligence, learning styles, and preferences. Including English learners in a grade-level classroom expands the differences by adding different language backgrounds, educational levels, cultural experiences, experiences of culture change, and sometimes the trauma of war, famine, or poverty. When learners are limited in their comprehension of English, providing input through other means—pictures, gestures, sounds, movement, graphics—helps provide them the "hook" they need to be included in the classroom conversation. Effective **differentiation** to include English learners involves expanding the dimensions of learning across different learning styles—verbal, auditory, kinesthetic—and different intelligences. Gardner's (1983, 1996) categories of intelligences include linguistic (language, e.g., writer), logical-mathematical (e.g., mathematician or engineer), musical (guitarist), bodily-kinesthetic intelligence (athlete, dancer), spatial intelligence (artist, designer), interpersonal intelligence (counselor, politician), intrapersonal intelligence (philosopher), and naturalist (oceanographer). Teachers differentiate the language they use and introduce in the classroom, the content they use, the classroom processes, the products that learners are asked to produce, and the assessment of those products. Many states and school districts are implementing a model called *response to intervention* (RTI) to provide early intervention for at-risk learners, but in this book, we also describe how it can be used within a framework of differentiated learning. We will introduce culturally and linguistically responsive RTI in this chapter, and throughout the book, we offer RTI Samplers to illustrate how the principles and practices we propose can be applied through culturally and linguistically responsive RTI.

Differentiation in Practice

Marie Matluck wanted to address a variety of learning styles while helping her kindergarteners learn letter names and sounds, so she provided opportunities for learners to learn these by differentiating the process—involving children in looking at pictures, singing, building with blocks, teaching one another, searching for letters in the environment outside schools, drawing letters and words that included the sounds of the letters, visualizing—making "mind pictures" associating letters with key words—and making letter shapes with their bodies. She sometimes gave learners choices as to which activities they used to practice their skills. With sounds that are used in both English and students' home languages, Marie provided pictures of key words that begin with the letter in both languages to take advantage of what children already knew and enhance transfer of learning from one language to another (Figure 1.2).

FIGURE 1.1 "Lion" / "León" Is a Key Word That Begins with the Same Letter in Both English and Spanish

Principle 6 Comprehensible Input with Scaffolding

Teachers provide rich input with appropriate context and support, to make that input comprehensible to learners, and appropriately and increasingly more challenging. English learners cannot learn from language they do not understand. **Comprehensible input** is a term first used by Steven Krashen (2003) that refers to language used by teachers and others in ways that English learners can understand as their language ability is developing. It ties back to Vygotsky's (1986) thinking about the social nature of learning. Oral and written input from teachers can be adapted to convey meaning to language learners at various levels and to be more understandable in a variety of ways. To make learners better understand oral language in the classroom, teachers make sure they face students when they speak (so that students can watch their mouths and facial expressions), speak slowly, and articulate clearly (so that students can hear the separate words), and increase **wait time** (the time after a question is asked before a student or students are asked to respond).

A scaffold is a metaphor for the way teachers provide support for language learners as they acquire English

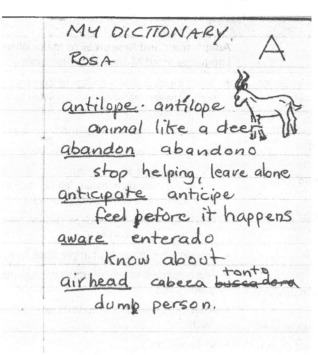

FIGURE 1.2 Rosa's Personal Dictionary

To improve the comprehensibility of written input, teachers choose texts with rich graphic elements and teach students how to understand and use these graphics; teach learners to use a variety of print and online sources to find word meanings, pronunciations, and examples of use; teach learners to organize and keep their own vocabulary notebooks or personal dictionaries (see example in Figure 1.2); provide alternate texts when texts are clearly beyond student comprehension; and use a variety of strategies to help students access texts that are near their instructional level. Table 1.2 suggests means to increase comprehensible input both orally and in writing. Strategies and techniques in Chapter 5, Oral Language Development, and in Chapters 8 and 9 on reading and writing will expand on these ideas to add to your repertoire of tools to support English learners by helping them to understand the language of your classroom.

Comprehensible Input with Scaffolding in Practice

When Jim Stalzer's sixth-grade class was studying the life cycle in science, he invited an ornithologist to come to speak to the class on the life cycle of birds. Jim wanted to make sure that all the students in his class, including newcomers who were beginning learners of English, could enjoy the visit. After the ornithologist accepted his invitation, Jim asked him for a short set of terms that he could preteach before the visit and supplied the speaker with a short list of suggestions (much like the ones in Table 1.2 for oral language input) that might help the ornithologist to be more easily understood in the multilingual, multicultural classroom. Jim also pretaught some of the terms to the newcomers and helped them practice questions to ask the guest.

Principle 7 Prior Knowledge

Teachers help learners use their prior knowledge of language, content, and the world to develop new language and increase learning. If we already know a lot about a topic—global warming, for example—we will find television programs, lectures, or written materials on global warming much easier to follow. If a student has learned a lot about a topic in his home language, it is easier to develop new language about that topic. **Prior knowledge** or background knowledge is key to comprehension for all learners (Marzano, Pickering, & Pollock, 2004), but it is of particular importance for English learners. If learners are less familiar with a topic and structures of the oral discussion or written text, they will have more difficulty with comprehension (Upala et al., 2007; Carrell & Eisterhold, 1988). Language difficulty increases

TABLE 1.2 Scaffolding Instructional Language

Adaptations to Make Oral Language Input Comprehensible	Adaptations and Resources to Make Written Language Input More Comprehensible
• Select topics that are familiar to learners and/or make connections between learners' prior knowledge and information they will read.	• Select topics that are familiar to learners and make connections between learners' prior knowledge and information they will read.
• Check comprehension often (use signals, cards, choral responses, questions, slates). When learners do not understand, demonstrate, explain, or rephrase.	• Use pictures, maps, and graphic organizers.
	• Preteach and reinforce key vocabulary.
• Use translation when this is the most efficient way to convey meanings of new words.	• Use and teach learners to use dictionaries and other word sources: picture dictionaries, learner dictionaries, translation dictionaries, and word source software.
• Adapt language of input to help learners understand:	• Teach learners to find and use picture, translation, and dictionary resources on the Web.
• Face students.	• Provide alternate texts at appropriate levels.
• Speak slowly (but naturally) and articulate clearly.	• Teach learners to select texts at appropriate reading/language levels.
• Pause frequently and increase wait time.	• Assign key selections from texts when entire text is out of reach.
• Use gestures, mime, facial expressions, pictures, props, and real objects to enhance meaning.	• Use audio texts.
• Model and provide student models of language to be used.	• Include reference links (to pronunciation, translation, pictures, background, etc.) in digital texts (McCloskey & Thrush, 2005).
• Monitor use of idioms and figurative language and explain them when needed.	• Use scaffolding strategies to support reading (e.g., reciprocal teaching, shared reading, guided reading).
• Use more direct sentence structures, articulate carefully, and adjust vocabulary.	
• Point out key ideas and vocabulary.	
• Use terms consistently; avoid overuse of synonyms for key terms.	

with cognitive difficulty, unfamiliarity, and lack of context. So, when developing language with English learners, teachers must work to *start where students are*. This includes finding out what students already know about a new topic and helping them to make connections between what they already know and what they are learning. It includes making connections

A teacher engages learners in a dialogue about nature

Prior Knowledge in Practice

Liz Bigler is introducing a lesson to her fourth-graders on Rosa Parks and the Montgomery bus boycott. She wants her beginning learners to understand the meaning of the word *fair* that is key to understanding the motivation for the boycott. She takes a bag of pennies and gives them out to a group of students. Three students get 10 pennies. The fourth gets 1. The children look puzzled, and Liz explains to them (with repetition, rephrasing, and gestures) that this is an example of something that is "not fair." The students then proceed with their total physical response (TPR) lesson, which includes acting out the boycott as the teacher tells the story. (See Bigler, 2006, for a complete description of this lesson.)

between learners' cultures and cultural knowledge and the new culture of the school and the community. It also may include, at beginning levels, selecting topics that learners are likely to be familiar with, providing necessary background information on new topics in home languages, preteaching key vocabulary to expand background knowledge before studying a topic, or helping learners make connections between what they know about language in their home language (L1) to uses of this knowledge in English (L2). It also might include providing background information in L1 before proceeding to study a theme or topic in L2. In a bilingual classroom, content could be taught in two languages. In a monolingual classroom teachers might, for example, have learners read or listen to a home language summary of a text before they will be reading it in English.

Principle 8 Content Integration

Language learning is integrated with meaningful, relevant, and useful content—generally the same academic content and higher-order thinking skills that are appropriate for the age and grade of learners. Teaching language along with age-appropriate academic content has several advantages: it is efficient because two goals—acquisition of language and

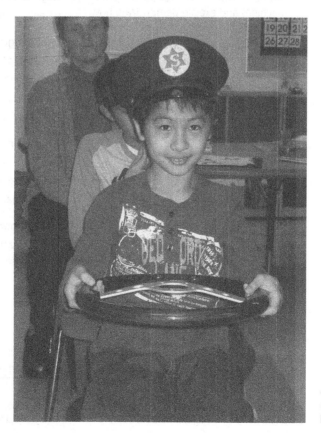

Children reenact the story of Rosa Parks and the Montgomery bus boycott

Content Integration in Practice

Julia Raca teaches in a multicultural, multilingual second grade with several English learners at different levels. She wants to make sure that everyone benefits from her science curriculum, including the new arrivals in her classroom, so she includes both language objectives and science objectives in all her lesson plans. (See Table 1.3.) When she teaches her "How Things Work" unit, her goals include students' understandings about tools, machines, and magnets, and she adds to them language goals including key vocabulary, giving instructions, and using verbs in the command form and future tense form. Julia starred objectives that she thought were appropriate for newcomers to achieve and others she expected them to work toward.

content learning—are accomplished at once. It is effective first because language is learned better when learners are doing something purposeful and important to them—and learning the content for their grade level is very important. It is also necessary because learners cannot afford to take a year or two off from content learning while they develop language: they will end up only further behind their peers. Content-based language learning can happen in a variety of settings: in a pull-out English language development (ELD) class (also called an *ESL class*), in which the teacher introduces content through integrated themes (this is often used with newcomers/ beginners); in a special section of a content class with a grade-level teacher with training in teaching ELD who teaches the content using approaches that make the content comprehensible to language learners and promote language development (this is sometimes done in middle and high schools with significant numbers of English learners); or in grade-level classes that include both English proficient learners and English language

TABLE 1.3 Including Language and Content-Learning Goals

Content Goals	Language Goals
• Learners name uses of various simple machines and explain/demonstrate how they work.*	**Key Vocabulary** wheels, gears, machine, parts, work*
• Learners identify certain machines and their parts (e.g., bicycle, gears, wheels).	**Oral Language** • Naming* • Retelling • Reporting • Asking for explanations
• Learners demonstrate and label the workings of simple machines (screws, wheel and axle, lever, pulley) on a compound machine, the bicycle.	**Grammar** • Future tense with "going to" • Helping verb "can/can't" • Commands*
	Comprehension • Visualization and description of information from text and charts
	Literacy • Use of alphabet to find information*
	Writing • Labeling of a diagram • Writing about how bicycles work

*Objectives appropriate for newcomers.

Source: Adapted from Freeman, D., Freeman, Y., Garcia, A. C., Gottlieb, M., McCloskey, M. L., Stack, L., & Silva, C. (2010). *On Our Way to English,* Grade 2, Unit 7. Copyright Rigby/Houghton Mifflin Harcourt. Used with permission.

Good teaching involves making assessment an integral part of every lesson

learners and in which teachers have training to attend to both content and language needs of learners and to differentiate instruction to include learners at different language and learning levels. These integrated models are used because research findings have shown that they are the most effective at both language learning and content learning for English learners (Cummins, 1986; Thomas & Collier, 2003). Teachers can differentiate through adapting the language, content, process, or product in classrooms (Tomlinson, 1999).

Principle 9 Clear, Appropriate Goals and Feedback

Teachers set and communicate attainable goals for learners and provide students appropriate and consistent feedback on their progress in attaining these goals. Setting clear goals helps both teachers and learners have a much greater chance to attain those goals. Goals begin our curriculum, inform our curriculum, and new, more advanced goals are the outcome of our curriculum. As John Dewey once said, "Arriving at one goal is the starting point to another."

We want English learners to attain the same high goals as their English-proficient peers, but to do this, we must set the right goals—goals that comprise the next step forward for individual learners. Learners want to do well, and will do much better when they understand what is expected of them and when our expectations are appropriate. We must establish clear language and content goals for learners and provide them feedback on their progress toward those goals. We can also, in developmentally appropriate ways, encourage learners to begin to evaluate their own progress toward accomplishing goals to help them become independent, self-motivated learners.

We must determine intermediary steps toward grade-level standards that are attainable at learners' language level. World-Class Instructional Design and Assessment (WIDA), a consortium of states dedicated to the design and implementation of high standards and equitable educational opportunities for English language learners, collaborated with the standards of the professional organization Teachers of English to Speakers of Other Languages International Association (TESOL) for school-age learners of English (Gottlieb, Cranley, & Cammilleri, 2007; TESOL, 2006). These *English language proficiency standards in the core content areas for grades PK-12* outline standards for teaching English learners the language they need to develop essential content concepts. The general standards are included on Table 1.4. The standards document offers expectations in the areas of language arts, science, math, and social studies for learners at five grade-level clusters of English language proficiency (PreK–K, 1–3, 3–5, 6–8, and 9–12) across the domains of listening, speaking, reading, and writing. Many states and districts have determined their own standards for English learners and selected instruments to assess their achievement.

But good assessment goes far beyond summative tests at the beginning or end of the year. Good assessment includes multiple assessments. Good teaching includes assessment as

TABLE 1.4 WIDA Consortium English Language Proficiency Standards in the Core Context Area (Gottlieb, Cranley, & Cammilleri, 2007)

English Language Proficiency Standard 1	English language learners communicate for *social and instructional* purposes within the school setting
English Language Proficiency Standard 2	English language learners communicate information, ideas, and concepts necessary for academic success in the area of *language arts*.
English Language Proficiency Standard 3	English language learners communicate information, ideas, and concepts necessary for academic success in the area of *mathematics*.
English Language Proficiency Standard 4	English language learners communicate information, ideas, and concepts necessary for academic success in the area of *science*.
English Language Proficiency Standard 5	English language learners communicate information, ideas, and concepts necessary for academic success in the area of *social studies*.

Source: Gottlieb, M., Cranley, M. E., & Cammilleri, A. (2007). WIDA English language proficiency standards. In *Understanding the WIDA English language proficiency standards: A resource guide.* Madison, WI: University of Wisconsin Board of Regents System. Retrieved from, http://www.wida.us/standards/Resource_Guide_web.pdf.

an integral part of every lesson so that children and teachers can clearly see the progress they are making. Teachers may assess in many ways that range from informal to formal: by asking questions of individuals, groups, and the whole class; by having learners give signs or signals; by having learners demonstrate their understanding with responses on slates; by giving a group

Clear, Appropriate Goals and Feedback in Practice

Scott Kessler teaches a middle school integrated mathematics class that includes seven early and late intermediate learners of English. His aim is to make the content of mathematics comprehensible to English learners in his class, and to do this he works to set incremental goals toward full achievement of content and language goals. He's consulted the WIDA standards (Gottlieb, Cranley, & Cammilleri, 2007), which have been adopted by his state, the Common Core Standards in Mathematics (Common Core State Standards Initiative, 2010), and adapted the rubric shown in Table 1.5 to use with his learners in a unit on decimals and measurement of central tendencies (mean, mode, median) in the domain of listening.

TABLE 1.5 Mathematics Rubric Using WIDA ELP Standard 3

Grade-level cluster: **6-8WIDA**   *Framework:* **Formative**   *Language Domain:* **Speaking**

ELP Standard 3: English language learners communicate information, ideas, and concepts necessary for academic success in the content area of mathematics

Curriculum Topic: Metric & Standard Units of Measurement

Correlated Common Core Standard for Mathematics: 5.MD.1. Convert among different-sized standard measurement units within a given measurement system (e.g., convert 5 cm to 0.05 m) and use these conversions in solving multistep, real world problems.

Level 1: Entering	Level 2: Beginning	Level 3: Developing	Level 4: Expanding	Level 5: Bridging
Name tools and units of standard or metric measurement from labeled examples (e.g., ruler-inches or cm; scale-pounds or kilos).	Estimate standard or metric measurement from pictures or real objects (e.g., "The dog weighs about 10 kilograms.").	Describe real-life situations in which measurement is needed from illustrated scenes (e.g., at the clinic or marketplace).	Discuss how measurement is used in real-life situations from illustrated scenes (e.g., construction, architecture, or cartography).	Explain how and when to convert standard or metric measurement in real-life situations (e.g., recipes, temperatures, or international sports)

TABLE 1.6 Nine Principles of ABC Language Teaching and Learning

Activity Based	Communicative
1. *Active Engagement.* Learners play enjoyable, engaging, active roles in the learning experience. 2. *Cultural Relevance.* Classrooms respect and incorporate the cultures of the learners and their families in the classroom while helping them to understand the new culture of the community, the school, and the classroom. 3. *Collaboration.* Learners develop and practice language in collaboration with one another and with teachers. 4. *Learning Strategies.* Learners use a variety of learning strategies to maximize learning in the classroom, to expand their learning beyond the classroom, and to become independent, lifelong learners.	5. *Differentiation.* Learning activities accommodate different language, literacy and cognitive levels and also incorporate many dimensions of learning: different learning styles, intelligences, and preferences. 6. *Comprehensible Input with Scaffolding.* Teachers provide rich input with appropriate context and support to make that input comprehensible to learners as well as appropriately and increasingly more challenging. 7. *Prior Knowledge.* Teachers help learners use their prior knowledge of language, content, and the world to develop new language and increase knowledge. 8. *Content Integration.* Language learning is integrated with meaningful, relevant, and useful content, generally the same academic content that is appropriate for the age and grade of learners. 9. *Clear, Appropriate Goals and Feedback.* Teachers set and communicate clear attainable goals to learners and provide students with appropriate and consistent feedback on their progress in attaining these goals.

quiz; by having learners score themselves along a rubric or on a checklist; by keeping checklists of learner accomplishments; by writing portfolios; by using state and national English language assessment instruments; and when learners are ready, by giving district, state, and national criterion-referenced or standardized tests designed for all learners.

We have now outlined nine principles included in two dimensions—principles that we hope will guide you toward supporting the learning of English language learners in your setting. Table 1.6 summarizes these principles for your review. The following chapters will show these principles at work in various aspects of your instructional program for English language learners in organizing your classroom, teaching oral language vocabulary, reading, writing, assessing, and putting it all together through content-based learning.

What Is Culturally and Linguistically Appropriate Response to Intervention (RTI)?

The RTI model is designed to meet government expectations for (1) quality instruction based on scientific research, (2) use of highly qualified teachers in the classrooms, and (3) instruction informed by regular assessment. The comprehensive model includes both regular and special education. RTI uses three tiers of instruction: Tier 1 includes research-based instruction in the general education classroom, Tier 2 involves intensive assistance as part of the general education support system, and Tier 3 provides special education. Because of this book's focus on the mainstream classroom, our focus will be the first two tiers of instruction (See Figure 1.3, Response to Intervention: Three-Tier Model for ELLs) (Brown & Doolittle, 2008; Baca, 2009),

In this book, we focus on Tier 1 and 2 instruction provided by general classroom teachers who may or may not be English language specialists. RTI is designed so that teachers do not wait for students to fail but provide appropriate, quality instruction from the beginning. Culturally and linguistically responsive RTI includes differentiation, accommodations, collaboration, and progress monitoring using appropriate assessment. Characteristics of effective RTI implementation for English learners include the following applications of the ABC model described earlier:

1. Active Engagement
   - Learners apply concepts to their own lives and to authentic tasks.
2. Cultural Relevance
   - Teachers incorporate the native language strategically. The model has been implemented successfully in bilingual settings in which native language is used strategically and/or as a first language for reading instruction (Vaughn et al., 2006).
   - Instruction builds on learners' home cultures

3. Collaboration
   • Learners have many opportunities to use language for interpersonal and academic purposes.
   • Learners collaborate to use higher-order thinking and active problem solving as well as to practice what they have learned.
4. Learning Strategies
   • Learners develop multiple ways to take responsibility for their own learning, including independent reading as well as reviewing and applying previously learned concepts.
5. Comprehensible Input with Scaffolding
   • New language is introduced in ways that support learning including rich vocabulary development, preteaching and reinforcing learning, and using organizers to build and support concepts and language
6. Prior Knowledge
   • Learners access prior knowledge, make connections between previous learning and new, and build new knowledge.
7. Content Integration
   • Learners use authentic content for development and application of language.
8. Clear and Appropriate Goals and Feedback
   • Teachers use appropriate diagnostic assessments before teaching, formative assessments while teaching to ensure that learners are acquiring concepts and to make them aware of what they are learning; summative assessments at key points in instruction to ensure that instruction is sufficient, appropriate, and well scaffolded and to provide clear feedback to learners on what they have achieved.

Response to Intervention: Three-Tier Model for ELLs

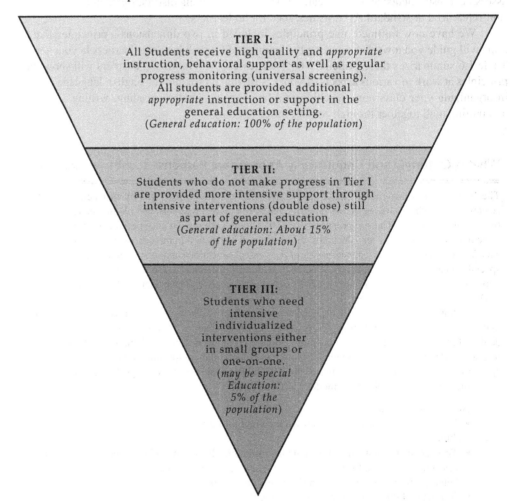

FIGURE 1.3 Response to Intervention: Three-Tier Model for ELLs (Brown & Doolittle, 2008, p.12).

Questions for Reflection

1. How is what a teacher believes about teaching reflected in how that teacher performs in the classroom?
2. What do you believe is important to best promote learning for all learners? What do you believe is important for enhancing the academic language of English language learners in particular?
3. Reflect on your own experiences of studying a new language.

Were you successful? What was most helpful? What was least helpful? What classroom principle and characteristics promoted your learning? Compare and contrast these principles with the ones outlined in this chapter.
4. Which of the principles outlined do you think is the most important? Why? Did any principle surprise you? If so, how?

Activities for Further Learning

1. Each "principle in practice" in this chapter describes teaching English learners in a particular grade-level classroom. Rewrite one of these vignettes to describe how this principle in practice might be changed to meet the needs of students at a different grade level.
2. Develop a lesson for a grade level that you teach or may teach. Focus your lesson on meeting one or more of the principles named in order to include learners of English. Exchange lessons with a partner and discuss how you have succeeded in teaching according to the principles and how you might take the lesson even further in that direction.
3. Observe an English learner in a content classroom over several days. Note what the student is doing, saying, and attending to during your observation. Does that learner seem to comprehend the language and expectations of the classroom? What does the learner seem to comprehend? What evidence from your observation indicates that the learner comprehends? What does the learner not seem to understand? What evidence from your observation indicates that the learner does not comprehend?
4. If a new student entered your class from a culture with which you were unfamiliar, outline preparation and processes that you might use to provide cultural relevance for that student in your classroom.
5. Interview two adults who learned English after starting school. Ask your interviewees about their educational history and experiences as early, intermediate, and advanced learners. Ask about the

difficulties they faced and what people, processes, materials, or strategies they feel helped them to learn English. How do these connect with the principles in this chapter?
6. Visit a community center, farmers' market, place of worship, or other location frequented by members of language minority groups in your area and where another language or languages are often spoken. Spend some time listening and observing. Reflect: What does it feel like to be the one who does not understand? If you can, begin a conversation with some individuals. Ask them how people in their community go about learning English and about challenges they face. Ask them what they wish for their children.
7. Choose a language that you do not know much about and that is spoken by one of your students/potential students. Search for information on the language you selected. See how much you can learn about that language in 20 to 30 minutes—just a little about pronunciation, writing system, grammar, vocabulary, related languages, words for greeting, and so on. What might speakers of that language find difficult when learning English? What connections to English might you capitalize upon?
8. Visit the Safe Schools Coalition web site on guidelines for avoiding bias in school curriculum materials (http://www.safe-schoolscoalition.org/guidelinesonbias-screen.pdf). Use its criterion to review your textbooks and/or materials that you are using or considering using in a future unit or theme.

Suggested Reading

Ariza, E. N. W. (2006). *Not for ESOL teachers: What every classroom teacher needs to know about the linguistically, culturally, and ethnically diverse student*. Boston, MA: Allyn & Bacon. Teachers of diverse learners are offered essential concepts for fully including those English learners in the mainstream classroom. Using many examples in the voices of students and teachers, Ariza considers the classroom settings, learning about cultures, specific information about cultural groups, language acquisition, and learning English through academic content, assessment, and connecting to the community.

Brown, H. D. (2000). *Teaching by principles: An interactive approach to language pedagogy* (2nd ed.). Upper Saddle River, NJ: Pearson ESL. This popular methodology text surveys a variety of language teaching options grounded in accepted principles of language learning and teaching.

Gibbons, P. (2002). *Scaffolding language, scaffolding learning: Teaching second language learners in the mainstream classroom*. Portsmouth, NH: Heinemann. Gibbons introduces the theory behind second-language learning in readable language and provides concrete classroom examples of applications along with classroom activities to implement to help English learners speak, listen, read, and write.

King-Shaver, B., & Hunter, A. (2003). *Differentiated instruction in the English classroom: Content, process, product, and assessment*. Portsmouth, NH: Heinemann. The authors clearly and concisely explain differentiation as a way of thinking about the classroom and a strategy for improving teaching. They provide both the rationale for differentiating and descriptions of differentiated teaching in the English classroom through modifications in learning content, learning process, and learning products and assessment.

Hoover, J. J., Klingner, J., Baca, L. M., & Patton, J. M. (2008). *Methods for teaching culturally and linguistically diverse exceptional learners*. Upper Saddle River, N.J.: Pearson/Merrill Prentice Hall. Written for the K-12 practitioner and other professional staff, this book offers rich information on instructional methods for culturally and linguistically diverse learners as well as assistance in differentiating between learning differences and learning disabilities.

Li, X., & Zhang, M. (2004). Why Mei still cannot read and what can be done. *Journal of Adolescent & Adult Literacy 48*:2. This case study explores the educational factors that failed a 14-year-old sixth grader from China, and how schools can prevent such students from failing in school.

References

Angelou, M. (Photographs by Margaret Courtney-Clarke) (1994). *My painted house, my friendly chicken, and me.* New York, NY: Clarkson Potter.

Baca, L. (2009, April). Implementing response to intervention with English language learners. Paper presented at the annual meeting of the Exceptional Education Graduate Research Symposium. Buffalo State College, Buffalo, NY. Retrieved from http://www.nysrti.org/docs/Implementing%20Response%20to%20Intervention%20with%20English%20Language%20Learners%20-%20Baca%202009.pdf

Bigler, L. (2006, March). Using TPR to illuminate stories: Reenacting the Rosa Parks bus protest. *TESOL in Elementary Education Interest Section Newsletter, 28*(1).

Bronfenbrenner, U. (1975). Is early intervention effective? In U. Bronfenbrenner (Ed.), *Influences on human development.* Hinsdale, IL: Dryden Press.

Brown, J. E., & Doolittle, J. (2008). A cultural, linguistic, and ecological framework for response to intervention with English language learners. Tempe, AZ: National Center for Culturally Responsive Educational Systems. Retrieved from http://www.nccrest.org/Briefs/Framework_for_RTI.pdf

Cameron, L. (2001). *Teaching languages to young learners.* New York, NY: Cambridge University Press.

Carrell, P. L., & Eisterhold, J. C. (1988). Schema theory and ESL reading pedagogy. In Patricia L. Carrel, Joanne Devine, and David E. Eskey (Eds.), *Interactive approaches to second language reading* (pp. 73–92). New York, NY: Cambridge University Press.

Chamot, A., & O'Malley, M. (1996). Implementing the cognitive academic language learning approach (CALLA). In R. Oxford (Ed.), *Language learning strategies around the world: Cross-cultural perspectives* (pp. 167–173). Honolulu: Second Language Teaching and Curriculum Centre, University of Hawaii.

Cummins, J. (1986). Empowering minority students: A framework for intervention. *Harvard Educational Review, 56*(1): 18–36.

Common Core State Standards Initiative. (2010). The Standards: Mathematics. Retrieved from http://www.corestandards.org/the-standards/mathematics

Delpit, L. (1995). *Other people's children: Cultural conflict in the classroom.* New York, NY: New Press.

Derman-Sparks, L., & Edwards, J. (2010). *Anti-Bias education for young children and ourselves.* Washington, DC: National Association for the Education of Young Children.

Freeman, D., Freeman, Y., Garcia, A. C., Gottlieb, M., McCloskey, M. L., Stack, L., & Silva, C. (2010). *On our way to English, K–5.* Austin, TX: Rigby/Houghton Mifflin Harcourt.

Gardner, H. (1983). *Frames of mind.* New York, NY: Basic Books.

Gardner, H. (1996, April). Multiple intelligences: Myths and messages. *International Schools Journal, 15*(2): 8–22.

Genesee, F. (2000). Brain research: Implications for second language learning. University of California, Santa Cruz: Center for Research on Education, Diversity & Excellence Occasional Reports. (ERIC Document Reproduction Service Paper 00 12.) Retrieved from http://pegasus.cc.ucf.edu/~gurney/BrainLearning.doc

Gottlieb, M., Cranley, M. E., & Cammilleri, A. (2007). WIDA English language proficiency standards. In *Understanding the WIDA English language proficiency standards: A resource guide.* Madison, WI: University of Wisconsin Board of Regents System. Retrieved from http://www.wida.us/standards/Resource_Guide_web.pdf.

Guthrie, J.T., Wigfield, A., Barbosa, P., Perencevich, K. C., Taboada, A., Davis, M. H., Scafiddi, N. T. Tonks, S. (2004). Increasing Reading Comprehension and Engagement Through Concept-Oriented Reading Instruction. *Journal of Educational Psychology,* 96(3), 403-423.

Heath, S. (1983). *Ways with words: Language, life and work in communities and classrooms.* Cambridge, UK: Cambridge University Press.

Jensen, E. (1998). *Teaching with the brain in mind.* Alexandria, VA: ASCD.

Kessler, C. (1991). *Cooperative language learning: A teacher's resource book.* Englewood Cliffs, NJ: Prentice Hall.

Krashen, S. (2003). *Explorations in language acquisition and use.* Portsmouth, NH: Heinemann.

Lessard-Clouston, M. (1997, December). Language learning strategies: An overview for L2 teachers. *The Internet TESL Journal, 3*(12). Retrieved May 2, 2008. http://iteslj.org/Articles/Lessard-Clouston-Strategy.html

Lightbown, P. M., & Spada, N. (2006). *How languages are learned* (3rd ed.). Oxford, UK: Oxford University Press.

Macaulay, D. (1975). *Pyramid.* Boston, MA: Houghton Mifflin.

McCloskey, M. L., & Thrush, E. (2005). Building a reading scaffold with WebTexts. *Essential Teacher, 2*(4): 48–51.

Marzano, R., Pickering, D. J., & Pollock, J. E. (2004). *Classroom instruction that works: Research-based strategies for increasing student achievement.* Alexandria, VA: ASCD.

Nunan, D. (1996). Learner strategy training in the classroom: An action research study. *TESOL Journal, 6*(1): 35–41.

Oxford, R. (Ed.). (1996). *Language learning strategies around the world: Cross-cultural perspectives.* Honolulu: Second Language Teaching and Curriculum Centre, University of Hawaii.

Reese, L., Garnier, H., Gallimore, R., & Goldenberg, C. (2000). Longitudinal analysis of the antecedents of emergent Spanish literacy and middle-school English reading achievement of Spanish-speaking students. *American Educational Research Journal, 37*(3): 633–662.

Robinson, F. P. (1970). *Effective study* (4th ed.). New York, NY: Harper & Row.

Slavin, R. E. (1995). *Cooperative learning: Theory, research, and practice* (2nd ed.). Boston, MA: Allyn & Bacon.

Snow, C. E., Burns, S. M., & Griffin, P. (Eds.). (1998). *Preventing reading difficulties in young children.* Washington, DC: National Academy Press.

Sprenger, M. (1999). *Learning and memory: The brain in action.* Alexandria, VA: ASCD.

TESOL. (2006). *PreK–12 English language proficiency standards in the core content areas.* Alexandria, VA: TESOL.

Thomas, W. P., & Collier, V. P. (2003). *What we know about effective instructional approaches for language minority learners.* Arlington, VA: Educational Research Service.

Tizard, J., Schofield, W., & Hewison, J. (1982). Collaboration between teacher and parents in assisting children's reading. *British Journal of Educational Psychology, 52*(1): 1–15.

Tomlinson, C. (1999). *The differentiated classroom: Responding to the needs of all learners.* Alexandria, VA: ASCD.

Upala, M. A., Gonce, L. O., Tweney, R. D., Stone, D. J. (2007). Contextualizing counterintuitiveness: How context affects comprehension and memorability of counterintuitive concepts. *Cognitive Science, 31*(3): 415–439.

Vaughn, S., Cirino, P. T., Linan-Thompson, S., Mathes, P. G., Carlson, C. D., Cardenas-Hagan, E., et al. (2006). Effectiveness of a Spanish intervention and an English intervention for English-language learners at risk for reading problems. *American Educational Research Journal, 43*(3:) 449–487.

Vygotsky, L. S. (1986). *Thought and language.* New York, NY: Wiley.

Yoon, B. (2007). Offering or limiting opportunities: Teachers' role and approaches to English-language learners' participation in literacy activities. *The Reading Teacher, 61*(3): 216–225.

MyEducationLab™

Go to the Topic, Comprehensible Input, in the MyEducationLab (www.myeducationlab.com) for your course, where you can:

- Find learning outcomes for Comprehensible Input along with the national standards that connect to these outcomes.
- Complete Assignments and Activities that can help you more deeply understand the chapter content.
- Apply and practice your understanding of the core teaching skills identified in the chapter with the Building Teaching Skills and Dispositions learning units.
- Examine challenging situations and cases presented in the IRIS Center Resources.
- Check your comprehension on the content covered in the chapter by going to the Study Plan in the Book Resources for your text. Here you will be able to take a chapter quiz, receive feedback on your answers, and then access Review, Practice, and Enrichment activities to enhance your understanding of chapter content.
- **A+RISE** A+RISE® Standards2Strategy™ is an innovative and interactive online resource that offers new teachers in grades K-12 just in time, research-based instructional strategies that meet the linguistic needs of ELLs as they learn content, differentiate instruction for all grades and abilities, and are aligned to Common Core Elementary Language Arts standards (for the literacy strategies) and to English language proficiency standards in WIDA, Texas, California, and Florida.

CHAPTER 2

Language Acquisition and Language Learning in the Classroom

Children's language development is wonderful, novel, creative, and awe inspiring. Children speak in order to tell us stories:

Adult: *What did you do yesterday at school?*

Leslie: *I listened to a story. Was a horse. And roses maked him sneeze. And his nose itched and his eyes itched. Sumpin' else. I had . . . uh I haved . . . a had a motorcycle and I sit down and thinking what I was doing and lookin' at all those kids and teacher goed by and she didn't ask me anything.*

Adult: *What might she have asked you?*

Leslie: *How come you're sittin' here?* (Weeks, 1979, p. 71)

They speak to amuse us:

Child: *(Sitting close to the teacher during Rug Time, an opening activity.) Hot. (Touches the microphone.)*

Teacher: *It's not hot. It's not hot. It's a microphone.*

Child: *(Takes the teacher's hand and places it on the microphone.) See hot?*

Teacher: *Cold. It's cold.*

Child: *See. Hot.*

Teacher: *No, it's not hot. It's cold.*

Child: *Ahm, hot.*

Teacher: *No, it's not hot* (Urzua, 1981, p. 56).

They sometimes speak to resist us:

Child: *Nobody don't like me.*

Mother: *No, say "nobody likes me."*

Child: *Nobody don't like me (eight repetitions of this dialogue).*

Mother: *Now listen carefully; say "nobody likes me."*

Child: *Oh! Nobody don't likes me* (McNeill, 1975, p. 27).

And they often speak to help themselves learn:

Wally: *The big rug is the giant's castle. The small one is Jack's house.*

Eddie: *Both rugs are the same.*

Wally: *They can't be the same. Watch me. I'll walk around the rug. Now watch—walk, walk, walk, walk, walk, walk, walk, walk, walk—count all these walks. Okay. Now count the other rug. Walk, walk, walk, walk, walk. See? That one has more walks.*

Eddie: *No fair. You cheated. You walked faster.*

Wally: *I don't have to walk. I can just look.*

Eddie: *I can look too. But you have to measure it. You need a ruler. About 600 inches or feet.*

Wally: *We have a ruler.*

Eddie: *Not that one. Not the short kind. You have to use the long kind that gets rolled up in a box.*

Wally: *Use people. People's bodies. Lying down in a row.*

Eddie: *That's a great idea. I never even thought of that* (Paley, 1981, pp. 13–14).

Developing and using language to promote learning is the focus of this book. We will describe the classroom conditions and teacher behaviors that promote language development and academic achievement for **English language learners (ELLs)** in grades K through 12. If you are a teacher with ELLs in your classroom, you have the double task of teaching those children content learning and the language they need to understand, speak, read, and write about that content. This is an exciting and challenging task.

To help us understand the kinds of classrooms we need to create for our English language learners, it is important to understand how languages are acquired. Although this discussion is limited, it will highlight the essential information you need to know.

What do we know about first language acquisition?

• What is the nature of the first language environment?

• How is learning a second language in the classroom different from the experience of acquiring the first language?

• What strategies do ELLs use to acquire languages?

• What can ELLs tell us about positive classroom environments and learning experiences?

WHAT DO WE KNOW ABOUT FIRST LANGUAGE ACQUISITION?

• First language acquisition is universal.
• First language acquisition is natural.
• First language acquisition does not require formal instruction.

Language Acquisition Is Universal

The birth of a child is a joyous event in all cultures of the world. Even so, parents worry about their soon-to-be born infant. They worry the child will be born healthy and with all fingers and toes intact and whether their children will see, hear, and function normally. It is very rare, however, for a parent to worry about whether a child will learn to talk. We all assume our children will learn to speak a language even though we may wonder if they will learn to read. Language acquisition is universal in all cultures of the world. All children with normal or near-normal mental and physical abilities learn to speak a language.

Although children in various parts of the world are spoken to in a variety of diverse languages, children within those language communities are able to acquire languages that many adult speakers in the United States find to be difficult. In addition, children accomplish much of their learning at an age when their cognitive abilities are not yet fully developed.

Language Acquisition Is Natural

Human beings are born with the biological predisposition to acquire languages. Language learning is part of our human nature. Children begin to acquire language by attempting to make sense of the language they hear around them. Somehow, in the first five years of life, children have figured out enough about sounds, words, sentences, and extended discourse to master most of the structures of their first language (Piper, 2006). Because this task is so natural to almost all children, we fail to appreciate the enormity of it.

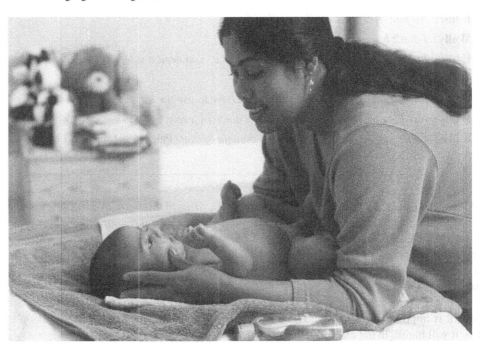

Parents the World Over "Talk" to Their Infant Children

Innate language theorists such as Noam Chomsky have speculated that children are born with mechanisms that predispose them to learn language systems (1957, 1975). Chomsky believes the human brain contains the basic structures for all rule-governed, human languages. As evidence of this, he notes that all languages contain components in common, such as categories of word classes, hierarchical structure, and linearity. He calls this innate device the *language acquisition device* (LAD) and proposes that it contains a "universal grammar" that enables all children to analyze the language spoken to them and construct grammatical rules for that language.

We believe the process through which children create languages is one of hypothesis testing. Children generate rules based upon the language input of the community: For example, the word *dat* refers to objects distant from the child, whereas *dis* refers to objects close by. In time, these rules are refined until most children have created the basic grammars of their first languages.

Children learn the language of the community around them. Those who live in multilanguage communities will sort through those languages and learn each in the specific language context in which it is used. For example, one author lived in a small town in the Philippines on the northern coast of Mindanao. The children of the town spoke Visayan with Christian shopkeepers, Maranao with Muslim schoolmates, and Tagalog and English with their teachers in school.

Children are known to create their own languages to communicate with others. The ten-year-old son of one author moved to the Peoples' Republic of China with his parents for a year's teaching assignment. Shortly after arrival in the country, the boy was observed playing ball with Japanese, Chinese, and American children of the university faculty. None of the children spoke the others' languages yet. But to play baseball, the children began to create a language mix from words used by each of them. They used Japanese for the word *throw*, English for *catch*, and Chinese words for *you* and *run*. In the absence of a common language, children will create one because it is natural for human beings to communicate with language (Figure 2.1).

First Language Acquisition Does Not Require Formal Instruction

If we taught children to speak, they'd never learn.

HOLT, *HOW CHILDREN FAIL*, 1964

It was once believed children acquired languages because they listened to and repeated the language of their parents. Imitation was seen as a form of tutoring for young children. We now

FIGURE 2.1 Children Often Acquire New Languages Because of a Need to Communicate during Play with Children Who Don't Speak the Same Language

know this behaviorist perspective is too simplistic an explanation for a complex and creative learning process. Children rarely repeat exactly what their parents say and often say things they have never heard said around them.

Even in the second language classroom, the creativity of children is apparent. When Marisol, a ten-year-old student recently arrived in the United States from Spain, raised her hand in class, we were surprised because the child spoke very little English and had never volunteered to speak. When called upon, she asked *Me go peepee?* Marisol was ignoring the structured lessons of the language classroom to create her own language system. She substituted *Me* for the first person pronoun *I* and simply used intonation for the request form. She was highly communicative and creative but could not be said to be imitating her teacher or any of her fourth-grade classmates.

In addition to not formally instructing their children in language, parents rarely make overt corrections of children's language. Instead, parents usually respond to the substance of their children's talk and ignore the grammar. One author watched two-year-old Anthony coloring with his mom (Levine, 1981). Anthony held up a crayon, and his mother said, *That's yellow.* Anthony then jumped up and said, *I get red.* His mother responded with, *You want to get the red? Show Mommy the red if you're gonna get it. What's red? It's like the red light. That's the same color as the red light when Mommy's gotta stop the car.*

Anthony's mother did not correct her child's grammar but responded to the topic of the conversation and used it as an opportunity to expand the child's utterance into a grammatical sentence: *You want to get the red?* She then continued to model a variety of other sentence forms all related to the subject of the red crayon. Her conversation does not resemble what we usually think of as language teaching, but her language input to her child is important to his growing language system.

Even though children's acquisition of a first language appears to be accomplished effortlessly, their growth in language skill in school requires considerable effort. We tend to assume that children are able to understand the highly abstract language of the school system, the text, and the standardized test when, in fact, they do not (Piper, 2006). Learning academic language—the variety of language that leads to school success—requires direct instruction and involves learning to read, write, and think at high cognitive levels. One of the reasons for this difference in ease of learning may be due to the nature of the learning environment in school versus the first language environment.

WHAT IS THE NATURE OF THE FIRST LANGUAGE ENVIRONMENT?

Children Are Immersed in Language

As we saw in the conversation with Anthony and his mom, parents immerse their children in a "veritable language bath" (Lindfors, 1987). Parents of newborns begin speaking to their infants in the delivery room. They continue the conversation with questions, exclamations, and commentary even though their babies are unlikely to answer a single question for at least two years. The lack of a child's response does not deter parents one bit. They keep on talking to their babies and attempt to engage their developing attention spans for increasingly longer periods of time.

Language Is Highly Contextualized

The language that parents and other family members use is thought to be helpful to language acquisition because it is highly contextualized. Contextualized language is accompanied by many visual cues as to its meaning. For example, pointing to a dog is one way to identify the meaning of the word *dog*. Caretakers use gestures such as pointing, touching, and making facial expressions to convey meaning to young children. They almost always speak about topics that young children are attending to at the moment of the utterance. Children can easily attach meaning to the language they hear because parents and family members are intent on helping their children understand their language. Children, then, acquire language within a context of use. They learn to ask for milk by pointing to the milk and approximating the "m" sound. They get picked up by raising their arms and saying *up*. They play with the doors on the cabinets and learn how to open and close them while also learning the words *open* and *close*.

Language Is a Tool for Purposeful Use

For children, language is a tool used to satisfy a purpose. Language helps children to get what they want, enables them to interact with other people, and allows them to report, have fun, imagine, and learn more about the world around them.

Children use language tools initially to satisfy their personal needs: *Want milk*. They quickly learn to use language as a tool for controlling others: *Gimme dat*. Informing and identifying objects is part of early language development: *Dat doggy*. Later, children develop these functions in more complex ways and add others as required. Imaginative play produces language such as *You be the mommy and I be the daddy*. Children's curiosity prompts them to ask *Why?* and is the precursor to higher-level reasoning skills.

Children Are Physically Active While Acquiring Language

The child acquiring a first language is physically very active in exploring the environment. Sucking, crawling, dropping, and throwing are learning activities for young children. Jean Piaget, a Swiss psychologist, explained how the physical activity of young children contributed greatly to the developmental stages of a child's conceptual growth. Children progress through several stages of development and capability, finally culminating in a stage called *formal operations*. In the early stages of language growth, the sensory-motor stage, children acquire knowledge by touching, grasping, looking at, and manipulating the objects around them (Labinowicz, 1980).

When children are not permitted to engage in active play, the cognitive and language losses that result are tragic. We have heard of these results in children who are confined to their cribs in orphanages and are unable to move outside a small space. Depression and retardation are some of the consequences of a lack of physical, active play in young children.

Active movement has been found to be central to learning. There seems to be a neurological basis to learning that occurs in activity-based environments. The cerebella system, which controls motor activity, is one of the first parts of the brain to mature and has been found to be central in the formation of memory, attention, and spatial perception. In other words, the same part of the brain that controls movement also processes and promotes learning (Jensen, 1998). It is highly likely that environment plays an important part in determining the cognitive and linguistic maturity of children. Active play is a critical element of a child's environment.

Acquisition Occurs within a Social Environment

The environment of a child acquiring language is predominantly social. Young children need caretakers for a long time. While parents are caring for their young children, they are also talking and playing with them. Daily activities such as feeding, bathing, and dressing take on the nature of games as parents encourage children to eat (*Open wide. Here comes the airplane!*) or to cooperate while putting on socks and shoes (*This little piggy went to market, this little piggy stayed home*).

Parents interact with children in a cycle of speech that is geared to the child's level of understanding. Most caregivers modify their speech in ways to help children understand the language. In English, for example, parents will eliminate pronouns (*Come to Mommy*), use redundancy (*You want the red? What's the red, honey?*), use diminutives (*See the doggy?*), simplify the topic and the length of the sentence, and exaggerate intonation in order to engage a baby's attention (Snow, 1977). Although other cultures may customize caretaker language in different ways, all cultures modify language for children to enable babies to understand and grasp meaning from the interactions they have with other children and adults (Figure 2.2). This customizing of language is finely tuned to the baby's beginning speech comprehension. The bond of love and trust between the parent and child ensures that parents will continue to speak to children and children will continue to take risks to develop linguistically even after the age of three when basic communication has been established.

Children Choose Those Aspects of Language That They Wish to Acquire

The young child's language environment is one where the child chooses the language topic. Children decide what is interesting to them, and parents begin to talk about those interests. For example, in an interaction between Anthony and his mother (to whom we were introduced earlier in this chapter), Anthony sat at a table coloring while his mother watched. The two of them talked about the colors. At one point, Anthony shifted his gaze from the coloring book to a truck on the toy shelf. His mother immediately changed the topic of the conversation to the truck and engaged Anthony in talking about it. Children direct the nature of their own language learning by choosing which grammar elements to focus on, deciding which words to learn, and even choosing the topics of the conversations they have with their caregivers (Levine, 1981).

FIGURE 2.2 Parents Modify Their Speech in Response to a Child's Linguistic Proficiency

Language Acquisition Is Emotionally Embedded

The language acquisition environment is an emotional one for children. The bond of love and trust between parents and children is the major impetus to the continuing conversations that occur for years between them. Recent brain research (Jensen, 1998) tells us that the emotional overlay to language learning has a neurological basis. Results from research that was begun in the mid-1980s upset our notions of the rational mind and the separation of emotion and reasoning. Emotions drive attention, create their own memory pathways, and create meaning. Although the amygdala, an almond-shaped organ in the central brain, seems highly involved in emotional thought, the expression circuitry of emotion is widely distributed in the brain. In fact, when the frontal lobe of the brain is destroyed through accident, human performance on intelligence tests drops very little. Removal of the amygdala, however, is extremely harmful; it destroys the capacity for decision making, creativity, humor, imagination, altruism, and love (Jensen, 1998, pp. 73–75). It appears that emotions are critical to all learning experiences and the formation of memory.

Language Acquisition Is an Integrated Learning Experience

The language environment of the young child is one where language is not separated from learning about the way the world operates. Although schools find it helpful to separate the math class from the social studies class, the learning of a young child is integrated. Children do not learn about the parts of language as described in a grammar book. They are completely uninterested in the names of word classes and verb tenses. Rather, children acquire language as a holistic experience while playing with objects and people around them. One-year-olds enjoy dropping objects into containers and spilling them out again (*in* and *out*). Two-year-olds explore every object in their environment while asking *What's dat?* Eight-year-olds are captivated by the world of nature and enjoy learning information about animals and their habitats. These children often report on their learning using the language of a biological scientist.

HOW DO ACQUISITION AND LEARNING DIFFER?

In our work with **English as a second language (ESL)** programs in the public schools, we have encouraged teachers to use children's natural, innate language-acquisition mechanisms to be successful language learners of English. In doing so, we acknowledge our belief in language acquisition driven by innate mechanisms interacting with the language-learning environment. Other factors driving language acquisition have equal importance, in our view, in content classrooms. The interaction between speaker-hearers is highly influential in the acquisition and learning of academic language; thus, we value the interactionist position as well. Explanations for both positions follow.

Stephen Krashen (Krashen & Terrell, 1983) was an early proponent of the innatist position as described by Chomsky and extended Chomsky's theory to second language acquisition research. Krashen believed that children learning the English language constructed their own grammars through a process of hypothesis testing, thus creating grammatical rules for the new language in a way similar to that of first language acquisition. Krashen explained the path of second language acquisition as a "natural approach," and has developed five hypotheses that have had an impact on classroom instruction of English language learners: the acquisition-learning hypothesis, the natural order hypothesis, the input hypothesis, the affective filter hypothesis, and the monitor hypothesis.

The Acquisition-Learning Hypothesis

The distinction between acquisition and learning is a critical one for classroom teachers. Krashen and Terrell (1983) define **acquisition** as "developing ability in a language by using it in natural communicative situations" (p. 18). When children play softball together on the playground or chat in the school cafeteria, acquisition may be coming into play. ELLs pay little attention to grammatical forms and instead concentrate on understanding and communicating meaningful messages. Language **learning,** however, requires "having a conscious knowledge about grammar" (p. 18). When learning about a language, children are taught word forms, suffixes and prefixes, spelling regularities, mechanics, and other aspects of a formal language system. Most learning about languages occurs in classrooms, but it is possible for classrooms to foster acquisition as well. Krashen's emphasis on the acquisition-learning distinction is not merely one of environment, however. The claim is that learners process language differently under the two conditions—acquisition focuses solely on meaning with subconscious internalization of language structures and forms while learning requires conscious awareness of the formal properties of language. (Piper, 2006).

Krashen believes children acquire their first language and "most probably, second languages as well." He says adults can also acquire languages although "they do not usually do it quite as well as children." Both learning and acquisition are important in classroom language development, but Krashen feels "language acquisition is the central, most important means for gaining linguistic skills even for an adult" (Krashen & Terrell, 1983, p. 18). Intuitively, the acquisition-learning distinction has appeal to teachers who have worked with ELLs. We recognize that students will not be effective or efficient learners when the focus of instruction is placed on rote repetition and grammar drills. Instead, effective teachers focus on meaningful communication related to purposeful content-learning activities.

The Natural Order Hypothesis

The natural order hypothesis claims that learners acquire language rules in a predictable order. This claim is based upon morpheme studies of second language acquirers (Dulay & Burt, 1974). These studies show that some of these structures, such as the progressive –*ing* ending and the plural, were acquired early in the grammars of both children and language-learning adults. Other structures, such as the regular past, the third person singular –*s,* and the possessive –*s* were acquired relatively late. This order prevailed when learners were acquiring (not learning) languages and focusing on meaning rather than form. Later work on the natural order hypothesis indicates that structures in a learner's first language may influence the order of morphemes acquired in the second language (McLaughlin, 1987). In spite of the evidence to indicate a natural order in the acquisition of morphemes, teachers do not base their language curriculums on this order and Krashen would not recommend that they do so. The reason is that language is acquired most efficiently in an environment of natural conversation that responds to children's interests and is structured for their understanding.

The Input Hypothesis

Language input in the form of oral language or reading is of primary importance for progress in the target language. Krashen asserts that the best input (*i*) is language that is understood by the learner but is a little beyond the learner's current understanding or competence (*i* + 1). The role of the teacher then is to provide abundant input to learners and to do so in ways that will help students understand the meaning of the communication. By providing a here-and-now context, instruction becomes **comprehensible input** and helps ELLs to negotiate the meaning of increasingly more complex structures and thus continue the acquisition process. Krashen considers comprehensible input the "most important part of any language teaching program" (Krashen & Terrell, 1983, p. 55). Teachers' experiences and classroom practice support the input hypothesis.

The Affective Filter Hypothesis

There are social and emotional variables that affect language acquisition. Those learners in a low-anxiety environment with motivation and good self-esteem have a lower **affective filter** and are more open to the input of others. This openness allows the learner to interact easily with proficient speakers and receive increasingly larger amounts of comprehensible input. Because acquisition proceeds under these conditions, it is important for teachers not to force ELLs to speak, thus creating a high-anxiety situation. Many children spend time in a **silent period** during which they attempt to understand the input around them and then choose to speak when they are ready. The silent period of some ELLs can be lengthy, depending on the personality of the student. Silence does not indicate acquisition is not taking place, however. Many ELLs begin to speak rather fluently at the end of their silent periods.

The Monitor Hypothesis

Krashen & Terrell (1983) assert that acquisition is primary to language development. As such, there is little emphasis on formal rules. When writing, however, ELLs are able to reflect upon the formal rules of language (if they know them), spend sufficient time in following those rules, and focus on the form of the language. This reflection process devoted to form is called the **monitor,** an internal grammatical editor that is called into play as students learn the formal structure and requirements of a language.

Krashen has had a major influence on the teaching and learning of second languages. He has been influential in showing teachers the importance of comprehensible input for oral and written language, the existence of the silent period, and the need for a low-anxiety classroom. These ideas in connection with techniques developed to increase academic competency in language have changed the nature of language classrooms.

The Interactionist Position

While acknowledging the importance of comprehensible input in language acquisition, interactionists stress the need for language interaction among speaker-hearers to promote language acquisition and language learning (Long & Porter, 1985; Swain, 1985; Pica, Lincoln-Porter, Paninos, & Linnell, 1996; Izumi & Bigelow, 2000; Klingner & Vaughn, 2000). Teacher interactions with ELLs have helped these students perform better academically. The reciprocal interaction model of teaching in which teachers participate in genuine dialogue with students has been shown to be more beneficial than the traditional teacher-centered transition model (Doherty, Hilberg, Pinal, & Tharp, 2003; Tikunoff, 1985). This model facilitates, rather than controls, student language while encouraging the development of higher-order cognitive thinking. High-quality exchanges between ELLs and content teachers who are trained in second language acquisition techniques also give students better access to the curriculum (Berman, Minicucci, McLaughlin, Nelson, & Woodworth, 1995; Doherty et al., 2003; Montecel and Cortez, 2002; Tikunoff, 1985).

Small-group work in classrooms between native speakers (NS) and ELLs or among pairs of native speakers has shown increased motivation and initiative among learners. Students produce more language in these conditions and are less anxious about their language usage (Long & Porter, 1985). Indeed, small groups of students, engaged in two-way tasks that require the exchange of previously unknown information, participate in a higher amount of language practice to produce a broader range of language functions, greater grammatical accuracy with frequent corrections, and more negotiation of meaning than those classes that are conducted by a teacher (Long & Porter, 1985). The use of cooperative learning has also been shown to be highly effective with ELLs, leading to higher achievement levels (Caldéron & Carreon, 1994; Caldéron, Hertz-Lazarowitz, & Slavin, 1998).

Negotiation of meaning is crucial to effective interaction in classrooms because it significantly aids the development of second language acquisition (Long & Porter, 1985). Negotiation of meaning occurs as learners receive comprehensible input and/or feedback on prior utterances. This input serves as data that enable learners to construct grammars while modifying and adjusting their language output, thus expanding their language development (Pica et al., 1996). Modified output results from signals from other speakers that communication has not been achieved, for example, open-ended questions such as *Glass? What about glass?* Requests such as these tend to generate modification in ELL language output that is more comprehensible and grammatically on target. Izumi and Bigelow (2000, p. 239) found that "extended opportunities to produce output and receive relevant input were found to be crucial in improving learners' use of the grammatical structure."

Even when the members of the small groups are language learners themselves, negotiation of meaning occurs that promotes language learning. "Teachers can be confident that the interaction can assist second language learning whether the source of that interaction is a NS [native speaker] or another learner" (Pica et al., 1996, p. 80). Klingner & Vaughn (2000) demonstrated negotiation of meaning among small groups of bilingual fifth-graders using a collaborative reading strategy (CRS). Interactions among the ELLs in their study led to semistructured vocabulary practice, negotiation of the meaning of text, and progress toward both language and content-learning goals.

It is clear that both innatist and interactionist theories have contributed to the nature of classroom instruction today. Teachers who "think language" while teaching content area objectives and who provide effective small-group work experiences with abundant comprehensible input in a low-anxiety environment, will be effective in enabling ELLs to both acquire and learn language. In spite of the gains made in helping teachers to create classrooms that take advantage of the brain's ability to acquire languages, there are still major differences in the first and second language experience. Table 2.1 illustrates some of the differences in the two environments.

TABLE 2.1 How Do Language-Learning Environments Compare?

	L1 Acquisition Environment	L2 Classroom Learning Environment
Opportunities for interaction	• Are constant and continuous • Focus on meaningful communication • Proceed from gestural responses to one-word utterances to phrases to sentence forms • Promote cognitive growth	• May be limited by large classes and restricted opportunities for interaction • May be teacher-directed lessons • Has limited time available for language practice • Includes unmovable furniture • May be few opportunities for language interaction outside the classroom
Language input	• Is abundant and frequent: teacher to student ratio often 1 to 1 • Has simplified syntax • Is highly redundant • Is well formed • Is semantically concrete	• May be limited in transmission-type classrooms • May not be at each student's level of ability • May be limited by lack of exposure to target language in the community
Language context	• Focuses on the here and now • Is highly meaningful to the child • Provides the meaning for most utterances	• May be removed from the here and now and focused on course book content • May be limited by lack of pictorial resources, gestural cues, and context clues
Topic selection	• Has learner-initiated topic • Had adult-adjusted language topics to capture the child's interest • Focuses on communication of meaning	• Has topics decided by curriculum or textbook, not the learners
Language output	• Has abundant output after a long, initial, silent period • Uses output for hypothesis testing and patterning • Is characterized by grammatical errors initially but still communicative • Is "authentic"	• May be extremely limited • May have delayed speech • Has large classes with full group instruction that limit opportunities for output • Discourages output errors • May not have "authentic" output opportunities
Love and trust (affective environment)	• Has language that is acquired in a highly trusting environment • Has high expectation of success. • Has affective environment that mediates the risk of language acquisition and motivates the speech act	• Must create trust, which does not occur naturally in the classroom • Has affective environment that depends on the skills of the individual teacher and the school setting • Has highly authoritarian classrooms that may increase learners' anxiety and decrease language growth

WHAT ARE FACTORS AFFECTING LANGUAGE ACQUISITION IN THE CLASSROOM?

Classroom language learning is very different from home first language acquisition. There are factors in the nature of classroom instruction that affect second language acquisition and ultimately, academic achievement, and are important for all teachers to understand.

Limited Language Input

Classrooms contain many children, and this may lead to limited language input to the learner. The ratio of speaker-hearer is increased from a one-on-one situation to a thirty-to-one situation. Without careful planning, the teacher cannot easily address children's language needs for abundant input. Whereas a child is immersed in language while acquiring a first language, many students are rarely spoken to in schools at all (Harklau, 1994, 2000). As children proceed through the grades, comprehensible input is reduced. Without abundant input of meaningful language, ELLs will not acquire language efficiently or quickly.

The emotional attachments that occur between parents and their children are not easily replicated in classroom experiences either. After elementary school, teacher interactions with students become more formal. Lectures increase and circle time decreases. These distinctions may lead to a classroom environment where ELLs are spoken to infrequently and receive little emotional support. Teachers who recognize the necessity for emotionally rich, input-abundant environments will need to restructure the typical classroom situation in order for children to acquire language more efficiently.

Classroom Organization

The way in which we organize our classroom has an impact on the amount of language learned. With all the demands of the content classroom, teachers of math, social studies, science, and language arts may report little time to teach to the specific language-learning needs of one or two children. Teachers tend to feel guilty about not spending enough time alone with ELLs to help them develop language skills. Teacher-centered, frontal teaching styles lead to more limited interaction between teacher and student and between student and student. There are times when this organizational style is necessary, for example when viewing a movie, listening to a speaker, or viewing a demonstration. But frontal teaching is only one of many classroom organizational patterns.

When we realize that teachers are not the only speakers of the language within a class, we can begin to understand how other students can be used to facilitate the language development of their peers. Classrooms that differentiate instruction through activities, projects, and group work are more easily able to manage the needs of a wide variety of learners. Because language acquisition occurs in a social environment, student-centered classrooms place the focus on activities that are multilayered, allowing for diverse kinds of learning and permitting children at all levels to integrate themselves within the classroom learning community. When ELLs are given purposeful opportunities to communicate about topics interesting to them, their language acquisition is facilitated.

High Content and Language Load

Language acquisition and content learning are difficult and demanding tasks. Content mandates now require students to learn content information and develop communication skills at increasingly higher standards. ELLs may not be able to read the textbook or easily comprehend teacher lectures or classroom discussions. But teachers expect that all students will become able to use language in complex ways and to pursue further learning. Teaching content in a way that supports the learner's efforts promotes both content learning and language acquisition. Differentiation of objectives, activities, and assessments helps ELLs to cope with the heavy language and content load of the typical classroom.

Language learning is a highly complex activity. Acquiring a language means acquiring the following:

- *Phonemes*: speech sounds that make a difference in meaning between words (such as pin pen).
- *Phonology*: rules governing the sound system of English, including sound-symbol relationships, intonational variations, stress, pitch, and juncture.

- *Morpheme*: a word or part of a word conveying a grammatical or lexical meaning (such as the *–ed* ending turning a present tense verb into the past tense).
- *Morphology*: the system dealing with the structure or form of words (want, wanted, wanting, unwanted).
- *Syntax*: the system describing the way in which words, oral or written, combine into sentences; grammar.
- *Lexicon*: the vocabulary of the language.
- *Semantics*: the scientific study of the meaning underlying a word, phrase, or sentence.
- *Pragmatics*: the conversational rules guiding the use of language in a social situation. These rules change as a variety of social factors change: context, age, purpose, and so on.

All of these can be acquired by ELLs in meaningful, communicative classrooms. But they will also need to learn aspects of language to extend their communication into academic discourse. Aspects of syntax, for example, can be acquired, but certain grammatical constructions that are rarely used in oral language can be learned only through classroom instruction.

In addition to the systems of language and their various components, speakers of a language are able to adjust their language usage between formal and informal application and use all four language skills: listening, speaking, reading, and writing in complex ways and for a variety of purposes. Academic **registers** and formal written **discourse** are examples of language requiring classroom instruction and learning.

Teachers assist ELLs the most in the early stages of language acquisition by helping them comprehend the language of the classroom and giving them time to attempt to make themselves understood. As ELLs feel more comfortable with and begin to use the language, we provide more opportunities for formal language learning and higher-level thinking and problem solving.

Academic Language and Social Language

In addition to the aspects of language mentioned earlier, the language of school is different from the social language used by students in the cafeteria or the playground. Cummins (1980, 1999) describes social language (**basic interpersonal communication skills**, or **BICS**) as language occurring within a **context-embedded** social environment. Social language is more easily understood because the speaker-hearer uses the context of the situation, gestures, and facial expressions to enable comprehension. A social setting that encourages natural interaction is helpful to the acquisition of social language. ELLs acquire this dimension of language within two years of schooling in an English-speaking environment.

Academic or school language (**cognitive academic language proficiency**, or **CALP**) is the language of the textbook and is **context reduced.** Learners will not be able to learn the verb forms, transitional and cohesion devices, and specific lexicon of this language dimension unless they receive targeted instruction. Academic language involves oral and written forms that are cognitively demanding but required for school success. The amount of time required to reach grade-level competency in academic context-reduced language is between five to seven years (Ovando, Combs, & Collier, 2006; Collier, 1989).

The distinction between social and academic language is an important one for teachers to understand. ELLs who speak social language are sometimes viewed as competent speakers of English. When they are slow to make academic progress, their delay may be ascribed to learning deficits. However, there is no relationship between academic achievement and social language. Unless students master academic language, including reading and writing, they will not achieve academically. When we involve students in appropriate grade-level content curriculum and experiences, support learning with context, and directly teach academic language forms, we are helping ELLs acquire and learn the language necessary to be successful in school.

Negative Bias

Although no one expects a young child to use language well, older students are expected to know languages. When children in school classrooms cannot use the language of their peers, the school community views them as nonknowers. These negative opinions can affect children by slowing the pace of their language development. Cohen and Garcia (2008) report that a negative social identity limits motivation to learn and creates a threatening environment that undermines achievement.

Interesting Content-Related Experiences Provide Excellent Language-Learning Opportunities

Rather than viewing the child as deficient or culturally deprived, we need to examine the school systems in which many of our children are failing. The native language abilities of ELLs are underutilized in many schools. The school community does not always view the cultural backgrounds of our students as resources. ELLs can achieve at higher levels with increased motivation when teachers integrate student experiences, interests, and cultures into the curriculum, the classroom instruction, and the educational experience in general.

Cognition, Age, and Social and Cultural Differences

School-age children do not always receive the abundant language input that very young children do when acquiring their first languages. But the cognitive level of school-age children is much higher than that of an infant. Thus, higher cognitive abilities can facilitate language-learning experiences in school. If the ELL has already acquired a first language and can read and write in that first language, the transition to a second language will be much smoother and more efficient. The ability to read in one language is an asset when learning to read in another. Aspects of reading transfer from language to language. For example, literate ELLs expect to retrieve meaning from the printed page and use strategies to find and retain information. Those who are writers in their first language can use writing as an aid to language learning, taking notes, and collecting vocabulary lists. The learning strategies used in first language schooling also transfer to the second language classroom. ELLs can use dictionaries, memorize vocabulary, compare grammatical rules, and focus on areas of the language that are problematical. Higher cognitive functioning is an asset to the older, literate, and educated ELL.

Underschooled ELLs are lacking in the first language academic skills that promote learning a second language. These children are usually placed in age-appropriate grade levels even though they may have had limited or no prior schooling. Age-level placement of these children is appropriate and desirable for affective and emotional reasons, but the learning curve for these youngsters is very steep and the challenges for their teachers are great. For children such as these, the entire school community is needed to plan a comprehensive educational program and carry it out.

The different social and cultural contexts of school are more difficult for older learners in general. As children advance through the grades, they may feel ostracized from social groups and friends. Newly arrived students will not understand the cultural and social patterns of U.S. adolescents. At times, the demands of school may be at odds with the demands of home and family. Older ELLs, for example, may be expected to earn money to help the family, which detracts from time spent studying. Isolation and loneliness can deter the progress of language development. The older ELL has less time overall to achieve language equality with peers in the classroom and older learners face higher expectations. For these reasons, many older ELLs are frustrated in their language-learning attempts.

Error Correction

Error correction of ELLs is problematical. Parents of very young children generally do not correct the grammar of their children's utterances. They concentrate instead on the meaning of the utterance. When Anthony tells his Mom *Here pot*, she corrects him by saying *No, that's a scoop* and ignores the fact that his sentence lacks a verb form. Instead she models a fully correct sentence form, *That's a scoop.*

In school, however, teachers are torn by their desire to correct an ELL's incorrect grammar and an unwillingness to embarrass the student. Teachers might take a cue from Anthony's mom who responded to her son's utterances with grammatically correct, expanded sentences.

STUDENT: *It go down.*

TEACHER: *Yes, the metal sank in the water.*

Errors are best dealt with on a case-by-case basis—adapting our responses to the context of the utterance, the content requirements, as well as students' age, level, and need.

Oral language errors are frequently made because speaking gives little time to think about the grammar being used. The intent of the utterance is on conveying meaning to the hearer, and the speaker is not focusing on accuracy. For this reason, it is good policy for the teacher to respond to the meaning of the statement rather than to the speaker's grammar. Teachers can respond, however, by providing good modeling of an expanded grammatical utterance. When Marisol asked *Me go pee pee?* we restated her request and responded to it at the same time. *You want to go to the bathroom? Yes, go right ahead.* This response is similar to the responses of caretakers to children's first language grammatical errors. The correct modeling provides the ELL with the grammatical information at the moment when it is needed.

Some oral errors in young ELLs are developmental. Native-English speakers aged five to seven often make similar errors. The overgeneralization of the past tense *–ed* ending (e.g., *bringed*) and the addition of the *–s* plural (e.g., *mans*) are two examples. These errors will correct themselves as students grow and receive more input.

Older English learners need to develop oral accuracy quickly to be successful both academically and socially. For this reason, older learners may be ready to focus on accuracy in their oral language and may be grateful for feedback or lessons about frequent errors. Older learners are embarrassed by speech errors and they will want to learn how to avoid them. In addition, errors that are not corrected lead to **fossilization**, that is, they persist in speech and become impervious to change (Selinker, 1972). Teachers can attend to these errors in sensitive ways. For example, a teacher who notices that students are having trouble with subject-verb agreement might develop a task in which learners use language frames to answer questions about a picture. For example, the teacher might use a picture of family members making tamales (from *Making Tamales* by Carmen Lomas Garza in McCloskey & Stack, 1996, p. 136). Learners use a variety of verbs (*wear, wrap, stand, sit*, and *play*) to describe the picture in the present and past tense with different persons and numbers and receive specific feedback on how they use the language.

Errors that persist past the beginning stages of language acquisition are best dealt with in writing. Written errors can be responded to more analytically. Teachers can note constant errors and focus on them in small group minilessons.

Culture Shock

One factor that affects almost all newly arrived ELLs is culture shock. Culture shock occurs when the ELL begins to be aware of the mismatch between the second culture and first culture expectations. The identity of the individual is disrupted when old ways of thinking, feeling, and communicating are not available or severely taxed by the new culture. The result is a feeling of resentment at the new culture, anger, loneliness, frustration, profound sadness, and, occasionally, physical illness.

Four stages of culture shock are universally acknowledged.

- *Stage 1:* Brown (1992) describes the first stage as a time of excitement. The ELL feels euphoric about the new culture and is excited by all the new experiences in the surroundings.
- *Stage 2:* The second stage occurs as the learner experiences more differences between the first and second cultures. ELLs feel uncomfortable in their new surroundings where everything is difficult and frustrating. During this stage, learners cling to other students from their culture or those who speak the same language for a respite from the frustrations and unpleasant associations of the new culture. This stage is the most difficult for children in our schools. They are often absent or tune out instruction if they are in class. The teacher will notice that work was not completed, and many times classroom disruptions occur as the ELL's anger mounts. It is important to provide comfort in the form of a buddy who speaks the same language, if possible, or at least an accommodating friend.
- *Stage 3:* The third stage of culture shock may last for a long time. The ELL has made some gradual progress to adapting to the new culture, but not all problems have been solved. Some feelings of empathy for others in the second culture begin to develop at this time. Children who are accepted into peer groups in school are better able to pass through this phase of culture shock than those who are isolated from other students.
- *Stage 4:* The fourth stage of culture shock occurs when ELLs accept both cultures and combine them into their lives. They acculturate rather than assimilate into the new culture. At this stage, students enjoy being in the new culture and function well there. They may adopt the mainstream culture at school and follow the values of the home culture outside of school.

Christine Igoa (1995) helped her students to adapt to the new culture academically, psychologically, and culturally. The result was that many of her students were able to reach this fourth stage of culture shock—recovery. "If the new immigrant child can get over the emotional hurdle of accepting the new culture without rejecting his or her home culture, if the child can free himself or herself from the emotional burdens of loneliness, isolation, fear of ridicule, helplessness, and anxiety, it then becomes very easy to reach and teach the child" (Igoa, 1995, p. 146). Chapter three provides many practical ideas for easing children into acculturation. Table 2.2 highlights some of the factors affecting language development in positive and negative ways in school.

TABLE 2.2 What Are Positive and Negative Effects of Language Development in School?

	Positive Effects	Negative Effects
Language input	Student peers can help ELLs to acquire language even if the teacher is occupied elsewhere.	Language delays will occur without sufficient comprehensible input.
Classroom organization	Differentiated, student-centered classrooms promote language and content learning.	Teacher-centered frontal instruction limits the interactive possibilities of classrooms.
Content and language load	Teacher and community expectations hold ELLs to a high standard .	The heavy load can be overwhelming for ELLs unless the content is differentiated.
Academic vs. social language	ELLs are capable of acquiring a variety of language registers.	Academic language takes a long time to acquire/ learn but is essential for academic achievement.
Negative bias	ELLs bring diverse cultural and social perspectives to our classrooms.	ELLs are viewed negatively because they cannot speak English even though they may speak other languages.
Cognition, age, social, and cultural factors	Older ELLs bring literacy skills and prior education to help them acquire the language.	Older ELLs have less time to be successful students and may be isolated socially and culturally from their peers.
Error correction	Errors are sometimes an indication of language growth; teachers can use them as opportunities to model correct grammar.	Public correction of errors is embarrassing to students.
Culture shock	At first, ELLs will be euphoric about the new language and culture.	ELLs will experience an emotional roller coaster during the first three stages of culture shock.

WHAT STRATEGIES DO ELLs USE TO ACQUIRE LANGUAGES?

Children use problem-solving strategies to acquire and learn languages. Teachers who are aware of these processes can accelerate the language-acquisition process through support of these strategies, which fall into two broad categories: learning strategies and communication strategies. Language-learning strategies are "the conscious thoughts and behaviors used by learners with the explicit goal of improving their knowledge and understanding of the target language" (Cohen, 1998, p. 68). Communication strategies are used to help learners understand and express meaning for the purpose of communication (Piper, 2006). Children use similar strategies in both first language and second language acquisition environments. Some of these strategies lead children to create incorrect utterances in the new language. Rather than view these as errors, we can recognize them as the result of the child's generating hypotheses about the new language and testing those hypotheses in her or his communication.

Learning strategies are general cognitive strategies such as memorization, generalization, and inference. Learners use these strategies to gain meaning from oral language words and structures and then remember them for later use. Communication strategies include *overgeneralization, language transfer,* and avoidance or *simplification.* What are these strategies and how do they assist acquisition?

- **Overgeneralization** occurs when ELLs perceive patterns of language usage, generate a rule from many examples heard in the environment, and use the rule in a speaker-listener conversation. On occasion, the rule may be incorrect or partially correct. For example, when children perceive the *–ed* ending of English verbs, they often attach the ending to irregular verbs in incorrect ways: *runned, bringed*, and so on. The *–s* plural may be added to generate *sheeps* and *deers*. This strategy occurs in both first and second language acquisition. As we hear students use these overgeneralized rule forms, we realize that they have made important learning gains. In time, with more opportunities for meaningful input of the irregular forms, ELLs will acquire accurate grammar.
- **Language transfer** is a communication strategy by which ELLs use rules from their home languages to understand and speak the new language. Spanish-speaking children use language transfer when they place adjectives after nouns when speaking English (*truck big*). ELLs use transfer in a positive way when they anticipate that the new language will contain similar structures to the home language. Thus, learners will anticipate that English contains noun and verb forms because Spanish contains these forms. When the new language contains forms such as articles that do not exist in the target language (e.g., Chinese), students tend to eliminate those forms in their earliest utterances.
- ELLs use a **simplification** or avoidance communication strategy when they avoid speaking about complex topics, avoid using full grammatical utterances, or avoid using word forms that they do not yet know. Young ELLs, responding to questions such as *How old are you?* use a simplification strategy by responding simply *ten.* The learner answers the question very simply, and thus continues the conversation, which may in turn lead to additional meaningful input. Younger learners more easily use simplification than older students do. Classroom conversations may require older ELLs to speak about complex topics even though they are not yet capable of doing so in grammatically correct forms. Teachers can promote academic language use by providing a variety of formats to scaffold responses to teacher questions such as sentence frames, signal responses, written responses, or group responses.

ELLs who actively use learning and communication strategies are more successful as language learners and acquirers. Teachers who encourage and teach strategy use are providing children the tools they need to learn and acquire language while also learning classroom content.

WHAT ARE THE CHARACTERISTICS OF A CULTURALLY AND LINGUISTICALLY APPROPRIATE RESPONSE TO THE INTERVENTION (RTI) MODEL?

Response to intervention (RTI) models have been developed as a way to prevent academic failure for linguistically diverse students by providing them quality instruction and support (Klingner & Edwards, 2006). In the past, ELLs were disproportionally overrepresented in special education classes (Artiles, Trent, & Palmer, 2004; Donovan & Cross, 2002) as schools struggled to find appropriate methods of educating students with limited English language skills. RTI provides a framework for assessing, instructing, and providing intensive interventions when needed for these students.

RTI models can differ in various ways, but the overall multitiered structure of these programs remains the same. A continuum of services that become increasingly intensive and specialized is provided to students. In Tier 1, the core curriculum is taught to all students in the general education classroom, and ELLs receive language instruction by an appropriately certified teacher. Tier 2 identifies students who require more intensive intervention to supplement classroom instruction. Intervention may be in the form of special instruction, small-group instruction, increased time for language instruction, specialized materials, or any combination of these. Tiers 1 and 2 are recursive in that students may move back and forth between these tiers at various points in the school year. Tier 3 may involve students who have an individualized education plan (IEP) and who receive specialized services for identified disabilities. These special interventions are more intensive than those possible in Tier 2 and are delivered by specially trained personnel.

RTI models that are effective with ELLs are culturally and linguistically responsive. They are characterized by (Echevarría & Vogt, 2011):

- High-quality, evidence-based, and language-rich classroom instruction that is consistent and effective, delivered by highly qualified content teachers who have received professional development to enable them to understand how to teach language to ELLs effectively.
- Frequent, continuous, and varied assessment for benchmark/screening, skill diagnosis, and progress monitoring of both language and content knowledge and skills.
- Documentation of assessment data in order to make decisions about placement, instruction, and nature/duration of interventions.
- Interventions that are implemented quickly with respect to cultural considerations and with fidelity to the specific research-based approach.
- Strong administrative support.

WHAT ARE THE CHARACTERISTICS OF AN EFFECTIVE CLASSROOM ENVIRONMENT FOR ELLs?

In an effective learning environment for English language learners, aspects of the first language environment are present: abundant and meaningful language input, atmosphere of trust and high expectation, and opportunities for output and interaction. In addition, teachers make connections to their students' cultures, prior learning, and learning styles. Instruction is differentiated in ways that will help ELLs to learn language as well as content. ABC language teaching and learning techniques combine aspects of first language acquisition and elements of school learning that help ELLs achieve success. RTI programs that encompass these aspects of language acquisition and language learning provide appropriate Tier 1 and Tier 2 environments for ELLs. Table 2.3 is illustrative of these effective learning environments.

WHAT ARE THE CHARACTERISTICS OF CULTURALLY AND LINGUISTICALLY APPROPRIATE TIER 1 INSTRUCTION FOR ELLs?

Tier 1 instruction for ELLs has all of the characteristics of the effective classroom environment described previously. Teachers can enrich their classrooms linguistically by incorporating aspects of first language acquisition in their instruction in Tier 1. See the RTI Tier 1 Sampler for selected specific ideas.

WHAT ARE THE CHARACTERISTICS OF CULTURALLY AND LINGUISTICALLY APPROPRIATE TIER 2 INSTRUCTION FOR ELLs?

After a few weeks, ELLs begin to understand basic commands and routines in the classroom. Soon they begin to speak in one to two word utterances to indicate personal requests, respond to greetings, and answer simple WH (what, when, where, who) or yes/no questions. In a few months, learners attempt to initiate language using simple sentence structures and comprehend one-step directions. If students are not making gains in their social language skills, a Tier 2 intervention may be appropriate. See the RTI Tier 2 Sampler for selected specific ideas.

TABLE 2.3 What Is an Effective Learning Environment for ELLs?

1. **Principles 1 and 2— Active Engagement and Cultural Relevance: A Positive, Supportive Learning Environment**
   - The teacher develops personal relationships with students and seeks to learn about their cultures, languages, ethnicity, family, and personal interests.
   - Multiple perspectives and viewpoints are honored so that students feel valued, supported, and respected in the class.
   - Classroom routines and rules are developed collaboratively and serve to help students feel secure.
   - The classroom climate enables students to feel comfortable when stating needs or requesting help, and the teacher fosters equal participation among all students in the class.
   - Students support each other's learning in small group and paired interactions.
   - All learners are actively engaged in the learning experience.

2. **Principles 3, 4, and 6—Collaboration, Learning Strategies, and Comprehensible Input with Scaffolding: Abundant Input and Output Opportunities**
   - The classroom is "language rich" in that many opportunities are structured for meaningful, comprehensible input from the teacher, peers, technology, texts, and other speaker-hearers in the school. Input is scaffolded to promote comprehensibility at an appropriate and challenging learning level.
   - The classroom is interactive with many structured opportunities for students to collaborate with academic language in partner conversations, small group assignments, teacher-supported conversations, oral reporting, role-plays, and debate.
   - Learners are taught strategies to increase their abilities to interact, collaborate, and share in the instructional conversation.

3. **Principle 5 Differentiation—Expectations of Success with Varied Approaches to Learning**
   - The teacher demonstrates a belief that all students are capable of learning academic language and content to a high level.
   - The teacher demonstrates that success is related to effort and praises students for effort and persistence.
   - Language lessons are structured to accommodate a variety of language, literacy, and cognitive levels to ensure that all learners will experience success.
   - The teacher uses a variety of instructional strategies to respond to students' various readiness levels, language proficiencies, cultures, interests, and learning styles.
   - Student tasks and texts are culturally relevant, interesting, and challenging but scaffolded effectively to ensure successful participation and maximum learning.
   - Classroom space, grouping patterns, use of technology, and instructional strategies are planned but flexible.

4. **Principles 7 and 8—Prior Knowledge and Content Integration: Engaging and Comprehensible Content**
   - The teacher has prioritized the curriculum to focus on the essential knowledge, understandings, and skills of the discipline.
   - Students are aware of what they should know or be able to do with language and content at the end of the lesson.
   - Content instruction integrates the academic language needed to read, write, speak, and understand the essential knowledge of the discipline.
   - Content is meaningful and relevant to student cultures and experiences and promotes high levels of thought.
   - Content is scaffolded to enhance comprehensibility, retention, application, and transfer to other disciplines.

5. **Principle 9—Clear, Appropriate Goals and Feedback: Frequent and Varied Assessment to Inform Instruction**
   - Assessment occurs before, during, and after instruction in order to determine student understanding of content objectives and growth in language objectives.
   - Multiple forms of assessment are used frequently and systematically to monitor student progress and to enable students to better demonstrate what they know or are able to do as a result of instruction.
   - Frequent feedback empowers students while the teacher encourages goal setting and self-assessment to help students develop responsibility for their own learning.
   - Assessment data are analyzed frequently, providing the teacher with a holistic picture of each student's learning style and development and to aid in designing future instruction.

RTI TIER 1 SAMPLER

- Learn the preferred names of your students and pronounce them correctly.
- Speak to new ELLs even when they are unable to respond. Embed your language with gestures related to "here and now" ongoing actions.
- Establish personal relationships with new non-English speaking students by using nonlinguistic gestures such as a smile, a wink, a "thumbs up" sign, a wave of hello or good-bye, a head nod, an "A-OK" sign, and so on.
- Assign a trustworthy student to accompany new learners to the playground, the next class, and the cafeteria.
- Take the time to personally show new students the location of bathrooms and other important areas of the school.
- Provide new students appropriate school materials if necessary and demonstrate how they can be stored in a desk or cubby.
- Name items that are used frequently in the class. Point to these objects and use repetition with directed eye gaze to help new learners focus on the vocabulary. Provide sentence frames for asking and answering: *What's this? That's a _____.*
- Write the class schedule on the side of the board. Use pictures to show special classes or events. Point to these pictures when lesson changes occur.
- Identify two or three patterned phrases that you use routinely to signify activities: *Clean up time! Time for lunch/gym/music. Take out your _____.*
- Communicate with parents frequently on the emotional and social progress of new English learners.

RTI TIER 2 SAMPLER

- Schedule daily language input sessions between you (or the ESL teacher) and the child for approximately 15 minutes.
- Sit quietly with a new student apart from the class. Talk in simple, short sentences about "here and now" topics. For example, for a young child: *Oh, you're wearing new shoes today. Two new shoes* (pointing and gesturing). *Your shoes are brown and white. Here's the brown color. Here's the white color. Your shoes have laces. Can you tie the laces? (Nodding yes response.)* For an older child you might say: *Oh, look* (pointing out the window)! *It's snowing. Can you see the snow? The snow is cold. The snow is white. Snow is white and cold. I like the snow. Do you like the snow?*
- Show a picture and talk about it, pointing to objects as you name them or comment on them. Try to use pictures that are integrated with content learning or with the student's native culture.
- Share pictures of yourself and family with a new learner. Point to the people and tell who they are. Encourage the student to bring in pictures of his or her own family. Provide sentence frames to identify family members: *This is _____. _____ is my _____.*
- Use directional language requiring an action response from the learner (e.g., *Show me the board. Show me the window. Do you see the door? Show me the door. Write your name on the board. Erase your name from the board. Give me the _____.* Integrate content related items if possible.
- Provide paper and markers and direct the student to draw simple pictures using the names of shapes and colors. Provide sample shapes in varied colors and say *Draw a yellow circle on the _____. Draw it here in the corner* (pointing). *Now draw a green square. Draw the square in the middle of the paper* (pointing). Relate this language to content learning if possible.
- Dictate simple math computation for a new student following a model. For example, *Write the problem 2 plus 7. Write the problem 22 plus 3.*
- Work with two or three learners to model simple requests with action responses: *Put your hands on your head. Clap your hands two times. Turn around.*
- Work with two or three learners who can give each other simple directions with an action response. *Pick up the pencil. Put the pencil on the book.* Use content-related pictures or objects if possible with sentence frames.
- Provide opportunities for learners to use language-learning programs on the computer.

Questions for Reflection

1. Why will children learning a second language in school find that task so difficult when we know that all children learn their first languages with almost no effort?
2. Of all the factors affecting acquisition in classrooms, which ones do you feel are the most difficult to overcome? Why?

3. What suggestions would you give to a new teacher in your school who is trying to create effective classroom experiences for new English language learners?

Activities for Further Learning

1. We have seen that language input is critical to language development. Discuss this notion with your classmates. Cite opportunities for language input in a primary classroom, an elementary classroom, and a secondary classroom. What obstacles do you foresee in providing sufficient input for ELLs? What are some practical suggestions for overcoming these obstacles?
2. Observe two children at play for fifteen minutes. Take notes on the language the children use during your observation. Bring your notes to class and compare your observations with your colleagues. What have you discovered about the children's language? What verb tenses are used? What question words? Do the children use many nouns and adjectives? Does the type of play change the nature of the language?
3. With your classmates, use your observation notes to design an activity for ELLs in the classroom that can be accomplished with similar, simple language items. Create a different activity for older learners.
4. Design a content-based card game for children that helps them to learn the following English verbs: *pick up, put down, take,* and *give.*
5. Interview a person who has learned English while attending a public school in the United States. Ask questions as to the effect of the following on her or his language development: age, home language, the classroom environment, the teacher, friends and social group, error correction, and literacy in the first language. Be prepared to describe the positive and negative effects of the factors on your interviewee.
6. Look at Table 2.2 and consider how each of the language development factors will affect the organization of your classroom and the way in which you instruct children. Consider an elementary classroom and a secondary classroom. How would the grade-level differences lead to a change in your classroom organization and instruction?
7. Krashen's definition of comprehensible input and Vygotsky's (1962) zone of proximal development are similar notions. They presuppose a teacher or knowledgeable peer can assist in language development. Describe how these notions could be practically implemented in a classroom.
8. Cummins's definitions of social language (BICS) and academic language (CALP) are useful in helping teachers understand different registers of English. Identify examples of social and academic language that might be encountered in a classroom. Provide examples of ways to scaffold the academic language so ELLs can understand it.

Suggested Reading

Cameron, L. (2001). *Teaching languages to young learners.* New York: Cambridge University Press.

Cowley, G. (1997). The language explosion. *Newsweek special edition: Your child:* 16–22. This is an informative and easy-to-read description of the first language acquisition process.

Cummins, J. (1992). Language proficiency, bilingualism, and academic achievement. In P. A. Richard-Amato and M. A. Snow (Eds.), *The multicultural classroom: Readings for content area teachers.* New York, NY: Longman. In this classic article, Cummins defines context-reduced academic language and offers implications for both teaching and testing.

Cummins, J. (1996). *Negotiating identities: Education for empowerment in a diverse society.* Ontario, CA: California Association for Bilingual Education. Cummins proposes a framework for analyzing the patterns of educational outcome observed in different world contexts. He argues that students in subordinated groups will succeed academically only to the extent that patterns of interaction in school challenge and reverse those of society at large that subordinate some communities.

Cummins, J. (2000). *Language, power, and pedagogy: Bilingual children in the crossfire.* Clevedon, UK and Buffalo, NY: Multilingual Matters. This is Cummins's latest effort to inform practice with theory and enable theory to be informed by practice. He searches here for coherence through an integrated interdisciplinary perspective that brings disparate fields into dialogue with each other.

Dudley-Marling, C., & Searle, D. (1991). *When students have time to talk: Creating contexts for learning language.* Portsmouth, NH: Heinemann. An academic but readable text describing both first language acquisition in home and at school. Topics include strategic approaches for teaching language, encouraging extended conversations, and using language for a variety of purposes and audiences. There is also a chapter about second language learners and their unique learning needs.

Heath, S. B. (1992). Sociocultural contexts of language development: Implications for the classroom. In P. A. Richard-Amato and M. A. Snow (Eds.), *The multicultural classroom: Readings for content area teachers.* New York, NY: Longman. Heath discusses the role of home and family in the development of literacy skills for language minority students. She presents examples from major language groups on the differences between language usage in the home and mainstream language usage of the school. She argues that success in school depends on a wide range of oral and written language usage.

Krashen, S. D. (2003). *Explorations in language acquisition and use: The Taipei lectures.* Portsmouth, NH: Heinemann.

Krashen, S. D., & Terrell, T. D. (1983). *The natural approach: Language acquisition in the classroom,* San Francisco, CA: Alemany Press. This gives Krashen's classic explanation of natural language learning coupled with ideas for incorporating this approach in schools.

Lightbown, P., & Spada, N. M. (2006). *How languages are learned* (3rd ed.). Oxford, UK: Oxford University Press. This clear and useful text explains language theory with the teacher in mind.

Scarcella, R. (1992). Providing culturally sensitive feedback. In P. A. Richard-Amato and M. A. Snow (Eds.), *The multicultural classroom: Readings for content area teachers.* New York, NY: Longman. This article provides many examples of the kinds of cross-cultural differences learners will encounter in our schools and communities. Scarcella offers ideas for giving helpful feedback to students in order to minimize cultural differences.

References

Artiles, A. J., Trent, S., & Palmer, J. (2004). Culturally diverse students in special education: Legacies and prospects. In J. A. Banks and C. M. Banks (Eds.), *Handbook of research on multicultural education* (2nd ed.) (pp. 716–735), San Francisco, CA: Jossey Bass.

Berman, P., Minicucci, C., McLaughlin, B., Nelson, B., & Woodworth, K. (1995). *School reform and student diversity: Case studies of exemplary practices for English language learner students.* Santa Cruz, CA: National Center for Research on Cultural Diversity and Second Language Learning and B. W. Associates.

Brown, H. D. (1992). Sociocultural factors in teaching language minority students. In P. A. Richard-Amato and M. A. Snow (Eds.), *The multicultural classroom: Readings for content-area teachers.* New York, NY: Longman.

Caldéron, M., & and Carreon, A. (1994). Educators and students use cooperative learning to become biliterate and bicultural. *Cooperative Learning Magazine, 4:* 6–9.

Caldéron, M., Hertz-Lazarowitz, R., & Slavin, R. (1998). Effects of bilingual cooperative integrated reading and composition on students making the transition from Spanish to English. *The Elementary School Journal, 99:* 153–165.

Chomsky, N. (1957). *Syntactic structures.* The Hague, Netherlands: Mouton.

Chomsky, N. (1975). *Reflections on language.* New York, NY: Pantheon.

Cohen, A. D. (1998). *Strategies in learning and using a second language.* London, UK: Longman.

Cohen, G. L., & Garcia, J. (2008). Identity, belonging, and achievement. *Current Directions in Psychological Science, 17:* 365–369.

Collier, V. (1989). How long? A synthesis of research in academic achievement in a second language. *TESOL Quarterly, 23:* 509–531.

Cummins, J. (1980). The construct of language proficiency in bilingual education. In J. E. Alatis (Ed.), *Georgetown University roundtable on languages and linguistics* (pp. 76–93). Washington, DC: Georgetown University Press.

Cummins, J. (1999). BICS and CALP: Clarifying the distinction. (ERIC Document Reproduction Service No. 438 551).

Doherty, R. W., Hilberg, R. S., Pinal, A., & Tharp, R. G. (2003). Five standards and student achievement. *NABE Journal of Research and Practice, 1*(1): 1–24.

Donovan, S., & Cross, C. (2002). *Minority students in special and gifted education.* Washington, DC: National Academy Press.

Dulay, H., & Burt, M. (1974). Natural sequences in child second language acquisition. *Language Learning, 24:* 37–53.

Echevarría, J., & Vogt, M. (2011). *Response to intervention and English learners: Making it happen.* Boston: Pearson.

Harklau, L. (1994). ESL and mainstream classes: Contrasting second language learning contexts. *TESOL Quarterly, 28:* 241–272.

Harklau, L. (2000). From the "good kids" to the "worst": Representations of English language learners across educational settings. *TESOL Quarterly, 34*(1): 35–67.

Holt, J. (1964). *How children fail.* New York, NY: Dell.

Igoa, C. (1995). *The inner world of the immigrant child.* Mahwah, NJ: Lawrence Erlbaum.

Izumi, S., & Bigelow, M. (2000). Does output promote noticing and second language acquisition? *TESOL Quarterly, 34*(2): 239–278.

Jensen, E. (1998). *Teaching with the brain in mind.* Alexandria, VA: ASCD.

Klingner, J. K., & Edwards, P. A. (2006). Cultural considerations with response-to-intervention models. *Reading Research Quarterly, 41:* 108–117.

Klingner, J. K., & Vaughn, S. (2000). The helping behaviors of fifth graders while using collaborative strategic reading during ESL content classes. *TESOL Quarterly, 34*(1): 69–98.

Krashen, S. D., & Terrell, T. D. (1983). *The natural approach: Language acquisition in the classroom.* San Francisco, CA: Alemany.

Labinowicz, E. (1980). *The Piaget primer: Thinking, learning, teaching.* Reading, MA: Addison- Wesley.

Levine, L. N. "Mother-child communication and the acquisition of deixis." PhD diss., New York University, 1981.

Lindfors, J. W. (1987). *Children's language and learning.* Upper Saddle River, NJ: Merrill/Prentice Hall.

Long, M., & Porter, P. (1985). Group work, interlanguage talk, and second language acquisition. *TESOL Quarterly, 19:* 207–227.

McCloskey, M. L., & Stack, L. (1996). *Voices in Literature: An anthology for middle/high school ESOL* (Bronze). Boston, MA: Heinle and Heinle.

McLaughlin, B. (1987). *Theories of second language acquisition.* London, UK: Edward Arnold.

McNeill, D. (1975). The contribution of experience. In S. Rogers (Ed.), *Children and language: Readings in early language and socialization.* London, UK: Oxford University Press.

Montecel, M. R., & Cortez, J. D. (2002). Successful bilingual education programs: Development and the dissemination of criteria to identify promising exemplary practices in bilingual education at the national level. *Bilingual Research Journal, 26:* 1–22.

Ovando, C. J., Combs, M. C., & Collier, V. P. (2006) *Bilingual and ESL classrooms: Teaching in multicultural contexts* (4th ed.). Boston: McGraw-Hill.

Paley, V. (1981). *Wally's stories.* Cambridge, MA: Harvard University Press.

Pica, T., Lincoln-Porter, F., Paninos, D., & Linnell, J. (1996). Language learner's interaction: How does it address the input, output, and feedback needs of L2 learners? *TESOL Quarterly, 30*(1): 59–84.

Piper, T. (2006). *Language and learning: The home and school years* (4th ed.). Upper Saddle River, NJ: Prentice Hall.

Selinker, L. (1972). Interlanguage. *International Review of Applied Linguistics, 10:* 209–231.

Snow, C. E. (1977). Mothers' speech research: From input to interaction. In C. E. Snow and C. A. Ferguson (Eds.), *Talking to children: Language input and acquisition.* New York, NY: Cambridge University Press.

Swain, M. (1985). Communicative competence: Some roles of comprehensible input and comprehensible output in its development. In S. M. Gass and C. G. Madden (Eds.), *Input in second language acquisition* (pp. 235–253). Rowley, MA: Newbury House.

Tikunoff, W. (1985). *Applying significant bilingual instructional features in the classroom.* Rosslyn, VA: National Clearinghouse for Bilingual

Education. (ERIC Document Reproduction Service No. ED 338 106).

Urzua, C. (1981). *Talking purposefully.* Silver Spring, MD: Institute of Modern Languages, Inc.

Vygotsky, L. S. (1962). *Thought and language.* Cambridge, MA: MIT Press.

Weeks, T. E. (1979). *Born to talk.* Rowley, MA: Newbury House.

MyEducationLab™

Go to the Topic, Listening and Speaking, in the MyEducationLab (www.myeducationlab.com) for your course, where you can:

- Find learning outcomes for Listening and Speaking along with the national standards that connect to these outcomes.
- Complete Assignments and Activities that can help you more deeply understand the chapter content.
- Apply and practice your understanding of the core teaching skills identified in the chapter with the Building Teaching Skills and Dispositions learning units.
- Examine challenging situations and cases presented in the IRIS Center Resources.
- Check your comprehension on the content covered in the chapter by going to the Study Plan in the Book Resources for your text. Here you will be able to take a chapter quiz, receive feedback on your answers, and then access Review, Practice, and Enrichment activities to enhance your understanding of chapter content.
- **A+RISE** A+RISE® Standards2Strategy™ is an innovative and interactive online resource that offers new teachers in grades K-12 just in time, research-based instructional strategies that meet the linguistic needs of ELLs as they learn content, differentiate instruction for all grades and abilities, and are aligned to Common Core Elementary Language Arts standards (for the literacy strategies) and to English language proficiency standards in WIDA, Texas, California, and Florida.

CHAPTER 3

Culturally Responsive Instruction: Connecting with Home Culture

Lynn King is a kindergarten teacher at an elementary school in Florida. Pelican Bay Elementary is located in an agricultural area, and many of its students come from migratory families. Lynn's classroom of eighteen children contains twelve children who are English language learners.

Although Lynn has been at Pelican Bay for ten years, she is constantly learning about the cultures of the children in her classroom. She recently recalled a parent conference with the father of one of her students, a child who was having difficulty conforming to classroom rules and routines. Lynn suggested to Miguel's father (through an interpreter) that she could send home a note when Miguel has had a bad day at school so that he would be able to follow through at home.

"What can I do to him at home?" the father asked.

"Well," Lynn responded, "you might take away one of his toys for a day or two."

"He doesn't have any toys," the father replied.

"Then don't let him watch TV for a while," Lynn said.

"The TV has been broken for a long time, and I don't have the money to get it repaired," the father said. "Miguel never watches TV."

"Okay, then don't let him ride his bike."

"He doesn't have a bike either, Miss King."

Lynn was running out of ideas but she finally said, "Then don't let him go outside to play."

The father explained patiently, "We don't have any air conditioning in our house and it's very hot. The kids have to play outside because it's too hot for them to stay inside."

Lynn told us this story because for her it was a turning point in her role as a teacher of migrant students. Lynn realized that she needed to learn more about the cultures of her students and to become a cultural mediator for them.

How do teachers make connections among their students, their families, the school, and the community?

··

- What is culturally responsive instruction?
- What are the attributes of teachers who are cultural mediators?
- How do teachers connect to the homes and families of their students?
- How can the school community support the education of English language learners?
- How can the community outside the school support the education of ELLs?

CULTURALLY RESPONSIVE INSTRUCTION

Lynn King's determination to become a **cultural mediator** for her students led her to start exploring the notion of culture and what it meant to her and to her students. Nieto and Bode (2007, p. 171) define **culture** as "the values, traditions, world view, and social and political relationships created, shared, and transformed by a group of people bound together by a common history, geographic location, language, social class, religion, or other shared identity."

For Lynn, **culturally responsive instruction** has begun to mean more than celebrating food, holidays, and clothing. Miguel's father taught her that family relationships, communication styles, values, and attitudes are also components of culture. Acquiring the skills, attitudes, and knowledge to enable her to effectively communicate and interact with individuals from other cultures would be an ongoing process that would engage her cognitively, affectively, and behaviorally during the rest of her teaching career.

As the Nieto and Bode (2007) definition indicates, **culture** is not a monolithic, stagnant concept. Nor are individuals from a common culture homogeneous. Culture is fluid, ever-changing, and nondeterministic. It consists of regularities in the experiences of individuals living in the world and in the schema of those people who share in those regularities. Culture is the summary of those regularities (Atkinson, 1999).

Teachers who are cultural mediators act as translators of culture and as guides to the invisible patterns that connect groups of people. Lynn's European American middle-class experiences did not prepare her well for teaching young migrant Mexican children of agricultural workers in the citrus industry of south Florida. She has resolved to explore the links between language, literacy, and culture and to change her instructional practices both in and out of the classroom in order to be a strong advocate for the children under her care.

Lynn is learning different ways of dealing with her students and with their families. She is learning to acknowledge the differences that her students bring with them to school. This includes differences in their genders, races, social classes, family structures, school experiences, religions, learning styles, and languages. She is learning that these differences affect the way that her students learn. And, finally, she is learning that accepting their differences also means making provisions for them in her instructional program (Nieto & Bode, 2007).

WHAT ARE THE FEATURES OF CULTURALLY RESPONSIVE INSTRUCTION?

Communication of High Expectations for All Learners

The social and cultural identities of students form the basis for school achievement and for their cultural identities. Cognitive development, academic development, and language development are all related to the extent to which individual students and their cultures feel valued by the school community (Collier, 1995). Students who feel a disconnect with the dominant school culture experience emotional and psychological distress leading to poor school achievement, behavioral problems, low motivation, and dropout status (Osterman, 2000).

Research indicates that the racial, ethnic, and gender stereotypes that lessen motivation in learners can be mitigated through simple teacher manipulations. Intellectual achievement is malleable (Aronson, Fried, & Good, 2002) and can be affected by subtle factors. Walton and Cohen (2007) found that students who felt a sense of belonging with high achievement groups had an increased motivation to learn. Students assigned to the "numbers group" or identified as having the same birthday as a math major increased their persistence in solving math puzzles by 70 percent. Other social bonds, such as being told they were "very good arithmetic students" (Miller, Brickman, & Bolen, 1975) led students to outperform their peers.

Subtle factors undermine achievement. Stereotype threats were found to exist for students in nondominant racial groups. When these students were given standardized tests said to measure intellectual ability, the group hearing this purpose performed worse than a control group that did not hear it (Steele, Spencer, & Aronson, 2002). Because people derive their self-worth from their racial, ethnic, or cultural group, students are vulnerable to any perceived threats to that group in ways that chronically damage their sense of identity. Even when others may not perceive a situation to be threatening, members of nondominant groups are hypervigilant to the threat of being viewed through the lens of a stereotype (Cohen & Garcia, 2005).

Learning within an Affirming Cultural Context

By creating a sense of cultural acceptance in the classroom, teachers validate their students' self-worth and show respect for their languages. They assist learners in developing new cultural identities in response to the new culture.

A student's cultural identity can be shaped from within and from without. It is both "self-given" and "other ascribed" (Sheets, 1999, p. 94). One's family and community contribute to a "self-given" identity. For example, a student may identify as White or Mestizo (mixed European and Indigenous ancestry) in Latin America only to become "colorized" when immigrating to the United States (Arriaza, 2004). Asian students also experience a change from White to non-White status and lose their ethnic identity as Japanese, Chinese, or Thai when they are lumped into the collective "Asian" pot in the U.S. culture (Lee, 1999). One Korean-American student recalled:

> *I used to think I was White . . . . This was when I lived in a small town . . . . Then in fourth grade I moved here. I saw that Asians were treated like the scum of the earth. I thought that wasn't going to happen to me. I don't have an accent. I have White friends. But . . . . people called me chink. They called me chink to my face* (Lee, 1996, p. 110).

The **cultural dissonance** that occurs when our deeply held values come into conflict with other, differing values leads to an uncomfortable sense of discord, confusion, conflict, and anxiety. These changes in cultural dynamics are often unexpected and not understandable, especially to children. Differing values conflict over a wide array of beliefs, but many of them relate to the differences between individualistic and collectivist cultures:

- The emphasis on the individual vs. the group.
- The student as an individual vs. a member of a family.
- The emphasis on personal property vs. shared property.
- The emphasis on impersonal (written) vs. personal (oral) communication.
- The emphasis on individual effort and reward vs. group effort and reward.
- The emphasis on independence vs. interdependence.
- The emphasis on efficiency vs. personal relationships.

Teachers can mitigate cultural dissonance in their classrooms when they recognize the differences in cultures and adapt their curriculum and instruction to include additional diverse practices.

The goal for our students is **acculturation**—the ability to be bicultural and live in a world viewed through two sets of cultural lenses. Acculturated students are able to take part in and understand the mainstream culture without giving up the traditions and values of their home culture. They have not traded one culture for another (**assimilation**) but have become enriched by the positive values that the new culture brings into their lives.

The good news is that racial attitudes are fairly fluid until late childhood (Branch, 1999). Because of this, teachers can affect the cultural identities of students from diverse cultures and shape identity development among students from the dominant culture by promoting equitable interactions within schools and by using culturally responsive instruction.

Culturally Responsive Instructional Practices

Culturally responsive instruction recognizes and utilizes students' language and culture. Teachers acknowledge their students' differences as well as their commonalities. They plan for instruction based on student experiences and strengths. They are committed to act as agents of change within the school and collaborate effectively with the wider school community to promote equity and sociocultural consciousness. Specifically, they do the following (Gay, 2000; Ladson-Billings, 1994; Nieto, 1996; and Banks & Banks, 2004):

- Revise curriculum to include a wide variety of viewpoints from differing cultural perspectives.
- Seek out instructional materials that portray the diversity of the classroom.
- Learn about their students' cultures and languages to form a basis for instruction.
- Utilize instructional practices that are compatible with their students' cultures and experiences.
- Promote equity and mutual respect in the classroom.

- Motivate students to participate actively in their learning.
- Share the constructionist view that all students can learn at a high level.
- Assess student achievement validly.
- Encourage students to think critically and independently.
- Challenge students to strive for excellence.

Teacher as Cultural Mediator

Teachers like Lynn develop the attributes that enable them to create effective learning environments for children of diverse cultures. These teachers actively seek to become cultural mediators by increasing their personal knowledge about diversity (Villegas and Lucas, 2002). They:

- **Explore their own personal histories** and membership in various groups.
- **Believe that difference is the "norm"** and that no one group is more competent than any other.
- **Learn about the histories** of the diverse groups in their classrooms.
- **Visit student families** and communities.
- **Understand how culture affects** the teaching/learning process.
- **Help students expand their knowledge** of their own culture and develop an appreciation for differences in others.
- **Create an atmosphere** in the classroom in which cultural differences are respected and explored.
- **Communicate that all cultures** have their own integrity, validity, and coherence.
- **Draw upon the cultural experiences** of children and parents, and include this authentic, relevant perspective in the curriculum.
- **Adapt instructional practices** to accommodate varied learning styles, building on students' strengths, and avoiding judgments that might negatively impact the achievement gains of students.

Gay (2000) has a similar outline of the roles and responsibilities of the teacher as a cultural mediator. These roles define teachers as the following:

Cultural organizers: creating a variety of learning environments in the classroom to reflect the styles and preferences of the learners.

Cultural mediators: honoring other cultures, clarifying new cultural concepts, combating prejudice, and talking about cultural differences.

Orchestrators of social contracts: helping children adapt to the culture of the classroom while creating a classroom culture that is compatible to the learners.

Culturally responsive instruction may provide the best learning conditions for all learners because it reduces student frustrations in the classroom and therefore limits the amount of unacceptable behavior occurring there (Hollins, 1996). Culturally responsive classrooms accomplish this by encouraging multiple viewpoints among learners. Instruction is based upon students' prior knowledge. Learning experiences that are highly relevant to the learners and differentiated for their language proficiencies are created. Teachers allow for diverse ways of knowing and learning as well as multiple possibilities for sharing knowledge and representing an understanding of the content.

Such changes are not easy to accomplish. North American classrooms are not traditionally structured to accommodate diversity. The lowering of cognitive challenge during instruction, the singular focus on basic skill development, and the limited exposure to sophisticated narrative structures in texts are some of the accommodations made for English language learners by teachers who have had little training in or experience with cultural diversity. ELLs in these classes may be called on less frequently, not encouraged to elaborate on their responses, and not challenged to develop higher-order thinking skills. They are rewarded for being "nice" but not expected to learn at a high level.

Some consequences of cultural illiteracy on the part of teachers are reported in a study by Willett (1995) of three first-graders, the children of Chinese families enrolled in an English-dominant classroom. The children (a boy and two girls) experienced differential access to achievement because of the socialization style of the classroom. The two girls were seated together and worked cooperatively throughout the year on their phonics workbooks. They were quiet and busy, supported each other in their learning goals, and appealed to other girls in the class to help them on occasion. The lone boy, Xavier, was seated apart from the girls and was not allowed to get out of his seat to solicit their help. In addition, the boys in the classroom were competitive rather than cooperative with each other and would not provide any help on the phonics seatwork. Xavier had to rely on the teacher for help far more often than the girls did. He came to be viewed as needy while the girls, who were seen as independent workers, held a higher status in the class. Eventually, Xavier was taken out of the classroom for extra help in an **English language development (ELD)** workbook, further reducing his status in the class. Although he scored the same as the two girls on the Bilingual Syntax Measure at the end of the school year, he was retained in the ELD class but the girls were not.

Why did the girls succeed while Xavier was deemed less successful? All of the children benefited from the routine nature of the task—completing pages in a phonics workbook—that was repetitive in its structure. But the girls had the additional assistance of a collaborative relationship and a cooperative learning environment. This greatly increased their confidence as learners and earned them esteem in the status hierarchy of the classroom.

What could a cultural mediator have done to change the outcome for these children? The teacher could have tried some of the following techniques:

- Create a safe environment by reducing competition and encouraging all of the children to negotiate meaning with their peers.
- Encourage children to use their native languages in class when seeking help with content learning.
- Talk to students about their learning and ask them to think of ways to help develop academic competency.
- Encourage children to use social interaction as a means of summarizing, organizing, brainstorming, and reflecting upon new learning.
- Talk to parents about their child's learning style and reactions to the classroom.

Indeed, changes in the organization of the classroom have dramatic effects on learners of every age. See Table 3.1 for an explanation of the five principles developed by the Center for Research on Education Diversity and Excellence or CREDE (2001). Classroom examples illustrate the CREDE principles in action.

Instructional Conversations Provide Excellent Opportunities for Students to Learn Academic Language

TABLE 3.1 CREDE Principles for Classroom Organization with Classroom Examples

CREDE Principles	Classroom Examples
1. *Joint Productive Activity:* This principle echoes the thinking of Vygotsky (1978) that learning occurs when an adult or expert peer assists a learner to higher achievement levels by working together toward a common goal or product. Through a focused activity, teacher and learner create a common culture grounded in the learning experience even though they do not share the same home culture.	When Shelly Sanders, a fifth-grade teacher at a migrant school in Florida, works in the school garden with the fifth-grade garden club, she is engaged in the type of joint productive activity that helps these children make the connections between their migrant agricultural experiences and their school science learning.
2. *Challenging Activities:* ELLs are able to learn at a high level when their teachers believe in their abilities and view them as "knowers" rather than as having a deficit. Children in classrooms today must be challenged to learn to high standards and supported in their achievement of those standards by carefully crafted lessons that build incrementally on a foundation of student success.	Xavier's experiences in first grade phonics occurred not because he was unable to learn phonics but because his teachers did not believe that he could and so did not structure the classroom to facilitate his learning. The cooperative, collaborative experiences of his Chinese female classmates helped them to achieve at a high level.
3. *Instructional Conversation:* Group discussions are usually not helpful to ELLs in mainstream classrooms. ELLs may lag behind the other students in their comprehension of the language that swirls around them. They feel disconnected from the group and hesitant to participate. The instructional conversation, however, can be an excellent technique for including all learners toward a learning goal.	The instructional conversation requires a classroom arrangement that accommodates a teacher meeting with a small group of students. They might be talking at a lab table in biology or meeting for a guided-reading session or working on a social studies project in the corner of the room. The teacher has a clear learning goal in mind and encourages all of the students to express their views and justify them. The teacher assists by questioning, restating, probing, encouraging, and praising. The students do most of the talking in these conversations and the teacher does a great deal of listening. The end of the conversation yields a resulting product: an oral summary, a listing of procedures, or a resolution of a problem.
4. *Language Development:* One of the most important changes in a content teacher's instructional load is the inclusion of language objectives in the content lesson plan. Purposeful instruction in the language of the academic content is required for students to learn at a high level. ELLs cannot be successful in math class without specific knowledge of the vocabulary and syntax of math. By incorporating academic language learning into classroom content, teachers further mediate for these students through the unknown culture of the classroom.	Janet Williams teaches second-grade math to a diverse classroom of learners. She knows that the language of math is a necessary piece of the content. She routinely plans for two or three language objectives to accompany her math lessons. Today, the students are learning to solve word problems using the phrase *more than*. Janet provides a model of this language pattern and has students in small groups asking and answering questions using the phrase *more than*. Eventually, students will write their own word problems using this pattern.
5. *Contextualization:* Classroom learning reflects the experiences and skills of the home and the community when teachers contextualize their instruction. In contextualized classrooms, activities derive from the experiences of the learners. They reflect community norms and make connections between the home and the school. Doing community-based learning activities in middle school, encouraging parent participation in literacy workshops, sending home books on tape for shared reading, growing vegetables in a school garden, and teaching cellular structure by decorating cookies are all examples of learning activities based upon student preferences and knowledge.	Richard Albaugh's fourth-grade students wrote their best essays of the school year when he asked them to write about "The Day the Crops Failed." His students, children of migrant agricultural workers, related to the freeze that killed the crops upon which their families' livelihood depended. They wrote and rewrote and delighted in reading their stories to multiple audiences. Their teacher had contextualized his writing instruction to facilitate his students' best efforts.

HOW DO TEACHERS CONNECT TO THE HOMES AND FAMILIES OF THEIR STUDENTS?

Why is it important that teachers reach out to parents? The answer is unequivocal. There is a strong link between parent involvement and children's success in school. The research is clear and abundant on the effects: higher grades and test scores, better attendance, fewer special education placements, higher graduation rates, and more enrollment and completion of postsecondary education (Bennett, 2004). Additional evidence indicates that school morale, teacher morale, teacher satisfaction, and school reputation all improve in districts with high parental involvement in education (Council of Chief State School Officers, 2006).

Studies show that student achievement grows in relation to the amount and duration of family involvement in the school. When low-income parents participate extensively in the school community, they see their children's test scores rise to the level of middle-class children, and the teachers' expectations rise for those students (Bennett, 2004).

Teachers and school administrators rank strong parenting roles in children's learning as the highest priority issue in education policy (Harris & Associates, 1993), and the lack of parent involvement as the biggest obstacle to school reform (Finn & Rebarber, 1992).

And yet, actual parent involvement in most schools is low. This is especially true in low-income communities and in schools with high ELL populations. As of 1997, only 18 percent of high-poverty school districts reported any efforts in their schools to involve parents in their children's education (U.S. Department of Education, 1997), and the great majority of teachers in those districts blamed academic failure on home and family life (Chen, 2001). This trend, happily, appears to be changing in that more recent data indicate increased involvement of parents and increased attendance at meetings for the general population of students (Child Trends Data Bank, 2010).

Individual teachers can make great differences with the children and families in their own classrooms. They can make the connections that count by viewing the linguistically and culturally diverse households of their students as repositories of "funds of knowledge" that can enrich classroom learning (Moll, Amanti, Neff, & González, 1992).

Teachers who seek to connect with the families of their students create a welcoming environment in the classroom. In addition to organizing the classroom and adjusting instructional practices, teachers who are cultural mediators seek to understand the hopes and concerns of families through the following strategies:

- Finding opportunities to talk to parents informally.
- Sending newsletters home with information about classroom events (translated into the language of the family).
- Using e-mail and the telephone to inform parents of student success stories.
- Conducting home visits to learn more about families and their cultures.
- Inviting parents to volunteer in the classroom.
- Hosting family nights at school to showcase student accomplishment, to introduce parents to new concepts such as bedtime reading, to inform parents of school activities, or to explain the school's report card.
- Researching the cultural backgrounds of families.
- Visiting local community centers and neighborhoods to learn more about community resources and norms.

The traditional parent-teacher conference is the most likely place for parents and teachers to start a relationship. Teachers who are aware of a parent's limited language skills in English make sure that the school provides appropriate translators for the conference. On occasion, schools have been forced to use children as translators, especially in the case of uncommon languages with few adult translators available. For the most part, this is not a desirable practice. Using children in a translation role diminishes the role of the parent and interferes with adult communication.

Teachers with strong communication skills are more effective at developing relationships with parents. They consider the following activities to be essential to their role as an effective parent partner:

- *Prepare in advance for the conference:* Collect student work samples and have a clear notion of what essential information is to be communicated and what information is to be learned from the parent.
- *Monitor nonverbal signals:* These signals convey a great deal to others, including notions of respect. Being on time, using eye contact, nodding while listening, and using peer-to-peer seating arrangements are techniques that send positive signals to parents.
- *Convey an attitude of acceptance, care, and concern:* This attitude should be directed to the parents and their child. Sharing success stories with parents will help to send these messages.

Relationship Building Between the Parents and the Teacher Can Begin at the Parent Conference

- *Listen to parents:* Let them tell their story and listen for the content and the level of feeling behind the words. Restate what you have heard and allow the parent to confirm your understanding.
- *Use open-ended questions:* These help you to learn more about the family and the child. For example, "Tell me what Irina is like at home" or "What does she enjoy doing with the family?"
- *Avoid placing blame on the family or making judgments about the family.*

The interventions and strategies mentioned here presuppose that the family is emotionally and culturally ready to relate to the school and cooperate in their child's education. There is a prevailing notion that parents of English language learners are not interested in assisting their children's school achievement because, statistically, their involvement with the school community is low. Teachers can be frustrated by families who make conference appointments and then do not come, or by parents who arrive late without any explanation. One author's experience with one such family required the help of the bilingual social worker in the district. We discovered a mother threatening suicide and a father who was physically abusive. This family needed extensive intervention. Their concerns were not at the level of school achievement. We learned that sometimes teachers need to be detectives to unearth information that can help us to advocate for our students.

There are other reasons for this lack of engagement, however. One explanation relates to the differences between Latin American and U.S. schools. In Latin American schools with large classes, teachers often administer "pass/fail" grades. Parents assume that, if a child has passed the grade, everything is fine. But U.S. schools are increasingly slow to retain or fail ELLs; therefore, passing from one grade to the next is not a signal that all is well.

Another explanation arises from the fact that many Asian and Latino families see the teacher as an education expert. Families from these cultures are not expected to offer opinions to the teacher or make suggestions. However, studies indicate (Goldenberg, 1987) and it has been our experience that when families are given specific tasks to perform at home, they are willing to comply. For example, when parents in one author's classroom were asked to listen to children's books on tape and coread with their children as a homework assignment, all of the parents accomplished this task and signed off daily on the worksheet that they had done so. Parents of our middle school students were eager to pick their children up from school so that the students could attend after-school tutoring sessions.

Non-English families are hesitant to participate in school events when their English skills are poor and the school has a limited bilingual staff. Parents and teachers both are uncomfortable in these situations, and communication difficulties impede a partnership between the two.

In addition to the barriers just mentioned, many newly arrived parents are not ready to take on responsibilities at school because they are still adjusting to a different culture. As parents proceed through various stages of adjustment, they are ready for different kinds of school involvement:

1. *Arrival/Survival stage:*   As new arrivals, parents need a basic school orientation and information about the school community. It is most helpful to give this information in the native language and in a face-to-face meeting. At this point, parents' interest in school is high but their participation may be limited.
2. *Culture shock:*   Parental energies are drained during this emotionally difficult period. Schools and teachers can support families by linking them to networks of other parents, initiating personal contact, minimizing demands on their time, and keeping lines of communication open.
3. *Coping:*   When parents have had time to become familiar with the new culture and begin to accept the cultural system, they may be ready to participate in school activities related to their children, assist in specific tasks to help learning at home, and participate in teacher-parent communication.
4. *Acculturation:*   In this final stage, parents feel comfortable in the culture. At this point they can be encouraged to participate in more school activities, including leadership roles and mentoring for other parents. Opportunities for wider community involvement are appropriate at this stage (Violand-Sanchez, Hutton, & Ware, 1991).

HOW CAN THE SCHOOL COMMUNITY SUPPORT THE EDUCATION OF ENGLISH LANGUAGE LEARNERS?

There has been a great deal of research in the past fifteen years on parent involvement and family-school partnerships. A framework for six different kinds of involvement has been developed to describe the range and complexity of these partnerships (Epstein, Sanders, Simon, Salinas, Jansorn, & Van Voorhis, 2002). Table 3.2 identifies the types of involvement, indicates what schools can do to assist at each stage, and suggests possible practices at each stage.

Of the six main types of school involvement in Table 3.2, the first three are the most common in schools:

- Parent as audience.
- Parent as home tutor.
- Parent as program supporter.

This was found to be true for groups of Anglo, African American, and Latino parents (Chavkin & Wiliams, 1993). The last three are less frequent:

Students Succeed Best When Parents Support Their Children's Education.

- Parent as colearner.
- Parent as decision maker.
- Parent as advocate.

Part of the reason for these types of school involvement may lie in the fact that these roles are nontraditional for all parents. Even for parents who are interested in school involvement, the last three categories require a commitment from the school and the community in order for this type of involvement to occur.

HOW CAN THE COMMUNITY OUTSIDE THE SCHOOL SUPPORT THE EDUCATION OF ELLS?

Fellsmere Elementary School on Florida's east coast is a migrant school within an agricultural county devoted to growing citrus crops. The school is composed of more than 90 percent bilingual students, many of whom are the children of migrant citrus workers. Fellsmere teamed with the wider community around the school to promote the health and welfare of the children in the school and their families.

The migrant specialist at the school worked with community health organizations to provide a medical clinic for families in the town. Migrant funding was obtained from Title I federal funds to create new pre-K classes for all of the four-year-olds in the community. The companies hiring migrant workers provided low-cost housing for its workers. The Catholic churches in the surrounding community began a fund-raising drive to enlarge the local church in order to include a learning center for instruction in language and computer technology and to provide a community center. Other local groups stocked pantries with nonperishable foods for those in need.

The school also reaches out to parents and reflects their cultural styles. There is a uniform dress code at the school with clothing sold at Walmart at reasonable prices. The PTA is 100 percent bilingual. The school hosts at least one family night per month with time for socializing, food, a presentation of school literacy events, and occasional presentations of literacy techniques that parents can use to encourage reading in the home.

Positive neighborhood environments such as the Fellsmere example have an effect on the academic achievement of children in that community (Ainsworth, 2002; Crowder & South, 2003; Fischer & Kmec, 2004). One of the authors saw the effects of community involvement in the support that community volunteers gave to an after-school homework club in a suburban New York school. Meeting twice a week for an hour per session, community members and teachers at the school provided personal, up-close help to ELLs struggling with homework demands. It didn't take long for teachers to begin reporting changes in classroom achievement as a result of the homework club.

Formal, after-school programs of all kinds—Boys' and Girls' Clubs, sports teams, game activities, and so on—have shown a positive effect in the form of increased achievement gains for ELL students. The "protective" function of the formal activity is highest for students who have no structured activities in their lives and for those students whose parents do not yet speak English (Cosden, Morrison, Albanese, & Macias, 2001). It remains unclear why sports teams might affect achievement gains. But for children who speak English only in school, there may be an increase in overall language competency that results from speaking English in a variety of settings.

Individual school districts throughout the United States have made concerted efforts to connect their schools to parents and the local community. One of these districts is the Anoka-Hennepin Independent School District in Minnesota. Anoka-Hennepin was awarded the 2005 Partnership District award from Johns Hopkins University to recognize the long-standing commitment and sustainable systemic approach to partnering family, school, and community.

A visit to the Anoka-Hennepin Parent Involvement web site (http://www.anoka .k12 .mn.us/education/dept/dept.php?sectiondid+10792) indicates the commitment this district has made to family involvement. The program began in the 1992–1993 school year when community education teamed with K–12 education to develop the Parent Involvement Program. Joyce Epstein's model (Epstein, Sanders, Simon, Salinas, Jansorn, & Van Voorhis, 2002) was selected to provide a research framework for the program. Funding was obtained for sixteen separate projects and for training parent groups.

TABLE 3.2 Suggested Practices for School, Family, and Community Partnerships

Type of Involvement	Schools and Teachers Can	Suggested Practices
Type 1 Parenting	Support parents in the maintenance of a home environment and parenting practices conducive to academic achievement.	• Discuss the school lunch and invite parents' comments on its appropriateness for their child. • If necessary, talk about climate changes and the clothing required. • Inform parents of necessary school supplies. • Encourage parents to read from native language children's literature at bedtime. • Suggest appropriate amounts of sleep for the age of the child. • Suggest a quiet study area at home stocked with resources for learning. • Encourage parents to praise their children's accomplishments. • Provide guidance on developmentally appropriate family activities. • Provide guidance on appropriate disciplinary practices. • Develop teen parenting programs.
Type 2 Communicating	Establish ongoing procedures for communication from school to home and home to school.	• Conduct at least two parent conferences per year. • Provide translations for oral and written communication as needed (determine literacy levels in the home). • Alert parents by telephone, e-mail, or in person of their child's successes and of upcoming classroom events. • Alert parents to important schoolwide events such as school picnics, shows, music concerts, and so on. • Alert parents to problems with behavior or academics, and ask for their suggestions and assistance. • Make home visits. • Maintain a parent-friendly office. • Post welcome signs in all languages spoken in the school. • Link new families with mentors. • Coordinate school tours and orientation for new families. • Hire a family coordinator/liaison.
Type 3 Volunteering	Recruit and organize parent help and support in the school and classroom.	• Invite parents to assist in a classroom project, activity, or field trip. • Invite parents to share a special skill with the children in the classroom. • Invite parents to share stories, photos, and artifacts from their culture. • Survey family and community members for prospective volunteers. • Provide access to English language programs for parents at night. • Set up networks of ELL parents with addresses and phone numbers. • Host an orientation program to prepare volunteers. • Help volunteers feel welcome and show appreciation for their efforts. • Announce volunteer activities throughout the year. • Provide volunteer information packets. • Develop a volunteer database and directory.

TABLE 3.2 Suggested Practices for School, Family, and Community Partnerships (*Continued*)

Type of Involvement	Schools and Teachers Can	Suggested Practices
Type 4 Learning at Home	Provide information and ideas as to how parents can help their children with homework and other curriculum-related activities.	• Encourage parents to talk to their children about their school experiences and peer relationships. • Encourage parents to review finished homework each night. • Encourage parents to ask their children to explain topics studied in the classroom. • Explain expectations for school behavior and learning. • Assign specific tasks for parents to assist their children in learning (e.g., play with math fact cards, listen to the child read, or share the contents of a child's journal or learning log). • Establish evening workshops to teach parents how to interpret a report card, read aloud to children, and establish appropriate disciplinary practices. • Offer opportunities for parents and children to learn together. • Encourage parents to explain to their children the importance of education in life.
Type 5 Decision Making	Include parents in school decision making and develop parent leaders.	• Encourage ELL parents to attend PTA meetings. • Develop networks of parents to work with teachers on school-related projects such as advisory councils. • Encourage involvement from every segment of the school community. • Provide classes for parents on topics of interest to them as parents and school partners. • Develop a parent resource center with books, multilingual videos, CDs, and other material to support parent leadership.
Type 6 Collaborating with the Community	Identify and integrate resources from the community to strengthen school programs, family practices, and student achievement.	• Provide parents with information on community organizations that provide health, recreation, and social support for families. • Invite community groups and industries to partner with the school for information sharing, grant assistance, developing laboratories for improved technology, scholarships, and internships in local business. • Provide opportunities for staff, families, and community members to learn together. • Bring together families, schools, and community organizations for mutual benefit. • Develop schools as community learning centers.

Source: Adapted from Epstein, Sanders, Simon, Salinas, Jansorn, & Van Voorhis, 2002, p. 3 and from Carter, 2003.

In the 2004–2005 school year, 9,000 parents and community members volunteered in the district. Halfway through the 2005–2006 year, 80,000 hours had been volunteered with a monetary value of $1,405,478. Forty-three of the district schools work in partnership with parents and community members and sponsor volunteer programs.

In the spring of 2006, eighteen workshops were offered to parents and community members. The workshops ranged from two-hour sessions to twelve-hour workshops and presented a diverse array of offerings:

- Raising Your Child's Self-Esteem.
- Unlocking Teen Conversations.
- How to Chill Out and Be a Cool Parent.
- Eating Disorders.
- Recognizing Illicit Drugs.

- Understanding the New Brain.
- Parenting on Purpose.
- What Girls Need/What Boys Need.
- Life as a Stepparent.

The district has a Parent Legislative Council and has developed a Parent Resource Center equipped with books, videos, audiotapes, and CDs available to parents. The center also offers resources for parent leaders to assist organizations in the district, such as the PTA, PTO, Booster Clubs, and advisory panels. The resources and contact people available help parent leadership with skill training, giving information on nonprofit management, issuing a monthly publication, and dispersing seventeen documents crucial for nonprofit management. Parents have access to the Parent Organization Directory and Citizen Involvement Handbook.

With strong leadership, necessary resources and conditions that foster collaborative relationships among the school, families, and the community, school districts can be assured that all students will have the support they need to achieve at a high level.

HOW DOES A CULTURALLY RESPONSIVE CLASSROOM CONNECT TO STUDENTS' CULTURES, LANGUAGES, AND FAMILIES IN A RTI MODEL?

RTI models seek to incorporate best practice for all learners within Tiers 1, 2, and 3. For language-learning students, "All practice needs to be culturally responsive in order to be best practice" (Moje & Hinchman, 2004, p. 321). Culturally responsive teachers understand the sociohistorical contexts that influence ELLs and their classroom learning (Klingner & Edwards, 2006). This means that the teachers are familiar with the "beliefs, values, and cultural and linguistic practices of their diverse students so that they can support their learning in positive ways" (Orosco & Klingner, 2010, p. 272). Because culturally responsive teachers appreciate the assets that ELLs bring with them to school, they are able to build upon their students' cultural and linguistic knowledge. The teachers use the relevance of the native culture to enhance comprehension and lead students to higher achievement levels. They have high expectations for their students and do not view their cultural differences as cultural disadvantages or their native language as evidence of cognitive deficit.

RTI TIER 1 SAMPLER

- Learn simple greetings and leave-takings in the languages spoken by children in the classroom. Consider placing these on a bulletin board in the classroom for use by all students.
- Create a classroom that is respectful of all customs. Explain differences in clothing, eating habits, hairstyles, and so on within the context of the dominant and the differing cultures.
- Allow use of the L1 for expressing or writing information. Encourage students who speak the same L1 to explain directions to less proficient English speakers.
- Display a map indicating the countries of origin of students in the class and display pictures reflecting their cultures.
- Learn the predominant learning style of the diverse students in the classroom and create several instructional practices based upon that style. For example, if students prefer to work cooperatively, use cooperative learning during instruction and pair students for partner learning.
- Use a wide variety of visuals and supplementary materials that relate to the home culture.
- Relate U.S. geography and history to that of other countries. Include the perspective of other cultures. For example, consider the varied perspectives of the Mexicans and the Americans during the Spanish American War.
- Encourage students to question assumptions from a variety of cultural viewpoints. For example, was the arrival of Christopher Columbus in the New World beneficial to the resident population?
- Send positive notes home in the L1.
- Visit students' homes and develop relationships with their families. Be sure to explain the reason for the visit and select a time that is convenient for the family.

RTI 2 SAMPLER

- Teach, reteach, and test in a variety of formats.
- Teach academic vocabulary directly with an emphasis on cognates in the languages of the students.
- Explicitly teach learning strategies that are congruent with the learning styles in the classroom, for example, partner vocabulary teaching and learning with word cards.
- Provide rubrics for classroom work and clear, posted objectives at varying language proficiency levels.
- Use problem-based and/or project learning among other formats.
- Assess the content of the student's learning rather than the language in which the learning is expressed.
- Infuse knowledge of student culture(s) into learning activities to make them more relevant.
- Use newspapers and authors from the cultures of the students.
- Relate current learning to past experiences, community events, and world issues.
- Develop a work and study plan for specific skill learning with the student's family members and provide weekly feedback on progress.

Culturally responsive teachers are informed as to the processes and strategies of second language learning in all four skill areas: listening, speaking, reading, and writing. They have acquired expertise in understanding how learning to read in a first language is different from learning in an additional language (August & Shanahan, 2006). Culturally responsive teachers are aware that not all evidence-based practices have been researched with language learners in the sample population (Klingner & Edwards, 2006). They are willing to monitor learning closely and modify instruction in ways that are culturally comfortable and promote achievement for their students.

Questions for Reflection

1. This chapter began with Lynn King's resolve to become a cultural mediator for her students. In what ways will she have to change her traditional role as a classroom teacher? What specific skills and knowledge will Lynn have to acquire? Do you think this type of change is necessary for all K–12 teachers in North American schools?

2. In what specific ways must a teacher relate differently to parents of language-learning students? Is the time and effort justified in a teacher's busy day? Give reasons for your answer.

3. Schools with large populations of language-learning children are often understaffed, crowded, and lacking in resources. In what ways could parent involvement change that situation?

Activities for Further Learning

1. Reread the vignette regarding Lynn King and the parent of the unruly boy. Identify areas of cultural confusion in the conversation. Next indicate in what ways Lynn could have resolved the situation in a more culturally sensitive way.

2. Evaluate the instructional materials in your classroom or the classroom of a colleague. Do the materials reflect the diverse students in the classroom? Tell why or why not.

3. Teachers have always had a mandate to connect to parents in order to report on student progress. This chapter suggests that teachers and schools must do a great deal more for ELLs and their parents. Prioritize the suggestions made for teachers and schools in their connections to parents of ELLs. Provide a rationale for your work.

4. Read Chapter 4 of *The Inner World of the Immigrant Child* by Christina Igoa (Lawrence Erlbaum Associates, 1995). This chapter entitled "Cultural/Academic/ Psychological Interventions" deals with balancing three aspects of the whole child. After reading about the CAP intervention, list the teacher strategies that a teacher of ELLs might use to help immigrant children achieve happiness and be successful in school.

5. Imagine that you are preparing for a teacher conference with the parent of a Latino student who has been in the United States for a year. Your student is creating minor behavior problems in the classroom, has not made any friends, and is not motivated to work hard academically. Work with a partner to write and perform a role-play in which you attempt to establish a relationship with the parent, convey unpleasant information, and encourage the parent to assist you in the education of the child.

6. Visit a local school that has ELL students among the school population. Look for evidence that the school is:

   - Creating a family-friendly environment.
   - Building a support infrastructure.

- Encouraging and supporting family involvement.
- Developing family-friendly communication.
- Supporting educational opportunities for families.
- Creating family-school partnerships.

7. Design a classroom that is both "student friendly" and "family friendly." Create a floor plan and describe the way that the room organization, the objects, pictures, and realia contribute to a "culturally friendly" learning environment.

8. Visit the Education World web site http://www.education-world.com/a_curr/curr200.shtml and read the article entitled "A Dozen Activities to Promote Parent Involvement!" For each of the activities mentioned, indicate how that activity could be changed to become appropriate for parents of ELLs.

9. Do research about your local community to determine whether local organizations or businesses are in partnership with the schools. After determining the level of involvement, research Joyce Epstein's model (Epstein, Sanders, Simon, Salinas, Jansorn, & Van Voorhis, 2002) to create a list of "Next Steps" for the school district and the community in their progress toward creating a school, family, and community partnership.

Suggested Reading

Epstein, J., Sanders, M. G., Simon, B. S., Salinas, K. C., Jansorn, N. R., & Van Voorhis, F. L. (2002). *School, family, and community partnerships: Your handbook for action* (2nd ed.). Thousand Oaks, CA: Corwin Press. This is a very comprehensive volume containing action steps for community partnerships with the school as a focus. It can be ordered from the Johns Hopkins web site publication list A: http://www.csos.jhu.edu/P2000/center.htm

Igoa, C. (1995) *The inner world of the immigrant child.* Mahwah, NJ: Lawrence Erlbaum. Igoa's work is unique in that it communicates to teachers the affective dimensions of immigrant children's experiences in a new culture and the impact of those experiences on academic achievement.

Nieto, S., & Bode, P. (2007) *Affirming diversity: The sociopolitical context of multicultural education* (5th ed.). Boston, MA: Allyn & Bacon. Nieto and Bode explain how personal, social, political, cultural, and educational factors interact to affect educational achievement of language-learning students. They provide a research-based rationale for multicultural education.

References

Ainsworth, J. W. (2002). Why does it take a village? The mediation of neighborhood effects on educational achievement. *Social Forces, 81*(1): 117–152.

Aronson, J., Fried, C., & Good, C. (2002). Reducing the effects of stereotype threat on African American college students by shaping theories of intelligence. *Journal of Experimental Social Psychology, 38,* 113–125.

Arriaza, G. (2004) Welcome to the front seat: Racial identity and Mesoamerican immigrants. *Journal of Latinos and Education, 3*(4), 251–265.

Atkinson, D. (1999). TESOL and culture. *TESOL Quarterly, 33*(4).

August, D., & Shanahan, T. (2006). *Developing literacy in second-language learners: Report of the National Literacy Panel on language-minority children and youth.* Mahwah NJ: Lawrence Erlbaum.

Banks, J. A., & Banks, C. A. (Eds.) (2004). *Handbook of research in multicultural education* (2nd ed.) San Francisco, CA: John Wiley & Sons.

Bennett, E. (2004). *Connecting families to schools: Why parents and community engagement improves school and student performance.* New York, NY: Fordham University, the National Center for Schools and Communities.

Branch, C. W. (1999). Race and human development. In R. H. Sheets & E. R. Hollins (Eds.), *Racial and ethnic identity in school practices: Aspects of human development* (pp. 7–28). Mahwah, NJ: Lawrence Erlbaum.

Carter, S. (2003). Educating our children together: A sourcebook for effective family-school-community partnerships. Consortium for Alternative Dispute Resolution in Special Education (CADRE) and New York State Education Department Office of Vocational and Educational Services for Individuals with Disabilities (VESID). Washington, DC: U.S. Office of Special Education Programs. Retrieved from www.directionservice.org/cadre/EducatingOurChildren_01.cfm

Center for Research on Education Diversity & Excellence. (2001). *Standards and indicators.* Retrieved from http://crede.berkeley.edu/products/print/occreports/g1.html

Chavkin, N., & Williams, D. (1993). Minority parents and the elementary school: Attitudes and practices. In N. Chavkin (Ed.), *Families and schools in a pluralistic society* (pp. 73–83). Albany, NY: State University of New York Press.

Chen, X. (2001). Efforts by public K–8 schools to involve parents in children's education: NCES 2001–676. Washington, DC: U.S. Department of Education, National Center for Education Statistics.

Child Trends. (2010). Parent Involvement in Schools. Retrieved from www.childtrendsdatabank.org/?q=node/186

Cohen, G. L., & Garcia, J. (2005). "I am us": Negative stereotypes as collective threats. *Journal of Personality and Social Psychology, 89:* 566–582.

Collier, V. P. (1995, Fall). *Acquiring a second language for school. Directions in language and education.* Washington, DC: National Clearinghouse for Bilingual Education.

Cosden, M., Morrison, G., Albanese A. L., & Macias, S. (2001). When homework is not homework: After school programs for homework assistance. *Educational Psychologist, 36*(3): 211–221.

Council of Chief State School Officers (CCSSO). (2006). Parent involvement at select ready schools. Retrieved from http://www.ccsso.org/content/pdfs/Parent_Involvement_at_Ready_Schools.pdf

Crowder, K., & South, S. J. (2003). Neighborhood distress and school dropout: The variable significance of community context. *Social Science Research, 32*(4): 659–698.

Epstein, J., Sanders, M. G., Simon, B. S., Salinas, K. C., Jansorn, N. R., & Van Voorhis, F. L. (2002). *School, family, and community partnerships: Your handbook for action* (2nd ed.). Thousand Oaks, CA: Corwin Press.

Finn, C. E., & Rebarber, T. (Eds.). (1992). Education reform in the '90s. New York, NY: Macmillan.

Fischer, M. J., & Kmec, J. A. (2004). Neighborhood socioeconomic conditions as moderators of family resource transmission: High school completion among at-risk youth. *Sociological Perspectives, 47*(4): 507–527.

Gay, G. (2000). *Culturally responsive teaching: Theory, research, and practice.* New York, NY: Teachers College Press.

Goldenberg, C. (1987). Low-income Hispanic parents' contributions to their first grade children's word-recognition skills. *Anthropology and Education Quarterly, 18:* 149–179.

Harris and Associates. (1993). *The American teacher: Teachers respond to President Clinton's education proposals.* The Metropolitan Life Survey. New York, NY: MetLife. (ERIC Document Reproduction Service No. ED 358082).

Hollins, E. R. (1996). *Culture in school learning: Revealing the deep meaning.* Mahwah, NJ: Lawrence Erlbaum.

Klingner, J. K., & Edwards, P. A. (2006). Cultural considerations with response-to-intervention models. *Reading Research Quarterly, 41:* 108–117.

Ladson-Billings, G. (1994). *The dreamkeepers: Successful teachers of African-American children.* San Francisco, CA: Jossey-Bass.

Lee, S. J. (1996). *Unraveling the model-minority stereotype: Listening to Asian American youth.* New York, NY: Teachers College Press.

Lee, S. J. (1999). "Are you Chinese or what?" Ethnic identity among Asian Americans. In R. H. Sheets & E. R. Hollins (Eds.), *Racial and ethnic identity in school practices: Aspects of human development* (pp. 107–121). Mahwah, NJ: Lawrence Erlbaum.

Miller, R. L., Brickman, P., & Bolen, D. (1975). Attribution versus persuasion as a means for modifying behaviour. *Journal of Personality and Social Psychology, 31:* 430–441.

Moje, E. B., & Hinchman, K. (2004). Culturally responsive practices for youth literacy learning. In T. L. Jetton & J. A. Dole (Eds.), *Adolescent literacy research and practice* (pp. 321–350). New York, NY: Guilford Press.

Moll, L. C., Amanti, C., Neff, D., & González, N. (1992). Funds of knowledge for teaching: Using a qualitative approach to connect homes and classrooms. *Theory Into Practice, 31*(2): 132–141.

Nieto, S. (1996). *Affirming diversity: The sociopolitical context of multicultural education* (2nd ed.). White Plains, NY: Longman.

Nieto, S., & Bode, P. (2007). *Affirming diversity: The sociopolitical context of multicultural education* (5th ed.). Boston, MA: Allyn & Bacon.

Orosco, M. J., & Klingner, J. K. (2010). One school's implementation of RTI with English language learners: "Referring into RTI". *Journal of Learning Disabilities, 43*(3): 269–288.

Osterman, K. F. (2000). Students' need for belonging in the school community. *Review of Educational Research, 70* (23): 323–367.

Sheets, R. H. (1999). Human development and ethnic identity. In R. H. Sheets & E. R. Hollin (Eds.), *Racial and ethnic identity in school practices: Aspects of human development* (pp. 91–105). Mahwah, NJ: Lawrence Erlbaum.

Steele, C. M., Spencer, S. J., & Aronson, J. (2002). Contending with group image: The psychology of stereotype and social identity threat. In M. Zanna (Ed.), *Advances in experimental social psychology* (vol. 34, pp. 379–440). New York, NY: Academic Press.

U.S. Department of Education. (1997). Overcoming barriers to family involvement in Title I schools. Report to Congress. (ERIC Document Reproduction Service No. ED407483).

Villegas, A. M., & Lucas, T. (2002). Preparing culturally responsive teachers: Rethinking the curriculum. *Journal of Teacher Education, 53*(1): 20–32.

Violand-Sanchez, E., Hutton, C. P., & Ware, H. W. (1991). *Fostering home-school cooperation: Involving language minority families as partners in education.* Washington, DC: National Clearinghouse for Bilingual Education.

Vygotsky, L. S. (1978). *Mind and society.* Cambridge, MA: Harvard University Press.

Walton, G. M., & Cohen, G. L. (2007). *Mere belonging.* Unpublished manuscript, Yale University.

Willett, J. (1995). Becoming first graders in an L2: An ethnographic study of L2 socialization. *TESOL Quarterly, 29*(3): 473–503.

MyEducationLab™

Go to the Topic, Cultural and Linguistic Diversity, in the MyEducationLab (www.myeducationlab.com) for your course, where you can:

- Find learning outcomes for Cultural and Linguistic Diversity along with the national standards that connect to these outcomes.
- Complete Assignments and Activities that can help you more deeply understand the chapter content.
- Apply and practice your understanding of the core teaching skills identified in the chapter with the Building Teaching Skills and Dispositions learning units.
- Examine challenging situations and cases presented in the IRIS Center Resources.
- Check your comprehension on the content covered in the chapter by going to the Study Plan in the Book Resources for your text. Here you will be able to take a chapter quiz, receive feedback on your answers, and then access Review, Practice, and Enrichment activities to enhance your understanding of chapter content.
- **A+RISE** A+RISE® Standards2Strategy™ is an innovative and interactive online resource that offers new teachers in grades K-12 just in time, research-based instructional strategies that meet the linguistic needs of ELLs as they learn content, differentiate instruction for all grades and abilities, and are aligned to Common Core Elementary Language Arts standards (for the literacy strategies) and to English language proficiency standards in WIDA, Texas, California, and Florida.

CHAPTER 4

Organizing the Classroom for Language Learning

M ary Le's fifth-grade class of mixed language speaking students has been studying a math unit on ratio and proportion. She wants the students to have hands-on practice with the language and the concepts of the unit. Today she has divided her twenty-eight students into seven groups of four and divided the roles among the students to ensure that all will participate equally. Mary's students are working with dry red beans, lima beans, and black-eyed peas—grouping the beans to reflect the math salad recipes she has created for the class. Mary has demonstrated that each salad has all three types of beans and she has presented several salad recipes on the overhead projector, modeling the language and the strategies to use when solving the problems.

Ms. Le: *This salad contains twelve beans. Half of the beans are red. How will we find out the number of red beans? Talk to your buddy.*

After the students have had a chance to discuss the problem, Mary asks one pair of students to tell the answer and how they arrived at it. Mary also illustrates the problem on the blackboard.

Ms. Le: *Lima beans make up one-fourth of the salad. How many lima beans are there? Talk to your buddy.*

After solving several problems in this manner, Mary gives red beans to one student in each group, lima beans to another, and black-eyed peas to another. She explains that the student with the red beans is responsible for determining the correct number of red beans in the salad. The fourth student in each group is the recorder of the math solutions. While the students are working on their problems, Mary floats around the room, listening to the language used and observing the social and learning strategies of her students. In the middle of the math activity, the principal arrives at Mary's door to introduce a new student recently arrived from Central America. Mary greets her new student and prepares a desk for the child to work, including pencils and a notebook. She then introduces the new student to a group involved in bean problems. She has chosen this group because the records indicate that the student is a Spanish-speaker and two students in the group can speak Spanish. (She knows that she needs to check because some students from Central and South America may not speak Spanish or Portuguese but one of a number of indigenous languages.) She asks one of the students to work as a buddy with the new child, explaining the math problem she is working on and engaging the new student in helping to find the solution to the problem. Mary makes a mental note to assess the new student's math skills at a later time and to ascertain information about prior schooling from the front office at the end of the school day.

How do teachers manage mixed language classrooms to promote efficient language and content learning?

- What must we as teachers consider when a new language learner enters the classroom?
- How can we organize the physical environment to promote language learning?
- How can we organize the social environment to promote language learning?
- How can we organize instruction to promote learning?

FIRST THINGS FIRST: FEELING READY TO LEARN

When English language learners (ELLs) arrive in a classroom, our first concern is to make sure that they feel safe and welcome in the class. ELLs come from a variety of places, some of them war torn and dangerous. Many of them want to be in our schools but others regret that their parents have taken them away from familiar family and friends. Usually, we know very little about our students when they first appear. But we know one thing—all of them are uncomfortable in this new environment and are anxious about how they will adapt to it.

We greet our new comers with a smiling face and a welcoming classroom. We are aware that even though our students cannot yet speak English, they can interpret our facial gestures.

Provisioning

What else can we do to make ELLs feel comfortable? A clear sign of welcome is to have a desk ready in advance for your new student. Learn how to pronounce the student's name correctly. Put a name tag on the desk with the student's name written in both the home language (if the student comes from a country that uses a different spelling or writing system) and in English. If the child arrives with no materials, find pencils and paper in the classroom to provision the new learner. Sit your new student near a friendly buddy—if possible, one who speaks the same language. The buddy system is useful to help new English language learners feel that they are not alone when they leave for the school cafeteria, the bathroom, the playground, or the bus to go home. Help the buddy to know that the new student will depend on their directions, and show the buddy ways to use gestures to communicate. We can do this best by modeling those gestures.

Gathering Information

As soon as possible after a new arrival, find out the information you'll need to teach the new ELL well. Some important things to learn are the following:

- Basic information.
- Previous schooling.
- Cultural information.

Basic information includes the child's name with correct spelling and pronunciation, native country and language, address, guardians or parents, telephone number, English speaking contacts and emergency contacts, and health history. It is important to know how children will arrive and depart from school—on the bus or with a parent—so that you can direct them safely at the end of the day. Find out, too, if your student is an immigrant, a refugee, or a migrant. Immigrants are permanent or semipermanent residents who have voluntarily entered the United States either on a documented or undocumented basis. Refugees may have been moved because of upheaval in their countries of origin. Sometimes refugees have been moved several times and may have stopped in semipermanent camps along the way. Migrants move in and out or around the country following seasonal work opportunities.

Often translators are available to help when parents first enroll their ELL children in school. Take advantage of this opportunity to find out as much as possible about students' school history. Be sure to find out what language(s) students speak and to ask how many days a year students went to school—not just how many years.

Previous schooling records are occasionally delayed and sometimes never arrive at all. When they do, they are usually in the child's home language. You will need translation help in some cases, as well as help in interpreting the meaning of terminology used in various other countries. (*Note:* Many schools, districts, and states have support resources to help you with this. Online support services are also available, such as the TransAct multilingual library of forms at www.transact.com.) Note the number of days present and absent, and the accumulated amount of instruction the child has received. This information will be important in preparing a plan of instruction for your student. Those children who have received instruction continuously in their countries of origin will understand how school functions, will have acquired literacy skills, and will be able to adapt to the classroom more easily. Those children who have received little instruction previously or whose instruction has been interrupted by war, sickness, migrant status, and other events will not have the skills expected of their peers. Some of these children are not able to use a pencil or a pair of scissors.

They will not be able to quickly adapt to the transitions of the classroom or find ways to help themselves learn. The learning plan for these children will be very different from the plan of a child with first language literacy and education.

Learning about *ELLs' cultures* is helpful for developing relationships with the child and avoiding miscommunication. It is also helpful in planning for their instruction. A child's culture includes the values, traditions, social and political relationships, and worldview shared by his or her family. The family culture is cemented by its shared history, geographic location, language, social class, and/or religion (Nieto & Bode, 2007). Culture determines many aspects of our personalities and ways of dealing with the world. Within some cultures, children rarely speak to adults unless asked to do so. These children, who remain silent in the classroom, will be waiting for us to invite them into the classroom conversation whereas others will jump into the mix without raising their hands. Some cultures teach children not to look at adults and are often misunderstood by European American teachers who require eye contact with students. In some cultures, touching on the head is disrespectful, and boy-girl groupings intolerable. We have taught children who laugh when embarrassed, respond poorly to praise, and view time far more fluidly than European Americans. Some of our students stand very close to us, refer to us as "teacher," and put their arms around our shoulders; others stand at a distance and never make physical contact. The more we learn about the cultures of our students, the better we are able to develop comfortable relationships with them.

ORGANIZING THE PHYSICAL ENVIRONMENT TO PROMOTE LANGUAGE LEARNING

Effective teachers plan carefully for the furniture, materials, and wall spaces in their classrooms. The physical environment can be structured in ways that limit our teaching choices and our ability to promote interaction, or it can contribute to learning efficiency and ease of socialization throughout the school day. If we use all the flexibility we can find or create, we can use the physical classroom to have a positive impact on instruction.

Furniture Is Important

Furniture structures much of what we do in classrooms. We realized how closely furniture defined classroom activities when we observed schools in rural areas of Egypt, China, and the Philippines. There the furniture consisted of heavy wooden benches shared by two or three students. The desktops were clean but rough, and the children could not easily get up and move around the room. The culture of those classrooms did not value students' movement, and so the furniture was appropriate to the school's educational philosophy. Instead, children worked together constantly. This was easy to do because of the close proximity of two or three classmates at all times. Individualized work assignments were not valued in these cultures; instead, children were encouraged to collaborate on their learning.

In U.S. schools in the last century, chairs and desks were sometimes bolted to the floor. This made group work very difficult and led teachers to rely mostly on individualized assignments for learners. Once again, the approach to learning was dictated by the constraints of the furniture.

We like furniture that allows teachers to create flexible groupings for students and have seen great variation in furniture arrangements in classrooms (Figure 4.1). Tom Silverman, a fourth-grade teacher, likes to place his students in a large U shape on days when he is showing a film or preparing for student presentations. The U shape allows all students to see and hear without obstruction. On other days, Tom places his students into groups of two. This is an organization that allows two students to work individually but still have access to a buddy whom they can call on for help. Many times, Tom places four students together into a learning group. This arrangement allows him to use cooperative learning, encourages group work, and promotes collaboration. During testing sessions, Tom resorts to the traditional pattern of rows of individual desks to provide privacy and security for the test results.

Sheila Arnow, a middle school teacher, also likes the versatility that moveable furniture gives her, but she has very little time between class changes to move all the furniture herself. She has devised a system of symbols; each symbol designates a classroom arrangement. When Sheila's students enter the room, they look to the chalkboard for the symbol of the day and immediately begin to arrange the desks into the appropriate placement. Sheila finds that this

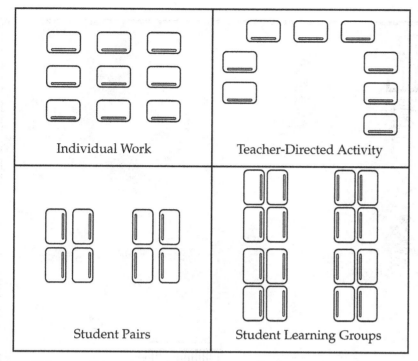

FIGURE 4.1 Furniture Arrangement Differs as Instructional Goals Change

technique is efficient and saves time. Her students have been taught to help with furniture placement quickly and quietly before beginning the lesson of the day. Sheila uses a U-shape arrangement, double desks, grouped desks, and individual desks. These arrangements meet most of her classroom needs.

Anita Brisken has enough space in her second-grade classroom for a very flexible furniture arrangement. For small-group and individual activities, her learners sit at tables. For teacher-directed activities, they have tiered benches in a semicircle. In that setting, all the children can see and hear well, and the teacher can easily monitor comprehension and participation.

Public Areas

Every classroom has public areas that all students share. One of these areas is the chalkboard (or whiteboard) where daily objectives and agendas are located (Figure 4.2). Students need to be aware of the purposes of board information and the information needs to be accessible to all learners in the class. We like to designate one area of the board as a daily calendar. We noticed that Cheryl Boynton does the same thing in her fifth-grade class. Her students look at the left side of the board daily to discover what they will do that day and the order in which each event will occur. Some of Cheryl's students who are new to literacy are able to comprehend the information because she writes her daily agenda using rebus pictures as clues to the activities. Cheryl draws a book for the language arts period, a math symbol for the transition to math class, a musical note, paintbrush, or soccer ball for the "special" of the day, and so on. The children in her class feel secure in knowing what will happen in the classroom that day, and they feel valued by their teacher because she includes all of her students in her preparation by differentiating her communication.

The bulletin boards inside and outside the classroom are public spaces that communicate needed information to students and to the school community. We have seen teachers use these boards to celebrate the successes of their students. Here is where we honor the best efforts of learners: the stories, tests, artwork, or projects that show academic achievement. Some of our ELLs will not have access to these celebrations unless we value their writing in their home languages and provide opportunities for them to be publicly successful.

Sharon Medford uses her bulletin boards to display information that students need to learn in her sixth-grade social studies classes. She turns her bulletin boards into "word walls" that contain the vocabulary of the content unit under study. By keeping the words on display, Sharon has the opportunity to point to the words as she is talking about them and to encourage students

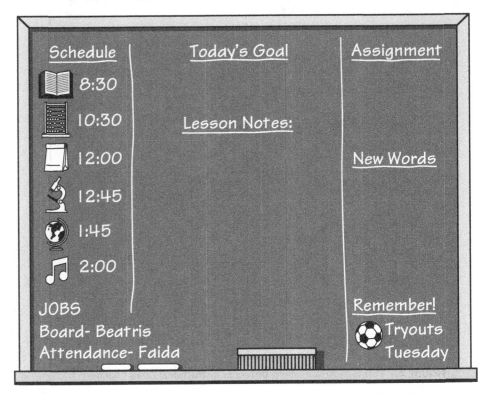

FIGURE 4.2 The Chalkboard or Bulletin Board is an Important Communication Tool

to use these words in oral discussions and in writing. The word wall gives language learners a better opportunity to be surrounded by the language of instruction.

Anne Marie Rice, a third-grade teacher, displays the language of mathematics on her bulletin board. She groups math function words pertaining to addition, subtraction, multiplication, and division around the symbol for each function (as shown in Figure 4.3). Her students are better able to solve word problems because they can refer to the vocabulary that signals the math function needed for the solution. This is one way that teachers can provide context for needed academic information.

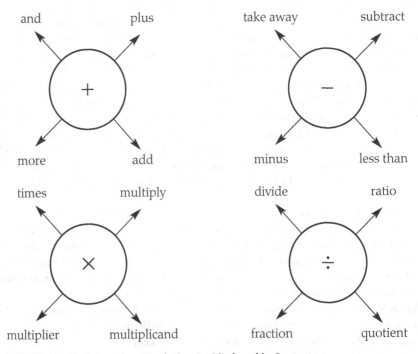

FIGURE 4.3 Math Function Words Can Be Displayed in Context

TABLE 4.1 Community-Building Activities Promote Collaboration among Learners

Name	Purpose	Description
Ball Toss	Greeting	Students stand in a circle greeting one another by name: "Good morning, Jack!" and then tossing a foam ball. Each student responds to the greeting and tosses the ball to another until all students have been greeted.
People Bingo	Get acquainted	Students circulate, searching for a person described in a box on a Bingo grid. Descriptions vary. For example: "Speaks another language; rollerblades every day," etc.
Structured Interview	Get acquainted	Teacher gives each student a list of questions to ask others in the class. Students are paired and rotate.
Birthday Line Up	Get acquainted	Teacher calls students to come to the front of the class and form a line beginning with students born in January. Students can arrange themselves in correct birthday order by asking each other: "When were you born?"
Guess the Fib	Get acquainted	Students tell three facts about themselves, one of which is a fib. The class guesses which one is the fib.
Class Calendar	Affirmation	Birthdays and perhaps one other important event are included on the calendar for each student. The special days are celebrated with interviews, favorite games played, favorite song played, memories of proudest moments, etc.
Spotlight (Seigle & Macklem, 1993)	Affirmation	A different child each day is called upon by the teacher to sit in the Spotlight. Other students take turns offering compliments by identifying specific examples: "I like the way you always offer to help me with my math problems."

Private Space

At times, we need to provide private space for students in our classrooms. Christine Igoa (1995) discovered that her students' desks began to mirror her own when the children began to bring meaningful symbols from home to decorate their desks. Just as the teacher's desk contained a flower, a pencil holder, and other personal mementoes, the children brought artifacts related to their homes and their cultures. She found that the children took comfort in being near reminders of their culture and were better able to focus on their work as a result.

You may want other areas of your classroom to function as personal space and to double as spaces for individual tasks students engage in while you work with small groups. Bill Harris, a second-grade teacher, was quite skilled as a carpenter and built a reading loft for his students. The soft carpet and throw pillows provided a comfortable spot for reading quietly, writing in a journal, or working with a buddy. A computer center/listening center with headphones helps teachers to provide learners with materials chosen for their levels for independent learning times. For those learners who are overwhelmed listening to a new language, a quiet reading spot could provide a restful time-out area.

No matter how you decide to organize your classroom, try to place ELLs in seats close to the area where most announcements and instruction take place. Our goal must be to integrate our ELLs into the work of the classroom as quickly and as easily as possible. We want to send the message that *What we are doing is important. You can do it. I will not give up on you.* The arrangement of furniture can help us to communicate those messages.

ORGANIZING THE CLASSROOM SOCIAL ENVIRONMENT TO PROMOTE LANGUAGE LEARNING

In the same way that teachers plan carefully for the physical environment of the classroom, they also plan for the social environment. Because much language learning occurs in social environments, our interactions with our students and their interactions with each other can affect learning efficiency. Let's consider some of the components of a classroom's social environment.

Social Integration

Activity-based communicative language learning requires active engagement and collaboration among ELLs. Integrating children physically in the classroom helps to promote active engagement.

But we also need to integrate them socially into the classroom community to encourage collaboration and promote academic achievement. Students need to feel safe in our schools, and they need to feel accepted socially before they will be ready to tackle the difficult job of learning in a new language. We can help to socialize ELLs in classrooms by including them in classroom activities enjoyed by English-speaking students and providing support for them to succeed. Assign jobs to a new student and an English-speaking buddy to accomplish together. Watering plants, cleaning the board, and delivering messages are some of these classroom tasks. Routines are another way to integrate ELLs. Activities such as distributing materials, collecting papers, taking roll, transitioning, lining up for outdoor activities, hanging up coats, finishing the lunch count, and beginning the morning's activities can be ritualized to help children adapt to a routine, patterned behavior. In this way, they can understand, anticipate, and begin to participate in these activities.

We think it is useful to use classmates to help socialize ELLs. Ask your students to teach playground games, hopscotch, jump rope, ball games, hand-clapping routines, and the fundamentals of baseball and basketball to the ELLs in your classroom. Children enjoy taking on these instructional roles, which provide needed language input to ELLs outside the classroom. Most importantly, however, they engage new learners in play with English-speaking classmates, an important first step in making a friend.

Community building can be accomplished through teacher-structured activities that help learners learn more about each other (see Table 4.1 for examples). Some teachers devise information surveys that require students to ask one another about hobbies, pets, favorite sports, and games. The more students know about each other, the more they will be willing to help each other learn.

Older ELLs may have a more difficult time fitting into the social life of the classroom. Adolescents form tight peer groups and are wary of others who look different and speak imperfectly. Group projects and cooperative learning provide excellent ways for a teacher to integrate ELLs into middle school and high school classrooms. Making expectations clear that everyone is to be included in your class, teaching learners specific behaviors for welcoming new students, and helping the new learners to learn to function in the class are also very important (Paley, 1993).

Presentation Formats

The social organization of our lessons will be more or less successful depending on how well they match the learners' needs. We have choices to make when structuring new input. We can choose formal presentations, such as lectures, or informal presentations, such as role-plays, interviews, and group inquiry. Some world cultures value the role of the teacher to a high degree, and children from those cultures may not realize that informal group work is a learning opportunity. They will be culturally acclimated to learn only from the teacher in a lecture format. Unfortunately, lecture format is a difficult presentation style for language acquisition. Cultural relevance, a principal of the ABC teaching and learning model described in Chapter 1, reminds us to teach ELLs to adapt to the culture of the school as we also attempt to incorporate student cultures into the classroom.

Grouping

We also have choices of whole-class, small-group, or individual formats for learning. There are cultural determinants for these choices as well. Whole-class formats can put a heavy comprehension load on ELLs unless the teacher scaffolds the oral language input. Gauging the level of student comprehension is difficult in these situations. Many listeners "tune out" when the listening burden becomes too heavy. Individualized formats are problematical when language learners need help in accomplishing tasks. If the teacher is not available, the learner has nowhere to go for assistance.

Buddy-group and small-group formats support ELLs if planned carefully. We need to consider the learner's gender, personality, language level, and educational level to make good matches for successful group work. These matches are more difficult to accomplish at the secondary school level. Unless the teacher has created a culture of cooperation and collaboration in the classroom, students may balk at working with a non-English speaker. We hope to avoid rejection of any youngster by teaching our students to work together from day one and sometimes including group support in the grading system. In a classroom of diverse learners, a variety of presentation and grouping methods will best match the needs of the all learners. Gibbons (2002, pp. 20–28) identifies the conditions in Table 4.2 for supporting ELLs during group work.

TABLE 4.2 Effective Strategies Lead to Successful Group Work with Language Learners

Essential Condition	Support Elements
1. Provide clear and explicit directions.	Directions are explained with clear contextual clues, modeling, pointing and gestures, written explanations, and picture clues.
2. Talk is a required part of the activity.	Students report to each other, to the teacher, or to other groups of children as part of the learning experience.
3. Group work has a clear outcome.	Something happens as a result of the group work. Information is shared or a problem is solved. The results are written or read.
4. The group work is cognitively appropriate.	The task is one that is cognitively challenging, requiring learners to think to accomplish the outcome.
5. The task involves content and language learning.	Language-learning objectives are aligned with grade-appropriate content-learning objectives.
6. All children are involved in the group.	Each child is assigned a task within the group to ensure that all learners are involved (timekeeper, manager, encourager, checker, recorder, reporter) or the content is jigsawed into separate pieces and assigned to individuals to learn and teach.
7. Children are taught how to accomplish group work.	Develop group rules collaboratively with the entire class. Before beginning, post rules and ask students to retell group procedures before each group experience.
8. Provide enough time for learning and language to develop.	Group work cannot be rushed. Recall the rules, state the purpose of the work, check for understanding, monitor the groups, and require summarization either orally or in writing.

Matching Learning Styles

Teaching would be a lot easier if our students were cut out with cookie cutters—each one an exact duplicate of the other. If this were the case, we could simply find the one instructional practice that best fits and use that practice consistently day after day. In our experience, however, our students were wonderfully surprising and diverse. No two were alike. They provided us with challenges and issues that continually required us to develop professionally and personally. Because our students and yours are children who learn in many different ways, we must ensure that our instruction includes a variety of learning experiences that will appeal to each of them. Every child can learn but not in the same way. Finding the learning styles of our students is like turning on the magic switch that enhances learning.

Khan was one English language learner who had us stumped for a while. Although he was a precocious leader of the other children and obviously curious, he could not learn to read. Many of our strategies failed until Khan reached the third grade and encountered a learning unit on animals. We discovered that Khan was an encyclopedia of knowledge about animals. He watched the Discovery Channel daily and remembered large amounts of factual information about animals, their habitats, and their behaviors that he heard there. We used that information to find colorful, fact-filled CD-ROMs about strange animals: spiders, wolves, and snakes. We sat with Khan as the CD-ROM read to him about the animals, and then we read aloud with him. Eventually, Khan began to read too. His world opened up that year as he quickly found his place among the grade-level readers in his class. For Khan, the combination of the colorful photos, his personal interest, the computer, and the auditory accompaniment on the CD-ROM was the key that eased him into reading.

Learning through multiple modalities has been shown to enhance long-term learning (Wolfe, 2001). Promoting visual, auditory, and kinesthetic experiences related to content and language objectives ensures that neural pathways in the brain will be activated and that new ones will begin to form. The visual components of memory are especially robust. Long-term memory for vocabulary, for example, can be greatly increased by associating words with pictures. Associating visual mapping with sounds and music activates all systems in the brain—those associated with patterns, emotions, sounds, images, and language. These multiple modalities enhance the ability of the brain to recall the information perhaps because information is not stored in only one area but in networks throughout the brain. Multiple pathways of neurons efficiently store and retrieve the networks of information.

ELLs from diverse ethnic communities and cultures will display strikingly different learning preferences from each other. We noticed these differences with children at very young ages as we observed their reactions to varying kinds of learning experiences: song and dance, artwork, projects, individual assignments, group role-plays, or memorization tasks. As preferences became apparent, we encouraged our students to participate in a variety of tasks—visual, auditory, kinesthetic, musical, artistic, and dramatic. Our strategy of using a variety of learning experiences was designed not only to captivate a diverse group of learners but also to enable all children in the classroom to develop capability in an increasingly wider range of learning experiences. So even though some of our Japanese students preferred not to speak aloud or participate in singing at first, we helped them with these skills, knowing that they are useful for language development. Even though our Guatemalan learners preferred to work in small groups with similar students, we supported their attempts to work individually as well, knowing that they would be tested in this way.

The learning preferences that students bring to our classrooms are often culturally determined. Individuals living within a culture and a family unit will develop learning styles that are congruent with others in their culture. ELLs who find themselves in North American schools will attempt to learn via the learning styles dominant in their home cultures. After years in North American schools, however, they tend to use learning styles of the mainstream students in their classrooms as well.

North Americans value individualism. They tend to raise their children with strategies of self-reliance. As an indication of this, nursery schools and kindergartens typically teach North American children to dress themselves by placing their coats on the floor with the collar facing them, inserting both arms into the sleeves, and flipping the coat overhead in one motion. Other cultures, such as the Chinese, value cooperation rather than individualism. In Chinese nursery schools, children are paired when it is time to put on coats. One child holds the coat for his or her partner to put on, and the partner does the same. Our European American students learn quite early to tie their shoes and eat by themselves. But Colombian parents whom we spoke to did all these things for their children. As a result, their children depended more upon their families, but that dependence led to strong bonding within the family unit.

Through many experiences such as these, children become predisposed to learn in generally similar ways. These culturally determined learning styles are modes of organizing, classifying, and assimilating information and are unique to cultural groups. Thus, Mexican-American and Chinese-American parents generally enculturate their children in a **field sensitive** style while European-American parents tend to use a **field independent** style with their children. This generalization is just that—a generalization. It is not meant to indicate that every person within a culture exhibits a similar learning style but that each culture has a tendency toward one style over another competing style. Witkin, Dyk, Faterson, Goodenough, and Karp (1962) first defined the terms *field sensitive* (or *field dependent*) and *field independent* in their work on perception. Field sensitive learners tend to perceive the organization of the field as a whole rather than its parts while field independent learners perceive discrete items as separate from the organized field. Field independent learners are often referred to as **analytical learners**, and the field sensitive learners are termed **global learners**.

As a result, children respond differently to a wide range of cognitive and affective learning conditions. Field sensitive/global learners prefer to learn within a social environment, helping and assisting others to reach a common goal and emphasizing the main idea of the topic—the "big picture." They tend to avoid analysis of words, sentences, and grammar rules. They enjoy using compensation strategies such as hypothesizing, and they employ synonyms and paraphrase (Scarcella & Oxford, 1992). These learners are sensitive to the feelings and opinions of others and welcome guidance and demonstration from the teacher. They understand best when new concepts are presented in a humanized story format and when the curriculum is relevant to their personal interests and experiences (Cox & Ramirez, 1981). Students from Puerto Rican, Caribbean, Chinese, Greek, Latino, and many African societies, among others, tend to be field sensitive.

Field independent/analytic learners enjoy working within an individualistic and competitive environment. They restrict their interactions with and dependence on the teacher, preferring to work out problems on their own. They prefer to focus on grammatical details and enjoy

TABLE 4.3 General Characteristics of Learner Styles in the Classroom

Field Sensitive/Global	Field Independent/Analytical
• Enjoys working with others to achieve a common goal	• Enjoys working independently
• Assists others and is sensitive to their feelings	• Competes with others
• Seeks guidance and direction from the teacher	• Interacts with the teacher only when necessary
• Learns concepts more easily in a humanized story format	• Prefers to learn specific details
• Functions well when curriculum is adapted to personal interests and experiences	• Pays little attention to the social environment of learning
• Prefers communicative activities	• Prefers to concentrate on grammatical rules
• Processes the whole picture	• Processes the separate pieces
• Processes simultaneously	• Processes sequentially
• Seeks patterns	• Seeks parts

analyzing language. They learn inductively, preferring to start with multiple examples and discrete facts and intuiting the principles and rules. They tend to work in a step-by-step, linear fashion focusing on details (Cox & Ramirez, 1981). European, Canadian, and U.S. cultures are field independent for the most part.

Teachers dominant in one learning style tend to teach to that style and value learners whose styles are congruent with their own. We tend to ascribe high intellectual ability to learners whose style matches our own. We have difficulty understanding the value of different paths to learning unless we have walked along those paths ourselves. Many grade-level teachers in North American schools are field independent, analytic learners. Many ELLs are field sensitive, global learners. It is important to know how to expand our teaching structures so that we are inclusive of all learners.

A review of the research by the Association for Psychological Sciences (Pashler, McDaniel, Rohrer, & Bjork, 2009) found that the evidence supporting incorporation of learning styles into instructional practice is weak. The study questioned the validity of these practices. Even so, activity-based communicative language learning emphasizes that ELLs should use a variety of learning strategies to maximize learning in the classroom and to become independent learners. We can assist ELLs in that goal by teaching and supporting learning strategies for a wide range of learners. Table 4.3 provides a brief description of global and analytical learners, and Table 4.4 indicates teacher behaviors that promote learning for each.

In addition to field sensitive/independent and global/analytical styles, other learning style categories affect the teaching/learning situation. More complex but more specific frameworks include Bernice McCarthy's 4MAT system (1987) and Gardner's multiple intelligences (2006) frameworks. Most useful for classroom teachers, however, are the visual, auditory, and kinesthetic preferences exhibited by learners. By using a variety of teaching techniques incorporating all three categories, we can accommodate learner differences and challenge learners in varied ways (Sprenger, 2008).

Approximately 40 percent of school-age students are visual learners. They recall most easily information they have seen or read. They benefit from diagrams, charts, pictures, films, and written directions. Another 20 to 30 percent rely on an auditory learning style. These learners attend well to traditional lecture-style instruction. They benefit from discussions, verbal directions, text Read Alouds, and nuanced teacher speech inflections. Tactile/kinesthetic learners learn best through a hands-on approach. They enjoy actively exploring, touching, and feeling the materials around them. These learners benefit from writing, using manipulatives in math class, drama, dance, lab activities, and field trips (Carbo, Dunn, & Dunn, 1986; Sprenger, 2008).

Most young children come to school as kinesthetic learners in kindergarten and then, after two or three years, become adept at visual learning. Some children, particularly girls, become auditory learners in late elementary school. However, many students, boys in particular, retain their kinesthetic/tactile learning style all of their lives (Dunn & Dunn, 1993; Sprenger, 2008).

TABLE 4.4 Teaching Suggestions for Teaching to Learning Style

Field Sensitive/Global	Field Independent/Analytical
• Give objectives in advance and incorporate short-term goals.	• Outline step-by-step procedures.
• Use visuals and graphic organizers, advance organizers, outlines, and study guides.	• List the known facts.
• Highlight the patterns.	• Allow written answers to oral questions.
• Use Think/Pair/Share in group discussions and presentations; encourage brainstorming.	• Provide wait time for oral responses.
• Base instruction on student interests and experiences.	• Encourage students to make guesses from known information.
• Use personal anecdotes to humanize instruction and include fantasy and mental imagery.	• Develop students' curiosity and encourage questions.
• Provide teacher modeling and guidance.	• Limit teacher explanations.
• Provide teacher reinforcement, interaction, and feedback.	• Use inquiry, discovery, and Socratic questioning.
• Use a deductive approach (rules first, followed by examples).	• Use an inductive approach (examples first, followed by student-determined rules).
• Encourage cooperation and collaboration.	• Provide competition.
• Include group projects, peer tutoring, and cooperative learning.	• Allow for independent projects.
• Provide group rewards.	• Provide individual rewards.

Traditional teaching in North American classrooms stresses the auditory modality as a preferred teaching/learning style. Teachers' use of this style prevails from late elementary through university education. ELLs—even those with a preferred auditory modality—are at a disadvantage in classrooms where auditory, lecture-style teaching predominates. ELLs and many other learners benefit from a classroom where a variety of teaching and learning opportunities are available.

ENGLISH LANGUAGE INSTRUCTIONAL PROGRAMS

Program models for language learning differ from state to state and also among districts within states. The great majority of the states (48) offer English-only instruction, and a majority of states (36) also offer programs taught dually in English and another language (Editorial Projects in Education, Inc., 2009). The most commonly reported programs are content–based English-as-a-second-language (ESL) and pull-out ESL instruction. These programs are offered in over 42 states (Editorial Projects in Education, Inc.)

English language program models include the following:

- *Content-Based ESL*: Content and language are taught together by a trained ESL professional. The goal is for academic growth in both content and language. In some cases, a team of one ESL and one content-certified teacher team teach these courses.
- *Pull-Out ESL*: This model usually has a goal of content and language learning although in some cases, only language is taught. ESL teachers meet with students outside their main-stream classes. These students are typically grouped according to language proficiency levels.
- *Sheltered English instruction*: The goal of instruction is to teach content and language to intermediate or advanced level ELLs. Grade appropriate, cognitively demanding instruction is tailored and taught in ways to make it comprehensible to the learner. In California, sheltered instruction is often referred to as **specially designed academic instruction in English (SDAIE)** (California Department of Education, 1994)
- *Structured English immersion*: Classes of ELLs are taught in English-only classes. Teachers have receptive knowledge of the students' native languages and adjust instruction to the proficiency levels of the students so that instruction is comprehensible.

- *Dual language instruction*: This program type aims to develop full literacy skills in English and in one other language.
- *Early exit transition instruction*: Although instruction begins in early elementary classes in the native language, students are transitioned into English-only classrooms as quickly as possible.
- *Late exit transitional, developmental bilingual, or maintenance education*: The goal of all three programs is to develop some proficiency in the native language and strong proficiency in English. Instruction in elementary school usually begins with native language instruction and gradually transitions to full instruction in English in mainstream classes with English-speaking peers (Editorial Projects in Education, Inc., 2009).
- *Two-Way immersion or two-way bilingual instruction*: These programs are designed for students with an English-only background and students from another language background. The goal is that both groups of students will become proficient in both languages. Two-way programs are typically started in early primary education with a small proportion of instruction in English and a large proportion of instruction in the non-English language. Gradually, English instruction increases as students gain equal proficiency in two languages.

ORGANIZING INSTRUCTION TO PROMOTE LANGUAGE LEARNING

Even in schools where English Language Development (ELD) teachers are available, ELLs spend most of their day with their classroom teacher. It is no longer possible to think of these learners as someone else's students. They are "our" students. We do not have the luxury of waiting until they learn English to instruct them. We need to teach them now, and we need to find ways to ensure that they will continue to learn while English-proficient students in our classrooms are thriving as well.

Given the external and internal pressures on teachers, Cummins (1984, 1996, 2000) has provided educators a theoretical framework to explain the dimensions relevant to the relationship between language proficiency and educational achievement in the classroom. The two dimensions displayed in Figure 4.4 are continuums. One is a continuum relating to a range of contextual support found within the learning situation for expressing and receiving meaning. The context-embedded extreme of the continuum allows for the ELL to actively negotiate meaning with a speaker-hearer, indicate a lack of communication, ask questions to enhance clarity, use facial gestures, and employ a range of behaviors that occur in face-to-face communication to enhance meaning. The other extreme, "content reduced," relies on "linguistic cues to meaning"

Sorting Tasks Are Appealing to Kinesthetic Learners

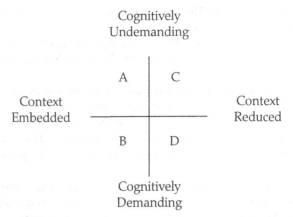

FIGURE 4.4 Range of Contextual Support and Degree of Cognitive Involvement in Communication Activities.

Source: California Association for Bilingual Education, 1996. Used with permission.

with no contextual support. The context-reduced situation thus requires higher-level knowledge of the language for communication to be successful (Cummins).

The second dimension in Cummins's theoretical framework consists of language tasks and activities that are **cognitively demanding/undemanding**. Those tasks termed "undemanding" are ones in which the "language tools have become largely automatized (mastered) and thus require little active cognitive involvement for appropriate performance" (Cummins, 1996, p. 57). Quadrants A and C represent undemanding tasks. Quadrants B and D represent tasks and activities requiring active cognitive involvement for successful completion. Many classroom tasks, such as presenting an oral report, writing an essay, or taking a standardized test, are cognitively demanding. Thus, quadrants B and D represent cognitively demanding classrooms. Quadrant B describes a classroom where tasks are cognitively demanding but teachers provide the contextual supports to aid ELLs in achieving success. These are the classrooms we describe as being effective for English language learners.

With an increasing number of English language learners entering our schools, we have seen the development of a variety of approaches for organizing the classroom to promote better learning for all students. These approaches are developed to make content information more accessible for ELLs (more context embedded), sometimes through the teacher's presentation techniques, use of content as a vehicle for learning, grouping techniques, and/or organization of the curriculum. The following approaches structure classrooms in ways to promote learning for all. It will be seen that there is overlap in the techniques and strategies used in many of these approaches and that overlap represents the best practice for all learners. We will describe these approaches briefly. To fully implement them, however, teachers should be aware that specialized training programs are the best way to gain thorough knowledge of any of them. The approaches are:

- Differentiated instruction.
- Culturally and Linguistically Appropriate response to intervention (RTI).
- The Cognitive Academic Language Learning Approach (CALLA)
- Sheltered instruction: Specifically Designed Academic Instruction in English (SDAIE) and Sheltered Instruction Observation Protocol (SIOP)
- Cooperative learning.
- Problem-based learning.
- Project learning.

Differentiated Instruction (DI)

Differentiated instruction (DI) is an instructional model for heterogeneous classes that provides multiple avenues of learning and differing challenges to a varied student population. Teachers learn to recognize the differences among their students and then plan and deliver instruction according to learner needs. Differentiated Instruction helps teachers to focus not on what they *teach* but on what their students *learn*.

Differentiated instruction operates from several premises that are central to the model (Tomlinson & Santangelo, 2010):

- One-size-fits-all instruction is no longer adequate to the needs of current learners.
- Effective DI teachers start with a mind-set that all students can learn the curriculum of the classroom when provided with appropriate support (Dweck, 2000, 2006).
- DI teachers plan instruction proactively, study their students and the content, and learn strategies to connect the two, a process called *instructional fit* (Tomlinson & Santangelo, 2010, p. 6).
- DI classrooms are marked by mutual respect and shared responsibility for learning.
- Classroom tasks focus on the essential understandings of the topic of study and require students to think at high levels and problem solve.
- Grouping is "purposeful, planned, and flexible" (Tomlinson & Santangelo, 2010, p. 8) to provide students the variety needed to match their interests and abilities.
- Teachers scaffold instruction to provide support for learners rather than reduce the complexity of instructional goals.
- DI incorporates a variety of best instructional practices and flexible classroom routines for a diverse learning community.

Those who have described Differentiated Instruction (Tomlinson, 1999; King-Shaver & Hunter, 2003), recommend four different areas of possible modification of instruction:

1. *Content*: What a student is to learn. Although we have clear standards and content for our curriculum, it is so full that we must make choices regarding what should be and is taught.
2. *Process*: How the student is to learn the content. Students can learn by speaking, listening, reading, writing, and doing. They can learn alone or together, and they can work independently or with the teacher.
3. *Product*: How the student is to display what she or he has learned. Learners can show what they have achieved in different ways: in oral responses, in writing, through a variety of projects, through a test, or by demonstration.
4. *Assessment*: How the teacher evaluates the learner's product. Teachers can choose to evaluate different components of the same assignment with the same objective or to use a different rubric.

We suggest that teachers of ELLs need to consider additional areas for modification relating to their students' *languages* and *cultures*. Within the DI model, teachers can assess the language proficiencies of their students and modify the language level of oral instruction, the materials used, the grouping practices implemented, the level of modeling and demonstration, and the visual and manipulative devices used to support comprehension and lead to essential understandings. Teachers can write clear language objectives related to the content learning, share these with students, and teach and assess the objectives within the context of a unit of study. Teachers can vary the language level of instruction and the language mode (oral, written, audio recording, role-play, debate, etc.). They can choose to use materials and/or instruction in learners' home languages when advisable and possible. They provide alternative texts more closely related to their students' reading levels and pair students to share learning experiences as listeners and speakers of the academic language taught in the classroom.

Student cultures can be accommodated through the learning environment of the classroom as well as through instructional processes. DI teachers work to create a classroom environment that allows students to feel safe, respected, and affirmed. At the same time, the classroom's physical arrangements are designed to accommodate a variety of individual, paired, and grouped learning situations. Instructional practices that incorporate a student's home language and culture as well as past learning and experiences ensure that the instructional fit is created for learners of varied languages and cultures.

To implement DI, teachers of ELLs need to have strategies for getting to know their students:

- Their interests (determined by interviews and forms, such as the About Me form in Figure 4.5).
- Their learning styles (determined by observations and interviews with families).
- Their language levels in whatever languages they use and are learning (determined by records, entry assessment, and ongoing class performance and test scores).
- Their academic levels (determined by records, test scores, and classroom performance).

About Me

Name _____ I like to be called _____

My favorite things to do are:

I speak this language (these languages): _____

My pet peeve (something that really annoys me): _____

My favorite book: _____

My favorite music or musician: _____

My favorite movie or game: _____

My favorite subject in school: _____

The hardest subject for me: _____

A goal I have is to: _____

In the summer, I like to: _____

Note: This inventory may need to be administered orally and/or made available in home languages for beginning learners. Younger learners might answer by drawing pictures. Older, more proficient learners might interview one another.

FIGURE 4.5 About Me Blank Worksheet

A one-size-fits-all delivery system is not optimal for any classroom and is not possible for a classroom with many differences in language, learning levels, and cultural backgrounds. DI is one instructional model that can accommodate these differences.

A Classroom Picture of Differentiated Instruction

Gabriela Kallal teaches eighth-grade language arts in a multicultural, multilingual classroom that includes five learners of English and two students designated as having special needs. A special education teacher is available in her class five periods per week to assist her. To implement differentiated instruction in her class, Gabriela has reviewed records and assessed interests, language levels, content levels, learning styles, and learning preferences of her learners. She includes ongoing assessment as part of her learning and keeps a roster nearby with key information about her learners that she can use in instructional decisions. One day in October, her students are studying a unit on character and point of view, reading two selections about Harriet Tubman: one from a biography by Ann Petry (1996) and the other a letter by Frederick Douglass (2001). Gabriela chooses to work with her class in four groups to use different processes for reading the text. On this day, the following activities are taking place:

1. An advanced group, after reading the text independently, works in the library with the support of a media specialist to research the Philadelphia Vigilance Committee and prepares to report to the class.
2. A group of English language learners first works with Gabriela. She discusses background vocabulary and introduces them to the story of Harriet Tubman and the Underground Railroad by viewing a series of paintings of Tubman's life by Jacob Lawrence (1993). Then she extends their understanding of the Underground Railroad by helping them use an interactive web site (http://www.national-geographic.com/features/99/railroad/). Finally, the group works independently, listening to an audio recording of the Douglass letter three times, each time for a different purpose: first time, listen for specific information; second time, list challenging terms; and third time, read along with the text.
3. A group of students, after exploring the Underground Railroad web site on their own, works with the teacher as she introduces a reciprocal teaching strategy for reading the text. Pairs will take turns reading a paragraph and questioning their partners, asking questions to summarize, clarify, identify details, and predict what will happen next.
4. A fourth group of students with special needs works with the special education teacher. This teacher has learners "read" the art first, trying to make guesses about what the story will entail. Next she helps learners with background information about Harriet Tubman and the Underground Railroad, and finally she works with learners to help them understand a targeted passage in the Percy selection that presents the essence of Harriet Tubman's mission.

Culturally and Linguistically Appropriate Response to Intervention

RTI is a theoretical and practical model for providing early detection and intervention for students who experience academic or behavioral difficulties (Fuchs & Deshler, 2007). Originally, the model was designed and implemented in elementary schools for improvement of literacy and math achievement and for limiting the numbers of students in special education. Later, the model was expanded to include students from differing linguistic backgrounds and to secondary schools. The underlying goal of RTI has been to move from an IQ-based, discrepancy model of identifying learning disabled (LD) students to a model in which early intervention and appropriate instruction could eliminate the disproportionate numbers of students (including ELLs) in special education (Orosco & Klingner, 2010).

RTI is a multitiered approach to intervention. In Tier 1, students are provided evidence-based instruction by a highly qualified classroom teacher. The instruction at this level may include modifications and accommodations for differing student language proficiencies, prior learning, and cultural differences, interests, and learning styles. Progress is monitored using valid formative and summative assessments.

For those students who are not achieving at expected levels, Tier 2 interventions are quickly put in place. These interventions include those applied in Tier 1 and, additionally, those that increase in intensity and/or duration. Tier 2 interventions may be implemented by a highly qualified classroom teacher or a specialist such as a qualified reading teacher, ESL teacher, or other qualified instructional professional. Monitoring is continued in Tier 2. Due to the recursive nature of RTI, many students may leave Tier 2 to return to Tier 1 after a short time as they achieve expected goals.

For those students who do not achieve at expected levels, further intervention and support is provided in Tier 3 through a special education evaluation and/or special education placement. In this way, the intensity of interventions increases as students move through the tiers.

Although RTI was developed to provide opportunity for achievement for many students, the implementation of the model for schools with culturally, linguistically, and socioeconomically diverse student populations has caused concerns (Orosco & Klingner, 2010). Some of those concerns and challenges include:

- The fact that many classroom teachers are inadequately prepared to teach ELLs (Education Week, 2009; Menken & Autunez, 2001). Teachers may be unfamiliar with appropriate instructional and assessment practices for ELLs. They may not understand the second language acquisition process or be aware of how to differentiate language acquisition from a learning disability (Au, 2005; Baca & Cervantes, 2004). Teachers may write content objectives for learners but fail to write language objectives for ELLs in their classrooms.
- The notion that classroom teachers should be familiar with the beliefs, values, cultures, and linguistic practices of their students (Orosco et al., 2010) to create culturally responsive classroom conditions that will promote learning,
- The flawed assumptions behind the notion of "evidence-based practices" for ELLs in RTI (Klingner & Edwards, 2006). Currently, most literacy instruction in elementary classrooms is based upon the recommendations of Reading First. These recommendations were in turn based upon the findings of the National Reading Panel (2000). The preface of this report, however, states that it "did not address issues relevant to second language learning" (p.3). Evidence-based practices for ELLs are difficult to locate in the research because English language learners are often omitted from participant samples due to their language differences (Ortiz, 1997). The external validity and applicability of these research-based practices limit their usefulness in classrooms for ELLs (Klingner & Edwards).

To make RTI culturally and linguistically appropriate for language learners, Echevarría and Vogt (2011) suggest consideration of the following:

- The use of interventions with fidelity to the specific way the approach was designed, the intended audience, and fidelity to the way it is meant to be implemented. Instructional personnel implementing the research-validated interventions are highly qualified in content-area instruction as well as in effective instruction for ELLs.
- The use of valid assessments for benchmarking/screening, skill diagnosis, progress monitoring, and decision making about student placement.

- Administration is highly supportive of a culturally responsive model of RTI. Administrators are aware of effective instructional practices and the research for teaching English language learners.
- Substantial professional development is provided for a long-term plan of providing culturally responsive RTI programs that address fidelity of instruction, intervention, and implementation.

The Cognitive Academic Language Learning Approach (CALLA)

CALLA is an instructional approach that integrates academic language development with content area instruction and learning strategies. It requires thoughtful planning on the part of the teacher in an effort to teach the essential elements of the approach as well as determine how individual ELLs will receive and act upon the instruction.

CALLA is used solely for content instruction. ESL teachers, bilingual teachers, content area teachers, and elementary or secondary teachers can use it. In any instructional setting where CALLA is used, teachers must first be familiar with and select appropriate content topics and concepts for the unit or the lesson. In addition, academic language skills and functions required to perform a specific content area task are itemized. CALLA instructional planning includes the following five steps (Chamot, 2005; Chamot & O'Malley, 1994):

1. Preparation
2. Presentation
3. Practice
4. Evaluation
5. Expansion

CALLA specifies that teachers select and teach learning strategies that are appropriate for tasks in different phases of the lesson. For example, in the *preparation* phase, when students are uncovering their prior learning, an appropriate learning strategy to teach is brainstorming. In the *presentation* phase, selective attention is needed for attending to new information either orally

A Classroom Picture of a CALLA Lesson

Sandy Chu teaches a thematic unit entitled "Life on Earth" to her class of multilingual sixth-graders. The unit is essentially a science unit, but Sandy also incorporates reading in the science fiction genre—a subject she knows will interest her students.

In the initial stages of the unit, she leads the students in the preparation phase with a challenging question. Sandy presents a rock and a plant to the class, divides students into work groups, and asks them "Which of these objects is alive and why?" Sandy requires that the students list reasons for their answers that they will share with the larger group. The group-work activity provides an opportunity for Sandy to encourage her students to develop the CALLA social strategy of cooperation. She provides lists of encouraging phrases and asks that each student use at least one of them during their discussions.

The reasons given by the students lead them into the presentation phase of the lesson, a reading on the characteristics of living things. Sandy will focus in this phase on the CALLA reading skill of selective attention. She asks students to search for six characteristics of living things in the article and to confirm or add to the lists that they have developed in their work groups. For those students requiring help with the reading, Sandy assigns buddy pairs to read aloud to one another.

In the practice phase of the lesson, Sandy pairs her students to work at the computer to create a table that describes the characteristics of living things and provide examples of those characteristics from the plant and animal kingdoms. Sandy teaches a CALLA grouping strategy—showing her students how to classify and organize the new information.

For the evaluation of this lesson, Sandy asks students to include the information on the tables they have made in two summary paragraphs describing the characteristics of living things and provide appropriate examples. In addition to displaying model sample paragraphs, Sandy also asks students to self-assess their written paragraphs by sharing a writing rubric appropriate to the task.

In the extension phase of the lesson, Sandy introduces a science fiction reading that describes an alien from another planet. She asks students to determine whether the alien is alive by using the characteristics they have learned. The CALLA cognitive strategy of deduction is appropriate to this phase of the lesson as Sandy encourages students to apply scientific characteristics to a fictionalized character.

or in print. The *practice* phase is a good time to teach cooperation strategies needed for group work. The *evaluation* phase lends itself to teaching students strategies for self-evaluation. And the *expansion* phase is the time when students use higher-order thinking and reflection skills to evaluate their learning in light of prior knowledge. A short summary of each phase of a CALLA lesson follows.

In the *preparation* phase of CALLA, teachers assess students' prior knowledge and experience with the curriculum concepts. CALLA suggests an exploration of ELLs' cultural, experiential, and educational background through a search of school records, talking with parents, discussing with colleagues, and sharing students' previous experiences through genuine conversation. Activities to help ELLs activate their own prior knowledge include brainstorming, using graphic organizers, doing hands-on activities, using manipulatives, holding teacher demonstrations, showing videos and films, and going on field trips (Chamot, 2005; Chamot & O'Malley, 1994). In many cases, ELLs have had no prior experience with content concepts; in this case, teachers plan concrete experiences designed to build prior knowledge for future learning.

The *preparation* phase also occurs when the teacher provides an overview of the content topic and explicitly communicates learning objectives. Many teachers preview and teach new vocabulary at this point while others prefer to wait until information is shared in the next phase of the instructional sequence.

The *presentation* phase of the lesson occurs when the teacher introduces new information, skills, and learning strategies to students. CALLA recommends that teachers use variety in their presentations to appeal to a range of learning styles. Questioning is encouraged during this phase, including questions to clarify understanding and to answer higher-level comprehension questions.

The *practice* phase of the lesson is student centered. Here, ELLs engage in hands-on exploration and practice of the new skills, strategies, and content; identify new vocabulary; and expand their language skills through interaction with other students in a group setting.

The *evaluation* phase is specifically designed to teach ELLs self-evaluation strategies to help them determine the effectiveness of their own learning efforts and lead them to become self-regulated learners. These activities can be either cooperative or individual.

The purpose of the *expansion* phase of CALLA is to help ELLs integrate their new learning into existing schemata or conceptual frameworks. Here, teacher-led discussion encourages ELLs to use higher-order thinking skills for purposes such as determining the importance of the content information, relating it to students' prior knowledge, and understanding applications of that learning to the world outside the classroom and to students' individual lives in particular.

The CALLA approach is notable for helping teachers to plan for and structure appropriate learning strategies in their content lesson plans. ELLs in particular need learning strategy instruction. ELLs learning in a new language and attempting to comprehend complex content knowledge and vocabulary require skill in a variety of cognitive, metacognitive, and social/affective strategies to be successful. The CALLA approach can be incorporated into any teacher's lesson planning.

Sheltered Instruction

Sheltered instruction (SI) promotes the use of second language acquisition strategies while teaching content-area instruction. It is typically used for ELLs who have achieved some aural-oral competency in English. The term *sheltered* refers to the assistance learners receive in the form of visuals, modified texts and assignments, scaffolding techniques, and attention to academic language development (Echevarría & Graves, 1998; Echevarría, Vogt, & Short, 2008). Sheltered instruction can be found in a variety of educational program designs. It may be part of an ELD or bilingual program, or it may be part of a secondary content course, such as a sheltered algebra course. Teachers using sheltered instruction include ELD and bilingual teachers, grade-level elementary teachers and secondary-level content teachers. The one thing they all have in common is their interest in promoting content area learning for all students while developing the academic language skills of English language learners.

The underlying theoretical basis of sheltered instruction is the notion that languages are acquired through meaningful use and interaction. The social, collaborative nature of learning as described by Vygotsky (1962), the emphasis on comprehensible input (Krashen & Terrell, 1983), the use of scaffolding techniques, and the integration of the four language skills (listening, speaking, reading, and writing) for learning school content are integral to this method of instruction.

Sheltered instruction is sometimes referred to as **specially designed academic instruction in English** or **SDAIE** (California State Department of Education, 1994). This program model has been used to promote cognitively demanding, grade-appropriate content curriculum for language learners who have an intermediate or advanced level of language proficiency. It has been particularly successful in addressing the needs of secondary-level learners of English, students who have little time to catch up with their peers in content learning. In a sustained professional development effort, sheltered teachers are taught to operationalize SDAIE through an observational protocol called the **sheltered instruction observation protocol (SIOP)** (Echevarría & Vogt, 2011; Echevarría, Vogt, & Short, 2008). The SIOP model specifically identifies those features of sheltered instruction that can enhance content learning and expand a teacher's educational practice. The model specifies 30 observable classroom behaviors grouped into three major categories:

- Preparation
- Instruction
- Review/Assessment

We will briefly discuss the characteristics of sheltered instruction specified in SIOP.

PREPARATION FOR INSTRUCTION   Sheltered instruction begins with clearly defined *content* and *language objectives* that focus on age-appropriate content concepts. Planning for instruction also includes the gathering of a wide variety of supplementary materials, sometimes called **explanatory devices**, which are used to promote clarity and meaning. Examples include visuals, graphs, charts, models, realia, and so on. It is at this time that teachers think of ways of adapting the content to ELLs. This could mean using a text outline or study guide, a graphic organizer, highlighting, or tape-recording the text and occasionally rewriting the text to shorten sentences or eliminate nonessential information. Meaningful activities are planned to assist learners in integrating the concepts of the lesson with language practice in listening, speaking, reading, and writing. Examples of these include role-plays, surveys, and presentations.

INSTRUCTION   During instruction, SIOP focuses on six areas that are considered essential. The first is *building a background* for learning. Building a background involves activating what students already know about the topic and explicitly linking the new topic to student background and to past learning experiences. At this time, target vocabulary is introduced using redundancy through oral repetitions, writing, and highlighting.

The second area of instruction involves the delivery of *comprehensible input.* Teachers moderate their speech to a slower rate for beginning learners. They enunciate clearly and use simple sentence structures. They explain academic tasks clearly and use a variety of techniques all dedicated to helping learners understand the content: demonstrations, gestures, body language, modeling, hands-on activities, and oral and written directions.

The third area to consider in sheltered instruction is the use of *learning strategies*. To promote higher-level thinking skills and to teach ELLs how to be effective learners, opportunities for strategy use are built into each lesson. Scaffolding techniques, both oral and procedural, are used to support understanding during instruction; various question types, especially those that promote higher-order thinking, are also used.

The fourth area of instruction concerns the *interaction* opportunities in the lesson. The sheltered lesson encourages ELLs to interact with the teacher and with peers concerning the lesson concepts. Grouping configurations are designed to support both language and content objectives. Teachers use wait time to allow enough time for ELLs to respond, and structures are used to help them clarify key concepts in the first language with their teachers and peers or through the use of the text.

The fifth area of instruction is *practice/application*. Sheltered teachers use hands-on materials whenever possible for guided practice of the new concepts. These manipulatives may be sorted, observed, created, or arranged, but they are to be used to help ELLs apply content and language knowledge. In other words, ELLs are to be doing something with the new content and using the four language skills of listening, speaking, reading, and writing as they learn.

The sixth area of instruction to consider is that of *lesson delivery*. During this phase of instruction, both content and language objectives are clearly supported by the structure of the lesson. ELLs are engaged 90 to 100 percent of the time, and the lesson is paced appropriately to the age and level of the learners.

REVIEW/ASSESSMENT   In this last phase, teachers provide for actively summarizing the target vocabulary and the key concepts of the lesson. ELLs are given feedback on their learning, and the teacher conducts an assessment of student comprehension of lesson objectives. The assessment need not be on paper with pencil but might consist of group responses, spot-checking, and asking many questions on the same topic to all learners throughout the lesson.

In the following classroom snapshot, we can see many examples that are described in SIOP. Ms. Fields has targeted the language necessary to teach the content objectives and included the use of passive voice constructions and content-specific vocabulary in her learning objectives. She has used a variety of techniques to teach target vocabulary (e.g., peer group, map pictures, and models) and oral scaffolding and differentiated questioning to help ELLs report on their state products. The grouping configurations provide further support for learners' comprehension, and the Numbered Heads Together technique used to check comprehension ensures that all students help each other. The students have opportunities to work hands-on with manipulatives, and a later reporting session will integrate the use of all four language skills.

Cooperative Learning

In both sheltered instruction and CALLA, group work is used to provide support for language learners. A specific kind of group work, **cooperative learning** can be used in mixed language

---

A Classroom Picture of Sheltered Instruction

Helen Fields is a fifth-grade teacher with a mixed language classroom. She is teaching an economics unit based upon the district curriculum. She has scheduled one month to teach the unit. She has structured her lessons to include content, language, and learning strategy objectives. In the following example, Helen has grouped her culturally and linguistically diverse students into heterogeneous groups of four. Each student has been assigned a state of the United States and must determine the major products of that state. This information will be used later when students learn economic principles such as supply and demand, and scarcity.

Helen has given each student an illustrated map of the United States showing the products produced by each state. There is an explanation key at the bottom of the map. Helen wants the students to work in small groups to interpret the product key and construct a model of each of the products in each student's state. Helen has collected art materials, fabric, popsicle sticks, and other materials to help students construct their products. After the products are made, Helen wants each student to report briefly to the entire class on the products produced in that student's state and then summarize her or his report in writing in her or his learning logs.

Helen begins her directions by checking the understanding of her students regarding their state assignments. When she is sure that students know their assigned states, can recognize their names when spoken, and locate them on the map, she begins to focus on the target vocabulary in the map key. Helen tells the students to work in their groups to identify all of the items in the map key and informs them that they will be assessed with **Numbered Heads Together**, one of the cooperative learning structures that Helen uses routinely to promote active learning among all of her students.

Helen assigns each small group a number from one to four and indicates that she will check their understanding by spinning for one of these numbers. As Helen poses a question, each group is responsible for "putting their heads together" to come up with the answer and ensure that all students in the group know that answer. When Helen spins a number, students with that number are required to answer.

As Helen floats around the classroom listening to the groups work, she is aware that some students are translating for their peers. Helen feels that judicious use of the target language helps solve many comprehension problems. During her comprehension check, however, the students will use English to explain each of the vocabulary items.

Helen next shows the students the various materials to use to construct a model of each of the products in the map key. She has constructed a few models herself to show the students what she wants them to do. While the students work, Helen has a chance to speak to her language-learning students and model the language she wants them to use when describing their products. She uses questioning techniques that are targeted to differing student language proficiencies to begin her dialogues.

- Tell me about your product.
- Is your product grown or manufactured?
- What is your product used for?
- Where is your product produced (grown, manufactured, mined, raised)?
- Was your product produced (grown, etc.) in Illinois or in Georgia?

classrooms to promote the kinds of collaborative social environments conducive to content and language-learning students. Peregoy and Boyle (2008, p. 90) define *cooperative learning* as "an instructional organization strategy in which students work collaboratively in small groups to achieve academic and social learning goals." The defining feature of cooperative learning is that "students develop knowledge through participation in curriculum-related tasks that demand participation and interaction by all group members (McGroarty & Calderón, 2005, p. 180). The emphasis on participation by all students distinguishes cooperative learning from group learning.

It may be that a cooperative structure is more supportive than the traditional competitive structure of classrooms for the current school population. The increase in racial and ethnic diversity in our school systems is a major reason why many large urban schools have invested heavily in professional development in cooperative learning. Another reason is that cooperative learning has been shown to promote higher achievement across all grade levels and all subjects for both minority and majority students (Johnson, Maruyama, Johnson, Nelson, & Skon 1981; Slavin, 1983; Kagan, 1994).

Cooperative learning is a particularly valuable organizational structure for language learners in that input to the learner is made comprehensible by team members, thus increasing the probability of improving language skills as well as of learning new content. The interaction required for cooperative learning increases not only the comprehensibility of the input but also the quality and quantity of language production. Through the collaborative negotiation process, one student's language production becomes the comprehensible input for another (Kagan, 1990). Thus, both language and content are understood and practiced simultaneously.

The strength of cooperative learning over group work rests on the method's basic principles, which Kagan (1994) cites as the following:

- Simultaneous interaction
- Positive interdependence
- Individual accountability
- Equal participation

BASIC PRINCIPLES Cooperative learning involves *simultaneous interaction*. Traditional classroom structures require that the teacher ask a question, wait for a student to respond, and then ask another question. The process takes a long time and, in a class of 30 students, this means that each student might be actively involved with learning for less than a minute. Language-learning students will rarely volunteer to respond to a teacher's question and may be left out of the conversation entirely. But cooperative learning classrooms involve all students simultaneously in discussion of the content concepts, thus maximizing active learning involvement.

Positive interdependence occurs when the gains of one member of a group are also seen as gains by all the members of the group. The stronger the positive interdependence, the more encouragement and tutoring is given to the lower-achieving members of the group. Thus, if each member of the group must perform well to receive an award (above 80 percent, for example), then group members are motivated to make sure that all learners can achieve at that level. This kind of group support is most helpful to language learners and low-achieving students. Not only do they receive tutoring help from their peers but the group structure creates a cooperative rather than competitive learning environment, possibly better suited to the learning styles of these students. Positive interdependence can be achieved by structuring the task or by establishing rewards. Teachers create task structures such as **Jigsaw** (Aaronson, Blaney, Stephin, Sikes, & Snapp, 1978) that lead to positive interdependence when they divide the information among group members, require a team product, limit the available resources (e.g., scissors, textbooks), or make a rule that no group member can proceed to the next step or station until all group members have completed the task. Rewards can determine positive interdependence by using the lowest score on the quiz as the group score, using the group average as a group score, or selecting at random only one test from each group as the group score.

Another way that cooperative learning is different from group work is the principle of *individual accountability*. This principle is important to prevent what Kagan (1994) calls a "freerider." This is an individual who lets others in the group do the work while accepting the reward or grade. Each member of the group must be accountable for his or her own contribution for achievement gains to occur. Teachers structure tasks that ensure individual accountability when they make each student in the group responsible for one portion of the project.

When group grades are averaged, each student in the group is made aware of the grades so that all know the contributions of each group member. In the Numbered Heads Together technique used by Helen Fields, students were responsible for answering on their own when their numbers were called. In the division of information Jigsaw, each student is responsible for becoming an expert in one area of knowledge and then teaching that information to others in the group. When cooperative activities require group roles such as recorder, reporter, illustrator, time keeper, manager, reader, and so on, care should be taken to assign roles based on the level of language required for the role. The reader, for example, should have competency in reading while the reporter must be able to speak in English with notes or a graphic organizer as support. Even though the roles are differentiated, all students are required to perform a role for the benefit of the group effort. In these ways, we can ensure that all students in the group are participating and contributing fully.

Equal participation is critical in groups containing language learners; otherwise, those who speak the language imperfectly will be dominated by their English-speaking peers and low-language-proficient students will be passed over by high-proficiency members of the group. Even in the case of buddy pairs, we cannot always be sure that there is equal participation (i.e., 50 percent) between the members of the pair. Buddy talk is an example of group work, not cooperative learning. To create equal participation between the pairs, we can use a cooperative learning structure called *Timed-Pair-Share* (Kagan, 1994). Partner A is called on to speak for a specified period of time, and then partner B has a turn for the same amount of time. This simple structure provides for simultaneous interaction and equal participation. It gives language learners the rare gift of uninterrupted speaking time, time to talk about a content concept, solve a problem, or express an opinion.

TEAMBUILDING   Cooperative learning teachers create teams rather than groups. Cooperative teams maximize heterogeneity. They mix achievers of all levels, genders, and ethnic and linguistic diversity. Teams build bonds of support through teambuilding activities and endure over an extended period of time. It is possible to create teams by chance, but more often they are carefully planned by teachers to distribute differences evenly throughout all groups and to separate learners who are too friendly, too dependent, or too volatile from one another. Kagan (1994) suggests changing teams after five to six weeks. This amount of time allows strong bonds to develop that promote learning. Changing teams after this period of time gives all team members the chance to practice their new social and language skills with other class members.

MANAGEMENT   Cooperative learning classrooms require a teacher skilled in classroom management and students who have been taught to respond to the management tools used to keep learning progressing efficiently. A great deal of modeling is used to teach students to modulate their voices, respond to an attention signal, and monitor time. Cooperative-learning structures, such as Timed-Pair-Share and Jigsaw, are taught so that students can use them in a variety of content areas. Cooperatively determined class rules help determine responsibilities for individuals as well as teams. Efficient methods of distributing and collecting materials are also incorporated into the teacher's management system. Although few teachers use cooperative learning 100 percent of the time, those teachers who are adept at using these management tools tend to use aspects of cooperative learning frequently. The group organization and management structures promote a more collaborative and efficient learning environment.

THE WILL AND THE SKILL TO COOPERATE   Teachers in classrooms of diverse learners quickly learn that they need to spend time creating a cohesive classroom environment—building the will to cooperate. Cooperative learning provides the structures to teach children how to work together with people from very different backgrounds. Teambuilding and classbuilding structures are aimed at creating a positive team identity and promoting respect and trust among group members. In this context, maximum learning can occur for all students. (See Table 4.5 for five examples of cooperative learning structures.)

Teambuilding structures are devoted to getting acquainted activities, creating a team identity, and team puzzles, projects and problems. Classbuilding activities involve the creation of class goals and rules, building a class identity, valuing differences, and providing mutual support (Kagan, 1994). Time spent on these kinds of activities pays off eventually when the diverse classroom unites into a supportive classroom.

The skill to cooperate does not come easily and naturally to children. We were not surprised to discover that the graduate school business programs attended by our own children included classes devoted to building skills in teamwork. These skills are essential in the business world as well as in the medical and legal communities. Most career paths require workers to cooperate and collaborate with others. The skills for efficient cooperative work need to be taught and learned. Our students need to learn how to listen to each other, resolve conflicts, and persuade and encourage each other. Cooperative learning, as opposed to group work, incorporates the learning of social skills. Teachers use modeling, role-playing, reinforcement, and self-assessment as some of the ways to teach specific social skills during cooperative content lessons.

TABLE 4.5 Five Cooperative Learning Structures that Promote Language Acquisition

Stand and Deliver	Pose a question or a topic to the class. Ask students to *think* about their answer to this question or their reactions to the topic. Wait for five to seven seconds or longer while students "think." Next ask students to stand up and find a buddy *(pair)* and talk about their answers or reactions. Finally, after several minutes of sharing, ask students to *share* their responses with the entire class. The brief opportunity to stand allows students some freedom of movement after sitting for long periods and provides more opportunities for buddy pairing.
Numbered Heads Together	This versatile activity can be used effectively for both memory-level and higher-order thinking activities. Instead of answering questions, learners can brainstorm ideas, solve a problem, draw a diagram, invent a product, etc. Place students in groups of four by numbering off from one to four. (If groups have five, two students take turns as one number; if groups have three, one student has two numbers). The teacher (or a student after students have learned the strategy well) asks a question about the reading and gives a time limit. Students take a few minutes to "put their heads together" to find and agree on an answer. (This may include looking up the page citation in the text.) The teacher calls a number to designate which student will answer for the team. Students with that number give their groups' answers (verbally, on paper, or on the board). Teacher gives feedback as appropriate; teams may receive points for correct answers, creative answers, correct spelling, etc. (Kagan, 1994).
Round Robin or Roundtable	This activity is useful for brainstorming, writing, and reviewing concepts and vocabulary learned. *Oral version:* Divide the students into groups of three or four. Write the topic on the board (e.g., "The Life Cycle of the Whale"). The first student names a stage in the life cycle. The next student adds to the description but cannot repeat something already said. Students continue to add responses until the teacher calls time (three to five minutes). The teacher asks one student from each group to summarize the group's work. Students are asked not to repeat an answer already stated by another group. The teacher charts each group's answers on the board or chart paper. In Roundtable (the written version), students pass around a sheet of paper and each student adds his or her contributions. Alternatively, place papers with questions on desks and have groups of students rotate from station to station answering the questions/ prompts. Create a class summary as above (Kagan, 1994).
Carousel Brainstorming; Carousel Reports	This is an efficient way to do either brainstorming or oral reports. Students all have a chance to present and discuss their work and discuss it with teacher and peers in a short amount of time. Arrange chart paper or notebook paper in four (or more) parts of the room. On the charts, write a series of questions to preview/review content that learners read and study. Form groups of about four students (one group per chart). Assign each group a chart. Give each group a different colored marker. Groups review their question and discuss their answers. Then one person writes the group's response. After five to ten minutes (or time needed), each group rotates to the next station. Students review questions and the answers other groups have given. They put a check by each answer they agree with or a comment on answers they do not agree with, and add their own new answers. Finally, groups share the information on their last chart with the rest of the class.
Line-Ups	This activity provides for authentic use of language learned, repeated practice of structures being studied along with opportunities to move around and interact. Have learners line up in order along some continuum (e.g., day and month of their birth, alphabetical or numerical order). Teach the language they will need to determine the order (e.g., what month and day were you born?). What number do you have? (In this case, students can interact but cannot show the number or words they have been given.) (Kagan, 1994).

Problem-Based Learning

In a local eighth-grade science class, students are learning to raise tilapia as part of an "Adventures in Aquaculture" thematic unit ("Gifford students," 2003). Mrs. Zielske, their teacher, has incorporated into the unit a wide range of activities:

- Testing water samples.
- Charting growth rates.
- Weighing and measuring the fish.
- Solving a problem (Why were the fish swimming into the drain and getting trapped there?).
- Taking a field trip to Sea World.
- Reading a nautical novel.
- Making metric measurements.
- Growing vegetables hydroponically.
- Hosting a fish fry.

The aquaculture unit is an example of **problem-based learning**. Creative teachers such as Mrs. Zielske are providing meaningful learning for their students by basing the curriculum on solving real-life problems facing our community and our world. Mrs. Zielske presented the following problem to her students:

> *You are a consultant with the Florida department of Fish and Wildlife. You have been asked to find a solution to the problem that Florida's rivers are not suitable to raising food fish.*

Examples of other topics used in problem-based intermediate and middle and secondary school classrooms include the protection of natural habitats, the allocation of scarce water resources, the homeless situation, highway congestion, and the effects of global warming. Even young children can be involved in problem-based learning when the problems affect them. We used this model to involve our students in designing the new playground for our school. Others have attempted to change the food offerings at lunchtime, find transportation for a field trip, or save a favorite tree from the sawmill.

The nature of the problems used for problem-based learning is complex and require students to delve into inquiry, information gathering, and reflection. These problems have no simple solutions and thus encourage students to take on the active role of problem solvers.

Because many of our strongest neural networks are formed by experience (Wolfe, 2001), problem-based learning leads to long-term retention of information as well as fostering skills of critical thinking and problem solving. Students are empowered by their ability to directly affect outcomes in the world around them, and ELLs increase their language growth by the collaborative nature of the learning experiences. The popularity of this system has led to many books and Internet sites offering suggestions for curricula at all grade levels (see Delisle, 1997; Brandt, 1998; Torp & Sage, 1998; Center for Problem-Based Learning (1993–2008) retrieved from http://www.samford.edu/ctls/archives.aspx?id=2147484112).

Project Learning

Our most memorable learning experiences relate to the projects of our childhood. Who could forget the three-dimensional map of Europe stuck to the dining room table with flour and water paste, and dripping with watercolors? These experiences stay in our memories because they engage learners in ways that simply listening cannot. Projects also offer many possibilities for ELLs to become involved in classroom learning because they enable these learners to acquire and share information in ways other than the traditional textbook reading or report-writing experiences that new English speakers find so difficult.

Student choice in **project learning** empowers and motivates them as they exert more control over their learning experiences. Some teachers use the **multiple intelligences** (Gardner, 1983) framework to provide variety and choice for student projects. Examples of reading projects might include:

Kinesthetic

- Construct a scene from the novel you read.
- Create a lifelike model of the story's hero.
- Create a three-dimensional model of the story's setting.

Verbal/Linguistic

- Choose one character from the book and create a series of letters written by the character during a difficult period of time.
- Choose one event in the novel and write the scene as a TV soap opera script.
- Write a newspaper article describing the most exciting event in the novel.

Intrapersonal

- Choose one character in the story and show the ways in which you and the character are alike. You may show the similarities through writing, drawing, or other appropriate means.
- Write a diary as if you were the main character of the story. Talk about your feelings as the events unfold.
- Express your reactions to the story—your feelings and responses—through music, art, or poetry.

Logical/Sequential

- Create a graphic organizer that visually shows the plot development of the story.
- Create a game board that represents the story's development.
- Create a series of puzzles or brainteasers about the major characters in the story.

Rhythmic

- Write a rap or song for the major character to sing.
- Create a mime dance to illustrate the major conflicts in the novel.
- Choose songs that represent the conflicts of the major characters in the book.

Visual

- Create a comic book representation of the story.
- Design a collage to represent the major character in the story.
- Take photographs of scenes that represent the setting of the story and create a collage with them.

Interpersonal

- Work with a friend to create a problem-mediation session between you and a major character in the book. Provide helpful alternatives to the character's problems.
- Work with a friend to role-play one of the events in the story in a way that makes sense to readers today.
- Work with a friend to interview class members on their reactions to the story and report to the class.

Naturalist

- Collect leaves, rocks, flowers, trees, and animal products that represent the setting of the story.
- Create a tape with sounds heard in the natural world to play while reading an outdoor scene of the novel.
- Identify the main character with a signature flower, plant, tree, and animal, and explain your choices.

Projects, to be successful, must be closely related to learning objectives and serve to increase student understanding of the content concepts. Wolfe (2001) gives an example of an interesting and engaging project in a California school that did not meet these criteria. Students were studying their state's history and were asked to build a replica of an early mission out of sugar cubes. The students enjoyed the project but it taught them nothing about the impact of the missions on California history or the contributions of the people who built them.

Linda Karl and Ray Kropp (Rutherford, 1998) designed a multidisciplinary math and English project for their students in Oak Lawn, Illinois, titled the "Invention Convention."

The project required students to identify a difficult task and create an invention that would make the task simpler. In the course of the unit, students:

- Created a scale drawing of the invention.
- Developed a scale model of the invention.
- Wrote a description including any math or physics formulas.
- Described the benefits of the invention.
- Designed a newspaper/magazine ad.
- Created a TV commercial.
- Wrote a feature article for the newspaper.
- Prepared an outline and a five-minute speech to be presented in class.

The many and diverse tasks required for this project called several skills into play, especially the language skills of listening, speaking, reading, and writing. At the same time, students had several choices concerning the nature of their invention and their depiction of it. Course objectives were also directly related to the tasks required for the project. Every student could find a task suited to learning style and interest in this stimulating and valuable project.

RTI TIER 1 SAMPLER

- Classroom observations of students will give insight to their learning styles. Make anecdotal observations of student reactions to varying presentation modes: lecture, pair work, individual or paired computer work, illustrations, project work, music and singing, role-plays, small group work, and so forth. Use these observations to devise learning opportunities for ELLs that match their learning styles.
- Talk to parents and/or use a survey instrument to determine the interests shared among your students. Use this information to construct learning opportunities that match student interest.
- Do research into the languages, cultures, and histories of the ELLs in your classroom. Use this information to make connections between new learning and student homes and cultures. The information can also be used to create a culture of acceptance among the various language groups in your classroom.
- Provide opportunities for students to work on "hands-on" projects with other students. They may make three-dimensional models to illustrate social studies concepts of geography and land formations, create models for experimentation of physics principles, or design dioramas to illustrate setting and character for language arts.
- Use the local community to design problem-based learning experiences for students. Relate the problems to those experienced by linguistically diverse families in your classroom: lack of transportation, lack of translation opportunities, lack of opportunities for network among families, information on safe and affordable housing, availability of medical care, and other issues of concern.
- Create cooperative learning teams in your classroom. Invest time in building team spirit through information-sharing opportunities. Have each team create a logo, a name, and a poster to introduce team members to others in the classroom. Encourage teams to identify team songs and mascots.
- Apply the preparation phase of the SIOP model by writing language objectives that arise from the content topic of instruction. Actively teach the language structures you have identified and assess them after students have had many opportunities to practice the new language.
- Pair a student with a partner who speaks the same home language during the building background, comprehensible input, practice and application, and lesson delivery phases of the lesson.
- Provide alternative reading texts relative to content learning topics: newspapers, diaries, computer web sites, magazine articles, and simplified texts.
- Provide outlines of the most critical concepts to be taught in the unit. Teach learners note taking by modeling the procedure on the OHP or the white board.

RTI TIER 2 SAMPLER

- After assessment has determined that some students have not learned to the desired level, group 3 to 5 students with similar academic profiles and reteach the concepts using a different format (demonstration, hands-on, visual, step-by-step, computer assisted, models, and so on).
- Select one of the CALLA learning strategies appropriate for your grade level and students. Directly teach, model, and assess the skill with students in small groups. Observe students in the days following instruction to check their correct use of the strategy. Choose another strategy and teach that one in the same way.
- Choose key vocabulary words or phrases required for content learning and academic writing. Directly teach them in small groups, and then designate pairs to work together as vocabulary tutors on a daily basis throughout the unit.
- For writing assignments, work with small groups or pairs of students to develop text organization using an outline or a graphic organizer. Provide opportunities for oral retelling of the content information using appropriate signal words. Pair students as writing buddies to provide specific help on writing assignments.
- As the class works on independent writing projects or on collaborative projects, group students who need reading interventions for 30-minute classes several times a week. Use these class times to isolate and teach core reading skills such as comprehension of main idea and details. Assess frequently.
- Prior to introducing a new content topic, group students in need of Tier 2 assistance to build their knowledge of prior concepts related to the topic. For example, when beginning a unit on the organization of the U.S. government, help students to determine how governments are organized in their native countries or assess their understanding of concepts related to the topic such as *democracy, representation, republic, congress, executive branch, legislative branch, judicial branch,* and so on. Build background using visuals, computer information, simplified texts, graphics, and other scaffolding devices.
- When determining background knowledge for a new topic, group ELLs and ask them to write what they know about the topic in their native languages. Even though you do not read/speak these languages, you can determine whether students have information to write about. If other students in the class speak the language, pair them to share what they know.
- Assign differentiated reading texts in a secondary English class related to a common theme. Meet with a book group for part of each class period but meet with the students needing Tier 2 assistance much more frequently than the other groups.
- For secondary learners, provide before- and after-school intervention programs, lunchtime interventions, or develop an intervention class period within a language arts block.
- Allow secondary students to have guided self-selection of reading materials related to their interests in an effort to increase motivation to read.

Questions for Reflection

1. Planning for classroom management and for instruction of language-learning youngsters is a complex task. As a teacher, your classroom will include monolingual English speakers in addition to language learners. How well will the suggestions given earlier work with English-dominant students? Where will you have to add to these suggestions or modify them?
2. The social environment of the classroom can help or hinder learning. How will language learners from different cultures change that environment? In what ways will their presence add to or detract from the classroom environment?
3. A basic premise of the organizing tools discussed in this chapter (CALLA, sheltered instruction, cooperative learning, problem-based and project learning, and differentiated instruction) is that language learners are active participants in all areas of classroom teaching and learning. What questions do you have about actively including these students in classroom lessons? What concerns does this notion raise?

Activities for Further Learning

1. Imagine that you are expecting a new student to enter your class next week. You have no information about the student. You need to find an efficient way to determine as much as you can in a short time. Create a form that can be used by the front office of the school to help you collect necessary information. Remember to include questions regarding basic information,

previous schooling, health information, and cultural information, if possible.

2. Create a floor plan for your ideal classroom of 25 mixed-language students. Indicate where and how students will be seated, the location of the chalkboard and the bulletin boards. Include other areas relative to the age of the students. For younger learners, you may want to include art areas, listening areas, bookshelves, and reading areas. For older learners, you will need to provide storage for reference materials. How does your classroom arrangement provide for flexibility of instruction?

3. Design a bulletin board that provides content-learning information to language learners in a contextualized format.

4. Create some community-building activities that can be used with mixed language populations at both the elementary and secondary grades. You may want to refer to *Cooperative Structures for Classbuilding* (1995) by M. Kagan, L. Robertson, and S. Kagan. San Juan Capistrano, CA: Kagan Cooperative Learning.

5. Create a list of teaching strategies and techniques that appeal to field sensitive learners. Create a separate list for field independent learners. Compare the lists. Which one best illustrates the classrooms that you attended as a child? Which list describes a classroom that you would like to be part of?

6. Choose a reading lesson that you have taught or select a reading lesson from a published program. Adapt the lesson for a group of mixed-language learners using a CALLA format.

7. Read again the teaching behaviors contained in the Sheltered Instruction Observation Protocol (SIOP). Check off the behaviors that are already a part of your teaching repertoire. Then list the ones that you need to learn more about to incorporate them into your teaching. Select two of those behaviors and research more about them. If you are currently teaching, start experimenting with these behaviors in your classroom.

8. Create a cooperative-learning content activity that incorporates the four principles of cooperative learning: positive interdependence, individual accountability, equal participation, and simultaneous interaction. Make sure that language skills are a focus of the activity.

Suggested Reading

Chamot, A. U., & O'Malley, J. M. (1994). *The CALLA handbook: Implementing the cognitive academic language learning approach.* New York, NY: Addison-Wesley. This is a classic text that should be required reading for every teacher.

Cummings, C. (2000). *Winning strategies for classroom management.* Alexandria, VA: Association for Supervision and Curriculum Development. The chapter on bonding and connecting offers many practical activities for creating a cohesive classroom community.

Echevarría, J., Vogt, M., & Short, D. J. (2008). *Making content comprehensible for English language learners: The SIOP model.* Boston, MA: Allyn & Bacon. An excellent description of sheltered instruction with many practical strategies clearly explained with classroom examples.

Meyers, M. (1993). *Teaching to diversity: Teaching and learning in the multi-ethnic classroom.* Reading, MA: Addison-Wesley. This slim volume offers chapters devoted to procedures for welcoming new students into the classroom. Blackline masters and sample information-gathering forms are included.

Scarcella, R. (1990). *Teaching language minority students in the multicultural classroom.* Englewood Cliffs, NJ: Prentice Hall Regents. Scarcella includes chapters on getting to know minority students, promoting interaction, and appealing to a variety of learning styles. The last chapter features teaching strategies for a variety of learning styles. The appendix contains descriptions of the major cultural groups in the United States—an excellent resource.

Ventriglia, L. (1982). *Conversations of Miguel and Maria: How children learn a second language.* Reading, MA: Addison-Wesley. This enjoyable and useful text describes the various strategies used by young children when acquiring a new language.

References

Aronson, E., Blaney, N., Stephin, C., Sikes, J., & Snapp, M. (1978). *The jigsaw classroom.* Beverly Hills, CA: Sage.

Au, K. (2005). *Multicultural issues and literacy achievement.* New York, NY: Routledge.

Baca, L., & Cervantes, H. T. (2004). *The bilingual special education interface* (4th ed.). Upper Saddle River, NJ: Pearson Merrill Prentice Hall.

Brandt, R. (1998). *Powerful learning.* Alexandria, VA: Association for Supervision and Curriculum Development.

California State Department of Education. (1994). *Building bilingual instruction: Putting the pieces together.* Sacramento, CA: Bilingual Education Office.

Carbo, M., Dunn, R., & Dunn, K. (1986). *Teaching students to read through their individual learning styles.* Englewood Cliffs, NJ: Prentice Hall.

Center for Problem-Based Learning. (1993–2008). Home page. Retrieved from http://www.imsa.edu/programs/pbln

Chamot, A. U., & O'Malley, J. M. (1994). *The CALLA handbook: Implementing the cognitive academic language learning approach.* White Plains, NY: Addison-Wesley.

Chamot, A. U. (2005). The Cognitive Academic Language Learning Approach (CALLA): An update. In P. A. Richard-Amato & M. A. Snow (Eds.), *Academic success for English language learners: Strategies for K-12 mainstream teachers.* White Plains, NY: Pearson.

Cox, B. G., & Ramirez, M. (1981). Cognitive styles: Implications for multiethnic education. In J. Banks (Ed.), *Education in the 80s: Implications for multiethnic education.* Washington, DC: National Education Association.

Cummins, J. (1980). The construct of language proficiency in bilingual education. In J. E. Alatis (Ed.), *Georgetown University roundtable on languages and linguistics* (pp. 76–93). Washington, DC: Georgetown University Press.

Cummins, J. (1984). Language proficiency, bilingualism and academic achievement. In P. A. Richard-Amato, *Making it happen: Interaction in the second language classroom from theory to practice.* White Plains, NY: Addison-Wesley.

Cummins, J. (1996). *Negotiating identities: Education for empowerment in a diverse society.* Ontario, CA: California Association for Bilingual Education.

Cummins, J. (2000). *Language, power, and pedagogy: Bilingual children in the crossfire*. Clevedon, UK, and Buffalo, NY: Multilingual Matters.

Delisle, R. (1997). *How to use problem-based learning in the classroom*. Alexandria, VA: Association for Supervision and Curriculum Development.

Douglass, F. (2001). Letter to Harriet Tubman. In A. Applebee (Ed.), *The language of literature*. Evanston, IL: McDougal Littell.

Dunn, R., & Dunn, K. (1993). *Teaching secondary students through their individual learning styles*. Boston, MA: Allyn & Bacon.

Dweck, C. S. (2000). *Self-theories: Their role in motivation, personality, and development*. Philadelphia, PA: Psychology Press.

Dweck, C. S. (2006). *Mindset: The new psychology of success*. New York, NY: Random House.

Echevarría, J., and Graves, A. (1998). *Sheltered content instruction: Teaching English-language learners with diverse abilities*. Boston, MA: Allyn & Bacon.

Echevarría, J., & Vogt, M. (2011). *Response to intervention (RTI) and English learners: Making it happen*. White Plains, NY: Pearson.

Echevarría, J., Vogt, M., & Short, D. J. (2008). *Making content comprehensible for English language learners: The SIOP model* (3rd ed.). Boston, MA: Allyn & Bacon.

Editorial Projects in Education, Inc. (EPE Research). (2009). *Perspectives on population: English language learners in American schools*. Bethesda, MD. Available: edweek.org

Education Week. (2009, January 8). *Quality counts*. Bethesda, MD: Editorial Projects in Education.

Fuchs, D., & Deshler, D. (2007). What we need to know about responsiveness to intervention (and shouldn't be afraid to ask). *Learning Disabilities Research & Practice, 22*(2), 129–136.

Gardner, H. (1983). *Frames of mind. The theory of multiple intelligences*. New York: BasicBooks.

Gardner, H. (2006). *Multiple intelligences: New horizons*. New York, NY: Basic Books.

Gibbons, P. (2002). *Scaffolding language scaffolding learning: Teaching second language learners in the mainstream classroom*. Portsmouth, NH: Heinemann.

Gifford students learn to grow fish. (2003, July 18). *Hometown News*.

Igoa, C. (1995). *The inner world of the immigrant child*. Hillsdale, NJ: Lawrence Erlbaum.

Johnson, D. W., Maruyama, G., Johnson, R., Nelson, D., & Skon, L. (1981). Effects of cooperative, competitive and individualistic goal structures on achievement: A meta-analysis. *Psychological Bulletin, 89:* 47–62.

Kagan, S. (1990). Cooperative learning for students limited in language proficiency. In M. Brubacher, R. Payne, and K. Rickett (Eds.), *Perspectives on small group learning*. Oakville: Ontario, Canada.

Kagan, S. (1994). *Cooperative learning*. San Clemente, CA: Kagan Cooperative Learning.

King-Shaver, B., & Hunter, A. (2003). *Differentiated instruction in the English classroom: Content, process, product, and assessment*. Portsmouth, NH: Heinemann.

Klingner, J. K., & Edwards, P. (2006). Cultural considerations with response to intervention models. *Reading Research Quarterly, 41:* 108–117.

Krashen, S. D., & Terrell, T. D. (1983). *The natural approach: Language acquisition in the classroom*. San Francisco, CA: Alemany Press.

Lawrence, J. (1993). *Harriet and the promised land*. New York, NY: Simon & Schuster.

McCarthy, B. (1987). *The 4MAT system: Teaching to learning styles with right/left mode techniques*. Barrington, IL: Excel.

McGroarty, M., & Calderón, M. (2005). Cooperative learning for second language learners: Models, applications, and challenges.

In P. A. Richard-Amato & M. A. Snow (Eds.), *Academic success for English language learners: Strategies for K-12 mainstream teachers*. White Plains, NY: Pearson.

Menken, K., & Autunez, B. (2001). *An overview of the preparation and certification of teachers working with limited English proficient (LEP) students*. Washington, DC: National Clearinghouse for Bilingual Education and ERIC Clearinghouse on Teaching and Teacher Education. Retrieved from http://www.eric.ed.gov/ERICDocs/data/ericdocs2sql/content_storage_01/0000019b/80/29/cb/0e.pdf

National Reading Panel. (2000). *Teaching children to read: An evidence-based assessment of the scientific research literature on reading and its implications for reading instruction*. Washington, DC: National Institute of Child Health and Development.

Nieto, S., & Bode, P. (2007). *Affirming diversity: The sociopolitical context of multicultural education* (5th ed.). Boston, MA: Allyn & Bacon.

Orosco, M. J., & Klingner, J. (2010). One school's implementation of RTI with English language learners: "Referring into RTI." *Journal of Learning Disabilities, 43*(3): 269–288.

Ortiz, A. A. (1997). Learning disabilities occurring concomitantly with linguistic differences. *Journal of Learning Disabilities, 30:* 321–332.

Paley, V. G. (1993). *You can't say you can't play*. Cambridge, MA: Harvard University Press.

Pashler, H., McDaniel, M., Rohrer, D., & Bjork, R. (2009). Learning styles: Concepts and evidence. *Psychological Science in the Public Interest, 9:* 105–119.

Peregoy, S. F., & Boyle, O. F. (2008). *Reading, writing, & learning in ESL: A resource book for K–12 teachers* (5th ed.). New York, NY: Longman.

Petry, A. (1996). *Harriet Tubman: Conductor on the underground railroad*. New York, NY: Trophy Press.

Rutherford, P. (1998). *Instruction for all students*. Alexandria, VA: Just ASK Publications.

Scarcella, R. C., & Oxford, R. L. (1992). *The tapestry of language learning: The individual in the communicative classroom*. Boston, MA: Heinle and Heinle.

Seigle, P., & Macklem, G. (1993). *Social competency program*. Wellesley, MA: Stone Center.

Slavin, R. E. (1983). When does cooperative learning increase student achievement? *Psychological Bulletin, 94:* 429–445.

Sprenger, M. (2008). *Differentiation through learning styles and memory*. Thousand Oaks, CA: Corwin Press.

Tomlinson, C. A. (1999). *The differentiated classroom: Responding to the needs of all learners*. Alexandria, VA: Association for Supervision and Curriculum Development.

Tomlinson, C. A., & Santangelo, T. (2010). Integrating differentiated instruction and response to intervention: From theory to practice [E-book]. Alexandria, VA: Association for Supervision and Curriculum Development. Retrieved from http://www.ascd.org/professional-development/pdquickkit-catalog.aspx

Torp, L., and Sage, S. (1998). *Problems as possibilities: Problem-based learning for K–12 education*. Alexandria, VA: Association for Supervision and Curriculum Development.

Vygotsky, L. S. (1962). *Thought and language*. Cambridge, MA: MIT Press.

Witkin, H. A., Dyk, R. B., Faterson, H. F., Goodenough, D. R., & Karp, S. A. (1962). *Psychological differentiation*. New York, NY: Wiley.

Wolfe, P. (2001). *Brain matters: Translating research into classroom practice*. Alexandria, VA: Association for Supervision and Curriculum Development.

MyEducationLab™

Go to the Topic, Instructional Programs and Planning, in the MyEducationLab (www.myeducationlab.com) for your course, where you can:

- Find learning outcomes for Instructional Programs and Planning along with the national standards that connect to these outcomes.
- Complete Assignments and Activities that can help you more deeply understand the chapter content.
- Apply and practice your understanding of the core teaching skills identified in the chapter with the Building Teaching Skills and Dispositions learning units.
- Examine challenging situations and cases presented in the IRIS Center Resources.
- Check your comprehension on the content covered in the chapter by going to the Study Plan in the Book Resources for your text. Here you will be able to take a chapter quiz, receive feedback on your answers, and then access Review, Practice, and Enrichment activities to enhance your understanding of chapter content.
- **A+RISE** A+RISE® Standards2Strategy™ is an innovative and interactive online resource that offers new teachers in grades K-12 just in time, research-based instructional strategies that meet the linguistic needs of ELLs as they learn content, differentiate instruction for all grades and abilities, and are aligned to Common Core Elementary Language Arts standards (for the literacy strategies) and to English language proficiency standards in WIDA, Texas, California, and Florida.

CHAPTER 5

Strategies for Oral Language Development

Mike Lawrence, a fifth-grade teacher, has been teaching a unit on the properties of liquids to his diverse class of language learners and native English speakers. Mike's students enjoy doing science because he teaches it using a hands-on method that involves all of his students in experiential learning. Yesterday the class predicted what would happen if Mike put his can of Coke into the freezer. They saw that the bottom and top of the can became convex and were able to report to Mike that this happened because the liquid froze and increased in volume. Today Mike has placed his students into small groups to perform experiments on the results of salt on the freezing temperature of water. Each group has a cup of fresh water, an ice cube, a saltshaker, and a piece of thread. They are trying to find ways to pick up the ice cube without using their hands. Marisol's group has figured out that the experiment has something to do with freezing and they are trying to determine how to freeze the thread onto the ice cube. Mike intervenes from time to time to comment and ask thought-provoking questions:

What is the freezing point of water?

That's right, water freezes at 32° F.

How would salt affect the freezing point of water?

Have you seen workers put salt on the streets in winter? Why do they do that? What would happen if you put salt on the ice cube?

If the ice cube melted slightly, how could you get the thread to freeze onto the cube?

As Mike moves around the room, he models the language he wants the students to use (*freezing point, fresh water /saltwater, melt/freeze, lower/higher, freeze, froze, frozen*). By the end of this lesson, he'll ask each group to report to him on what they have discovered. This will give him further opportunities to help the language learners in the group use the scientific terms and the correct verb tenses. Before groups report their findings to the rest of Mike's class and write their summaries, they rehearse by reporting to one another.

What kinds of classroom conditions and activities lead to oral language development in language learners?

- What are the necessary classroom conditions for academic language learning?
- What stages do learners go through before they become proficient in oral language?
- How does the teacher's clarity affect oral language development?
- What structured question and response patterns promote oral language development?
- How do teachers scaffold oral language learning and provide for teacher-guided collaborative dialogue opportunities in classrooms?

CONDITIONS FOR ORAL LANGUAGE LEARNING

Is learning to speak a new language easy or difficult? It seems the answer to this question, as to so many others, is "it depends." There is general agreement (Goodman, 1986, p. 8; Enright & McCloskey, 1988, pp. 21–29; Hernández, 1997, pp. 162–164; Goldenberg, 2004) that learning is easier when certain conditions are present. Some of these conditions include the following criteria:

- **Language learning is social learning.** Students learn language when teachers provide plentiful, collaborative experiences with peers, teachers, and others in the community. These experiences provide the interest and enjoyment that sparks learners to achieve at higher levels. They also help learners develop the social skills necessary to become bilingual.
- **Language learning proceeds most rapidly when the environment is supportive and accepting,** and when there are multiple opportunities for success. All learning, not only language learning, is accelerated when these conditions are present. A supportive, accepting classroom can still be a rigorous classroom as long as instruction is scaffolded to ensure learner success.
- **Language learning proceeds incrementally, starting from what the learner already knows from prior cultural and linguistic experiences:** English language learners do not come to school as blank slates. Every child has already acquired some knowledge when they enter our classrooms. We need to determine what our new students already know and plan our instruction based upon their cultural experiences, their language experiences, and their school learning experiences.
- **Language learning requires plentiful comprehensible input:** Language learners strive to derive meaning from the language they hear about them. When the language is contextualized in ways to make it meaningful, language learning is accelerated.
- **Language learning requires that students use the language:** Language learners seldom learn without opportunities to use the language—to speak to others in purposeful ways. Structuring output requires learners to think about grammatical aspects of language and word choice in order to be understood by others.
- **Language learning is purposeful, authentic, and important to the learner:** The purpose of the language-learning task should be a real, authentic purpose. Completing a workbook page does not qualify as a real purpose for learners. But writing a letter to a pen pal, debating a topic, or presenting a science project are examples of authentic and purposeful uses for language. If English language learners (ELLs) see these events as important to their own learning—to their peer group, to their class, to their school, family, or communities—they will be motivated to work diligently.
- **Language learning integrates and explores the development of subject matter, cognition, and language.** Because language is integral to learning anything, and because cognitive development is inextricably linked to language development, these processes cannot be separated. Indeed, the role of school is to integrate and develop learning, cognition, and language because there is no institution outside of school that is dedicated to that goal.

ACADEMIC LANGUAGE LEARNING

Unfortunately, these conditions for optimal language learning are not part of many classroom experiences for language learners. Language learning is increasingly difficult even for some of our best students. Fillmore and Snow (2002, p. 30) report that in 1997, 60 percent of the freshmen at the Irvine campus of the University of California who took the English composition competency test failed. One-third of these students eventually enrolled in ESL classes at the university because their level of academic English was not sufficient to support college-level instruction. These students were not new arrivals to the country—95 percent of them had lived in the United States for eight years or more. Most of them were honor students, and 65 percent of them had taken honors and Advanced Placement English courses.

At UCLA, students who had been in mainstream classes throughout elementary and secondary school were shocked to find they were required to take ESL classes. Carlos reported:

I felt kinda bad, I thought that I knew how to write and stuff, but I guess I didn't. But then I go, well I need the help. My writing is really bad.

Martha, a student in the United States since kindergarten, had a more extreme reaction:

Oh, I remember they told us and I was so—I am going to cry—it's happening again. . . . So we get into a group and everybody in my group, I just started talking to them. . . . I just wanted to see their reaction—and everybody felt just the same . . . they made a mistake, they just want to fill people in the classes (Brinton & Mano, 1994, p. 14).

What went wrong? Although most of these students had spent more than eight years in elementary, middle school, and high school classrooms, they were not linguistically prepared to succeed in higher education or in the workplace. Although able to speak English well enough to graduate from high school, the English skills they had acquired were not sufficient for a freshman college class. These students needed "well-designed instructional intervention" with "explicit instruction" in academic language (Fillmore & Snow, 2002, p. 31).

What, specifically, is academic language? In Chapter 2 we define cognitive academic language proficiency (CALP) as Cummins (1996) defined it: language that is cognitively demanding, decontextualized, and relying on a broad knowledge of specific vocabulary, specialized grammar, and academic discourse structures. Textbooks are written in academic language, and standardized tests are designed to measure it. The amount of time needed for ELLs to become proficient in this language averages from five to seven years (Thomas & Collier, 2002).

Children become adept at academic language usage through their interactions with their teachers, their course materials, and their peers. Gibbons (2003, p. 252) demonstrates the range of school language **registers** in her description of the following four texts:

Text 1: *Look, it's making them move. Those didn't stick.*

Text 2: *We found out the pins stuck on the magnet.*

Text 3: *Our experiment showed that magnets attract some metals.*

Text 4: *Magnetic attraction occurs only between ferrous metals.*

It is possible that you will not understand what the child is talking about in text 1 because the language is restricted to a here-and-now situation. If we tell you that the child is talking in a small group that is experimenting with magnets to determine which objects they will attract, the language becomes clearer. This language is context embedded. The use of the pronouns (e.g., *it, those*) is unclear unless you are standing near the speaker. Text 1 is an example of informal speech that is not appropriate for academic talk or written text.

Text 2 is also oral language and indicates what the child reported to the teacher after the experiment was complete. This shift in register shows that the child is able to identify elements of the language that must be specified for the teacher to understand. Thus, the words *pins* and *magnet* help to make the communication more explicit. This text is still highly personal, however, with the use of the pronoun *we* and the general word forms *stuck* and *found out*. This text begins to approach the style of academic, written language.

Text 3 represents the child's written report of the experiment. This version reads like an academic and scientific generalization. The verb forms are more specific (*attract*) and the results are qualified (*some metals*).

Text 4 is taken from a child's encyclopedia and is more generalized than text 3. Rather than talking about *our experiment*, the encyclopedia uses the term *magnetic attraction*. The verb form *occurs* is far more representative of scientific texts than the child's original statement (*the pins stuck*). *Ferrous metals* replace *some metals*.

The transition from text 1 to text 4 represents the process of linguistic and cognitive development that formal education is all about. The role of the teacher in this process is to provide the support that students need to make this kind of growth. A teacher can assist ELLs in moving from the social language of text 1 to the academic language of texts 3 and 4 by utilizing the following effective teaching strategies:

• Teacher repeats learner's utterances and then **recasts** them using academic vocabulary.

Teacher: *The magnets stuck to each other. They attracted each other.*

When students attempted to report on what happened in the magnet experiment, they used informal language such as *stuck* and *pushed*. The teacher repeated their language, *stuck to each other*, and then provided the technical terms necessary, *attract/repel*.

- Teacher signals how to **reformulate** student utterances in ways that are more academically acceptable.

Teacher: *Okay, can I just clarify something? You've got two magnets? They're in line? When you put the two together like that (demonstrating), they attracted each other. Is that right? Okay, can you tell me what you had to do next?*

In this example, the teacher supplied a demonstration of magnetic attraction and modeled the language needed to explain the process. Next the teacher **prompts** the student to continue with the explanation in a similar fashion.

- Teacher prompts a need for reformulating utterances.

Teacher: *Wait just a minute. Can you explain that a little bit more, Julianna?*

Here the teacher provided opportunities for the student to restate her learning using the models and prompts provided during the dialogue. On some occasions, learners attempted to restate several times, improving each time with the support of the teacher's reformulations and encouragement (Gibbons, 2003).

The result of this kind of learning conversation exposes ELLs to a great deal of redundancy. After working in inquiry groups with other students, they are then asked to report to the teacher or to classmates on their results. During this oral reporting phase, teachers recast the informal language of the students into the formal academic language of the classroom. Teachers also demonstrate their meanings, model the academic language, and urge learners to explain using the academic terminology of school. The oral reporting phase of the lesson, in which ELLs must actually use formal school language while being supported by teacher scaffolding, is critical for building an ELL's ability to learn academic language.

Culturally Diverse Language Patterns

Students from other cultures may come to school with different oral traditions than those that are expected and valued by North American teachers. This can be true even when the children are

Teacher Language Provides the Academic Model Required for Effective Content Learning

born in the United States. The ethnographic research of Heath (1983, 1986) indicates that learners from diverse cultural and economic groups are enculturated to use language in ways that are different from school language. In North America, middle-class parents use conversations with their children to enable them to become competent language users for the purposes of reporting on details, hypothesizing, linear storytelling, drawing inferences, generalizing, and evaluating.

In other cultures, parents use language to socialize and to teach respect for family and/or authority figures. Although storytelling is valued, the form of the oral narrative may vary depending on the culture. Stories in English tend to be linear with the plot directing the progress of the narration. Asian cultures may use a circular structure with the subject approached from a variety of different viewpoints. These stories tend to emphasize character over plot (Gadda, 1994). In the blue-collar African American families studied by Heath (1983), stories were valued if they showed creativity and were clever or verbally inventive. These stories were closer to performances than oral narratives.

The use of parental questioning varies from culture to culture as well. Middle-class North American parents tend to ask many **display questions.** These are questions whose answer is well known to the questioner. Schools value display questions as a way of assessing children's learning. In other cultures, display questions are rarely asked. Heath (1986, p. 161) reports that the working-class Mexican American parents that she studied "seldom ask questions that require children to repeat facts, rehearse the sequence of events, or foretell what they will do." Their questions focus on information within the family circle, seldom from outside that circle, and are rarely display questions.

Teachers of diverse learners, aware of the range of language patterns that children bring with them to school, need to expand the repertoire of these patterns to include those that the schools value. ELLs can achieve academic success if they are exposed to and taught a range of oral and written language usage. Using language to talk about math problems and solutions, discussing historical events and their effects, talking about characters and events in stories, and questioning processes in science will support our students' mastery of academic language as well as aid their comprehension and retention of content learning.

ORAL LANGUAGE DEVELOPMENT

In the progression of developing language skills, listening and then speaking (the aural-oral skills) are usually the first to be acquired. If ELLs are literate in their first language and have studied English as a foreign language, it is possible they will arrive in our classrooms with some reading and writing skills in English, although their comprehension and production may still be limited. Most beginning ELLs in the United States, however, are young, may have been born here, and have limited or little literacy in the home language. These students will need to develop their English capabilities by listening, developing understanding, and then beginning to speak.

The four language skills of listening, speaking, reading, and writing are related to each other and complement each other. Although listening and reading are receptive skills, learners must still be cognitively active to engage in them well. The learner acts upon input that is either oral or written, hypothesizes meaning, and interprets the message. For ELLs who are not literate in their home language, listening comprehension generally precedes reading comprehension. The two processes are related in that the ability to interpret oral language is useful in supporting reading comprehension and vice versa. These are internal processes that are difficult to observe and assess. They are not passive processes, however. ELLs use strategies of various kinds to access meaning. While listening, students may use a strategy of watching carefully for gestural cues to meaning, may listen selectively for words that are stressed or repeated, may repeat certain words with a questioning intonation, nod in agreement, ask clarifying questions (e.g., *What is . . . ?* or *Can you repeat . . . ?*) or ask an informant for a translation. While reading, students may use strategies including previewing the pictures and charts in the text, using a dictionary, making an analogy to what is already known, or searching for specific information.

Speaking and writing are productive processes. They require ELLs to create rather than interpret a sentence orally or in writing. Here, young English language learners unconsciously hypothesize the correct language form based upon the rules they have created for the language. This is a process of induction—creating a rule based upon the data analyzed through listening and reading. In this way, the four skills support each other and promote language development.

Because of the "dynamic interrelationship" (Peregoy & Boyle, 2008) of the four skills, it is helpful to language learning if teachers plan to integrate skill use during instruction. The ability to read target vocabulary on the chalkboard assists listening comprehension. Oral practice in the use of new vocabulary assists reading comprehension. Oral role-plays assist in the development of grammatically correct writing. Time spent in written composition helps ELLs to negotiate the rules of grammar that can then be used in oral speech. Efficient teachers know that learning accelerates when the four language skills are integrated within their lessons.

In this chapter, we will discuss the growth of oral language within the classroom. We will describe the beginning and intermediate stages of language development and suggest procedures for supporting language growth in a variety of contexts.

STAGES OF ORAL LANGUAGE DEVELOPMENT

To plan lessons appropriately, we need to be aware of the level of English understood and spoken by our students. Krashen and Terrell (1983) defined four stages of language development: preproduction, early production, speech emergence, and intermediate fluency. All ELLs progress through these four stages but not at the same rate.

Teachers of English to Speakers of Other Languages, Inc. (TESOL) has identified five language levels that overlap somewhat with the Krashen and Terrell levels (TESOL, 2006):

Level 1 Starting: ELLs can communicate basic needs and use high-frequency vocabulary.

Level 2 Emerging: ELLs can communicate about routine experiences and use generalized academic vocabulary, phrases, and short sentences.

Level 3 Developing: ELLs can communicate on familiar matters and use some specialized academic vocabulary and expanded sentences in writing.

Level 4 Expanding: ELLs can use language in abstract situations and for new experiences and specialized vocabulary as well as a variety of sentence lengths with varying complexity.

Level 5 Bridging: ELLs can use a wide range of texts and recognize implicit meaning and use technical academic vocabulary in a variety of sentence lengths and with varying linguistic complexity.

The TESOL levels apply to both oral and written language whereas the Krashen and Terrell levels apply only to oral language. TESOL does not include a preproduction level but has expanded the intermediate fluency level into three separate levels (3, 4, and 5). Level 5, the bridging level, occurs when ELLs are very close to becoming fully English proficient but still require modifications for grade-level material. In the discussions that follow, we refer to both the TESOL and Krashen/Terrell levels.

Preproduction

The preproduction stage is usually the shortest stage with most ELLs emerging into beginning speech in a couple of months. However, individual differences occur among learners; we have had students who began to speak in "chunks" of memorized language on their second day of school. We have also had experiences with students who did not speak for an extended period of time. One student, Virgine, was silent for an entire year! At the end of that year, however, she began to speak, not in one-word utterances but in sentences. Although Virgine was silent, she was still learning English.

During the preproduction stage, it is important to engage ELLs in classroom learning experiences even if they are unable or unwilling to speak. We send important expectation messages to learners when we treat them as functioning classroom members. During this time, teachers need to provide comprehensible input and to lower affective filters. Engaging ELLs in social interactions in the classroom will help to fulfill both of these criteria. In our experience, ELLs respond to instruction more quickly if they feel socially secure in our classrooms. Having a friend or a buddy provides that security. English-speaking students who are not accustomed to having a non-English speaker in the classroom may need some help in providing assistance to the ELLs. Show students how to use gestures to provide context to oral speech. Help students to develop empathy for the ELLs and monitor their interactions to avoid misunderstandings or conflict.

Preproduction ELLs can usually understand more language than they are able to produce and are actively learning through listening to our language input. Teachers can support student comprehension at this stage with gestures, scaffolding devices, abundant context clues, lesson outlines projected on the wall, drawings, and simple commands requiring a nonlinguistic response. It is important to model all expected behavior, including simple procedures such as lining up, accessing a locker, or requesting a bathroom pass. Learners at this stage respond well to peer instruction and a buddy's directions. Without forcing students to speak, we can encourage speech emergence at this stage through the use of classroom chants, group songs, raps, and whole group responses. Total physical response (TPR), a strategy in which learners show their understanding of new language by responding to teachers' series of commands to perform actions, is highly successful with beginners (Herrell & Jordan, 2007). Predictable books with repeated choral responses are effective in the early elementary grades. Older learners are attracted to rap chants. These activities are even more appealing to many learners when we combine them with rhythmic clapping, finger snapping, or toe tapping.

Although ELLs may not be able to speak English yet, it is important that we continue to speak to them in English. Smiling, making eye contact, and being aware of body language will carry a great deal of meaning at this stage of language development. It is also helpful to provide modeling of the kinds of language forms learners need during the preproduction stage. The following forms are suggestive:

What's this/that?

Good morning.

Good-bye.

How are you? Fine, thanks.

I want . . .

I need . . .

I don't understand.

Can I . . . ?

Modeling two or three language forms, writing the forms on a note card for literate learners, and using context clues to meaning will help ELLs to proceed into the next stage of development, the early production stage.

Level 1: Starting—Early Production

The starting/early production stage is a continuation of the preproduction stage. At this time, ELLs still require comprehensible input and a low affective filter. They still require social interactions that are supportive and friendly. ELLs are able to attend more to language input at this stage, and they are able to respond with one-word answers and then simple phrasal responses.

Reading and writing are not to be delayed until learners can speak English. Reading and writing provide important elements of comprehensible input, and these skills can be included in a school program from the very beginning.

The techniques used in the preproduction stage can be continued at this time. Teachers can also use targeted questioning techniques to include ELLs in the instructional conversation. *Yes/no questions* are the easiest for learners to respond to:

Teacher: *Is this a map?*

Student: *Yes.*

Teacher: *Yes, it is. It's a map of the United States.*

In this example, the teacher asks a simple yes/no question and then expands the student's response in a way that provides more vocabulary and grammatical information to the learner.

Either/or questions also require a one-word response but are supportive in that they supply the vocabulary item needed as well as the pronunciation.

Teacher: *Is this a map of the United States or Canada?*

Student: *United States.*

Teacher: *That's right. It's a map of the United States.*

TABLE 5.1 Language Development Stages

Stage	Sample Student Behaviors	Sample Teacher Behaviors	Questioning Techniques
Starting • Students totally new to English • Generally lasts 1–3 months	• Points to or provides other nonverbal responses • Actively listens • Responds to commands • May be reluctant to speak • Understands more than one can produce • Needs survival language	• Makes gestures • Focuses language on conveying meanings and vocabulary development • Uses repetition • Does not force student to speak • Models all expected behavior • Encourages students to participate in group songs, chants, and choral responses • Checks comprehension frequently	• *Point to . . .* • *Find the . . .* • *Put the . . .next to the . . .* • *Do you have the . . .?* • *Is this a . . .?* • *Who wants the . . .?* • *Who has the . . .?*
Emerging • Students are "low beginners." • Generally lasts several weeks	• Uses one- or two-word utterances • Uses short phrases • Initiates conversations by gesturing or using single words • Can work with rhymes and rhythms • Continues to rely on buddies	• Asks questions that can be answered by yes/no and either/or responses • Models correct responses • Ensures a supportive, low anxiety environment • Does not overtly call attention to grammar errors • Asks short-answer WH questions	• Yes/no: *Is the light on?* • Either/or: *Is this a screwdriver or a hammer?* • One-word response: *What utensil am I holding in my hand?* • General questions that encourage lists of words: *What do you see on the tool board?* • Two-word response: *Where did he go? To work.*
Developing • Students are "beginners" • May last several weeks or months	• Speaks in short phrases and sentences • Participates in small-group activities • Demonstrates comprehension in a variety of ways • Begins to use language more freely but makes many errors in grammar • Enjoys role-playing • Uses present tense almost exclusively • Can dictate 3–5 word sentences	• Focuses content on key concepts • Uses expanded vocabulary and responses • Models language structures • Asks open-ended questions that stimulate language production • Provides frequent comprehension checks • Uses performance-based assessment	• *Why?* • *How?* • *How is this like that?* • *Tell me about . . .* • *Talk about . . .* • *Describe . . .* • *How would you change this part?*
Expanding • Students are "high beginners, intermediate, or advanced" • May require several years to achieve native-like fluency in academic settings	• Engages in discourse and communicates thoughts more effectively • Participates in reading and writing activities to acquire new information	• Fosters conceptual development and expanded literacy through content • Continues to make lessons comprehensible and interactive	• *What would you recommend/suggest?* • *How do you think this story will end?* • *What is the story mainly about?*

TABLE 5.1 Language Development Stages *(Continued)*

Stage	Sample Student Behaviors	Sample Teacher Behaviors	Questioning Techniques
	• Uses language for concrete problem solving	• Teaches thinking and study skills	• *What is your opinion on this matter?*
	• Can use present and past tenses	• Continues to be alert to individual differences in language and culture	• *Describe/compare . .*
	• Can begin to write independently with teacher support	• Uses sheltered instructional strategies	• *How are these similar/ different?*
	• Can use grammar for substitutions, deletions, and rearrangements of words		• *What would happen if . . . ?*
	• May experience difficulties in abstract, cognitively demanding subjects at school, especially when a high degree of literacy is required		• *Which do you prefer? Why?*
			• *Create . . .*
Bridging • Students approach skill development comparable to that of English-only peers	• Engages in debates and explanations with increasing linguistic complexity	• Teaches language skills through a focus on content	• *Justify...*
	• Engages in research using longer written texts with implicit meanings	• Teaches thinking and study skills	• *Assess...*
	• Writes in multiple genres in a variety of grammatical structures	• Continues to be alert to differences in language and culture	• *Persuade...*
		• Continues to promote comprehension through selected sheltering techniques	• *Speculate...*
			• *Propose...*
			• *Evaluate...*

Source: Adapted with permission from Grognet, Jameson, Franco, & Derrick-Mescua (2000). *Enhancing English language learning in elementary classrooms: Study guide* (p. 43). Washington, DC and McHenry, IL: Center for Applied Linguistics and Delta Systems.

WH questions are the next in difficulty. They ask questions such as *What? When?* and *Where?* These questions require only a one-word response but the response must be supplied by the learner.

Teacher: *What is this?*

Student: *A map.*

Teacher: *That's right. It's a map of the United States.*

In addition, teachers can ask "predictable questions" such as:

How are you?

What's your name?

How old are you?

Do you like ice cream?

These questions are predictable in that ELLs are usually asked about their name and age. Other predictable questions presuppose the answer. Even so, questions of this sort open up conversations and promote interactions with language that lead to further oral development.

Even when ELLs can only say one word, teachers can use that one word to develop opportunities for comprehensible input. Consider this example from Urzua (1981, p. 9) of a teacher with a five-year-old child:

Child: *Fish.*

Teacher: *Yes it is a fish. A tiny fish. A fish the color of your shirt.*

The teacher in this example is responsive to the child's attempt to interact in the new language and provides additional vocabulary and information in an effort to keep the conversation moving.

In the following example (Urzua, 1981, p. 22), note the repetitions used by the teacher reading a book with a child.

Child: *(Pointing to a picture in the book) Look at that!*

Teacher: *He's sweeping the floor. Oh, he's cross. Show me. He's cross. Yes, he's cross.*

Child: *(Singing a child's song) Na-na-na . . .*

Teacher: *I like that song. It makes me happy. I like it very much.*

Child: *(Pointing to a picture) Cry.*

Teacher: *Cry. The elephant's going to cry. Why? Why did the elephant cry?*

Child: *Lion there.*

Teacher: *Oh the lion is there. The elephant is afraid of the lion. He's afraid.*

Repetition and vocabulary information are evident in the following example (Urzua, 1981, pp. 40–41) in which the child wants to paint a red picture but has chosen the orange paint.

Teacher: *Do you want to paint red?*

Child: *Huh?*

Teacher: *Do you want to paint with red?*

Child: *Yeah.*

Teacher: *All right, here's red. There's just a little bit.*

Child: *Okay. This red?*

Teacher: *Uh huh. A little bit of red . . . Is it the red you want?*

Child: *Ah, this a more?*

Teacher: *I'm gonna put a little water with your red. Then you'll have enough red.*

In addition to providing vocabulary, repetition, and information about the structure of the language, teachers also give effective feedback to learners through their conversations. In the following example (Urzua, 1981, p. 30), note the persistence of the teacher as she tries to understand the child. Her final question enables the learner to understand that she needs to elaborate on her message in order to be understood.

Child: *I got a bathing suit . . . A new one.*

Teacher: *You have a what?*

Child: *A bathing suit.*

Teacher: *A baby shoe?*

Child: *A bathing suit.*

Teacher: *Soup?*

Child: *Bathing suit.*

Teacher: *Baby soap?*

Child: *Bathing suit.*

Teacher: *What do you do with it?*

Child: *I put it on and I go swimming.*

Teacher: *A bathing suit. You put it on and you go swimming.*

Level 2: Emerging—Speech Emergence

The emerging/speech emergence phase usually lasts longer than the preceding stages. During this time, ELLs experiment with language although they may make many grammatical errors. As in the preceding examples, however, teachers do not overtly correct errors in oral production. Because the goal is comprehension, it is frequently best to provide the learner with extensions of his or her own language attempts (e.g., *a tiny fish* or *the elephant's going to cry*) and continue the conversation. Modeling the correct language serves many purposes. Teacher modeling provides vocabulary, structure, and feedback to learners. But most importantly, it sends the message "I want to talk with you and help you to understand my language."

Teachers can continue to target their questioning to ELL proficiency levels at this stage, asking questions requiring more than a one-word response. If we are aware of the student's ability to use language, we can target our questioning to a level slightly higher than the learner is capable of producing alone. In this way, we challenge ELLs to continue to develop, and we support them while they are learning.

The teacher strategies from earlier stages are still important at the emergence/speech emergence stage. In addition, we need to be more aware of checking the comprehension of ELLs. We can check comprehension through a variety of questioning techniques: pair and group reports as well as nonverbal means such as illustrations, signals, and labeling of diagrams or graphic organizers. At this time, it is also helpful to involve ELLs in performance-based assessments such as role-plays, projects, and investigations.

Levels 3, 4, and 5: Developing, Expanding, Bridging—Intermediate Fluency

This is the longest period of the language development process. Intermediate-level ELLs take years to achieve an academic language level that is comparable to their grade-level peers. In Thomas and Collier's final report on their longitudinal study of various models for developing English language in schools (2002, p. 270), they found that when ELLs are "schooled all in second language" in a high-quality program, the process takes, on the average, from five to seven years but may take much longer for learners with interrupted education or for those who are in programs that are not well implemented. The implications of this amount of time are staggering. ELLs entering an English language school during the middle school years may never have enough time to catch up. Indeed, language learning is a process that will last throughout our students' lifetimes. They will continually be confronting new language demands as they progress through school into work or into college, where each new course will overflow with vocabulary challenges.

We can discern three levels within the intermediate fluency stage (developing, expanding, and bridging), but the strategies used at each of these levels are similar. Teachers continue to focus on comprehensible input, expanding the input to wider content contexts, readings, and genres. Questioning techniques are also widened, and *open-ended questions* requiring expanded responses become routine at the developing stage. Grade-appropriate learning objectives will help to ensure that ELLs develop conceptually as well as linguistically. It is important to continue to use sheltered learning strategies throughout all three stages because the learning and language demands increase.

Learners at the intermediate fluency level are capable of producing social conversation that is comparable to grade-level peers. This presents a dilemma for teachers who have had little experience with English language learners. It is not unusual for a student to be fluent in social language while still lagging far behind in academic skills such as oral debating, persuasion, reading, writing, and test taking. In our experience, teachers who teach these youngsters are often baffled as to why the academic problems persist, often throughout the elementary school years. Because their interpersonal language seems so fluent, teachers tend to view the ELLs as proficient speakers even though teachers may know that the learners are developing English as a second or third language. It is at this stage that teachers might initiate diagnostic testing to determine why the ELL is not yet proficient and perhaps even if the student has special needs. Tests written in academic language—the same language that requires five to seven (or more) years to learn—may not reveal the language development needs of the ELL.

When learners are able to communicate with social language, their motivation to continue to acquire academic language may falter because the academic language is not necessary to achieve communication. Those ELLs who read widely can acquire a great deal of language from written materials. Unfortunately, for many ELLs, reading without careful scaffolding and support can be a difficult and frustrating experience because of the challenge of academic language along with the large number of unknown words. The most important thing teachers can do for ELLs at this stage of learning is to continue to challenge them cognitively and linguistically while supporting their learning with a variety of sheltering techniques. Consciously instructing with language objectives is crucial at this stage to spur the development of academic language. Learners need explicit instruction in language structures and vocabulary found in the content curriculum. Even in the final bridging stage when learners are considered to be proficient language users and may exit from ESL support programs, they will still require close monitoring and language support for a period of time.

TEACHER TOOLS FOR ORAL LANGUAGE DEVELOPMENT

For oral language to develop in classrooms, students must "interact directly and frequently with people who know the language well enough to reveal how it works and how it can be used" (Fillmore & Snow, 2002, p. 31). The primary person fitting this description is the teacher. In the following section, we describe the kind of language that teachers need to use in classrooms to give clarity to their explanations and directions. Then we describe ways to improve the nature of teachers' question-and-response interactions with students.

Increasing Clarity in Teacher Language

Clarity is the process of delivering clear instructions to students—of explaining things well (Saphier & Gower, 1997). It is the primary task of most teachers. We need clarity to introduce new subject matter, to give directions, explain concepts, clear up confusions, and help learners make connections between old and new concepts.

CLEAR SPEECH   The bottom line of clarity is clear speech. The following are aspects of effective teacher language:

- Repetition.
- Slower rate of speech with occasional pauses.
- Gestures, context, and explanatory devices.
- Stress on important vocabulary items.
- Modeling of correct forms.
- Avoidance of unnecessary slang, idioms, and jargon.

  To this list, we add the following caveats:

- Avoid unknown references.
- Avoid sarcasm.

   Referring to people, places, or things that have no meaning for our ELLs is confusing rather than clarifying. We are always reminded of the second graders who stared blankly as the teacher referred to an object in a story as being *as flat as a phonograph record*. It had not occurred to the teacher that these children were too young to have ever seen a phonograph record. The rest of the lesson was spent correcting that error as the teacher pulled her old record player out from the back of the closet and showed the wide-eyed youngsters how the record magically dropped onto the turn table and played.

   Unknown, unexplained referents may turn learners' minds away from the focus of the lesson. These referents can become more a distraction than a tool for learning. ELLs will not have the same experiences as students growing up in North America. Although they may be familiar with current pop music stars, they might not understand why George Washington is pictured cutting down a cherry tree or what the relationship is between a groundhog and the weather. Teachers can avoid the use of unfamiliar referents, or, when necessary, build the background knowledge necessary for ELLs to understand what they learn. Frequent comprehension checks will alert teachers as to whether referents they are using are familiar or unfamiliar.

   Using sarcasm in classrooms is seldom appropriate. Students love humor, and ELLs can appreciate visual and physical humor as well as some humorous language. But sarcasm is very difficult to understand and is often at someone's expense. What's more, when ELLs see everyone laughing and they do not understand why, they're likely to assume that people are laughing at them. ELLs can be the victims of an inappropriate joke without ever understanding the meaning of the comment.

   In addition, effective teachers enunciate classroom language clearly. Teaching talk is different from social conversation. When we misunderstand a friend or cannot quite catch a meaning, we feel free to say *Excuse me?* or *Huh?* Those kinds of cues are not available to children in classrooms. If teachers do not use clear diction, enunciate properly, or pronounce words clearly and appropriately, ELLs have no easy way to retrieve the missing information.

Clear, Specific, and Fluent Teacher Language Enables ELLs to Learn Academic Concepts and Vocabulary

Teachers can also be excellent models for grammar and sentence formation. Long, rambling, or run-on sentences are not as communicative as short, simple sentences. And because vocabulary is such an important element of subject matter learning, teachers need to use appropriate vocabulary—content-specific vocabulary—rather than substitute more general and vague terminology. ELLs in math classes need to hear the words *numerator* and *denominator* rather than *the number on the top* or *the number on the bottom*. They need to learn specific vocabulary items, such as *magnet, attract, force,* rather than generic ones, such as *thing, stuff,* or *what-cha-ma-call-it.*

Modeling academic speech routinely for students assists them in understanding meaning through context and aids them in acquiring the necessary academic terms needed to achieve at a high level. Often teachers will use social speech in classrooms in an effort to be understood. Compare the differences between the two:

Academic Language	Social Language
• Conclude and analyze	• Figure out
• Categorize and classify	• Group
• Predict	• Guess
• Infer	• Think
• Observe	• Watch
• Demonstrate	• Show
• Report and explain	• Tell
• Record	• Write down
• Differentiate	• Sort
• Research	• Find out
• Create	• Make

A teacher's speech assists cognitive academic language learning when it is specific. The following are examples of nonspecific and confusing utterances (Saphier & Gower, 1997):

- Kind of, sort of, mostly, somewhat
- Basically, in a nutshell, so to speak, you know, actually, and so forth
- I guess
- A bunch, a little, some
- Possible, perhaps, maybe
- Generally, ordinarily, sometime
- Somehow, somewhere, someplace, something

Unclear language in the classroom might sound like the following:

This science lesson may help you to understand a bit about several aspects of photosynthesis. Maybe you remember something about photosynthesis from yesterday's lesson?

The teacher could have improved clarity and comprehension in the following way:

Today we're going to learn the three elements that contribute to photosynthesis. First, what is the definition of photosynthesis that we learned yesterday?

The second example is clear as to what the students will learn (three elements). The teacher's question indicates what they want to know (the definition of photosynthesis) and gives learners a clue that it was learned yesterday. The use of markers such as *first* provides ELLs with transition points in the teacher's language, again promoting the clarity and comprehensibility of the language.

Finally, teacher language must be as free as possible of false starts and hesitations. These occur when the teacher has not completely thought out what to say or is not really clear about what is being taught. An example might be:

Today, we're uh . . . going to . . . I'll help you to understand what we me . . . , or what we defined yesterday, as photosynthesis. We're going to review or present . . . , I'll present the ele . . . three prerequisite elements that go wi . . . , that contribute to photosynthesis.

Teacher language is the instrument that we use to play our instructional music. In addition to our form and word selections, volume, stress, and intonation enable us to capture the attention of our students.

EXPLANATORY DEVICES   Explanatory devices contribute to the clarity of our instruction by providing visual clues to the meaning of our oral language. In the preparation phase of instruction, teachers collect the materials they will use to make the input comprehensible to their ELLs. These materials include the following:

- Objects, photos, props, and materials to be used as examples.
- Visual organizers such as the Venn diagram, time lines, flowcharts, semantic maps, and tree diagrams. (See Figure 5.1 for examples.)
- Demonstrations.
- Role-plays.
- Teacher-created notes or an outline of the lesson to be used by students for later review.
- Teacher-created outlines or graphic organizers projected on the wall or monitor—especially useful in upper elementary and secondary school classes where students are expected to write summaries in their notebooks. A visual provides a written clue to the structure of the text and the meaning of the oral language.

COGNITIVE EMPATHY   To explain things well to ELLs, we must first understand what is inside their heads. Saphier and Gower (1997, p. 190) call this "cognitive empathy"—knowing the information, feelings, and goals learners bring with them into the classroom. When teachers have cognitive empathy with their students, they are able to recognize the moment when misunderstandings occur and then focus on exactly what is not understood in ways that clear up confusion. Cognitive empathy requires teachers to check for the understanding of *all* students, *frequently*, throughout the lesson. One moment in particular when checking is critical is when giving directions.

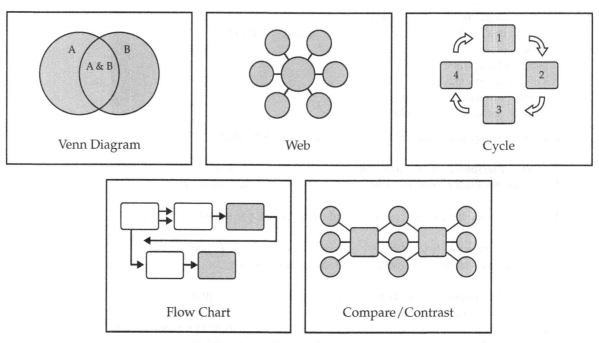

FIGURE 5.1 Graphic Organizers Present Visual Pictures That Support Language and Thinking Concepts

GIVING DIRECTIONS AND STATING REASONS FOR LEARNING   Clarity requires that teachers clearly think through the steps of their directions. We can do this by imagining our students as they follow our instructions—running a movie in our minds as we watch them proceed. By doing this, we can avoid directions such as the following:

Get into small groups and think of an ending for the story we wrote this morning.

In this example, the teacher has not indicated the number of students in the group nor indicated the roles they will play, such as recording and reporting. She has suggested they *think of* an ending but has not told them to write it. These learners will also need some modeling of ways to reach consensus, offer suggestions, and use the language of agreement and disagreement. They need written directions in addition to the teacher's oral statements. Without these supports, it is unlikely that the activity will be successful for all learners. Clearer instructions might include these steps:

1. *First, form groups of three. Count off by three.*

    Number 1 is the leader—you get the group started and ask questions.
    Number 2 is the recorder—you take notes.
    Number 3 is the reporter—you tell your group's ideas to the class.

2. *Second, retell the story to one another. You can take turns.*
3. *Third, brainstorm a new ending. Then select the best one and write it down.*
4. *Finally, your reporter will report your answer to the class.*
5. *Now watch as Candace, Araxy, Paul, and I show you how the activity looks.*

Finally, the teacher needs to provide the students a reason for doing the activity. Students should have a clear understanding of how the activity contributes to the objective of the lesson, the learning from the past, or the learning that will occur in the future. Learners will have more engagement and effort when they understand the value of their activities.

Question and Response Patterns

The teacher-learner dialogue forms the basis of the instructional conversation in classrooms. We have argued for collaborative classrooms where teachers and students negotiate meaning through dialogues that are clear, comprehensible, promote higher-order cognitive skills, and are representative of all students in the classroom.

In fact, there is evidence that teacher talk far outweighs student talk in most classrooms (Goldenberg, 1996; Harklau, 1994). The instructional pattern that predominates in classes from K to grade 12 is recitation. This is a pattern of:

- Teacher question
- Student response
- Teacher evaluation

Without knowledge, experience, and motivation to teach differently, teachers will teach the way they were taught. Because many teachers have gone to schools where a recitation pattern prevailed, it is difficult to dislodge this pattern from the repertoire of many teachers in classrooms today. Why is a preponderance of recitation problematical for students? Ramirez, Yuen, and Ramey (1991) conducted a study of more than 2,000 language-learning students in bilingual and immersion classrooms. They were asked if the classrooms of these learners provided an ideal language-learning environment. They responded:

No. Consistently across grade levels . . . students are limited in their opportunities to produce language and in their opportunities to produce more complex language. Direct observations reveal that teachers do most of the talking in classrooms, making about twice as many utterances as do students. Students produce language only when they are working directly with a teacher, and then only in response to teacher initiations. Of major concern is that in over half of the interactions that teachers have with students, students do not produce any language as they are only listening or responding with nonverbal gestures or actions. Of equal concern is that when students do respond, typically they provide only simple information recall statements. Rather than being provided with the opportunity to generate original statements, students are asked to provide simple discrete close-ended or patterned (i.e., expected) responses. This pattern of teacher/student interaction not only limits a student's opportunity to create and manipulate language freely, but also limits the student's ability to engage in more complex learning (i.e., higher order thinking skills) (Ramirez, Yuen, & Ramey, 1991, p. 8).

The recitation pattern is often referred to as IRF (initiation, response, feedback). An example might be the following:

- Initiation   TEACHER: *Digestion: Who knows what digestion means?*
- Response   STUDENT: *I know. I know. When you eat.*
- Feedback: TEACHER: *That's right. When we eat we digest our food. That's digestion* (Fillmore & Snow, 2002, p. 24).

Too often, teachers evaluate an incorrect response as in the preceding example without probing for more accurate information. The answer given by the student here is imprecise and does not indicate that processes of digestion occur in the mouth, stomach, and intestines and involve the processing of food. However, the teacher's response indicates that this definition is adequate. The IRF pattern is responsible for preventing the language output of the sentence-length discourse structures that lead to language growth. In these cases, teacher question-and-response patterns inhibit the ideal conditions known to lead to increased language achievement.

STICKING WITH YOUR STUDENTS   Environments in which ELLs' use of language is highly restricted will result in less language development. ELLs need opportunities for extended conversations with knowledgeable language users in order to develop the high level of academic language necessary for school success. The recitation classroom limits learners to one-word responses as in the following dialogue (MacLure & French, 1980, as cited in Simich-Dudgeon, 1998, p. 3):

Teacher: *Matthew, what do you think hedges are useful for?*

Matthew: *Corn (quietly).*

Teacher: *Can't hear you, Matthew.*

Matthew: *Corn.*

Teacher: *Hedges are useful for corn? No. Karen?*

Matthew: *So the things can't get out.*

Teacher: *So the things can't get out. (Three-second pause.) Stop the animals getting into the cornfield to eat all the corn—wouldn't it?*

The teacher in this exchange evaluated Matthew's one-word response (*No*) and went on to the next student. Matthew had no opportunity to explain his response. Although it is very likely that he knew that hedges were related to corn cultivation, he simply couldn't express the relationship without some scaffolding from the teacher. For example, the teacher could say, *Corn? Tell me a little more about that, Matthew.*

If Matthew could not tell more about his answer, the teacher had other options. She could ask pinpoint, specific questions to isolate the point of confusion or to provide supportive language structures: *The hedges grow around the corn, don't they? Corn grows behind the hedges.* Sticking with a student sends a clear message that we know they can do it and we are there to help them do it successfully. What message does it send when we respond *no* and move on to another student?

WAIT TIME   Sometimes we need to slow down the rapid-fire question-response recitation pattern to provide enough time for ELLs to think about the question and formulate a response. This time lag is most critical for ELLs who may still be trying to translate the teacher's question while others are answering it. The answer will never be heard, and the ELL slips further from becoming a participant in the instructional conversation.

According to Simich-Dudgeon, McCreedy, & Scheleppegrell, one sixth-grader verbalized this in the following way:

> *[My friend] knows what [the answer is] but he can't actually say it out, and sometimes that happens with people who don't know English, you know. It's just that you can't phrase it right* (Simich-Dudgeon, 1998, p. 6).

Using sufficient **wait time** (Rowe, 1986) helps learners to process questions and to begin to formulate a reasoned response. Wait time requires that we wait for at least three to five seconds before calling on a student to answer a comprehension question. This is sometimes harder than it seems. Most teachers are uncomfortable with silence in the classroom. The average wait time is 0.5 seconds (Saphier & Gower, 1997).

But the results of using wait time make waiting worthwhile. We have noted that more students attempt to respond when we wait a little. We have also noted that the quality of the responses improves. Perhaps when students have more time to formulate answers, they process their responses and refine them—not blurting out the first thing that pops into their heads.

Bob Hunter, a middle-school teacher, experimented with wait time in his classroom. He thought that the message he had been sending to his students was a faulty one: *Answering fast shows that you're smart.* In fact, Bob valued thoughtfulness and wanted to curb the impulsiveness of the youngsters in front of him. He also worried about the ELLs in his class who never answered a question, the shy students who never raised their hands, and the learning disabled students who were similarly not included in class discussions.

But Bob's initial experiments with wait time were disastrous. His students became impatient with not being called on promptly. They began to call out, make hooting noises, and in other ways try to get their teacher's attention. Finally, Bob decided to include his students in the experiment. He explained that he was using something called *wait time* with them and told them the reason why: *We all need to participate and be more thoughtful in our class discussions and comments.* From then on, Bob saw a great improvement in the quantity of responses he received from students who had not participated before. He also noted that responses were more thoughtful. He sent a message to his students through the use of this technique: *What we're talking about is important and I'm going to help you join in this conversation.*

Scaffolding Oral Language Development

As children progress through school they have opportunities to interact with teachers and with other adults in ways that increase cognitive levels and **linguistic competence**. Vygotsky (1962) described a collaborative, social context as being the critical component of all learning.

He rejected the view that learning occurs by the teacher's transmitting information to the student. He also rejected the view that learning occurs through the individual learner's attempts at discovery and inquiry. Rather, he saw all learning and development as a process of collaboration between the teacher and the learner. Through this collaboration, learners are supported in their language use to speak and perform tasks at a level beyond their competency—beyond their **zone of proximal development (ZPD)**.

Scaffolding is a term first used by Bruner (Wood, Bruner, & Ross, 1976) to metaphorically describe the temporary, yet essential, nature of the structures that teachers use to support learning. Oral scaffolding helps maintain the learner's interest, reduce choices, maintain goal orientation, highlight critical aspects of the task, control frustration, and demonstrate a potential activity path (Wood et al., 1976). Gibbons (2002, p. 10) defines *scaffolding* as "a special kind of help that assists ELLs to move toward new skills, concepts, or levels of understanding." Scaffolding is thus the temporary assistance by which a teacher helps a learner perform so that the learner will later be able to complete a similar task alone. It is future-oriented—as Vygotsky has said, what a child can do with support today she or he can do alone tomorrow.

Teacher-guided **collaborative dialogues** scaffold oral language usage in content classrooms and provide academic language-learning opportunities for ELLs. Primarily, they provide opportunities for ELLs to use the language purposefully and then support that language use. However, simply listening to a new language is not sufficient to be able to learn and use it for academic purposes. ELLs need to be able to talk either to their teachers or to their peers about what they are learning. During teacher-guided collaborative dialogues, teachers may ask students to report to them on what they have read or learned. Open-ended questions are helpful to begin the conversation. They allow ELLs to select the information they will talk about.

Tell me what you know about . . . ?

What did you discover about . . . ?

What did you find out about . . . ?

What can you tell me about . . . ?

As ELLs begin to report, their utterances will be filled with false starts and hesitations. At this point, they need time to express themselves adequately. It is difficult to wait in these situations, but we need to wait rather than jump in and solve the language dilemma for the student. We can support language development by the use of questioning that focuses on the meaning the student is trying to convey. Table 5.2 provides an example of scaffolding of oral language for reporting on a middle-school science experiment related to density. In Table 5.2, the teacher slows down the conversation and waits while the student struggles to report what happened when he placed various items in a bowl of water. The teacher's questions accomplish several purposes: They pinpoint the exact area of confusion in the student's language (e.g., *What goes down?*). They model grammatically correct sentences (e.g., *The wood floats.*). They provide the needed content vocabulary and grammatical structures to report on the experiment (e.g., *The screw sinks because it's more dense or less dense?*), and they probe for fuller, complete explanations (e.g., *What else? What goes down? What causes the screw to sink?*). The student leads the conversation and is given the time to develop the language he needs to express his knowledge. Scaffolding in this way enables language learning to occur.

Teachers can create opportunities for collaborative dialogues in classroom interactions with ELLs by using a pattern of interaction (Simich-Dudgeon, 1998, p. 3) characterized by

- Teacher question
- Student response
- Teacher-facilitated negotiation of meaning, or feedback

Teachers use a variety of strategies to facilitate and negotiate meaning and/or provide feedback to students. We have discussed the importance of wait time to provide opportunities for learners to construct language. We have also mentioned the variety of questioning techniques that can be used to support collaborative conversations. In the dialogue on density, the teacher begins the conversation with an open-ended question: *What did you find out?* The teacher follows up with a series of WH questions to pinpoint the areas where miscommunication may occur: *What goes down?* The WH questions are followed by an either-or question that models the target vocabulary and grammatical structure of the comparative: *The screw sinks because it's more dense or less dense?*

TABLE 5.2 A Teacher-guided Collaborative Dialogue Can Be Used to Scaffold a Science Experiment

Commentary	Teacher	Student
The teacher begins the dialogue with an open-ended question.	*What did you find out?*	*If you put a wood in the water . . . it . . . stay up.*
The teacher supplies the target vocabulary item "float," restates the student's sentence, and probes for more information.	*The wood floats? Okay. What else?*	*The thing . . . you put the thing . . . and it . . . it go down.*
The teacher's question indicates the specific noun needed for communication to continue.	*What goes down?*	*The screw . . . the screw go down in a water.*
The teacher provides the vocabulary item "sink," and asks a cause-and-effect question.	*What causes the screw to sink?*	*The screw sink because it . . . too . . . it too . . . screw too . . .*
The teacher provides two choices for the student to select the appropriate word.	*The screw sinks because it's more dense or less dense?*	*More dense . . . The screw sink because it more dense.*
The teacher restates the student's sentence while confirming the meaning.	*Yes, the screw is more dense and so it sinks in the water. What about the wood?*	*The wood less dense. The wood float because it less dense.*

In addition to questioning, teachers use a series of strategies to keep the conversation going:

- **Repetition:** The teacher repeats and may expand the student's utterance.
- **Recasting:** The teacher provides needed technical or academic vocabulary.
- **Reformulation:** The teacher models the necessary academic language.
- **Prompting:** To address a need for a student reformulation, the teacher provides opportunities for the students to restate using academic language.

The density conversation shows examples of each of these strategies. Repetition of student language with an expansion is seen in the question *The screw sinks because it's more dense or less dense?* Recasting is seen in the utterance: *The wood floats?* in which the teacher supplies the vocabulary for *float*. Reformulation occurs when the teacher says: *Yes, the screw is more dense and so it sinks in the water.* Finally, the dialogue has several examples of teacher prompting: *What else? What about the wood?* Each of these prompts sends the clear message: *You can do it and I'm not going to give up on you.*

Teacher questioning can also signal text organization. The density experiment is based upon a cause-and-effect reaction. When students restate their results and write them in the lab report, their language needs to reflect this form of text organization. The teacher models several examples of cause and effect during the dialogue: *What causes the screw to sink? Yes, the screw is more dense and so it sinks in the water.* The signal words *causes* and *so* are used appropriately for the content and foreshadow the text organizational structure that will be necessary for a written report.

The teacher's clarity, pinpoint questioning, repetition, reformulation, prompting, and use of wait time provide learners both the language and the content learning they need to achieve. We especially appreciate the fact that this conversation represents ways in which teachers can help students use language to analyze, reflect, and think critically. Although occurring in a classroom, the conversation is closer to being a real discussion than to being a lecture. Talk is used to explore ideas, and the teacher is responsive to what the students have to say. In many ways, this conversation exhibits many of the attributes of an instructional conversation.

INSTRUCTIONAL CONVERSATIONS These conversations are similar to conversations that take place between adults and children outside of school in that they "appear to support children's advancing linguistic and communicative skills" (Rogoff, 1990, p. 157). The social nature of learning described by Vygotsky (1962) is evident here in that the teacher acts as a facilitator who encourages students to produce many different ideas and fosters a great deal of student involvement. Teacher talk is minimized as students are encouraged to share ideas and then are guided to an understanding of the focus of the discussion that the teacher has planned ahead of time. There are rarely correct or incorrect answers in these collaborative discussions, nor is there any evaluation by the teacher. Rather, the teacher guides learners to a consensus or a common foundation of understanding (Goldenberg, 1991, 2004).

Some of the instructional elements (Goldenberg, 1991, 2004, p. 7) found in instructional conversations include:

1. Thematic focus for discussion.
2. Activation of prior knowledge.
3. Direct teaching when necessary.
4. Encouragement of complex language and expression.
5. Encouragement of students to determine a basis for statements.

The conversational elements (Goldenberg, 1991, 2004, p. 7) are:

1. Few display questions when the teacher knows the answer.
2. Teacher responsiveness to student contributions.
3. Connected discussion in which one utterance builds upon another.
4. Challenging, nonthreatening atmosphere.
5. General participation with students self-selecting their turns.

Because of their collaborative nature and their ability to involve many students in creating the understanding of concepts, instructional conversations are very effective vehicles for teachers of ELLs in content-learning classes.

INTERACTIONAL STRUCTURES   Collaborative dialogues with individual students and instructional conversations with small groups of students have a definite place in the content classroom. But there are occasions when all students in the class need structured opportunities for oral language development. These occasions invite ELLs into the instructional conversation and allow their English-speaking peers to model the necessary academic language. The following suggestions are appropriate for all learners:

- *Use cooperative learning principles as a way to provide more input and negotiated output in small-group learning experiences.* Structuring group activities to create positive interdependence and individual accountability ensures that all learners will have simultaneous opportunities to be heard in the classroom.
- *Organize instruction in ways that will create an audience for learning.* Classroom presentations, for example, require learners to acquire both the content and the academic language related to the content in order to report to classmates, schoolmates, parents, teachers, and others in the community. One of the most impressive presentations we have seen at a board of education meeting was accomplished by four ELLs, recent arrivals to the United States, who described their participation in the new high school physics program. Formal presentations are not the only way to promote language growth, however. Informal oral reporting to the teacher is a necessary phase of the lesson that gives ELLs an opportunity to rehearse the content vocabulary and grammar needed for academic learning.
- *Establish long-term dialogues with your students.* We know one teacher, Amy Luray, who met on a scheduled basis, one on one, with each student in her class throughout the year. They talked about progress in learning, set goals for the future, determined ways to provide for support, and prepared for parent-teacher conferences. Other teachers carry on long-term dialogues with their students through dialogue journals in which they converse in writing over the school year.
- *Encourage students to discuss and process new content during the input phase of the lesson.* One technique for doing this in a structured way is called *10-2* (Saphier & Haley, 1993). To use the 10-2 structure, the teacher presents new material for no more than ten minutes at a time. After ten minutes of oral input, the teacher pauses and students share their notes with a buddy, summarizing the concept or discussing a question posed by the teacher. Following the two-minute pause, the teacher may resume ten more minutes of input.

Ten minutes does not seem like a long time, but when listening to complex subject matter in a new language, ten minutes can seem like an hour. We like the fact that 10-2 provides ELLs a stress-free opportunity to clarify their thinking and understanding with a classmate—and the clarification takes only two minutes. Those two minutes are well spent by the teacher who floats around the classroom, assessing the comprehension of learners.

Opportunities to organize thinking ensure better conceptual development for all learners. The research on 10-2 shows that English-speaking experimental groups performed better on complex test items and had better retention of the material and more positive attitudes toward the subject matter (Saphier & Haley, 1993). It seems that the 10-2 structure affords all students the time needed to organize new learning into the schema of what they already know and understand—one of the requirements for meaningful learning.

- *Encourage students to discuss and process new content at every phase of the lesson.* Sometimes it is not sufficient to simply encourage students to participate; we must also require their participation. Cindy, a student from Hong Kong, recalled her school silences this way:

> *[School] was so difficult. I mean, everybody was in on the conversation. They had class discussions and communicated with each other. . . . I felt alone because there weren't that many people that could communicate with me. I was pretty quiet, I think. There was only one student besides myself who was Chinese . . . we didn't talk that much in the beginning . . . she's also kind of shy (Igoa, 1995, pp. 86–87).*

Another student, Alice, came to the United States from China at the age of eight. She remembers:

> *I didn't participate in a lot of stuff. I wanted to. You know, the other kids were doing certain things and I looked at them. I said, "Oh they're having fun. I want to do that." But then, I was reluctant to do that because I felt maybe I couldn't do that, right? Maybe I thought I wasn't good enough to do what they were doing. It was really bad to just sit there and look at what they were doing with the feeling that I wanted to do it but just couldn't (Igoa, 1995, p. 83).*

Cindy and Alice longed to participate more fully in classroom discussions. They needed a teacher who structured the class in ways that invited all learners to contribute and scaffolded them to feel secure in their contributions.

Harklau's case study of high school-level language learners (1994, p. 250) noted that "opportunities to engage in extended interactions with mainstream teachers during classroom instruction were rare." In addition, teachers rarely called on ELL students to speak in class. We have found this to be true in many elementary classrooms as well (Schinke-Llano, 1980).

The benefits to structuring interactional opportunities around content learning are so great for both language and content learning that we recommend using short interactional structures at every phase of the lesson. Examples of these interactional structures are described in Table 5.3.

TABLE 5.3 Interactional Structures Promote Oral Language Use in Content Classrooms

1. Learning Buddies	Learning Buddies is a simple structure uniting two learners for a brief period of time to summarize or review learning (Saphier & Haley, 1993). The pairing can be accomplished periodically and can be used to stimulate learning when students appear to be "tuning out" of a presentation. Some teachers like to have students get up and move in order to pair with a buddy. If this is the case, students need to know ahead of time who their buddies will be to save time and avoid confusion. Methods of pairing students vary. Saphier and Haley (p. 29) suggest the following ideas:

- Teacher-assigned learning buddies who change from time to time. By assigning buddies strategically, teachers can pair ELLs with language speakers and avoid pairing students who do not work well together. Rotating buddy pairs will ensure that students have opportunities to meet with a variety of partners.

- Randomly selected buddies provide novelty and prevent arguments about buddy assignments. Some teachers use question-and-answer matching, asking students to match themselves with a student whose answer card matches their question card. For example: *What is the capital of New York state?*

- Another technique for random selection is to create card pairs related to the content learning: word opposites, states and capitals, chemical elements and symbols, dates and historical events.

(Continued)

TABLE 5.3 Interactional Structures Promote Oral Language Use in Content Classrooms *(Continued)*

2. Round the Clock Learning Buddies	Student-selected buddies are problematical in that one student may be left out of a pairing. One technique we like to use to decrease the likelihood of this is Round the Clock Learning Buddies (Saphier & Haley, 1993). Students are given a version of a clock face (following) with lines drawn for each number on the clock. Students are instructed as follows: *Put your name on the paper. You will get up (in a minute) and walk around the class making an appointment with twelve other students. Write your name on your 1 o'clock buddy's clock and ask her or him to write her or his name on your clock. You won't have a lot of time, so you have to work quickly. Complete all twelve appointments on the clock.* After about three minutes, call time and ask students to return to their seats. If some have not finished and need an appointment at specified times ask: *Who needs a 1 o'clock buddy?* Pair the students in this way so that all clocks are complete. Students should be told to keep their clocks with them in class every day. Once completed, the clocks can be used at any time during a lesson when you want to provide language support for learning: *Meet with your 5 o'clock buddy to share . . . , name . . . , identify . . . , read . . . , or recall three important ideas from today's class.*

Name _____

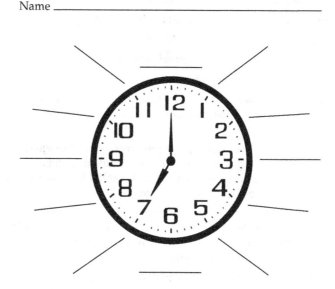

Teachers we have worked with have modified the Clock Buddies structure in many ways to adapt the technique to their classes.

- Our elementary colleagues reduced the clocks in size and laminated them, attaching them to the top of their students' desks.

- Our high school colleagues printed the clocks on neon colored paper for easy access. One physics teacher made a wall chart of all clock buddies to eliminate time wasted looking for the clocks.

- Other teachers have adapted the technique to their content learning. The fifth-grade teachers in one school created maps of the New England states and used New England Buddies and selected a buddy for each state. They rotated to other regions of the country and were pleased at the amount of map knowledge their students had acquired by the end of the year.

- A chemistry teacher created Chemistry Apparatus Buddies at the beginning of the school year to help learners quickly learn the names of the equipment. Others in her department used the structure for Chemical Symbol Buddies.

- The French teacher used a map of France and the Spanish teacher quickly followed suit with a map of Spain.

- Kindergarten teachers knew that twelve appointments were too many for their young students, but they adapted the technique to Shape Buddies (circle, square, triangle, and rectangle) and then to Primary Color Buddies. There seems to be no end to the variations.

3. Think-Pair-Share (T-P-S)	T-P-S is the simplest structure for brief classroom interactions. At appropriate times (to activate, summarize, or problem solve), teachers ask students to *think* about a question. After a minute or two, learners are asked to *pair* themselves with a nearby buddy and discuss what they have thought about. Finally, learners are asked to *share* with another pair or with the large group. We have found that this structure provides language learners with rehearsal time and/or practicing or experimenting with the structure of their language. Frank Lyman reports that during the sharing time, students may be emboldened to respond, either talking about their own thinking or the thinking of their buddy (Kagan, 1994).

TABLE 5.3 Interactional Structures Promote Oral Language Use in Content Classrooms *(Continued)*

	Think-Pair-Write is an adaptation that allows for more reflective learners to write their responses before sharing with others.
4. Paired Verbal Fluency (P-V-F)	P-V-F is another structure that provides ELLs oral language practice. It requires students to listen to a buddy speak and then speak themselves in alternating rounds. The entire structure takes only a few minutes but can be used for a variety of purposes. P-V-F can be used as an activator to help students recall previous learning or to connect to learning that will come in today's lesson. It is also effective as a summarizer when students need to check their understanding of a concept, to process and organize new input, or to clarify misunderstandings. Saphier and Haley (1993, p. 45) describe the basic stages of this structure as follows: **Set Up:** Students pair up and identify who is A and who is B in each pair. **Round I:** A speaks for 45 seconds while B listens. B speaks for 45 seconds while A listens. **Round II:** A speaks for 30 seconds while B listens. B speaks for 30 seconds while A listens. **Round III:** A speaks for 15 seconds while B listens. B speaks for 15 seconds while A listens. At the end of each round, the teacher signals (with a bell or hand clapping) the time, and students switch speakers. P-V-F provides ELLs one of those rare moments in a classroom—45 seconds of talking time with no interruptions.
5. Paraphrase Passport	Paraphrase Passport is an excellent technique to encourage ELLs to take part in classroom discussions. In our adaptation of Kagan's (1994) structure, a student contributes a response to a teacher's question. The teacher then asks another student in the class: *What did Tony say?* The student called upon must paraphrase or repeat what the prior student has said. In our experience, students are surprised when we introduce this gambit into discussions. In most cases, they haven't listened to each other's responses. This is a great loss. We can teach our students to listen if we use Paraphrase Passport from time to time during discussions. The value for ELLs is that it provides a model for language and encourages those students to become a part of the instructional conversation.
6. Talking Chips or Talking Tokens	Talking Chips (Kagan, 1994) is another technique for encouraging oral language use. When students work in small groups to solve a problem or answer a question, we give them a certain number of tokens to use during talking time. Each time a student speaks, he or she must deposit a token in a container in the middle of the table. At the end of the discussion, all tokens must have been used. In this way, ELLs who are new to the language are encouraged, even required, to say something to their group members. Kagan describes a simpler form of Talking Chips. He asks each student to put a chip (such as a pen) in the middle of the table when she or he talks. That student may not speak again until all other students in the group also have deposited their chips. The dominating members of the group are thus controlled from taking talking time away from others.
7. Stir the Class	Stir the Class (Rutherford, 1998, p. 98) is another structure that involves ELLs in oral language interactions. We have seen this structure used with beginning-level learners with good results even though the learners had very little language. Here's how it works: Each student has a sheet of paper and is asked to write three names, reasons, examples, causes, etc. about the topic under study. At a signal, the students walk around the class collecting ideas from classmates and sharing their ideas. When the teacher calls time, students return to their groups and share their lists with each other. They could prioritize, categorize, or sort the lists if appropriate. We saw a teacher use this structure in a fifth-grade classroom preparing to study the geography of the United States The teacher asked students to write the names of three states on their papers. Basra, a newly arrived student, was able to do this with group help. He then walked around and shared information. He was able to participate because the language demands of the task were not high. One thing that was notable was the big smile on Basra's face as he shared his information with fellow students.

ASSESSMENT OF ORAL LANGUAGE DEVELOPMENT

Oral language development impacts content learning, reading achievement, and writing skill development. For example, Hart and Risley (1995) found that differential exposure to parental language input created a gap of 30 million words in a child's vocabulary by age 3. This language accumulation at age 3 was a strong predictor of academic achievement in third grade. Little research has been conducted on the direct relationship between oral language instruction and reading achievement for ELLs. However, in one study, oral language intervention activities had a positive influence on English reading outcomes (Pollard-Durodola, Mathes, Vaughn, Cardenas-Hagan, & Linan-Thompson, 2006).

In a culturally and linguistically appropriate Tier 1 classroom model, ELLs are required to receive explicit instruction in language forms and functions from a qualified instructor who is aware of the process of language acquisition and the range of language proficiency levels. Oral language proficiency can be accelerated when teachers are aware of the level of proficiency attained by the ELLs in their classes. Through frequent progress monitoring, teachers can chart student progress and more closely match instructional targets to developing language forms.

The Student Oral Language Observation Matrix (SOLOM) (San Jose Unified School District, n.d.) in Table 5.4 is a useful tool for recording observations of ELLs' oral language progress. The SOLOM gives holistic descriptors of language behaviors at five different levels. We might relate level 1 of the SOLOM to the starting stage, level 2 to the emerging stage, level 3 to the developing stage, level 4 to the expanding stage, and level 5 to the bridging stage.

The SOLOM is useful in that it provides descriptors for five different elements that comprise language development: comprehension, fluency, vocabulary, pronunciation, and grammar. It is not unusual for an ELL to progress quickly in one area, such as pronunciation, but lag behind in another area, such as grammar. The SOLOM helps us to be aware as teachers that there is no single language developing but a plurality of language elements that develop over time.

TABLE 5.4 Student Oral Language Observation Matrix (SOLOM)

s	1	2	3	4	5
A. Comprehension	Cannot understand even simple conversation	Has great difficulty following everyday social conversation, even when words are spoken slowly and repeated frequently	Understands most of what is said at slower-than-normal speed with some repetitions	Understands nearly everything at normal speed, although occasional repetition may be necessary	Understands everyday conversation and normal classroom discussion without difficulty
B. Fluency	Speech so halting and fragmentary that conversation is virtually impossible	Usually hesitant; often forced into silence because of language limitations	Everyday conversation and classroom discussion frequently disrupted by student's search for correct manner of expression	Everyday conversation and classroom discussion generally fluent with occasional lapses while student searches for the correct manner of expression	Everyday conversation and classroom discussion fluent and effortless; approximately those of a native speaker
C. Vocabulary	Vocabulary limitations so extreme that conversation is virtually impossible	Difficult to understand because of misuse of words and very limited vocabulary	Frequent use of wrong words; conversation somewhat limited because of inadequate vocabulary	Occasional use of inappropriate terms and/or rephrasing of ideas because of limited vocabulary	Vocabulary and idioms approximately those of a native speaker
D. Pronunciation	Pronunciation problems so severe that speech is virtually unintelligible	Difficult to understand because of pronunciation problems; must frequently repeat speech in order to be understood	Concentration required of listener; occasional misunderstandings caused by pronunciation problems	Always intelligible, although listener conscious of a definite accent and occasional inappropriate intonation pattern	Pronunciation and intonation approximately those of a native speaker
E. Grammar	Errors in grammar and word order so severe that speech is virtually unintelligible	Difficult to understand because of errors in grammar and word order; must often rephrase or restrict speech to basic patterns	Frequent errors in grammar and word order; meaning occasionally obscured	Occasional errors in grammar or word order; meaning not obscured	Grammar and word order approximately those of a native speaker

Source: San Jose Unified School District (n.d.). Sacramento: California Department of Education.

The authors have used the SOLOM as an assessment tool to record aural-oral progress. We tape-recorded student oral language responses twice during the school year: once in the fall and once in the spring. In the recordings, our ELLs responded to a series of questions designed to elicit a variety of grammar and vocabulary elements. After taping, we charted the results using the SOLOM as a guide. The descriptors for each of the five levels on the SOLOM enabled us to achieve a numerical score for each language component and finally, a total score. To improve the usefulness of the scores, we used two teachers to listen and record results for the same students. In that way, we were able to establish a more reliable score.

The information we gain from planned observations and from unplanned observations in a natural classroom setting provides us with a picture of progress that may be more helpful than a numerical score on a standardized test. This is information that we can share with parents, other teachers, and the students themselves. It is a form of feedback not biased by test validity and shows a clear picture of how language is used within the classroom for a variety of different tasks.

Clipboards can be utilized to record informal observations of student language progress during teacher-student dialogues or during small-group work sessions. We like to keep a list of students on our clipboard and carry it with us as we float around the room, questioning, listening, and interacting with a variety of students. With the clipboard in hand, we can quickly note progress or jot down an area for future instruction for each of our students. This clipboard also helps us monitor our attention—keeping track of who's had a chance to speak, and whom we have helped individually that day.

Student self-assessment is a technique that helps to promote reflection among ELLs as to their skill development. Simple self-assessment instruments can be used to determine the level of comprehension after a science video, the grammaticality of speech following an oral presentation, or comprehension of a reading passage during social studies. Self-assessment is also useful for helping students to reflect on the social skills needed for classroom cooperative work. Self-assessment can become a routine factor in the content classroom and provide additional information to that gathered by the teacher during formal and informal assessments.

RESPONSE TO INTERVENTION

RTI TIER 1 SAMPLER

- Communicate oral language objectives to students orally and in writing. Ask students to restate the objective to a partner.
- Use a variety of 10-2 structures such as Think-Pair-Share throughout instruction. Use these structures to help students explain concepts to each other or to answer questions posed orally.
- Provide time for opportunities for extended discourse. For example, use Paired Verbal Fluency to have students orally summarize content information acquired through lecture, the textbook, or the computer.
- Reduce the number of display questions asked during class. Instead, ask questions that students can answer in buddy pairs. Observe these verbal interactions and take notes on student involvement.
- When giving directions to students, scaffold the oral language with modeling, explanatory devices, and/or written steps. Have partners restate the directions to each other.
- Use wait time after asking conceptual questions to individuals, small groups, or the class as a whole.
- Structure oral language use between partners or within small groups by providing sentence frames as a guide to academic language. For example, in an economics lesson, use a sentence frame such as: _____ is/are produced/grown/manufactured in _____.
- Structure small group work so that all students in the group are required to participate orally without being interrupted. One way to teach this social skill is to put a cup with labeled wooden sticks in the center of the table. A child may speak when taking his or her stick out of the cup. All sticks must be used before students have a second chance to pull a stick and speak.
- Provide time for teacher-guided collaborative dialogues as students work at tasks in small groups, in partner pairs, or on individual assignments.
- Monitor progress frequently through informal classroom observations, holistic rating scales, anecdotal evidence, and assessments of student language performances (such as retellings, role-plays).

RTI TIER 2 SAMPLER

- Work with a small group of ELLs to preteach academic vocabulary prior to a reading lesson. Require students to use the language orally by defining vocabulary in their own words, stating similarities and differences between words, telling what the words do not mean, giving an example of the word from their own experience, and other oral language tasks.
- Activate learning by requiring students to make predictions orally to a partner. Provide extra time during the class for these predictions.
- Have students tell what they know about a new topic. Ask them to relate the new topic to prior learning or to prior experiences. Provide extra time for these stories to be told.
- Help students to create and conduct surveys related to new content learning. Have the ELLs conduct the surveys by asking oral questions and listening to the responses, taking notes on the responses, and reporting the information back to the class or the small group orally.
- Jigsaw the new vocabulary among a group of ELLs. Have them teach the vocabulary to each other and then to other students in the class.
- Provide explicit instruction in academic language structures to small groups. For example, in a lesson organized around comparison and contrast, teach the signal words required for retelling major concepts and identify a sentence frame that is useful to that task.
- Teach the skill of oral summarization. Provide outlines to help students identify the main ideas in a reading and support those ideas with details. Provide time for students to retell the ideas orally using the outline.
- Prior to reading from the text, teach small groups of students the major points of the text organized on a graphic organizer. Provide time for students to retell these ideas to a partner using appropriate signal words required by the text organization.
- Model "I" statements for a small group of students while performing a task. Provide an opportunity for students to model "I" statements for the small group.
- Teach students to tell what steps they would go through in order to solve a math problem. Provide rehearsal time to practice the process and then have students report on the process to the class.

Questions for Reflection

1. In many North American classrooms, children spend much of class time listening while the teacher or a few other students talk. Is it your belief that learning is accomplished through listening? Has this been true in most of the learning experiences you have had in school? What should be the appropriate amount of teacher talk versus student talk in a classroom? Does this vary depending on the age of the students? Why? How should the ratio change for English language-learning students?
2. This chapter introduces levels of language proficiency that describe ELLs on their way to full language proficiency. Which of these language levels is most difficult for teachers to assess and instruct? Is grade level a factor? Give reasons for your choice.
3. How is learning oral language in a classroom similar to acquiring a first language? Review the suggestions for oral language development in this chapter and relate how these activities promote learning that is similar to the learning processes that occur when children acquire a first language.

Activities for Further Learning

1. ELLs generally proceed through levels of oral language proficiency. Talk to others in your group to determine: What difficulties do these stages present to the classroom teacher? Which level do you find most difficult to teach? What are the specific problems presented at each of these levels? Does the age of the learner affect the difficulty in teaching learners at each of these levels?
2. Work with your group to determine teaching and communication techniques that are effective for ELLs at each of the oral language development levels. It may be useful to think of techniques for very young learners, for those in the intermediate grades, and for those in secondary school.
3. Talk to members of your group about the kinds of oral language activities you have experienced in your elementary and secondary school years. Did your teachers engage you in oral presentations, role-plays, puppet shows, songs and poetry, debates, or drama? Did your classroom experiences involve a great deal of individualized

work? Was the classroom a silent place or were students involved in collaborative learning? How did your experiences affect your own learning? What kinds of classroom activities are most helpful for language learners? Should activities become more individualized as learners move into middle school? Why or why not?

4. What would Vygotsky say about the amount of teacher talk versus student talk in a classroom? When is teacher talk helpful and when does it become harmful to learning? How can student talk be useful to learning? When is student talk not helpful?

5. Observe a classroom teacher and note the kinds of language used in presentations and input to learners. Is there evidence of modeling of academic language? Record that language and be ready to report to the class about it.

6. Review the list of teacher tools for oral language development included in this chapter. Prioritize the list, putting the most useful tools at the top and the least useful at the bottom. Be able to give reasons for your ordering.

7. Observe a teacher in a classroom engaged in a small group discussion and/or learning. Listen to the teacher's language for examples of questioning and response patterns or collaborative dialogues. Record the language that you hear and be ready to report on it in class.

8. Observe an English language learner in a classroom setting where interaction is taking place—either a small group discussion or project work session. Use the SOLOM assessment chart to determine the quality of the child's oral language development. At which language proficiency level would you place this student? Does the child's teacher concur with your assessment?

Suggested Reading

Anstrom, K. (1998). Preparing secondary education teachers to work with English language learners: English language arts (NCBE Resource Collection Series #10). Washington, DC: Center for the Study of Language and Education, George Washington University. Ideas for incorporating oral language development into secondary literature instruction are presented in this brief report.

Goldenberg, C. N. (1991). Instructional conversations and their classroom application (Cooperative Agreement No. R117G10022). Washington, DC: Office of Educational Research and Improvement. This short report provides an excellent overview of instructional conversations with practical ideas for application and a rating scale to assess the use of the technique in the classroom. Other more recent Goldenberg citations expand on teaching and learning in classroom settings for ELLs.

Goldenberg, C. N. (2004). *Successful school change: Creating settings to improve teaching and learning.* New York: Teachers College Press. Practical suggestions are included here which expand on Goldenberg's (1991) report.

Goldenberg, C. N. (2006, July 26). Improving achievement for English-learners: What the research tells us. *Education Week.*

An excellent and brief analysis of relevant research for English language learners.

Harper, C., & de Jong, E. (2004). Misconceptions about teaching English-language learners. *Journal of Adolescent & Adult Literacy, 48*(2): 153–162. Authors explore four common misconceptions about teaching English language learners and offer recommendations for effective teaching.

Krashen, S. D. (2003). *Explorations in language acquisition and use: The Taipei lectures.* Portsmouth, NH: Heinemann. Krashen continues to explore the nature of language acquisition and learning within the classroom context—an update of his classic 1983 work with Terrell.

Rosenshine, B., & Furst, N. (1973). The use of direct observation to study teaching. In R. M. Travers (Ed.), *Second handbook of research on teaching.* Chicago, IL: Rand McNally. This report includes a classic discussion of Clarity—one of nine variables discussed by the authors that correlate to student growth on standardized tests.

References

Brinton, D., & Mano, S. (1994). "You have a chance also": Case histories of ESL students at the university. In F. Peitzman and G. Gadda (Eds.), *With different eyes: Insights into teaching language minority students across the disciplines* (pp. 1–21). White Plains, NY: Longman.

Cummins, J. (1996). *Negotiating identities: Education for empowerment in a diverse society.* Ontario, CA: California Association for Bilingual Education.

Enright, S., & McCloskey, M. (1988). *Integrating English: Developing English language and literacy in the multilingual classroom.* Reading, MA: Addison-Wesley.

Fillmore, L. W., & Snow, C. E. (2002). What teachers need to know about language. In C. T. Adger, C. E. Snow, and D. Christian (Eds.), *What teachers need to know about language* (pp. 7–53). McHenry, IL: Delta Systems.

Gadda, G. (1994). Writing and language socialization across cultures: Some implications for the classroom. In F. Peitzman and G. Gadda (Eds.), *With different eyes: Insights into teaching language minority students across the disciplines* (pp. 43–56). White Plains, NY: Longman.

Gibbons, P. (2002). *Scaffolding language, scaffolding learning.* Portsmouth, NH: Heinemann.

Gibbons, P. (2003). Mediating language learning: Teacher interactions with ESL students in a content-based classroom. *TESOL Quarterly, 37:* 247–273.

Goldenberg, C. N. (1991). Instructional conversations and their classroom application. (Cooperative Agreement No. R117G10022). Washington, DC: Office of Educational Research and Improvement.

Goldenberg, C. N. (1996) The education of language minority students: Where are we and where do we need to go? *Elementary School Journal, 96*(3).

Goldenberg, C. N. (2004). *Successful school change: Creating settings to improve teaching and learning.* New York, NY: Teachers College Press.

Goodman, K. (1986). *What's whole in whole language?* Portsmouth, NH: Heinemann.

Grognet, A., Jameson, J., Franco, L., & Derrick-Mescua, M. (2000). *Enhancing English language learning in elementary classrooms.* McHenry, IL: Center of Applied Linguistics and Delta Systems.

Harklau, L. (1994). ESL versus mainstream classes: Contrasting L2 learning environments. *TESOL Quarterly, 28:* 241–272.

Hart, B., & Risley, T. R. (1995). The early catastrophe: The 30 million word gap. *American Educator, 27*(1): 4–9.

Heath, S. B. (1983). *Way with words: Language, life, and work in communities and classrooms.* Cambridge, UK: Cambridge University Press.

Heath, S. B. (1986). Sociocultural contexts of language development. In *Beyond language: Social and cultural factors in schooling language minority students.* Bilingual Education Office, California State Department of Education, Sacramento. Los Angeles, CA: Evaluation, Dissemination and Assessment Center, California State University, Los Angeles.

Hernández, H. (1997). *Teaching in multicultural classrooms: A teacher's guide to context, process, and content.* Upper Saddle River, NJ: Merrill.

Herrell, A. L., & Jordan, M. (2007). *Fifty strategies for teaching English language learners* (3rd ed.). Upper Saddle River, NJ: Pearson Education.

Igoa, C. (1995). *The inner world of the immigrant child.* Mahwah, NJ: Lawrence Erlbaum.

Kagan, S. (1994). *Cooperative learning.* San Clemente, CA: Kagan Cooperative Learning.

Krashen, S. D., & Terrell, T. D. (1983). *The natural approach: Language acquisition in the classroom.* San Francisco, CA: Alemany Press.

Peregoy, S. F., & Boyle, O. F. (2008). *Reading, writing, and learning in ESL: A resource book for K–12 teachers* (5th ed.). Boston, MA: Allyn & Bacon.

Pollard-Durodola, S. D., Mathes, P. G., Vaughn, S., Cardenas-Hagan, E., & Linan-Thompson, S. (2006). The role of oracy in developing comprehension in Spanish-speaking English language learners. *Topics in Language Disorders, 26*(4): 365–384.

Ramirez, J. D., Yuen, S., & Ramey, D. R. (1991). Final report: Longitudinal study of structured English immersion strategy, early-exit and late-exit transitional bilingual education programs for language minority children (Contract No. 300-87-0156). Washington, DC: U.S. Department of Education.

Rogoff, B. (1990). *Apprenticeship in thinking: Cognitive development in social context.* Oxford, UK: Oxford University Press.

Rowe, M. (1986). Wait time: Slowing down may be a way of speeding up. *Journal of Teacher Education, 37:* 43–50.

Rutherford, P. (1998). *Instruction for all students.* Alexandria, VA: Just Ask Publications.

San Jose Unified School District. (n.d.). *Student Oral Language Observation Matrix (SOLOM).* San Jose, CA: Author. Retrieved from http://www.cal.org/twi/evaltoolkit/appendix.Solom.pdf

Saphier, J., & Gower, R. (1997). *The skillful teacher: Building your teaching skills.* Carlisle, MA: Research for Better Teaching.

Saphier, J., & Haley, M. A. (1993). *Summarizers: Activity structures to support integration and retention of new learning.* Carlisle, MA: Research for Better Teaching.

Schinke-Llano, L. (1980). Foreigner talk in content classrooms. In H. W. Seliger and M. H. Long (Eds.), *Classroom oriented research in second language acquisition* (pp. 146–165). Rowley, MA: Newbury House.

Simich-Dudgeon, C. (1998). Classroom strategies for encouraging collaborative discussion. *Directions in Language and Education, 12:* 1–19.

TESOL (Teachers of English to Speakers of Other Languages, Inc.) (2006). *PreK–12 English language proficiency standards.* Alexandria, VA: TESOL.

Thomas, W. P., & Collier, V. P. (2002). *A national study of school effectiveness for language minority students' long-term academic achievement.* Retrieved from http://repositories.cdlib.org/crede/finalrpts/1_1_final/ or http://crede.berkeley.edu/research/llaa/1.1_final.html

Urzua, C. (1981). Talking purposefully. In C. W. Hayes and C. Kessler (Eds.), *The teacher idea series: A practical resource library for second language teachers* (vol. 1). Silver Spring, MD: Institute of Modern Languages.

Vygotsky, L. S. (1962). *Thought and language.* Cambridge, MA: MIT Press.

Wood, D., Bruner, J., & Ross, G. (1976). The role of tutoring in problem solving. *Journal of Child Psychology and Psychiatry, 17:* 89–100.

MyEducationLab™

Go to the Topics, Speaking and Listening and Instructional Strategies, in the MyEducationLab (www.myeducationlab.com) for your course, where you can:

- Find learning outcomes for Speaking and Listening and Instructional Strategies along with the national standards that connect to these outcomes.
- Complete Assignments and Activities that can help you more deeply understand the chapter content.
- Apply and practice your understanding of the core teaching skills identified in the chapter with the Building Teaching Skills and Dispositions learning units.
- Examine challenging situations and cases presented in the IRIS Center Resources.
- Check your comprehension on the content covered in the chapter by going to the Study Plan in the Book Resources for your text. Here you will be able to take a chapter quiz, receive feedback on your answers, and then access Review, Practice, and Enrichment activities to enhance your understanding of chapter content.
- **A+RISE** A+RISE® Standards2Strategy™ is an innovative and interactive online resource that offers new teachers in grades K-12 just in time, research-based instructional strategies that meet the linguistic needs of ELLs as they learn content, differentiate instruction for all grades and abilities, and are aligned to Common Core Elementary Language Arts standards (for the literacy strategies) and to English language proficiency standards in WIDA, Texas, California, and Florida.

CHAPTER 6

Oral Language Development in the Content Classroom

Shelly Sanders is a fifth-grade science coordinator and classroom teacher at Pelican Bay Elementary School in Florida. All of her students are native Spanish speakers, the children of migrant workers in the citrus industry. Shelly enjoys teaching hands-on science to her students. Today she is teaching a grade-level lesson concerning the components and functions of plant and animal cells. She has chosen a cookie-decorating activity to help her students practice and learn the concepts and language of the lesson.

Shelly places the students into lab groups and asks each group to choose a materials' handler to help her distribute the materials. As the students begin to work, they talk about the project using both English and Spanish. Dayelle's group includes Gustavo, Janet, Arielli, and Victor, a non-English speaking student. Dayelle confers with Gustavo before translating for Victor.

Gustavo says, *The green one is chloroplasts. It goes close to the nucleus.* Gustavo checks his science text and then says, *Your nucleus goes in the middle and ours goes on top.* Dayelle and Arielli translate the information for Victor. Since the girls have never studied cell structure in Spanish, they don't know the scientific terms in that language. Instead, they use the English terms they are currently learning.

Shelly circulates around the room while the students work. She observes and listens to the group conversations, occasionally asking questions of each group, *If you have an animal cell, are you going to use chloroplasts? If you have a plant cell, will you need vacuoles? Who needs mitochondria?*

When the cookies are complete, Shelly says, *If you have a plant cell, stand in front of the room with your cell.* Eleven students come to the front. *Animal cell people, check their cells. Are they correct?* The students check each other and determine that the plant cells are all correct.

Animal cell people come on up. Now check these. Some of these look different. Why are they different? Selene volunteers, *That one* (pointing) *shouldn't have a . . .* (Selene checks her chart) *a plant vacuole. That's right*, says Shelly, *this cell shouldn't have a plant vacuole because it's a what? That's right; an animal cell. Animal cells don't contain plant vacuoles.* Elissa and Justin quickly remove the plant vacuoles from their cells (Lacina, Levine, & Sowa, 2006, pp. 20–21).

What kinds of classroom conditions and activities lead to oral language development in the content areas of the language arts, social studies, math, and science?

- What language requirements are determined by the content areas of language arts, social studies, math, and science?
- What instructional strategies are effective in each of the content areas?
- How can songs, poetry, chants, and raps be used effectively?
- What are the active listening activities that help to foster the development of oral language?

CONTENT LEARNING AND ORAL LANGUAGE DEVELOPMENT

In content classrooms, students are introduced to new concepts and language by listening to content presentations and interacting with others concerning the content concepts and vocabulary. English language learners (ELLs) need to be included in these aural-oral activities in order to develop the academic language skills necessary for success. Each of the content areas presents challenges and opportunities for English language learners—opportunities to participate in the oral language of the classroom.

The Common Core State Standards in English Language Arts for Kindergarten through 12th grade make reference to College and Career Readiness Anchor Standards for Speaking and Listening, Reading, Writing, and Language. These standards are meant to align curriculum, instruction, and assessment. As such, they emphasize the need for educational equity, setting high expectations for all learners, including ELLs. "Teachers should recognize that it is possible to achieve the standards for reading and literature, writing and research, language development and speaking and listening without manifesting native-like control of conventions and vocabulary" (Applications of Common Core Standards for English Language Learners, p. 1) In the following sections, we will describe culturally and linguistically appropriate instructional practices in the content classroom and reference appropriate standards from the Common Core State Standards.

Language Arts

A great deal of the content of the language arts curriculum is learned through reading a text. Written texts are difficult to comprehend because the rich context of conversation is missing, vocabulary is often difficult, and sentences are longer and of greater complexity than speech. In addition, literacy skills must be in place to access texts.

A wide variety of literature genres appears in the language arts curriculum. For example, students are taught poetry, biography, personal narrative, drama, short stories, novels, various nonfiction texts, and speeches. In addition, language arts programs presume visual and multimedia literacy, with expectations that learners are able to access and understand graphic texts, electronic texts, and film or video. Not all of these genres may be common in the cultures of our ELL students. ELLs may come from cultures in which oral storytelling is more prevalent than written narrative. Youngsters who come from homes where books are not available and where no one has ever read to them may have limited knowledge of the typical problem/resolution structure in North American stories. Yet, ELLs need to learn language arts content in spite of their reading skill proficiencies and cultural differences. How can teachers teach this content while accelerating academic oral language development?

STORYTELLING   Storytelling is a good way to help ELLs learn the linear structure of English expository reading and writing. One effective strategy for assisting new learners is reading aloud. Simple, familiar stories accompanied by many pictures are best for beginning-level ELLs. Folk tales from other cultures, including those set in and/or written by authors from your students' cultures, provide a familiar context that will engage student interest.

Picture books are useful in helping ELLs to retell an oral story narrative. Some teachers encourage their ELLs to write their ideas on sticky notes, and use these notes and pictures as **scaffolds** when retelling the story in the picture book.

Teachers can model telling stories for their students using specific strategies to communicate meaning and to move the plot. Story elements can be made more explicit by using graphic organizers. Simple graphic organizers that support storytelling may include categories for setting, characters, problem, and outcome (see Figure 6.1).

The cyclical nature of a story or event can be illustrated through a cycle chart. These charts are particularly useful for children's circle stories. *A Pocketful of Opossums* (Almada, Nichols, & O'Keefe, 2004) is one example of an appealing cyclical story that can be graphically represented on a cycle chart.

To emphasize the linear nature of the plot, a graphic such as Figure 6.2 can be used. Pictures may be included in the graphic to assist meaning and embed context into the story elements.

After reading stories to students and charting them on a graphic, the teacher can demonstrate an oral retelling and ask students to use the graphic as a scaffold when retelling the story

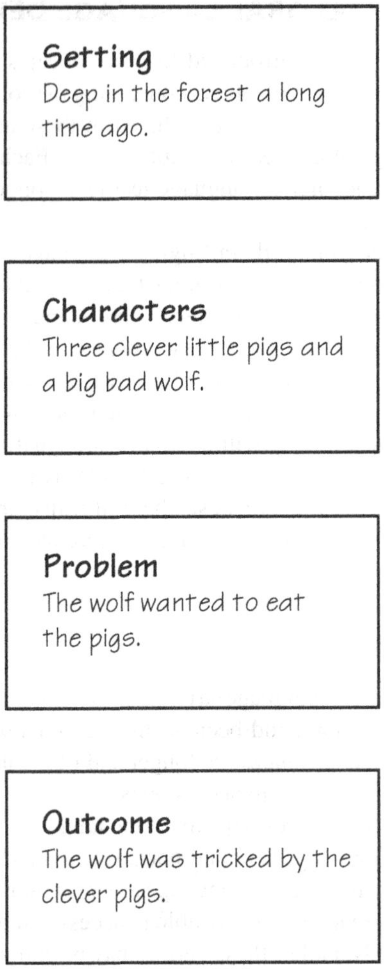

Setting
Deep in the forest a long time ago.

Characters
Three clever little pigs and a big bad wolf.

Problem
The wolf wanted to eat the pigs.

Outcome
The wolf was tricked by the clever pigs.

FIGURE 6.1 Graphic Organizers Create a Visual Image of the Elements of a Story

to a buddy or to a small group of learners. Inserting signal words of chronology (e.g., *first, next, after a while*) or cause and effect (e.g., *because, so, as a result*) into the graphic will enable students to use these important transition words in their retellings. Later, the same graphics will support a written summary of the story.

Older learners can tell stories about their families, their lives, admired or unusual characters, or immigration stories. When students interview family members, this encourages parents to participate in their children's school experiences. Other stories might include tales from the neighborhood or an adventure shared with a friend. Teachers also can schedule oral interviews with community members during class time. Before each interview, the ELLs can assist in developing a list of questions to be asked. Next, ELLs can practice interviewing each other in order to improve their oral questioning skills and to practice note-taking.

The newspaper provides a wealth of material for storytelling. ELLs can select interesting stories from their city, state, or another country. The teacher can help them to extract critical information from the story and insert it into a graphic organizer (such as the one in Figure 6.1). Important vocabulary can be explained at this time and appropriate signal words chosen for a retelling. The newspaper accounts and the graphics act as scaffolds for the language needed to relate the narratives.

Relevant Common Core Anchor Standards (http://www.corestandards.org/the-standards/ english-language-arts-standards) for storytelling include:

- Prepare for and participate effectively in a range of conversations and collaborations with diverse partners, building on others' ideas and expressing their own clearly and persuasively.
- Integrate and evaluate information in diverse media and formats, including visually, qualitatively, and orally.

Narrative Stories Can be Graphically Represented on a Cycle Chart

My Story
Setting
Characters

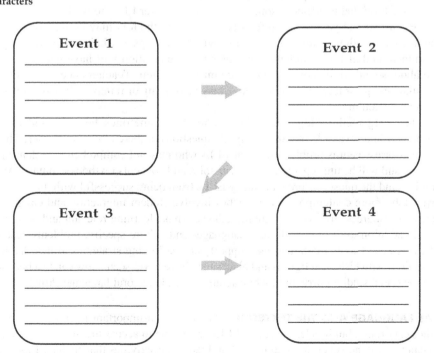

FIGURE 6.2 **A Graphic Organizer Depicts the Linear Nature of the Story's Plot**

- Present information, findings, and supporting evidence such that listeners can follow the line of reasoning and make sure the organization, development, and style are appropriate to task, purpose, and audience.
- Adapt speech to a variety of contexts and communicative tasks, demonstrating command of formal English when indicated or appropriate.

READER'S THEATRE   The Reader's Theatre technique (Black & Stave, 2007) offers opportunities to incorporate oral language development into literature study. In this technique, teachers help learners turn a story into a script and then dramatize the action. Even beginning ELLs can learn to comprehend the story and participate in small roles in Reader's Theatre. The teacher supports learners by creating a script (or helping learners to do so), assigning characters, collecting props, and mapping out minimum stage action. Rehearsals provide needed language practice for ELLs with beginning language proficiency. Finally, the production is presented to an audience, perhaps to parents, staff, another class, or the other half of the class.

Literate ELLs can be encouraged to develop a script for the production, with the source of the dialogue usually coming from the original storybook or folk tale. In this way, all four language skills are integrated into the lesson. New learners are supported in their skill development and benefit from learning about story structure in English.

Relevant Common Core Anchor Standards (http://www.corestandards.org/the-standards/ english-language-arts-standards) for Reader's Theatre include all of those listed for storytelling in addition to standards related to writing a script:

- Write narratives to develop real or imagined experiences or events using effective technique, well-chosen details, and well-structured event sequences.
- Produce clear and coherent writing in which the development, organization, and style are appropriate to task, purpose, and audience.

Social Studies

The social studies present a challenge for ELLs. Textbooks are filled with abstract, multiple-meaning vocabulary and complex, compound sentence forms. Words such as *table, mean*, and *party* take on whole new meanings in a social science context—meanings that are confusing and unfamiliar to ELLs. Passive voice verbs are common while subject referents are often found in the middle (not at the beginning) of sentences. A great deal of the social studies content is communicated through program materials (textbooks and ancillaries). These texts are usually written at a level that is difficult (sometimes impossible) for ELLs to read.

Historical and geographic referents assumed by the text may be unknown to students. If educated in other countries, students will have gaps in their understanding of U.S. government and history. Students with interrupted education will have gaps in their knowledge about social studies of their home countries, as well. Teachers need to carefully probe their students' prior learning—knowledge may be missing or it may be based upon an entirely different curriculum.

Teaching methodology in social studies has sometimes been limited to accessing information in a textbook and answering the questions at the end of the chapter. This style of input and assessment is problematical for ELLs who may not comprehend the dense prose of a textbook and will be unprepared for the principles and concepts textbooks contain. An inability to understand the questions prevents many ELLs from being successful with this teaching style. Fortunately, more contemporary approaches involve student interaction and engagement, and the use of resources, artifacts, and multimedia can make learning relevant and bring it to life.

In addition to dealing with these language- and culture-specific problems, teachers must address issues of motivation, and use support and scaffolding strategies to help learners make connections with historical figures and places they have never seen. How can teachers help ELLs learn the social studies curriculum while acquiring academic oral language skills?

ORAL LANGUAGE AND THE TEXTBOOK   The text is an important learning tool in the social studies classroom, but it is less useful if ELLs are unable to access the information it holds. The text can be used, however, for a number of oral language activities that enable ELLs to gradually acquire basic principles, concepts, and academic and technical vocabulary while practicing oral language skills. Activities such as the following take advantage of text graphics:

- Describe what you see in the pictures.
- Describe what you can understand about the charts, maps, and graphs.
- Change the chapter headings into questions. For example, *Volcanoes:* W*hat are volcanoes? Where are volcanoes located? Why are volcanoes important?* Try to ask and answer these questions with a buddy (prior to reading).
- Change the chapter subheadings into questions, and ask and answer these with a buddy.
- Ask and try to answer any focus questions found at the beginning of the chapter.
- Tell what you know about the questions at the end of the chapter.
- Find boldfaced or italicized vocabulary, and try to use these words in a sentence or ask a question using the words.

Social studies chapters usually include lists of questions at the end that highlight the important learning in the chapter. These are followed by Application and Expansion activities to help students make connections between the content knowledge and their own prior knowledge and experiences. We suggest that teachers use a strategy called **Teach the Text Backward** (Center for Applied Linguistics, 1998), beginning with hands-on activities in the application and expansion section and followed by group discussion and perusal of the questions at the end of the chapter. Only then do students prepare to read the text. Teach the Text Backward progresses from the concrete to the conceptual, from the known to the unknown, and from simple concepts to more difficult ones. The steps for this technique are as follows:

1. Have students complete application and expansion activities at the end of the chapter to help them make connections with the concepts discussed in the chapter. If the activities are not connected to your students' lives, adapt them to ensure closer cultural connections. Make use of "hands on" experiences at this time.
2. Engage students in discussion of the topic, helping them to make explicit their understandings of the major concepts.
3. Enable students to read the questions at the end of the chapter and answer them or make guesses based upon the level of their current understanding.
4. Help students to read and comprehend the text.

Application and expansion activities help students to develop a rudimentary understanding of the underlying concepts in the chapter while making connections to what they already know. For example, in a chapter on immigration, the application activity at the end of the chapter may require students to share some basic facts about their own or their family's immigration history. With the Teach the Text Backward strategy, the teacher would use this activity as a starting point. Students write the date of their family's immigration on a large note card and then line up in the classroom in the order of earliest immigration to latest. Students can also answer basic questions about their immigration history such as *How did you or your ancestors immigrate to the United States? Where did you immigrate from? Why did you immigrate?* (Students whose ancestors are Native Americans, or students who can't find out when their families arrived might instead tell stories of the migration of others from their ethnic group.) Teachers might be mindful of students for whom this topic is a sensitive one (for example undocumented immigrants) and make modifications in the type of information to be shared with the class.

ELLs can be supported in this activity with key sentence frames written on the back of the note card:

- *"My family immigrated from _____."*
- *"My family immigrated in the year _____."*
- *"My family came to America by _____."*
- *"My family immigrated because _____."*

After reporting on the basic immigration information, teachers can use this opportunity to help students learn basic concepts about immigration. Then they can ask students to determine when most of their classmates immigrated to the United States and why. From these observations, teachers can develop additional concepts about U.S. immigration.

Hands-on application events also give the teacher the opportunity to teach language forms and provide time for their practice. In this lesson, students learn and practice the various forms of the word *immigrate* along with the prepositions that accompany these forms: *immigrate from, immigrate to, immigrate between* _____ *and* _____.

By approaching the text through oral language development, teachers can take advantage of prior knowledge and concrete learning experiences that lead youngsters into new, abstract learning. Their oral language knowledge can be transferred into a written format and the abundant context of the application activities is gradually removed for the more limited context of the printed text.

The Common Core Anchor Standards for English Language Arts Listening and Speaking also apply to oral language use in the social studies classroom. The Anchor Standards listed for oral storytelling can be used to teach and evaluate oral language listening and speaking skills related to Teach the Text Backward and to the following discussion of oral history.

ORAL HISTORY   Given the reasons presented above, many teachers are using a teaching approach to social studies that views history as a series of stories. Students link their prior experiences to the curriculum, with their backgrounds providing the raw historical data around which the curriculum is structured. Oral history helps students to view themselves and their communities as players on the historical stage (Olmedo, 1993). Because of the oral nature of this learning, ELLs can strengthen their oral language skills while learning content concepts. Oral history relates the students' experiential knowledge, the people and events that have filled their lives, to important social studies concepts and events.

A Classroom Picture of Teach the Text Backward

Jane Sorenson's middle school science class is studying a unit on ocean ecology. As part of the unit, students will learn about ocean food chains, consumers and producers, the role of algae and bacteria in ecological systems, and the delicate balance that keeps ocean waters healthy. Jane begins the unit with an application activity using the technique, Teach the Text Backward. Jane creates picture cards, each one displaying an ocean organism. She distributes these cards to fifteen students in the classroom and asks them to come to the front of the class and *line up in order*. Jane doesn't tell her students what *the order* of the line-up is, but she tells the student with the picture of a shark to stand at one end of the line. As the students determine their order, Jane asks the other students to watch carefully and tell a partner if they think the order is correct or incorrect and why. Jane's students quickly determine that the large fish should be at one end of the line and the smaller ones at the other end. But they have difficulty deciding what to do about the *bacteria, algae,* and *kelp* cards. They notice that *bacteria* and *algae* are represented by several members of the group. These students finally decide that they should stand at the end of the line.

Next, Jane asks the students to tell about themselves using the sentence frames she has written on the back of each card. Beginning with the end of the line, students say:

- *I am called (a)* _____.
- *I live in the* _____.
- *I consume* _____ *and* _____. Or
- *I am consumed by* _____ *and* _____.

After all students have reported, Jane conducts a comprehension check with the class. She models true/false statements about the ocean organisms and asks students to respond with a Thumbs Up/Down. Next, Jane introduces the vocabulary words *producers* and *consumers*. She asks students to predict with a partner which organisms are producers and which are consumers. Jane has color coded the cards to scaffold this task. All of her students are able to confirm that the blue cards are consumers and the green cards are producers. Jane checks students' understanding of these words by asking them to respond in chorus with the appropriate term as she points to and names an organism.

Jane has made sure that more students are producers, and she asks students to infer with a buddy why this is so. Next, Jane puts all students into small groups with a set of ecology cards. The small groups sort the cards into the appropriate order and write sentences using the target vocabulary and the passive voice sentence structure *am consumed by.* After this task, each of the small groups will give oral reports to the class.

Anstrom (1999, pp. 6–7) provides two examples of relating oral history to students' lives:

1. In preparation for a Civil War unit, ask students about their personal experiences of being different from others in the group. Talk about the fact that these differences can sometimes lead to conflict. Expand the discussion into the political, social, ethnic, and economic differences among people. Relate those differences to those existing between the North and the South at the start of the Civil War.

2. For a unit on westward expansion, open with a discussion on immigration. Ask language learners to interview their family and/or friends for immigration stories. Relate these in a class discussion to migration patterns to and within the U.S. Ask students to think about how they fit into these patterns as new immigrants to the U.S.

Oral history is best taught within a thematic curriculum structure where topics are studied in depth. Some of the concepts that lend themselves to this approach include: dependence and interdependence, scarcity, migration, acculturation, the impact of change on society, causes and results of war, rights and responsibilities of citizenship, climatic change and the economy, and lifestyles of specific peoples (National Council for the Social Studies Task Force, 1989). Thematic instruction is described more fully in Chapter 12.

Olmedo (1993, p. 9) has the following suggestions for getting started when teaching oral history:

1. *Identify the concept* you will teach. Make sure that it is grade appropriate and based upon the scope and sequence of the social studies text.

Shared Family Experiences Help Students to See Themselves as Players on the Historical Stage

2. *Preview an interview guide* that your students can use to collect the data necessary for the unit. Your students will benefit from constructing the guide with you, suggesting questions, and manipulating question structures.

3. *Translate the guide,* have students translate it, or use the foreign language teachers in your school to help you put the questions into the native languages of the students. Note: Free online translators such as Babelfish (http://babelfish@yahoo.com) are available for many languages. Although these translators are not yet able to produce clear and accurate text, they can translate many words and help those speaking that language to gain a general understanding of the text. They can also give a head start to a translator. Over-the-phone translations are also available for a fee (e.g., http://www.languageline.com/, which is available for 150 languages).

4. *Practice and record interviews* before sending students into the field. They will need experience in note-taking as they interview, using the tape recorder, and being familiar with the questions.

5. *Invite guest speakers* to be interviewed by the class. Record these interviews and help the students to transcribe them afterwards.

6. *Select an interviewee* for students to question. Older relatives are excellent resources. If not available, look for community or church members. Search various institutions, such as hospitals and work sites. Remember that not all ELLs will have family members who are still alive or who are living in this country.

7. *Assign tasks* for students such as interviewing, recording, transcribing, summarizing, or reporting to the class.

8. *Select themes* from the oral interviews that match the concepts in the social studies curriculum and present these to the class.

9. *Compare and contrast experiences* among the interviewees and relate these experiences to readings based upon the experiences of historical figures. Find the similarities and differences among both groups of people.

Our experience with oral history in the upper elementary and secondary grades was very rewarding. Our ELLs were highly motivated to tell their stories to each other and later to write these stories for a class book. When the local radio station asked for people to submit their immigration stories for a special immigration week, we encouraged our students to send theirs. The children were invited to the radio station to record their stories, which were later aired on the radio.

DIALOGUES The social studies curriculum lends itself to prepared dialogue presentations among and between ELLs of various language proficiencies. Teacher-prepared dialogues conform to the content learning objectives of the lesson but are presented in the familiar context of a conversation. ELLs can practice these dialogue role-plays in preparation for presentation to the entire class. The activity aids in oral language development as well as content learning. Audience members may be prompted to ask questions of the presenters in order to engender more attentive listening, or the teacher may ask questions of the audience to recap the material presented in the dialogue.

Dialogues can be differentiated for language levels and can be structured to include important grammatical elements such as past tense verbs and question forms, adverbial clauses, and complex sentences.

Examples of dialogues might include:

- Antony explaining his conquests to Cleopatra.
- Lewis and Clark's conversation while planning their expedition.
- Two citizens of Boston observing the Boston Tea Party.
- Rosa Parks talking to her husband after her arrest for civil disobedience.

Dialogues lend themselves to the following Common Core Anchor Standard (http://www.corestandards.org/the-standards/english-language-arts-standards) for Listening and Speaking:

- Evaluate a speaker's point of view, reasoning, and use of evidence and rhetoric.

Math

Mathematics has a language of its own. The language is specific (definite), precise (clearly expressed), and logical. Indeed, the National Council of Teachers of Mathematics (NCTM) included math communication as one of its five goals for all students (NCTM 2000, 2006). Math assessment is often dependent on knowledge of specific math vocabulary (e.g., *minuend* and *subtrahend*) as well as an understanding of the text structures used to communicate mathematically, most obviously in word problems. Consider the following problem:

Number *a* is five less than number *b*. Express the equation for this problem.

Students who have learned that the words *less than* have a specific mathematical meaning and are familiar with the syntax of equations might correctly express the above equation as:

$$a = b - 5$$

An ELL might use the word *less* as it appears in a nonmathematical sentence context and express the equation incorrectly as:

$$a = 5 - b$$

FACTORS AFFECTING ACHIEVEMENT There are a variety of factors influencing the math achievement of ELLs. The level of English language development is an obvious one. An intermediate level of English is necessary for understanding most math word problems. The age of the learner, including developmental level, also is a factor. More importantly, however, is the amount of previous learning the ELL has acquired in math.

When Dulce entered our school, she had never been to school before. Although she was placed in the third grade because of her age, she was way behind the other children in language, literacy, and math. Dulce could not participate in the third-grade math class until she acquired some basic math skills and language. She needed tutoring in number recognition and naming, counting, and grouping. She had to learn basic math symbols such as =, −, +, < and >. She also needed to learn the language that clustered around these symbols:

Two plus three equals five.
Five minus two equals three.
Five is greater than three.
Three is less than five.

Dulce was able to learn these concepts fairly quickly because she was eight years old rather than five. Although they may need to learn the basics, older learners will acquire them more quickly than younger learners because they are cognitively more mature. It is important that teachers are aware of students' prior learning so that the gaps in knowledge can be filled and students can begin to participate in grade-level appropriate instruction.

Another factor affecting achievement is the difficulty of the material. Math knowledge is cumulative and, as students advance in school, the amount of math information they are required to know increases while new skills build upon ones previously learned.

Some teachers are surprised that ELLs who have been educated in a native language in another country sometimes surpass North American curriculum standards for math. These advanced students are able to compute at a higher level, but may not be able to express their thinking and communicate it to others. And so, the ability to convey ideas to others is a factor in their achievement. Some of our ELLs conveyed their thinking in a nonverbal way through computation on the board. It was interesting to see that not all math computation is done in the same way. Division, for example, is taught differently in other countries and yet the answers are the same. When ELLs have opportunities to show what they know in math, we empower their learning and prompt them to achieve more.

A final important factor in math achievement is the amount of primary language support children receive for their math learning. In schools with bilingual programs, ELLs are taught in their native languages until they understand the concepts. At that point they transition their knowledge into English. Those ELLs who are taught math in a second language will be at a disadvantage. However, many families are eager to provide support for their children's learning, and math is one area where parents can support school instruction through the use of the native language. We encourage parents to incorporate math concepts into daily life at the elementary level. Telling time, counting, measurement, money, and basic math operations (addition, subtraction, multiplication, and division) are appropriate at this level. Upper elementary and secondary students can be included in discussions of sales percentages, nutritional components of food, interest payments, and car lease agreements. These math-related topics affect the daily life of the family and become more important to English learners as they see their families using math to make decisions.

The Common Core State Standards for Mathematics rely on eight Standards for Mathematics Practice. These standards describe the processes, proficiencies, and varieties of expertise that mathematics educators at all levels should seek to develop in their students (www.commoncorestandards.org). In the following sections we will describe and make reference to the Standards for Mathematics Practice that apply to individual instructional techniques.

INSTRUCTIONAL TECHNIQUES FOR MATH CLASS   Techniques for teaching math to ELLs are also useful in teaching math to all learners. One of the differences will be found in the emphasis on extensive oral and written language practice needed to communicate mathematical reasoning. Specifically, students will need to learn the following oral skills (Buchanan & Helman, 1993):

1. Responding to questions
2. Initiating questions
3. Using English to discuss math
4. Using math vocabulary and grammar
5. Explaining mathematical reasoning

TEACH REQUIRED LANGUAGE STRUCTURES   The oral language required for success in math class can only be attained if teachers are explicit in their instruction, creating language objectives for math alongside their content objectives. Teachers will need to teach not only the language required by the math objective but also any additional language skills required for communication in math class. For example, when teaching Dulce the symbols < and >, it was also necessary to teach her the comparative use of the term *greater than*. To help Dulce remember these, the teacher helped her visualize a hungry alligator that always tried to eat the larger number (shown in Figure 6.3).

When teaching the processes required for a subtraction problem, it will be necessary to explain the use of words such as *first, next, then, finally,* and other words that signal the steps needed to solve a problem. Word problems often require the use of the question words *how much* and *how many*. Students choose the appropriate question depending on whether they are working with mass nouns or count nouns.

THINK-ALOUD MODELING   Presentation techniques in the math class include "think-aloud" modeling of the thought processes and language required for problem solving. The overhead projector (OHP) or the Smart Board are useful tools when teachers need to talk about the steps of problem solving while presenting the steps visually for students. Wall charts with sample problems, solutions, steps needed for problem solving, and math terminology are also helpful for making math reasoning visible to students (as shown in Figure 6.4).

Think-aloud modeling is a technique that supports the development of the following Common Core State Standards for Mathematical Practice (http:www.corestandards.org/the-standards/mathematics/introduction/standards-for-mathematical-practice/):

• Make sense of problems and persevere in solving them
• Reason abstractly and quantitatively
• Construct viable arguments and critique the reasoning of others
• Attend to precision

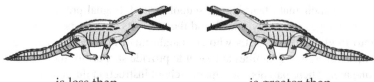

is less than   is greater than

FIGURE 6.3 Visuals Help Children Internalize Concepts Such as "Less Than" and "Greater Than"

How to Solve a Math Problem in Four Steps
1. Try to understand the problem.
   - Explain it using your own words.
   - Find the important information.
   - Draw a picture.
   - Make an estimate.
2. Determine how to solve the problem.
   - Look for signal words that signal addition, subtraction, multiplication, or division.
   - Look for a pattern between this problem and others you have solved.
   - Break the problem into parts.
   - Write a math sentence.
3. Solve the problem.
   - Record your work carefully and neatly.
4. Check the work.
   - Do the calculations again.
   - Use the proper label (feet, dollars, pounds, etc.).
   - Work the problem backwards.

FIGURE 6.4 Students Can Better Recall the Problem-Solving Process If the Steps Are Displayed Prominently

RELATE LEARNING TO PRIOR EXPERIENCES AND CULTURE   Building on a student's prior experience is especially helpful because math knowledge is cumulative and sequential. Different cultures use different algorithms for solving math problems, and learners may have acquired correct processes and solutions for problem solving that are different from those taught in our schools. We need to look carefully at our learners' work and listen to what they have to say before we assume their work is in error. If, through this process, teachers discover gaps in learning, it may be necessary to modify learning objectives and to differentiate learning in order to help students achieve in the math class.

When Jorge entered our fifth-grade math class, we discovered that he didn't know the multiplication tables past five. This slowed down his learning as he attempted to count on his fingers whenever a calculator was not available. Tutoring in multiplication, along with frequent opportunities to listen to a recording of multiplication fact songs, soon caught him up to the rest of his peers. Jorge needed a variety of techniques to learn multiplication tables in a new language. Flash cards, multiplication charts, and learning to count by six, seven, and so on, were all helpful as well. The biggest help was a learning buddy who practiced daily with him for short periods.

Effective math teachers relate their learning objectives to the daily lives and interests of their students. Our students always enjoyed learning word problems related to decimal placement by using menus from popular fast food shops. Our older middle school and high school students enjoyed using information related to car purchases, online shopping, and sports statistics.

The Common Core Standard (http:www.corestandards.org/the-standards/mathematics/introduction/standards-for-mathematical-practice/) related to this principle is:

- Model with mathematics

REQUIRE ORAL LANGUAGE REPORTING   Oral language reporting is an important part of small-group work in math. It provides a need for students to make the effort to learn the appropriate academic language. ELLs can be grouped to work on tasks and then asked to report orally on the results. For example, when teaching addition of fractions, students can convert to the lowest common denominator, add the numbers together, and organize math sentence strips into the appropriate order from the largest to the smallest number, as shown in Figure 6.5.

$$2 \ 1/2 + 13/4 =$$

$$5/2 + 13/4 =$$

$$10/4 + 13/4 =$$

$$2 \ 3/4 =$$

$$5 \ 3/4 =$$

FIGURE 6.5 An Activity for Organizing Fractions by Size (Short, 1991)

Individual group members, holding the sequenced strips, can read the fractions aloud and ask other class members if they agree with the order they have chosen. Similar tasks include sequencing fractions on a **semantic gradient,** as in Figure 6.6.

We have known teachers who placed children in pairs to practice their oral language reporting on how they solved a math problem. The language of math is an integral part of understanding math.

The Common Core Standards (http:www.corestandards.org/the-standards/mathematics/introduction/standards-for-mathematical-practice/) related to these activities include:

- Attend to precision
- Look for and express regularity in repeated reasoning

USE MANIPULATIVES Although there has been occasional controversy regarding math methods, current practice recommended by the NCTM includes frequent use of manipulatives prior to paper-and-pencil tasks. Manipulatives provide students with opportunities to experience learning in an active way and then to reflect on their experiences. This is constructivist thinking. Constructivism is a theory of learning that stresses the active role of the student in the construction of knowledge and meaning from experiential learning (Bruner, 1996; Dewey, 1966; Piaget, 1973; Vygotsky, 1986).

Even older learners benefit from active learning and the use of manipulatives, models, and visuals to help foster comprehension. We saw one teacher use a drink can very effectively to

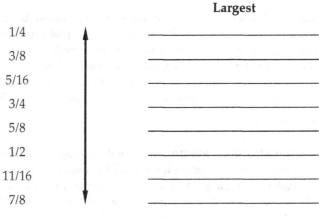

Sequence the fractions in order from the largest to the smallest.

Largest

1/4

3/8

5/16

3/4

5/8

1/2

11/16

7/8

Smallest

FIGURE 6.6 An Activity for Sequencing Fractions on a Semantic Gradient

FIGURE 6.7 A Drink Can Is Used to Help Students Determine the Formula for the Volume of a Cylinder

help learners understand the formula for the volume of a cylinder (Figure 6.7). The students had learned a formula for the area of a circle ($\pi \times r^2$). Then the teacher showed a drink can and asked how they could use that formula to determine the volume of the can. The students realized that the shape of the can is similar to a series of disks piled one on top of the other. They said, *If we could measure the area of a series of disks that were 1 cm high, we could combine them to find the answer.* The teacher asked the students to measure the height of the can and then told them they had discovered the formula they needed: $\pi \times r^2 \times h$.

The Common Core Standards (http:www.corestandards.org/the-standards/mathematics/introduction/standards-for-mathematical-practice/) related to the use of manipulatives include:

- Model with mathematics
- Make sense of problems and persevere in solving them
- Reason abstractly and quantitatively

DRAW PICTURES   Note how the drawing of the can clarifies the process of solving the problem. Drawing pictures to represent a word problem or concept is another helpful strategy to assist comprehension of the language of the problem. Effective teachers draw simple, illustrative pictures while reading the problem aloud, emphasizing, clarifying, and scaffolding the acquisition of mathematical terminology and concepts. Practice continues as ELLs create their own drawings and use the drawings to explain the problem orally to a math buddy. Pictures assist learners in forming the mental images that provide context for problem solving in a new language.

The same Common Core Standards related to the use of manipulatives also apply to drawing pictures.

ISOLATE THE QUESTION AND THE SIGNAL WORDS   The next step in problem solving is to determine which operation is necessary to solve the problem. Determining the question or questions of the problem is the first step. Many word problems that appear to have only one question actually are asking several questions embedded into one. An example might be the question *How many Toyotas, Fords, and Hondas are in the parking lot?* There are actually three questions in this problem. We can help student comprehension by writing all three separately.

Isolating the signal words for math operations helps to determine how to proceed with the problem. We like the graphic organizer for math operations shown in Figure 4.3 in Chapter 4. When teachers display this necessary vocabulary on the bulletin boards, ELLs can access it to determine which math operations are appropriate. Eventually, students will learn that when they see the signal word *altogether* the problem is asking for an addition operation while the words *fewer than* are probably signaling subtraction.

Teaching students these techniques helps to implement the Common Core Standards (http:www.corestandards.org/the-standards/mathematics/introduction/standards-for-mathematical-practice/) related to comprehension and abstract reasoning:

- Make sense of problems and persevere in solving them
- Reason abstractly and quantitatively

USE ROLE-PLAYS Students can participate in role-plays to demonstrate math problems. To illustrate a number sentence in addition (e.g., 3 + 2 = 5), the teacher can have three boys stand up, who are then joined by two girls. The reversed algorithm (2 + 3 = 5) can be demonstrated by presenting two girls joined by three boys. Children will see that the total is the same in both versions. Additionally, students can role-play word problems to gain better understanding of the concepts involved. Role-play a restaurant scene to find the correct tip for the waiter, a car showroom scene to calculate the interest rate on a lease, or a department store scene to determine the interest on the store credit card. There are other ways to make math more communicative and personal. Learners can make graphs of their own hair and eye colors using pictures of themselves, or chart their improvement in typing speed using ratios. Learning new concepts in this way is motivating to students and results in better comprehension and more efficient learning. Role-plays help students to achieve standards of:

- Make sense of problems and persevere in solving them
- Reason abstractly and quantitatively

USE VARIED GROUPING Small-group work is essential in math class to help learners generate the negotiation of meaning needed to develop language and to communicate and reason in English. Our fifth-grade math students participated in joint problem solving with manipulatives followed by paper-and-pencil tasks. They also worked in groups to practice choral recitations of large denominations of money (e.g., *three hundred fifty-seven dollars and eighty-two cents*) before they learned to spell and write the numbers. Secondary school students will need to practice the reading of numbers written in scientific notation:

$$8.3 \times 10^3 = 8,300$$

Eight point three times ten to the third power equals eight thousand three hundred.

Working together, students can check one another's work, create word problems, explain how to solve problems, report to the teacher, dictate numerals, and practice the vocabulary of math or keep a log of new math processes and the explanations that they have learned.

Group work emphasizes the Common Core Standard (http:www.corestandards.org/the-standards/mathematics/introduction/standards-for-mathematical-practice/) of:

- Construct viable arguments and critique the reasoning of others

USE VISUALS Charts, graphic organizers, and visuals or drawings help ELLs comprehend mathematical thinking. The simplest visuals can be created on the chalkboard, OHP, or Smart Board. When teachers model their thinking with a visual component, ELLs can begin to understand the order of the math task. Important concepts can be color-coded to stand out to learners. Graphic organizers are helpful in modeling distinctions such as *before/after* and *more/less*.

Charts and graphs are useful supports for problem solving. When teaching place value and the position of digits, use a place value chart (Figure 6.8). The chart will help students to read

Place Value Chart

	thousands	hundreds	tens	ones
45			four	five
873		eight	seven	three
3,279	three	two	seven	nine
8,930	eight	nine	three	zero

FIGURE 6.8 A Place Value Chart Enables Students to Read Numerals Correctly

Scalene Triangle   Isosceles Triangle   Equilateral Triangle

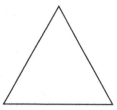

FIGURE 6.9 Visuals Support the Oral Descriptions of Three Types of Triangles

the numbers correctly. When learning the characteristics of triangles, use visuals or geoboards (Figure 6.9) to help ELLs describe each triangle orally using math vocabulary (words such as *sides* and *congruent*).

The 100s Board helps beginning math students understand basic number concepts such as *even/odd*, and counting by twos, fives, or tens. Cuisenaire rods, dice, and multilink cubes are also helpful in counting. Some numbers are "close confusers" (numbers with similar pronunciation, e.g., 13 and 30, 14 and 40, 15 and 50). ELLs may need a great deal of practice to learn to hear the small differences in pronunciation between the numbers in each pair.

The visuals we have described enable students to achieve the following Common Core Standards (http:www.corestandards.org/the-standards/mathematics/introduction/standards-for-mathematical-practice/):

- Look for and make use of structure
- Look for and express regularity in repeated reasoning

USE FREQUENT AND VARIED REPETITION   We're not suggesting that teachers repeat the same words over and over. Rather, we believe that teachers need to represent material frequently in many different ways. This recycling of information can be restatements using different words, visual representations to support oral explanations, or repeating activities with modifications. In each repetition, modeling the language of math will ensure that our students will begin to acquire that language.

In addition, students will be closer to achieving the following standards from the Common Core (http:www.corestandards.org/the-standards/mathematics/introduction/standards-for-mathematical-practice/):

- Make sense of problems and persevere in solving them
- Reason abstractly and quantitatively
- Model with mathematics
- Attend to precision

DEMONSTRATE   Another way to increase comprehension in the math class is to demonstrate all processes and products. When folding paper for a Bingo game involving multiplication facts, show and tell how to fold the paper and set up the game. When collecting data for statistics, demonstrate the method of dice rolling and note-taking required for the final math calculations.

Successful achievement in math involves ELLs in:

- Joint problem solving
- Communication of math reasoning (oral and then written form)
- Developing and using the language of mathematics
- Making connections to daily life

When these criteria are met, ELLs can successfully enter the classroom math conversation.

Science

Children are curious about and drawn to scientific investigation. Many of the questions they ask about the world focus on the world of science. The motivation to learn science is an excellent basis for the development of the mental skills and academic language so essential for further achievement. Also, science is best done in the way that children most enjoy learning—in a "hands-on" manner. Reading about science is not the same as "doing" science. ELLs need not be prevented from learning by their inability to read dense pages of scientific discourse. Rather, they can engage in processes of questioning, observing, measuring, organizing information, making predictions, and drawing conclusions within a social framework of talk: questions, giving directions, sharing, and comparing information. Such experiential and constructivist learning provides the context necessary for comprehension of scientific concepts and academic language. The group nature of the inquiry provides scaffolding that supports further achievement.

The National Science Education Standards (NSES), under the auspices of the National Research Council (NRC) (1996), emphasize the theme of "Science for All." The goal is scientific literacy for all learners. The nature of scientific literacy can be summarized by the NRC definition (NRC, 1996). All students need to be taught to:

- Make observations
- Ask questions
- Investigate solutions
- Communicate results

In the process of engaging in hands-on scientific inquiry, ELLs also learn metacognitive and cognitive skills needed for future learning: questioning, observing, recording information, predicting results, hypothesizing, gathering and organizing data, documenting positions, analyzing, and concluding. These skills are so critical to academic achievement that it would be difficult to imagine a learner being successful in school without their mastery.

FACTORS AFFECTING ACHIEVEMENT The factors that affect math achievement also affect achievement in science:

- Previous learning
- Age and developmental level
- Level of English
- Difficulty level of the material
- Ability to understand and communicate ideas symbolically
- Native language support

Teachers should be aware that previous science instruction in another country may not be similar to the science taught in North American schools. For this reason alone, it's important to activate ELLs' prior knowledge as much as possible to determine what learners already know, as well as any inconsistencies, knowledge lags, or misunderstandings they may have.

It will be more difficult to instruct those ELLs who have had little or no previous science instruction in grade-level appropriate skills and knowledge. Resources in the home language, including written materials and multimedia, and opportunities to speak and work with speakers of their language are very useful in helping ELLs understand new concepts. Parents with some science background might be helpful in home language discussion of basic science concepts. Teachers can also scaffold the development of science language and concepts through demonstrations, drawings with labeled vocabulary, science lab sheets formatted for easy comprehension, science vocabulary notebooks, word walls, graphic organizers that visually display processes and procedures, and a variety of vocabulary learning activities.

INSTRUCTIONAL TECHNIQUES FOR SCIENCE CLASS Many of the same general techniques used to teach math are also helpful in teaching inquiry-based science.

- Model and/or demonstrate procedures, products, and processes.
- Use varied grouping that integrates experiential learning and oral reporting.
- Relate learning to the ELLs' prior experience, culture, and knowledge.
- Use manipulatives, real objects, or models as much as possible.

The oral language skills of comprehending, answering and asking questions, communicating scientific information, explaining scientific concepts, and using specialized vocabulary are also comparable to those required for math learning. In the following section, we will describe instructional techniques that are specific to science instruction and that serve the dual function of developing scientific thinking and concepts while encouraging the production of oral language skills related to scientific inquiry.

1. **Use visuals**—charts, diagrams, and drawings—that contain important information that can be labeled. ELLs who excel in visual representation can offer their drawings as models for the class. Sample tasks include:

   - Draw a group of simple machines and label them.
   - Draw the layers of the Earth and label them.
   - Draw a picture illustrating the process of evaporation. Label the parts and describe the process using the picture as a guide.
   - Use maps and globes for demonstrations and provide blank maps that students can color code for temperature, rainfall, and so on.
   - Use various graphic organizers to record the stages in the life cycle of various creatures (frogs/toads, butterflies) and processes (weather and erosion). Label each stage. Describe how changes occur at each stage.
   - Create tree diagrams of food categories, microbes, and animals. Report to the class, giving examples of each category.
   - Complete a flow chart that describes the process of sound transmission. Label each stage in the process and describe the process to the class.

2. **Use graphs and charts** that contain descriptive information as a resource for language development. Provide key questions on the screen or chalkboard to help students ask and answer questions using the chart. For example:

   - *How tall is the _____ tree? It's _____ feet tall.*
   - *How much does a _____ weigh? A _____ weighs _____ pounds.*
   - *What does the symbol _____ stand for? The symbol _____ stands for _____.*
   - *In what state can _____ be found? _____ can be found in _____.*
   - *Is _____ a metal or a non-metal? _____ is a _____.*
   - *What is _____ used for? _____ can be used for _____ and _____.*
   - *What does a/an _____ measure? A/an _____ measures _____.*
   - *How is _____ measured? _____ is measured in _____.*

3. **Demonstrate the scientific method**. Design simple experiments that require ELLs to work in small groups to observe and record data. Model talking about and proceeding through the steps:

   - State the problem or question.
   - Form an hypothesis of the cause of the problem and make predictions for results based upon the hypothesis.
   - Test your hypothesis by doing an experiment or study (with proper controls).
   - Check and interpret your results.
   - Report your results to the scientific community.

4. **Design and implement experiments** and require students to report orally to the class on their results. For example:

   - Throw a ball into the air. Count how many seconds it takes to fall to the ground. Record the time. Estimate the height of the throw. Record the height. Report your data to the class. What can you predict about a ball thrown 50 feet into the air? Five feet?
   - Record your partner's pulse beat in minutes on a chart for three situations: resting, after walking for two minutes, after running for two minutes. Switch places. Report your results to the class.
   - Estimate your partner's height, foot length, and arm length. Record the estimates on a chart. Measure the lengths using a ruler. Record on a chart. Switch places. Report your results to the class.
   - Line a shoe box with white paper. Line another shoe box with black paper. Place a glass of water inside each box and put the boxes in direct sunlight. Hypothesize about which box will make the water hotter. After two hours, measure the temperature of the water. Record your results and report to the class.

5. Use **sort tasks** of various kinds to reinforce scientific concepts and help to teach vocabulary. ELLs can sort words by writing them in two columns or by arranging word cards into two groupings. The second method is appropriate for pairs of young learners or any student who enjoys manipulating objects in order to learn. For example:

- Sort animal names (or pictures of animals) into two groups: warm blooded/ cold blooded or vertebrate/invertebrate. Compare with others in your group and give reasons for your choices.
- Sort igneous/sedimentary/metamorphic rocks into three groups. Compare and give reasons for your choices.
- Sort all the food eaten by group members in the last two days into seven food groups. Compare with others in your group. What conclusions can you come to about your group's choices?
- Sort pictures of animal feet, paws, hooves, or teeth into categories. How do the feet and the teeth help the animal?

6. **Use advance organizers**. These are organizational frameworks that emphasize the essential ideas of the lesson or unit. They help students to understand and focus on what they are about to learn. Advance organizers (Ausubel, 1960; Brookbank, Grover, Kullberg & Strawser, 1999; Schoen & Schoen, 2003; Stone, 1983) give learners the "big picture" of the learning topic before instruction begins. For language learners, graphic advance organizers are most easily understood because they are primarily visual and nonlinguistic. They help students to more clearly see the relationships among the concepts presented in the text and they aid in the understanding of academic vocabulary. Examples of advance organizers most useful for science class include:

- *semantic feature charts:* indicating the central features of organisms, rock forms, atoms, etc.
- *concept maps:* indicating the identifying features of a central concept
- *cycle graphs:* indicating the correct sequence of a process such as a life process, weather process, erosion, etc.
- *flow charts:* indicating the steps in a process such as a scientific experiment

As each of these suggestions indicates, scientific inquiry in the classroom is achieved through the following:

- Asking questions
- Forming hypotheses
- Investigating solutions
- Communicating results

Science and math are related in their concern for all four elements as well as in the strategies used to teach and promote language competency.

ORAL LANGUAGE DEVELOPMENT EVERY WHICH WAY

The content subject areas provide excellent opportunities for oral language development utilizing teacher-guided collaborative dialogues, instructional conversations, varied grouping options, and interactional language structures. Other ways in which ELLs can grow in their language skills within the context of content learning involve techniques using rhythm, music, creative role-play, and technology.

Songs and Chants/Poetry and Rap

Music is motivating to many learners. The rhythms of songs and chants entice ELLs to want to participate in group efforts even though their oral language skills are limited. We have observed new learners who memorize rap songs and television jingles because of their infectious rhythms and melodies. These songs are often memorized in "chunks" of language that are unanalyzed by learners on a word-for-word basis. The meaning is understood in a global way, but ELLs may be unaware of exactly how many words make up the lyrics or what the individual words mean.

This kind of learning is helpful to ELLs for a few reasons. It gets them into the language immediately, using it for a pleasurable purpose. As such, they often join with others in singing or chanting, and feel a part of the group. In this way, they are eased into the pronunciation, intonation, and rhythms of the new language. Eventually, ELLs will begin to analyze the songs, at a time when they can better comprehend the meaning. At that point, they will often use these chunks of language in their productive speech for communicative purposes.

At the early elementary level, songs are used with hand motions that express the meaning of the song. In this way basic concepts of *up/down, over/under, right/left, in/out,* can be taught. We think it's important to incorporate this kind of music into classrooms of diverse learners— even if the teacher is not skilled in singing. The songs bring unity to the class and create a happy feeling among the learners. In addition, ELLs can learn real language in this way. We were always amazed at the amount of language learned by elementary second grade ELLs who participated in our school's chorus. In spite of the complexity of some of this music, the children were able to perform with gusto, and they acquired a great deal of academic language along the way.

Many teachers use songs and chants to reinforce classroom learning. We have seen social studies teachers use chants to reinforce lessons in history. Some of these teachers told us that they use commercially produced materials that help ELLs to sing about the American Revolution or the Boston Tea Party. Other teachers have used music, and specifically rap, to help learners memorize information such as the periodic table of the elements. Sue Quinn and Joann Fusare-White from Roth Middle School in Henrietta, New York, use music to help their students memorize mathematical formulas. Some examples of formulas, which are sung to the tune of "Wheels on the Bus," are (as cited in Rutherford, 1998, p. 122):

For *perimeter* of a figure you add the sides,
Add the sides, add the sides.
For *perimeter* of a figure you add the sides
All the way around!

Circumference of a circle is $\pi \times d$, $\pi \times d$, $\pi \times d$.
Circumference of a circle is $\pi \times d$. π is 3.14!

Area of a rectangle is length $\times$ width,
Length $\times$ width, length $\times$ width.
Area of a rectangle is length $\times$ width
Only for this shape!

Even without writing musical notation, teachers can take advantage of this technique through the use of rhythmic chants to reinforce learning. A chant is similar to a rap but doesn't necessarily include rhyming. Each statement is said to a rhythmic beat accompanied by toe tapping or finger snapping. Various elements of language can be learned in this way. Imagine the following question and answer format chanted in chorus with one-half of the class asking the questions and the other half answering in a rapid and rhythmic two-beat-per-line cadence:

Group A: *What's the Constitution?*

Group B: *It's the law of the land.*

Group A: *When was it written?*

Group B: *In 1787.*

Group A: *What does it state?*

Group B: *That we are a nation of checks and balances.*

Group A: *Checks and balances.*

Group B: *With three main branches.*

Group A: *Three main branches.*

Group B: *To govern the land.*

Group A: *How many branches?*

Group B: *Three main branches.*

Group A: *What's the first branch?*

Group B: *The legislative branch.*

Group A: *What's the second branch?*

> **Group B:** *The executive branch.*
> **Group A:** *What's the third branch?*
> **Group B:** *The judicial branch.*
> **Group A:** *The legislative branch.*
> **Group B:** *That's the first branch.*
> **Group A:** *The executive branch.*
> **Group B:** *That's the second branch.*
> **Group A:** *The judicial branch.*
> **Group B:** *That's the third branch.*
> **Group A:** *Three main branches.*
> **Group B:** *Three main branches.*
> **Group A:** *Who's in charge of the legislative branch?*
> **Group B:** *The Congress. The Congress.*
> **Group A:** *Who's in charge of the executive branch?*
> **Group B:** *The President. The President.*
> **Group A:** *Who's in charge of the judicial branch?*
> **Group B:** *The Supreme Court. The Supreme Court.*

Teacher and students together can create chants and display them on the wall or board, or provide copies for each student. Performances could be formally presented to other classes or informally practiced in class when a break in routine is needed. Literate learners could be called upon to work in small groups to write chants as a way of summarizing learning. This is a novel form of assessment that appeals to diverse student learning styles.

The motivations for poetry and rap are similar to those for songs and chants. Students enjoy these forms of expression. Adolescents, in particular, are drawn to the rap style. The difference between the two techniques is that poetry and rap tend to be more stylized and often use rhyming. These techniques can be explored in much the same way as songs and chants, and can be related directly to content learning.

It is best to present a poem, song, chant, or rap within a meaningful context. We like to write the poem or song on a large sheet of chart paper, the OHP, or the board and include rebus pictures or drawings to indicate unknown words. We read the poem to our ELLs with enthusiasm and emotion, and invite them to join us in subsequent readings. We have found it helpful to reproduce these writings for students to include in poetry/song/chant books that they make and illustrate with their own pictures.

One teacher we know has a Poetry Month to encourage all of her students to carry a "Poem in Your Pocket." Each student chooses a favorite poem and carries that poem in a pocket. All of the other teachers and students in the school can ask to hear any of these poems throughout the month. They get many repeated readings as others in the school join in the fun of poetry sharing. The ELLs in this classroom benefit from the repetitions of the poetry and the communicative nature of the task.

Role-Plays, RAFTs, and Simulations

Role-plays are excellent tools for providing oral language practice of subject matter content. There are a variety of ways to include role-play into classroom learning but basically, teachers we have observed have used student-made role-plays or teacher-prepared role-plays. The advantage of writing a role-play for ELLs to perform is that teachers can be sure to include in the language and concepts that are important to the unit. This takes time, however, and when presented to students, can be perceived as only a script to follow, with little learner investment.

When ELLs write their own role-plays, they become more invested in the activity. The role-play also works as an assessment of learning. Teachers can see what students have taken from the learning unit as the role-play unfolds. Careful planning is needed to be sure that students are successful in their role-plays. It is best if the writing is done in small groups and the teacher presents a **RAFT** (**R**ole, **A**udience, **F**orm, **T**ime) to guide the writing. A RAFT is a type of

A Classroom Picture of a RAFT

Cindy Liang, a fifth-grade teacher in a mixed classroom of ELLs and native English speakers, uses a Thanksgiving Dinner RAFT to help her students learn about the history of the Pilgrims. Each child in the class is assigned the name of a real Pilgrim to research. As the month continues, students plan a Thanksgiving dinner of authentic foods that they cook themselves and serve to each other and invited guests. Each child, dressed in authentic costume, reacts on that day as the real person in history: speaking of events in their lives and answering questions of those invited to share the feast. More than a simple cooking project, Ms. Liang's class becomes highly engaged with the academic content and learning. In later history units, these students will be able to recall their first-person experiences and view historical events in a different way—as events that affected real people and impacted their own lives. This is the kind of transferable skill learning that we aspire to in all of our teaching.

Ms Liang created a RAFT to help structure the Thanksgiving role-play:

Role: You are a Pilgrim named _____ living in the New World.

Audience: You are responding to people from another time and telling them about your life.

Form: You are to answer questions addressed to you as completely as possible about your life and your dreams for the future.

Time: The fall of 1621 after the harvest.

role-play in which the teacher creates a scenario about the content being studied (Rutherford, 1998). The teacher assigns a role to the students, determines an audience, a format for the presentation, and a time frame. For example:

- You are a newspaper reporter (role and audience). Your job is to interview (form) Meriwether Lewis, William Clark, and Sacagawea as they reach the Pacific Ocean on November 17, 1806 (time) after exploring the territory between the Mississippi River and the Pacific Ocean. Be sure to determine from each person which aspects of the trip were most momentous for them.
- You are a cloud seeder (role). Your job requires you to fly an airplane, seeding the clouds to promote rainfall for a spring crop (time). Write a presentation (form) that you will give to a group of drought-ridden farmers (audience) explaining the rain cycle and how you will help them to get rain. Answer their questions and convince them to hire you.
- You are a doctor in the local hospital (role and time). Your patient has a heart problem but doesn't understand how the heart is involved in circulation. Role-play an office visit where you explain (form) the circulatory system to your patient (audience).

These role-plays can be presented within the classroom or to another class of students. They can be copied for each student to read and preserved in a book of role-plays created by the class.

SIMULATIONS   are similar to role-plays but in the former, the teacher structures the learning more concretely for learners. For example, students might be asked to set up a store in the classroom and then assume the roles of clerk and customer. Some teachers encourage students to write the script for these simulations, especially when they are based upon a story read in class, a fairy tale, or a retelling of an event in history.

Potential products for simulations, role-plays, and RAFTs are limitless. Students can express their learning in many ways other then through paper-and-pencil tasks. A quick run through the alphabet can highlight at least 26 products for learning:

1. Advice column
2. Banner
3. Comedy act
4. Documentary
5. Eyewitness account
6. Flannel board
7. Greeting card
8. Hand puppet
9. Interview

10. Jingle
11. Kite
12. Letter to the editor
13. Mnemonic
14. Nursery rhyme
15. Owner's manual
16. Puzzle
17. Quilt
18. Radio commentary
19. Slide show
20. Tall tale
21. UFO
22. Venn diagram
23. Web page
24. X-ray
25. Yearbook
26. Zodiac chart

WebQuests

A **WebQuest** is an inquiry-oriented lesson format in which most or all the information that learners work with comes from the web. The model was developed by Bernie Dodge at San Diego State University in 1995, with early input from SDSU/Pacific Bell Fellow Tom March, the Educational Technology staff at San Diego Unified School District, and waves of participants each summer at the Teach the Teachers Consortium. Information and a database of WebQuests by other teachers as well as products by learners are available at www.WebQuest. org. The web site allows teachers to access WebQuests on a wide variety of content topics. Once found, those topics are identified by content area and grade level. Each WebQuest is further divided into an Introduction, Task, Process, Evaluation (with completed rubrics), Conclusion, Credits, and a Teacher's Page with information to help teachers identify the most effective WebQuests for their students.

Increasing the kinds of learning experiences and the products of learning can provide ELLs with a more inclusive classroom experience as well as tap the many diverse learning styles of native English learners.

LISTENING IN WHILE NOT TUNING OUT

Comprehending language is very different from simply hearing it. The former is an active mental processing skill, whereas the latter is a function of the ability of our ears to transmit sounds. In Chapter 5, we talked about the importance of listening during the preproduction stage of oral language development. However, it's not only during preproduction that listening is important to learning. Listening is an essential skill for subject matter concept learning as well as for the development of academic language. Students at all grade levels benefit from structured listening activities.

We were visiting a friend with a twelve-month-old grandchild recently. As we watched little Jack play with his toys and interact with his mother and grandmother, it was obvious that he understood a great deal of language. Jack followed his mother's commands and questions to *Come here, Give me the giraffe, Do you want your bottle? Pick up those papers*, and so on. During all this time, Jack rarely uttered a word. Indeed, his mother indicated that Jack only spoke two words: *bot* (bottle) and *no*. In spite of his lack of productive language, Jack is learning language at a normal rate.

Noticing that children learned their first languages by listening and responding to language, James Asher, a psychologist at San Jose State College in California, determined that language could be learned through kinesthetic responses to auditory commands. The many studies conducted to test this hypothesis showed that the **Total Physical Response** (TPR) method resulted in long-term recall of the language (Asher, 1979). TPR reminds us that listening to language should not be a passive activity. We will get better language learning results if students are asked to move their bodies or react in some way as a result of the listening activity.

In Chapter 8 we discuss how to assist ELLs in the sound discrimination so necessary for phonemic awareness and phonics. In this chapter, we will focus on listening comprehension in the content classroom.

Listening for Understanding

The best way to promote listening for understanding is to be sure to talk to ELLs individually every day. Even when students are unable to comprehend much language, they will attempt to understand and use context clues to guess at meanings. Teacher language that is interspersed with various kinds of questions is very helpful in promoting listening skills. Questions, with their rising intonational formats, are quickly identified and they call out for a response. In the beginning, teachers supply the responses for their learners.

Hi Carlos. How are you? What's this? Is this your book bag?

It's a really big book bag. It feels heavy. Is it heavy? No? Not too heavy?

Good.

The repetitions in these conversations, the use of the question words and rising intonation, and the obvious reference (book bag) help to put the language learner at ease. These dialogues send the message: *My teacher wants to talk to me!* They also send the message that understanding English might not be too impossible a task.

We have included specific tasks for developing skill in listening with understanding. The tasks range from the easiest to the most difficult. These tasks are adaptable for a variety of subject matter content, and the language can be aligned to the proficiency level of the learner. The important element of each is that teachers focus on the development of listening skills even after ELLs have acquired social language.

1. **Use gestures.** As we have discussed earlier, hand, facial, and body gestures contribute to the meaning of oral language in the classroom. Routine classroom language that can easily be communicated with gestures includes these expressions: *good morning, stand up, sit down, listen, look, give me . . ., let's go, come here, open your books, put down your pencil,* and *good-bye.*

2. **Teach classroom routines** and directional language by playing Simon Says. You can also ask students to perform an increasingly more difficult series of actions:

    *   *Walk to the chalkboard.*
    *   *Pick up the chalk.*
    *   *Write the numeral _____ on the chalkboard. (or Write the formula for _____.)*
    *   *Put down the chalk.*
    *   *Walk to your desk and sit down.*

3. **Play Picture (or number) Bingo,** directing students to place a token on a picture of a new vocabulary item. The pictures might be simple, such as animals of the desert, or more complex, such as chemistry apparatus.

4. **Play Airport** to help ELLs listen for specific information related to numbers and time. Draw a grid on the chalkboard such as the one shown in Figure 6.10. The grid should contain columns for flight numbers, cities, and countries (in mixed-up order), boarding gate numbers, and times of departure. Call out the information in a way similar to an announcer at an airport:

    Flight number 13 for Cuernavava, Mexico, leaving Gate 28 at 9:15 pm.

    The student must listen to, remember, and point out the specific times called by tapping on or pointing to the chalkboard grid. It's important that the student not respond until the announcement is finished. By requiring ELLs to wait before responding, you enable them to develop increasingly longer memory spans. The announcer can control the speed and the quantity of items called according to the ability of the class. The airport activity can also be accomplished in pairs and students can write their responses on paper.

    This activity can be used with any content information that is contained on a chart: the periodic table of elements, the thirteen original colonies with their founders, dates and locations, animal families, and many others.

5. **Listen and choose.** Present students with a group of vocabulary items related to the unit under study. Write the words on the chalkboard or project them on a screen and accompany

Flight no.	City	Country	Gate no.	Departure Time
17	Bogotá	Colombia	28	2:45
40	Cali	Guatemala	30	4:32
13	Mexico City	Mexico	17	8:30
70	Cuernavaca	Panama	39	9:15

FIGURE 6.10 A Grid Format Activity, "Airport," Teaches Receptive Listening Skills

them with pictures, if necessary. Then describe one of the items, one sentence at a time. Begin with very general sentences and gradually become more specific. The students must identify the item you are describing. For example:

It's a scientific instrument.
It contains a glass lens
It has a knob to focus the view.
It enlarges microscopic items on a slide.

At some point, ELLs will recognize that you are describing a microscope and indicate the correct word by pointing to or naming the item. If the class is very diverse, you may ask learners not to call out but simply raise their hands when they know the answer. In this way you can recognize those who are able to make early guesses but still provide more input for those who are not sure.

The important element of this exercise is the input that ELLs are receiving as you define the objects. Terms such as *scientific, contains, focus*, and *microscopic* are all part of the academic language of the unit. As ELLs listen, they are required to attend to this language and attempt to understand it. The result is that they have more exposure to academic language in a way that requires them to actively process the language.

6. **Play "If I Were . . . ."** Complete the phrase with a statement related to the unit under study. Students vote on the correctness of the statement, perhaps by showing a signal card labeled True/False or signaling Thumbs Up/Down.

   If I were a reptile, I would have fur.
   If I were a plant, my leaves would always contain chlorophyll.
   If I were Balboa, I would discover the Pacific Ocean.

7. **Sequence the pictures.** Describe an event in history or a scientific process based upon a sequence of four or five pictures. Give the pictures to a group of ELLs who have listened to the description and ask them to sequence the pictures correctly. Later, they can retell the event or process.

8. **Use dictation** to help ELLs extend their memories, develop cognition, listen attentively, and listen with discrimination. Begin with simple sentences containing known grammatical structures and vocabulary. Tell students you will say the sentence only once. They are to listen with their pencils resting on their desks. Hold up your finger, a ruler, or a colorful flag as a signal that they may begin writing. Say the sentence at a normal conversational speed, then count under your breath to ten before giving the signal. After the dictation, correct the sentence immediately by writing the correct form on the board. If students are not

correct, they can use the model to make corrections. ELLs are challenged by this activity and thus motivated to succeed. The ten-second wait will help ensure that they understand and have time to process the oral language before writing. The time wait also helps them develop longer memories for oral language.

9. **Teach note-taking.** Even when ELLs are adept at listening and understanding the language of their teachers and friends in conversations, they may have difficulty understanding more formal language presentations such as a lecture, assembly program, or speech. Having skill in note-taking is essential to learning from these formal presentation formats. We can help students develop listening and note-taking skills in this way:

- Distribute copies of a content-related paragraph containing ten to fifteen sentences or refer ELLs to a paragraph in their textbooks. Read the paragraph aloud to the students while they read silently.
- Next, ask them to close their books and listen to the same paragraph a second time. During this second reading, ask students to take notes on the contents of the paragraph.
- After the note-taking, go to the whiteboard or OHP and ask students to tell you the notes they have taken. Write these down. If the students have omitted any important information, include it on the board summary at this time.
- Next, distribute copies of the same paragraph to students with key words or phrases omitted. Read the complete paragraph again and ask students to fill in the blanks as they listen to the reading. After this third reading, you can check the correctness of the students' answers in a variety of ways. Students can read the filled-in sentences aloud, or pair up and compare their answers to those of a buddy. Finally, students can refer to the text or the original reading.

As ELLs advance in their cognitive and linguistic skills, you can use this same technique to teach outlining skills by reading a three- or four-paragraph narrative to the class.

Listening and oral language are related skills. Listening is receptive but not passive. Oral language is a productive skill. Development in one skill increases the development of the other related skill. When we consider the amount of time spent listening in classrooms, we begin to understand the need to make those listening experiences productive ones for all learners.

ASSESSING LISTENING AND SPEAKING SKILLS IN THE CONTENT CLASSROOM

When assessing listening and speaking skills in the content classroom, teachers need to be clear about their goals and objectives. Many classroom activities include both language skill goals and content learning goals.

Consider the following directions: *Describe the appearance and composition of two planets in the solar system.* This objective includes both an oral language skill (describe) and content knowledge (appearance and composition of two planets in the solar system). In order to assess a student's performance, the teacher needs to separate the content learning goals from the language goals. It is possible that a student has good knowledge of the composition and appearance of the two planets in question, but is unable to fluently and grammatically describe them.

Rubrics are one way to separate the assessment of language skill from content knowledge. Rubrics are scoring scales using numbers or letters that identify the specific criteria used to evaluate a product or presentation. They are most effective when shared with students at the beginning of the learning unit and clearly explained or explicitly modeled. Through a rubric, target performance can be clearly explained, describing several levels of proficiency.

For example, the rubric in Table 6.1 is one that can be used for description in a variety of content subjects. What is important is that the teacher scaffolds the oral reporting task so that all learners can approximate the Proficient level. ELLs might use a graphic organizer or note cards as scaffolds during their descriptions and be given ample opportunity for practice before assessment.

The content knowledge portion of the learning objective can also be assessed through the use of a rubric. This rubric, however, would be specific to the content and learning requirements. Students will need to see the rubric before the learning unit begins and understand each of the components specified there. It is helpful to show well-prepared models of products and to demonstrate processes in order to make assessment clearer to ELLs. Provide opportunities for students to reference the rubric throughout the lesson.

TABLE 6.1 Rubrics are Useful for Oral Language Assessment

	Novice	Developing	Proficient	Expert
Fluency	Speech is halting and fragmentary. There is no continuity in the presentation.	Usually hesitant; description contains long periods of silence.	Description is occasionally disrupted by the student's search for correct manner of expression.	Description is generally fluent with rare lapses for correct expression.
Vocabulary	Vocabulary limitations are so extreme that no content is communicated.	Difficult to understand because of misuse of words, missing vocabulary, lack of signal words, and very limited academic vocabulary.	Occasional use of incorrect wordage: there is evidence of both academic and technical vocabulary and signal words required for logical description of the content.	Academic and technical vocabulary are used appropriately to describe the content. Signal words are in evidence as required.
Pronunciation	Pronunciation problems are so severe that speech is virtually unintelligible.	Difficult to understand because of pronunciation problems; must frequently repeat in order to be understood.	Language is comprehensible with few misunderstandings caused by pronunciation problems.	Description is always intelligible, although listeners may be conscious of an accent.
Grammar	Errors in grammar and word order are so severe that speech is virtually unintelligible.	Difficult to understand because of errors in grammar and word order; must often rephrase or restrict speech to basic patterns.	Meaning is clear with simple grammar and word order. There is evidence that the grammar is tailored to the content.	Grammar is correct. Language structures are appropriate to the content.

RTI TIER 1 SAMPLER

- Establish aural-oral language objectives related to the content of the instruction. For example, if students are listening to a fairy tale, help them to recreate the story with puppets. If students are reading chapter books connected to social studies, set up media interviews with the lead characters to ask and answer questions about the content.
- Provide graphic organizers to illustrate the text organization of literature and content readings. Include the necessary signal words found in the text or the graphics. Use these graphics to scaffold student retelling of the major points of the reading.
- After a period of oral language input, check comprehension through signals (Thumbs Up/Down), Buddy Talk, or Think-Pair-Share-Write.
- After checking comprehension for oral input, have each student in the class write a question about the content. Place all questions in a bag and ask buddy teams to pull a question, confer, and answer the question. Allow students to use notes for this activity or a textbook.
- Before assigning a reading in a textbook, ask partners to skim through the text to look at pictures, captions, graphs, maps, bold glosses, and other graphic scaffolds. Have students take notes on information they have learned or on questions they want answered in the text.
- Relate the concepts in the social studies text to the lives of the students in the classroom by telling a story about yourself relating to the topic. Encourage students to tell stories about their connections to the topic, about their parents or family or extended relatives. For example, when studying ancient civilizations, tell of a visit to see objects from King Tut's tomb in the history museum. When studying World War I, tell how that war affected members of your extended family.
- Create oral language dialogues relating to classroom content that can be performed on YouTube. Be sure the dialogues incorporate the vocabulary and grammatical structures necessary for the content.

- Require students to draw pictures or graphics of word problems and use these graphics to support an oral retelling of the problem's solution.
- Demonstrate or prepare a science lab for each major topic in the curriculum. Structure student work on a lab sheet and demonstrate how to complete the lab and the lab sheet on the Smart Board or the OHP.
- Create a RAFT as a social studies or language arts project that involves every student in using oral language to role play a part.

RTI TIER 2 SAMPLER

- Work with students who need oral academic language practice in small groups. Target specific vocabulary and grammar structures for each small-group session. Model the language within the context of the content you are teaching. Pair the students or work one-on-one with a student to structure oral language conclusions about the content topic. Provide an outline or graphic organizer to structure the language. Encourage all attempts to speak. Persist in helping students to be successful.
- Take anecdotal records of student oral language use in the content classroom. If students do not speak in front of the class, monitor language use while they are working in small groups.
- As students master academic language structures related to content learning, help them to record the language in a journal or learning log. Review these records at each small-group meeting.
- Meet with students in small groups to preview the graphics, pictures, glossed vocabulary, charts, and maps in the text prior to teaching the material to the class. Have students tell you what they can infer from each picture and graphic in the text. Create a series of questions generated from the section headings in the text. For example: Isaac Newton and the Laws of Physics will become: *Who was Isaac Newton? Why is Isaac Newton famous? What are the laws of physics? How many laws are there? etc.*
- While other students are reading the text assignment, meet with ELLs and read some portions of the text together. After each short paragraph, encourage the students to retell orally what they have read in the text. After each section, retell the information and record major ideas and concepts on an outline. These outlines can then be used for written summaries.
- Work with students in small groups to create a series of questions related to the content learning. Teach students to find the answers to the questions in the text (using the index) or on the web using a search engine. Provide time for students to ask and answer the questions. When all students have asked their own questions, exchange the questions and ask and answer them again.
- When teaching content vocabulary to ELLs, provide multiple contexts for each word. Model the usage. Give nonexamples. Expand each word into related word families such as the noun, verb, adjectival, and/or adverbial form. Help students to create vocabulary charts where the various forms can be written. Revisit the word forms frequently, providing opportunities for students to use the words actively in oral language.
- After presenting new information to the class, meet with ELLs and re-present the information, breaking it down into smaller steps and providing opportunities for the students to retell the information in an oral format.
- Prior to introducing a new topic, create an outline of the critical information and concepts to give to ELLs. As students progress through the learning unit, ELLs can use these outlines to structure their learning, oral reporting, and writing.
- During small-group work, be explicit when ELLs are making progress and when they are not. If a student falls short of expectations, provide models, demonstrations, and oral scaffolds to bridge the learning gap. Provide opportunities for many correct responses and slow down the rate of learning until the student is able to be successful.

Questions for Reflection

1. What supports do classroom teachers need in order to become academic language teachers in content classrooms in grades K through 12? How can they make considering language development part of their daily thinking and lesson planning?
2. We have suggested incorporating language objectives for knowledge and skill development into all content classes with ELLs. Which content do you think will be the most difficult for you? Why? Which content class will be the least difficult? Why?

3. Students at all grade levels spend a good deal of class time listening. This is a particularly difficult skill for ELLs to learn. Develop this argument further with reference to various grade levels and then support your thinking with examples of techniques that will ease the load, and promote the language development, of ELLs in content classrooms.

Activities for Further Learning

1. Look back at the instructional techniques recommended for the content areas of language arts, social studies, math, and science. For each content area identify two or three techniques that you consider most helpful to all learners. Share your conclusions with others in your group. Are your choices similar or different? Discuss why each of you has made your choices. Are there other techniques not mentioned that you would include? Share these with your group members.
2. Consider the following lesson plan for an elementary-level science lesson on electricity. The plan is designed for students working in small groups. The purpose of the lesson is student investigation of electrical circuits.

> **Materials:** Cell batteries, insulated wire (with insulation removed at the ends), flashlight bulbs
> **Directions:** Experiment to find ways to connect the batteries, bulbs, and wires so that the bulbs will light.
> **Vocabulary:** Connect, battery, bulb, wire, predict, circuit

Predict what the students will report at the conclusion of the experiment. Identify the technical and academic language you want the students to use. Note the kind of grammar needed to use academic language to report on the experiment. Talk with your group members about techniques you could employ to help students use this formal, academic, and scientific language prior to writing a report.

3. Work with your group to create a rap or a chant in academic language that reports on the learning about electrical circuits.
4. Consult a curriculum guide or the Common Core State Standards for Mathematics to devise a lesson plan for a diverse first-grade math class. Identify the technical and academic language you want the students to use. Note the kind of grammar needed to communicate about the math learning. Talk with your group members about techniques you could use to help students practice and use this formal, academic math language in the classroom.
5. Consult a curriculum or standards guide to create a social studies lesson for a mixed-language sixth-grade classroom. Select the specific objectives (content, language, and learning strategies) and create activities that will promote oral language practice and use within a content learning context.
6. Consult a curriculum guide or the Common Core State Standards for the English Language Arts to develop a language arts lesson for an eighth-grade classroom of mixed-language proficiencies. Develop specific objectives (language, content, and learning strategies), and devise classroom experiences that will require all students to be active participants, practicing and using the target language with appropriate scaffolds.
7. Develop activities that infuse one of the above lessons with music, dance, or artistic expression.
8. Create a RAFT for content learning for each of the above lessons (science, math, social studies, and language arts).

Suggested Reading

Calderon, M. (2007). *Teaching reading to English language learners, grades 6–12: A framework for improving achievement in the content areas*. Thousand Oaks, CA: Corwin Press. This practical guide is filled with tools for secondary teachers with English learners in their classes. It includes lesson templates, rubrics, sample lesson plans in mathematics, science, language arts, and social studies, and descriptions of successful programs.

Fathman, A. K., & Crowther, D. (2006). *Science for English language learners: K–12 classroom strategies*. Arlington, VA: NSTA Press. This book, written by a language specialist and a science teacher, provides a comprehensive guide to teaching language and science together using inquiry-based practices. The text includes an overview of principles that both content areas share, practical strategies and models for lesson and curriculum development, and a review of standards in both areas, along with many resources.

Gomez, S., McKay, H., Tom, A., & White, K. (1995). *Eureka! Science demonstrations for ESL classes*. Reading, MA: Addison-Wesley. This book contains 66 science demonstrations

suitable for learners from upper elementary to middle school. There are reproducible pages for student use, excellent and simple line drawings, suggestions for language learning, and detailed instructions for each demonstration. Questions for analysis and application are provided as well as activities promoting student explanations. The demonstrations are grouped into science units including the scientific process, air, force and motion, electricity and magnetism, visual perception, sound, properties of liquids, chemistry, and heat. Teachers with limited knowledge of how to teach either science or ELLs will benefit from this material.

Johnston, J., & Johnston, M. (1990). *Content points A, B, C: Science, mathematics, and social studies activities*. Reading, MA: Addison-Wesley. These three slim workbooks present many valuable ideas for teachers who are interested in learning ways to scaffold instruction in the content areas. The materials are aimed at students from upper elementary to middle school. The language requirements and subject matter concepts increase in difficulty from Book A to Book C.

References

Almada, P., Nichols, A., & O'Keefe, L. (2004). *A pocketful of opossums*. Barrington, IL: Rigby.

Anstrom, A. (1999). Preparing secondary education teachers to work with English language learners: Social studies. Washington, DC: NCBE Resource Collection Series #13, Center for the Study of Language and Education, Graduate School of Education and Human Development, The George Washington University.

Applications of Common Core Standards for English Language Learners. Retrieved from http://www.corestandards.org/assets/application-for-english-learners.pdf.

Asher, J. (1979) *Learning another language through actions: The complete teacher's guidebook*. San Jose, CA: Sky Oaks Productions.

Ausubel, D. P. (1960). The use of advance organizers in learning and retention of meaningful material. *Journal of Education Psychology, 51*(5), 267–272.

Black, A., & Stave, A. M. (2007). *A comprehensive guide to readers' theatre: Enhancing fluency and comprehension in middle school and beyond*. Newark, DE: International Reading Association.

Brookbank, D., Grover, S., Kullberg, K., & Strawser, C. (1999). Improving student attention through organization of student learning. Chicago: Master's Action Research Project, Saint Xavier University and IRI/Skylight. (ERIC Document Reproduction Service No. ED435094.)

Bruner, J. (1996). *The culture of education*. Cambridge, MA: Harvard University Press.

Buchanan, K., & Helman, M. (1993). *Reforming mathematics instruction for ESL literacy students*. Washington, DC: National Clearinghouse for Bilingual Education.

Center for Applied Linguistics (CAL). (1998). *Enriching content classes for secondary ESOL students: Trainer's manual and study guide*. McHenry, IL: Delta Systems.

Common Core State Standards: Anchor Standards for English Language Arts. (2010). Retrieved from http://www.corestandards.org/the-standards/english-language-arts-standards

Common Core State Standards for Mathematics. (2010). Retrieved from http://www.corestandards.org/assets/CCSSI_Math%20Standards.pdf

Dewey, J. (1966). *Democracy and education*, New York: Free Press.

Lacina, J., Levine, L. N., & Sowa, P. (2006). *Collaborative partnerships between ESL and classroom teachers: Helping English language learners succeed in pre-K–elementary schools*. Alexandria, VA: TESOL.

National Council for the Social Studies Task Force on Scope and Sequence. (1989, October). In search of a scope and sequence for social studies. *Social Education, 53*, 376–387.

National Council of Teachers of Mathematics (NCTM). (2000). Principles and standards for school mathematics. Retrieved from http://www.nctm.org/standards/

National Council of Teachers of Mathematics (NCTM). (2006). Curriculum focal points for prekindergarten through grade 8 mathematics. Retrieved from http://www.nctm.org

National Research Council. (1996). *National science education standards*. Washington, DC: National Academy Press.

Olmedo, I. M. (1993). Junior historians: Doing oral history with ESL and bilingual students. *TESOL Journal* (2): 7–10.

Piaget, J. (1973). *To understand is to invent*. New York: Grossman.

Rutherford, P. (1998). *Instruction for all students*. Alexandria, VA: Just ASK Publications.

Schoen, F., & Schoen, A. A. (2003). Action research in the classroom. *Teaching Exceptional Children, 35*, 16–21.

Short, D. J. (1991). *Integrating language and content instruction: Strategies and techniques*. Washington, DC: National Clearinghouse for Bilingual Education.

Stone, C. L. (1983). A meta-analysis of advance organizer studies. *The Journal of Experimental Education, 51*(4), 194–199.

Vygotsky, L. S. (1986). *Thought and language*. New York: Wiley.

MyEducationLab™

Go to the Topic, Speaking and Listening, in the MyEducationLab (www.myeducationlab.com) for your course, where you can:

- Find learning outcomes for Comprehensible Input along with the national standards that connect to these outcomes.
- Complete Assignments and Activities that can help you more deeply understand the chapter content.
- Apply and practice your understanding of the core teaching skills identified in the chapter with the Building Teaching Skills and Dispositions learning units.
- Examine challenging situations and cases presented in the IRIS Center Resources.
- Check your comprehension on the content covered in the chapter by going to the Study Plan in the Book Resources for your text. Here you will be able to take a chapter quiz, receive feedback on your answers, and then access Review, Practice, and Enrichment activities to enhance your understanding of chapter content.
- **A+RISE** A+RISE® Standards2Strategy™ is an innovative and interactive online resource that offers new teachers in grades K-12 just in time, research-based instructional strategies that meet the linguistic needs of ELLs as they learn content, differentiate instruction for all grades and abilities, and are aligned to Common Core Elementary Language Arts standards (for the literacy strategies) and to English language proficiency standards in WIDA, Texas, California, and Florida.

CHAPTER 7

Teaching Vocabulary to English Learners

$\mathbf{M}$r. Reed, a chemistry teacher at an urban high school, believes that science classes introduce many more words than language arts classes do. While he takes the teaching of vocabulary very seriously, he makes every effort to ensure that it is also interesting and fun for his learners. At a recent training event, he had found out about a cooperative learning strategy called "Clock Buddies" that helped teachers mix up the class for activities. In the activity, he gave students a sheet with the numbers on a clock face, and they signed up a partner for each "hour," providing 12 different pairings of students in the class for short, paired activities. So, for the first week of school, Mr. Reed created "Chemistry Buddies." He passed out an illustrated list of 12 pieces of apparatus that students needed to know, and for each item, students found a different "buddy" and wrote that person's name next to the term (see Table 7.1). Now students had a list of partners for paired activities for the first week of school, and all Mr. Reed had to say was, "Find your *Bunsen burner* (or other apparatus) buddies." Students worked in different pairs to identify the apparatus, draw and label it, remind one another of safety rules, prepare and assess their lab notebooks, and quiz one another on names and procedures for using the apparatus. Each time they found a new partner, they were also reviewing the apparatus terms. Mr. Reed found that the students learned the terms faster than any group he had ever taught. What's more, the strategy worked beautifully for both his English-proficient learners and his ELLs—all of whom were learning lots of new vocabulary.

Chemistry Lab Apparatus Buddies for (your name): Finn		
 **Bunsen burner** buddy: Leo	 **Condenser** buddy: Marta	 **Beaker** buddy: Khan
 **Graduated cylinder** buddy: Mohamed	 **Crucible tongs** buddy: Scarlett	 **Burette** buddy: Madison
 **Erlynmeyer flask** buddy: Luis	 **Volumetric flask** buddy: Amy	 **Mortar and pestle** buddy: Deepa
 **Microspatula** buddy: Ciaran	 **Ring stand** buddy: Ara	 **Florence flask** buddy: Ronin

FIGURE 7.1 Chemistry Lab Apparatus Buddies

How do teachers help English learners build vocabulary?

- Why is learning vocabulary important for English learners?
- What do we mean when we speak of vocabulary? How many words do students need to learn?
- What words should we teach?
- What are the characteristics of effective vocabulary instruction?
- How should we provide direct vocabulary instruction?
- How can we help learners develop their own tools to deal with unknown words independently?
- What are active, interactive strategies to support vocabulary development?
- How can we assess vocabulary development of English learners?

WHY IS LEARNING VOCABULARY IMPORTANT FOR ENGLISH LEARNERS?

If you ask English learners what they want and need most of all in their language development, their answer would be "More words." Of course they need many other aspects of language, but words are essential to their language development and learning in all content areas. Research shows that second language readers rely heavily on vocabulary knowledge, and that a lack of vocabulary knowledge is the largest obstacle for second language readers to overcome (Huckin & Block, 1993). One of the most robust findings of reading research is how vocabulary knowledge contributes to reading comprehension, fluency, and academic achievement in all areas (Lehr, Osborn, & Heibert, 2004; National Research Council, 2010). Vocabulary knowledge leads to better reading comprehension, but also results from it. Vocabulary serves as a bridge between the word-level processes of phonics and the cognitive process of comprehension (Heibert & Kamil, 2005). Knowing words makes readers more fluent, able to read more quickly and easily than those who know fewer words. Learners who have a lot of words in their oral vocabulary are better able to comprehend their reading and receive higher test scores than their peers who know fewer words. That is the challenge the classroom teacher must face—and the challenge is greater with ELLs who know so many fewer words in English. It is the goal of this chapter to provide tools and strategies to address the vocabulary needs of English learners in content classrooms, and to provide wide, rich, deep learning of these building blocks of English according to the principles of the activity-based, communicative model we describe in this book.

WHAT DO WE MEAN WHEN WE SPEAK OF VOCABULARY? HOW MANY WORDS DO STUDENTS NEED TO LEARN?

When we speak of vocabulary, we are not talking only about individual words. Vocabulary includes much more—combinations of words like phrasal verbs (*stop by, stand up*), compound and hyphenated words (*breakfast, go-between*), phrases (*red-hot coals, ball of wax*), idioms (*beyond the pale; eat your heart out*), and collocations. Collocations are the company words keep—the ways that words are used in certain order, with certain other words. For example, we say *strong coffee,* not *powerful coffee,* but *powerful engine,* not *strong engine.* We include not only the thousands of words we use in everyday interpersonal conversation, but also the tens of thousands more that are used for academic learning. In many ways, these sets of words overlap: The most common 2000 words make up about 80 percent of general academic texts (Nation & Waring, 1997). In other ways, they do not overlap—many academic words are used only in their specialized contexts, and the academic meanings of terms like *angle, function, table, cycle,* or *stock* can differ greatly depending on the context and discipline in which they are used. Words are also challenging because they have multiple meanings and uses. A simple word like *run* can be used in so many forms and in so many ways. How many ways do you see the word *run* used in the following narrative?

I hate it when my nose *runs,* because I always *run* out of cold medicine and I have to *run* out for more. Plus I *run the risk* of catching pneumonia and I feel too *run-down* to go for my daily *run.* One time I *ran* to the pharmacy in my hybrid (you know it *runs* on both gasoline and electricity—and it really *runs* like a charm!). I also needed to *run by* the office to *run off* some copies. Anyway, it was raining so hard it was *running* off the roof so my jacket got all wet in the rain and the colors *ran.* Then I tripped on the wet sidewalk (I really think clumsiness *runs* in my family) and got a *run in my stocking* and had to change it so I was *running late* and then I discovered I'd *run low* on gas. I was so nervous I *ran* a red light and *ran right into* a Lincoln Navigator. The guy I *ran into* was that baseball player who scored a winning *home run* for the Braves last Saturday. When I told my kids, they were so impressed that I was *running around with* a celebrity—even if what I really did was *run across* – or was it *run into* him. But I do *run on...*

It might help us know how many words to teach if we had an estimate of how many words there are in the English language, but it is surprising how difficult that is to figure out. Do we count all the words there have ever been, or only words that are still in use? Do we count only root words (*station*), or every form that words can take (*stationed, stationary, stationery...*). Do we count every meaning of a word (like all those meanings of *run* above) as a word? Do we count word families (a base word plus the words derived from that word, for example, *excite, excitement, excited, excites, exciting*). The *Oxford English Dictionary* lists about one quarter million words— English has more words than any other language because when English speakers come across a word in another language that they find useful or interesting, they just adopt it. English has three times as many words as German and six times the number of words as French (Bromley, 2007). But not even a native speaker can know them all. And what does *know* mean? Does it mean *recognizes* or *actively uses*? Depending upon the parameters used, the estimates of how many words an educated person knows vary widely (Nagy & Anderson, 1984; Pinker, 2002). When children enter school, the number of words they know varies greatly depending upon the language environment of their early years (Hart & Risley, 2003). The average native-speaking two-year-old knows about 300 words. The average native-speaking five-year-old knows about 4000–5000 words at the start of school but there is a wide range, related strongly to parent educational achievement. Native speakers acquire about 1200 word families a year throughout school (Anglin, 1993), leading to about 11,000 word families at the end of high school and about 20,000 at the end of college (Biemiller, 2001; Goulden, Nation, & Read, 1990).

How can humans learn so many words at school? And how on earth can new learners of English learn them all? English learners have a great challenge to learn enough words to be able to understand their grade-level content textbooks! Although we cannot directly teach all of the words our learners need to know, we can make a significant difference by directly teaching as many important words as we can and by helping learners develop tools to keep acquiring vocabulary throughout their lives. We must develop a multifaceted approach for vocabulary development that includes: (1) motivating learners to want to learn words, (2) selecting highly useful and important words for direct teaching and thorough practice, (3) making them highly aware of words they encounter and how words function and are constructed, (4) developing the skills of learners to use tools and strategies to learn and use new words on their own, and (5) ensuring that learners have opportunities to increase the breadth and depth of their vocabulary knowledge through listening, speaking, writing, and extensive choice reading.

WHAT WORDS SHOULD WE TEACH?

What are the important words we should teach? We recommend considering three important criteria: (1) words that are used and encountered frequently in school, (2) words that are used in academic texts across different content areas, and (3) words that help students become effective learners in the classroom.

The availability of large databases of words, along with tools to analyze them, has helped us to locate important words to teach. Words in the first 2000 word families make up about 85 percent of the words we speak and 80 percent of the words in the texts students will read in school (Nation & Waring, 1997). We should help beginners acquire these most frequently used words quickly. The General Service List (West, 1953, updated by Bauman & Culligan, 1995, http:// jbauman.com/gsl.html) compiles these 2000 frequently used words in English. This list includes all kinds of words, but the easiest to teach are picturable words like *family, money, book,* or *eye.* But note that many of the highest frequency words are function words that can't be easily learned except through exposure and use with other words in a meaningful context. (For example, the first 10 words are *the, be, of, and, a, to, in, he, have,* and *it*). Another source of word frequencies for American English is Davies & Gardner's *A Frequency Dictionary of Contemporary American English* (2010). The authors used an enormous corpus of words from television, documents, and other sources to compile their frequency list, a version of which is posted at www .wordfrequency.info/free.asp.

Academic words are used frequently in academic texts across the disciplines. Several researchers and practitioners have developed lists of key academic words. Marzano and Pickering (2005) have listed key words by subject area. Jim Burke (2012) has assembled a cross-subject area list for secondary learners that is available at www.englishcompanion.com/ pdfDocs/academicvocab.pdf. Beck, McKeown, and Kucan (2002) have organized vocabulary a bit differently, dividing words into three tiers. Tier 1 words are the basic words that are reasonably easy to teach, usually because there is some kind of physical referent (*clock, baby, happy,* and *walk*). These words need to be taught to young learners/beginners because they are high-frequency words that they will see many times. But because they are easier to teach, and because they are encountered frequently, less time needs to be spent on these words than on those in the other two tiers. Tier 2 words are the important words. These high-frequency words are found and used across many content areas. Teaching these words deeply requires time and effort but will have a lasting impact on students' learning and communication. Examples of Tier 2 words include *parallel, scale, plateau, range,* and *relief.* The words may have particular meanings in certain content areas (these examples have specific meanings in geography), but are used in a variety of ways by proficient language users. Tier 3 words are lower-frequency words that are specific to one content area. For example, the geographical terms *archipelago, azimuth, estuary, tundra,* and *sinusoidal projection* are Tier 3 words. These are important words to be taught within the context and content in which they are used. The researchers suggest that teachers should consider these criteria when choosing words to teach: (1) How important and useful is the word? (2) What is the instructional potential of the word? and (3) What role does the word play in communicating the meaning of the context in which it is used, and in access to learning in school?

Averil Coxhead (2000) analyzed a large corpus (an online collection) of millions of words to determine which words were commonly used across academic areas. She created the Academic Word List (AWL), a set of 570 word families that are used frequently across a broad range of academic texts. The list can be found at simple.wiktionary.org/wiki/AWL. Coxhead excludes from the AWL the 2000 most frequently used words from the General Service List because they are usually learned early from the many times they are used and encountered. She divides the AWL into 10 sublists, ordered from most frequently used to least frequently used. Although they are found frequently in academic texts, these words are used infrequently in informal conversations, and rarely in the homes of ELLs. This makes the AWL words highly valuable words to be taught. The order of frequency of the sublists also suggests an order in which the words might be taught, so that the most useful words will be available to learners first. Note that as we said above, the first 2000 words provide 80–85 percent of the words encountered in academic texts. But learners need to know 95 percent of the words for comfortable independent reading with comprehension, and need to be able to use contextual clues to determine the meaning of new word families (Biemiller, 2001). Academic words make up the 10 percent difference that makes the text comprehensible. If they are frequently used and highly useful, and 570 is not an unteachable number of words, then it makes great sense to focus intensive instruction on these academic words.

Kinsella (2005) discusses another category of words—she uses the term *portable words* to describe words and phrases that are highly useful in academic discourse in a variety of disciplines. These include words in the AWL such as *symptom* or *prevalence,* but also words, phrases, and sentence frames that give learners ways to participate in oral and written discourse. Portable words also include ways to state a point of view such as *In my opinion..., I agree..., According to....* as well as the language ELLs need to be successful in the classroom—for example, language to ask for clarification or assistance from a teacher or a peer, such as, *Could you please say that again?* or *I still have a question about...* or language for holding the floor in a discussion, such as *As I was saying ... Please let me finish ...* (cited in Walter, 2004, p. 96).

Thomas Cobb (2012) has assembled a remarkable set of tools for learning about words and their use on his website, The Compleat Lexical Tutor www.lextutor.ca. One of the tools, the Vocabulary Profile (VP) (www.lextutor.ca/vp/), provides a color-coded profile of a text that shows which words are in the first 1000 frequency group, which are in the second 1000 frequency group, which are words on the AWL, and which are off-list words (these would include names, places, rarely used words, and technical terms for a content area). The output provides a rich, color-coded array of information about the selected text that, once a teacher knows the age and language levels of learners, can be useful in selecting texts that might be appropriate for learners to read as well as important words from the texts for direct teaching. Table 7.1 provides an example of text analysis by the VP, with only part of the actual data that was produced.

TABLE 7.1 Example of Text Analysis Using the Vocabulary Profile

Beavers		Word Families	Total Words	Percent
Beavers are very busy animals who work as engineers to change the environment. They work primarily at night to build dams, canals and their home structures, called lodges. They work in groups called colonies to create one or more dams that provide deep, quiet water. These ponds protect them against predators and help them float food and building materials. The beaver population was once very large but has declined due to factors such as extensive hunting for fur and the killing of beavers because beavers harvest trees and cause flooding that interferes with human land and water uses.	K1 Words (1-1000):	49	74	75.51%
	K2 Words (1001-2000):	10	10	10.20%
	1k+2k	50	84	(85.71%)
	AWL Words (academic):	6	6	6.12%
	1K + 2k + AWL	56	90	(91.83%)
	Off-List Words:	8	8	8.16%
	Total Words:	72	98	100%

FREQUENCY:

- First 500 function (39): and and and and and and and are as as as at because but for for for has in of or that the the the the their their them they they they to to to to to was who with

- First 500 content (23): build building called called change food groups home large more night once one provide such used uses very very water work work work

- Second 500 content (13): against animals caused colonies deep due extensive human land materials population protect trees

- 1001-2000 (11) busy canals engineers floating flooding fur harvesting hunting interfered medicine quiet

ACADEMIC WORD LIST (6): create declined environment factors primarily structures

- Sublist 1 (4): create environment factors structures

- Sublist 2: primarily

- Sublist 5: declined

OFF LIST WORDS (8) beaver beavers dams dams glands lodges perfume predators (Cobb, 2012; Heatley & Nation, 1994)

WordSift (Hakuta & Weintjes, 2012, www.wordsift.com) provides a visual way to analyze texts in a number of ways. It illustrates word frequency by creating a *word cloud,* in which the size of words indicates their frequency in the text. The tool also links to selected words in the online Visual Thesaurus, an excellent source of related words. In addition, WordSift provides links to an array of images from which teachers may choose to enhance learners' understanding of the word. A sample text analysis is included in Figure 7.2.

Teachers need to make sure that ELLs learn: (1) the words that are most frequent in English, (2) the words that are most frequently used in academic language, (3) the words that are important for the academic content they are studying, and (4) the words and phrases that provide access to the academic discourse in the classroom. Many researchers, educators, and textbooks have provided us assistance in determining what words these are, but in the end, it is the teacher who must know his or her learners and determine what vocabulary they need most.

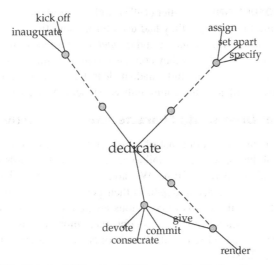

FIGURE 7.2 Sample displays from WordSift (Hakuta & Wientjes, 2012), using the Mother Goose rhyme "As I was Going to St. Ives" and "The Gettysburg Address," by Abraham Lincoln

WHAT ARE THE CHARACTERISTICS OF EFFECTIVE VOCABULARY INSTRUCTION?

What Doesn't Work?

Keith Folse (2004) has explored myths regarding teaching vocabulary to ELLs. Four interesting myths apply to what *doesn't* work:

GUESSING WORDS FROM CONTEXT Many teachers believe that guessing and learning new words from the context of the reading is an excellent strategy for learning second language vocabulary. This strategy is frequently used by native speakers, but research has shown that ELLs can fail to comprehend passages, infer incorrect meanings, and forget meanings quickly. They also may not know enough words in a passage to be able to infer meanings of new ones (Nation & Waring, 2004). Teachers should be certain that learners have a vocabulary level sufficient to make a text manageable before expecting them to independently infer words from context. They should directly teach vocabulary to prepare learners for challenging texts, while continuing to develop learners' skills in using context to infer meaning.

TEACHING VOCABULARY IN SEMANTIC SETS Teachers often find it convenient and intuitive to teach vocabulary in semantic sets. (By semantic sets, we mean organizing words around a simple vocabulary topic—for beginners, those might be colors, family members, days of the week, etc.) But research evidence suggests that it is just the opposite—semantic sets may actually confuse learners and hinder learning (Tinkhan, 1993, 1997; Waring, 1997). A better way to organize vocabulary is to organize words around themes. For example, rather than teaching beginners the words for numbers and foods and days of the week as sets to be memorized, we might teach a unit around Eric Carle's (1986) story of *The Very Hungry Caterpillar,* in which the new words are used in a story context: "On Monday, he ate through one apple." The rhythm and repetition of the story, along with the spectacular illustrations make all the words come alive—and the children learn the science of the life cycle of butterflies to boot! With older learners, we still must think of connecting words under a superordinate theme—we teach words in our weather unit through the story of the water cycle, which we relate to experiences of farming, storms, floods, and droughts that learners might have experienced or may recall.

TOO MUCH INFORMATION TOO SOON Many, many words in English have multiple meanings and uses. Learners (and teachers) can only deal with a limited amount of information about a word at a time. So, teachers should expect limited learning from a single meeting, and expect to return to words both to build deeper meaning and to provide practice in recalling and using the words that have been taught.

EXPOSURE ONLY Miller (1993) studied eighth graders in Australia to learn how well they had acquired math terms they had used throughout the year. Out of twenty key terms (such as *sum, digit, quotient, remainder,* and *diameter*), learners were only able to define four correctly at the end of the year. When they could use symbols, diagrams, or examples, they averaged eleven correct definitions. The study made it clear that vocabulary, even terms that are essential in a content course, is difficult to acquire unless teachers place strong emphasis on vocabulary instruction.

What Does Work: Characteristics of Effective Vocabulary Instruction

Often students learn a list of words and score well on a multiple-choice vocabulary test at the end of the week, but they fail to be able to use the words in speaking or writing, or even to recall them after a period of time. We have discovered from the psychology of memory that in order to acquire vocabulary in depth, in their permanent memory: (1) learners must notice words—they must bring the words to conscious awareness, (2) they must process words deeply—encoding the information in a variety of contexts in more and more elaborate ways, and (3) they must have repeated, spaced retrieval of the words—encountering them many times at different intervals (Folse, 2004).

Beck, McKeown, and Kucan (2002) describe three characteristics of what they call "robust vocabulary instruction." In the instruction these authors describe, teachers create an environment in which words are valued and celebrated. Teachers choose important words to introduce, contextualizing the target words in ways that make sense to the learners, providing student-friendly explanations, giving many examples, and asking learners to give examples as well. Then teachers post the target words, use them often, and encourage learners to find appropriate uses for them in the classroom as well. After introducing a term, teachers might ask questions like these to develop depth and nuance of meaning:

What day was *previous* to today?

What word is *previous* in alphabetical order, *bear* or *badger*?

Why might an historian want to know about *previous* events?

What word is the opposite of *after*?

Would you prefer to hire a plumber with *previous* experience?

Would you trade for a player who scored 20 goals the *previous* year?

Does *previous* mean *prior* or *before?*

Does *previous* mean *small?*

We believe that high-quality, permanent, in-depth vocabulary learning will happen with daily, frequent, brief, and active interactions with new vocabulary. In these interactions, teachers should work to:

1. ***Develop word awareness.***   Develop learner awareness, curiosity, and enthusiasm about words by creating a rich classroom environment, making learning active and interactive, and incorporating many games and opportunities to collaborate.

2. ***Teach important words directly.***   Choose important words—both general words and key words across academic subjects—to teach directly and systematically, providing descriptions more than definitions and using both linguistic and nonlinguistic representation, and varying instruction for the type of words. Realize that word meanings will be shaped gradually and cumulatively.

3. ***Analyze and explore words.***   Provide many experiences analyzing words—teaching about word parts, uses, and relationships, and taking advantage of cognates in learners' languages.

4. ***Build learner control.***   Help learners develop strategies for solving and learning new words independently to take control of their own vocabulary learning.

5. ***Expand exposure.***   Promote extensive opportunities to use words in active, interactive ways and to expand exposure through listening, writing, speaking, and choice reading. Reading aloud to learners and providing them with extensive reading have been shown to make a particularly important contribution to learners' vocabulary development (Krashen, 2004; Trelease, 2006).

We devote the rest of the chapter to strategies and tools for implementing a vocabulary program with these characteristics in mind.

HOW SHOULD WE PROVIDE DIRECT VOCABULARY INSTRUCTION?

English learners have a special need for direct vocabulary instruction, because they have not had the opportunities proficient speakers have to encounter the words throughout their lives and through extensive reading in English. Several authors have proposed steps for the direct teaching of vocabulary in school (for example, Beck, McKeown, & Kucan, 2002; Marzano & Pickering, 2005).

We recommend the following six steps for direct vocabulary instruction for English learners.

Steps for Direct Vocabulary Instruction

1. ***Present, pronounce, and define the word.***   If it is appropriate, display and point to a picture that shows the meaning of the word. Write the word on the board. Pronounce the word and provide a brief definition or explanation of its meaning. "Our new word is *site*. A site is a place, like a space of ground where something is built. It can also be a place where an event is held. Our school was built on this site 23 years ago. The site of our performance yesterday was the auditorium. Plymouth Rock was the site where the pilgrims landed in 1620." It is not always necessary to present a new word entirely in English. Sometimes it is more efficient to help the learner grasp the meaning quickly by using his or her L1. If the word has a cognate in a language known by English learners, make the connection. When appropriate, provide a translation that can serve as a quick bridge from L1 to L2. "*Site* is *sitio* in Spanish." Whenever possible, present the word in a context that is meaningful and known to the learner.

2. *Help the learners read and pronounce the word a number of times.*   Have learners count the syllables in the word and tap out the syllables on their desks. Include action games, call and response, and other techniques to make this activity lively and motivating.

> *Ok, everyone, let's read this word:* **site**.
> *Say it soft:* **site**
> *Say it loud:* **site**
> *Say it slow: s-i-t-e*
> *Left side of the room:* **site**
> *Right side of the room:* **site**
> *Whisper* **site** *to the person next to you:* **site**.

3. *Provide examples of the word used in several different contexts—beginning with contexts familiar to learners, and adding newer and more sophisticated contexts as their knowledge of the word develops.*

> What do you think? Does this look like a good *site* for a picnic?
> The beavers found the right *site* on the creek to build a new dam.
> Sharon Creech has a really cool *website*.
> Gettysburg is the *site* of an important battle in the Civil War.

4. *Carry out many activities that help learners engage with the word.*   The activities should progress from less demanding responses (such as signal responses) to more active participation with oral and written responses. They should provide a variety of encounters with the word that lead to rich, deep understanding. The games and activities discussed below offer many examples. Help learners find ways to use the word appropriately in the classroom context, and celebrate when they do so.

5. *Have learners create their own visual representations of the target word.*   They may choose to use Pictures, Word Squares, Word Circles, a Semantic Map, or other graphic organizers. Have them keep their notes on important words in their personal dictionaries or on their personal word walls (see below).

6. **Discuss alternate forms of the word,** for example, for the word *hope*:

noun	hope, hopes
verb	hope, hopes, hoping
adjective	hopeful
adverb	hopefully

Alternate parts of the word, for example for the word *contradiction*:
contra (against) dict (speak) tion (noun ending)
How the word is and is not used, for example, we say: *make a mess, not do a mess.*
Other interesting features of the word, for example, that it has a homophone:

> *Site* is pronounced just like *sight*. Isn't that interesting? How are the meanings different? Can you think of a sentence that uses both words correctly? What is special about a *website*? How is it like the *site* of a building or a convention or the *site* of a party?

HOW CAN WE HELP LEARNERS DEVELOP THEIR OWN TOOLS TO DEAL WITH UNKNOWN WORDS INDEPENDENTLY?

Your students will become more independent and effective learners if they can develop strategies for dealing with new words they meet. Good learners don't employ just one strategy—they have a repertoire of many strategies and are able to make good decisions about the right one to use for the current text. The flow chart in Figure 7.3 provides a series of questions and steps that you can teach learners to use independently when they find words they don't know. Take time to teach and have learners practice each strategy with your help. Make sure learners know that they can use the strategies in different order, depending on the text and the situation. Help them develop their skills in knowing what strategy is best to use when.

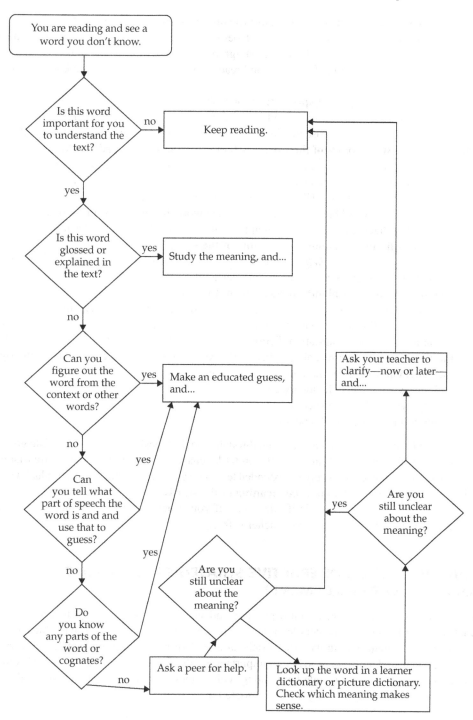

FIGURE 7.3 New Word Decision-Making Flow Chart

Following are suggestions for teaching the flow chart questions and strategies:

1. **Do you need to know this word? Can you understand the meaning without knowing it?**

   If the word is in bold or italics, it might be a key word for the text you are reading. If it is capitalized, it might be an unfamiliar name. If looking further for the meaning of the word doesn't seem important to your reading of the text, don't spend a long time and slow your reading by studying the word. *Skip it and keep reading.* If the word is used many times, or you find out that you need to know what it means, come back later to find its meaning.

2. **Is the word explained in the text? Is it in the glossary?**

   If the word is explained in the text or included in the glossary, it's probably important to understanding the text. *Read the definition/explanation carefully* to make sure you understand. Then continue your reading.

3. **Can you figure out the meaning from the other words and the context?**

    Read the words around the word. Does one or more of them give a hint to the meaning of the unknown word? Read the paragraph containing the word. Make an educated guess about the meaning of the word and read on. Check it later if you think you still need to know what it is.

4. **Can you tell what part of speech the word is?**

    Look at how the word is used and decide *if it's a noun, verb, adjective, adverb, or other kind of word.* Then use that information to improve your guess about the word.

5. **Do you know any parts of the word? Is there a cognate to a word you know?**

    Look at the parts of the word. Does it have a root word or prefix or suffix that you recognize? Is it a compound word? Does it have a prefix or a suffix? (Use your prefix/suffix list [Stall & Shiel, 1999] to help.) Do you recognize the root from another word you know? Does the word have a cognate—a related word that you know in another language? (Remember that cognates are often helpful, but occasionally are "false friends.")

6. **Are you still unclear about the meaning of the word?**

    Ask your peers for help with the word. Someone may be able to offer a synonym or translation or picture that can help you understand.

7. **Are you still unclear about the meaning of the word?**

    If you can't make a reasonable guess, and you're pretty sure it's an important word, *use a learner dictionary* (one written for students learning English, with clear and simple definitions) and/or a translation dictionary (or online translation) to look up the word. If the word has multiple meanings, check the text again to make sure you choose the right meaning. Online learner dictionaries can be found at:

    http://www.learnersdictionary.com/

    http://www.ldoceonline.com

    http://nhd.heinle.com/home.aspx

    Online translations can be found through Google Translations (http://translate.google.com/), which currently translates to/from 64 languages. Although most online translations are not yet reliable, especially for extended text, they are often helpful with individual words.

8. **Are you still unclear about the meaning of the word?**

    Ask your teacher to clarify the word. If your teacher is busy, continue on with the reading and ask later when your teacher is free.

WHAT ARE ACTIVE, INTERACTIVE STRATEGIES TO SUPPORT VOCABULARY DEVELOPMENT?

In addition to direct teaching, we must provide students with many rich ways to learn and interact with words as part of content learning. There are many more strategies available (see our resources and references), but we offer a rich sample of strategies to provide engaged learners deep processing and multiple exposure to important words. Table 7.2 outlines the baker's dozen strategies we had room to include here, along with suggestions about what students and what stages of vocabulary learning they are appropriate for.

TABLE 7.2 A Baker's Dozen Tools and Strategies for Active, Interactive Vocabulary Development

A Baker's Dozen Tools and Strategies for Active, Interactive Vocabulary Development							
	For K-6 learners	For 5-12 learners	For beginners	For intermediate	For advanced	For introducing words	For extending understanding of words	For enhancing word memory
Drawing Pictures	x	x	x	x	x	x	x	x
Semantic Map	x	x	x	x	x	x	x	
Word Square	x	x	x	x	x	x	x	x
Word Sorts	x	x	x	x	x		x	x

A Baker's Dozen Tools and Strategies for Active, Interactive Vocabulary Development

	For K-6 learners	For 5-12 learners	For beginners	For intermediate	For advanced	For introducing words	For extending understanding of words	For enhancing word memory
Word Splash	x	x		x	x		x	
Word Wall	x	x	x	x	x		x	x
Semantic Feature Analysis		x		x	x	x	x	
Read, Retell, & Summarize	x	x	x	x	x	x	x	
I Have, Who Has?	x	x	x	x	x		x	x
Conga Line	x	x	x	x	x		x	x
Sentence Machine	x	x		x	x		x	x
Personal Dictionary	x	x	x	x	x	x	x	x

Drawing Pictures

One of the most effective vocabulary development techniques we have used with our students is a method that we came upon by accident. We had been asking our students to evaluate their own learning of vocabulary, a useful learning strategy. The students were asked to work with a buddy to determine how well they knew each of the new words. If they could define the word, they checked "I Know It" on the practice sheet. If they were unsure of the meaning, they checked "I Kind of Know It," and if they could not guess at all, they checked "I Don't Have a Clue." We used these self-evaluation charts to help learners focus on the words they needed to learn. After talking about the meanings and having the students share these meanings with their classmates, we asked the students to draw pictures of the words they didn't know to help them remember them for the next day. An example from one student (Table 7.3) shows the scribbled word balloon for *muttering,* the little twins for *resembles,* and the sad face for *frown.* At the end of the unit, students indicated that the self-drawn pictures helped them the most in retaining the meaning of the new vocabulary.

Teach learners to make simple drawings with stick figures, and help them resist spending a lot of time creating great works of art. The important element in all of these activities is that learners are actively participating in the experience, an important principle of learning. Active

TABLE 7.3 Leaders Can Self-Assess Learning and Draw Pictures to Learn and Remember Unknown Words

	I Know It	I Kind of Know It	I Don't Have a Clue
muttering			√
electricity	√		
frown			√

TABLE 7.3 Leaders Can Self-Assess Learning and Draw Pictures to Learn and Remember Unknown Words *(Continued)*

	I Know It	I Kind of Know It	I Don't Have a Clue
earned	√		
resemble 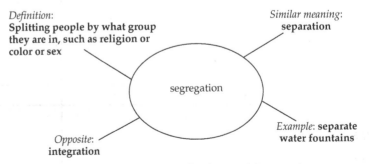			√

participation does not always mean moving around the classroom. But it doesn't mean sitting passively either. For students to learn most efficiently, we believe they must be actively engaged in the learning experience. Sometimes, this means writing, drawing, and talking about the new vocabulary, as the examples in Figure 7.5 (next page), where students were asked to create word squares with buddies. Sometimes it means drawing pictures or completing a graphic organizer with new terminology. Sometimes it means asking students to respond with Thumbs Up/Thumbs Down as we define a new word or place markers on new words on a Bingo card in response to definitions read aloud. Or it might mean placing students into small groups and assigning four new vocabulary words to the group—one per student. Students each select a word and draw a picture of the word on a sticky note. When finished, the teacher can call out the words at random and students raise their pictures as the word call gradually increases to a faster pace. Students exchange words and the teacher continues calling out. Students can stand, place the picture on their heads, or form pairs or conga lines to teach each other their words. Students exchange pictures again and the teacher moves on to call out word definitions, word opposites, or word forms. All of these are examples of active student involvement with 100 percent participation.

Semantic Mapping

Semantic Mapping is a tool for providing meaning to new vocabulary. We like to write the new word in the center of the map and ask students to answer questions like these:

- *What is another word that has a similar meaning?*
- *What is an example of this word?*
- *What is the opposite of this word?*
- *What is a definition of the new term in your own words?*

Then we draw lines to link the related terms to the word. Remember that for English learners the word may be very unfamiliar and you may need to provide related terms when they can't think of them. Figure 7.4 shows a semantic map for the word *segregation*.

Definition:
Splitting people by what group they are in, such as religion or color or sex

Similar meaning:
separation

segregation

Opposite:
integration

Example: **separate water fountains**

FIGURE 7.4 Semantic Map for the Word *Segregation*

Word Square

The **word square** graphic organizer (Figure 7.5) is a multidimensional tool for deepening understanding of new vocabulary. Students use a variety of ways to explore and remember a new

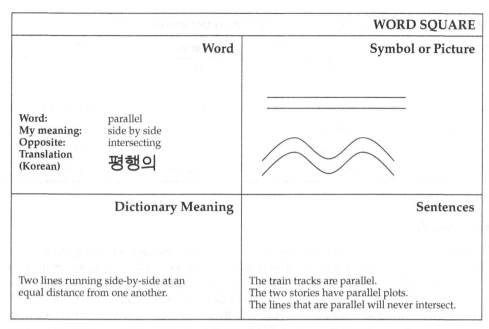

FIGURE 7.5 Word Square for *Parallel*

term. To teach the strategy, have students help you create a word square for an unfamiliar word in one of their texts. Show them how to find a translation, how to write the meaning in their own words (they may need to look up the word first), and how to think of an opposite or negative example of the word. Have students look up the word in a picture dictionary, learner dictionary, or translation dictionary (depending on their level), and ask them to come up with several sentences that illustrate the meaning of the word. Then encourage them to create a pictorial symbol for the word that will help them remember it. After learners have tried word squares with their teacher, they're ready to try with a partner or in a small group, and eventually on their own. Learners can use their word squares to teach one another new, challenging terms.

Word Sorts

Word Sorts, in which learners organize sets of words into categories, help learners to reflect on meanings of words and extend their understanding. There are two types of word sorts: in *closed sorts* the teacher supplies the categories for sorting; in *open sorts* the learners choose the categories. Use a word wall or pocket chart to introduce the concept. Choose a set of terms that you have introduced. At first, pick the category names for closed sorts—categories such as letters of the alphabet (words that start with *a*), sound/spelling patterns (*-ight* words), spelling pattern type (consonant-vowel-consonant [CVC], CVCC, VC, VCCV, etc.), formality or register of words (*Hello* is more formal than *Hey*), uses of words (for example, transition words that change direction, like *however,* or *but . . .*), number of syllables, parts of speech, etc. Have learners make suggestions as you manipulate word cards into categories. Later, provide a set of words and have learners suggest the categories. See Table 7.4 for an example of a word sort by initial sound. See Table 7.5 for an example of a word sort by parts of speech.

TABLE 7.4 Word Sort of Words with *ee* Sound by Spelling Pattern

-ee words	-ea words that say ee	-y words that say ee	-e words that say ee
tree			
bee	pea	happy	be
see	sea	baby	me
fee	flea	candy	he
feed	lead	lovely	
weed			

TABLE 7.5 Word Sort of Physical Education Terms by Parts of Speech

Nouns	Compound nouns	Verbs	Adjectives
efficiency	volleyball	jog	frequent
circuit	sportsmanship	exert	spatial
benefit	overload	stretch	intramural
awareness	overtraining	train	respiratory
reduction	overuse	coordinate	fast-twitch
health	warmup	visualize	irregular

WordSplash

WordSplash activates vocabulary learning as it introduces or summarizes a reading. Learners are challenged to discover relationships among important words in a text. The terms represent important ideas that the teacher wants learners to attend to when they read. Choose important words from a text learners will be reading, along with some words they can use in making connections between the words. On a chart, transparency, or board, "splash" key words for a text random design. Some of the terms will be familiar to the learners, but they must connect them in new ways to predict or summarize the text. In Figure 7.6, the text is *Planting the Trees of Kenya: The Story of Wangari Maathai,* by Claire A. Nivola. Before the reading, introduce several unfamiliar words using the eight steps described above. Invite learners to study the words using a glossary, dictionary, peer advice, and teacher help as needed. Preview the story using a strategy such as a "picture walk." Then challenge learners, individually, in pairs, or in small groups, to predict connections between the words by writing complete sentences that connect two or more of the words or phrases on the WordSplash. For example, learners might use the words in Figure 7.6 to write, "In Kenya, fig trees are sacred." Have learners share sentences and use the opportunity to discuss and clarify meanings and uses of the words. After they read the text, they can review their predictions to see how accurate they were. And the same WordSplash can be used as an assessment at the end of the lesson. Ask learners to write sentences that connect the words and correctly tell about the reading. You can also use a

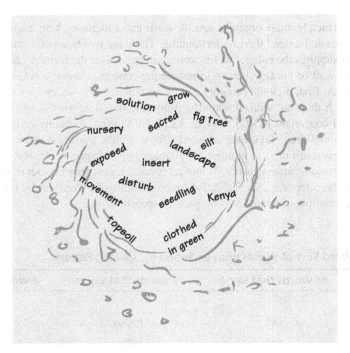

FIGURE 7.6 WordSplash for *Planting the Trees of Kenya: The Story of Wangari Maathai,* by Claire A. Nivola

WordSplash for other purposes, for example, to prepare learners to watch a film or to have a guest speaker; or to have students create a WordSplash for younger learners (Saphier & Haley, 1993).

Word Wall

An interactive **word wall** is a systematically organized collection of words displayed in large letters on a wall or other large display place in the classroom. It is a tool for use, not just for display. Words are added, removed, and rearranged frequently. The wall is discussed and referred to every day. Many teachers add a certain number of words each week, depending upon the lesson focus and student needs. Frequently, words in the chart are reorganized according to skills and concepts being developed.

For example, on the first day of school in primary grades, the word wall might include only the letters of the alphabet with students' names listed under the initial letter. Later, the wall might include words with certain vowel or consonant sounds. Teacher and students might pull words with the same endings (*make, take, bake*), or beginnings (*think, through, that*), or certain parts of speech, or words that are pronunciation challenges, or words that are Spanish cognates, or words that are useful in writing about the topic they are currently studying.

In a middle school or secondary classroom, the word wall might highlight key signal words to use for a certain type of writing. For example, if students are writing up an experiment, they may need technical words to describe how they used the scientific method as well as academic language for their descriptions. In the word wall sample in Table 7.6, a science teacher has included key words used in writing about experiments.

TABLE 7.6 Section of a Word Wall in a Science Class

Words for writing about your experiment	
Question:	Why does . . . What will happen if. . . . How . . .
Hypothesis:	If . . . then . . .
Experiment:	Equipment, procedure, variables, control, results
Results, Discussion:	Data, data table, reducing data (e.g., mean), analysis
Conclusion:	Accept, reject hypothesis, reasons

All students, but particularly English learners, will find the word wall a tremendous resource when they are writing. In addition, the teacher can save time when asked how to spell words by simply pointing to the word, or a similar word, on the wall. For example, "Do you want to spell *lake*? Look at the word *take* on the Word Wall. Look under *T* for *Take*. *Lake* ends like *take*. How would you change *take* to *lake*? Right, write *take* but start it with an *l* instead of a *t*. They are both -*ake* words."

If you do not have a permanent classroom, there are a variety of ways that you can still use word walls. You might borrow a small space in the room, or carry the wall with you. For example you can bring words on cards in a pocket chart, you can put words on sticky notes and have students place them on the wall. You can also have learners create their own portable word walls to keep in their notebooks—a new page for each unit of study. Learners divide a page into a 3 x 4 grid with 12 boxes, one box for each two letters of the alphabet (and one for WXYZ). As new words are introduced, learners write them on their word walls, with definitions and other cues to help them remember.

Semantic Feature Analysis

With **semantic feature analysis**, learners use a grid to explore relationships between terms and concepts. Make a list of related terms down the vertical axis of the grid. Make a list of features or characteristics across the horizontal axis of the grid. Then, have learners make a check (√) in the box when the terms/concepts have that characteristic. Table 7.7 is an example of a semantic feature analysis in which learners in a math class explore the properties of whole numbers. In the process of completing the analysis, they strengthen their understanding of key terms such as *multiple, prime,* and *square.*

TABLE 7.7 Semantic Feature Analysis for Properties of Whole Numbers

Number	Features/properties	Multiple of 2	Multiple of 3	Multiple of 4	Multiple of 5	Prime	Square
	Semantic Feature Analysis Topic: Properties of Whole Numbers						
1						✓	
2		✓				✓	
3			✓			✓	
4		✓		✓			✓
5					✓	✓	
6		✓	✓				
7						✓	
8		✓		✓			
9			✓				✓
10		✓			✓		
11						✓	
12		✓	✓	✓			
13						✓	
14		✓					
15			✓		✓		
16		✓		✓			✓
17						✓	
18		✓	✓				
19						✓	
20		✓		✓	✓		

Read, Retell, Summarize

The **Read, Retell, and Summarize** strategy is a way for learners to practice using new vocabulary as they apply their comprehension of text and process what they have read (Duff & Maley, 2007).

PREPARE FOR THE ACTIVITY   Choose a passage for learners to study. Select a set of terms from the passage that are key to its meaning.

THE ACTIVITY   Read the passage aloud to the students. Dictate the key words and have the learners make a list. Discuss meanings as needed. Have learners read the passage. If they have a copy of the text they can write on, they can highlight or underline the key words. Then, working with partners, learners retell the reading, using only the list of words as a reference. Walk around to listen to the retellings and make notes of words that you should further clarify.

I have, who has?

"I have, who has?" is an active way to practice vocabulary and content concepts. Learners match descriptions/definitions and terms (or questions and answers) in a fast-paced, cooperative oral activity.

PREPARE THE CARDS   Choose a set of terms and definitions on a theme or topic. After teaching students the new terms, prepare a set of *I have, who has?* cards. (See Table 7.8 for an example.) Start by writing the topic at the top of the first card, for example, *Smoking,* and the word *START*. On the bottom of that card, write *Who has?* and the description of one of the chosen terms. On the top of the second card, write *I have* and the term. On the bottom of the second card, write *Who has?* and the description for the next term. The third card has *I have* and the term described on the second card at the top, and *Who has?* and the description of a new term at the bottom. Continue with this pattern to make as many cards as you like. On the last card, write the term at the top and *Last Card* at the bottom. (Alternately, you can create a card that links the last card to the first and have the activity cycle.) Make enough cards so that each student in the group or class has a card. Some students may have two, as all the cards must be included in the activity.

PLAY THE GAME   Pass out all the cards, making sure that each student has at least one. Give the learners time to discuss terms and look them up in class notes or in a dictionary. Then the student with the *START* card reads, *Who has* and his/her description. The student who has the word that was just described on his/her card answers: *I have,* and reads the term. Then the second student says *Who has* and reads the description on his/her card. Continue play until all cards have been matched. Then have learners trade cards and play the game again. After some practice, you might time how long it takes to complete the series; the goal is to be able to do it faster and faster.

TABLE 7.8 I Have/Who Has? Cards on Tobacco Use

I Have/Who Has? Cards on Tobacco Use

USING TOBACCO Start Who has *a poison found only in tobacco leaves*?	I have *nicotine.* Who has *what you have developed when you need to smoke more and more for an effect*?	I have *tolerance to nicotine.* Who has *physical and psychological discomfort when people try to give up smoking*?
I have *withdrawal symptoms.* Who has *a gas that replaces oxygen in your blood when you smoke*?	I have *carbon monoxide.* Who has a degenerative (keeps getting worse) lung disease caused by smoking that destroys your ability to breathe?	I have *emphysema* Who has *unborn child that may be harmed by smoking*?
I have *fetus.* Who has *a habit that can lead to cancer of the mouth and addiction to tobacco*?	I have *chewing tobacco.* Who has *constricts blood vessels, cutting down flow of blood and oxygen through your body*?	I have *effects of nicotine.* Who has *dangerous exposure to cigarette smoke of other person that may increase the risk to several diseases caused by active smoking*?
I have *second-hand smoking.* Who has *a reason that many young people between the ages of 10 and 18 begin experimenting with smoking*?	I have *peer pressure.* Who has *when you do this, the body begins to repair some of the damage caused by cigarette smoking*?	I have *quit smoking.* LAST CARD

(This sample has 12 cards — follow the pattern to create any number of cards on any topic.)

Conga Line

Conga Line is a vocabulary game named after a popular Cuban line dance. The game provides a highly interactive way to study and review important terms.

PREPARE THE GAME   Choose recently taught or review words for study. A day ahead, each student prepares one card with a term on the front and the definition, description, and example on the back. Teachers should collect and check the cards, and then edit or ask for revisions to make sure that the information on each term is accurate. Then the teacher returns the cards to learners, who carefully study their cards so they are prepared to teach their terms to someone else.

PLAY THE GAME   Learners stand with partners in two parallel lines. At a signal, learners turn to the partner opposite them in the other line and take turns teaching one another the word they have on the card. At the next signal, the two partners exchange cards. Then the last student in one line goes to the front of that line and everyone in that line moves back one. At the next signal, the new partners teach one another their new terms. This pattern continues until everyone has partnered with everyone else.

Sentence Machine

In **Sentence Machine**, learners cooperate to form sentences using key content vocabulary in response to questions created by the class. This activity can be used to review and "cement" concepts and language being developed in their studies (McCloskey & Stack, 2011).

PREPARE FOR THE ACTIVITY   Display a list of key terms related to the concepts/topic being studied. Have learners work in groups of about four. Assign terms to each group and ask them to construct questions, each including one of the terms assigned to their group.

THE ACTIVITY   Each group sends one person to the front of the class. They stand in a line facing the class. Introduce the process by having the front group practice the process of answering questions with sentences, with each person speaking one word at a time in order. When an unfinished sentence gets to the end of a line, it "wraps" around back to the first person. Use general questions to help students get started. For example, ask, "What is your name?" Students answer the question in a complete sentence, one word at a time, e.g., student #1 says "My," student #2 says "name," student #3 says "is," student #4 says "(her first name)," student #5 says "(his last name)." (Now everybody laughs.) Class members then take turns asking their group's questions, one at a time. Learners are to answer questions, using the key terms correctly, in the same way— each learner speaks only one word of the answer at a time. As a result, learners have to think "on their feet" not only about the terms and the correct answers, but also about many aspects of language, including grammar (what form of words to use and in what order), collocation (what words "go together"), and word choice. The teacher is available to prompt or suggest the correct form when a student gets stuck. You will also find that students in the line and the class will all be processing the sentences themselves as they are being constructed, and will be eager to make suggestions. Continue as time allows or until all the questions are answered.

Personal Dictionary   Encourage learners to be word collectors—finding useful and important words and putting them into their own dictionaries. They can use a loose-leaf notebook and organize words alphabetically, or prepare a spiral notebook by writing the letters of the alphabet on the top of pages (several pages for each letter). When learners (or you) find words they want to be sure to remember, they can create an entry for their personal dictionaries. For simple words, they might write a synonym, translation, or draw a little picture. For more complex concept words, they might create a word square or word wheel that shows more of the complex meaning of the word. Encourage students to use these words in word games and activities and in their writing. They can use a number of the vocabulary strategies in this chapter for their entries, e.g., pictures, word squares, word circles. See the personal dictionary example in Figure 1.2.

HOW CAN WE ASSESS VOCABULARY DEVELOPMENT OF ENGLISH LEARNERS?

Vocabulary has traditionally been assessed using multiple-choice questions. These are limiting for a variety of reasons: They often don't show the learners' depth of vocabulary knowledge because they focus on a specific meaning in one context; they show only learners' recognition of words, not their use; and the definitions are limited by the quality of the distracters (wrong answers), which may be very different or very similar to the word. We would like to take a different tack in looking at assessment of vocabulary. Our goal in this section is not to offer summative tools like those on formal and standardized assessments. These are available—because there is no language without vocabulary, vocabulary is actually part of every assessment in every subject area—but learners can't understand the questions or give answers to show what they know unless they know what the words mean. Vocabulary assessment is imbedded in English Language assessments like Access (WIDA, 2012), in specialized instruments like the Peabody Picture Vocabulary Test (Dunn & Dunn, 1997), and in the standardized instruments used nationally and by and for states and consortiums of states. Rather, we offer an array of formative assessment tools that are an integral part of instruction—tools that teach as they assess. We also offer tools that learners can use to assess their own vocabulary growth.

Curtis (1992) found that the depth of understanding of words, not just recognition of words, differentiated high- from low-performing college students. Since our goal is depth of understanding and actual use of the words our students learn, we want to suggest a range of assessment tools that show understanding of nuances of meaning and multiple meanings and uses of words. With the additional goal of learner autonomy in mind, we also want to share some ways that learners can take responsibility for assessing their own learning. Since our goal is active engagement, we offer assessment tools for the classroom that are fun and interesting, and that help students learn while teachers find out what they know.

Note that many of the activities we have described above are effective for assessment as well as for introducing, expanding, and using words. For example, when the class plays *I have/Who has?* it is clear which students know the terms and descriptions, and when the activity is repeated several times, which students have learned to recognize them. It is also clear if there are certain terms or concepts that are giving many learners trouble, and these can be retaught directly. When the class plays *Sentence Machine,* you have a great opportunity to observe inevitable errors learners make in finding and choosing words as well as in determining what forms of the words to use in the particular sentence. These can point toward concepts that need more attention with the full class, or with certain individuals or small groups. When learners do *Word Sorts,* keep examples of learners' work over time to see how their understanding of words grows, and the kinds of classifications they are capable of changes. Following are formative assessment/ teaching activities focused on vocabulary.

GIVE SIGNALS FOR VOCABULARY ASSESSMENT   We have mentioned the value of signals before for keeping everyone in the class engaged and participating. Learners can use signals to indicate what they know about words. For example, you can ask students if they know a word and have them reply with thumbs up (I know it), thumbs sideways (I sort of know it), or thumbs down (I don't have a clue). Or you can ask specific questions to which learners reply with the signals: *Would you like to pet a **savage** dog? Do you need dark glasses when the sun is **brilliant**?*

USE PICTURES FOR ASSESSMENT   Learners can select pictures to show their understanding of vocabulary. They can also draw pictures on paper or white board slates to show that they understand words. This is an excellent strategy for beginners using easily picturable words and Total Physical Response (TPR): *Draw a picture of a **house**. Draw a **flower** growing in front of the house. Draw the **family** that lives in the house. Show that it is **raining** at the house.* More advanced learners can also draw pictures that show what more abstract words mean. In response to *Draw a picture that shows what **encounter** means,* a learner might draw two stick people meeting one another, or a knight confronted by a dragon.

DEMONSTRATE MEANINGS   Ask learners to devise a short skit that illustrates the meaning of a word. For example, to answer the question *How would you act if you were **irresponsible**?* small groups might perform little plays. One group might show someone littering; one group might show someone forgetting her homework; another might show someone leaving a mess in the kitchen.

DISTINGUISH BETWEEN EXAMPLES AND NONEXAMPLES   Offer learners examples and non-examples of words and ask them to choose the positive example. *Our team won the game this week. Our team lost the game last week. Which time did we **prevail**?* Be sure to discuss the reasons why learner answers are right or wrong.

SHOW OR TELL HOW WORDS ARE ALIKE OR DIFFERENT   Ask learners to tell how two words are alike or different. *How is it different to say that someone is **beautiful** rather than **gorgeous**?*

PLACE WORDS ON A CONTINUUM   Ask students to place word phrases on a scale. How would you line these words up, from *most* or *strongest* to *least* or *weakest*? *assault, pick on, attack, bully, conflict with, fight.* There may not be an absolute right order, but there will be rich opportunity to observe learners' levels of understanding of the words.

INTERPRET WORDS USED IN CONTEXT   Ask learners to interpret a word used in a context. *If you were lost in a **desolate** place, what might you see?*

ANALYZE LEARNER WRITING USING THE VOCABULARY PROFILER (VP) HTTP://WWW.LEXTUTOR .CA/VP/ Enter short pieces of learners' academic writing into the Vocabulary Profiler. (You can have older learners do the entry themselves.) What do you learn about the kinds and levels of words that students use? Do they use any words from the Academic Word List? What percentages of the words they use are at the 1-1000 word level, the 1001-2000 level, or beyond those levels? *Note:* With younger learners, try using the VP-Kids http://www.lextutor.ca/vp/kids/, which evaluates children's texts against ten 150-word lists generalized from children's oral language.

CLOZE PROCEDURE Create a cloze passage by choosing a passage learners have been studying and making a copy with certain terms left out. Classic cloze leaves out every *n*th word, but you may choose to leave out key terms for the subject or topic. You may choose to give supports such as providing a list of words for filling in the blanks, or including the first letter of the words in the blanks. Table 7.9 shows a challenging example from mathematics about the Pythagorean Theorem.

SELF-RATING SCALE Have learners rate how well they know words on a matrix, choosing one of these answers for each word: I know the word very well, I kind of know the word, I know the word a little, I don't know anything about the word. They can use a grid like the one in Table 7.3 above, or they can write their ratings on a white board slate and hold it up for you to see. Or they can have cards with ratings of 1, 2, 3, and 4 that show their level of understanding, and they can hold one up when you say the word.

SELF-ASSESS WHILE READING Ask learners to read with a sticky note on which they write unknown words they encounter. After reading, they can compare with a partner to see if others can explain the words they jotted down. If some words that seem important are still unclear, they can then check them in a learner dictionary and/or translation dictionary, as well as their teacher. This activity serves the added purpose of informing the teacher about which words are important to teach.

ASSESS VOCABULARY IN FREQUENCY SETS An interesting set of online tools for self-assessment and for self-study for upper elementary through high school learners can be found through Tom Cobb's (2011) Compleat Lexical Tutor Website http://www.lextutor.ca/tests/. For example, there are online multiple-choice tests that assess knowledge of vocabulary at different frequency levels—the first 1000 words, the second 1000 words, up to the 14,000 word level. (Try that one yourself—it's quite challenging!) Because all learners tend to learn words in about the same order—most frequent words first, these tests help learners find the words that are important for them and at the right level for them to study. The lists of words at each level are also available through the site as a resource for learners and teachers.

CONCLUSION

In this chapter, we have discussed the prime importance of vocabulary for English learners. We have defined vocabulary in a broad sense, including words, forms of words, idioms, collocations, and uses of words. We discussed which of the hundreds of thousands of words in the English language are most important to teach and learn. We determined that effective vocabulary instruction should have five components. Teachers should: (1) develop word awareness, (2) teach important words richly and directly, (3) help learners to analyze and explore words, (4) build learner control and responsibility for their own vocabulary development, and (5) expand learners' exposure to words. We have provided a wide range of activities and strategies for introducing vocabulary and

TABLE 7.9 Cloze Passage on the Pythagorean Theorem

Directions: **Complete the passage below, filling in the blanks with the correct word from the word menu at the bottom**

In any right _____, the area of the _____ whose side is the _____ (the side _____ the right angle) is equal to the _____ of the areas of the squares whose sides are the two _____ (the two sides that meet at a right angle).

Word Menu: *hypotenuse legs opposite sum*   *square triangle*

supporting vocabulary development, with some directed by the teacher, some supported by the teacher, and some for learners to use independently after instruction. We have also offered a set of formative strategies for teachers and learners to use to assess vocabulary growth and development.

Table 7.10 offers ways to apply the concepts in this chapter with Tier 1 and Tier 2 RTI.

TABLE 7.10 Teaching Vocabulary to English Learners — RTI Samplers

RTI Tier 1 Sampler:

- Make a list of cognates and borrowed words that come from the countries of learners in your classes on your WordWall. Encourage ELLs to be aware of ways that the language they know can help them learn English.

- Ask the English learners to tell you about situations where they really needed a word but did not know it.

- Make sure that your ELLs have access to both a learner dictionary and to translation dictionaries for the languages they speak.

- Teach a lesson about phrasal verbs, which English learners find so difficult. How can they learn the differences in meaning of *look up, look over, look down on, look forward to, look back on, look out,* and *look up to?*

- Help learners set up their personal dictionaries. Remind them to make entries for important words you cover in class. Have them choose words in their notebooks to study with partners for a week. Partners give one another a quiz at the end of the week.

- Develop a classroom library, or section of the school library, where ELLs can find materials suited to their age, interests, cultural backgrounds, and reading proficiency. Promote the use of this library with classroom tasks, such as choosing a book, reading from it with a partner.

- Read aloud to your students daily, and take time to teach three or four important words from the selection.

- Make learners aware of *academic words*—words that they don't often use in ordinary conversation but that are important for learning in school.

- Play with words every day—study root words, prefixes, and suffixes. Make a list of common word parts (and meanings) that learners can refer to when they encounter new words.

- Teach learners that words can have multiple meanings. Have them collect multiple meanings for some common words such as: *like, run, play,* or *lock.*

- Every day, assess the learning materials you will use to determine vocabulary needs of learners.

- Demonstrate a number of vocabulary games to learners. Have learners make a list of their favorites. Play those often.

- Guide learners through the New Word Decision-Making Flow Chart. Make sure they understand how to use all of the learning strategies included.

- Have learners make word cards of words they want to learn. Use the Conga Line activity to have learners teach one another the words. Play I have/Who has with the word cards.

RTI Tier 2 Sampler

- Assess the vocabulary level of English learners individually. With them, make a list of important words they want to study and learn.

- Teach learners ways to study words with a partner, like *test, study, retest.*

- Teach small groups of learners how to draw simple pictures to help them understand and remember words.

- Observe small groups of learners as they do a word sort—how well do they choose the categories for the sort? Does the sort show that they understand the words?

- Use semantic maps to show small groups of learners different meanings of words along with related words.

- Before assigning a reading, preteach important words from the reading for a lesson to an individual or small group including ELLs.

- Teach learners how to select for study words that will be important for them to succeed in their academic work.

- Have a small group create a Sentence Machine to answer questions about the topic you are studying. Give them specific terms they must include in their sentences.

- Begin a lesson with a WordSplash activity about the passage you will read.

- Create a cloze passage from a recent class reading. Devise different levels of support for different levels of learners.

Questions for Reflection

1. How might you go about determining important words to teach directly to your learners in a grade-level content class?
2. What are the key elements that help learners remember words? How can you facilitate these in the classroom?
3. What are the key characteristics of effective vocabulary instruction? Which characteristic do you think is the most important and why?
4. Sort the vocabulary strategies and activities introduced in this chapter into three categories: (1) strategies for introducing new words to learners; (2) classroom strategies that help learners practice and use words they are learning; and (3) strategies for learners to use independently to take responsibility for their own learning. (Alternatively, create your own categories for the word sort.)
5. What are the purposes of formative assessment of vocabulary in the classroom? How can they best be carried out?
6. How does the approach to teaching vocabulary in the classroom outlined in this chapter meet the principles of the Activity-Based Communicative Model described in Chapter 1?

Activities for Further Learning

1. Visit a content classroom to observe a lesson. Which words seem important to understanding the content of this lesson? Which strategies does the teacher use to find out how well learners understand these words? Which strategies does the teacher use to teach them?
2. Try out some of the vocabulary assessment tools available through the Compleat Lexical Tutor http://www.lextutor.ca/tests/. Test your own lexis (the words you know and use) at the 10,000 word level or above. What did you learn about your own vocabulary? Then try out the assessment with an English learner, starting with one of the first 1000 word tests, and moving higher as long as they are comfortable. What did you learn about their lexis? How could you learn more? How might you use this information in planning for teaching this learner?
3. Analyze a chapter of a content textbook. Look for vocabulary that is crucial to this content in three categories: (1) terms specific to the content area that are important for this lesson; (2) key academic words, not specific to this content but nevertheless necessary for being able to learn from the text; and (3) portable language—phrases and structures needed to ask questions, discuss, and write about this content for the class.
4. Analyze a paragraph of an academic text using two tools: WordSift [www.wordsift.com] and VP http://www.lextutor.ca/vp/ or http://www.lextutor.ca/vp/kids/. How is the output from the two tools alike? How is it different? What can you use from this information to inform your teaching? How might you use it?
5. Plan a series of lessons to introduce, enhance, and have learners practice several items from each category of words in the activity above. What activities will you use for each part of your instruction? How will you ensure that the lessons are engaging to learners? How will you assess the depth and breadth of their vocabulary learning?

Suggested Reading

Allen, J. (2007). *Inside words: Tools for teaching academic vocabulary, grades 4–12*. Portland, ME: Stenhouse Publishers. Allen provides a quick overview of the importance of vocabulary teaching and research on effective instructional strategies for vocabulary development. The greater part of the book consists of rich examples of tools and strategies for vocabulary development in the content classroom. A CD included with the book includes graphic organizers in English and Spanish.

Beck, I. L., McKeown, M. G., & Kucan, L. (2002). *Bringing words to life: Robust vocabulary instruction*. New York: Guilford Press. The authors present a clear and practical approach for choosing words for instruction, motivating learners, and providing deep understanding of important vocabulary, with many classroom examples and activities.

Cobb, T. (2011). The Compleat Lexical Tutor http://www.lextutor.ca/ Cobb provides amazing tools and resources for teachers of vocabulary: Vocabulary Profile (VP), Academic Word List, General Word Lists, Concordancer, and many more. The experimental VP-Kids http://www.lextutor.ca/vp/kids/ offers word family lists and online text assessment for younger learners.

Fillmore, L. W., & Snow, C. E. (2000). What teachers need to know about language. Washington, DC: ERIC, U.S. Department of Education Clearinghouse on Languages and Linguistics. http://citeseerx.ist.psu.edu/viewdoc/download?doi=10.1.1.92.9117&rep=rep1&type=pdf. The article outlines what teachers should know about language, including the units of language which are so important in teaching vocabulary.

Folse, K. S. (2004). *Vocabulary myths: Applying second language research to classroom teaching*. Ann Arbor: University of Michigan Press. The author compiles research and effective practice in vocabulary teaching in the English language classroom by searching out and debunking myths; e.g., guessing words from context is an excellent strategy for learning L2 vocabulary, or "the use of translations to learn new vocabulary should be discouraged."

Helman, L., Bear, D. R., Templeton, S., Invernizzi, M., & Johnston, F. R. (2011). *Words their way with English learners: Word study for phonics, vocabulary, and spelling* (2nd ed.). Upper Saddle River, NJ: Pearson. Based on research on literacy development, the authors provide assistance to teachers in helping learners use what they know from their home language, and developing paths towards literacy and vocabulary development.

Nation, I. S. P. (2001). *Learning vocabulary in another language*. New York: Cambridge. Nation's classic guide to teaching vocabulary is both well informed by research and highly practical and useful in the classroom.

References

Anglin, J. M. (1993). Vocabulary development: A morphological analysis. *Monographs of the Society for Research in Child Development, 58*(10, Serial No. 238).

Bauman, J., & Culligan, B. (1995). *The general service list.* http://jbauman.com/gsl.html.

Beck, I. L., McKeown, M. G., & Kucan, L. (2002). *Bringing words to life: Robust vocabulary instruction.* New York: Guilford Press.

Biemiller, A. (Spring, 2001). Teaching vocabulary: Early, direct, and sequential. *American Educator.* http://www.aft.org/newspubs/periodicals/ae/spring2001/biemiller.cfm

Bromley, K. (April, 2007). Nine things every teacher should know about words and vocabulary instruction. *Journal of Adolescent & Adult Literacy, 50*:7.

Burke, J. (2012). The English companion website. http://www.englishcompanion.com/pdfDocs/academicvocab.pdf

Carle, E. (1986). *The very hungry caterpillar.* New York: Philomel Books.

Cobb, T. *Compleat Lexical Tutor* and *Web Vocabprofile* [accessed 15 February 2012 from http://www.lextutor.ca and http://www.lextutor.ca/vp/]. The *Web Vocabprofile* is an adaptation of Heatley & Nation's (1994) Range.

Coxhead, A. (2000). A new academic word list. *TESOL Quarterly 34*(2): 213–238.

Curtis, M. B. (1999). *When adolescents can't read: Methods and materials that work.* Brookline MA: Brookline Books.

Davies, M., & Gardner, D. (2010). *A frequency dictionary of contemporary American English.* New York: Routledge.

Duff, A., & Maley, A. (2007). *Literatur* (2nd ed.). New York: Oxford University Press.

Dunne, L. M., & Dunn, L. M. (1997). *Peabody Picture Vocabulary Test-Third Edition (PPVT-III).* Upper Saddle River, NJ: Pearson.

Folse, K. S. (2004). *Vocabulary myths: Applying second language research to classroom teaching.* Ann Arbor: University of Michigan Press.

Goulden, R., Nation, P., & Read, J. (1990). How large can a receptive vocabulary be? *Applied Linguistics 11*: 341–363.

Hakuta, K., & Weintjes, G. (2012). WordSift. www.wordsift.com.

Hart, B., & Risley, T. R. (Spring, 2003). The early catastrophe: The 30 million word gap by age 3. *American Educator.* http://www.aft.org/pdfs/americaneducator/spring2003/TheEarlyCatastrophe.pdf

Hiebert, E. H., & Kamil, M. L. (2005). *Teaching and learning vocabulary: Bringing research to practice.* Mahwah, NJ: Erlbaum.

Huckin, T., & Block, J. (1993). Strategies for inferring word-meanings in context: A cognitive model. In T. Huckin & J. Coady (Eds.), *Second language reading and vocabulary learning* (pp. 153–178). Norwood, NJ: Ablex.

Kinsella, K. (2005). Teaching academic vocabulary. Sonoma County Office of Education Brief. http://www.scoe.org/docs/ah/AH_vkinsella2.pdf

Krashen, S. D. (2004). *The power of reading: Insights from the research.* Portsmouth, NH: Heinemann.

Lehr, F., Osborn, J., & Hiebert, D. H. (2004). *A focus on vocabulary.* Research-Based Practices in Early Reading Series published by the Regional Educational Laboratory at Pacific Resources for Education and Learning. http://www.prel.org/products/re_/ES0419.htm

Marzano, R. J., & Pickering, D. J. (2005). *Building academic vocabulary: Teacher's manual.* Alexandria, VA: Association for Supervision and Curriculum Development.

McCloskey, M. L., & Stack, L. (2011). *Teaching tolerance through English.* Unpublished workshop handout. Balatonlelle, Hungary.

Miller, D. L. (1993). Making the connection with language. *Arithmetic Teacher, 40*:6: 322–313.

Nagy, W. E., & Anderson, R. C. (Spring, 1984). How many words are there in printed school English? *Reading Research Quarterly, 19*:3, 304–330.

Nation, P., & Waring, R. (1994*). Vocabulary size, text coverage and word lists.* http://www.fltr.ucl.ac.be/fltr/germ/etan/bibs/vocab/cup.html

Nation, P., & Waring, R. (1997). How much vocabulary does a second language learner need? In N. Schmitt and M. McCarthy (Eds.): *Vocabulary: Description, acquisition and pedagogy* (pp. 6–19). Cambridge: Cambridge University Press.

National Research Council. (2010). Language diversity, school learning, and closing achievement gaps: A workshop summary. M. Welch-Ross, Rapporteur. Center for Education, Division of Behavioral and Social Sciences and Education. Washington, DC: The National Academies Press.

Nivola, C. A. (2008). *Planting the trees of Kenya: The story of Wangari Maathai.* New York: Farrar, Straus, and Giroux.

Pinker, S. (2002). *The blank slate: The modern denial of human nature.* New York: Viking.

Saphier, J., & Haley, M. A. (1993). *Activators: Activity structures to engage students' thinking before instruction.* Carlisle, MA: Research for Better Teaching, Inc.

Stahl, S. A., & Shiel, T. G. (1999). Teaching meaning vocabulary: Productive approaches for poor readers. Read all about it! Readings to inform the profession. Sacramento: California State Board of Education.

Tinkham, T. (1993). The effects of semantic clustering on the learning of second language vocabulary. *System, 21*(3), 371–380.

Tinkham, T. (1997). The effects of semantic and thematic clustering on the learning of second language vocabulary. *Second Language Research, 13*(2), 138–163.

Trelease, J. (2006). *The read-aloud handbook,* 6th ed. New York: Penguin.

Walter, T. (2004). *Teaching English language learners: The how-to handbook.* White Plains, NY: Longman.

Waring, R. (1997). The negative effects of learning words in semantic sets. *System, 25*(2), 261–274.

West, M. (1953). *A general service list of English words.* Harlow, Essex: Longman.

WIDA. (2012). Access for ELLs, Developed by the Center for Applied Linguistics. http://www.wida.us/assessment/ACCESS/

MyEducationLab™

Go to the Topic, Vocabulary Development, in the MyEducationLab (www.myeducationlab.com) for your course, where you can:

- Find learning outcomes for Vocabulary Development along with the national standards that connect to these outcomes.
- Complete Assignments and Activities that can help you more deeply understand the chapter content.
- Apply and practice your understanding of the core teaching skills identified in the chapter with the Building Teaching Skills and Dispositions learning units.
- Examine challenging situations and cases presented in the IRIS Center Resources.
- Check your comprehension on the content covered in the chapter by going to the Study Plan in the Book Resources for your text. Here you will be able to take a chapter quiz, receive feedback on your answers, and then access Review, Practice, and Enrichment activities to enhance your understanding of chapter content.
- **A+RISE** Visit A+RISE. A+RISE® Standards2Strategy™ is an innovative and interactive online resource that offers new teachers in grades K-12 just in time, research-based instructional strategies that meet the linguistic needs of ELLs as they learn content, differentiate instruction for all grades and abilities, and are aligned to Common Core Elementary Language Arts standards (for the literacy strategies) and to English language proficiency standards in WIDA, Texas, California, and Florida."

Developing Literacy with English Learners: Focus on Reading

Nadia El Naggar works with a multilingual, multicultural second-grade class. Eight of her twenty-four students, who come from five different countries, are being served by the ESOL program, and eight others have exited from the program, but still need her support in continuing to improve their reading skills. Nadia is the reading teacher of record for all. Let's view a snapshot of one of her full-class mini-lessons in language arts.

In science, the class has been building an understanding of the growth cycle through the theme, "the circle of life." On this day, Nadia demonstrates the shared reading strategy with a big book called *A Pocketful of Opossums* (Almada, Nichols, & O'Keefe, 2004). The title page is shown in Figure 8.1. She begins the lesson by reviewing with the class a poster that shows four stages in the life of a lion, a chicken, a frog, and a butterfly and having learners label the pictures. She asks new learners to label the animals and more proficient English speakers to label the stages. Students take turns acting out the four stages for each animal as the class names the animal and the stages. Some children respond with gestures for *yes* and *no* questions; others respond with short answers that Nadia accepts and expands upon.

Next, Nadia asks the children if any of them has ever seen an opossum. Many have not. She shows the children the picture of an opossum on the cover of a big book, and asks the children to practice saying the word. She then explains that opossums grow from babies to adults, just like people, and this is what the book is about. She introduces the book, models making predictions about what the class will learn with questions (e.g., "How big is an opossum?" or "Where do the baby opossums live?") and encourages the children to make other predictions and ask questions starting with *why, what,* and *where.* They ask:

"What in the pocket?"

"Why no hair?" [on the baby]

"Why is it on its mama's back?"

"Where does possum live?"

After this introduction, Nadia uses the shared reading strategy to support learners as they read and share the text in many ways over several days. With a pointer, she draws the children's attention to the text as it is read. The first time through, she reads aloud to the children, but on successive readings, more and more children read along. Each reading includes questions and discussion to monitor children's comprehension and maintain their attention. For example, she checks to make sure that all students understand the meaning of *pocket*, and has several students show their own pockets.

Following several readings of the story, with children participating more each time (some reading along, some reciting along, some combining reading and reciting, and a few newcomers just watching with keen interest), the teacher uses the text for a variety of literacy-building activities, including letter-sound connections, vocabulary development, summarizing and restating, and plotting life cycles on a time line.

FIGURE 8.1 Previewing Pictures from a Book, Such as This One, Helps to Set the Stage for Guided Reading

Source: A Pocketful of Opossums, Almada, et al. (2004).

At the end of the week, the teacher sends home a page with the main events in the story pictured and captioned. Children read the story to their parents in English, then retell it in the home language. Parents are proud to listen to and discuss the stories with their children, and they sign their children's papers; they're also glad to understand and be involved in what their children are learning.

How do effective teachers develop literacy with English learners?

• What are current definitions of literacy and approaches to developing literacy?
• What are the unique characteristics and needs of English language learners (ELLs) who are developing literacy in English?

- What are effective strategies for literacy development of ELLs at different language-learning and literacy stages?
- What are recommendations for schools to ensure that all ELLs are participating in a comprehensive and appropriate literacy program?
- How can we address the unique literacy development needs of older learners whose education has been interrupted?
- What types of reading assessments are used with ELLs in schools?

WHAT IS LITERACY?

Literacy is not just reading. It actually involves all modes of language—listening, speaking, reading, and writing. When learners develop literacy, they acquire the ability to construct and convey meaning from their own written texts and the texts of others. They begin to have effective ways to learn about the world, to interact with people in the world, and to be able to influence what happens in the world through the written word. Our goals for English learners are to help them develop beyond merely being *able* to do these things—we want our students to become learners who *choose* to read and write, who *delight* in reading and writing. This chapter focuses on teaching English learners to read, but readers will find many connections to speaking, listening, and writing as well.

Reading is taught in a variety of ways that are often grouped into **top-down approaches** and **bottom-up approaches**. In top-down approaches (Figure 8.2), the focus is on what readers bring into the process, helping them use their world knowledge to bring meaning to the text, then expanding it to develop decoding and comprehension skills in the context of the meaning. In "bottom-up" approaches (Figure 8.3), the focus is placed on developing building blocks in sequence—focusing first on developing the ability to hear sounds, then on building decoding skills (associating sounds with letters and letter combinations), and then continuing on to develop word study skills, fluency, and comprehension.

Top-Down Approaches

Top-down approaches to reading include emergent literacy, which was pioneered by Don Holdaway (1979) and Marie Clay (1997) in Australia and New Zealand, and expanded by proponents of the Whole Language philosophy and guided reading. This approach views children as beginning to develop written language knowledge from the moment they are first exposed to reading and writing. Literacy development, like oral language development, is a process in which learners act out reading and writing, and gradually—with guidance, instruction, and

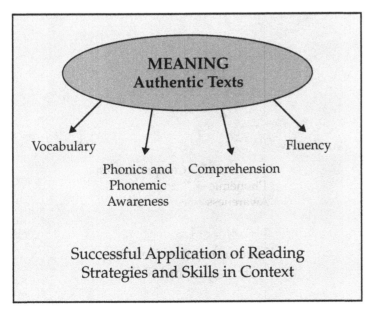

FIGURE 8.2 Top-down Approaches to Reading

feedback—begin to approximate increasingly conventional reading and writing to get meaning from text. This approach employs literacy development strategies that parallel effective oral language development (Moustafa, 1997). These strategies include providing comprehensible input, scaffolding, and social interaction around literacy that lead students toward mature reading and writing. Emphasis is placed on developing motivation and purposes for reading, helping learners understand the context, gaining meaning from reading, and making meaning with writing. Marie Clay describes reading as "a message-gaining, problem-solving activity that increases in power and flexibility the more it is practiced" (1997, p. 6). Kenneth Goodman (1967) used "a psycholinguistic guessing game" as a metaphor for reading. In this "game," learners develop abilities in using phonemic (letter sounds), semantic (word meaning), and syntactic (word order and grammar) cues to get meaning from a page. The approach does not, as critics have often said, omit the teaching of literacy skills but rather promotes the introduction of literacy skills such as phonics, grammar, and spelling in context as students are ready for them and need them, and in a way that is compatible with their cognitive development. The approach is most effective when the curriculum and well-prepared teachers support the development of the strategies and skills children need, understand the usual sequences of development, and are knowledgeable about effective methods for the introduction and use of the skills and strategies. Top-down elements of curriculum are important for helping ELLs acquire meaning. ELLs need to learn what texts mean either before or as they learn to read them.

Bottom-Up Approaches

By contrast, there has been recent renewed interest in what are called "bottom-up" approaches (Figure 8.3), influenced by such publications as that of the Reading First initiative of the No Child Left Behind Act (NCLB) (U.S. Department of Education, 2002). It is important to note that although the research reviewed by the National Reading Panel (National Institute of Child Health and Human Development, 2000) did not include studies focusing on the literacy development and needs of ELLs, the results have been widely disseminated as appropriate recommendations for all readers, regardless of their language background (Stahl, 2002). Likewise, NCLB did not include provisions to accommodate the different language development and content achievement of ELLs, although recently "flexibilities" have been incorporated into the testing requirements for ELLs (U.S. Department of Education, 2002). These "bottom-up" approaches emphasize explicit development of the component skills of literacy, including developing phonemic awareness, phonics, word study, fluency and comprehension skills, and then putting these together to develop reading proficiency. The Reading First Program (U.S. Department of Education, 2009) is based on the findings of the National Reading Panel and is designed to implement the use

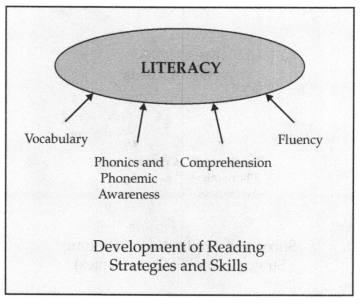

FIGURE 8.3 Bottom-up Approaches to Reading

of scientifically based research promoted by NCLB. Reading First is a state grant program in which states are eligible for federal funds if they demonstrate how they plan to improve reading instruction and student achievement using scientifically proven methods.

It is important to note that most explicit literacy approaches in use in grade-level classrooms are dependent on prerequisite oral language proficiency of learners. They assume that learners have acquired the sound system, vocabulary, structures, and patterns of the English language, and are able to use this knowledge to develop the skills of reading. Learners of English do not meet these prerequisites. The National Literacy Panel, convened to "identify, assess, and synthesize research on the education of language-minority children and youth with regard to literacy attainment and to produce a comprehensive report on this literature" (August & Shanahan, 2007, 2008), found evidence to show that learners of English benefitted from bottom-up approaches, but primarily for reading at word level; more complex, top-down approaches were important for developing oral language needed for reading and reading fluency, and for comprehension ability.

Integrated Approaches

Integrated approaches (Figure 8.4) view reading as constructing meaning. Children begin to become readers long before entering school, and they use invented forms of literacy on their way to conventional reading and writing. In integrated approaches (Figure 8.4), meaning is central, and teachers work to integrate top-down and bottom-up approaches, integrating comprehension and decoding, reader and text, and reader and writer (Birch, 2006). They teach the component skills of reading within the context of authentic, connected texts—texts that are simple and repetitive at first, and then gradually more complex. They sequence skills within thematic units that include relevant, age-appropriate content. They may include the use of leveled readers— texts at levels that very gradually increase in difficulty by carefully and deliberately introducing a few new reading skills and new vocabulary at each level. They may use a guided reading approach (August & Shanahan, 2008; Fountas & Pinnell, 1996, 2001), in which teachers work with small, leveled groups, guiding students to read books at progressively more difficult levels and introducing new features of text and reading strategies along the way, all in the context of a variety of rich literacy experiences.

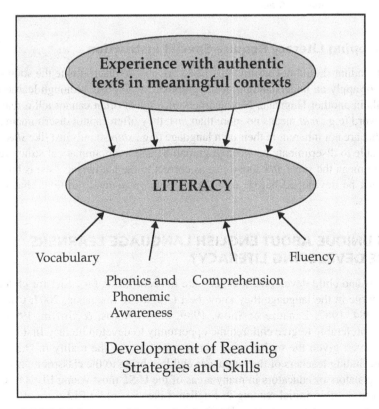

FIGURE 8.4 Integrated Approaches to Reading

This Girl, Like Many ELLs, Developed Literacy in Her First Language—Arabic

ELLs Developing Literacy Require Special Instruction

Teachers of reading should not assume that ELLs are able to discriminate the sounds, know the vocabulary, or apply an understanding of the grammar of English, although learners may have parallel skills in another language. New learners of English often cannot tell a real word from a nonsense word (e.g., *mat* means no more than *jat*); they often cannot discriminate new sounds of English that are not inherent in their own language (e.g., *ship* sounds just like *sheep*); and they may not be able to discriminate between grammatical and nongrammatical structures (e.g., "he happy" might mean the same and sound just as correct to the learners as "she is happy"). These elements must be developed before or as learners learn to read the texts that require such discriminations.

WHAT IS UNIQUE ABOUT ENGLISH LANGUAGE LEARNERS WHO ARE DEVELOPING LITERACY?

Most linguists and child development experts are in accord: It is far easier for children to learn to read and write in the language they know best (August & Shanahan, 2007; Cummins 2010; Hudelson, 1984, 1987; Lanauze & Snow, 1989; Snow, Burns, & Griffin, 1998). So, when possible, it is preferable to give children the opportunity to develop literacy first in their mother tongue. However, given the multilingual classrooms that are the reality in U.S. schools, the challenges in finding teachers of the languages children bring to the classroom, and the policies chosen by legislators or educators in many areas of the U.S., most young ELLs in U.S. schools are expected to develop initial reading in English. Likewise, older ELLs are often expected to continue their literacy development in English. This presents unique challenges for school-age

ELLs and their teachers. Although the development of ELLs who are acquiring literacy in a new language has many parallels to first language literacy development, there are a number of important distinctions for teachers to keep in mind.

What ELLs Bring

ELLs bring a great deal with them to the literacy table. They already know at least one language, and they use it in sophisticated and age-appropriate ways. They have the same cognitive maturity as their native-English speaking peers. They may have had some exposure to literacy in their mother tongue, and they may have acquired many literacy skills and strategies as applied in another language system. They bring with them rich experiences in one or more cultures. Each day they move between a home culture and a school culture that have wide differences in values and expectations. As teachers, we must discover, respect, use, and celebrate what English learners already know and the unique contributions they bring to our classrooms. Culturally sensitive and responsive programs are important supports for teachers who want to build on the strengths their language learners bring with them (Jiménez, 2010; Jiménez & Teague, 2009).

TRANSFER OF LITERACY FROM NATIVE LANGUAGE TO SECOND LANGUAGE Although much research is still needed about the similarities and differences between the native-language and second-language reading processes, researchers have found that processes seem to be more alike than they are different. Heath (1983) refers to transferable generic literacies; Krashen (2003) proposes that second-language reading entails the same basic processes as first-language reading, and Fitzgerald's (2003) research indicates that the cognitive reading processes of English language learners in the U.S. were similar to those of native-English speakers. Literacy skills from L1 **transfer** to L2. Such skills might include phonological knowledge, topical knowledge, general background knowledge, problem-solving strategies, and inferencing skills. Generalized examples of positive transfer from L1 to L2 reading include positive past experiences as a learner, for example, effective strategies for reading academic texts, appropriate purposes for reading, successful experiences with task completion, ability to monitor comprehension, and skill in analyzing and learning new vocabulary (Grabe & Stoller, 2002). Knowing the level of literacy in L1 can be helpful in determining expectations in L2 reading instruction. Most teachers we have worked with are confident that learners who come with considerable literacy in L1 have a strong advantage in developing reading skills in English. We encourage you to do what you can to find out about your learners' previous schooling. If you are able to locate and use L1 reading and writing assessments for the languages of your learners, these tools will help you in knowing whether you are introducing first-time literacy or helping learners to transfer literacy skills they already have to a new language. If no standardized tools are available, you can still get an idea about your learners' level of literacy development by asking them to read to you from a book written for their age group in the language they know. Does the student know how to handle a book? How fluent is the reading? Likewise, you can ask your ELLs to write something for you in their native language (Figure 8.5 shows one such example). Ask questions like these about your writing samples. Does the handwriting look as if the learners have had considerable instruction and practice? Do they write fluently? Is there organization to the way words are arranged on the page? Can the learners read to you what they have written? Whatever information you can glean on what literacy skills your learners bring to the classroom will help you to teach them better.

What ELLs Need

Language development takes time. Researchers estimate that although children learning a second language can be effective in social language in one to two years, the average time that they take to acquire native-like academic language is about five to seven years (Cummins, 1994; Thomas & Collier, 1997). Native speakers who have experienced rich language input may have a vocabulary of more than 5,000 words by age five or six (Nation, 2001). They have usually acquired the basic syntax of their first language as well by this age. This provides a rich basis for learning to encode and decode and comprehend the language they already know orally into written form. We certainly cannot wait for ELLs' full acquisition of oral language before we begin literacy instruction, as we do with native speakers. In fact, in order to help these students eventually acquire native-like academic language, we need to provide instruction in which oral

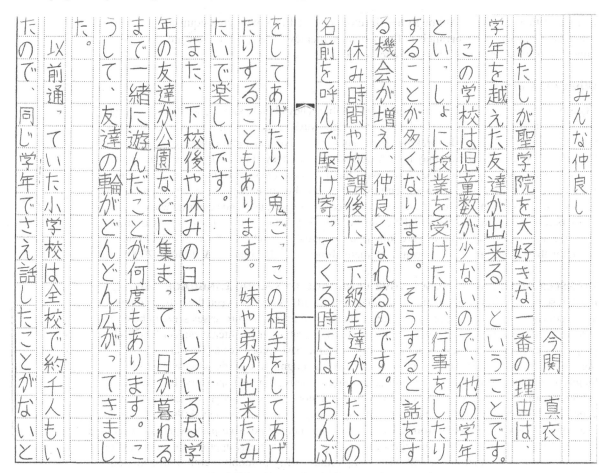

FIGURE 8.5 What Does the Eight-Year-Old Who Wrote This Know About Reading and Writing?
Reprinted with permission from Teruko Imazeki.

language development, literacy development, and content learning all support one another. As we provide scaffolded, supportive instruction for students' literacy development, we offer many opportunities for oral language development through rich conversations about the materials learners read and the content they read about. And we remain conscious of the various aspects of language that learners are acquiring—including words and word meanings, sounds and sound systems, language patterns, and cultural and social contexts.

WORDS AND MEANINGS (LEXICAL ASPECTS OF LANGUAGE)　Native speakers generally learn to read using language they already employ in speech. Learners of English have additional tasks: They must also learn the **lexical aspects of language**. They need to learn what the words mean and how to say them, often using sounds they have never encountered before. While we do not delay reading instruction until oral language is well developed, especially for older learners, we must be alert about integrating oral language development with literacy instruction. We carefully assess our students' oral and reading comprehension and employ direct teaching of needed vocabulary. We introduce new words in contexts that make them more easily understood, recycling and re-using new words through thematic instruction to provide the many encounters students will need to learn these terms thoroughly. We also provide background knowledge to make new terms understandable to learners who have not had the experiences needed for comprehension.

SOUND PATTERNS AND SPELLING (GRAPHOPHONEMIC ASPECTS OF LANGUAGE)　As they learn to read and write, native speakers learn to connect sound patterns of words and word parts—ones they already use in listening and speaking—with spelling patterns. These are the **graphophonemic aspects of language**. So when a native-speaking child learns to read "A clock is a circle," the child connects sounds and a spelling pattern to words and concepts she is very familiar with—she knows what a clock is and what the word for clock means; likewise with a circle. A new learner of English may know what a clock is and what a circle is (although in this digital age, he may not have seen many clocks with circular faces), and even the concept that *is* can mean "is an example of," but not the English names for these items or concepts. Learners of English have to do more: They do not just learn how to make connections between letters/syllables and sounds they already use to identify words they know. Rather, they hear the sounds (which may not all be present in their home language), know what the words mean, and read those sounds and patterns. Therefore, it is very important to introduce these new sounds in meaningful contexts using words students know or are learning along with pictures and other contextual cues that provide support.

Learners of English should encounter concepts of **phonemic awareness** and **phonics** in the context of meaningful, purposeful, culturally respectful language use, and real words (Enright & McCloskey, 1988). Strategies for developing phonemic awareness for native speakers include shared reading of books that play with sounds, writing with invented spelling, and teaching onsets and rimes (onsets are initial sounds and rimes are the word family endings, e.g., *c -at, r -at, m – at*) using a variety of activities (Cunningham, 2008; Cunningham, 1999; Helman, 2009). With ELLs, additional care must be taken that the language used in these activities is comprehensible to learners or that the learners have the opportunity to acquire the language before or as they are expected to read it. For example, look at the sample phonics page depicted in Figure 8.6 and note how the development of phonics skills is complicated when the learners are ELLs. Native speakers are likely to recognize the objects and associate the appropriate words with a few reminders from a teacher. On the other hand, although ELLs may recognize the pictures, they may not have the cultural experience of jumping rope, playing a flute, or seeing a mule. Even more likely is that these learners have no idea what the English word for the picture depicts (*mug, tube,* or *June*) and may not be able to hear all the phonemes (sounds with differences in meaning in a language) used. Spanish speakers, for example, would be unfamiliar with the English sound for "*j*" or the initial consonant blends, or the short "*u*" sound.

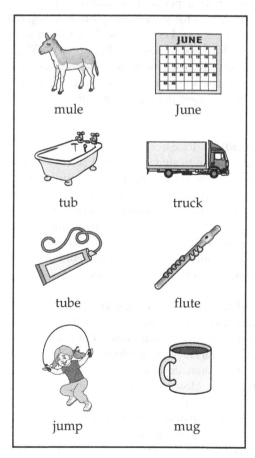

FIGURE 8.6 Sample Pictures from a Phonics Text

LANGUAGE PATTERNS AND GRAMMAR (SYNTACTIC ASPECTS OF LANGUAGE) Learners of English (as well as speakers of "non-school" dialects) do not always connect print to patterns they recognize, but rather must learn new patterns for constructing grammatical language. They must learn the **syntactic aspects of language**. For these students, it is even more important than for native English speakers that the texts they are learning to read use meaningful language that is both linguistically and culturally accessible. For beginning learners, print should have characteristics that make it easier to remember and learn such as rhyme, rhythm, and repetition; content should be familiar to learners and respectful of their cultural heritage; language patterns should be those frequently encountered in their school and community experiences. Stories such as *Brown Bear, Brown Bear, What Do You See?* (Martin & Carle, 1992) introduce language with universal appeal to new learners of English. Older learners may enjoy age-appropriate, school-appropriate rap songs or jazz chants (Graham, 1978, 2003). Reading selections, songs, and chants with these characteristics all provide rich ways to introduce language patterns. For intermediate and advanced learners, texts should be at students' independent reading or instructional level. If the books are not at this level, teachers should provide adequate scaffolding, or support for learners so that they can make sense of the text and the lesson. (Scaffolding strategies will be discussed in the next section.)

CULTURAL AND SOCIAL CONTEXTS (SOCIOLINGUISTIC ASPECTS OF LANGUAGE) First-language learners are often familiar with different ways that language is used with different conversation partners and in different settings. (Linguists call this **register**.) We use different language with family members of different ages, with friends, with teachers and administrators, and in different settings: on the phone at home, in reporting an experiment in a presentation before the class. New learners of English who come from other countries and cultures do not just learn to read the words and language forms that are appropriate in various sociolinguistic contexts; they must learn what language is appropriate and when, and then learn the terms and language structures that are used as well. Native speakers intuitively internalize these **sociolinguistic aspects of language**. But ELLs must learn appropriate language and nonverbal behaviors for a very new cultural setting (North American schools) in new cultures (in North America). For example, ELLs from some cultures have learned that making eye contact with adults is rude and disrespectful. Their "polite" behavior may be interpreted by North American teachers as showing lack of interest and disrespect. These differences require teachers to be culturally aware and sensitive, and to use curricula and materials that take into account the wide range of cultures now represented in North American schools.

HOME-SCHOOL CONNECTIONS Research evidence has led to a wide consensus concerning the value of parental participation in students' school achievement, social development, and specifically reading and language development (Cummins, 1994; Heath, 1983). Although parents and teachers may not speak the same language, there are many ways that teachers can support parent participation in their children's literacy development. By integrating oral language development in the context of thematic instruction, phonological awareness, and phonics instruction, contextualized grammatical instruction, and home-school connections with best practices in literacy instruction, we can help children discover the joy of reading as well as the power of access to school and community resources.

DIFFERENCES BETWEEN ORAL LANGUAGE DEVELOPMENT AND LITERACY DEVELOPMENT In many ways, oral language and the language of print are the same—we use similar words, our sentences have similar syntax. But there are a number of ways in which literacy development is unlike oral language development. While children learn the oral language of their community, not every culture develops a written language, and not all children learn the written language of their culture. Most children require explicit instruction for successful literacy development. So, effective, balanced literacy instruction requires a print-rich environment in which teachers continue the development of oral language, teach text processing and production strategies, insure cultural background knowledge, and develop decoding and encoding skills (Cloud, Genesee, & Hamayan, 2009). The classroom setting provides input—both oral and print—that is understandable to learners and at the right instructional level. It provides social

Nonverbal Behavior Has Very Different Meanings in Different Cultures, Which Requires Teachers of ELLs to Be Culturally Aware and Sensitive

interaction with and about texts, and explicit instruction in strategies and processes used to make meaning from text. As they introduce language learners to print, teachers demonstrate the pleasure and usefulness that literacy offers us in our lives.

INTEGRATED LITERACY APPROACH   An Integrated Literacy Approach involves combining meaningful reading and writing, conversations with and about reading, and instruction in reading and writing skills and strategies used in authentic contexts. It meets the needs of a wide range of English language learners for developing literacy. A basic element is providing a print-rich classroom in which students' oral language and literacy development are valued and put to use. The literacy strategies we will recommend gradually move from providing more teacher responsibility to promoting shared responsibility between teacher and learner, to facilitating learner independence in reading.

THE LANGUAGE/LITERACY MATRIX

Language and literacy skills do not necessarily develop in parallel with ELLs. Some learners may have good first-language (L1) literacy and English language instruction focusing on reading and writing, but still may have had little practice with oral language and be unfamiliar with the sounds of U.S. English. Other learners may have acquired some oral proficiency in English but have not had an opportunity to learn to read in any language. These students may have English oral skills that are more advanced than their reading skills. Teachers who are responsible for the reading development of ELLs should have access to assessments of both types of language learning.

TABLE 8.1 The Language/Literacy Matrix (Freeman et al., 2010)

Stages of Language Acquisition	Levels of English Literacy Development			
	Emergent Literacy	Early Literacy	Early Fluency	Fluency
Stage 1: Starting (Preproduction)				
Stage 2: Emerging (Early Production)				
Stage 3: Developing (Speech Emergence)				
Stage 4: Expanding (Intermediate Fluency)				
Stage 5: Bridging (Advanced Fluency)				

Table 8.1, the Language/Literacy Matrix (Freeman, Freeman, McCloskey, Stack, Silva, Gottlieb, & Garcia Colon, 2010) can help teachers to track both the language and literacy levels of ELLs. Using the results of English language assessment instruments and appropriate reading assessments, place the names of the ELLs in your class in the appropriate boxes. Use these dual assessments in making materials choices and grouping choices, and in setting expectations for ongoing assessments.

Levels of oral language development (described in detail in Chapter 5) are listed down the left-hand column. Levels of English literacy development are listed across the top row. Note that your knowledge of childrens' L1 literacy, obtained through formal and/or informal assessment, will also be useful in determining your expectations, your instruction, and your grouping for reading instruction.

The following are descriptions of the four literacy levels:

EMERGENT LITERACY   Learners at the **emergent literacy** level understand that print can carry meaningful messages, but they are still learning to encode, decode, and understand these messages. They learn basic concepts about books, print, letters, sounds, and writing. They read books that have many kinds of support: for example, they are short and they often have elements of repetition, rhythm, and rhyme with direct match between the words and the pictures. Learners at this level begin to realize that they can get meaning from text and that they can write texts for others to read.

EARLY LITERACY   Learners at the **early literacy** level understand that books have messages that do not change and that there are certain conventions regarding how print is presented. They begin to read and write simple fiction and nonfiction texts. They know that reading involves finding meaning through using certain problem-solving skills. At this level, learners usually read word-by-word, often with a finger pointing at each word.

EARLY FLUENCY   At the **early fluency** level, learners begin to use multiple clues to make meaning from text and are able to understand the main ideas of texts as well as their emotional impact. They rely more on the text and less on the illustrations to understand the author's message. They use a wider range and variety of problem-solving strategies for reading and determining the meaning of new words.

FLUENCY   At the level of **fluency**, learners are becoming mature readers. They make sense of longer and more complex texts approaching or at the level of their native-speaking peers; they use a variety of strategies flexibly to accomplish their reading purposes. They orchestrate all the clues available to them to make meaning: letter-sound relations, the grammar of English, the meanings of words, and the background information and context of the text. When needed, they use self-correction as they read to maintain the meaning of the text. Upper elementary, middle, and secondary school readers at this level develop high-level vocabulary and rich comprehension skills to use with their grade-level academic texts.

WHAT TOOLS AND STRATEGIES CAN WE PROVIDE TO HELP ELLS DEVELOP LITERACY?

Table 8.2 summarizes strategies that support ELL literacy development. We use the metaphor of **scaffolding**, first introduced by Jerome Bruner (Wood, Bruner, & Ross, 1976) to describe the support that teachers offer to English learners. When workers construct a tall building, they often erect scaffolding—supportive structures around the building to enable them to do their construction work. As the building progresses, scaffolding that is no longer needed is removed. Likewise, teachers provide useful tools and strategies to support learners in developing new language and concepts. And as students become proficient and independent, they begin to use tools and strategies for learning on their own as teachers dismantle unneeded scaffolds and create new, more challenging ones to guide learners toward even higher achievement. This approach is called the *gradual release of responsibility model* (Brown, Campione, & Day, 1981; Fitzgerald & Graves, 2004) and is shown in Figure 8.7. At early levels in this approach, teachers take most of the responsibility for making the reading task successful; but as learners acquire more skills, they take on more and more of the responsibility for their success.

TABLE 8.2 Strategies for Developing Literacy for English Language Learners (ELLs)

	Emergent/Early Literacy (Stages 1–3)	Early Fluency/Fluency (Stages 3–5)
Scaffolding Throughout Literacy Lessons	• Provide comprehensible input, checking comprehension frequently. *(Read Aloud)* • Build oral language vocabulary and fluency in meaningful contexts with rich literacy experiences. *(Shared Reading)* • Monitor and develop learners' ability to hear and reproduce English phonemes. *(Choral Reading)* • Develop/reinforce abilities to associate the sounds with spelling patterns of English with letters and word parts. *(Adapting Phonics for ELLs)*	• Provide comprehensible input, checking comprehension frequently. • Continue to build more complex oral language vocabulary and fluency in meaningful contexts. *(Anticipation Guide, Question-Answer-Response or QAR)* • Expand phonics into word study. • Continue to develop listening comprehension, awareness of the differences between L1 and English.
Choosing Texts	• Texts with rhyme, rhythm, repetition. • Illustrations are closely related to text. • Themes are comprehensible across cultures. • Scaffold texts, use selections from texts, or select alternate texts when needed. *(Choosing Texts)*	• Interesting, well-written texts. • Texts have gradually increasing complexity and length. • Texts in which culturally and linguistically diverse learners can see themselves. • Gradually expand to a variety of fiction and nonfiction genres. • Modify texts, use selections from texts, scaffold texts, and select alternate texts when needed. *(Choosing Texts)*
Before the Reading	• Motivate: build concept of reading as a purposeful process of making meaning; develop learners' understanding of purposes for reading. • Review, reread, recite previous texts, chants, and songs. • Teach key vocabulary. *(See Chapter 7)* • Build background knowledge of concepts needed to comprehend text. *(Graphic Organizers, Picture Walk-Through)* • Make connections to learners' own experience and learners' families and communities. *(Language Experience)* • Recommend reading strategies for the text. *(Think Aloud, Guided Reading)*	• Motivate: expand purposes for reading and understanding of a range of genres. • Teach key vocabulary, academic vocabulary, and vocabulary development strategies. • Build background knowledge of concepts needed to comprehend text *(Teaching text structure, i.e., how text is organized). (Also see Chapter 9)* • Make connections to learners' own experience and to learners' families and communities. *(Home-School Connections, Take-Home Reading)* • Focus attention on one or two key reading comprehension strategies. *(Think Aloud, Guided Reading, Teaching Comprehension Skills)*

TABLE 8.2 *(Continued)*

	Emergent/Early Literacy (Stages 1–3)	Early Fluency/Fluency (Stages 3–5)
During the Reading	• Use gradual release of responsibility for reading from teacher to learner: Reading to learners, reading with learners, supporting learners' independent reading. • Teach/reinforce key comprehension skills, literacy skills, and phonics in context through the text. *(Adapting phonics for ELLs)* • Use read aloud, shared reading, and guided reading techniques.	• Use a variety of supportive structures to scaffold during the reading: • *Read aloud, audio texts* • *Shared reading* • *Reciprocal teaching* • *Guided reading* • *Jigsaw reading* • *Silent reading* • *Text selection/modification* • *Graphic organizers* • Teach/reinforce key comprehension skills and literacy skills for identifying words and developing sentence and text-level skills. *(Semantic Feature Analysis)* • Develop oral skills for talking about text and for fluent and expressive reading. *(Reciprocal Teaching)*
After the Reading	• Develop comprehension through questioning and discussing. *(QAR)* • Teach and apply word-solving tools in meaningful contexts. *(Graphic Organizers)* • Build writing experiences from the reading: e.g., using sentence frames from the text. *(See Chapter 9)* • Support learners as they respond to texts orally, in writing, and expressively. *(See Chapters 5 and 9)* • Make literacy connections with the home. *(Home-School Connections, Take-Home Reading)*	• Continue to develop comprehension and problem-solving through questioning and discussing. *(Anticipation Guide, QAR)* • Continue word, sentence, and text-solving during reading. *(See vocabulary strategies in Chapter 7)* • Build writing workshops around the genre of the selection. *(See Chapter 9)* • Support learners as they respond to texts orally, in writing, and expressively. • Make literacy and literary connections with the home. *(Home-School Connections, Take-Home Reading)*

We will describe the scaffolding strategies for use throughout literacy lessons (Table 8.2) as well as specific strategies for use before, during, and after the reading. We have combined the stages of literacy development into two groups because of the space limits in this chapter, but encourage readers to think of these supports as located along a continuum: from more support to less support; from expectations that the teacher does most of the work in reading to expectations that learners are responsible for making meaning from the text on their own. A number of specific strategies are suggested in parentheses. These are not comprehensive, but are *examples* of the types of strategies to use.

Next, we include brief descriptions of the strategies mentioned for the two reading level groups: Emergent/Early Literacy and Early Fluency/Fluency. We have listed the strategies in alphabetical order to help you find them easily. Then we include a section with additional recommendations for older readers in third grade and above, both those who are literate in their first language and transferring literacy skills to English, and those who have low-literacy in their first language and are developing initial literacy in English. Table 8.3 lists all the strategy descriptions included in this chapter.

Strategies to Support ELL Reading Development

1. **Adapting Phonics for ELLs**
   Levels: Emergent/Early literacy
   Grades: All if developing initial literacy

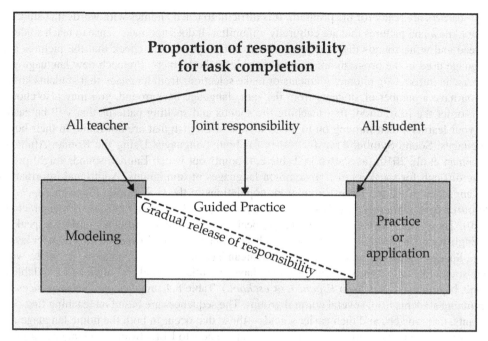

FIGURE 8.7 Gradual Release of Responsibility Model

Source: Brown, Campione, & Day (1981); Fitzgerald & Graves, (2004).

ADAPTING PHONICS FOR ELLS   Phonics is one of the important components of literacy development at emergent/early literacy levels, but traditional phonics often does not fit the needs of ELLs. If your school provides a phonics program for learners of English, you may need to make adjustments to the program in order to include these students. First, make sure that

TABLE 8.3 20 Strategies for ELL Literacy Development
Focus on Reading
1. Adapting Phonics for ELLs
2. Anticipation Guide
3. Choice Independent Reading
4. Choosing/Adapting Texts for ELLs
5. Choral Reading
6. Feature Analysis
7. Graphic Organizers
8. Guided Reading
9. Home-School Connections
10. Instructional Conversations
11. Intensive Reading
12. Jigsaw Reading
13. Language Experience
14. Picture Walk
15. Point of View
16. Question-Answer-Response (QAR)
17. Reading Aloud to ELLs
18. Reciprocal Teaching
19. Shared Reading
20. Think-Aloud

your learners are ready for the program. It is difficult to teach phonics with words that students do not know and pictures that are culturally unfamiliar. It does not make sense to teach students to read and write sounds they cannot yet hear. Before you begin, check that the pictures and language used in the program are comprehensible to the learners. Preteach new language you will use in introducing phonics elements or make selections from language that students know. If you have a number of students from the same language background, you may also choose to re-order the instruction, first teaching the sounds and spelling patterns that will be easier for your learners, then moving on to those sounds of English that are not found in their home languages. Sound-Symbol Transfer Issues for Four Languages Using the Roman Alphabet (Freeman et al., 2010), as shown in Table 8.4, points out which English sounds might prove more difficult for speakers of five common languages of immigrants. Additional information on languages of the ten largest immigrant populations in the U.S. can be found in *Teacher's Resource Guide on Language Transfer Issues for English Language Learners* (Freeman et al., 2010). These include grammar issues (e.g., speakers of Arabic use articles more than speakers of English, and are likely to make errors, such as "I like the sports.") and phonics transfer issues (e.g., Spanish, Vietnamese, Cantonese, and Korean have no short *a* sound as in *hat*, so the word may sound like *hot;* Spanish speakers do not have an initial *s* sound and often add a syllable to words beginning with *s,* as in *Espanish* or *eschool.*). Table 8.4 suggests phonics sequences for beginning students from several cultural groups. The sequences are based on teaching first consonants, then vowels, and then easier sounds—those that occur in both the home language and English—first and then moving on to sounds that are new to ELLs from each language group.

UNDERSTANDING AND ACCOMMODATING LEARNERS WITH DIFFERENT LANGUAGE BACKGROUNDS   There are many ways that languages differ and it is valuable for teachers to understand a bit about the first languages of the learners in their classrooms. For example, they may have different writing systems. In a **logographic language**, one symbol represents the meaning of a concept, individual word, or part of a word. Arabic numerals and mathematical symbols are examples of logographic symbols. Chinese, Japanese (Kanji), and Korean use logographic systems. In a **syllabic language**, one symbol represents a syllable, or consonant-vowel combination. Japanese and Korean languages both use syllabic writing systems. In **alphabetic**

TABLE 8.4 Sound-Symbol Transfer (Freeman et al., 2010)

Issues for four languages using the Roman Alphabet. Sounds with transfer issues (from a given language to English) are indicated by bullets.

English Sounds/ Symbols	Spanish	Vietnamese	Hmong	Haitian Creole
b as in bat			•	
c as in cat		•	•	•
c as in cent		•	•	
d as in dog				
f as in fish				
g as in goat	•		•	
g as in giant			•	
h as in hen	•			
j as in jacket	•	•	•	
k as in kite			•	
l as in lemon				
m as in moon				
n as in nice				
p as in pig				
qu as in queen	•		•	•

(Continued)

TABLE 8.4 (*Continued*)

Issues for four languages using the Roman Alphabet. Sounds with transfer issues (from a given language to English) are indicated by bullets.

English Sounds/ Symbols	Spanish	Vietnamese	Hmong	Haitian Creole
r as in rabbit	•		•	
s as in sun			•	
t as in teen			•	
v as in video	•			
w as in wagon		•	•	
x as in x-ray				
y as in yo-yo				•
z as in zebra	•	•	•	
sh as in shoe	•			
ch as in chair				•
th as in think *th* as in that	•			•

Source: From Morganthaler, L. (Ed.) (2004). *On our way to English: Teacher's resource guide of language transfer issues for English language learners.* Austin, TX: Rigby/Houghton Mifflin Harcourt. Used with permission.

systems, one symbol generally represents one sound. The Roman alphabet is used in most European languages as well as Vietnamese and many African languages. Greek has its own alphabet. The Cyrillic alphabet is used in Serbo-Croatian and Russian. In addition to writing systems, languages also have very different vocabularies, grammatical systems, and sounds.

Although it might be very useful, we know it is not likely to be feasible for you to learn to speak all the languages of your English learners. You can, however, learn a little about how their languages work to help you predict what features of language may be easily confused, and what aspects of English may be new to students from certain groups so that you can prepare to focus lessons on these issues as appropriate. Wikipedia (http://en.wikipedia.org) has brief introductions to most languages you will encounter in the classroom. Another useful source is *The Human Languages Website* by Tyler Chambers, which includes links to rich resources on 209 languages (http://www.ilovelanguages.com/).

EXPLICIT PHONICS AND PHONEMIC AWARENESS Remember that phonics should be developed in the context of language that is meaningful and purposeful for learners. Although young learners tend to acquire new sound systems easily, sometimes oral development activities are needed to help some learners—especially middle school and older learners, and individuals who seem to have trouble with the sound system—develop the ability to hear new English sounds, and to recognize similar sounds such as rhyming sounds. Phonics sequenced from easy to difficult may be adapted for different language groups. Focus first on hearing differences. Begin sound-letter associations with consonants (in easy-to-difficult order) and then teach vowels through word families. Phonics programs developed for middle and high school students may focus only on sounds—and not word knowledge. These programs have a downward spiral effect in that, after several weeks of exposure, they no longer have a positive effect on student learning (Calderón, 2007). In order to avoid this problem, use known words to teach phonics elements and teach reading skills through engaging, motivating, texts chosen to be at learners' instructional level. Your school's speech/language assessment process should also include processes for detecting whether ELLs have speech/language issues (e.g., auditory or articulation problems) separate from their language development needs, and for serving those special needs. Keep in mind that learners with special needs will be found with the same frequency among ELLs as among other groups.

2. **Anticipation Guide**
   Level: Early fluency/fluency
   Grades: 3–12

The **anticipation guide** (Herber & Herber, 1993) helps students to develop background information about a topic they will read about as well as to explore their own ideas about the topic and to report on the author's main ideas. First, prepare a list of true-false statements about a reading. Before they read the text, have learners complete the "you" column on the chart with their own opinions about the statements. They discuss their answers in small groups and explain why they answered as they did. After they read the text, they rethink their responses to the statements according to the information provided in the text and write their answers in the "text" column. Have the students discuss their answers, and encourage students to support their opinions by returning to the text. See the sample Anticipation Guide in Table 8.5.

3. **Choice Independent Reading**
   Levels: All
   Grades: All

Choice reading is a powerful tool for improving ELL literacy. Teach students to select books for independent reading that interest them and that are at their comfort reading level. (Note that reading levels can vary with learners' interest and motivation.) Provide children with books to choose from and structured, regular time to read alone and to one another. Model by reading your own book during choice reading time. Create opportunities for learners to share and discuss the books they read, and to develop their thinking about what they have learned. Beginning readers may choose wordless books, class-made books, picture books, books in their first languages, or audiotapes. With success, support, and guidance, learners will move on to more and more challenging texts and begin to love to read.

4. **Choosing/Adapting Texts for ELLs**
   Levels: All
   Grades: All

Teachers whose classes include English learners must learn how to work with multilevel, multilingual, multicultural groups of wide diversity (Cloud, Genesee, & Hamayan, 2009). They must choose texts carefully to meet the range of students, attending to the following:

- A variety of texts should accommodate students' many purposes for reading, e.g., texts for thematic study, texts for intensive instruction in guided reading, or texts available for students' choice during independent reading.
- Texts should include relevant material that is aligned with mainstream content learners will need for academic courses.

TABLE 8.5 Anticipation Guide for "Dealing with Bullying"

Directions:

1. Read the statements below.
2. Before you read the selection, fill out the "you" column. Write "T" if you think the statement is true or "F" if you think it's false.
3. After you read, write your answers in the "text" column. Write "T" if you think the answer is true according to the text. Write "F" if you think the answer is false according to the text.

You (True or False)	Text (True or False)	Statement
		Bullying can be verbal, nonverbal, psychological, or physical.
		Walking away from a bully is a sign of cowardice.
		Only boys can be bullies.
		Bullies are always people who are big, brave, and secure.
		Body language can help you stand up to a bully.
		Never make jokes with a bully.
		If your friends act like bullies, you should join them.
		Talking about bullying—with peers and adults—is often a good thing to do.
		If you see someone being bullied, you should stand up and speak up.

Based on the reading "Dealing with Bullying" at TeensHealth (http://kidshealth.org/teen/your_mind/problems/bullies.html).

- Texts should include appropriate cultural aspects—content that the students have the background to understand. They should have positive, accurate, empowering representations of students' cultural groups that avoid stereotypes or stereotypical settings. (Some groups of American Indians may have lived in tepees, but historically Indians have lived in many types of homes, and most live in contemporary homes today; likewise, members of other groups should not be stereotyped by income level, jobs, and so on.)
- Illustrations should show the varieties and contemporary realities of members of ethnic groups.
- Texts should provide contextual support, such as diagrams and illustrations that are interesting, closely complement, and support the text, or glossaries that define unfamiliar terms.
- Texts should, as much as possible, meet the proficiency demands of learners in terms of vocabulary, length, grammatical complexity, and background information required. Several leveling systems are in use for determining the demands of a text (e.g., Fountas & Pinnell, 1996, 2001). One system (Freeman et al., 2010) has been developed with the needs of English language learners in mind.
- Early texts should offer language authenticity—natural, predictable language based on oral language familiar to students, often with elements of rhyme, rhythm, and repetition that make texts memorable.
- Text content and illustrations should be appropriate for the age level, background, knowledge, and cultures of learners.
- Texts such as powerful stories, memorable language, purposeful content, and fine art should provide intellectual, aesthetic, and emotional satisfaction (Cloud et al., 2009).

Useful resources for finding appropriate books for Kindergarten to eighth grade learners include the following review journals: *Book Links, Horn Book Guide to Children's and Young Adults' Books,* and *Interracial Books for Children Bulletin,* as well as *Notable Books for a Global Society* (www.clrsig.org/).

SPECIAL CONSIDERATIONS FOR CHOOSING TEXTS AT THE EMERGENT/EARLY LITERACY LEVEL   In addition to the considerations for all EL students, the following aspects refer specifically to learners at the emergent/early literacy level.

- Select texts that incorporate features that make language memorable, such as rhyme, rhythm, and repetition. This type of text is particularly important for younger learners and individuals who have not learned to read in another language. *The Grouchy Ladybug*, by Eric Carle (1996), uses a patterned, repetitive story that introduces values about getting along, as well as concepts of size and telling time.
- Find books in which illustrations closely parallel the text to support comprehension. Elisha Cooper's *Beach* (2006) uses quiet illustrations that carefully parallel the story of a family's day at the beach. Graphic novels, like *Zebrafish* (Reynolds, 2010) or *The Complete Persepolis* (Satrapi, 2007), or books with graphic elements like *Doodlebug* (Young, 2010) are powerful with English learners, because the graphic elements are equally comprehensible to everyone.
- Ensure that themes of texts are comprehensible across cultures, or provide background to understand them. *Everybody Cooks Rice* (Dooley, 1991) illustrates how cultures are both alike and similar—how one food can be shared among many cultures, but prepared and eaten differently—and allows learners from a number of different cultures to see characters like themselves in a book.
- When grade-level texts are too difficult or too long for English learners, provide scaffolding in a variety of ways, including: reading the text aloud to learners; providing "walk through" introductions to texts; engaging in shared reading, shared reading with audio texts, and guided reading; having learners read along silently as you read and then read the next word aloud when you pause; and requiring independent reading of selected sections of a text. These scaffolding strategies are described in more detail in the following section.

Choosing Texts at Early Fluency/Fluency Levels

- For learners at the early fluency levels, texts should be well written and of high interest. Whenever feasible, provide learners with opportunities to select texts.
- Texts should generally have gradually increasing complexity and length. Many schools are "leveling" books using designated leveling criteria, such as that developed by Fountas and

Pinnell (1996) or Freeman et al. (2010). Levels enable teachers to select books at students' instructional levels when students know about 90 percent of the words. Students can select books at their independent reading level when they know about 95 percent of the words. Keep in mind that the percentages developed for instructional and independent reading levels have been established for English-proficient students, and that English learners would be expected to be challenged by many new words in reading. Also keep in mind that students' high interest and motivation can help them conquer very challenging texts, so children should be encouraged to range beyond their expected levels on occasion.

- Linguistically and culturally diverse learners and their peers should also have opportunities to read books in which they can see people like themselves, people from cultures with which they are familiar, and characters with whom they can identify. *Samir and Yonatan* (Carmi, 2002), for example, with characters from Israel and Palestine who room together in a hospital, provides middle school readers with insight on these cultures and on the experience of being an outsider.
- Learners at these levels can be encouraged to expand their reading to a wide range of fiction and nonfiction genres and should be provided with time for choice reading in school.
- To make challenging grade-level texts more comprehensible, use a variety of strategies, including reading aloud, shared reading, reciprocal reading, guided reading; and reading selections from texts, modified texts, alternate texts, translated summaries, and audio or multimedia support (McCloskey & Thrush, 2005). Scaffolding strategies are described in greater detail in the next section.

5. Choral Reading
Levels: All
Grades: Primary, Intermediate

In **choral reading,** students have their own copies of a text, and they all read together. Often the teacher or a student stands in front of the class to lead the oral reading. When reading dialogues, plays, or stories with dialogue, different groups often read different parts of the text. Assessment suggestion: After students are comfortable with a text, have a student lead the choral reading and walk around the room, standing behind individuals as they read. Note their progress on self-stick notes attached to individual folders or on a class checklist.

6. Feature Analysis
Levels: All
Grades: All

Learners use a grid to explore how terms and concepts are related to one another and to make distinctions between them—performing a **feature analysis**. The first column lists terms; the first row lists categories. Terms receive a plus sign ("+") if they fit in that category, and a minus sign ("−") if they do not. (See Tables 8.6 and 8.7.)

TABLE 8.6 Semantic Feature Analysis Category: Types of Books We Read

	Early/Emerging to Primary				
	Features				
Terms	**Nonfiction: Biography**	**Historical Fiction**	**Fantasy**	**Reader Liked It**	**Takes Place in the U.S.**
Roberto's book: *Tutankhamen's Gift*	−	+	−	+	−
Mikhail's book: *Abiyoyo*	−	−	+	+	−
Niki's book: *Story Painter*	+	−	−	+	+
Raga's Book: *The Librarian of Basra*	+	−	−	+	−

TABLE 8.7 Semantic Feature Analysis Category: Quadralaterals

| | Early Fluency/Fluency to Intermediate + | | | | |
| | Features | | | | |
Terms	Only Two Parallel Sides	Two Sets of Parallel Sides	All Sides Are Congruent	Two Sets of Congruent Sides	All Angles Are Congruent
Square	–	+	+	–	+
Rectangle	–	+	–	+	–
Parallelogram	–	+	+	–	–
Rhombus	–	+	+	–	–
Trapezoid	+	–	–	*	–

7. **Graphic Organizers**
   Levels: All
   Grades: All

Use pictures or designs with graphics to outline text and to illustrate principles within a text. The storyboard, story map, character web, time lines, Venn diagram, ranking ladder, and many other **graphic organizers** can be used effectively (see Figure 8.8). After demonstrating and teaching graphic organizers, encourage students to develop their own to learn from what they have read and to prepare to write.

During reading, use graphic organizers aligned to the structure of the text to assist learners in taking notes and clarifying their comprehension. For example, when reading about a central concept or character, use a semantic map as students search the text for identifying attributes. When reading a text organized chronologically, use time lines or flow charts for note-taking about

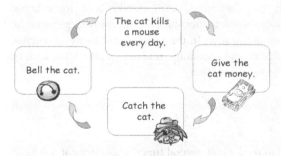

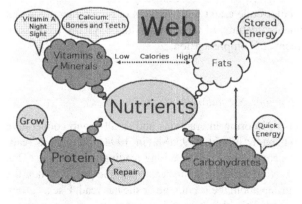

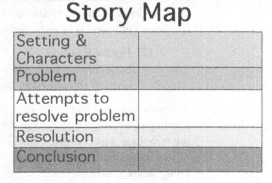

FIGURE 8.8 Sample Graphic Organizers

important events and/or stages. For cause-and-effect texts, use graphics that clearly identify the cause or causes and the resulting effect(s). Finally, comparison-and-contrast text organizations can be made more comprehensible with a Venn diagram or double bubble comparison graphic. (See Chapter 5, Figure 5.1, for examples of these graphic organizers.) These graphics can be useful for an oral retelling of the text or as a support for a written summary.

8. Guided Reading
Levels: All
Grades: Primary and Intermediate; Middle school and secondary for early reading.

For **guided reading** (Fountas & Pinnell, 1996), work with small groups with similar reading processes. Books are carefully, progressively leveled to introduce new vocabulary, phonics elements, features of print, and sophistication and length of content. Select and introduce new books and support children reading the whole text to themselves, making teaching points during and after the reading, based on close observation of students' reading performance.

9. Home-School Connections
Levels: All
Grades: All

Teachers and schools work to make connections among the school, classroom, and family to help families become engaged in the learning process and to support learners. For ELL families who may have had very different experiences of school, it is important to make efforts toward home-school connections culturally relevant. One example of a culturally and linguistically relevant activity is *At-Home Reading*. After children have mastered texts at school, send the texts home in an envelope with a chart for parents to initial. Students read the books aloud to family members in English, and then summarize the books in the home language. Parents initial the chart and return the book to school. This practice has been shown to have a powerful effect on the development of reading fluency and comprehension, as well as on home-school relations (Tizard, Schofield, & Hewison, 1982).

10. Instructional Conversations
Levels: All
Grades: All

Through a challenging but nonthreatening process called **instructional conversations**, students learn to discuss readings at a high level (Tharp & Gallimore, 1988). Provide background knowledge, teach skills or concepts when necessary, and promote students' use of text, pictures, and reasoning to support arguments or positions about text. In the process, ask many open-ended questions, respond to student insights and ideas, and encourage students to take turns with one another—as you act as a senior participant in the discussion.

11. Intensive Reading
Levels: Early Fluency/Fluency
Grades: Middle school, Secondary

In **intensive reading**, students are directed to read a text several times, each time for a different purpose, using duplicated copies of texts they can write on (McCloskey & Stack, 1996). By asking students to underline, annotate, and color-code a text with markers or highlighters, you can draw students' attention to literary elements, features of the sound/symbol system, patterns of language, conventions of print, and elements of comprehension.

12. Jigsaw Reading
Levels: Early Fluency/Fluency
Grades: Intermediate, Middle school, Secondary

Research evidence shows positive effects of tutoring interactions and small-group cooperative learning tasks (Kagan, 1994; Samway, Whang, & Pippitt, 1995; Slavin, 1994). The **jigsaw** reading technique was first researched by Aronson (1978). Divide a long reading into sections. One or two individuals in a group read each section and prepare to teach it to the group. When the group meets, each individual teaches the group about the section he or she has read. Use a "group quiz" or the "numbered heads together" cooperative learning strategy to assure group responsibility for the content and to assess comprehension.

13. Language Experience
Levels: Emergent/Early literacy
Grades: Primary, Intermediate, Secondary

Ashton-Warner (2002) first used the **language experience approach** with Maori children in New Zealand, and it has been the subject of considerable subsequent research. After a discussion of a shared or recalled experience, students dictate a narrative as you write it on a chart, projected computer screen, or transparency. Revise and edit the text together with students. Use opportunities to teach vocabulary text structures, language structures, and conventions of print. Later, students can use copies of the text as reading texts and as the basis for a series of follow-up activities, including practice with vocabulary, phonics, language structures, comprehension, independent reading, and creative expression.

14. Picture Walk
Levels: Emergent/Early literacy
Grades: Primary, Intermediate, All who are developing literacy

A procedure frequently used in guided reading, a **picture walk** (Fountas & Pinnell, 1996) helps to build learners' interest in a story and set up expectations about what they will enjoy. In addition, a picture walk helps learners focus on using visual cues as they read. This is a valuable skill for English learners who may find context information in picture cues that will help them comprehend the story. To lead a picture walk, "read" through the pages of the story without reading the words. As you look at the pictures, point out, and have students point out, key characters, aspects of the setting, and events, and have them ask questions and make guesses about them. A picture walk will activate ELLs' prior learning, help learners develop familiarity with the story, enable teachers to introduce and discuss new vocabulary, and make teachers aware of background information that language learners may need to know to understand the story.

A picture walk through *Mrs. Wishy-Washy* (Cowley, 1999) might look like this:

- We're going to read *Mrs. Wishy-Washy.* Here's the title, *Mrs. Wishy-Washy*, and here's the author's name. It's Joy Cowley.
- Let's look at the front cover. What do you think this story will be about? Who do you think will be in the story?
- Do you know what this is? (A pig.) What do you know about pigs? What is this pig doing? Why? Who else do you see?
- Let's turn the page. Look, there are the same characters again. Who are they?
- Now what is happening? What do you think will happen next?
- We're almost at the end of *Mrs. Wishy-Washy.* How do you think it will end?
- Now, what do you want to find out when we read the story?
- I wonder what Mrs. Wishy-Washy will say to all the animals?

15. Point of View
Levels: All
Grades: All

For **point of view**, students take on the role of characters in a fiction or nonfiction text, and work to understand the motivation behind the actions of the characters (McCloskey & Stack, 2003). Divide the students into groups of three or four. Assign each group a character from the reading. Ask the group to think of at least three questions they could ask that character. Then one member from each group comes to the front of the room and takes on the role of the character. Group members ask the "character" their questions. Other groups may also ask questions of that character. The character answers the questions based on the reading and his or her background knowledge.

16. Question-Answer-Relationships (QAR)
Levels: Early Fluency/Fluency
Grades: Intermediate, Middle school, Secondary

With **question-answer-relationships (QAR)** (Raphael, 1982), students learn to ask different types of questions and to locate answers in a text. First, model, teach, and practice the four levels of questions of QAR. (These questions are based on *Story Painter: The Life of Jacob Lawrence*, by John Duggleby and Jacob Lawrence [1998]):

- *Right there questions.* For these questions, the answer is stated in the text—The question asks for facts from the text (e.g., "Where was Jacob Lawrence born?").
- *Think and search questions.* For these questions, students must look for the answer in more than one part of the text. The question asks the reader to bring together and think about information from different parts of the text (e.g., "In what different places did Jacob Lawrence live while he was growing up? How did moving around affect him?").
- *Author and you questions.* For these questions, the answer is a combination of information from what the reader knows and what the author has written. The question asks for information from both the reader and the text (e.g., "What outside influences helped Jacob Lawrence to develop his talent? What did Jacob Lawrence do himself? Which do you think the author sees as most important? Which do *you* think is most important?").
- *On your own questions.* For these questions, the answer comes from the reader's knowledge and experience. The question asks for an opinion from the reader (e.g., "What talent would you like to develop? How might you do that?").

Prepare a list of questions in the four areas for the students to answer based on a selection from the text. In small groups of 3 to 4, have students read the selection from the text and answer the questions. They should indicate the QAR category for each question and justify their decisions. Next, the students read another selection from the text and write their own QAR questions. Groups exchange their questions with other groups, answer them, and categorize them into QAR levels. Eventually, learners develop their own questions in the four categories and use them to discuss the readings.

17. Reading Aloud to ELLs
Levels: All
Grades: All

Reading aloud provides motivation, access, background information, and vocabulary development, and it builds comprehension skills (Trelease, 2006). After an oral discussion to develop the schema (the organizational plan or structure of the text) and explain background information needed to understand a text, introduce the book by reading it aloud to students. If you are reading a picture book or other shorter text, you may choose to read through the text the first time for flow. Then stop to ask and answer questions when needed during the second and subsequent repetitions.

Reading Aloud Can Provide Learners with Access to a Text That Is Slightly Above Their Instructional Reading Level

Ask students which words they do not understand and provide pictures, translations, or definitions as needed. If you are reading a chapter book, such as *Where the Moon Meets the Mountain* (Lin, 2011), you might have learners summarize the previous day's chapter before beginning the next one. Reading aloud is a good way to make students familiar with a text to prepare them for other kinds of reading or to provide access to a text that is slightly above their instructional level. Reading aloud a nonfiction book like *Me... Jane* (The life of Jane Goodall) (McDonnell, 2011) is an excellent way to introduce learners to a new genre—biography. Reading aloud also provides a good model for pronunciation, phrasing, and expression. Audiotapes provide a different, though related, type of reading support for ELLs, and can help them with independent reading. Repeated reading with audio support has been shown to help ELLs improve their reading.

18. Reciprocal Teaching
Levels: Early Fluency/Fluency
Grades: Intermediate, Middle School, Secondary

Palinscar (1986) found that when **reciprocal teaching** was used with learners for just 15 to 20 days, assessments showed that students' reading comprehension increased from 30 percent to 80 percent. Follow-up research on the strategy (reported in Oczkus, 2003) has shown it to be effective in many situations. Reciprocal teaching (Palinscar & Brown, 1984) helps students to focus intently on what they are reading by using four key strategies. By consciously asking questions and summarizing content, they learn to understand and remember what is read. English language learners must listen to one another's questions and comments, and teach each other the material. In preparation for reciprocal teaching, instruct students about strategies of *summarizing, clarifying, question-generating,* and *predicting.* Model the "teacher role." Then the student "teacher" uses these strategies in questioning and leading the group discussion as readers participate in a dialogue about the text. Each person takes a turn as "teacher," reading a short passage and asking questions about it to the group. Turns may rotate after a paragraph or a longer section.

19. Shared Reading
Levels: Emergent/Early Literacy
Grades: All

For **shared reading**, use engaging, enlarged texts (such as big books, charts, or projected texts) that all learners can easily see to involve learners in reading together as you use a pointer to direct students to look at the text being read. A typical shared reading lesson might look like this: (a) With students, "warm up" by rereading together texts that students have studied previously and are comfortable with. (b) Lead prereading activities, including building anticipation for the book; discussing the parts of the book, author, and title; reviewing reading skills and strategies, and previewing the pages and making predictions about the text. (c) Do multiple readings of the text, with you reading the text aloud the first time and having learners chime in on more and more of the reading with successive repetitions. Occasionally, or as the need arises, stop to discuss needed reading strategies, comprehension skills, elements of phonics, or conventions of print. (d) Have the class participate in a variety of activities to follow up on the group reading, such as retelling (with your help and then by themselves) and discussion of the story; mini-lessons on certain reading strategies (e.g., letter-sound relationships, text features, or the writer's craft). (e) Engage students in a variety of group or individual extension activities, including small-group reading and instruction; listening to the story on audiotape with follow-up activities; creative expression in art, drama, or music; or writing activities using patterns from the text to create new variations.

In **shared-to-guided reading**, designed for ELLs, first "walk" learners through the text, using picture cues to develop vocabulary. Then set the scene, read and reread the text aloud, and help students recall and discuss the content. Students read the book independently or with partners and follow up on reading with recall, skill development, and expressive responses to the literature.

20. Think-Aloud
Levels: All
Grades: All

In the **think-aloud strategy**, you model the internal thinking involved in reading and allow students to observe learning strategies in action. First, determine the learning strategy to be taught and the content you will use; for example, sequencing with a work of fiction, such as *Momotaro: The Peach Boy* (Shute, 1986) at the emergent/early literacy level, or historical fiction, such as

Sacajawea (Bruchac, 2002). Determine what you want students to know about the strategy; for example, how to place events along a time line. Plan an assessment to determine if students are successful with the strategy, such as a "numbered heads" activity in which learners construct a time line for a chapter of the book. Plan your think-aloud carefully—think about the strategy to be taught, the central concept and key themes of the text, and your own experiences related to the themes. Put notes in the text where you might stop to think aloud.

Introduce the lesson by explaining that in a think-aloud, someone says out loud what they are thinking about how to go about learning. Demonstrate the think-aloud as you read the text. Stop and look at the ceiling or otherwise show when you're stopping to think as you read. For sequencing, use key words such as "Now, what happened first? Second? Third? What was the final event? I am using this sequencing strategy because ...." (Note: this may take many repetitions before the students understand it thoroughly.) When students understand the strategy you are using, ask them to practice it using a short section of the reading.

ISSUES IN LITERACY DEVELOPMENT WITH OLDER ENGLISH LEARNERS

A recent case study, "Why Mei Still Cannot Read and What Can Be Done" (Li & Zhang, 2004) explores the factors involved in a Chinese student's failure to develop proficiency in reading and writing in a U.S. public school. Mei, a fourteen-year-old sixth grader, has failed to learn to read despite spending two years in elementary school with a pullout ESL program four times a week. The authors reveal that much of Mei's problem came from the lack of communication and collaboration among Mei's classroom teachers, her ESL teacher, and her parents. They conclude that teachers—preservice classroom teachers, inservice classroom teachers, and English language development teachers—must learn to work with one another as well as with support staff, administration, and parents to plan, implement, and supervise an adequate program for each ELL student, taking into account all of the variables: educational background, native language ability, age of arrival, parents' education and occupations, and personal experiences.

Older learners of English have special issues in developing English reading skills that must be taken into account in all the school situations that require reading (de Jong & Harper, 2004). First of all, these learners are not all alike—they have remarkable differences in the background and personal characteristics they bring to your class. Although each student is unique, we will generalize our descriptions into three groups for clarity (Freeman, Freeman, & Mercuri, 2003). One group includes recent arrivals with adequate formal schooling in their first language. They have academic and literacy skills, and need to transfer these skills to English, while continuing to develop and maintain their content knowledge. A second group includes recent arrivals who, for

Older Learners of English May Have Special Issues in Developing English Reading Skills

various reasons (living in rural areas, poverty, war, membership in language minority, etc.), have had limited or interrupted formal schooling. These students often do not have a strong academic background or reading skills in their home language and, of course, need to develop these in English along with conversational skills. These students are often referred to as Students with Interrupted Formal Education (SIFE). A third group, sometimes referred to as "Generation 1.5" learners, includes long-term English learners whose schooling has all or nearly all taken place in the U.S., but who have never developed strong literacy either in their first language or in English; in addition, although these individuals may have good conversational skills in two languages, they do not have strong academic skills in either (Roberge, 2002; Robertson & Lafond, 2008).

So, learners of English may differ on their:

- Level of schooling in any language.
- Level of literacy in their home language or English (or in additional languages—some learners, such as indigenous Guatemalans, may speak different languages at home from those spoken in their schools in Guatemala).
- Level of cultural adaptation—many older students' characteristics, experiences, and educational needs lie somewhere between first-generation adult immigrants and U.S.-born second-generation children of immigrants.
- Motivation and interest in developing English literacy.

There are several additional issues that present special challenges to developing literacy with older learners. First, there is much more language for them to learn—the content is much more complex for a sixth grader or tenth grader than for a first or second grader: The texts are much longer and the language is more advanced. Second, often secondary schools are ill equipped to assist nonliterate students. They have fewer resources and a shorter amount of time in which to teach both literacy and content knowledge. Third, students tend to acquire the social language needed to communicate with peers, teachers, and the greater community in a few years (Cummins, 1994; Hakuta, Butler, & Witt, 2000; Thomas & Collier, 1997; Hakuta, Butler, & Witt, 2000), but they take a much longer time to perform academically like their English-proficient peers. Teachers often misinterpret learners' oral conversational fluency and expect that students should be performing like grade-level native-speaking peers within this time frame; however, research shows that the average length of time for learners to perform like native speakers is five to seven years. Fourth, assessments used at these grade levels are frequently inappropriate because so much of content assessment is confounded with language assessment, and it is therefore difficult for these learners to show what they know about the content on such assessments. Recent development of specific standardized assessments for English learners may prove helpful in this area, but nevertheless have the same limitations as standardized tests. Fifth, researchers have found that developing literacy in the first language is often a more efficient route to second-language literacy, but few programs for older learners provide such opportunities, so students must deal with developing initial literacy in a language they do not know very well. Finally, home environment has an important impact on the learning of these students. Adolescent ELLs are more likely than English speakers to live in families that fall below the poverty line; in addition, some of these students are undocumented (Short & Fitzsimmons, 2007). Both of these factors may affect literacy development.

What Are Our Recommendations for Developing Literacy with These Older Learners?

While applying the principles and strategies we have outlined in this chapter, pay particular attention to these recommendations:

1. ***Find out who your students are.*** Recognize their unique needs and differences. Interview students, family members, and other relatives or community members to find out about students' histories, their ethnic groups, their educational backgrounds, and the languages they know and use. Students often show up with a translator on their first days—take advantage of this opportunity to learn whatever you can. Avoid making assumptions, for example, that a student who arrives from Kenya speaks Kiswahili. There are many indigenous languages in Kenya; in addition, there are refugee centers in Kenya where families may have arrived from other countries, e.g., Somalia, Ethiopia, or the Sudan. Or a student from Latin America may speak an indigenous language, and not Spanish. There are many such situations parallel to these throughout the world.

2. ***Look for and work with your learners' strengths.*** Although older learners may lack literacy, they bring a great deal to your classroom. Do not make the mistake of considering a student to be a "tabula rasa." As you learn about your students, discover their strengths. What literacy, preliteracy, or literacy awareness do they have in any language? What languages do they know, and how well do they know them? What experiences have they had with English? What writing system/s do they know? Many of these strengths are avenues for transfer of learning to their new language. What are their habits? What can you learn about their cultures? What are their interests? What needs do they have for English literacy in their daily lives as well as their school lives? This is all information you can capitalize on in planning your instruction to engage and motivate these learners. Background knowledge—what students have learned from prior schooling or from personal experience—can then be built upon and related to current instruction. Short and Fitzsimmons (2007) suggest explicitly discussing how a student's background knowledge relates to the topic at hand. For example, while studying the Civil War, relate that conflict to a military conflict in the native country and use video clips, demonstrations, and field experiences to make the connection explicit.

3. ***Assess your learners carefully and continuously.*** Expect the unexpected. Students at this age, particularly those with strong educational backgrounds, can progress very quickly and should not be held back by the need to follow a lockstep curriculum. On the other hand, students who are developing initial literacy may take more time and will be likely to need specialized reading instruction from an instructor who understands both reading development and English language development. The ongoing informal assessment techniques presented in Chapter 11, in addition to the formal English language assessments expected by your school, will help you to discern what your learners know and can do, what you should be teaching them, and how quickly they can progress. Be aware, as well, that there will be students with special needs among your English learner population. RTI can be very helpful in developing an appropriate learning path at any stage of referral. If a student's progress is clearly not typical, do not wait long to make a referral for further assessment. Watch learners carefully and keep track of your observations. Ask parents if learners exhibit developmental differences in the home. English learners who are gifted or who have certain learning issues may need special education assessment and services. Minimally, specialists can help you develop pre-referral strategies to serve the child appropriately and to continue assessing the child to determine special needs. Be sure to talk to parents or guardians as well about how learners perform in their first language and in interactions at home. These actions can provide very helpful information when determining whether further evaluation is needed.

4. ***Teach the sounds and symbols of language directly, but contextually.*** Use pocket charts and word walls with key words and important content words to display and discuss sound and spelling patterns. Beginners can study sophisticated alphabet books (e.g., *The Graphic Alphabet* [Pelletier, 1996]; *The Museum Alphabet* [Metropolitan Museum, 2002]; *Alphabet City* [Johnson, 1995]; or *Discovering Nature's Alphabet* [Castella & Boyl, 2006]), and then create their own alphabet books about topics of their own choosing. Ideally, these topics will be related to content learning objectives. Spelling tasks are also an excellent way for older learners to develop the sound/writing system for English. Group words that share a sound/spelling pattern for study each week and have learners analyze and study these words together and quiz one another periodically. Use word walls so these learners can sort and analyze content words they are learning by sounds and spelling patterns.

5. ***Provide age-appropriate literature and content materials with a suitable amount of challenge.*** Although finding appropriate materials for older students has been very difficult in the past, many more materials are available that support older learners who are developing literacy, both through specialized literacy programs and through fiction and nonfiction library materials. These often correlate to grade-appropriate content-area concepts so that English learners can focus on the same standards as their English-proficient peers, but with reading materials at an appropriate level. Look for materials that will interest learners; that are related to what their content classes are studying; that they can access, given their educational backgrounds; and that are at an appropriate reading level. Because English learners are just developing their English vocabulary, you may find that you will use books that are slightly more difficult for them than ones where they know 90 or 95 percent of the words. They may require more scaffolding support in the form of such strategies as graphic organizers, pictures, audio recordings, or book talks.

- *Use picture books.* Do not make the mistake of avoiding picture books because they are not generally used by older learners. If carefully chosen to be appropriate to learning needs and age level, fiction and nonfiction picture books can be context-rich sources for learning. And in our experience, older learners are delighted to find interesting, important books that they can read and understand. *Beyond Words*, by Benedict & Carlisle (1992) outlines many ways to use picture books with older readers and writers.

- *Access readings online.* You can locate content-rich readings accompanied by graphics, pictures, and glosses that help to increase comprehensibility (e.g., for storybooks, see http://www.wegivebooks.org/; for science, see some of the many resources of the National Science Foundation: http://www.nsf.gov/news/classroom/education.jsp).

- *Use online text-to-speech software.* Find software with read-aloud applications that enable learners to listen to and read text simultaneously (e.g., Natural Reader: http://www.naturalreaders.com/, iSpeech: www.ispeech.org/, ReadPlease: www.readplease.com/, eSpeak: http://espeak.sourceforge.net/, or Dspeech: http://dspeech.en.softonic.com).

- *Seek out materials in which learners can see themselves;* look for accessible literature from and about your students' cultures. Hadaway and McKenna (2007) have written a rich resource for using global literature.

- *Look for rich and engaging, but shorter texts for instruction.* New learners of English read slowly, and they have twice as much to learn as their proficient peers—content AND language. Provide learners with instructional texts that include the content and academic vocabulary they must learn, but do not overwhelm them with volume. Campbell (2007) provides helpful suggestions for shorter readings, along with strategies to teach them in the classroom.

- *Analyze texts carefully for accessibility* and, if you choose to use them, to determine important words and background information to preteach before asking learners to read them independently.

- *Provide a wide range and large quantity of reading materials and time* for learners to engage in extensive choice reading, and encourage learners to interact with and about the materials they choose. Research indicates that this engagement with materials that interest learners, that they choose, is a powerful contributor to language development (Krashen, 2004).

6. ***Provide encouragement and design instruction for success.*** Affect is important to helping students with interrupted education. This is the age at which English learners who are developing literacy may become discouraged with school and either stop trying or drop out, or both. If you scaffold tasks at which your learners can succeed, and through which they see themselves learning, and you offer students encouragement as they attempt more and more challenging learning opportunities, they will see the possibilities for learning and not be discouraged by their temporary limitations. They will have the hope and support they need to become successful.

- Incorporate cooperative learning tasks into literacy instruction and ensure that 100 percent of your students are interacting with the new language in all skill areas: listening, speaking, reading, and writing. Too many secondary students sit silently in classrooms with little opportunity to speak or be spoken to by teachers or fellow students (Harklau, 1994). Peer acceptance is high in importance for students in grades 9 to 12. By promoting interaction among learners, teachers can increase motivation for student learning.

- Explicitly instruct students in reading comprehension skills and strategies that can be generalized to other applications and academic reading situations (Slavin, Madden, Chambers, & Haxby, 2008; Tierney & Readence, 2004). Explicit instruction is different from skill practice. The components of comprehension skill instruction include the following (Calderón, 2007):

  1. Students are told the relevance or purpose of the strategy.
  2. The teacher defines the strategy, models its use, explains where it can be used, and gives an illustration of what it is not (for example, showing how *inferring* is different from *guessing*).
  3. Students are led in guided practice of the strategy, and are given feedback on their performance.
  4. Students are given time to try out the strategy independently and urged to monitor their performance.
  5. The teacher engages in a gradual release of responsibility model as students increasingly assume more responsibility for strategy use.

Bae Meh, Robika, and Foziya Are Students of the Global Village Project in Decatur, Georgia (a school creating a pilot for refugee teens with interrupted educations from many refugee camps worldwide)

6. Students are routinely given opportunities to apply strategy use in independent learning tasks.

- Work to develop meaningful, rigorous learning tasks that provide the content learners need and are comprehensible to each learner in the group. Kinsella (2008) has developed rich resources for developing the academic discourse skills of English learners. For example, she recommends explicitly teaching and practicing strategies and language for students to actively participate in classroom discussions such as the language in Table 8.8 below. English Language Development (ELD) standards, such as WIDA's (2012) standards, (currently used in 27 states), or your own institution's or region's standards, are an essential source of guidance in developing learning paths for older learners developing literacy (www.wida.us). The Common Core Standards, adopted by most states in the United States, are also useful for literacy development. High school teachers may find examples of early literacy development lessons in the Common Core Curriculum Maps Project located at http://commoncore.org/maps/index.php. Here, specific student objectives relating to the standards of English Language Arts are integrated into units of study to serve as exemplars for standards use.

7. *Make learning purposeful and meaningful and give learners ownership.*   Garcia (1999) found that successful teachers focused on topics and concepts that have meaning and relevance for students, and organized their instruction around themes. Researchers have found

TABLE 8.8 Explicit Language for Participating in Classroom Discussions (Kinsella, 2008)

Expressing an Opinion	Predicting
I think/believe that . . .	I predict/imagine that . . .
In my opinion . . .	Based on . . ., I infer that . . .
Based on my experience, I think . . .	I hypothesize that . . .
Asking for Clarification	**Paraphrasing**
Excuse me, what do you mean?	So you are saying that . . .
Would you please explain that again?	In other words, you think . . .
I have a question about that.	What I hear you saying is . . .

that theme study is important for helping older English learners develop language and content together (Echevarria & Short, 2010; Enright & McCloskey, 1988). Through theme study, students build confidence and competence by becoming "experts" in a particular area. They can integrate information and vocabulary across content areas. Teachers are able to recycle vocabulary, reading skills, and concepts as they focus on answering theme questions that are important to learners. Students are able to make choices and develop learning of concepts and skills around learning that is important to them.

8. *Make learning culturally relevant.* Learn both with and from your students about their home cultures. Culture is deeply embedded in our personalities and psyches—it defines who we are. By valuing the cultures of your students and making these cultures part of what you learn in school, you are affirming your students as people and you are building their senses of self-worth. By providing background information and cultural bridges learners may need to understand the material you teach in class, you help them to learn that they will be able to bridge two cultures successfully and keep what is valuable in both.

ASSESSING ELL LITERACY DEVELOPMENT

Our motto for assessment is, "assess what you teach, the way you teach it." By this, we mean that your teaching and your assessment should be part of the same process, and should work together to promote your students' learning, to inform your teaching, and to monitor progress for your parents and your school. To do this, you will use a variety of types of assessment. We address assessment in depth in Chapter 11, but briefly explain here the types of literacy assessment:

1. *Standardized reading achievement or performance-based assessments.*
2. *English language proficiency tests:* standardized assessments designed specifically for ELLs. (These include, for example, the CELDT in California, ACCESS in a consortium of 16 U.S. states, TELPAS in Texas, and a variety of "off the shelf" assessments determined by individual districts in Florida.)
3. *Holistic measures* of literacy development.
4. Widely used *assessments of specific literacy skills.*
5. *Assessments from a reading ELD program.*
6. *Teacher-developed assessments* to be used as part of the teaching process.

Standardized Reading Achievement Tests

Many schools are required to use standardized assessments with ELLs. Teachers who work with ELLs should be aware of important issues regarding the use of these tests with ELLs. First, it is very difficult to separate whether these instruments are actually assessing literacy development or language development because these are often confounded. Second, results may be influenced by issues of cultural background or previous experiences of learners, which may result in instruments not accurately assessing skills. Third, the process of taking an inappropriate assessment may not be harmless—students are often very frustrated and upset when asked to perform beyond their capabilities. Know that many districts and states provide accommodations for ELLs to offer a more level playing ground when students are taking these assessments. And know that the scores students receive on these tests may not tell you much about their learning or your teaching.

English Language Proficiency Tests

As a result of NCLB (2002), states are required to develop or adopt assessments of English language proficiency that can be used to assess learners' and schools' progress toward meeting standards. A consortium of 27 states (the WIDA consortium) uses the W-APT (Wida ACCESS Placement Test) and the ACCESS test (Assessing Comprehension and Communication in English State-to-State for English Language Learners). This test is based on the WIDA/TESOL Standards and assesses listening, speaking, reading, and writing of English learners at appropriate grade levels. Other states have their own assessment programs. For example, ELLs in California take the California English Language Development Test (CELDT); in Texas, they take the Texas English Language Proficiency Assessment System (TELPAS); in New York, the New York State English as a Second Language Achievement Test; and in Florida, learners take the Comprehensive English Language Learning Assessment (CELLA), a four-skill language proficiency assessment developed under contract by Educational Testing Service (ETS). Most of these assessments include reading sub-scores to show ELL reading proficiency. These tests are usually administered upon a learner's initial entrance into a school district for placement, and then administered annually to show progress. Because they are given so infrequently, and because of the time lag in scoring, they are not as useful for informing teaching as they are for measuring school progress over the long term.

Holistic Measures of Reading Development

Many teachers have found holistic measures of reading, which often provide sub-scores of specific skills, to be very useful in understanding how readers are developing. They can be time-consuming, as they are often individually administered, but provide very rich information about how learners' reading is developing. Remember that the scoring methods for any of these may not be developed with ELLs in mind, and that instructions may state that a pronunciation error, for example, should be scored as a reading error. You may have to make accommodations in interpreting results for ELLs. Three types of holistic measures are:

- *Informal reading inventories.* Several **informal reading inventories** are used to get a close look at students' reading. Teachers with training in their use can get a picture of learners' development, and often a grade-level equivalent score that is comparable across schools and programs. These tools, often administered individually, use progressively more difficult passages. Learners read each passage as teachers score their oral reading; then teachers ask a series of questions, or ask for a summary or retelling to assess comprehension.
- *Miscue analysis.* In **miscue analysis**, developed by Kenneth Goodman (Goodman, Watson, & Burke, 2005), learners read set passages and teachers score various aspects of student reading, trying to see how the reader approaches the task. The instrument looks, for example, at self-corrections learners make and at errors that indicate the reader's thinking. Errors might indicate whether learners are attending to syntactic, semantic, or phonemic cues (or some combination) in solving new words.
- *Running record.* The **running record assessment**, developed by Marie Clay (2000), has been used in Reading Recovery and other programs. Teachers can use a variety of texts at appropriate levels for learners and use a coding system to record exactly what learners read, including repetitions, corrections, mispronunciations, and so on. Teachers also ask for a retelling to assess comprehension. The resulting data are then analyzed to determine a number of sub-scores in learners' reading.

Reading Skills Tests

A number of tools have been developed to look at specific skills of reading, for example, phonemic awareness, phonics, vocabulary, fluency, and comprehension. All of these can be useful, but all can also have limitations when working with English learners. The Dynamic Indicators of Basic Early Literacy Skills (DIBELS) (http://dibels.uoregon .edu) for example, is widely used to measure primary learners' development of early skills in phonological awareness, alphabetic principle, and fluency with connected text. The tool does not look at how learners' thinking about reading is developing, and uses items such as nonsense words (Nonsense Word Fluency NWF) that are particularly confusing for ELLs. To add to the confusion on this test, a number of the English words and nonsense words used on the Dibels are *real* words in Spanish, so Spanish-speakers can read these words correctly in their own language but be marked wrong on the Dibels.

Other instruments look at reading fluency, and the speedy recognition of letters and words with accuracy of decoding and expressiveness (prosody). Assessments of fluency include tests such as the Oral Fluency Assessment from Scholastic (1999) (http://content.scholastic.com/browse/article.jsp?id=4445) that measures the number of words read correctly per minute (WCPM) rate. Other fluency assessments are holistic, such as the Multidimensional Fluency Scales (Rasinski, 2003). These four scales provide rubrics at four levels to evaluate a learner's expressiveness, phrasing, smoothness, and pace while reading text. Ratings of fluency do not take English language development into account. The evaluations of expressiveness and phrasing are highly dependent upon comprehension of the reading passage. For example, a lack of expression or improper stress, intonation, and phrasing are penalized. All of these elements are dependent upon the reader's comprehension of the vocabulary, grammar, and context of the passage.

Vocabulary development assessments include the Peabody Picture Vocabulary Test-4 (Dunn & Dunn, 2007), a test of receptive vocabulary development that the authors claim can be used to evaluate learning in ELLs. We are aware, when using receptive vocabulary tests, however, that the norms of these tests may be affected by cultural differences among learners, their educational gaps, and their language development.

Publisher-Made Reading Assessments

Reading programs (often used with advanced/exited ELLs) and reading components of ELD programs (which can provide comprehensive reading instruction to beginning/intermediate learners) often include assessment packages that can help teachers with appropriate placement of learners in levels of the program as well as with knowing whether the goals of a unit or chapter have been achieved. We encourage you to look at the quality of learner responses as well as at the final score, because, as with other assessments, language development issues may influence results; and also, as with other assessments, learners may have very good, logical, intelligent reasons for giving answers that are scored as "incorrect."

Teacher-Made Reading Assessments

Teachers can develop tests, quizzes, comprehension checks, dipsticking activities, and rubrics and checklists for assessing learner products. They can also use systems for observing student reading and reading habits. These tools all can be used to apply assessment as part of teaching and are highly useful in making sure that your focus is on what learners actually *learn*. Teaching is not, after all, a matter of covering the content, but of working with learners to uncover knowledge, strategies, and skills.

Student Self-Assessment

Learners also can play an important role in the assessment of their reading. They can keep a record of their extensive reading, listing books and authors they have read, along with brief summaries. (Some classes include brief book reviews by class members on the class blog or web site.) They can fill out a checklist of their reading habits and strategies or complete an inventory about what kinds of materials they enjoy reading. All of this information can be used to motivate good reading and to inform the teaching of reading.

TABLE 8.9 Developing Literacy with ELLS: Focus on Reading – RTI Samplers

Developing Literacy with ELLS: Focus on Reading: RTI Samplers

RTI Tier 1 Sampler:

- Use the Word Wall to outline a sequence of sounds and spelling patterns that will work best with your language learners. Refer to the wall daily as you discuss what you are reading.

- Use learners' names to introduce sounds and symbols of the language for beginners.

- Develop an Anticipation Guide for an important text that learners will read. Guide them through the process of using the guide before and after they read. Use their post-discussion to assess their comprehension of the reading.

- Help learners create and learn to use a reading journal to track the books they read. Have them make recommendations to classmates.

- Develop a classroom library, or section of the school library, where ELLs can find materials suited to their age, interests, cultural backgrounds, and reading proficiency. Promote the use of this library with classroom tasks, such as choosing a book and reading from it with a partner.

- Read aloud a picture book related to a content topic learners are studying, or to their own cultural or immigrant experiences. Have them make a book map of key information in the book.

- Help learners find books they can read that are from or about their home cultures. Encourage learners to compare the book to their own experience and share their ideas with the class. Whenever possible, connect learners' cultures and countries to topics you are studying in social studies, e.g., history, geography, political organization, or culture, and encourage ELLs to share their own knowledge.

- Create oral language dialogues relating to classroom content that can be performed on YouTube. Be sure that the dialogues incorporate the vocabulary and grammatical structures necessary for the content.

- Find song lyrics or a poem of interest to learners, e.g., "Famous," by Naomi Shahib Nye. Introduce it with a background discussion about what it means to be famous and present relevant vocabulary. Read it aloud together every day for a week. Discuss its meaning again. Perform it for a visitor or another class.

TABLE 8.9 *(Continued)*

RTI Tier 2 Sampler

- Demonstrate how to do a feature analysis with current classroom vocabulary in front of the class, using a projector or board. Then assist learners in doing another feature analysis with a partner.

- Use graphic organizers to outline/summarize class readings. Keep a list on the wall of the kinds of graphic organizers learners know about. Ask them to use one of them in preparing a report for the class.

- After an important event (a trip, a natural disaster, a visitor to the class, something in the news), take dictation from learners and create a narrative about the event. Have learners help you expand, clarify, and organize the text. Then use it for reading activities.

- After reading a text, have students think of questions they have for characters in the story. Then use "Point of View" to have learners take the roles of characters in the text while other learners interview them.

- Use a think-aloud to share your thinking processes as you prepare to read a challenging content-area text. Talk about how you skim the text, looking at the pictures and reading the captions. Then read all the bold print headers. Then look at the questions at the end. Finally, read the text and check your comprehension as you read.

- Work individually with students who read at low levels. Learn about their sound and writing systems in order to make comparisons and contrasts.

- Teach small groups of learners how to ask questions about a text: details, clarification, prediction, and summary. Pair learners to do reciprocal reading with an accessible text.

- While learners are reading chorally, listen carefully to a targeted student or two and take notes on reading strengths and needs. Use these to plan individual guided reading sessions.

- Help learners create individual lists of key content words they need to learn. For first grade science, they might be words about force and motion, like *push, pull, faster, force*. For seventh grade math, they might be words about algebraic equations, like *linear equation, non-linear, simplify the expression, input/output*. Have them analyze the words with a feature analysis.

- While other students are reading the text assignment, meet with ELLs and read some portions of the text together. Create an instructional conversation to develop background, teach needed skills of concepts, and help them use text, pictures, and reasoning to discuss their ideas about the text.

- Work individually with students to help them learn to choose from the class or school library books that are interesting to them and that they can read with little assistance. They might like to read along with an audio book.

- With individuals or a small group, use intensive reading to study an important text. Provide copies of the text they can write on, using colored pencils or highlighters, and have learners read the text several times for different purposes. If the text is a story, they might look for the lead and discuss whether it was a good one that caught their interest. If they are learning about characters, they might look for descriptions about a particular character (different group members could choose different characters). If they are studying sentence combining, they might look for sentences with two parts and see how they are joined.

- Using a rich and well-illustrated historical or biographical text, such as *Planting the Trees of Kenya: The Story of Wangari Maathai (Nivola, 2008)*, take a group of ELLs on a picture walk to develop interest in the story, vocabulary to understand it, and expectations about what will occur. Then read the book aloud to the full class and lead a discussion about the *who, what, when, why, where,* and *how* of the story, using a graphic organizer.

- Use a story that the class has dictated and revised and that you have written on chart paper as a text for a shared reading with a small group of ELLs.

- Provide a supplementary reading curriculum that is in addition to the core reading program in general education. The supplementary curriculum should be designed to address the student's specific learning needs. Monitor progress frequently and share with all teachers involved.

- Incorporate intensive instruction into programs for secondary students who are developing literacy. Ensure that the instruction is systematic and explicit with modeling, multiple examples, and feedback. Require that the reading teacher, ESL teacher, and content teachers are sharing goals and objectives so that all learning is integrated.

CONCLUSION

Although this one chapter might not offer a comprehensive preparation for teaching reading to your English learners, it can serve as an introduction to the topic and encourage further study of this important area. The resources listed in Table 8.9 are intended to guide deeper exploration. In the next chapter, we continue the literacy discussion with a focus on writing—and look at how writing can be both the cause and the result of English language development.

Questions for Reflection

1. What do you need to know about the ELLs in your classroom in order to effectively teach them reading? How can you obtain the information you need to know?
2. Reflect on the additional challenges presented by older learners who are developing literacy in English. What suggestions would you make to content-area teachers for scaffolding the reading that students are expected to do in a content class?
3. Review the reading strategies outlined in this chapter. With which ones are you already familiar? With what you know about teaching English learners, how might you change the way you use these strategies? Which strategies would you target for further study? Why?

Activities for Further Learning

1. Summarize the differences between native speakers' literacy development and ELLs' literacy development in one of these areas: alphabetics (phonemic awareness and phonics), vocabulary, fluency, and comprehension. Describe some different instructional techniques that might accommodate the learner differences you discuss. Evaluate the materials used in your school to determine adaptations that would improve instruction for ELLs.
2. Observe and take careful notes on a reading lesson with a group that includes English language learners, focusing on the teacher. What strategies does the teacher use? Do you observe differences in the way the teacher works with ELLs? Does the teacher adapt oral language? Does the teacher introduce vocabulary differently? Does the teacher adapt teaching strategies? Does the teacher encourage learners to use certain reading strategies? Is there evidence of cultural relevance?
3. Observe and keep an anecdotal record (noting any interactions with the teacher and the speech and actions of the learner) on a reading lesson with a group that includes English language learners, focusing on one ELL. Afterwards, analyze your notes. How was the learner successful? What were the learner's challenges? What were the learner's strategies? What would you like to know more about as a result of this activity?
4. Explore the tools available at the Compleat Lexical Tutor web site (http://www.lextutor.ca/). Look at the word lists available. Enter a text that students are expected to read (type the text or cut-and-paste a text file) into the Vocabulary Profiler, the Concordancer, and the Hypertext Builder. Describe how these tools might support you in developing your learners' literacy.
5. Select a target age and language level. Visit your school or community library to look for multiethnic books on appropriate themes for the learners you have selected. Create an annotated bibliography and give your rationale for including each book on the list.

Suggested Reading

Campbell, K. (2007). *Less is more: Teaching literature with short texts, grades 6–12*. Portland, ME: Stenhouse. In addition to great questions and strategies for teaching a variety of short-text genres, Campbell also offers excellent suggestions for texts to use with older students, including short stories, memoirs, graphic novels, poetry, children's literature and picture books, and essays.

Cappellini, M. (2005). *Balancing reading and language learning: A resource for teaching English language learners*. Portland, ME: Stenhouse. Cappellini uses the framework of a balanced reading program to outline a complete program for establishing, planning, conducting, managing, and assessing literacy development.

DeCapua, A., & Marshall, H. W. (2011). *Breaking new ground: Teaching students with limited or interrupted formal education in U.S. secondary schools*. Ann Arbor: University of Michigan Press. The authors do not view teaching students with limited or interrupted education as remediation. They share the processes and procedures for the implementation of an instructional model developed to work with these students successfully.

Fitzgerald, J., & Graves, M. F. (2004). *Scaffolding reading experiences for English language learners*. Norwood, MA: Christopher Gordon. Scaffolding is the theme for a comprehensive course in teaching reading to English learners.

Gibbons, P. (2009). *English learners, academic literacy, and thinking: Learning in the challenge zone*. Portsmouth, NH: Heinemann. Gibbons presents and discusses in detail five broad areas that enable English learners to participate in high-quality learning across the curriculum: engaging deeply with intellectual contexts, developing academic literacy, employing reading strategies and improving comprehension, gaining writing independence, and learning content-area genres.

Hadway, N. L., Vardell, S. M., & Young, T. A. (2002). *Literature-based instruction with English language learners*. Boston: Allyn & Bacon. Describes the nature of English language learners in classrooms, as well as language acquisition and literature-based instruction to develop oral language and reading and writing skills, and to assist learners in responding to culture.

Herrell, A. L., & Jordan, M. (2008). *Fifty strategies for teaching English language learners* (3rd ed.). Upper Saddle River, NJ: Pearson. Authors provide fifty carefully selected strategies to help ELL students understand content materials while developing their speaking, reading, writing, and listening skills in English. Strategies include definitions, rationales, and step-by-step implementation instructions; all are specifically tied to Teachers of English to Speakers of Other Languages (TESOL) standards.

Peregoy, S. F., & Boyle, O. F. (2004). *Reading, writing and learning in ESL: A resource book for K–12 teachers* (4th ed.). Boston, MA: Allyn & Bacon. A classic resource for ESL educators that explores contemporary language acquisition theory while providing suggestions and methods for instruction.

Young, T. A., & Hadaway, N. L. (Eds.). (2006). *Supporting the literacy development of English learners: Increasing success in all classrooms*. Newark, DE: International Reading Association. The section on reading instruction includes chapters on developing comprehension strategies, using guided reading, and teaching ELLs about expository text structures—all based on research but written with practitioners in mind.

References

Almada, P., Nichols, A., & O'Keefe, L. (2004). *A pocketful of opossums*. Barrington, IL: Rigby.

Aronson, E. (1978). *The jigsaw classroom*. Beverly Hills, CA: Sage Publications.

Ashton-Warner, S. (2002). *Teacher*. New York: Simon and Schuster.

August, D., & Shanahan, T. (Eds.). (2007). *Developing literacy in second-language learners: A report of the national literacy panel on language-minority children and youth*. Mahwah, NJ: Lawrence Erlbaum.

August, D., & Shanahan, T. (Eds.). (2008). *Developing reading and writing in second language learners: Lessons from the report of the National Literacy Panel on language-minority children and youth*. New York: Routledge.

Benedict, S., & Carlisle, L. (1992). *Beyond words: Picture books for older readers and writers*. Portsmouth, NH: Heinemann.

Birch, B. M. (2006). *English L2 reading: Getting to the bottom* (2nd ed.). Mahwah, NJ: Lawrence Erlbaum.

Brown, A. L., Campione, J. C., & Day, J. D. (1981). Learning to learn: On training students to learn from texts. *Educational Researcher, 10*, 14–21.

Bruchac, J. (2002). *Sacajawea*. New York: Scholastic.

Calderón, M. (2007). *Teaching reading to English language learners, grades 6-12*. Thousand Oaks, CA: Corwin Press.

Campbell, K. (2007). *Less is more: Teaching literature with short texts, grades 6-12*. Portland, ME: Stenhouse Publishers.

Carle, E. (1996, reprint edition). *The grouchy ladybug*. New York: HarperCollins.

Carmi, D. (2002). *Samir & Yonatan*. New York: Scholastic.

Castella, K., & Boyl, B. (2005). *Discovering nature's alphabet*. Berkeley, CA: Heyday Books.

Clay, M. (1997). *Becoming literate: The construction of inner control*. Portsmouth, NH: Heinemann.

Clay, M. (2000). *Running records for classroom teachers*. Portsmouth, NH: Heinemann.

Cloud, N., Genesee, F., & Hamayan, E. (2009). *Literacy instruction for English learners*. Portsmouth, NH: Heinemann.

Common Core Curriculum Maps: English Language Arts. (n.d.). http://commoncore.org/maps/index.php.

Cooper, E. (2006). *Beach*. New York: Scholastic.

Cowley, J. (1999). *Mrs. Wishy-Washy*. Aukland, New Zealand: Shorthand Publications.

Cummins, J. (1994). Knowledge, power and identity in teaching English as a second language. In F. Genesee (Ed.), *Educating second language children* (pp. 33–58). New York: Cambridge University Press.

Cummins, J. (June, 2010) Rethinking monolingual instructional strategies in multilingual classrooms. *Canadian Journal of Applied Linguistics* (CJAL)/*Revue canadienne de linguistique appliquée* (RCLA), North America, 221–240.

Cunningham, J. W. (1999). How we can achieve best practices in literacy instruction. In L. B. Gambrell, L. M. Morrow, S. B. Neuman, & M. Pressley (Eds.), *Best practices in literacy instruction* (pp. 34–45). New York: Guilford.

Cunningham, P. M. (2008). *Phonics they use* (5th ed.). Boston: Allyn & Bacon.

de Jong, E., & Harper, C. (2004). Misconceptions about teaching English language learners. *Journal of Adolescent & Adult Literacy, 48*, 2.

Dooley, N. (1991). *Everybody cooks rice*. Minneapolis: Carolrhoda Books.

Duggleby, J., & Lawrence, J. (1998). *Story painter: The life of Jacob Lawrence*. San Francisco: Chronicle Books.

Dunn, L. M., & Dunn, D. M. (2007) *Peabody picture vocabulary test* (4th ed.). Bloomington, MN: NCS Pearson.

Echevarria, J., & Short, D. (2010). Programs and practices for effective sheltered content instruction. In California Department of Education (Ed.) *Improving Education for English Learners: Research-Based Approaches*. Sacramento, CA: CDE Press.

Enright, D. S., & McCloskey, M. L. (1988). *Integrating English: Developing English language and literacy in the multilingual classroom*. Reading, MA: Addison-Wesley.

Fitzgerald, J. (2003). New directions in multilingual literacy research: Multilingual reading theory. *Reading Research Quarterly, 38*, 118–122.

Fitzgerald, J., & Graves, M. F. (2004). *Scaffolding reading experiences for English language learners*. Norwood, MA: Christopher Gordon.

Fountas, I. C., & Pinnell, G. S. (1996). *Guided reading: Good first teaching for all children*. Portsmouth, NH: Heinemann.

Fountas, I. C., & Pinnell, G. S. (2001). *Guiding readers and writers (grades 3–6): Teaching comprehension, genre, and content literacy*. Portsmouth, NH: Heinemann.

Freeman, D., Freeman, Y., McCloskey, M. L., Stack, L., Silva, C., Gottlieb, M., & Garcia Colon, A. (2010). *On our way to English teacher's guide*. Austin, TX: Rigby/Houghton Mifflin Harcourt.

Freeman, Y., Freeman, D., & Mercuri, S. (2003). Helping middle and high school age English language learners achieve academic success. *NABE Journal of Research and Practice, 1*(1), 110–122.

Garcia, E. (1999). *Student cultural diversity: Understanding and meeting the challenge* (2nd ed.). Portsmouth, NH: Heinemann.

Goodman, K. (1967). Reading: A psycholinguistic guessing game. *Journal of the Reading Specialist, 6*(1), 126–135.

Goodman, Y., Watson, D., & C. Burke. (2005). *Reading miscue inventory*. Katonah, NY: Richard C. Owen Publishers.

Grabe, W., & Stoller, F. L. (2002). *Teaching and researching reading*. England: Pearson Education Limited.

Graham, C. (1978). *Jazz chants*. New York: Oxford University Press.

Graham, C. (2003). *Children's jazz chants old and new*. New York: Oxford University Press.

Hadaway, N. L., & McKenna, M. J. (2007). *Breaking boundaries with global literature: Celebrating diversity in K–12 classrooms*. Newark, DE: International Reading Association.

Hakuta, K., Butler, Y. G., & Witt, D. (2000). *How long does it take English learners to attain proficiency?* (Policy Report). The University of California Linguistic Minority Research Institute.

Harklau, L. (1994). ESL versus mainstream classes: Contrasting L2 learning environments. *TESOL Quarterly, 28*, 241–272.

Heath, S. B. (1983). *Ways with words: Language, life and work in communities and classrooms*. New York: Cambridge University Press.

Helman, L. (2009). *Literacy development with English learners: Research-based instruction in grades K–6*. New York: Guilford Press.

Herber, H. L., & Herber, J. N. (1993). *Teaching in content areas with reading, writing and reasoning*. Boston: Allyn & Bacon.

Holdaway, D. (1979). *Foundations of literacy*. Portsmouth, NH: Heinemann.

Hudelson, S. (1984). Kan yu ret an rayt en ingles: Children become literate in ESL. *TESOL Quarterly, 18*(2), 221–248.

Hudelson, S. (1987). The role of native language literacy in the education of language minority children. *Language Arts, 65*, 287–302.

Jiménez, R. (November/December 2010). Knowing how to know: Building meaningful relationships through instruction that meets the needs of students learning English. *Journal of Teacher Education, 61,* 403–441.

Jiménez, R. T., & Teague, B. L. (2009). English language learners and literacy development. In L. M. Morrow, R. Rueda, & D. Lapp, (Eds.), *Handbook of research on literacy instruction: Issues of diversity, policy, and equity.* New York: Guilford Press.

Johnson, S. (1995). *Alphabet city.* New York: Viking.

Kagan, S. (1994). *Cooperative learning.* Riverside, CA: Kagan.

Kinsella, K. (2008). Developing academic discourse skills for English learners in grades K–12. Santa Clara County Office of Education Institute. http://www.sccoe.k12.ca.us/depts/ell/kinsella.asp

Krashen, S. D. (2003). *Explorations in language acquisition and use.* Portsmouth, NH: Heinemann.

Krashen, S. D. (2004). *The power of reading: Insights from the research* (2nd ed.). Portsmouth, NH: Heinemann.

Lanauze, M., & Snow, C. (1989). The relation between first and second language writing skills: Evidence from Puerto Rican elementary school children in bilingual programs. *Linguistics and Education, 1,* 323–329.

Li, X., & Zhang, M. (2004). Why Mei still cannot read and what can be done. *Journal of Adolescent & Adult Literacy, 48*(2), 92–101.

Lin, G. (2011). *Where the moon meets the mountain.* New York: Little Brown.

McCloskey, M. L., & Stack, L. (1996). *Voices in literature: An anthology for middle/high school ESOL.* Boston, MA: Heinle & Heinle.

McCloskey, M. L., & Stack, L. (2003). *Visions: Language, literature, content—books A, B, & C.* Boston, MA: Heinle & Heinle.

McCloskey, M. L., & Thrush, E. (2005). Building a reading scaffold with web texts. *Essential Teacher, 2*(4), 49–52.

McDonnell. P. (2011). *Me . . . Jane.* New York: Little Brown.

Martin, B. J., & Carle, E. (1992). *Brown bear, brown bear, what do you see?* New York: Henry Holt.

Metropolitan Museum of Art (New York). (2002). *Museum ABC.* Boston: Little, Brown.

Moustafa, M. (1997). *Beyond traditional phonics: Research discoveries and reading instruction.* Portsmouth, NH: Heinemann.

Nation, P. (2001). *Learning vocabulary in another language.* Cambridge, UK: Cambridge University Press.

National Institute of Child Health and Human Development. (2000). Report of the National Reading Panel. Teaching children to read: An evidence-based assessment of the scientific research literature on reading and its implications for reading instruction: Reports of the subgroups (NIH Publication No. 00-4754). Washington, DC: U.S. Government Printing Office. http://www.nationalreadingpanel.org.

Nivola, C. A. (2008). *Planting the trees of Kenya: The story of Wangari Maathai.* New York: Farrar, Straus and Giroux.

Nye, N. S. (1995). *Words under the words: Selected poems.* Portland, OR: Far Corner Books.

Oczkus, L. D. (2003). *Reciprocal teaching at work: Strategies for improving reading comprehension.* Newark, DE: International Reading Association.

Palinscar, A. S. (1986). The role of dialogue in providing scaffolded instruction. *Educational Psychologist, 21,* 73–98.

Palinscar, A. S., & Brown, A. L. (1984). Reciprocal teaching of comprehension-fostering and comprehension-monitoring activities. *Cognition and Instruction, 1*(2), 117–175.

Pelletier, D. (1996). *The graphic alphabet.* New York: Orchard.

Raphael, T. (1982). Question-answering strategies for children. *The Reading Teacher, 36*(2), 186–191.

Rasinski, T. V. (2003). *The fluent reader.* New York: Scholastic.

Reynolds, P. H., & FableVision. (2010). *Zebrafish.* New York: Athaneum.

Roberge, M. M. (2002). California's generation 1.5 immigrants: What experiences, characteristics, and needs do they bring to our English classes? *The CATESOL Journal, 14*(1), 107–127.

Robertson, K., & Lafond, S. (2008). How to support ELL students with interrupted formal education (SIFEs). http://www.colorincolorado.org/article/27483/F.

Samway, K. D., Whang, G., & Pippitt, M. (1995). *Buddy reading: Cross-age tutoring in a multicultural school.* Portsmouth, NH: Heinemann.

Satrapi, M. (2007). *The complete Persepolis.* New York: Pantheon.

Scholastic. (1999). *Oral fluency assessment.* New York: Scholastic.

Short, D., & Fitzsimmons, S. (2007). *Double the work: Challenges and solutions to acquiring language and academic literacy for adolescent English language learners—A report to Carnegie Corporation of New York.* Washington, DC: Alliance for Excellent Education.

Shute, L. (1986). *Momotaro: The peach boy.* New York: Lothrop, Lee & Shepard.

Slavin, R. E. (1994). *Cooperative learning: Theory, research, and practice* (2nd ed.). Boston: Allyn & Bacon.

Slavin, R. E., Madden, N. A., Chambers, B., & Haxby, B. (2008). *Two million children: Success for all* (2nd ed.). Thousand Oaks, CA: Corwin Press.

Snow, C. E., Burns, S. M., & Griffin, P., (Eds.). (1998). *Preventing reading difficulties in young children.* Washington, DC: National Academy Press.

Stahl, S. (2002). *What the NRP report doesn't say.* Keynote address at the Michigan Reading Recovery Conference, Detroit, January. Available at www.ciera.org.

TeensHealth. Dealing with Bullying. http://kidshealth.org/teen/your_mind/problems/bullies.html

Tharp, R. G., & Gallimore, R. (1988). *Rousing minds to life: Teaching, learning, and schooling in social context.* Cambridge, UK: Cambridge University Press.

Thomas, W. P., & Collier, V. P. (1997). School effectiveness for language minority students [Electronic Version]. *NCBE Resource Collection Series.* http://www.ncela.gwu.edu/pubs/resource/effectiveness/

Tierney, R. J., & Readence, J. E. (2004). *Reading strategies and practices: A compendium* (6th ed.). Boston: Pearson College Division.

Tizard, J., Schofield, W. N., & Hewison, J. (1982). Collaboration between teachers assisting children's reading. *British Journal of Educational Psychology, 52,* 1–15.

Trelease, J. (2006). *The read-aloud handbook.* New York: Penguin.

U.S. Department of Education. (2004). Fact Sheet: NCLB provisions ensure flexibility and accountability for limited English proficient students. http://www.ed.gov/nclb/accountability/schools/factsheet-english.html.

U.S. Department of Education. (2009). Reading First program description. http://www2.ed.gov/programs/readingfirst/index.html.

U.S. Department of Education, Office of Elementary and Secondary Education. (2002). Public Law 107–110. Elementary and secondary reauthorization: The No Child Left Behind (NCLB) Act of 2001 (Enacted in 2002). http://www.ed.gov/policy/elsec/leg/esea02/index.html.

WIDA. (2012). English language development standards, 2012 Edition. www.wida.us.

Wood, D., Bruner, J., & Ross, G. (1976). The role of tutoring in problem solving. *Journal of Child Psychology and Psychiatry, 17,* 89–100.

Young, K. R. (2010). *Doodlebug: A novel in doodles.* New York: Feiwel and Friends.

MyEducationLab™

Go to the Topics, Reading and Writing and Assessment, in the MyEducationLab (www.myeducationlab. com) for your course, where you can:

- Find learning outcomes for Reading and Writing and Assessment along with the national standards that connect to these outcomes.
- Complete Assignments and Activities that can help you more deeply understand the chapter content.
- Apply and practice your understanding of the core teaching skills identified in the chapter with the Building Teaching Skills and Dispositions learning units.
- Examine challenging situations and cases presented in the IRIS Center Resources.
- Check your comprehension on the content covered in the chapter by going to the Study Plan in the Book Resources for your text. Here you will be able to take a chapter quiz, receive feedback on your answers, and then access Review, Practice, and Enrichment activities to enhance your understanding of chapter content.
- **A+RISE** A+RISE® Standards2Strategy™ is an innovative and interactive online resource that offers new teachers in grades K-12 just in time, research-based instructional strategies that meet the linguistic needs of ELLs as they learn content, differentiate instruction for all grades and abilities, and are aligned to Common Core Language Arts standards (for the literacy strategies) and to English language proficiency standards in WIDA, Texas, California, and Florida.

Developing Literacy with English Learners: Focus on Writing

Diana Bela has been teaching a science unit on plants to her fourth-grade class at an urban school in the Southeast. Her 28 students come from ten different countries, and they have had varied educational experiences and opportunities. Many have had little or no experience with expository writing, and most find their fourth-grade textbooks difficult to read. Diana has used several of the reading strategies discussed in Chapter 8 to help her learners access the text. Today she wants them to orally recall what they have learned in science while developing their skills in writing a summary report. She uses the shared writing strategy to encourage a rich academic conversation as she guides learners through the writing process.

The first step in writing is brainstorming. Diana explains that scientists need to write carefully and clearly to explain scientific findings, and that the students, too, can write like scientists. They are concluding their science unit on plants, and the topic today is the contribution that plants make to our lives. To model the first step, Diana asks, "How do plants help us?" Learners are encouraged to skim the science chapter and come up with possible answers. Most of the suggestions are single words or phrases: "wood houses," "cotton clothes," "food," "medicines." Diana offers encouragement as she writes learners' ideas on a graphic organizer on the board (see Figure 9.1).

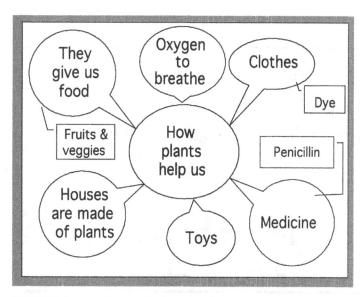

FIGURE 9.1 How Plants Help Us: A Graphic Organizer

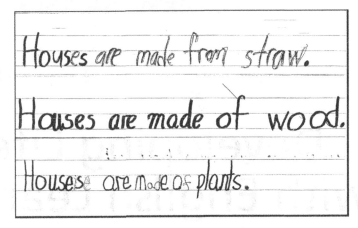

FIGURE 9.2 How Plants Help Us: Sentences

Diana asks learners to categorize, color-code, and group their suggestions. She assigns pairs of students to write a sentence about each idea, encouraging them to be specific. For example, she says, "It's not very clear to say that plants give us medicine. Let's give an example. What kind of medicine can we get from plants? Right, penicillin is one kind."

Student pairs select ideas from the Web and write drafts of ideas for the essay on sentence strips, which Diana puts in a pocket chart. Students help her to group the ones about similar ideas together to start to build paragraphs. Several students come up with sentences about how plants contribute to our homes (see Figure 9.2).

This gives Diana an opportunity to introduce sentence combining. "This is a little boring to say three times, 'Houses are made of. . . .' How can we combine these sentences into one, more interesting, one? Are straw and wood examples of plants? How can we say that?" Students come up with, "Houses are made of plants, like straw and wood."

As the students read the sentences they have written, they come up with ideas to improve them. Diana gives a little "mini-lesson" on how to "cut and paste" and "insert" words to improve their writing (see Figure 9.3).

After the piece is revised, learners work together to suggest the best sequence for the sentences by physically rearranging the sentence strips. Then they work with the teacher to compose an introductory and a concluding sentence. Finally, each individual suggests a title and writes it on a sticky note, and the class votes on the best one (see Figure 9.4).

The final piece is carefully written on a chart and posted in the hall outside the classroom. Students are proud of what they have produced and want to read it over and over again to one another and to anyone who visits. They copy the text to take home to read to their families, adding their own illustrations (see Figure 9.5).

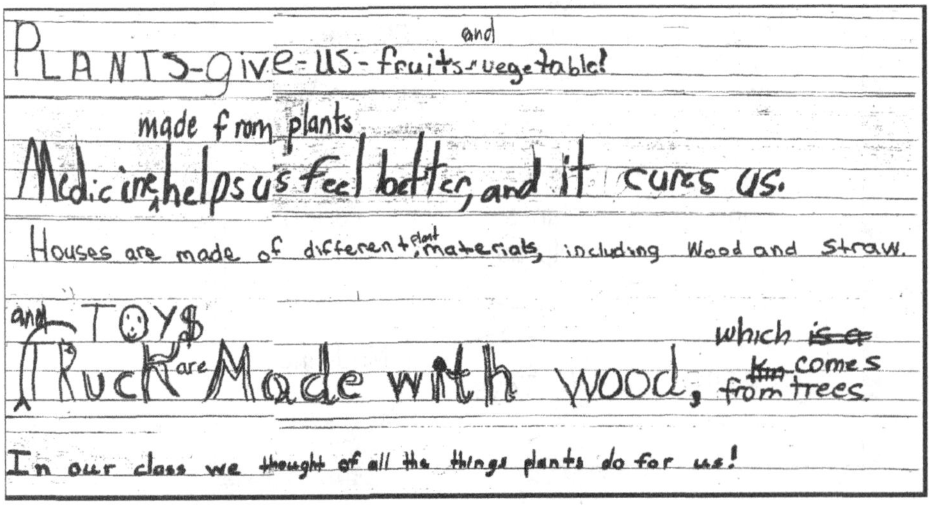

FIGURE 9.3 How Plants Help Us: Revised and Combined Sentences

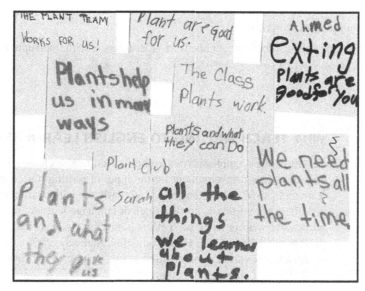

FIGURE 9.4 How Plants Help Us: Possible Titles

The Plant Team Works for Us

Plants help us in many ways in our everyday lives. Plants give us oxygen and we need oxygen to breathe. We need cotton from plants to make clothes to wear. We use plant dye to make things more colorful.

Plants give us fruits and vegetables. Medicine made from plants makes us feel better and it cures us. Houses are made of different plant materials, including straw and wood. Toy trucks are made with wood, which comes from trees.

In our class, we thought of all the things plants do for us!

FIGURE 9.5 The Finished Piece: The Plant Team Works for Us

How can writing help to develop English learners' literacy?

- Why should we use writing with ELLs?
- How does second language writing develop?
- How can we connect writing to active, interactive learning?
- What are the challenges we face in teaching writing to ELLs?
- How can we establish a rich writing environment?
- What are effective strategies for helping ELLs learn to write?

- How can we use the writing process with ELLs?
- How can we address the unique writing development needs of older learners with interrupted education?
- What are ways to assess writing for ELLs?

WHY TEACH WRITING TO ENGLISH LEARNERS?

Recent national emphasis on reading has led to less classroom time, less curriculum emphasis, and less teacher development on the topic of writing. Often in the past, programs for English learners focused on oral language skills early on, with instruction of writing introduced later with a skills-based emphasis so that English language learners had few opportunities for authentic, purposeful writing in class. Yet, as both Diana's class and research on writing development illustrate (Edelsky, 1993; Hudelson, 1984; Samway, 2006), English learners can clearly benefit from rich and varied opportunities to use writing to construct meaning in their new language at all stages of language development.

HOW DOES WRITING DEVELOP WITH ELLs?

Young learners pass through similar stages in writing development in both first (L1) and second (L2) languages (Hudelson, 1984). They begin with scribbling, making random marks, and drawing; then they begin to use the letter names and initial letters to represent words (e.g., "R EU HP?" [Are you happy?]), move on to phonetic spelling (e.g., "I thot hee waz crazie." [I thought he was crazy.]), and gradually progress to more sophisticated writing with traditional spelling and usage. Older learners who have not mastered writing in their first language will pass through similar stages. But there are many unique aspects for English learners who are beginning to write. One of these is **positive transference**—when learners use aspects of their first language to help them learn to write in their new language (Olivares, 2002). For example, if learners already know how to write in another language, they can make use of many concepts and organizational frames or **schemas** they have developed in that language and apply them to the new one. A student who already knows how to write a summary in Russian, for example, can transfer the schema for writing a summary into English (Carrell & Eisterhold, 1988). Learners who have studied a content area can also use cognates they have learned. For example,

English Learners Benefit from
Opportunities to Use Writing to
Construct Meaning in Their New
Language

TABLE 9.1 Writing Development of English Learners

Writing Aspect	Beginning EL	Intermediate EL	Advanced EL
1. Vocabulary/Word Choice	Vocabulary is limited. Learners translate, avoid words they don't know, use vocabulary sources such as dictionaries and/or ask for help.	Learners know most of the first 2,000 most frequent words, may have trouble with infrequent or "academic" words.	Learners' vocabulary is approaching native proficiency.
2. Sentence Fluency	Writes a few words or sentences.	Writes several sentences.	Writes several paragraphs (depending on age).
3. Sentence Variety	Learners can use one or two sentence patterns.	Learners use several sentence patterns.	Learners vary sentence patterns and have a large repertoire.
4. Organization	Writing does not have evidence of sequencing, or is so short that organization is not apparent.	Writing shows evidence of an organizational plan.	Learners use appropriate organization for the genre chosen.
5. Genre	Learners use the same format for most writing.	Learners know several different writing forms or "schemas" and choose among them.	Learners know many different genres and choose appropriately among them to match the purpose of the piece.
6. Grammar	Writer often uses the present tense, and has trouble with word order.	Writer uses more standard word order but makes typical learner errors and interference errors, e.g., -s endings on verbs, articles.	Grammar is similar to that of native speakers with occasional learner errors.
7. Conventions	Attempts at spelling using letter names, L1 sound system. Spaces between letters and words. Punctuation, capitalization, and paragraphs not used consistently.	Writer uses phonetic spelling, with some errors due to differences in sound system between L1 and L2. Generally uses paragraphs, spacing, capitals, and punctuation.	Most high-frequency words are spelled correctly; others are close. Capital letters, punctuation, indentation, and other genre format used accurately and consistently.

scientific terms in many languages use Latin or Greek roots and are similar across languages (particularly Romance languages such as Spanish, French, Italian, Portuguese, and Romanian), so words will be very similar; with some instruction and encouragement, learners can use these similarities to figure out the new terms. Sometimes this application of knowledge from L1 to L2 writing may also lead to **interference errors**, in which the rules of one language are applied incorrectly in another; these can be explained and resolved, and the process of doing so can increase understanding of the structure of the new language. For example, many Asian and Slavic languages do not use articles, and learners from these groups often have trouble understanding how and when to use them. Teachers will need to find out what their students know about writing in both L1 and L2, as well as their English proficiency levels, and set expectations accordingly. Table 9.1 outlines writing expectations of learners across three English language levels according to seven traits of writing (Culham, 2003, 2005). Of course, expectations will also vary according to the learner's age and grade level. Other useful descriptions of writing expectations by language level and grade level are included in the WIDA Can-Do Descriptors (http://www.wida.us/standards/CAN_DOs/).

CONNECTING WRITING TO ACTIVE, COMMUNICATIVE LANGUAGE TEACHING AND LEARNING

For ELLs at all levels, writing is an excellent environment for implementing the principles outlined in Chapter 1 of this book. Because writing involves productive skills, young writers can be highly active in developing their own creations. They can write about their own knowledge and experiences, providing cultural relevance. They can use collaborative tools in gathering ideas and in responding to one another's writing. Writing builds comprehension because learners better understand how texts are constructed as they put their own texts together. Writing also reveals who the learners are and what they know, to better enable their teachers to connect new knowledge to learners' previous experiences. Writing in content classes can help to develop and cement content learning, enabling learners to work with and apply the content concepts and skills they are developing. Leki (2003) notes that content-based writing, in which learners develop knowledge about a topic over time and then make decisions about what to include and how to write about that topic, is useful in preparing English learners for success in the writing they will use in school and beyond. Writing is also adaptable for a multilevel class that includes ELLs. Because learners write at their own levels, writing is an ideal activity for differentiation of instruction for students with different needs, learning styles, backgrounds, and abilities. Through careful use of assessment tools and processes, small group work, and teacher feedback, teachers can respond to learners where they are, and lead them toward achieving successive levels in their writing development. Writers in a class do not all have to be at the same level; they simply must know where they are in their writing development, and where they are going.

Writing can help language development at early stages (such as when learners know a few words and phrases, and are just beginning to decode and encode the language) by presenting an authentic need to negotiate the meanings of letters and sounds and to apply the phonics skills they are developing. At later stages of language development, writers can develop and polish their productive skills, and better comprehend various genres by trying to compose in them. Well-developed writing lessons and tasks, accomplished at appropriate, increasingly challenging levels, make demands on learners that lead them to build their development of writing ideas, vocabulary/word choice, sentence fluency, sentence variety, organization, grammar, and conventions.

CHALLENGES OF TEACHING WRITING TO ENGLISH LEARNERS

Writing is a tremendous challenge for learners of English. They have to develop ideas and try to express them in new words, using everything they are acquiring in the new language at once: the words, the sentence patterns, the grammar, the genre, and the conventions of print. In addition, writing involves understanding sociocultural expectations that may be very different and new for the learners. Even if learners understand a genre such as letter writing or essays in one culture, expectations may be very different in another culture. In Spanish, letters are typically more formal and elaborate than in English, and a polite introduction is expected. In Japanese, because everyone in that island culture shares many expectations, it is appropriate to leave cultural understandings unstated—in fact it is demeaning for the reader to state some concepts too explicitly. In English, on the other hand, writers are expected to be so clear that any reader can understand what they mean. Writing is likely to be the last language area for learners of English to master—teachers should not be surprised to see "language learner errors" in students' writing for many years, and to need to spend instructional time addressing them.

DEVELOPING A WRITING ENVIRONMENT

Samway (1992, 2006) describes important characteristics of classrooms that foster rich writing development. Teachers provide learners with opportunities to use writing for real purposes for real audiences, across the curriculum, so that they become enthusiastic and experienced in effectively communicating their ideas. Teachers help learners to develop their knowledge of the craft of writing, to understand the relationship between oral language and writing, and to use that knowledge to discuss what they read. Writing is also closely tied to thought processes. Children use writing to help them think and use thinking to improve their writing. Effective teachers of writing develop a "learning community" in which learners see one another as valuable resources and sources of support in the writing process.

Students use their previous experiences with oral and written language to construct new meanings and to further develop their language capacities. For ELLs, using previous experiences manifests itself in two ways (Enright & McCloskey, 1988). First, learners implement the "tie back" strategy when they use their previous experiences from their home countries' cultures and language to develop English language and literacy capacities. A second, "tie in" strategy is used when learners use their experiences in one of the four language processes of listening, speaking, reading, and writing in English to help them develop their capabilities with the other processes. Thus reading does not precede writing and listening does not precede speaking: The four modes support one another. Writing key words on the blackboard may help a student listen better; reviewing a concept through paraphrasing it with a partner may cement reading comprehension; writing key words and concepts may prepare a student to talk about them.

To create a writing environment, classrooms both celebrate and connect reading and writing. Teacher and students read together, talk about what they read, write about what they learn and what they think; the classroom reflects their work—student's written work is prominently displayed along with a celebration of books and authors. The environment is print-rich, with labels, instructions, and procedures for readers and writers at various stages. Students are encouraged to read and review books for the class. The classroom provides rich access to words via translation dictionaries, English dictionaries, picture dictionaries, and online sources (see Chapter 7).

GETTING STARTED: INTERACTIVE WRITING

Support your learners' early efforts through interactive writing. Interactive writing works well to introduce concepts of writing to beginners. Writing begins as a dialogue, a conversation between writers that can provide a bridge between the informal and interactive nature of conversation and the more formal and solitary nature of writing. Learners can have a natural means to negotiate meaning through real, purposeful written exchanges. Four examples of interactive writing are message boards/mailboxes, interactive journals, content learning logs, and literary logs.

MESSAGE BOARDS/MAILBOXES   Set up a bulletin board where learners can stick messages, or stack and label milk-carton mailboxes where folded notes can be tacked or placed with the name of the intended recipient on the outside. If you have the resources, use e-mail or classroom messaging software for message exchange. Begin writing short notes to students, asking questions about them or what they are learning, commenting on their successes, relating interesting events, or perhaps just drawing and labeling a little picture. (If your class is large, you may choose to write some of your messages on the board to the group in general, or to post or send a message to the class and have learners write individual responses.) Encourage learners to use the message board/mailboxes/e-mail to communicate with one another as well as with you. Monitor the message board and set up clear expectations for kindness and good etiquette in its use.

Exchanging Messages Is Motivating and Effective for Beginning Writers

INTERACTIVE/DIALOGUE JOURNALS   Dialogue journals and letters help to engage learners in the personal process of negotiating meaning (Hadaway & Young, 2006). The focus of the dialogue can be personal narrative or can be related to content learning. Encourage learners to write frequently in a bound journal, notebook, or folder about topics of their own choosing. (You may also provide a few suggestions or prompts on a chart or the board for when learners feel "stuck.") Exchange questions, report personal ideas or experiences, make promises, evaluate classroom activities, offer contributions to the class, apologize, give directions, complain, review learning, or state opinions. In your responses to student writing, remember these basics:

- Use a direct conversational style, matching the length and level of reasoning to the student's proficiency and cognitive ability.
- Offer new and interesting information in your responses, and model writing slightly more complex than that of your students.
- Ask real questions that seek student opinions and information that you do not know.
- Direct corrections may not be appropriate in writing intended to be a conversation. You may choose to correct indirectly by using the same language of your learners with errors "fixed" in your responses. Note common types of errors that occur and provide the class with "mini-lessons" on these topics.
- Some older learners, on the other hand, may be eager to have you point out their errors. Discuss this with the writers to determine some aspect of writing on which they want your feedback, and, if the writer requests it, make a few corrections in that area when you respond.

In the interactive journal excerpt in Figure 9.6, which shows the correspondence between Thuy, a fifth grader from Vietnam, and her homeroom teacher, Ms. O'Brien, note how Ms. O'Brien provides indirect feedback for spelling, grammar, conventions, and format by modeling correct forms. Notice, too, how she raises the level of language just a little, challenging Thuy to raise her reading and writing to a slightly higher level.

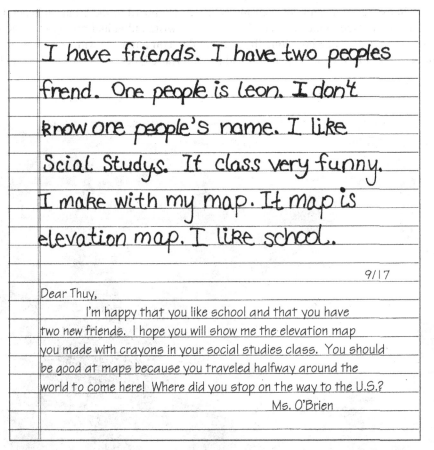

I have friends. I have two peoples frend. One people is Leon. I don't know one people's name. I like Scial Studys. It class very funny. I make with my map. It map is elevation map. I like school.

9/17

Dear Thuy,

I'm happy that you like school and that you have two new friends. I hope you will show me the elevation map you made with crayons in your social studies class. You should be good at maps because you traveled halfway around the world to come here! Where did you stop on the way to the U.S.?

Ms. O'Brien

FIGURE 9.6 Excerpt from Interactive Journal

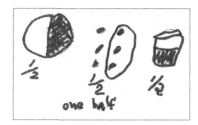

FIGURE 9.7 Excerpt from Grade 2 Math Journal: Fractions

Web tools, used creatively and responsibly, can greatly expand the potential of interactive journals. Web publishing and information gathering tools can help learners create content for the Internet and interact with it. Tools for the Internet that can contribute to all types of journaling include blogs, wikis, podcasts, and many others (Richardson, 2010). Learners are motivated to write clearly and well for online presentations. Radio WillowWeb (http://mps.wes.schoolfusion.us/) is an example of a program series in which learners prepare and present podcasts for the school and for archiving on the school web site. Repeated types of broadcast segments (e.g., Fun Facts, Just Jokes, Did You Know? Wonderful Web Sites) provide authentic purpose for writing in different genres about content learning as well as schemas that are accessible and interesting for both writers and audience. Moreover, the process of reading their writing for radio integrates students' language skills of reading, writing, and speaking.

CONTENT LEARNING LOGS   Writing regularly about content concepts and content helps learners remember what they are learning as they deepen their understanding. Have learners keep a log of what they are learning in their content classes—in math, science, social studies, art, or music, for example. At the end of each class, learners write in their logs a statement summarizing something important they want to remember from the day's lesson. Figures 9.7 and 9.8 show learning log entries from units on fractions at different grade levels.

The log might also include pictures about what certain fractions look like. Or learners might document processes they used to do computations with fractions. For example, in a math lesson on fractions, learners might illustrate fractions in various formats; they might document the processes they use to compute fractions; they might summarize lessons, write main ideas or main points, or write directions to teach someone else a process.

Remember this!   February 23

When you add things, they have to have the same name.

3 kids + 2 kids = 5 kids

The name is kids. The total is five kids.

When you add fractions, they have to have the same name, too.

2/8 + 5/8 = 7/8.

2 eighths plus five eights is seven eights.

The name is eighths. The total is seven eighths.

FIGURE 9.8 Excerpt from Grade 4 Math Journal: A Rule for Adding Fractions

An algebra teacher might provide sentence frames to help learners to self-assess their math understanding. For example, the teacher might ask learners to:

Reflect on where you are in the course and complete two of the following statements:

Now I understand _____.
I still do not understand _____.
I can help myself by doing _____.
You can help me by _____.

Or, the teacher might provide key terms and a challenge for a journal entry, e.g.: "Write a story that tells which is larger, *n* or -4*n*. Use these terms: *if, then, integer, negative number, positive number, variable.*"

LITERARY JOURNALS   As part of your independent choice reading program (see Chapter 8), encourage your students to keep literary journals. Have learners write down in a section of their notebooks or in a separate bound composition book the title and author of each book they read along with a brief review. Provide sharing times for students to read their reviews and make recommendations to one another for future reading. Read aloud to the class brief reviews of books for their ages and levels. Keep a literary journal yourself and model giving "book talks" from your written reviews. In order to provide comprehensible input to different levels of learners in your class, your model book talk might include showing the class your favorite picture spread from a fiction or nonfiction picture book, giving a very short summary, stating a thought about the theme or themes of the book, and offering a curious question that readers might like to find the answer to by reading the book. Hadaway and Young (2006) suggest that more advanced learners make a new journal (five to ten pages folded in half and stapled) for each book they read and write an entry after they finish every three to four chapters. Teachers provide open-ended prompts such as, "I predict . . .," "My favorite part . . .," "I connect . . .," or "I would change . . .," (p. 203). Before class discussions, students circle or highlight particular parts of their journals they want to share with the group.

SCAFFOLDING LEARNERS THROUGH THE WRITING PROCESS

An integrated, process approach to writing has many advantages for students' language learning. For beginning readers, reading their own writing or that of their peers gives them the opportunity to practice reading texts written with words that are part of their speaking vocabularies and target words for content writing. In this way they are challenged by reading words they know, not by trying to learn the meanings of words at the same time as they are learning to read them. Students learn reading and writing skills, such as encoding and decoding the sounds of the language, in a purposeful, meaningful context and so are more prepared to comprehend what they read. Writing also helps learners to become more independent language learners—they must use many resources—peers, teachers, books, dictionaries, word walls, word analysis skills, and understanding of genre. Writing gives teachers the opportunity to show how these skills serve real purposes for written communication. ELLs who write frequently learn spelling and grammar skills better, and gain a better understanding of the types of writing as they use them in their composition, beyond what they can learn from focused lessons.

Writing educators (e.g., Calkins & Mermelstein, 2003; Graves, 2003; Hudelson, 1984; Samway, 2006) used observations of the way professional writers work to describe the **writing process** as the various steps a writer goes through in the process of developing a final piece. This process is not always the same for each writer or each piece, however, and does not always proceed in a linear pattern through all the steps. Nevertheless, guiding learners through these stages can help them understand the processes involved in careful writing. The steps can serve as a guideline for teachers in helping ELLs discover effective writing processes to use to achieve their own goals for writing as they meet their school's and state's writing standards, such as WIDA's 2012 ELD standards, used by a consortium of 27 states (www.wida.us). The steps can also be adapted to different genres, including

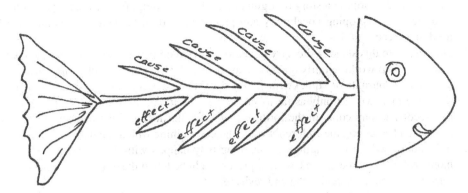

FIGURE 9.9 Fishbone Graphic Organizer Showing Cause and Effect

various types of writing that students use in different content areas: for example, writing in time sequence or cause and effect in social studies (e.g., the fishbone graphic organizer in Figure 9.9) or writing about a scientific cycle (e.g., the graphic organizer for the water cycle in Figure 9.10).

Steps in the Writing Process

1. *Pre-writing.* This is the stage in which the learner has experiences, reads, listens, conducts experiments, interviews people, comes up with ideas, and then reviews and collects his or her thoughts about the piece to come. Preparation for writing might include engaging in rich conversations, jotting down lists, selecting and using graphic organizers for the writing genre chosen, studying features of a certain genre, researching

FIGURE 9.10 Cycle Graphic Organizer Showing the Water Cycle

a topic and developing a story or argument, and/or outlining. For ELLs, preparation will also include developing vocabulary and practicing certain language forms that will be used in a piece.

2. *Drafting.*   In this stage, writers try to get ideas down on paper, attending more to content than form, and working fairly quickly so as to keep the train of thought going. They might use content journals or "quickwrites," for this process. Very young, beginning learners may take their writing only as far as this stage. The initial draft might be the final draft. The feedback may come in the form of general "mini-lessons" the teacher creates after reading and assessing the children's work and determining which standards and skills need to be addressed. Incorporating new learning may happen with the next draft. For older, more proficient learners, some writing pieces might be left at the draft stage; others will be selected for intensive reviewing and revising.

3. *Sharing and reviewing drafts.*   During this stage, writers read their writing to themselves and to others, and think about and discuss how they might improve the writing. For example, they might review how to make it more complete, sequence it better, organize it more clearly, use words well, include the right amount of detail, make arguments convincing and logical, and/or make the piece interesting. Learners may refer to standards, criteria, or checklists to assess their works in progress. Teachers of English learners help to develop the language needed for students to talk about their writing and may also introduce peer learning strategies such as Encourage, Question, Suggest (EQS) (see the explanation in Table 9.3) to help learners respond effectively to each other's writing.

4. *Revising.*   In this stage, learners try to include the ideas for improvement that came up in sharing and reviewing their drafts. Some teachers use individual or small-group writing conferences to help learners plan their revisions and to give them feedback and encouragement. ELLs may need extra support in this stage as their writing usually reveals areas in which their language is still developing. Teachers cannot focus on all the errors learners make, but must choose important and developmentally appropriate concepts to teach.

5. *Editing.*   When the content of the piece is determined, writers go back once more to edit and polish the piece, checking their capitalization, usage, punctuation, and spelling. Rog (2007) includes an editing mini-lesson for young learners to help them edit their own writing, referring to these four elements as "CUPS." We have included several editing checklists that can be adapted for your learners and used for this stage of the process. (See Tables 9.4, 9.5, and 9.6.)

6. *Publishing.*   The final stage in the writing process is a celebration of the accomplishments of writers. Writing can be published in many ways: the student, the teacher, or others might read their works aloud; the works might be posted in the classroom or on the class web site; writings might be collected into classroom books; learners might take their pieces home to read aloud to family members and then retell in the home language; or the pieces might be sent in to a children's publication or writing contest.

The Shared Writing Process

Before we ask ELLs to write, we need to provide them with some of the tools they will need. They will need good sources for ideas, lots of words and phrases about their topic, and appropriate language structures and patterns to express their ideas. But it is not enough to tell them how to access and use these tools; we need to *show* them by modeling the tools in use. In the opening vignette to this chapter, Diana used **shared writing** to model and guide learners through the process. Let's take a careful look at the strategies she used in this way of modeling writing.

Shared writing is a collaborative process through which learners provide content for a text and the teacher provides scaffolding for the text's construction. The teacher takes the lead in showing learners that when they have an experience, learn something, or think about something, they can talk about it, write it down, refine their writing, and share it with others. Shared writing shows learners how writing is done, and helps them understand how it is possible for them to be writers. It can help to:

- Develop interest in and enjoyment of writing.
- Demonstrate the purposes of writing.

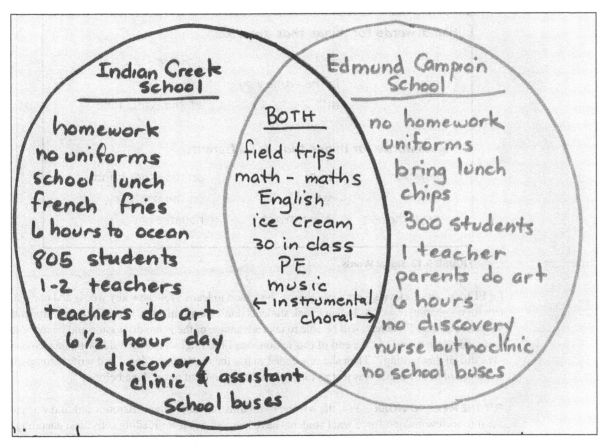

FIGURE 9.11 Venn Diagram Comparing Indian Creek and Edmund Campion Schools

- Provide participation in all stages of the writing process.
- Enable learners to understand the planning and organization involved in constructing various kinds of texts.
- Provide opportunities to teach language—vocabulary, grammar, usage, and conventions of spelling and punctuation.
- Provide models for students' independent writing.

BUILD BACKGROUND   Begin with a shared experience, a memory, a read-aloud text, or a content concept you're studying. You might, for example, share and discuss a story or non-fiction text, take a walking field trip, or interview a visitor. Have learners dictate as you take notes. Generate words and ideas for the writing as you construct your piece. One U.S. class had a visitor from the United Kingdom. They asked about elementary schools there and compared the visitor's answers with their own school using a Venn Diagram (see Figure 9.11).

READ THE DRAFT AND DISCUSS REVISIONS   As you discuss revisions, incorporate teaching/ review of appropriate strategies and skills of the reader/writer. Introduce features of the text structure you are using. Use your assessment of students' independent writing to determine skills to be addressed in shared writing. For the compare/contrast lesson, the class reviewed **signal words** and frames for comparing and contrasting (see Figure 9.12).

Demonstrate organizational features and elements of the writer's craft. The teacher at Indian Creek explained that there were two ways to write a compare/contrast essay. One way is to write about one thing, then write about the other. The other way is to compare the two in each category. The teacher also helped learners to see that using a variety of different signal words helped. (See Figure 9.13 for Indian Creek's finished essay.)

Revise the writing in front of everyone, referring to editing and revision tools. You may want to physically cut and paste the piece so the writers can see how that can be done. Work to have everyone involved in the writing. You will need to vary your questioning and your task expectations

---

Signal words for things that are alike:

both	and	likewise
like	in the same way	
	still	at the same time

Signal words for things that are different:

however	but	on the other hand
rather	yet	on the contrary
nevertheless	in contrast	nonetheless

FIGURE 9.12 Signal Words

for ELLs at various levels—some might use the lesson to learn a few new key words and one pattern for comparing (e.g., "At Indian Creek students don't wear uniforms, but at Campion, students do wear uniforms."). Others will be able to take advantage of the genre discussion and be ready to write their own pieces. At the end of this lesson, one little English learner said, with amazement, "We did all that writing!" Then she proceeded to use the model to sit down and write a comparison piece of her own that was just as long—something she had never done before.

PUT THE PIECE TO WORK   Post the writing (with illustrations) in the classroom and find ways to use it to review and reinforce what students have learned: use it for reading activities; encourage

---

**Comparing Our School with
Edmund Campion School in England**

We had visitors from England. They helped us compare Indian Creek School in the United States to Edmund Campion School in England.

We learned that both schools have field trips. Children at both schools study math (they call it "maths" in England), English, music, and PE.

There are some ways both schools are different. At Indian Creek, students do not wear uniforms but at Edmund Campion they do. Children have homework at Indian Creek, but they don't at Edmund Campion.

Students in England bring their lunch. At Indian Creek, most students eat in the cafeteria. Our school has a clinic with a nursing assistant. They have no clinic, but they do have a nurse.

Our school is much larger. We have 805 students and Edmund Campion has 300. At Edmund Campion parents help with art, but teachers do art at Indian Creek. We study only English. They study English and French. Most students walk to school but we have one bus at Indian Creek. There are no busses at Edmund Campion School.

We like going to school at Indian Creek, but we'd love to visit Edmund Campion!

FIGURE 9.13 Comparing Indian Creek and Edmund Campion Schools

learners to copy the writing in their notebooks; have a student read it to anyone who comes in the room; send home copies for students to read to their families.

Preparing Learners for Different Text Types

For learners new to academic language, particularly students with interrupted formal education, teaching explicit features of different types of writing is essential, because they may not otherwise have had opportunities to learn about them, or even have been exposed to them. Table 9.2 outlines several text types that learners will be asked to produce in school, as well as key features of these types.

Additional strategies for scaffolding writing are included in Table 9.3.

ISSUES IN TEACHING WRITING TO STUDENTS WITH INTERRUPTED FORMAL EDUCATION (SIFE)

English learners face multiple challenges in middle and high school: They are faced with difficult content that they must grapple with in a new language, they are negotiating a new culture and educational system, they may find themselves as beginning readers and writers in

TABLE 9.2 Writing Types and Features

Type of Text	Personal narrative, recount (e.g., my new baby sister)	News Report (e.g, report on class trip)	Narrative (e.g., a fairy tale or fable)	History Report (e.g., social studies research paper)	Procedure (e.g., science lab report, math process)	Discussion or argument (e.g., Do teens get enough sleep?)
Purpose	To tell what happened	To tell what happened	To teach and/or entertain	To give and analyze information	To tell how a procedure was done and analyze results	To persuade others, to justify a position
Organization	Orientation: who, where, when Sequence of events	Orientation: who, what, when, where, how, why Sequence of events May relate to other events, discuss significance	Orientation: who, where, when Sequence of events Problem, resolution	General statement Characteristic 1 & discussion (may have sub-headings) Characteristic 2 & discussion Characteristic 3 & discussion Documentation	Introduction & purpose Materials Process Observations & data Analysis Conclusions	Statement of position Arguments and supporting evidence Arguments against and evidence Conclusion
Commonly used Connectives	Time terms: First, then, next, afterwards, finally	Time terms: First, then, next, afterwards, finally	Time terms: Upon a time, later, afterwards, in the end	For example As a result To summarize Therefore Because of In addition to Also	First, second, third, finally; if . . . then;	First, second, in addition, therefore, however, in order to, on the other hand
Other language features	Past tense, descriptive language	Specific dates and times	Past tense, action verbs, descriptive language, dialogue	Use of forms of the verb "to be" Specialized vocabulary of subject & topic	Procedural verbs: This lab demonstrates; My hypothesis is; I observed; My data shows; As a result of . . .' In conclusion Specialized vocabulary of subject & topic	Persuasive language: it is logical to conclude that

TABLE 9.3 More Strategies for Scaffolding Writing

Strategy	Writing Stage	Procedure
Reading Aloud Examples of the Genre/Skill	Pre-writing	Provide good examples of the genre you ask learners to use. For example, when they are writing a narrative, you will want to teach them to use a strong lead—one that invites readers into the story and "grabs" them with questions they want answered. Collect strong leads from professional writers and from student works (to use anonymously). Offer learners some good examples of strong leads and discuss why they work. E. B. White starts *Charlotte's Web* with, "Where's Papa going with that ax?" (White, 2004). A newspaper article begins, "Let's talk about tattoos." (Gartner, 1993).
Semantic Mapping/Graphic Organizers	Pre-writing/ drafting	Use graphic organizers to make the structure and organization of a piece of writing visible and clear to all learners. For example, learners might use the "Fishbone" graphic organizer to outline a piece that describes cause and effect. Graphic organizers can be found on the web at sites such as these: http://www.eduplace.com/graphicorganizer/ http://edhelper.com/teachers/graphic_organizers.htm http://www.educationoasis.com/curriculum/graphic_organizers.htm
Quickwrite	Drafting	A Quickwrite is an activity to help learners generate ideas and develop fluency. Ask learners to write about their topics for a limited time (3–5 minutes) without stopping. Assure students that spelling and grammar are not important in a Quickwrite. What is important is to get as many ideas down on paper as possible. If someone does not have anything to write, she can just write her name over and over until she gets a new idea.
EQS	Sharing and reviewing drafts	EQS (Encourage, Question, Suggest) helps learners develop skill in responding to others' writing. Over time (several days to several weeks, depending upon age and language level), help learners develop the three skills of *encouraging, questioning,* and *suggesting.* With each skill, first model the skill yourself, then model with a student partner, and directly teach the language that learners will need to use the technique. Below are descriptions of the skills and the language that learners will need to apply that skill. **E:** *Encourage:* Offer the writer interest and encouragement by telling her specific things you like and why. Language samples for encouraging: • "The giant is a funny character." • "I could tell that you read a lot about penguins." • "I liked the surprise at the end." • "The first sentence made me want to read more." Words for encouraging: *Good, great, interesting, funny, detail, read, happy, silly, laugh, sad, curious, surprise, suspense, mystery, choose* **Q:** *Question:* Ask questions to help the writer be clear and include important details. Language samples for questioning: • "What does the giant look like?" • "What happens to the penguins in the winter?" • "Did you give any hints of (or foreshadow) the surprise?" • "Why did the story end that way?"

TABLE 9.3 More Strategies for Scaffolding Writing *(Continued)*

Strategy	Writing Stage	Procedure
		Words for questioning:
		• Who went . . . ?
		• Why did . . . ?
		• Did you . . . ?
		• Where did . . . ?
		• How will you . . . ?
		• When will . . . ?
		S: *Suggest:* Gently suggest different choices and possible improvements. Language samples for suggesting:
		• "Could you tell me more about what the giant looked like and what clothes she wore?"
		• "What about adding a picture of the penguins?"
		• "Maybe you could put something in earlier about how she was afraid to fly. What do you think?"
		• "What verb could you use instead of 'is'?"
Sentence Combining	Revising	Sentence combining helps students make their writing clearer and more sophisticated. It provides teachers a chance to show how to create more complex sentences by taking out repetition, creating adjectives, and using "signal words" to create phrases and clauses within sentences.
		Before sentence combining: I have a brother. He is four. He likes to play soccer with me. When he can't score he gets mad. He won't go home. Sometimes I let him score.
		After sentence combining: My four-year-old brother loves to play soccer with me, but he gets so mad when he doesn't win that sometimes I let him score just so we can go home.
Computer Reformulation	Revising/ editing	This is a variation of *reformulation* (Allwright, Woodley, & Allwright, 1988; Tocalli-Beller & Swain, 2005), a strategy in which native speakers reformulate language learners' texts and then the two discuss the process and the results. Use an online translator such as Babel Fish, which translates between many European languages, as well as Chinese, Japanese, and Korean. http://babelfish.altavista.com.
		Have learners write in L1 on the computer (or have someone enter their writing) and translate by computer into English. (The results will be inaccurate, but helpful in getting you started.) Then collaborate with the class and the writer to revise the piece into a translation of what the writer intended to say.
Writing Conferences	Revising/ editing	Set aside time while students are writing to meet with individuals to talk about their writing. Spend most of your time listening, encouraging learners to share their writing and explain how they want to improve it. Focus your comments on a few writing traits and skills you have covered or are working on in class. Work toward improvement, not perfection.
Spellchecker/ Writing Software	Editing	Online spell-check and grammar-check programs and thesauruses can be very helpful to EL writers if the writers learn that these tools only provide guidance, not authoritative answers. Take time to teach learners how to use the tools to help them rethink and question their writing choices. After electronic checking, they may need to go on to use other resources, such as a dictionary.
Author's Chair	Publishing	Every writing day, provide an opportunity for a young writer to sit in the "author's chair" to read aloud from his or her work. Lead the class in providing feedback in the form of encouragement and questions about the work.

(Continued)

TABLE 9.3 More Strategies for Scaffolding Writing *(Continued)*

Strategy	Writing Stage	Procedure
Classroom Library/ Web Site	Publishing	Set up a library for student publications in your classroom or in the school library. Make this library available during choice reading times and encourage parents to come to school to read and listen to their children's works. Alternately, put your learners' writing (with scanned artwork) on a secure class web site, where students and parents can read and enjoy the works.

classes with students functioning at college levels, and they are also coming of age—perhaps one of the most challenging aspects of their situation. They are at the peak of their sensitivity to identity issues and peer relations at a time when it is difficult for them, and relations with domestic peers are often difficult. It is the responsibility of schools to meet these students where they are; sadly, much of the research indicates that many are not successful (Leki, Cumming, & Silva, 2008).

Bunch, Lotan, Valdés, and Cohen (2005) describe units of study for secondary students revolving around challenging social studies concepts and concluding with all students writing persuasive essays demonstrating their comprehension of the concepts taught in the unit. The primary pedagogical technique, complex instruction, was used to promote academic and linguistic achievement. Complex instruction evolved from over 20 years of research by Elizabeth Cohen, Rachel Lotan, and their colleagues at the Stanford School of Education (Cohen & Lotan, 1997). (See http://cgi.stanford.edu/group/pci/cgi-bin/site.cgi for a description, videos, and research.) Complex instruction is effective for secondary language learners in that it uses multiple ability curricula, providing access for diverse linguistic abilities, instructional strategies that scaffold learning, and attention to classroom status problems that can impede learning for many diverse, secondary learners.

Bunch and colleagues (2005, p. 15) identified effective features of the instructional unit for secondary students from mixed academic and linguistic backgrounds. These included:

- creating "group worthy" tasks that could not be completed by a single individual.
- providing textual support and scaffolds to enable learners to comprehend primary source materials and complex text.
- modeling academic language for social studies by providing models and rubrics for a persuasive essay, sentence starters, and outlines.
- allowing for additional time and support in class for writing.
- delegating responsibility and authority for learning to students.
- facilitating peer support.
- treating problems relating to unequal classroom status.

Providing routes to success at complicated tasks is therefore the requirement. Scaffolding, using strategies such as the ones described in this chapter, must start with what learners know and can do and build on that base. For example, if you are preparing learners to write a research paper, you might design a sequence of scaffolded tasks that prepare learners for this type of writing. Leki (1992) outlined a series of such tasks, beginning with personal narrative and leading eventually to referenced research papers. For each step, the teacher carefully prepares learners to apply the skills involved with focused mini-lessons. Steps might include:

1. Choose a topic in which you have a personal interest and investment. (For example, a teen likes to play video games but her parents think they are a waste of time.) Do games help or hurt the school learning of high school students?
2. Write about your personal experience with the topic.
3. Make an appointment, prepare questions, and interview someone who is an expert on the topic (in person, on the phone, or online). If possible, tape the interview. Summarize the interview and include several direct quotations that are important.
4. Read three published pamphlets, articles, or other works about the topic. Take notes on your reading and highlight important passages. Keep track of reference information. Learn the right way to cite a personal essay, an interview, a pamphlet, a web page, a newspaper article, or any other source you use.

5. Develop your main ideas and outline your paper. Learn about when to cite a source and how to use direct quotations.

6. Write your paper. Cite the references you have used.

ASSESSING WRITING

Today's teachers and learners are feeling the pressure of high-stakes writing exams, often with cutoff scores required for secondary school graduation. The learning curve required for English learners is very sharp, but we cannot focus on everything at once: We must pace our day-to-day writing expectations on what learners can do now and what they can learn to do next, keeping the final proficiency goal in mind. Ongoing assessment tools can help teachers and learners to observe and document writing progress, determine short-term goals for the next challenge to tackle, and provide feedback to learners and parents.

Mini-Lessons and Checklists

When Diana first started teaching writing, she felt that she was not a good writing teacher if she did not find and mark every mistake in a student's paper. The result of this level of correction for an ELL is a paper with so many red marks that it "bleeds," discouraging the student and preventing her from wanting to try again. Meanwhile, the teacher hesitates to assign writing tasks and then face still more piles of papers to correct. A guide who was helping a group of climbers attempt the overwhelming task of climbing Mount Everest asked his group, "How do you eat an elephant?" The answer was, of course, "one bite at a time." A mountain climber, after very careful planning, must take one step at a time up Everest. To an English learner, learning to write and climbing Mount Everest may both seem like unachievable goals, but the solution is to take one bite at a time—to conquer small goals in writing development (and retain them) and to celebrate one's progress along the way. When we learn to target certain criteria for a piece of writing—criteria that learners understand, want to meet, and are able to succeed at—the process becomes achievable and pleasurable.

When new learners of English come into your classroom, try to get samples of the students' writing in their first languages. You will know a lot just from looking at that text. Does the handwriting indicate that the child has written a lot? Is there a clear sense of organization and order to the page? Is the child confident or hesitant? Is the writing fluent? This information, though just an introduction, can help you begin to learn about your students, their history, and their educational backgrounds.

Determining Goals: Standards for ELL Writing

World-class Instructional Design and Assessment (WIDA) Consortium has recently updated its 2012 ELD standards for its 27 member states. TESOL, an international professional organization for teachers of English to speakers of other languages, updated its K–12 ESL standards to become the TESOL PreK–12 Proficiency Standards, incorporating the use of language to achieve content goals and meet content standards (TESOL, 2006).

The WIDA standards documents are organized by grade level and by five English language proficiency levels (Entering, Emerging, Developing, Expanding, and Bridging), and four core content areas (language arts, math, science, and social studies) plus a feature strand (e.g., art, music, health) at each grade level.

Information on the standards, sample descriptors, and ways to use the standards can be accessed from the WIDA web site (http://www.wida.us). The sample descriptors shown in Table 9.4 are adapted from the WIDA classroom framework for grade levels 3 to 5 in writing and social studies. The descriptors give an idea of how the standards can be aligned to both content goals for writing and levels of proficiency of your English learners.

Once the focus standards and descriptors for a unit have been determined, it is time to develop "mini-lessons" for the "elephant bites" that will become your writing lessons. Lucy Calkins (Calkins, 1994; Calkins & Mermelstein, 2003) first used the concept of "mini-lessons" to model and teach aspects of writing. A mini-lesson is a short, five- to ten-minute lesson at the beginning of writing time that provides explicit instruction on a specific writing technique or skill. Assessment is an ongoing part of every lesson: You can teach learners how to use various assessment tools as they write, conference, revise, and edit. In the vignette at the beginning of this chapter, Diana conducted several mini-lessons to build the skills learners needed, including

TABLE 9.4 WIDA English Language Standards: The Language of Social Studies

Writing Domain: Engage in written communication in a variety of forms for a variety of purposes and audiences.

Standards	Level 1 Entering	Level 2 Beginning	Level 3 Developing	Level 4 Expanding	Level 5 Bridging
Social Studies	Reproduce historical highlights from time lines or visually supported newspaper headlines.	Produce entries for historical journals from time lines or visually supported newspaper headlines.	Maintain historical journals in chronological order based on time lines or newspaper headlines.	Produce reports from historical journals (using technology).	Produce historical documentaries from multiple sources (using technology).

Source: WIDA ELP Standards © 2004, 2007 Board of Regents of the University of Wisconsin System. Used with permission.

TABLE 9.5 Writing Self-Assessment

How I Write

What I think	☹	😐	☺
Details			
Beginning, middle, end			
Makes sense			
Punctuation: (.), (!), (?)			
Capital letters			
Spelling			
I like my story			

TABLE 9.6 Editing Checklist: Spelling and Word Choices

1. I checked the spelling of the following words in the textbook, in a dictionary, or with a friend: ☐

2. I asked (name and relationship, e.g., my sister Marta) _____ to check my spelling. ☐

3. I used a computer spell checker. I had misspelled the following words: ☐

4. I chose appropriate and specific words. Three specific words I used are: ☐

5. I looked up the following words in the dictionary: ☐

6. I used the following strong verbs instead of "to be": ☐

7. Other: ☐

one on inserting and cutting and pasting text, one on sentence combining, and another on writing a title.

Checklists are useful for helping learners understand the expectations for writing, encouraging learner self-assessment, and giving teacher feedback. For beginning learners, the purpose is to focus attention on aspects of writing. For example, the checklist in Table 9.5 is designed for beginning learners in primary grades to assess their own writing. As learners develop, they can use more details in their assessment tools. The checklist in Table 9.6 helps them consider issues of spelling and word choice. As learners progress, they can use more sophisticated rubrics to assess their writing. Rubrics, such as the persuasive essay rubric in Table 9.7, can be designed to fit the genre that learners are using. And after more advanced learners have been taught key grammar points, they can be expected to proof for them in their writing, using a tool like Table 9.8, Checklist of Key Grammar Points.

TABLE 9.7 Persuasive Essay Rubric

Criteria	Quality 1	2	3	4
My Position	I do not say what my position is.	I define my position, but it is confused or unclear.	I define my position clearly.	I clearly define my position and explain why it is controversial.
Reasons Supporting Position	I do not give reasons that support my position.	I give one or two reasons that support my position somewhat, but provide little evidence for it.	I give three reasons that support my position and provide evidence, examples, or statistics for all three.	I give clear and compelling reasons (at least three) that support my position and provide many examples, statistics, or other evidence.
Reasons Against the Position	I do not give arguments against my position.	I admit that there are arguments against the position, but don't explain them.	I discuss arguments against my position, and provide some evidence to support the arguments.	I thoroughly discuss arguments against my position and provide examples or statistics as evidence.
Organization	My writing is disorganized.	My writing shows evidence of organization, but sometimes gets off topic. There are few transitions between paragraphs.	My writing has a clear beginning, middle, and end. I generally use appropriate transitions between paragraphs to support the logic of the argument.	My writing is well organized, has a strong opening, strong supporting evidence, and a satisfying conclusion. There are logical transitions betweens paragraphs.
Closing	I forgot to write a closing.	My closing does not remind my audience of my argument.	My closing reminds the audience of my argument and restates the most compelling piece of evidence for it.	My closing restates my argument and cites the most compelling evidence for it.
Sentences	Too many confusing sentences make my essay hard to read.	My sentences are often awkward. There are some run-ons and fragments.	I wrote well-constructed sentences that show evidence of variety.	My sentences are clear, well constructed, and varied with compound and complex construction evident.
Conventions	Multiple errors in spelling, punctuation, and grammar make my paper hard to read.	Too many errors are distracting to the reader, but do not impede communication.	My spelling is correct. I make few errors in grammar and punctuation.	I use first-person form, with grammatical sentences, correct punctuation, and spelling.

TABLE 9.8 Checklist for Key Grammar Points

1. Do all sentences have at least one main subject and one main verb?
2. Did I use formal words for formal writing or informal words for informal writing?
3. Did I use idioms correctly?
4. Did I use the correct verb tense? Did I use the tense consistently?
5. Did I use verb phrases (e.g., verbs with prepositions like *turn up, turn over,* or *run down*) correctly?
6. Did I use plurals for count nouns (cows) and not non-count nouns (sheep)?
7. Did I use articles correctly?
8. Did I use nouns for nouns, verbs for verbs, adjectives for adjectives?
9. Do my subjects agree with my verbs: singular for singular, plural for plural?

TABLE 9.9 Running Record of Writing Pieces

					Name
Topics	Date of 1st Draft	Date of Questions	Date of 2nd Draft	Date of Final Draft	Rating: E = Excellent VG = Very Good G = Good NW = Needs Work
1.					
2.					
3.					
4.					

TABLE 9.10 Developing Literacy with ELLs: Focus on Writing: RTI Samplers

RTI Tier 1 Sampler

- Find out what your learners can do through writing assessments and writing samples.
- Set up a physical or online message board for your classroom. Use it to communicate with learners and answer their questions.
- Help learners to recognize what they know about writing from their first language and to transfer those skills to English.
- Work to create a writing environment by creating many reasons and uses for writing, celebrating authors, and celebrating writing as students learn.
- Have learners use content logs to document what they are learning.
- Have learners document the books they have read and share their reviews with the class.
- Model writing with learners using shared writing, in which you act the scribe to write down their ideas and then help them to organize and edit them into a final piece.
- Help learners choose topics for their writing that are important to them and that they can connect to their own experience.
- Scaffold writing development using the writing process.
- Use a quickwrite to develop fluency in the drafting stage of writing.
- Teach sentence combining to help learners understand and use compound and complex sentences.
- Help learners develop good keyboarding skills as soon as they are old enough. Make sure they know about tools such as spell checkers and grammar checkers. Introduce them to writing support software. Most of the writing for this generation will be by computer.
- Use graphic organizers to outline/plan class writings. Keep a list on the wall of the kinds of graphic organizers learners know about. Model how to use each one. Ask learners to choose the best one for the writing they plan to do.
- Teach Encourage, Question, Suggest (EQS) to help learners give one another useful, constructive feedback on writing.
- Use a multistep process to scaffold learners' movement from more personal writing toward academic writing.
- Assess learner writing and develop mini-lessons to address frequent writing issues. Collect quality examples of various aspects of writing and use them to illustrate the skills.
- Have learners keep a running record of their writings throughout the year, and note what stage in the writing process each reached.
- Teach learners how to assess their own writing, and encourage them to use a variety of rubrics and checklists to do so.
- Introduce different types of writing and key organizational features and language structures for each.
- Use the Word Wall to display key vocabulary and signal words for different types of writing.
- Hold writing conferences with individuals or small groups to provide personal encouragement and feedback for their writing.
- Publish students' writing in a variety of formats, both paper and electronic.

TABLE 9.10 Developing Literacy with ELLs: Focus on Writing: RTI Samplers *(Continued)*

RTI Tier 2 Sampler

- Assess learners individually. Look in particular for their strengths and work to build on these to create meaningful writing experiences.

- Use interactive journals to have personal written conversations with learners to encourage them to write, learn about them and what they know, and provide a model for language they are learning.

- Find out who learners' favorite authors are and feature them in the classroom. Coach learners to write and present a book review on the author to prepare to sit in the "Author's Chair."

- Have learners support the writing in their learning logs with illustrations and graphics that help to communicate the information.

- Model having a writing conference using EQS. Then work with individuals who have more trouble with the process while others are working in small groups.

- Help learners create individual lists of key signal words they need for their writing.

- While other students are writing, take dictation from ELLs and help them turn their ideas into a finished piece. Help them find a topic that relates to their own experience. Share the piece with the class.

- Meet with ELLs to review the genre they will be using for writing.

- Give ELLs a tour of the classroom writing center and make sure they know about the resources that are available to them.

- Provide a tutorial on helpful writing software (e.g., Inspiration/Kidspiration, Secret Writer's Society, The Write Connection, The Story Wizard).

- Provide an area of the word wall for reference words for ELLs. Put up words they need and are learning for writing; change and add others when the words have been mastered.

- Break down the writing genre you are teaching to ELLs into steps. Start with a step at which they can clearly succeed and progress from there.

- Tell ELLs which aspect of writing you will be looking for in their papers. Focus on one or two aspects at a time.

- Set achievable goals for ELLS. Discuss with ELLs your goals for them so they clearly understand where they are going and the progress they are making.

Writers can also keep track of their own process, noting which pieces they are working on, which ones they complete, and their self-assessment of the selections. Stack (2001) has her students keep notes on a form called a "running record of writing pieces," shown in Table 9.9.

Writing is clearly a key aspect of teaching ELLs. Writing helps us "start where students are," because all learners write at their own levels. Learners at all levels can write right away; at beginning levels, this writing may include drawing, writing in another language, or pointing to pictures or telling the teacher words to write down. With lots of practice and exposure, feedback from teacher and peers, careful ongoing assessment, and rich responses to their writing, each child can steadily grow as a writer. Writing provides powerful ways for learners to construct, remember, and communicate in the language they are learning, and to apply what they know in their first language to a new one. Writing works best when understood as a developmental process: We can communicate to learners that they do not have to get everything right the first time; they just need to work to do something a little better each time. And we can celebrate each small step of the way as our learners become powerful, fluent, resourceful, and imaginative writers.

Questions for Reflection

1. What aspects of writing were addressed in Diana's lesson? What elements of "the writer's craft" did she teach, and how did she do that?
2. Why is writing an activity that is particularly suited for helping ELLs acquire English? How does it connect to the principles outlined in Chapter 1?
3. What are differences in the writing process across various content areas, e.g., language arts, social studies, science, math, health, or the arts?
4. Given the limitations of time and the large number of students in classrooms, how might you organize writing instruction to use your and your students' time efficiently?
5. What are some ways you can use student writing to enhance school-home connections?
6. How can you adapt your writing instruction to address the needs of students with interrupted formal education (SIFEs)?

Activities for Further Learning

1. Develop a writing "mini-lesson" to scaffold one of the aspects or traits of writing in Table 9.1. How will you include modeling, explaining, scaffolding practice, and independent practice? How will you design your lesson to include learners at various language levels?
2. A new ELL enters your class. This student is from a language background that no one else in the classroom speaks. How might you begin to assess this learner's knowledge of writing in L1 and English? What assessment tools might you develop/use? What other resources might you need? What rubric might you use or create?
3. Create an annotated list of Internet resources for students to use in their writing and/or for teachers to use in teaching writing. You might search for dictionaries/translation sites in various languages, including English; useful graphic organizers; and rubrics for assessing writing at your chosen grade levels.
4. Plan and conduct a shared writing lesson series about a particular genre (e.g., thank you letter, personal narrative, persuasive essay, compare/contrast essay, report of an experiment, analysis of data, or explanation of a process). Assess and evaluate your lesson. Did learners progress toward achievement of the goals? Were you able to include learners at a variety of levels in the class? Did you make adaptations of the task to meet the levels/needs of ELLs?
5. Create a collection of good examples of a trait or genre you plan to teach, such as a collection of strong first sentences, a collection of good endings, examples of conversation, examples of transitions, advertisements, letters, reports, essays, and so on. You may use published work, student work, or your own examples. Develop a rubric and use it to analyze each piece, evaluating elements such as appropriateness for the grade/level of your learners, qualities of the writing, and so on.
6. Plan a word wall to assist a specific class that includes English learners. What will you include on the first day of school? How will the word wall change through the school year? What activities will you incorporate into your class to make use of the word wall? What are some lists of words that you plan to add over the year? (Note: There are many word wall lists available on the Web that you might consult.) How might you adapt/enhance your word wall for the ELLs in your class?
7. Design a writing center for a classroom that includes specific resources to meet the needs of the ELLs in that class. You might consider picture dictionaries and other vocabulary sources, translation tools, and software, as well as a variety of writing and drawing materials, stationery and envelopes, models and examples of genres of writing, rubrics, various writing prompts/task cards, and journals. Explain the purpose of the materials and resources you include and the procedures you will establish for using the writing center.

Suggested Reading

Barrett-Dragan, P. (2005). *A how-to guide for teaching English language learners in the primary classroom.* Portsmouth, NH: Heinemann. This book, written by a classroom teacher, takes the reader through the first twenty days of school, showing how to get ELLs started in their language acquisition, as well as how to build an inclusive classroom community that supports their learning.

Chen, L., & Mora-Flores, E. (2006). *Balanced literacy for English language learners, K–2.* Portsmouth, NH: Heinemann. The authors focus on seven aspects of balanced instruction to help ELLs develop and expand literacy skills: interactive read-aloud, emergent story book read-aloud, shared reading, reading workshop, writing workshop, guided reading, and word work.

Franklin, E. (Ed.). (1999). *Reading and writing in more than one language: Lessons for teachers.* Alexandria, VA: TESOL. This book discusses issues in K through 12 literacy with bilingual learners. Ten chapters from various contributors offer different viewpoints speaking from real classroom experiences, offering evidence and examples from teachers and students.

Hadaway, N. L., & Young, T. A. (2006). Negotiating meaning through writing. In T. A. Young & N. L. Hadaway (Eds.), *Supporting the development of English learners.* Newark, DE: International Reading Association. Hadaway and Young's chapter provides a clear explanation of the issues in ELL writing development, and offers principles and examples for helping beginning learners start to write, particularly by using interactive writing.

Hudelson, S. (1984). Kan yu ret an rayt en ingles: Children become literate in ESL. *TESOL Quarterly, 18*(2), 221–248. The author shares and carefully analyzes the writing of young bilingual students who are developing English language skills, offering recommendations for effective practice.

Leki, I. (1992). Building expertise through sequenced writing assignments. *TESOL Journal,* Winter, 1991–1992.

Leki, I., Cumming, A., & Silva, T. (2008). *A synthesis of research on L2 writing in English.* Mahwah, NJ: Erlbaum. This text synthesized 25 years of the most important findings in the field of second language writing in English in North America.

Richardson, W. (2010). *Blogs, wikis, podcasts, and other powerful Web tools for classrooms* (3rd ed.). Thousand Oaks, CA: Corwin. A guide to harnessing the power of Web 2.0 tools for classroom learning for teachers who want to bring social media to the classroom. Each chapter of the book describes and provides examples and links to a Web 2.0 tool.

Samway, K. D. (2006). *When English language learners write: Connecting research to practice, K–8.* Portsmouth, NH: Heinemann. Samway connects the latest research on ELLs and language acquisition to effective classroom practices and gives steps to take in providing writing instruction that is responsive to ELLs' needs.

References

Allwright, R. L., Woodley, M. P., & Allwright, J. M. (1988). Investigating reformulation as a practical strategy for the teaching of academic writing. *Applied Linguistics, 9,* 236–256.

Bunch, G. C., Lotan, R. A., Valdés, G., & Cohen, E. G. (2005). Keeping content at the heart of content-based instruction: Access and support for transitional English learners. In D. Kaufman & J. Crandall (Eds.), *Content-based instruction in primary and secondary school settings* (pp. 11–25). Alexandria, VA: TESOL.

Calkins, L. M. (1994). *The art of teaching writing* (New ed.). Portsmouth, NH: Heinemann.

Calkins, L. M., & Mermelstein, L. (2003). *Launching the writing workshop.* Portsmouth, NH: FirstHand.

Carrell, P. L., & Eisterhold, J. C. (1988). Schema theory and ESL reading pedagogy. In P. L. Carrell, J. Devine, & D. E. Eskey (Eds.), *Interactive approaches to second language reading* (pp. 73–92). Cambridge, UK: Cambridge University Press.

Cohen, E. G., & Lotan, R. A. (1997). *Working for equity in heterogeneous classrooms: Sociological theory in practice.* New York: Teachers College Press.

Culham, R. (2003). *6 + 1 traits of writing: The complete guide for grades 3 and up.* New York: Scholastic Professional Books.

Culham, R. (2005). *6 + 1 traits of writing. The complete guide for the primary grades.* New York: Scholastic.

Edelsky, C. (1993). *Writing in a bilingual program: Había una vez.* Norwood, NJ: Ablex.

Enright, D. S., & McCloskey, M. L. (1988). *Integrating English: Developing English language and literacy in the multilingual classroom.* Reading, MA: Addison-Wesley.

Gartner, M. (October 7, 1993). Tattoos and freedom. *The (Ames, Iowa) Daily Tribune.*

Graves, D. H. (2003). *Writing: Teachers and children at work* (20th anniversary ed.). Portsmouth, NH: Heinemann.

Hadaway, N. L., & Young, T. A. (2006). Negotiating meaning through writing. In T. A. Young & N. L. Hadaway (Eds.), *Supporting the development of English learners* (pp. 150–167). Newark, DE: International Reading Association.

Hudelson, S. (1984). Kan yu ret an rayt en ingles: Children become literate in ESL. *TESOL Quarterly, 18*(2), 221–248.

Leki, I. (1992). Building expertise through sequenced writing assignments. *TESOL Journal,* Winter, 1991–1992.

Leki, I. (2003). Research insights on second language writing instruction [Electronic Version]. *CAL Digest.* http://www.cal.org/resources/digest/0306leki.html.

Leki, I., Cumming, A., & Silva, T. (2008). *A synthesis of research on L2 writing in English.* Mahwah, NJ: Erlbaum.

Olivares, R. A. (2002). Communication, constructivism and transfer of knowledge in the education of bilingual learners [Electronic Version]. *International Journal of Bilingual Education and Bilingualism,* 5(1). http://www.multilingual-matters.net/beb/005/0004/beb0050004.pdf.

Richardson, W. (2010). *Blogs, wikis, podcasts, and other powerful Web tools for classrooms.* Thousand Oaks, CA: Corwin.

Rog, L. J. (2007). *Marvelous minilessons for teaching beginning writing, K–3.* Newark, DE: International Reading Association.

Samway, K. D. (Spring, 1992). Writers' workshop and children acquiring English as a nonnative language [Electronic Version]. *NCBE Program Information Guide Series.* http://www.ncela.gwu.edu/pubs/pigs/pig10.htm.

Samway, K. D. (2006). *When English language learners write: Connecting research to practice, K–8.* Portsmouth, NH: Heinemann.

Stack, L. (2001). *An introduction to writers' workshop for English language learners.* Unpublished manuscript, San Francisco.

TESOL. (2006). *PreK–12 English language proficiency standards.* Alexandria, VA: Author.

Tocalli-Beller, A., & Swain, M. (2005). Reformulation: The cognitive conflict and L2 learning it generates. *International Journal of Applied Linguistics, 15*(1), 5–28.

White, E. B. (2004). *Charlotte's web.* New York: HarperTrophy.

WIDA. (2011). *WIDA's CAN DO Descriptors by grade level cluster.* http://www.wida.us/standards/CAN_DOs/

Young, T. A., & Hadaway, N. L. (Eds.). (2006). *Supporting the development of English learners.* Newark, DE: International Reading Association.

MyEducationLab™

Go to the Topics, Reading and Writing and Assessment, in the MyEducationLab (www.myeducationlab.com) for your course, where you can:

- Find learning outcomes for Reading and Writing and Assessment along with the national standards that connect to these outcomes.
- Complete Assignments and Activities that can help you more deeply understand the chapter content.
- Apply and practice your understanding of the core teaching skills identified in the chapter with the Building Teaching Skills and Dispositions learning units.
- Examine challenging situations and cases presented in the IRIS Center Resources.
- Check your comprehension on the content covered in the chapter by going to the Study Plan in the Book Resources for your text. Here you will be able to take a chapter quiz, receive feedback on your answers, and then access Review, Practice, and Enrichment activities to enhance your understanding of chapter content.

- **A+RISE** A+RISE® Standards2Strategy™ is an innovative and interactive online resource that offers new teachers in grades K-12 just in time, research-based instructional strategies that meet the linguistic needs of ELLs as they learn content, differentiate instruction for all grades and abilities, and are aligned to Common Core Language Arts standards (for the literacy strategies) and to English language proficiency standards in WIDA, Texas, California, and Florida.

CHAPTER 10

Structuring and Planning Content-Language Integrated Lessons

Kathy Gill is teaching her fourth-grade class a unit on fables. Her students have read many of Aesop's fables, and Kathy has asked them to interview family members for examples of fables from their native cultures. The students have brought these stories to class and shared them with the group. Kathy has gathered the stories together and produced copies for the class.

Today, Kathy is distributing two brief stories to each of her six classroom groups. The first is one of Aesop's fables and the second is a fable brought by a student from home. Kathy wants the students to find commonalities in each of the stories, eventually defining the characteristics of a fable.

Kathy has assigned jobs to each of the four children in every group. One child is the reader and has the job today of reading the stories to the others. One student is a reporter and will report the results of the group work to the class as a whole. One student is the writer who will write the results, and the fourth student is the manager and timekeeper. This student's job is to keep the work moving along, and to make sure everyone understands his task and finishes the work on time. Kathy has assigned her English language learners (ELLs) to groups where she knows they will be supported by their classmates. She has assigned tasks to these students based upon their language abilities. For example, her beginning-level ELL is assigned to be a timekeeper in a group in which another student can speak her language.

Kathy has provided job tents for each student. The folded oak tag "tent" states the job name and pictures it as well. There are descriptions of what the job entails on each card, along with "frames" suggesting language these learners might use. The class has used these cards before—Kathy is sure many of the students understand their jobs—but she wants to check to be sure.

Kathy: *Mario, you are the reader today. What will you do?*

Mario: *I will read the stories to my group.*

Kathy: *Okay, and what will you do, Marta?*

Marta: *I listen to the stories and find the thing in common.*

Kathy: *(nodding) What does Marta mean by "in common"?*

Several children raise their hands and Kathy waits for five seconds for all to think about her question. Then she says, "Turn to your buddy and tell your buddy what Marta means by "finding the things in common" in the two stories."

How do teachers structure lessons for content-language integrated classes?

- What are the six characteristics of lessons that support learning?
- What are the three kinds of objectives for integrated lesson planning?
- Why do we activate prior knowledge?
- What are the essential elements of effective language and content input?
- How can we support guided practice?
- What activities are appropriate for independent practice?
- How can students summarize what they have learned?
- How can we conduct assessment throughout the learning experience?

LESSON CHARACTERISTICS THAT SUPPORT LEARNING

Lesson planning for a grade-level classroom of diverse English language learners requires careful thought and structure in order to integrate the content and language learning needs of all students. Effective teachers make adjustments to their lessons that lead to achievement gains for ELLs. These teachers carefully structure their language use, teach grade-appropriate content, integrate all learners heterogeneously in instructional groups that support practice, and provide corrective feedback. The element that sets apart these classrooms more than any other may be the conscious planning for language development that occurs in mixed language content classrooms. Whether our subject matter is science, math, language arts, or social studies, the language of the content is an important part of the learning of the content.

In our discussion of lesson planning, we will keep in mind the elements of good lessons that have been found to relate to achievement gains for English language learners. The following six factors are critical features (Fillmore, Ammon, McLaughlin, & Ammon, 1985, pp. 125–143).

Teacher-Directed Instruction

The language of the teacher during instruction can provide valuable input to ELLs and better access to the curriculum. High-quality student-teacher exchanges have been found to exist in exemplary math and science programs in California in which teachers were trained in second language techniques (Minicucci, 1996). But these high-quality exchanges are not the norm in mainstream classrooms. Teachers in one study (Stoops Verplaetse, 1998) commonly used imperative directives ("Open your books to page 45"), asked few questions, and rarely asked high-level cognitive or open-ended questions of ELLs. Lindholm-Leary (2001) found a high number of directives in math classrooms. Harklau (1994) found that by secondary school, teachers rarely adjusted their lectures to increase comprehensibility for ELLs. Students tuned out of the lessons for the most part and busied themselves by working on homework assignments or reading the text. Elementary and middle school classrooms additionally exhibit "astonishingly low levels of oral engagement and academic talk among 'at risk' Latino students in both mainstream and ESL classes" (Arreaga-Mayer & Perdomo-Rivera, 1996, p. 251). The authors report that academic talk occurred for only 2 percent of the day for ELLs in classrooms they studied.

The result of this impoverished language environment over a period of time is diminished comprehensible input and decreased access to the curriculum. Teachers who have limited or poor language interactions with students have very little notion of their students' language levels. Since they rarely hold extended conversations with them, they can be widely off the mark when asked to rate their language abilities. Teacher-guided collaborative dialogues (described in Chapter 5) enable teachers to engage in genuine dialogue with their students. This technique is beneficial to the development of higher-order cognitive skills and language skills, and provides better access to the curriculum than a traditional transmission teaching model (Berman, Minicucci, McLaughlin, Nelson, & Woodworth, 1995; Doherty, Hilberg, Pinal, & Tharp, 2003; Tikunoff, 1985).

Content teachers can accelerate content comprehension and language growth by adjusting their language patterns in order to model the language forms related to the specific content area studied. These forms change from one area of content to another. Science lessons may stress present tense verbs, passive voice forms, measurement terms, and specific vocabulary: *Cut thin slices of a beet so that they can be placed on a microscope depression slide and viewed with the lowest power (4X).* Social studies texts contain many present perfect and past tense forms, use adverbials of time, and are language dense: *The March on Washington for Jobs and Freedom on August 28, 1963 riveted the nation's attention. Rather than the anticipated one hundred thousand marchers, more than twice that number appeared, astonishing even its organizers.* Math word problems use specific language closely related to the processes required for problem solution: *Measure the following objects using the metric scale. Convert the measurements to the English scale by multiplying or dividing.* Effective teachers isolate this language, create language objectives to teach it, model it, and provide opportunities for their students to use it appropriately.

Heterogeneous Grouping

When grouped with English-speaking peers, ELLs are able to hear more correctly formed language than when isolated in ELL-only classes. In integrated classrooms, the language input of both the teacher's directions and the students' responses create a range of English proficiency that, if comprehended, provides a source of content-related grammatical structures and vocabulary. Students are expected to participate more in mixed classes than in ELL-only groupings, and if the teacher has planned effectively, they will have reason and opportunity to produce language output. In addition, mixed groupings build redundancy into activities and provide opportunities for extended dialogues (Calderon, Hertz-Lazarowitz, & Slavin, 1998; Gersten, 1996; Saunders, O'Brien, Lennon, & McLean,1996). This output potential is essential to language acquisition (Izumi & Bigelow, 2000; Swain, 1985). As learners use what they know in the new language, their fellow students help them to determine whether their communication is effective. In studies of small-group interactions among ELL-only groups (Pica, Lincoln-Porter, Paninos, & Linnelli, 1996), researchers found that the group interactions assisted language learning even when the source of the interaction is another ELL. Help from other students, whether native speakers or ELLs, apparently provides the language practice that can assist learners in developing new grammar forms and learning academic vocabulary (Fillmore, 1989; Pica et al., 1996).

The integration of technology into the content curriculum provides other opportunities for ELLs to work in heterogeneous groupings with English-only classmates. Cummins, Brown, and Sayers (2007) report on implementing approaches to promote literacy and engagement among minority learners using technology as a means to develop higher-order learning. Dixon (1995) reports effective learning for middle school students on spatial visualization tasks and concepts of reflection and rotation when compared to a traditional textbook approach. It appears that well-managed cooperative learning, on the whole, promotes higher achievement levels in ELLs (Calderón & Carreon, 1994; Calderón et al., 1998; Calderón, Tinajero, & Hertz-Lazarowitz, 1992). Negotiation of meaning and adjustment of output relates to language gains. But perhaps the most important element of heterogeneous grouping is the assurance that English language learners will work on grade level and with cognitively appropriate content.

Appropriate Content

Fillmore et al. (1985) found a relationship between the level of instruction, the level of language, and the academic outcomes of classroom programs (p. 129). ELLs excelled when the level of instruction provided was high and when the teachers were demanding. This outcome was especially notable in the Hispanic students in the study. In certain classrooms, teachers were skilled at organizing and presenting grade-appropriate materials in ways that engaged English language learners and aided their comprehension. Content-free, simplified materials could not hold learner interest as keenly as appropriate grade-level content. Many studies have agreed that a meaningful and academically challenging curriculum is a core component of effective programs for ELLs (Berman et al., 1995; Doherty et al., 2003; Montecel & Cortez, 2002; Ramirez, 1992; Tikunoff, 1985). An emphasis on learning basics such as the alphabet, numbers, and colors does not provide appropriate content learning for older learners. Engaging learners in age-appropriate content material will provide them with the basics as well as a great deal more.

Attention to Language

Effective teachers place an emphasis on communication and comprehension, and they plan ways to help ELLs enter the instructional conversation of the classroom. Using consistent language patterns for regular routines, teachers help their students quickly learn the transitions that occur in any lesson or school day. We saw this clearly in one kindergarten class where we observed a newly arrived Chinese student. Although he did not yet speak or understand English, he participated loudly by sing-songing his teacher's announcement: *It's clean-up time. It's clean-up time* at the end of the play period.

The location of the instruction in the classroom and the materials used help to mark transitions between lessons. Formulaic expressions and routine beginnings and endings of lessons are further aids to English language learners' comprehension. Clearly labeled daily agendas and lesson outlines provide the patterned routine so necessary for older learners. Consistent lesson formats for instruction help learners to anticipate what will come next and be prepared to participate. Merchant and Young (2000) create a weekly syllabus called the *Sci Fire News* at the beginning of each week for their mixed language science classes. The syllabus alerts students to activities, announcements, and assignments for the coming week.

Attention to language occurs when teachers plan for the content language necessary for students to learn the content. In Dana Richmond's middle school algebra class, many of the students were not able to explain how they solved problems using appropriate math vocabulary. Dana knew the vocabulary was crucial to understanding the algebraic concepts and that it would be tested at the end of each unit. She provided opportunities for groups of learners to work together in creating their explanations and then presenting them to the class, along with the correct problem solutions. Learning these terms in isolation, Dana discovered, was not effective. The language and content learning had to be integrated and Dana needed to plan for that integration.

The integration of language and content objectives has been explored (Berman et al., 1995; Echevarria, Short, & Powers, 2003; Minicucci, 1996) as a way of providing better access to the curriculum and higher achievement for ELLs. Research indicates that content-language integration is a key component of successful literacy development for English language learners (Gersten, Baker, Shanahan, Linan-Thompson, Collins, & Scarcella, 2007). By creating language objectives, content teachers and their students become aware of the desired language outcomes, language proficiencies, vocabulary usage, and grammatical elements necessary for the content to be communicated. Language objectives signal that teachers are directly and explicitly teaching language to second language learners. Indeed, we advocate for the addition of a language development component in every content classroom containing ELLs.

Supported Practice

Teachers support language learning when they provide students with opportunities to practice the language within a content context. Language output is as important as language input (Izumi & Bigelow, 2000; Swain, 1985). The form of support can be visual, verbal, graphic, or interactional. When students work in groups or enter into teacher-guided collaborative dialogues with their teachers, the interactional support enables them to use newly acquired language in a variety of ways. They are able to determine what works, and they are supported by more experienced listeners to negotiate what they want to say. Fillmore (1989) says teachers need to plan their elicitation questions carefully in order to engage learners at each level of proficiency. This "response tailoring" might mean the teacher plans to ask simple *yes-no* or *either-or* questions of beginning English learners while presenting intermediate learners with open-ended questions.

Planning for supported practice also means teachers plan in advance not only the kind of language they will use for various levels of learners but also the language output that will result. They plan how to support the output through a visual, graphic, or interactional context. And so, intermediate ELLs may describe the process of metamorphosis using a graphic organizer to structure their language and vocabulary. Beginning learners will describe the same process with the same organizer but may answer only by pointing to pictures in response to the teacher's questions: *Where is the butterfly? Show me the caterpillar. What happens after the caterpillar makes the cocoon?*

Corrective Feedback

Learners can receive feedback from the teacher on their language use in ways that encourage learning, and do not lead to embarrassment. These include:

- repetition,
- recasting language into correct academic vocabulary,
- modeling correct answers in responses that address the meaning learners were trying to convey,
- providing elaboration with this modeling to expand and improve language used (reformulation),
- asking questions to help learners clarify what they mean,
- prompting learners to explain more fully and completely,
- noting common errors and using them to develop mini-lessons for individuals, small groups, or the whole class,
- providing rubrics to help learners detect their own errors, and
- pointing to models or rules on the wall to help learners correct errors and promote learner self-evaluation.

Sometimes it might be important to simply ignore the language error and attend solely to the meaning a learner is trying to convey. Olivier (2003) reports that the ways in which teachers use language affect how learners modify their language. If teachers give constructive feedback, learners tend to use the feedback to rephrase. Feedback and open-ended questions from fellow students in small-group settings also provide the data for modification of output and development of grammar (Pica et al., 1996).

A LESSON FORMAT FOR INTEGRATED LEARNING

Keeping in mind the six characteristics of lessons that work, we propose a lesson format for integrated content and language instruction that is based upon a three-part structure: *Into, Through, and Beyond* (some teachers call this structure *Before, During, and After*). The organization of our lesson is based upon work in cognitive psychology, particularly on the view that knowledge is constructed and that the focus of instruction should be helping students to develop learning and thinking strategies rather than helping them memorize and acquire facts. Mayer's cognitive model of knowledge construction (1992) lists three learning processes necessary to meaningful learning:

1. *Selection* of information to be learned and added to the "working memory"
2. *Organization* of information in the "working memory" into a coherent whole
3. *Integration* of the organized information into prior knowledge structures already existing in the "working memory" and the permanent memory

For meaningful learning to occur, learners must proceed through all three processes (see Table 10.1). They first select information that is necessary to the learning experience, focusing on this information and not attending to other information in the environment, the textbook, or lecture. In order to select appropriately, learners must comprehend the information and make their selections based upon their understanding of the new information. In reading a textbook passage, for example, learners must understand some of the information in the text before they are able to select the information that is most important for the learning experience. In listening to a lecture, learners must pay close attention to the information they need to learn and remember and ignore all other auditory input.

After the selection process, learners organize the selected information into a coherent whole. Organizing the totality of a story might mean learners are able to answer specific questions about the story and retell the story according to an organizing principle. The organization of auditory input might mean that learners are able to take notes and organize that information into an outline according to an organizing principle. Or it might mean that they are able to summarize the major concepts orally.

The final step is integration of the whole topic into the schema of what learners already know about the topic—their prior knowledge and information already existing in permanent

TABLE 10.1 A Three-Part Lesson Format for Comprehensive Lesson Planning

Theme: What "big idea" or topic will connect this lesson to others I will teach this week or month?

Lesson Phase	Lesson Components	Questions for Lesson Planning
Into the Lesson	Content Objectives	What *specifically* do I want my students to know or be able to do at the end of the lesson? How can I *communicate* the objective to my students? Is my objective *measurable?* What contextual *supports* can I provide for learning?
	Language Objectives	What specifically do I want my students to be able to understand, say, read, or write by the end of my lesson? How can I communicate the objective to my students? Will I be able to measure this objective? What contextual *supports* can I provide for learning?
	Learning Strategy Objectives	What learning strategy will I teach or *demonstrate* to help my students learn better? How can I *communicate* the objective to my students? Is my objective *measurable*? What contextual *supports* can I provide for learning?
	Activating Prior Knowledge	How will I help students to focus their attention on what they *already know* about the information or the skill in today's lesson?
Through the Lesson	Vocabulary	What vocabulary will the students be using? How will they *use the vocabulary*? Does the vocabulary reflect the *content* I am teaching?
	Language and Content Input	How will the new information be conveyed to my students? Will they listen to it, read it, or engage in research to discover it? How can I support the input with *context* and *scaffolding?*
	Guided Practice	How will I help my students *practice* the new information or skill in a way that will help them to be successful? Can I incorporate a *collaborative activity* into this practice? How will I *check their comprehension* of the new information?
Beyond the Lesson	Independent Practice	What assignments or homework shall I have my students complete to facilitate long-term *retention?* Does the assignment reflect the *variety* in my students' learning styles?
	Summarizing	How can I help my students to *demonstrate, tell, or write* what they have learned today?
	Assessment	How will I know what *each* of my students has *learned* in this lesson?

memory. This presupposes learners are aware of what they already know and their current information has been activated through classroom experiences, such as interactions with the teacher or their peers. Integration of the information requires learners to arrange the new information in some way, perhaps hierarchically, temporally, or spatially. For example, in learning about Juan Ponce de Leon, learners might place his name within the category of known explorers. The timeline of de Leon's life and the location of his explorations also can be meshed with known histories of other explorers and areas of exploration in the New World. Without this integration of the new information, long-term learning does not take place.

The three-part lesson format described here corresponds to Mayer's description of the cognitive processes leading to meaningful learning.

INTO THE LESSON: DEFINING OBJECTIVES, ACTIVATING, AND PREPARING FOR LEARNING

In the *Into* phase of the lesson, teachers prepare for the new learning. Preparation involves determining and clearly communicating objectives, activating what learners already know about the topic, motivating them to learn more, providing a perspective for the learning, and stimulating learners to begin processing the new information.

Defining Content Objectives

This is the first step in planning a lesson. When teaching English language learners, we want to think about three different kinds of objectives:

1. Content objectives that are grade appropriate and cognitively challenging
2. Language objectives that identify the language needed for the content to be processed, learned, and communicated
3. Learning strategy objectives that promote thinking about learning, analysis, and reflection

As shown in Table 10.1, the questions we ask ourselves when planning for instruction concern the specificity of the objectives, our ability to communicate them and measure their effectiveness, and the degree to which we can support the learning.

- *Content Objectives:*   What specifically do I want my students to know or be able to do at the end of the lesson? Is my objective measurable? How can I communicate the objective to my students? How can I support their learning?
- *Language Objectives:*   What specifically do I want my students to be able to understand, say, read, or write by the end of my lesson? How will I communicate the objective to my students? Will I be able to measure this objective? How can I support their learning?
- *Learning Strategy Objectives:*   What learning strategy will I teach or demonstrate to help my students learn more effectively? How can I communicate the objective to my students? Is my objective measurable? How can I support their learning?

Specificity in defining objectives helps us to focus more clearly on what it is we want students to learn during our lessons. This is more effective than thinking about the activities we are going to use or how to get the students involved in the learning. We have to think about those aspects of the lesson, too, but they do not determine learning outcomes in the same way as specific and clearly communicated content and language objectives.

Objective writing is best done in terms of what the students will do and not what the teacher will do. Thus, we like to think in terms of language where the student is the subject of the objective, for example: *The students will be able to state three causes for the fall of the Roman Empire*, or *Learners will illustrate the four stages in the life cycle of a frog*.

We advocate the use of Bloom's Taxonomy of Thinking Skills (Bloom, Englehart, Furst, Hill, & Krathworl, 1956) to bring more specificity to our thinking about objectives. Table 10.2 lists the Taxonomy or six levels of cognitive thinking defined by Bloom and his colleagues; the next columns indicate cue words that are highly specific to that level of thinking. These cue words are active verbs. When used to write content or language objectives, they bring clarity to our thinking and to the thinking of our students concerning what they are going to learn or be able to do. For this reason, we prefer not to use cue words such as *review* when writing objectives. This verb does not specifically tell us what the students are going to know or be able to do. More likely it refers to what the teacher is going to do—and that is still not very clear.

The six levels of cognition on the Taxonomy begin at the Knowledge level, the level of naming and labeling, equivalent to the level of the two-year-old who asks Mom *What's dat?* This is the level of vocabulary learning and it is a good place to start content lessons. As we proceed through our lessons, we move through the hierarchy, giving students opportunities to comprehend and apply knowledge. It would be a mistake to end learning at this point, however. Students will not achieve meaningful learning unless they also analyze the information, synthesize the learning to form a new whole, and evaluate the material for a given purpose. Although it may not be possible to achieve each level of the hierarchy for every lesson, it is essential to teach

TABLE 10.2 Bloom's Taxonomy of Thinking Levels

Thinking Level	Cue Words		
Recall Remembering previously learned material	• Observe • Repeat • Label/Name • Cluster	• List • Record • Match • Memorize	• Recall • Recount • Sort • Outline (format stated) • Define
Comprehension Translate Grasping the meaning of material	• Recognize • Locate • Identify • Restate • Paraphrase	• Describe • Tell • Report • Express • Explain	• Cite • Document/Support • Summarize • Precise/Abstract
Application Generalize Using learned material in new and concrete situations	• Select • Manipulate • Sequence • Organize • Imitate	• Use • Frame • Apply • How to • Show • Demonstrate	• Dramatize • Illustrate • Test/Solve • Imagine (information known)
Analysis Break down/Discover Breaking down material into its component parts so that it may be more easily understood	• Examine • Classify • Distinguish • Differentiate • Outline (no format given)	• Map • Relate to • Characterize • Analyze • Conclude • Question	• Compare and Contrast • Research • Debate and Defend • Refute • Infer
Synthesis Compose Putting material together to form a new whole	• Propose • Plan • Compose • Formulate	• Create • Invent • Design	• Construct • Imitate • Imagine • Speculate
Evaluation Judge Judging the value of material for a given purpose	• Compare (Pro/Con) • Prioritize/Rank • Judge • Decide	• Rate • Evaluate • Criticize • Argue • Justify	• Convince • Persuade • Assess • Value • Predict

Source: Adapted from Zainuddin, Yahya, Morales-Jones, & Ariza (2002, pp. 257–258).

to the higher levels for a substantial part of each learning unit. Standardized testing requires students to compare-contrast, compose, persuade, and argue—all higher-order skills. And it is through teaching at these higher levels that ELLs are able to develop the language and cognitive skills they need to communicate about complex content.

Defining Language Objectives

Language objectives are essential for English language learners to become language users (Gersten, 1996). We cannot assume that learners will develop language through classroom immersion. Academic language is used primarily in schools and textbooks, not in casual conversations. In order for learners to acquire it, teachers must create language objectives and provide opportunities for structured practice of the language.

The kinds of language objectives we focus on are determined by the age of the students, the standards, and the nature of the content learning. Although there are general similarities embedded in learning all content (the ability to read, to construct meaning, to understand oral discussions, to make inferences, and determine causation), there is also a great deal of knowledge variation among subject areas, which requires a high degree of differentiated knowledge by teachers and students. This differentiated knowledge is so complex and abstract that generalities "are not sufficient to leapfrog the middle ground of differentiated knowledge" (August & Hakuta, 2002, p. 27). In other words, students need to learn and be taught specific academic language proficiencies that are aligned with specific subject matter content. Science uses language that is structured quite differently from that of language arts and mathematics. Teachers who are aware of the language requirements of each content course will be better able to create language objectives for teaching those language structures and functions.

The social studies are particularly challenging for language learners. If, for example, the lesson is devoted to the Gold Rush, we will expect learners to use past tense verbs and adverbial clauses to describe historical events. The description of the Gold Rush will likely include complex sentences with independent and dependent clauses. The topic may also include cause and effect structures in addition to a chronological text structure. Vocabulary related to the Gold Rush may include words with multiple meanings: *mine, pan,* and *prospect* for example. The language of maps entails place names and passive voice verb constructions (e.g., *The center of gold panning was located in the Yukon. The Yukon is situated in . . .).* Communicative functions will also be utilized during the course of study, and these can be included in the language objective. Students may be asked to *describe, explain, sequence,* or *analyze* aspects of the Gold Rush. They will also be required to develop language skills related to these functions: speaking, listening, reading, and writing.

Writing language objectives is one of the hardest skills that classroom teachers of ELLs have to learn. For one thing, teachers are excellent English language users, but they may be unused to working with students who are multilingual or limited in English proficiency. Because of this, they find it difficult to identify the academic language and grammatical structures that will pose problems for their students. In much the same way that a fish is unaware of water, teachers may be unaware of the grammatical structures that are required to explain a math word problem. In addition, teachers may not have had opportunities to speak to their language-learning students and may be unaware of the levels of their language proficiency. If this is the case, designing appropriate language objectives for a content lesson will be guesswork. Some teachers feel they have little time during their content classes to also teach language. They feel this is the job of a specialist such as the ESL teacher. The truth of the matter is that many schools have limited ESL teacher services and ELLs are with their grade-level teachers for most of the day. For these reasons, increasing numbers of school districts require teachers to be proficient in delivering content instruction and language development lessons to their students. The following section will structure the process of developing language objectives.

We like to determine language objectives by thinking backwards. After determining content objectives and the activities required to achieve those objectives, we think about what students need to do with language to complete those activities successfully. For example, students may read a passage in a textbook, report on information either orally or in writing, listen to and communicate with others in small-group work, or take notes from an oral presentation. Each of these activities involves a **language skill** such as listening, speaking, reading, or writing.

Language content such as performing a language function, using content-specific vocabulary, or required grammatical constructions is also involved. We like to run the lesson through our minds as if viewing a movie. We imagine our students working on the activities we have chosen and try to identify the language they will need to be successful at these tasks. Often, we will discover the language we want to teach in the textbook or in other materials used to inform the class. All students need to understand this language, regardless of whether they are English language learners.

In addition to the language required by the content subject, students also need language to communicate with others in the classroom environment. For example, when discussing a text passage, group members may be asked to indicate their level of word knowledge, to predict what the article will be about, or to summarize major concepts. Not all students will have the academic language skills to respond to these tasks appropriately. The teacher can teach appropriate responses and structure language objectives to communicate the purpose of the language task. Examples are:

- *Students will be able to ask for and respond to questions in the present tense regarding word knowledge.*
- *Students will be able to make predictions about informational text using specific verbs in the present tense.*
- *Students will orally summarize the one major concept in the text reading using the present tense and appropriate academic modifiers* (primarily, mainly, on the whole).

In addition to writing language objectives for communication purposes, it is always helpful to provide students with sentence frames that will scaffold their language attempts. After identifying the language requirements of the lesson, we suggest writing a sentence frame that is an ideal response, suited to the grade-level requirements and the language proficiencies of the students:

- *Do you know what _____ means?*
- *Are you familiar with the word _____?*
- *I (don't) know what _____ means.*
- *I am (not) familiar with the word _____.*
- *I predict that the article will be about_____.*
- *I predict that the article will discuss/focus on _____.*
- *I believe that the article is mainly about _____.*
- *The overall thesis of this article appears to be that _____.*

Effective language objectives describe what Kate Kinsella (2011) calls "portable" language. That is, academic structures, grammatical forms, and functions that are used routinely in academic discourse. She suggests the following characteristics of language objectives (Kinsella, 2011). They:

- stem from the linguistic demands of a standards-based lesson task
- focus on high-leverage (portable) language that will serve students in many contexts
- emphasize expressive language domains: speaking and writing (but not excluding listening and reading)
- use active verbs to explain functions and tasks
- name the specific language students will use

The language of school requires that students learn both grammatical forms and language functions. **Form** describes the internal grammatical structure of words. **Function** relates to the purpose for which language is being used. Examples of grammatical forms include:

- *comparative adjectives* (greater than, less than, more complicated)
- *prepositions* (divided into, multiplied by)
- *active or passive voice* (The people vote…Cars are manufactured in…)
- *past and present perfect tenses* (it was, they have gone)
- *historical present* (Lewis writes in his journal that…)
- *pronoun referents* (he, she, they, them, her, our, their)
- *agreement of subject and verb* (she was, they were)
- *signal words* (however, also, finally, for example, due to)
- *compound sentences* (Evaporation is part of the water cycle, and so is condensation.)
- *complex sentences* (Evaporation, which is part of the water cycle, is a process…)

Language functions include the following, among others:

- *retelling, describing, explaining*
- *matching, labeling, illustrating*
- *summarizing*
- *identifying characteristics*
- *sequencing*

- *outlining*
- *comparing and/or contrasting properties and entities*
- *classifying*
- *inferring*
- *persuading*
- *asking, requesting*
- *predicting outcomes*
- *identifying cause and effect*
- *researching*

When teachers combine both form and function in a language objective, they can be very precise about the language they intend their students to learn. Kinsella (2011) proposes that teachers refer to a group of precise, active verbs that indicate language functions. For example, the verb *articulate* indicates that students will be *retelling, explaining,* or *describing* in an oral modality. The verb *compare* indicates that students will be *identifying similarities among entities* or *characteristics of entities.* These active verbs correlate to the listing of cue words on Table 10.2—Bloom's Taxonomy of Thinking Levels. On Table 10.2, it is clear that certain verbs are appropriate for comprehension level tasks and others more suited to analysis tasks. For this reason, we advocate using the Taxonomy listing when creating language objectives.

The cue words, all active verbs describing language functions, can be combined with language forms—grammatical structures—that are necessary for academic communication. Therefore, teachers might imagine a sentence frame such as (Kinsella, 2011):

Students will (function: active verb phrase) using (language target: grammatical form).

From this frame, we can generate language objectives with sentence frames for various content classes that are precise and clear.

- *Students will define target vocabulary using precise noun and verb phrases in the present tense.*
  The word _____ means to _____ or to _____.
- *Students will sequence events in a narrative using chronological signal* words (first, next, soon, finally).
  First, (noun phrase + past tense verb). Next, (noun phrase + past tense verb).
- *Students will summarize experimental results using precise terminology in the present and past tense where appropriate.*
  The problem of my experiment was _____. I hypothesized that _____. The method of the experiment included the following steps: _____. The result of the experiment was _____. I can explain the results by stating/showing _____.
- *Students will use mathematical terminology to express an equation in the present tense. _____ to the third power equals _____.*
- *Students will describe a geographic diagram in the text using the passive voice, the terms* longitude *and* latitude, *and numbers in the 100s.*
  Serbia is _____ at _____ degrees longitude and _____ degrees latitude.

Examples of unclear language objectives usually do not refer to the form or the function of the language that is being taught. Many of these objectives are confused with typical language arts objectives:

Students will write a summary of the reading in the text.

Students will determine the main idea of the text reading.

Students will deliver an oral report.

Language arts objectives are content objectives. As such, they describe the kinds of learning that will take place around the skills of reading, speaking, and writing about written text. These content objectives generally indicate a language skill involved in the lesson outcome, but they usually do not mention the form and functions involved. In this way, language arts objectives are different from language objectives.

English Language Arts objectives may be derived from standards and resemble them closely. For example, the language arts objectives cited above relate to the following Common Core Anchor Standards (http://www.corestandards.org/the-standards/english-language-arts-standards):

- *Write informative explanatory texts to examine and convey complex ideas and information clearly and accurately through the effective selection, organization, and analysis of content.*
- *Determine central ideas or themes of a text and analyze their development; summarize the key supporting details and ideas.*
- *Present information, findings, and supportive evidence such that listeners can follow the line of reasoning and make sure the organization, development, and style are appropriate to task, purpose, and audience.*

The Common Core Standards and most language arts objectives in general will cite a language function (write, speak, read, describe, record, etc.) because these functions are related to the use of language for learning purposes. However, language arts objectives and standards differ from language objectives in that they do not specify the form of the language to be used for oral and written purposes—the productive language.

The next step in defining lesson objectives is to communicate the content and language objectives to students both orally and in writing. Communication of learning goals is critical to achieving those goals. We have been told by principals and supervisors that the most effective teachers are very clear about the goals of their lessons. After spending five minutes in their rooms, you are sure to know exactly what the learners are being taught to know or do. In addition to orally informing students, it is important to write the objectives on the board where they can be referred to easily. ELLs who cannot clearly understand the oral language will have a second chance to understand the written communication. Once learners know what they need to learn to be successful, they are able to set about learning. Communicating this information gives all students the opportunity to be a part of the instructional conversation.

Determining how to assess your objectives is another part of the preparation phase of the lesson. You may want learners to end the lesson by writing a short summary in their learning logs, sharing their summary with a partner, creating an illustration, answering a quick question on a sticky note, responding to your summary questions through signals (such as "thumbs up" and "thumbs down" signals), or writing a "Dear Teacher" letter. Remember that you will be assessing both content and language knowledge, and the nature of the lesson determines the nature of your assessment. If you have a reading-skill goal in mind, you may want learners to demonstrate comprehension by completing a graphic organizer that summarizes the text passage. Assessing oral skills will require an oral response either in large- or small-group format. Listening skills can be the most difficult language mode to assess because you cannot see inside your students' heads. You can, however, ask students to produce language orally or in writing that demonstrates comprehension.

Defining Learning Strategy Objectives

Learning strategies are an important part of lesson preparation for all students. These strategies form the core of the CALLA approach, which is described in Chapter 4. For English language learners, learning strategies are particularly important. ELLs use these strategies to help them compensate for their lack of classroom language proficiency. Strategies that help them become better learners include:

- organizing main ideas
- planning how to complete a learning task
- listening to information selectively
- checking their own comprehension
- planning when, where, what, and how to study

    Learners also need to know how to:

- use reference materials
- take notes
- summarize
- relate new learning to prior learning
- predict and infer meanings

During class, they must be able to:

- ask questions of the teacher and their peers
- work with others in a group

Once again, we cannot assume our students have learned these essential strategies. If we want learners to use learning strategies to achieve, we have to plan for their use.

Rona Wilson begins each year with her seventh-grade students by concentrating on social learning strategies of questioning, praising, participating, and cooperating. She plans lessons in which she defines the social skill, models the skill, and then sets up situations that require her students to practice each of the skills. Rona supports the English language learners in her class by writing the language necessary to the skill on large charts that she keeps hanging on the wall. For praising, she writes items such as *That's a good idea, Well done*, and *Good job*. Question starters might include phrases such as *What do you call . . .? How can I . . .?* and *Do you have . . .?* After a while, students no longer need the wall words as they incorporate the language into their growing language systems.

Performance Indicators

Performance indicators are observable, measurable language behaviors that teachers can assess as students engage in classroom tasks (TESOL, 2006). Performance indicators are similar to language or content objectives, but they contain three elements of classroom progress critical to the success of ELLs:

1. *Content information* derived from the content curriculum, state, and national standards. Examples include: math operations, human body systems, or initial consonant clusters.
2. *Language functions* that indicate how the language is used in communicating. Examples of functions include: persuade, defend, and interpret.
3. *Support or strategy* that scaffolds the communication act enabling ELLs to be successful with developing language skills. Examples include: using manipulatives, visuals, graphic organizers, or working in small groups (TESOL, 2006, p. 43).

Performance indicators provide the three essential elements needed for successful instruction of ELLs in content classrooms. Both content and language objectives are clearly specified. In addition, an element of support, a scaffold, is indicated to ensure that the learning experience is structured in a way to help ELLs be successful. Examples of supports and strategies for content and language learning include social (interactional) supports, material supports, and learning supports.

Social Supports

- Small group learning
- Interactive structures that encourage discussion and active participation (Buddy Talk, Think-Pair-Share, and so on)
- Cooperative learning structures (Numbered Heads Together, group work with designated roles, Roundtable/Round Robin, Jigsaw, and so on)
- Study buddies
- Study groups

Material Supports

- Graphic organizers, diagrams
- Pictures, props, and gestures
- Advance organizers, outlines, structured notes, T-lists
- Picture dictionaries, learner dictionaries, translation dictionaries, word source software
- Alternative and modified texts

Learning Supports

- Learning strategies (note-taking, selective listening and reading, summarizing, organizational planning, effective memorization, prediction, advance organization, and so on)
- Vocabulary learning tools (personal dictionaries, Word Squares, visualization, and so on)

When supports and scaffolds are combined with language and content objectives, teachers can modify instruction for differing proficiency levels. For example, a performance indicator targeting the content of plants (grade levels 1 to 3) might require beginning level learners to:

> *Draw and label local plant or animal species from real life observations, experiences, or pictures* (TESOL, 2006, p. 65).

The same content for an intermediate level learner might require a different language function and a different support structure such as:

> *Compare physical attributes of local plant or animal species from real-life observations, experiences, or pictures, using graphic support* (TESOL, 2006, p. 65).

In this last example, the language function (compare) requires a comparison graphic organizer as a support structure. As teachers respond to multiple levels of language proficiency in classrooms, they modify the language functions and support structures while teaching the required content to all learners.

Note that performance indicators as defined by TESOL (2006) do not require that the *form* of the language be specified. In our opinion, adding the form in addition to the function of the language provides more specificity and assists teachers in being aware of precisely what kind of language is to be taught and learned. Let us look again at the performance indicators described earlier with the addition of the form of the language and a sentence frame to make that language explicit:

- *Draw and label local plant or animal species with proper nouns using real life observations, experiences, or pictures* (TESOL, 2006, p. 65).

  > *White Oak, Red Maple, Elm, White Ash, Spruce, Red Cedar*

- *Compare physical attributes of local plant or animal species from real-life observations, experiences, or pictures, using graphic support, precise adjectives, and comparative signal words* (TESOL, 2006, p. 65).

  > *White Oak leaves have _____ lobes while Red Maple leaves have _____ lobes. (rounded, pointed)*

Activating Prior or Current Knowledge

Activation takes place while proceeding *Into the Lesson*, immediately after the communication of objectives. It is one of the most important ways teachers help learning to occur. The educational psychologist, David Ausubel (1968), has said it is the "single most important factor influencing learning." Why is this so? Once learners are aware that they already know something about a topic, it is no longer viewed as totally new. Learners won't give up on themselves before they start, but will be willing to continue the learning dialogue, especially once they have made an initial contribution to the conversation. Learners feel empowered at the outset of instruction.

Learners also feel cognitively engaged and focused on the new learning. We like to think of it as attaching Velcro to the brain. The new learning "sticks" because our students have become participants in the exploration of knowledge in our classrooms.

Activation also serves the teacher's purpose of finding out what learners already know about the topic and clearing up any misconceptions they may have about it. This information helps teachers to adjust instruction to learners' previous knowledge as well as to their interests and cultures. The teacher may discover her students mistakenly believe all rivers flow from the north to the south or seasons occur because of the distance of the Earth from the Sun. This misinformation will need to be clarified before further learning can take place.

The question that needs to be asked during this phase of the lesson is: *How will I help students to focus their attention on what they already know about the information or the skill in today's lesson?* There are many techniques used by teachers to activate learning. All of them have in common the effect of getting learners cognitively engaged and ready to accept the new learning. Let us look at a few we have found to be useful at a variety of grade levels.

SEMANTIC MAPPING   This is sometimes called Spider Mapping. We like to use large pieces of chart paper to create our semantic maps (Figure 10.1). We draw a circle with the content topic printed in the center and then lead students in a brainstorming session to tell what they know about the topic. With ELLs, you'll notice that few of them will raise their hands to contribute to these

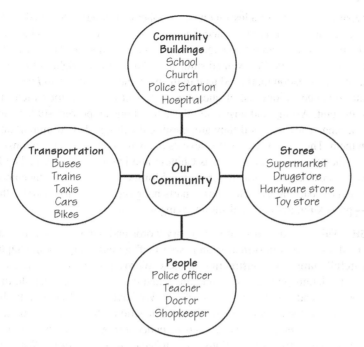

FIGURE 10.1 The Semantic Map Is a Visual Picture of How the Vocabulary in the Unit Is Related

brainstorming sessions. In order to overcome this problem, we like to ask students to brainstorm in buddy pairs first, setting a goal of two to ten ideas per pair depending on the age of the students. This rehearsal time gives our students more opportunity to prepare their language and then contribute to the group. Once the semantic maps are complete, we can begin the process of grouping ideas. In the *Our Community* map, the various vocabulary words relating to the community have been grouped under headings such as *Stores, People, Transportation*, and *Community Buildings*. The grouping process teaches an important learning strategy to young learners; and the language used to process the grouping leads to vocabulary and grammatical structures, such as *Trains go under transportation*, and *The policeman belongs in the People group*.

THE K-W-L CHART   The chart (Ogle, 1986) shown in Figure 10.2 is a fixture in many classrooms. It works as a useful activator asking students about the lesson content: *What I Think I Know What I Want to Know What I Learned*. We like to use it with students at every grade level. The first question, *What do I think I know?* is similar to the question we ask when brainstorming semantic maps. In this situation, however, we may need more than a one-word answer. We used the K-W-L

What I Think I Know	What I Want to Know	What I Learned
Christopher Columbus was an explorer.	Where did he live?	
	When did he live?	
He was Chinese?	Where did he explore?	
He lived in 1957?	Why is he famous?	
He sailed on a ship.		

FIGURE 10.2 The K-W-L Chart Provides a Framework for All Phases of the Lesson

chart when preparing students for a lesson on Christopher Columbus. We asked students to tell us all they knew about the famous explorer and then wrote their answers on the chart. In some cases, we modeled the fact that we weren't sure about some of our own ideas. We placed these ideas on the chart with a question mark. We wanted students to know it is all right not to be sure of all of their answers, and the question marks led us into the next question: *What do I want to know?* This question usually produces a long list of questions, a perfect road map for structuring the rest of our lessons in the unit. Asking and answering these questions empowers students to take charge of their own learning. They feel as if they are learning the things that are important to them, not imposed upon them. The K-W-L Chart also reveals many different misconceptions—some of our students told us they thought Columbus was Chinese and lived around 1957! The last question, *What did I learn?* provides the summarizer we need for the learning experience and allows us to assess each student's learning as well. These charts hang on the classroom walls throughout the learning unit—provoking, guiding, and summarizing learning.

WORDSPLASH　This is a collection of vocabulary words and phrases taken from a text that the students will read for content information and "splashed" across a large chart (Saphier & Haley, 1993a). We carefully tailor the construction of these Wordsplashes to both the content we wish to focus on and the language necessary to express that content. In the example in Figure 10.3, students are about to read about chemical reactions. We have included the verb phrases needed to make cause-and-effect statements about chemical reactions shown on the chart, for example: *Chemical reactions are caused by interactions of molecules. Rust is caused by iron molecules combining with oxygen. Chemical reactions occur when molecules interact.* We instruct students to work in buddy pairs to write sentences using the vocabulary on the chart.

Students must predict the relationships between the words and the concepts in order to write their sentences. Many learners make guesses because they have limited understanding of the vocabulary on the chart. Nevertheless, all learners can be mentally involved in the activity of trying to use these words and become familiar as a preparation for later learning. After writing the sentences, we read the textbook and determine whether our guesses are correct. At this point, we like to ask our students to change their sentences to make them correct. For young learners, we write student sentences on the board and correct them in small groups.

CORNERS　Merchant and Young (2000) use this cooperative strategy to assess their students' prior knowledge in their unit on scientific measurement. Students are divided into four groups and proceed to the four corners of the room, where they are given a task. In the measurement unit, they are asked to take their science journals with them and record their answers to the questions written on the chart in each corner. Students work together to create answers and then move on to the next corner at a signal. In other versions of corners (Kagan, 1994), students are asked to take a stand in response to a question, such as *What causes air pollution?* The four corners of the room are each labeled with a different response: *Car exhaust fumes, Cigarette smoke, Factory emissions,* and *Wildfires.* Students choose one of the four answers and then go to that corner to share their reasons for making the choice. Some teachers then ask students to visit other corners and listen to the reasons behind the other choices. Another option is to appoint a spokesperson for each group who shares the reasons with the class.

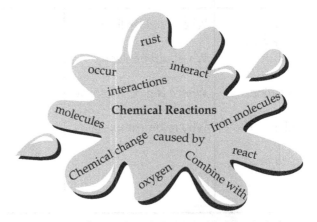

**FIGURE 10.3 The Words and Phrases on the Wordsplash
Can Be Combined to State Important Concepts from the Unit**

CAROUSEL BRAINSTORMING   (Saphier et al., 1993a). This is a good activator to use at the beginning of a unit of study. It can also be used as a summarizer at the end of the learning unit. For this activity, we place charts around the walls of the room. Each chart has a heading or questions related to a sub-unit of the major topic. For example, when fifth graders are about to study the regions of the United States, we might ask questions such as:

- *What are the major crops of the Pacific Northwest region?*
- *What important historical events happened in the Pacific Northwest region?*
- *What do you know about the geography of the Pacific Northwest region?*
- *What states are located in the Pacific Northwest region?*
- *What natural resources are located in the Pacific Northwest region?*
- *What manufactured products are produced in the Pacific Northwest region?*

Students move in small groups around the room, attempting to write what they know on each chart. We like to give each group a different color marker to distinguish itself. At the end of the activity, each group returns to the original chart and proceeds to read what others have written there. If charts cannot be hung on the wall, pass the charts around to table groups.

The *Input* phase of the lesson requires students to comprehend new information and collaborate with others in learning tasks. Several of the Common Core Anchor Standards (http://www.corestandards.org/the-standards/english-language-arts-standards) relate to this phase of the lesson:

- *Prepare for and participate effectively in a range of conversations and collaborations with diverse partners, building on others' ideas and expressing their own clearly and persuasively.*
- *Integrate and evaluate information in diverse media and formats, including visually, quantitatively, and orally.*
- *Evaluate a speaker's point of view, reasoning, and use of evidence and rhetoric.*

THROUGH THE LESSON: INPUT FOR ACTIVE UNDERSTANDING, VOCABULARY DEVELOPMENT, AND PRACTICAL PURPOSE

During the *Through* phase of the lesson, a great deal of learning occurs. This is the lesson delivery phase. It is also the phase where the teacher continues to connect new learning to previous knowledge and to the learners' interests and cultures. Practice and application of learning take place during this phase of the lesson, with emphasis on interaction among the learners, comprehensible input, and scaffolding of the learning.

Vocabulary Learning

We like to ask the following questions when planning for the *Through* phase of the lesson with regard to vocabulary:

- *What vocabulary will the students be using?*
- *How will they use the vocabulary?*
- *Does the vocabulary reflect the content I am teaching?*

Vocabulary selection occurs as we think about the nature of the content and the language we want to teach. There is an important distinction to be made in the kinds of vocabulary selected for our lessons. Content-specific, technical vocabulary represents terms necessary to learning the content (Beck, McKeown, & Kucan, 2002; Genesee, 2006; Snow, Met, & Genesee, 1989). For example, in a unit on the Civil Rights movement, the terms *segregation, desegregation, boycott,* and *integrate* must be included. These words must be taught to the entire class, as they will likely be new to most learners, even those who speak English.

In order to talk about civil rights, however, there are other vocabulary items, and academic or textbook language that are not specific to the civil rights content, but are part of an educated speaker's vocabulary. For the Civil Rights example, we might want to use adverbial phrases, such as:

- *in 1957 ...*
- *after the arrest of Rosa Parks ...*
- *when the Supreme Court ruled ...*

Certain verb phrases are also necessary, such as:

- *ensure basic freedoms*
- *abolish slavery*
- *amend the constitution*
- *enact laws*

When choosing the vocabulary to teach, be aware of both the technical and the academic vocabulary needs of students. Different content subjects require different academic language. By reading the science, math, and social studies texts used in schools, you can familiarize yourself with the language necessary to talk about each of these subjects.

Methods of teaching vocabulary are described more completely in Chapter 7.

Language and Content Input

The questions to ask with regard to the content and language input phase of the lesson are:

- *How will the new information be conveyed to my students?*
- *Will they listen to it, read it, or engage in research to discover it?*
- *How can I support the input with context?*

Input that is comprehensible and conveyed to the learner as clearly and as concretely as possible is the goal for this phase of the lesson. Additionally, if the new learning can be connected to what our students already know or to their cultural backgrounds, we can increase their understanding in ways leading to long-term retention.

How can we make new learning comprehensible? For oral instructional input, it's important to be aware of the **clarity** of our language input to students. We try to avoid idiomatic expressions, jargon, and slang as much as possible. We speak clearly, not too rapidly, and underline all that we say with repetition of the important phrases and ideas. We accompany our oral language with gestures that lead to meaning: pointing to words, pictures, or objects, demonstrating with body gestures (with a smile, a shrug, a frown, or with fatigue), and using word stress and pauses to highlight important language.

We incorporate as many **explanatory devices** as possible into our input. These devices include visual aids, writing on the chalkboard, charts, drawings, graphs, maps, real objects, graphic organizers, and models. We bring objects from home and use objects in the classroom to help students comprehend our oral language.

Teacher **modeling** is an important part of how we help students understand new input. Effective teachers provide models of the processes and products they want their students to engage in and create. One teacher we know used classroom objects, such as a ruler and a small block, to help her students understand the concept of a lever. She placed the block on the windowsill and inserted the ruler under the sill using the block as a fulcrum to lift the window. The simple machine was then diagrammed on the chalkboard as students recalled what they had seen her do. The parts of the machine were labeled (*load, effort, fulcrum, lever*) and students made their own drawings with labels. Next, students used rulers and blocks to work in small groups and determine other jobs this simple machine could accomplish in the classroom. The modeling by the teacher and the later hands-on learning opportunity ensured that all learners in the class understood the nature of the lever as an example of a simple machine.

If we have begun teaching with an **activator** that causes students to ask questions, such as those on the K-W-L chart, we can begin the *Input* phase of the lesson using those questions as a guide. Working in small groups, learners can use picture books, texts, maps, and other resources to find answers to their questions.

In a sixth-grade unit on the Middle Ages, Barbara Agor (2000) used a picture walk and brainstorming as activators for her lessons. She began by having students ask questions based upon their exploration of the many picture books she had provided. Barbara wrote these questions down and used them to help guide her instruction. She introduced activities to aid her students' comprehension of the period. The class created time lines, stretching from the Middle Ages to the present. They added important events to the time line throughout the unit as learners became aware of the major changes occurring during this period of history. Students also made lists comparing and contrasting *Things we have today* and *Things they had then*. They used these lists to write personal letters to a time traveler from the Middle Ages, alerting him to the changes he would encounter in this century.

Interaction between learners provides a further help to comprehension of new learning. We try to use buddy pairs and small groups frequently. We determine ways to help the students interact positively with one another (positive interdependence) and to assess each learner's individual growth (individual accountability). In a unit on Guatemala, Betty Wein, with the help of her third graders, first gathered many books and artifacts from the country. She then divided her class into groups of four and used the Jigsaw strategy to divide up the learning. Each student was responsible for determining one of the following:

- food products
- clothing and housing
- geography
- weather

Betty asked all of the students in the food product group to work together using books, pictures, and home interviews to learn about the major food products of Guatemala. She did the same with the other three groups. By the end of their research, students were able to return to their "home" groups and report on what they had learned. Students took notes on a chart that was later used to create essays about Guatemala. The essays helped Betty determine what each student had learned as a result of her unit.

Content and language input that is characterized by student comprehension and interaction is effective input. We can be assured our students understand the concepts and language of the topic. Comprehension alone is not sufficient to ensure long-term learning, however. Next, we need to guide students in practice and application of the new knowledge and skills.

Guided Practice

With regard to the guided practice phase of the lesson we ask:

- *How will I help my students practice the new information or skill in a way that will help them to be successful?*
- *Can I incorporate a collaborative activity into this practice?*
- *How will I check their comprehension of the new information?*

During guided practice, provide scaffolding to help students be successful in their first practical use of the new skills or knowledge. This kind of guidance at the beginning of the practice session greatly increases the rate and degree of learning. Scaffolds also help to support the learner's first attempts to express or write about the new learning.

At this stage of the lesson, students should be guided step by step through the processes of the task. If we want learners to write about what they have learned about the history of the historic Navajo people, for example, we need to show ways to talk about Navajo characteristics.

The Jigsaw Strategy

Jigsaw is a technique that aids language and content input by fostering interaction among learners. Content is broken up into related parts, like interlocking pieces in a jigsaw puzzle, in order to stimulate interaction among learners and improve student comprehension. Learners become experts on one portion or piece of a topic and share their expertise with others. Learners are also able to study a portion of a large amount of information and hear summaries of the rest from peers. Everyone shares responsibility for learning.

Procedure:

- Divide participants into "home groups" of about four students.
- Assign each person in a home group an "expert number."
- Assign each expert number a section of the reading.
- Students reassemble into "expert groups," based on their numbers.
- They read their assigned section of the text and determine how best to teach the material to their home groups.
- Experts return to their home groups and take turns teaching the content learned in their expert groups to their home groups.

Using a semantic map listing Navajo characteristics, we can model sentences that describe the Navajo lifestyle then invite students to orally describe the Navajo, using the same **key sentence frames**, while being supported by the semantic map.

The Navajo _____ for _____.

used bows and arrows	hunting
rode and tamed horses	work
wore woven headbands	decoration
raised cattle and sheep	food

Further practice occurs as students interact with each other using the new language. Instructing students to *Tell your buddy four characteristics of the historic Navajo people* is an opportunity to provide English language learners with supported practice in using the new language and structures.

Nancy Wong provided guided practice for her third-grade students in their science unit based on the life cycle of the salamander. After students had opportunities to observe the animals, listen to stories about them, and leaf through many picture books, Nancy wanted her students to become responsible for the care and feeding of the animals. Each day, she gave a mini-lesson on one aspect of care such as feeding, cleaning the aquarium, handling, and so on. She supported the major points by writing them on a chart. She then gave her students opportunities to tell each other what they had learned about the care of their classroom pets. Eventually, Nancy wanted the students to create a Salamander Care and Feeding manual to be used in the third grades in the school. The daily oral language practice helped her students not only to learn the information but also to be able to talk about it and write about it.

We can clearly communicate the need for classroom activities if we create a *practical purpose* for learning. Betty Wein accomplished this goal by helping her students to present the results of the Guatemala unit at an open school night. Barbara Agor (2002) invited interested groups from the school to see and hear her students talk about the Middle Ages. Nancy Wong created a practical purpose for her third graders when she suggested her students use their Salamander Care and Feeding manual to teach the classroom next door how to care for the salamanders they would have in their own classroom for the following month.

Teachers such as Betty Wein, Barbara Agor, and Nancy Wong are able to guide their students' learning step by step because they are always aware of what their students understand and what they do not. They *check for comprehension* throughout the lesson. This is an important element in teaching that is sometimes forgotten because of the lack of time and the large number of students in classrooms. But checking for comprehension is essential to knowing which students are with us and which ones are not.

Keep in mind the need to check *everyone's* comprehension in the classroom. If you ask a question and one learner answers well, it does not mean that the rest understand. Many ELLs might not choose to raise their hands in class or might not volunteer quickly enough after attempting to comprehend the teacher's question. So we need strategies to include them in our comprehension checks and in classroom learning in general.

We need to find ways to check comprehension:

- of all of our students
- frequently
- on the same topic or concept
- during instruction

Madelyn Hunter has called this kind of checking **dipsticking** (Saphier & Gower, 1997). In the same way that mechanics use a dipstick to check for oil in a car's engine, teachers use techniques to check for comprehension in the minds of their students.

Dipsticking can be accomplished using either recall or comprehension questions or both. If we use only recall questions, however, we may not be sure students have a good understanding of the concept. ELLs may be able to recall a one-word answer for the teacher, but they may not really understand how that word relates to the whole topic. Comprehension questions are better at assessing complete understanding. To answer a comprehension question, students must understand the concept or guiding principle that is being assessed. For example, in order to answer the question *What have we read about Geronimo that tells us he was not a Navajo?* students must understand the characteristics of the historic Navajo people. The question, *Does refrigeration represent a physical or a chemical change?* also requires an understanding of an underlying principle of chemistry. Thus, we may need to ask a number of questions at several different levels, both recall and comprehension, so that each student can communicate the extent of his or her current understanding and also achieve success with the realization of that learning.

Checking every student in the class frequently may seem an impossible task. But there are techniques that can help us to accomplish this goal. The **one-question-quiz** is used when the teacher wants to check comprehension of all students. The teacher asks a summarizing question and students write the answer while she circulates through the room noting which students can respond correctly.

Asking questions to the entire class and telling them to answer with a *buddy* is another way to check understanding. We have seen teachers who float around the room listening to answers and then say, *Tell me what your buddy told you,* to assess students they haven't yet heard from.

Thumbs up/thumbs down is a signal response that provides a quick check of which students are confident in their answers and which ones are hesitating. The teacher says, *Paul Revere was a silversmith who made a midnight ride to warn that the British were coming,* and students respond with thumbs up. If she says, *John Paul Jones once said, "Give me liberty or give me death,"* students respond with thumbs down.

Other signal responses involve the use of **response cards** (Cavanaugh, Heward, & Donelson, 1996; Heward, Gardner, Cavanaugh, Courson, Grossi, & Barbetta, 1996). These are cards or other items such as pictures held up by learners simultaneously in response to teacher prompts. The use of response cards greatly increases student participation in the class (Heward et al., 1996). They give the teacher instant feedback on the level of student understanding, and they provide a form of scaffolding to students who can use pictures and the responses of other learners to support their own learning.

One third-grade teacher we know gives her students cards with a multiplication sign on one side and a division sign on the other. She reads word problems and asks her students to show the appropriate sign for solving the problem. In English class, her students use cards to identify correct punctuation, parts of speech, or run-on sentences (RO).

We like to use *hand signals*, too. We teach a letter from sign language such as *r* to signify *reptile* and *m* to signify *mammal*. Students enjoy using these signals to identify animals or animal characteristics. We model sentences such as *These animals are cold blooded,* and students use the sign for the letter *r*. Or we say, *These animals provide milk for their young,* and students show the *m* sign.

Checking vocabulary can be done quickly using signals. Write two words on the chalkboard labeled number 1 and number 2. Define one word and ask students to show the correct number by raising one or two fingers. As students listen to the teacher definitions, there is opportunity for modeling of academic language required for the topic. Students will listen carefully at these moments because they want to participate in the group activity and they are supported by the responses of other learners. Imagine describing the word *reptile* by using more general and then more specific clues to the meaning: *This is a class of vertebrates. These vertebrates frequently crawl on stubby legs or on their bellies. These vertebrates are cold-blooded. A crocodile is an example of these vertebrates. A snake is another example.*

One of our favorite comprehension checking devices is using the **slate**. We have used slates with students of all ages and found them to be one of the most effective techniques for gauging comprehension of simple recall information; assessing math computation; and practicing phonics skills, language mechanics, or spelling. We model the process by holding our own slates, asking a question, quickly writing the answer, and then asking students to *Show your slates*. We take a quick scan of the room and show our slate with the correct answer. Students can quickly self-correct with this immediate feedback. Our students are strongly motivated to participate in this task. It is low stress and fun, and even beginning English language learners will feel comfortable participating.

Individual slates resembling miniature chalkboards are sold in educational supply stores. These can be expensive and require the use of chalk and an eraser that may be messy. We have also used dry erase board cut into 9-inch by 12-inch rectangles as a cheaper alternative. These require the use of special dry erase markers and are bulky. The cheapest and easiest slate we

Signals are Quick Assessment Tools That Encourage Students to Be Actively Involved in the Learning Experience

have used is a piece of white paper slipped into a see-through page protector. Most of these can be written on and erased with a tissue (we suggest you check before buying, though, as they can be made of many different materials). If the page protector has been three-hole punched, students can keep these in their ring binders for easy access.

As they listen to teacher input in the form of definitions, sentences, or characteristics, all of our students are involved in learning and all of them are listening to our language. This is an important time in the classroom. These moments create excellent opportunities for language input. The students are attentive, they are listening, and they are primed to respond to our language. Even though the time spent in checking is registered in minutes, the gains for learners are enormous. There is 100 percent participation. We, too, learn a great deal about our students at these moments. This learning helps us to know if students need additional guided practice or if they are ready to move into the next phase of learning—independent practice.

The *Through* phase of the lesson requires using language in multiple ways. Examples of related Common Core Anchor Standards (http://www.corestandards.org/the-standards/english language-arts-standards) for this phase of the lesson include:

- *Apply knowledge of language to understand how language functions in different contexts, to make effective choices for meaning or style, and to comprehend more fully when reading or listening.*
- *Determine or clarify the meaning of unknown and multiple-meaning words and phrases by using context clues, analyzing meaningful word parts, and consulting general and specialized reference materials, as appropriate.*

BEYOND THE LESSON: PROVIDING REASONS FOR FURTHER COMMUNICATION

Independent Practice

Independent practice is the phase of the lesson during which we want our students to internalize the new learning by integrating it into the other knowledge structures or **schemas** that they already have. During this phase we ask ourselves:

- *What assignments or homework shall I have my students complete to facilitate long-term retention?*
- *Does the assignment reflect the variety in my students' learning styles, interests, knowledge levels, and proficiency levels?*

The arena of the classroom is a "here and now" situation. We have advocated for the use of situational activities with scaffolding supports, such as visuals and realia. We have also called for a great deal of peer interaction within the classroom to provide opportunities for real language use. At some point, our learners need to move beyond this "here and now" context in order to expand language use into more abstract arenas and promote learning retention.

Billows has described the learner's situation as "four concentric spheres with the learner at the center" (1961, pp. 9–12):

- Sphere no. 1: This is "what the learner can see, hear, and touch directly." This is the arena of the classroom.
- Sphere no. 2: This is "what the learner knows from his own experience, his daily life, what he has seen and heard directly but cannot see or hear at the moment." This might describe the student's neighborhood, home, or native country.
- Sphere no. 3: This sphere represents what the learner "has not yet experienced directly, but what he can call to mind with an effort of the imagination, with the help of pictures, dramatization, charts and plans."
- Sphere no. 4: The fourth sphere is "what is brought into . . . mind through the spoken, written or printed word alone, without help through audio-visual aids."

The role of the teacher is to support learners as they move outward through these four spheres to achieve the last sphere, where learners can read printed text with no visuals or contextual supports and achieve comprehension through the language alone. Billows' work precedes the gradual release of responsibility model (Brown, Campione, & Day, 1981; Fitzgerald & Graves, 2004) described in Chapter 8 (Figure 8.7). Teacher scaffolding is abundant in the initial learning spheres where teachers take on most of the responsibility for student success. This scaffolding is gradually reduced as students acquire more skills and display competency in the learning task.

The progress of this movement is in line with what we know about good teaching. We suggest effective teachers begin instruction with the "here and now" and attempt to help learners activate what they already know about the topic from prior learning or experience. As learners progress in their understanding, teachers use techniques and materials to promote learning beyond the realm of the classroom—starting with concrete experiences and leading into abstract learning. The final outcome results when learners can read a text or take a standardized examination and comprehend the material well.

The movement from Sphere number 1 to Sphere number 4 requires careful planning, as we have suggested. In addition, it is helpful to think about the movement of the language growth occurring as learners move through these four spheres. Mohan (1986, p. 110) describes this progress as an increase in the distance between the speaker and hearer of the language. He arranges the discourse in order of increasing distance:

1. Reflection   **2.** Conversation

3. Correspondence   **4.** Publication

Reflection occurs within the learner. There is no distance because the speaker and hearer are one. Conversation occurs between a speaker and hearer who are face to face. Correspondence is writing for a known audience—for example, a letter to a pen pal or an essay for the teacher. Publication is "impersonal communication" for an unknown audience where feedback does not exist, as in a newspaper article. As the distance between the speaker and hearer grows, the level of difficulty of the language increases. The lack of feedback at the fourth level requires the highest level of language skill because there is no context other than that created by the language itself. As our learners progress in their language skills and cognitive growth, their goal is the level of publication.

In another kind of distance, Mohan (1986, p. 110) describes the distance from the speaker to the topic of the language. The levels reflect the "increasing abstraction" created between the experience and the description or verbalization of the experience.

1. Drama   **2.** Narrative

3. Exposition   **4.** Argumentation

Drama, for example, in the form of a role-play, is closely related to telling a story about content experience. Narrative is more abstract as students attempt to report back on a learning experience. Exposition relates to generalizing about learning, perhaps in the form of an essay. Finally, argumentation is the most abstract, at the theory level. Here students might engage in a debate.

These two kinds of distances reflect growing cognitive and language abilities in our students. Mohan (1986) describes the "Show and Tell" experience of kindergarten or first-grade students as a face-to-face, conversational exchange "somewhere between drama and narrative." This experience also reflects Spheres 1 and 2 in Billows' (1961) scheme. The child makes a transition between home experience and school experience.

Older English language learners still require concrete classroom experiences characteristic of "Show and Tell," such as science experiments, but these experiences need to be reflective of appropriate grade-level content learning. Older learners also need to move beyond the level of face-to-face conversation and role-play into the world of interviews, reporting, research, generalization, and theory.

During the *Beyond* phase of the lesson, we attempt to move our students beyond the "here and now" aspect of practice and application, and into a more abstract realm of using language to communicate beyond the classroom. We have discussed a few examples of teachers who took their learners beyond the classroom experience and created culminating activities at the end of a unit to communicate to a wider audience in a more abstract form of discourse. Barbara Agor's (2000) students reported on the Middle Ages to members of the school community. Nancy Wong's students taught other third graders how to care for salamanders and wrote a Care and Feeding manual to support their instruction. Fifth-grade teachers we have worked with created opportunities for *Beyond* classroom experiences when they culminated their experiential science unit with a science fair. The fair was attended by parents, school board members, and members of the community. Each student was responsible for presenting a science experiment visually in the form of a display and also for reporting to others about the experiment, answering questions, and clearing up misunderstandings.

Another interesting and challenging form of *Beyond* the classroom experience is called **service learning**. Service learning gives students the chance to apply the content of their studies to real problems in their communities (Allen, 2003). Service learning is more than volunteerism because of the academic goals that are integral to the program. In the most rigorous forms of service learning, students analyze real problems in their communities, such as traffic congestion or pollution, and then plan ways to create social change. Planning bus routes to save fuel, doing research on plants that will reduce pollution, and convincing local authorities to plant drought resistant plants in states with water shortages are some of the projects students might tackle. The language requirements of these projects help students to communicate beyond the level of the classroom and connect them with the real world in which they live.

The *Beyond* phase of the lesson allows learners to participate in lesson formats that are varied and that provide novelty. For many of our students, paper-and-pencil tasks do not relate to their learning styles and may not reflect their intelligence and creativity. The notion of variety in learning is an important one when there are diverse language learners in the classroom. The variety of languages and cultures will surely reflect a variety in learning styles as well. If we can appeal to our students to use language to communicate, tease, entertain, and inform, we are enlarging their levels of discourse. Using language to create songs, poetry, plays, radio shows, and debates for an audience ensures our students will retain their learning over time.

Examples of Common Core Anchor Standards (http://www.corestandards.org/the standards/english-language-arts-standards) related to the *Independent Practice* phase of the lesson include:

- *Integrate and evaluate content and media presented in diverse media and formats, including visually and quantitatively, as well as in words.*
- *Delineate and evaluate the arguments and specific claims in a text, including the validity of the reasoning as well as the relevance and sufficiency of the evidence.*

Summarizing

The summary phase of the lesson relates back to our content, language, and learning strategy objectives. In this phase of the lesson, we ask:

- *How can I help my students to tell or write what they have learned today?*

Summarizing learning can be done by students at the end of each lesson. We want our students to expect to be challenged on their learning each day. Summarizing sends a strong message to students that they are responsible for the learning of the objectives that were communicated at the start of the lesson.

Too often, teachers skip this stage of the lesson because of time constraints. But summarizing need not take up a lot of class time. Some of the techniques we enjoy using take no more than five minutes, but they help all learners to integrate their new learning with what they already know about the topic. Summarizing also helps students to self-assess their own learning—an important strategy.

3-2-1 is an easy but effective summarizing activity (Saphier et al., 1993b). Write the three requirements for the summary on the board: recall information from the lesson, show understanding of the topic, and analyze the concept. Then, students respond in writing that is collected. Notice how the 3-2-1 elements increase in cognitive complexity. In the following example, the "3" requests students to simply recall. The "2" asks for a comprehension level of understanding. The "1" is at the level of analysis in Bloom's (1956) Taxonomy of Thinking Skills.

3 events in the history of the Navajo people

2 major differences between the historic Navajo and the Apache people

1 reason why you would have preferred to be either a Navajo or an Apache in the past

The **Ticket to Leave** (Saphier et al., 1993b) is an excellent summarizer when little time remains at the end of the class. Students are asked to respond to the teacher either in writing or orally. You can collect the "tickets" as students leave the class or stand at the door listening to student responses. Examples of inquiries might be:

* *Answer the question on the board* (written as the day's objective).
* *Write one thing about today's content that leaves you puzzled.*
* *Name the most important thing you learned in today's class.*
* *Be able to give three reasons why . . .*

Learning Logs are student notebooks that record short summaries of a lesson. Some teachers like to use them at the end of every lesson, collecting them from time to time to check on their students' comprehension. Learning logs can be freely written as a summary or can be structured; it depends on the age and ability of the students. It is best to use open-ended questions to structure a learning log question. Recall questions tend to be answered in short phrases that limit the development of language skills and fall short in helping students to structure their own comprehension of the lesson.

Some open-ended inquiries useful in promoting a lesson summary are:

* *Tell what you learned today about . . .*
* *What do you know now about . . . that you didn't know before?*
* *What did you understand about today's lesson? What don't you understand yet?*
* *What were the most important points from today's discussion?*
* *Explain your understanding of . . .*

Draw a Picture/Diagram (Saphier et al., 1993b) is most effective with topics that can be represented visually. You can give students a blank piece of paper and ask them to draw or diagram a topic, or you can provide a diagram, outline, or graphic organizer for students to complete. Some examples of this technique are the following:

* *Complete the flow chart to include all of the steps in the process.*
* *Draw a picture of the main character as described in today's reading.*
* *Draw a diagram of the process of photosynthesis.*
* *Indicate where each of the three battles occurred on the map.*
* *How does an apple grow? Draw the main stages.*

The summarizing phase of the lesson can be used to support at least two of the Common Core Anchor Standards (http://www.corestandards.org/the-standards/english-language-arts-standards) for the English Language Arts:

* *Present information, findings and supporting evidence such that listeners can follow the line of reasoning and make sure the organization, development, and style are appropriate to task, purpose, and audience.*

> • *Write routinely over extended time frames (time for research, reflection, and revision) and shorter time frames (a single sitting or a day or two) for a range of tasks, purposes, and audiences.*

Assessment

The assessment phase, although written here as the last phase of the lesson, really takes place throughout the learning experience. The question we ask about assessment is:

> • *How will I know what each of my students has learned in this lesson?*

We have previously discussed comprehension checking or **dipsticking**, which takes place with all students throughout the lesson. Dipsticking is an important source of **formative assessment** information for teachers—ongoing knowledge of student performance to guide instruction. It may be too late to assess at the end of a lesson or at the end of the unit. At that point, we have no time to reformulate our lesson, change our techniques, or provide for additional guided practice. Assessment needs to be ongoing and classroom based.

Another kind of assessment—**summative assessment**—is used at the end of the learning experience—at the end of a unit of study, or often at the end of the school year, to provide information to report to parents as well as to evaluate programs, schools, districts, and states. Summative assessment is sometimes done in the form of district-level testing, departmental testing, or standardized testing.

The type of assessment we are primarily addressing here is formative assessment. This kind of assessment is the ongoing collection of information gathered both during and after instruction in order to determine how well a student is progressing. Formative assessment is often built into the lesson itself using tasks that are familiar to students—for example, writing in a learning log on a daily basis or summarizing from a graphic organizer. The use of a **rubric** ensures that students are aware of what will be assessed and how they can achieve at the highest levels in the class.

The more frequent and varied our assessment is, the better it will be able to determine achievement. If we only rely on weekly quizzes to assess students, we will have a limited picture of achievement. If, however, we use weekly quizzes, learning logs, dipsticking, student reporting, group quizzes, role-plays, and group presentations, we will have a variety of ways to inform our instruction and to create a clear picture of the learner's achievement. Active learning strategies, for example, can be used as assessment tools in every phase of the lesson. Table 10.3 lists some of the strategies we have recommended in this book for checking student comprehension *Into, Through,* and *Beyond* the target lesson. Assessment issues are described in more depth in Chapter 11.

TABLE 10.3 Active Learning Strategies for Every Phase of the Lesson

Lesson Stage	Assessment Technique
Into the Lesson: Activate Prior Knowledge/Assess Pre-knowledge	• K-W-L chart • Wordsplash • Semantic map • Corners • Carousel brainstorming • Picture previews • Open-ended questions • Buddy talk • Line ups • Stir the class

TABLE 10.3 Active Learning Strategies for Every Phase of the Lesson *(Continued)*

Lesson Stage	Assessment Technique
Through the Lesson: Input for Active Understanding	• Signals • Think-pair-share • Buddy talk • Teacher questioning • Jigsaw the information • Anticipation guides • Wordsplash
Through the Lesson: Guided Practice	• Reciprocal reading • One question quiz • Thumbs up • Slates • Signal cards • Sort tasks • Line-ups • Cooperative learning groups • Numbered heads together
Beyond the Lesson: Independent Practice	• Cooperative learning groups • Biopoems • Sort tasks • Project learning • Inside-outside circle • Journal entries
Beyond the Lesson: Summarizing	• Ticket to leave • Homework • Journal entries • ABC summary • 3-2-1 summary • Slates

RESPONSE TO INTERVENTION

RTI TIER 1 SAMPLER

- Adjust the language of instruction to increase comprehension for ELLs. Use an outline of the lesson on the overhead projector or the chalkboard and point to target language while teaching. Connect with students through eye contact and proximity during oral input. Change location from the front to the back of the room as necessary and when possible.
- Place language learning students in heterogeneous groups of three or four students. Provide many opportunities throughout the lesson for group members to share

oral information, respond to questions, provide examples, decide on truth value of statements, and create summary statements. Rotate response opportunities among group members to ensure that all students are responding. An excellent structure for this activity is called *Numbered Heads Together.*

- Pair ELLs with English-speaking peers at computer stations to gain information from the Internet, outline a project, create a survey, or research a topic.
- Create daily agendas with pictures of each activity in elementary classrooms. Place the agenda in the same location each day. Begin the day by pointing to each activity, naming it, and indicating the time of the activity. In secondary classes, use an outline of the daily lesson placed on the board or the overhead projector. Begin the lesson by identifying the content, language, and learning strategy objectives. Then indicate the activities that will accomplish these goals in the lesson.
- Provide variety in the lesson delivery by supporting student learning in varied ways. For limited proficient students, provide pictures, graphs, maps, hands-on projects, or computer visual input. For more proficient learners, provide some of the above options to support textbook reading.
- Explain and post content, language, and learning strategy objectives in the classroom. Provide examples of products. Demonstrate processes that will be required in the course of the lesson. Make the objectives small enough to be accomplished during the lesson or break down the objectives into incremental steps that can be accomplished over time. Provide sentence frames to scaffold the language to be taught and to help learners understand the language lesson objective. Model the sentence frames and provide opportunities for students to practice them with a partner.
- Determine learning supports (social, material, or learning strategy) for each lesson objective. Use these to differentiate instruction for various language proficiencies in the classroom.
- Activate prior or current knowledge of the learning concept using one of the strategies presented in this chapter. Determine which students have misconceptions or no prior knowledge of the topic and plan for additional support for these students.
- Plan to input the language and content of the lesson through several modalities (listening, speaking, reading, writing). For oral input, provide an outline of major topics and target vocabulary. At ten-minute intervals, partner students to summarize, respond to a question, or determine a question to ask about the oral input. If possible, rewrite written input to conform to student reading levels. Provide limited readers with a partner to read the text together.
- Check student comprehension of the content input frequently throughout the lesson. Use response cards for recall questions and answers. Use learning partners for questions related to conceptual understanding of the topic.

RTI TIER 2 SAMPLER

- When preteaching or reteaching with students in small-group sessions, use consistent routines to structure the lessons. Begin with objectives and an outline of the session. Follow up with instruction in the vocabulary of the lesson, opportunities to practice, presentation of the new content related to prior knowledge, and guided practice. Use patterned, routine language for directions and explanations to increase comprehensibility.
- Adapt the instructional delivery to students by preteaching the concepts to be taught during the classroom lesson. Preteach individually or in a small group session. Model and explain vocabulary with visual or graphic supports. Provide opportunities for students to use the target vocabulary and state their understanding of the major concepts.
- Identify the key concepts of the lesson and make them explicit to students in a small-group session. Outline the concepts on a graphic organizer to indicate the text organization of the reading to follow. Have students use their prior knowledge of the concepts to make a connection with the new information. For example, if students have

studied the government of a native country, ask them to explain what they know about that government and then make explicit comparisons to the new government to be studied. If students have knowledge of a fairy tale or animal fable in another language, ask them to retell that narrative. Then make explicit connections to the new narrative to be taught.

- When checking for understanding during a large-class lesson, identify those students who need further instruction in the concept or skill. Meet these students in small groups and reteach the concept using a different approach. For example, increase the use of manipulatives for math concepts, use a role-play or demonstration to increase comprehension of word problems, provide opportunities for oral practice in explaining the steps to solve an equation.
- Meet with students in small groups and provide them with examples of a finished product prior to beginning project or writing work. For example, if students are to create a PowerPoint presentation to explain a concept, show examples of excellent PowerPoint presentations. Providing a rubric to explicitly state project requirements is another way to explain project excellence.
- When giving directions for an assignment, write the steps clearly and explain each to small groups of students. Increase comprehension by providing visuals or exemplars for the assignment directions.
- During guided practice using reading material, use audiotaped texts or peer readers for students who have limited reading proficiency.
- When assessing learners, provide concept maps, outlines, and study guides as advance organizers. Meet with these students individually or in small groups and teach them to use the advance organizer as an aid to comprehension of the lesson concepts. If necessary, assess these students on segments of the lesson unit rather than the entire unit at one time.
- During the independent practice phase of the lesson, place students with a knowledgeable and supportive partner for modeling and assistance.
- Provide many opportunities for students to summarize learning, orally and in writing, with the teacher, in a small group, or with a knowledgeable peer.

Questions for Reflection

1. Reflect on the six lesson characteristics supporting and promoting achievement for language learners. Arrange these in a hierarchy of priority from most important to least important. Defend your choices with examples from life experience.
2. The lesson format described here (*Into, Through, Beyond*) is based upon a cognitive model of knowledge construction. Does this model imply that knowledge is constructed rather than memorized or learned? What are the differences in these viewpoints?
3. Essential to this chapter's view of learning is the integration of language activities in every part of the lesson and language objectives in every content lesson. Can this be done with learners who are newcomers and beginners in English? How?

Activities for Further Learning

1. Two teaching characteristics that support learning for language learners are heterogeneous grouping and appropriate grade-level content. Teachers who are not familiar with techniques for working with diverse classes have difficulty teaching challenging and grade-level content to students of mixed achievement levels. What problems can you foresee in these situations? What problems might teachers have? Students? Parents? What strategies and suggestions can you offer to teachers to support achievement gains for all learners in heterogeneous learning situations?
2. Teacher language has been mentioned as an important characteristic of effective instruction for English language learners. Teacher language that is unclear leaves students confused as to what is expected of them. Too often, this leads to inattention and discipline problems. Think about the language you use with students in the arena of giving instructions. Create a series of instructions for students that incorporate the aspects of clarity mentioned in this chapter: body gestures, simple language, repetition, explanatory devices, and oral and written support.
3. We have said lessons for English language learning students need to have specific, measurable objectives for content, language, and learning strategies. Use the Bloom Taxonomy in this chapter to create content, language, and learning strategy objectives for two different lessons: elementary science and middle school social studies.
4. Checking for understanding becomes more important when English language learning students are in our classrooms.

Teachers cannot assume all learners will understand the directions for an activity or the new content information. Talk in your group about the suggestions given here for dipsticking activities. Which ones are you already familiar with? Which ones can you imagine using in a class of mixed-language users? What other methods can you suggest for checking the understanding of your students?

5. Vocabulary learning is crucial for academic success. Students need to learn both technical vocabulary and academic vocabulary. In order to have some hands-on experience with both kinds of vocabulary, review typical teacher language in the area of

- classroom routines
- directions

You might find examples of this language in teacher manuals, textbooks, or in the directions used for standardized testing. What aspects of this language are typical of academic language? Which words are used routinely but may need clarification? How could you help students understand this language?

6. Select a textbook passage used by students. Analyze the language of the text and isolate the technical vocabulary and the academic vocabulary (or grammar). How could you help students understand and learn this language?

7. Imagine you are teaching a third-grade class in multiplication. You are entering the Guided Practice phase of the lesson. What scaffolds could you use with students to help them be successful in their first experiences with multiplication?

Now think about a sixth-grade social studies lesson on the topic of latitude, longitude, the equator, and the Tropics of Cancer and Capricorn. How could you support students in their guided practice of these concepts?

8. Describe examples of "Beyond the Classroom" communication that could be incorporated into each of the lessons described in question number 7.

Suggested Reading

Echevarria, J., Vogt, M., & Short, D. J. (2003). *Making content comprehensible for English language learners: The SIOP® model* (2nd ed.). Boston: Allyn & Bacon. An excellent description of sheltered instruction with many practical strategies clearly explained with classroom examples.

Hill, J. D., & Flynn, K. M. (2006). *Classroom instruction that works with English language learners.* Alexandria, VA: ASCD. Authors review research on effective teaching, and particularly effective teaching of ELLs, and show how these strategies can be implemented in multicultural, multilingual classrooms. Strategies include cooperative learning, summarizing and note-taking, reinforcing effort and providing recognition, using nonlinguistic representations, and involving parents and the community.

Mohan, B. A. (1986). *Language and content.* Reading, MA: Addison-Wesley. One of the classic books relating to the integration of language and content in classrooms. We appreciate the knowledge framework described here, which advances students in the growth of language and in cognition as they explore content.

Piper, T. (2002). *Language and learning: The home and school years* (3rd ed.). Upper Saddle River, NJ: Merrill. This book has much to delight those who are interested in the subject of language and children. Chapter 9 is relevant in its discussion of the relationship between language and cognitive growth. Chapter 10 discusses school language in both its positive and negative aspects. The discussion of teacher language is especially relevant here. Chapter 12 details ten principles for language learning.

References

Agor, B. (2000). Understanding our past: The middle ages. In S. Irujo (Ed.), *Integrating the ESL standards into classroom practice grades 6–8,* (pp. 1–27). Alexandria, VA: TESOL.

Allen, R. (2003). The democratic aims of service learning. *Educational Leadership, (60)*6, 51–54.

Arreaga-Mayer, C., & Perdomo-Rivera. C. (1996) Ecobehavioral analysis of instruction for at-risk language-minority students. *Elementary School Journal, 96,* 245–258.

August, D., & Hakuta, K. (Eds.). (2002). *Educating language-minority children.* Washington, DC: National Academy Press.

Ausubel, D. P. (1968). *Educational psychology: A cognitive view.* New York: Holt, Rinehart and Winston.

Beck, I. L., McKeown, M. G., & Kucan, L. (2002). *Bringing words to life: Robust vocabulary instruction.* New York: The Guilford Press.

Berman, P., Minicucci, C., McLaughlin, B., Nelson, B., & Woodworth, K. (1995). *School reform and student diversity: Case studies of exemplary practices for English language learner students.* Santa Cruz, CA: National Center for Research on Cultural Diversity and Second Language Learning, and B. W. Associates.

Billows, F. (1961). *The techniques of language teaching.* London: Longman.

Bloom, B., Englehart, M., Furst, E., Hill, W., & Krathworl, D. (Eds.). (1956). *Taxonomy of educational objectives: The classification of educational goals. Handbook I: Cognitive domain.* New York: David McKay.

Brown, A. L., Campione, J. C., & Day, J. D. (1981). Learning to learn: On training students to learn from texts. *Educational Researcher, 10,* 14–21.

Calderón, M., & Carreon, A. (1994). Educators and students use cooperative learning to become biliterate and bicultural. *Cooperative Learning Magazine, 4,* 6–9.

Calderón, M., Hertz-Lazarowitz, R., & Slavin, R. (1998). Effects of bilingual cooperative integrated reading and composition on students making the transition from Spanish to English. *The Elementary School Journal, 99,* 153–165.

Calderón, M., Tinajero, J., & Hertz-Lazarowitz, R. (1992). Adapting cooperative integrated reading and composition to meet the needs of bilingual students. *Journal of Educational Issues of Language Minority Students, 10,* 79–106.

Cavanaugh, R. A., Heward, W. L., & Donelson, F. (1996). Effects of response cards during lesson closure on the academic performance of secondary students in an earth science course. *Journal of Applied Behavior Analysis, 29*(3), 403–406.

Common Core State Standards: English Language Arts Anchor Standards. (2010). http://www.corestandards.org/the-standards/english-language-arts-standards.

Cummins, J., Brown, K., & Sayers, D. (2007). *Literacy, technology, and diversity: Teaching for success in changing times.* Boston: Pearson.

Dixon, J. K. (1995). Limited English proficiency and spatial visualization in middle school students' construction of the concepts of reflection and rotation. *Bilingual Research Journal, 19*(2), 221–247.

Doherty, R. W., Hilberg, R. S., Pinal, A., & Tharp, R. G. (2003). Five standards and student achievement. *NABE Journal of Research and Practice, 1*(1), 1–24.

Echevarria, J., Short, D., & Powers, K. (2003). *School reform and standards-based education: How do teachers help English language learners?* Technical report. Santa Cruz, CA: Center for Research on Education, Diversity & Excellence.

Fillmore, L. W. (1989). Teaching English through content: Instructional reform in programs for language minority students. In J. Esling (Ed.), *Multicultural education and policy: ESL in the 1990s* (pp. 125–143). Toronto, Canada: OISE Press.

Fillmore, L. W., Ammon, P., McLaughlin, B., & Ammon, M. S. (1985). *Learning English through bilingual instruction: Executive summary and conclusions.* (Final report to National Institute of Education). Washington, DC: U.S. Department of Education.

Fitzgerald, J., & Graves, M. F. (2004). *Scaffolding reading experiences for English language learners.* Norwood, MA: Christopher Gordon.

Genesee, F. (2006). *Educating English language learners: A synthesis of research evidence.* New York: Cambridge University Press.

Gersten, R. (1996). Literacy instruction for language minority students: The transition years. *The Elementary School Journal, 96*(3), 228–244.

Gersten, R., Baker, S. K., Shanahan, T., Linan-Thompson, S., Collins, P., & Scarcella, R. (2007). *Effective literacy and English language instruction for English learners in the elementary grades: A practice guide* (NCEE 2007-4011). Washington, DC: National Center for Education Evaluation and Regional Assistance, Institute of Education Sciences, U.S. Department of Education. http://ies.ed.gov/ncee.

Harklau, L. (1994). ESL versus mainstream classes: Contrasting L2 learning environments. *TESOL Quarterly, 28,* 241–272.

Heward, W. L., Gardner III, R., Cavanaugh, R. A., Courson, F. H., Grossi, T. A., & Barbetta, P. M. (1996). Everyone participates in this class: Using response cards to increase active student response. *Teaching Exceptional Children, 28,* 4–10.

Izumi, D. S., & Bigelow, M. (2000). Does output promote noticing and second language acquisition? *TESOL Quarterly, 34*(2), 239–278.

Kagan, S. (1994). *Cooperative learning.* San Clemente, CA: Kagan Cooperative Learning.

Kinsella, K. (2011, March). *Writing appropriate language objectives: A lesson-planning tool kit.* Paper presented at the 45th Annual TESOL Convention, New Orleans, LA.

Lindholm-Leary, K. J. (2001). *Dual language education.* Avon, UK: Multilingual Matters.

Mayer, R. E. (1992). Cognition and instruction: Their historic meeting within educational psychology. *Journal of Educational Psychology, 84,* 405–412.

Merchant, P., & Young, L. (2000). Investigating how much: Linear, volume, and mass measurement. In S. Irujo (Ed.), *Integrating the ESL standards into classroom practice grades 6–8* (pp. 55–84). Alexandria, VA: TESOL.

Minicucci, C. (1996). *Learning science and English: How school reform advances scientific learning for limited English proficient middle school students* (Educational Practice Report No. 17). Santa Cruz, CA: National Center for Research on Cultural Diversity and Second Language Learning.

Mohan, B. A. (1986). *Language and content.* Reading, MA: Addison-Wesley.

Montecel, M. R., & Cortez, J. D. (2002). Successful bilingual education programs: Development and the dissemination of criteria to identify promising and exemplary practices in bilingual education at the national level. *Bilingual Research Journal, 26,* 1–22.

Ogle, D. M. (1986, February). K-W-L: A teaching model that develops active reading of expository text. *The Reading Teacher, 39*(6), 564–570.

Olivier, R. (2003). Interactional context and feedback in child ESL classrooms. *Modern Language Journal, 87*(87), 519–533.

Pica, T., Lincoln-Porter, F., Paninos, D., & Linnell, J. (1996). Language learners' interaction: How does it address the input, output, and feedback needs of L2 learners? *TESOL Quarterly, 30,* 59–84.

Ramirez, J. D. (1992). Longitudinal study of structured English immersion strategy, early-exit and late-exit transitional bilingual education program for language-minority children (Executive Summary). *Bilingual Research Journal, 16*(1–2), 1–62.

Saphier, J., & Gower, R. (1997). *The skillful teacher: Building your teaching skills.* Carlisle, MA: Research for Better Teaching.

Saphier, J., & Haley, M. A. (1993a). *Activators: Activity structures to engage students' thinking before instruction.* Carlisle, MA: Research for Better Teaching.

Saphier, J., & Haley, M. A. (1993b). *Summarizers: Activity structures to support integration and retention of new learning.* Carlisle, MA: Research for Better Teaching.

Saunders, W., O'Brien, G., Lennon, D., & McClean, J. (1996). Making the transition to English literacy successful: Effective strategies for studying literature with transition students. In R. Gersten & R. Jimenez, (Eds.), *Effective Strategies for Teaching Language Minority Students* (pp. 99–132). Monterey, CA: Brooks Cole.

Snow, M. A., Met, M., & Genesee, F. (1989). A conceptual framework for the integration of language and content in second/foreign language instruction. *TESOL Quarterly, 23*(2), 210–217.

Stoops Verplaetse, L. (1998). How content teachers interact with English language learners. *TESOL Journal, 7*(5), 24–28.

Swain, M. (1985). Communicative competence: Some roles of comprehensible input and comprehensible output in its development. In S. M. Gass & C. G. Madden (Eds.), *Input in second language acquisition* (pp. 257–271). Rowley, MA: Newbury House.

Teachers of English to Speakers of Other Languages, Inc. (TESOL). (2006). *PreK–12 English language proficiency standards.* Alexandria, VA: Author.

Tikunoff, W. (1985). *Applying significant bilingual instructional features in the classroom.* Rosslyn, VA: National Clearinghouse for Bilingual Education (ERIC Document Reproduction Service No. ED 338 106).

Zainuddin, H., Yahya, N., Morales-Jones, C., & Ariza, E. (2002). *Fundamentals of teaching English to speakers of other languages in K–12 mainstream classrooms.* Dubuque, IA: Kendall/Hunt.

MyEducationLab™

Go to the Topic, Planning, in the MyEducationLab (www.myeducationlab.com) for your course, where you can:

- Find learning outcomes for Planning along with the national standards that connect to these outcomes.
- Complete Assignments and Activities that can help you more deeply understand the chapter content.
- Apply and practice your understanding of the core teaching skills identified in the chapter with the Building Teaching Skills and Dispositions learning units.
- Examine challenging situations and cases presented in the IRIS Center Resources.
- Check your comprehension on the content covered in the chapter by going to the Study Plan in the Book Resources for your text. Here you will be able to take a chapter quiz, receive feedback on your answers, and then access Review, Practice, and Enrichment activities to enhance your understanding of chapter content.
- **A+RISE** A+RISE® Standards2Strategy™ is an innovative and interactive online resource that offers new teachers in grades K-12 just in time, research-based instructional strategies that meet the linguistic needs of ELLs as they learn content, differentiate instruction for all grades and abilities, and are aligned to Common Core Language Arts standards (for the literacy strategies) and to English language proficiency standards in WIDA, Texas, California, and Florida.

CHAPTER 11

Assessment Tools for the Integrated Classroom

Annie Watt's second-grade class takes a district-developed reading test twice a year to evaluate the effectiveness of reading instruction in the grade. Annie had been hopeful that Julio, an English language learner in her class, would do well on the test. She watched him as he attempted to read the text passages and answer the questions, and cringed as he became outwardly upset.

Waving his hand wildly to get her attention, he called out, "Ms. Watts, Ms. Watts, what's this word mean?"

Annie knew she couldn't help Julio with word meanings and suggested that he "take his best guess."

The test seemed to take forever. Julio gave up after a half hour and put his head on his desk until others in the class were finished. Annie breathed a sigh of relief when she could send the children out to the playground at the end of the session.

When test results arrived weeks later, Annie was dismayed to see that even simple reading passages and questions were too difficult for Julio. For example, Julio responded incorrectly to the following questions:

1. Joe and Jim are playing football. Joe runs the ball to the goalpost. Who do you think is the winner of this game?

2. Select a breakfast food from this list:
   (a) pancakes   (b) a sandwich   (c) rice

3. Sandy and Tim want to play baseball after school. Sandy is bringing his bat and ball. What do you think Tim will bring to the game?
   (a) a net   (b) a glove   (c) a wicket

4. Jane knew that spring had arrived when she saw her first
   (a) tulip   (b) icicle   (c) pumpkin

Annie began to rethink her earlier evaluations of Julio. Perhaps he wasn't making as much progress as she had thought. Why were these questions so difficult for Julio?

How do teachers assess the progress of English language learners in their classrooms?

- What is assessment?
- What are the fundamental principles of assessment for ELLs?
- What are the critical factors affecting assessment of ELLs?
- What are examples of authentic, performance-based classroom assessment?
- How do standards affect classroom assessment?
- What are the implications for assessment of ELLs in the RTI model?

WHAT IS ASSESSMENT?

In our discussion on assessment, we focus on teachers and practitioners who instruct English language learners in content and language learning in classrooms of many different types: ESL **pull-out**, ESL **push-in**, **bilingual**, **dual language**, and multilingual, multilevel content classrooms in elementary and secondary schools.

The measurement issues in these classrooms are complex because various kinds of measurement are used for different purposes in public schools. In this chapter, we will begin by describing three types of assessment:

- Standardized Testing
- Classroom-Based Assessment
- Program Evaluation

STANDARDIZED TESTING   The narrowest in focus of the three types of assessment, standardized tests are designed by test developers to measure discrete skills at one moment in time. Tests are developed for **reliability**—that students will score the same on different administrations of the test, and **validity**—that tests really measure what they are designed to measure. Standardized tests have been developed by states and national companies for many content areas. Specific tests have also been developed for ELLs to show their levels of English-language development.

CLASSROOM-BASED ASSESSMENT   This type of assessment refers to the gathering of information on an ongoing basis over a period of time. Formats for classroom-based assessment use authentic classroom curriculum, are varied, and may include teacher observations, teacher-developed tests, comprehension checking, and rubrics for student products (writing projects, presentations, and multimedia products), checklists, surveys/questionnaires, and anecdotal records. Classroom-based assessment is directly linked to student need, is integrated into instruction, and can determine progress toward specific skills. The purposes of classroom assessment include:

- monitoring student achievement
- planning and improving instruction
- providing communication to parents and school personnel
- providing students with information and feedback about their progress

PROGRAM EVALUATION   With the broadest scope of the three, program evaluation seeks information about schools, teachers, and large groups of students for the purposes of:

- monitoring the effectiveness of an educational program
- determining the effectiveness of teaching and learning in a school district
- attaining accountability for state standards and reporting summary information
- ensuring equitable educational opportunities on the national level

Standardized testing, which often takes place in the spring in public schools, is frequently used in program evaluation. Other kinds of school data (e.g., attendance, drop-out rates, etc.) may be included as well. It is possible to use many other kinds of information in program evaluation, such as classroom-based assessment, but in today's schools, standardized tests dominate. Following recent education legislation in the United States, standardized tests are used to determine school effectiveness. Schools must demonstrate levels of achievement and improvement or they will be subject to escalating levels of consequences, one of which might be the "restructuring" of the school (which could lead to a new administration and the requirement that teachers reapply for their jobs). This legislation has put tremendous pressure on schools and teachers to be sure that students perform well on standardized tests. At present, a number of states are beginning to employ a growth model using data from standardized tests that evaluates learners on their yearly growth rather than their achievement of grade-level equivalent scores.

DIFFERENT TYPES OF ASSESSMENT   Assessment for ELLs can be categorized further by type and purpose of assessment. Table 11.1 compares criterion-referenced to norm-referenced, language proficiency to content proficiency, and direct performance to indirect performance assessments (TESOL, 2001, p. 12).

TABLE 11.1 Comparing Assessment Test Types, Purposes, and Formats

Criterion-Referenced	Norm-Referenced
Student performance is compared and rated against a set of predetermined criteria. The criteria might be determined by a state or content standard, a teaching objective, a performance indicator, or a teacher-created rubric.	Student performance is compared and ranked relative to similar populations in the state or the country.
Language Proficiency	**Academic Proficiency**
Student language performance is assessed globally in regard to listening, speaking, reading, and writing skills.	Student performance of curricular content and skill is assessed.
Direct Performance	**Indirect Performance**
Student performance for specific knowledge is assessed through a demonstration of ability. An example is an oral report or a written essay.	Student performance gains are assumed through assessment of one aspect of a skill. For example, answering comprehension questions or taking a vocabulary quiz assesses aspects of reading. Often, listening comprehension is assessed indirectly.

Adapted from *Scenarios for ESL standards-based assessment*, TESOL (2001, p. 12).

WHAT ARE THE FUNDAMENTAL PRINCIPLES OF CLASSROOM-BASED ASSESSMENT FOR ELLS?

We propose four fundamental principles for ELL classroom-based assessment. Assessments should:

- provide fair, reliable, and valid information.
- inform teaching and improve learning.
- use multiple sources of information.
- use familiar instructional techniques.

Conduct a Fair, Reliable, and Valid Assessment

Fairness is an essential attribute of the teacher/student relationship. Most children ask for and respond well to a teacher who is fair. Fairness in assessment occurs when all students have an equal chance to show what they know and can do. Fairness does not mean that all students must be treated exactly the same. In fact, treating all students the same may be very unfair. For example, it is unreasonable to require beginning ELLs to take standardized tests that do not provide any meaningful information and that result in the learners having an experience of failure and frustration.

To achieve this goal of fairness in assessment for ELLs, teachers often need to provide accommodations. For example, when working with math word problems, teachers can scaffold the tasks by providing models of appropriate problem solving that students can then apply in other situations. Teachers can ask students to work in buddy pairs so learners have a chance to negotiate the meaning of questions. Teachers can provide oral language practice in describing problem solutions before moving to the writing phase of the lesson. If we ask ourselves the following questions, we may be better able to adjust our assessments to pass the "fairness test":

- Did the student understand the question sufficiently to answer it?
- Did the student, in fact, answer the question that was asked?
- Am I evaluating the student's content understanding or the student's language development?
- Is my assessment reflective of my instructional practices?
- Did I provide the student with the support needed to respond to my assessment (support in terms of a peer, an outline, a cloze passage, a list of terms, a graphic organizer, pictures or realia, native language translation, etc.)?
- Have I told students what I am evaluating and modeled a desired product?
- Have I clearly specified the criteria on which evaluation is based?
- Am I evaluating the process or the product, or both?

By answering and responding to these questions, teachers will be assured that all students in the class will have the opportunity to show what they know or are able to do.

RELIABILITY Reliable assessment occurs when there is consistency and dependability in results that occur over a period of time, when scored by different raters. Holistic assessment of writing, for example, is reliable when the raters are trained in the same holistic scoring technique and achieve consistency among themselves when scoring the same writing passages. Reliability in assessment of oral language occurs when trained raters use taped oral language samples with a criterion-referenced rating scale, such as the Student Oral Language Observation Matrix or SOLOM (see Table 5.4 in Chapter 5) to mutually assess vocabulary, fluency, syntax, and other aspects of oral language.

VALIDITY When assessment instruments measure what is intended, they are said to be valid. The interpretations made from valid tests or assessments are deemed adequate and appropriate, and curriculum and instructional decisions can be adjusted based on the results. When learners do not understand the language of a test, then it is not valid to use that test to determine their knowledge of content. It is difficult to achieve valid results with one-shot testing. Rather, effective teachers use multiple, appropriate measures to get a rich picture of what learners know and can do. Classroom-based, informal assessment that is varied and reflects the classroom teaching style can best achieve a broad and valid picture of the learner's skills and knowledge.

The issue of validity is probably the most compelling issue in assessing ELLs. Poor language proficiency may prevent ELLs from displaying their content knowledge gains adequately. Cultural differences may confuse ELLs who come from cultures with experiences that are dissimilar to those of test developers. Therefore, when assessing content, teachers should assure that they are measuring content learning and not assessing ELLs' cultural understanding or language proficiency. The following questions help to pinpoint the problem:

- Am I assessing language knowledge or knowledge of the world?
- Am I assessing knowledge of the world available to all cultures or only to particular cultural groups?
- Am I assessing the content objectives or the language skills of the student?

Valid assessment occurs when teachers evaluate the content objectives they intend to assess regardless of the language used to express that content. Creating specific objectives and rubrics for assessment is helpful in ensuring valid assessment.

Consider the issue of validity in the assessment example in Figure 11.1, which is a seventh-grade student's response to the teacher's request for a paragraph summarizing what he had learned about the pyramids of Egypt. Reading this paragraph, you cannot help but note the many grammatical errors, as well as the influence of the student's native Spanish in the word choice and word order of the language. In order to evaluate the work, however, the teacher needed to refer to the directions given for the task and the rubric distributed to students for assessment. The teacher's directions were the following:

- Use the information on your graphic organizer to write at least one paragraph summarizing what you have learned about the pyramids of Egypt.
- Include a topic sentence, supporting details, and a conclusion.

Miguel's teacher used the rubric in Table 11.2 to assess his pyramid paragraph. When evaluated according to the task directions and the rubric, we can see that a valid assessment concerning the content, organization, and neatness of the paragraph gives this student a passing grade. He has comprehended the information about the building of the pyramids, their location, and their time frame, and provided an example of the greatest pyramid, in Giza. In addition, the student has learned and used the vocabulary necessary for the concept of pyramid building: *Pharaoh, pyramid, Egypt, sled, slaves, barge, tomb*, and *stone*. The assessment of the paragraph according to the rubric is a **product grade**.

The additional assessment of the language of the paragraph is a **process grade**. The teacher should note grammatical errors in the paragraph, such as the lack of past tense verbs, and lessons must be planned to help the student learn to use verbs correctly in discussions of history. These types of ELL writing errors (e.g., verb tenses, word choice, word order, and articles) are persistent for many years, even after ELLs have exited from English Language Development (ELD) programs, and it is important that classroom teachers be comfortable dealing with them. In this situation, lessons addressing common issues can be integrated into the instructional plan as part of future learning about Egypt. An assessment can be made on this learning objective

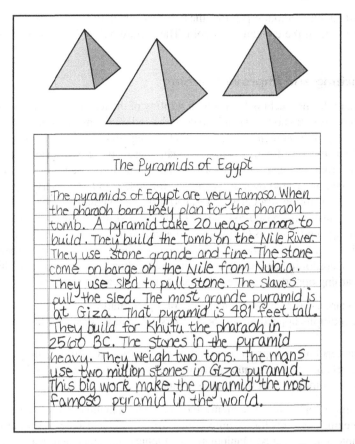

The Pyramids of Egypt

The pyramids of Egypt are very famoso. When the pharaoh born they plan for the pharaoh tomb. A pyramid take 20 years or more to build. They build the tomb on the Nile River. They use stone grande and fine. The stone come on barge on the Nile from Nubia. They use sled to pull stone. The slaves pull the sled. The most grande pyramid is at Giza. That pyramid is 481 feet tall. They build for Khufu the pharaoh in 2560 BC. The stones in the pyramid heavy. They weigh two tons. The mans use two million stones in Giza pyramid. This big work make the pyramid the most famoso pyramid in the world.

FIGURE 11.1 Summary of What a Seventh-Grade Student Had Learned About the Pyramids of Egypt

separate from the content that the language conveys. Assessment of content knowledge is thus accomplished separately from assessment of language ability.

Separating product grades from process grades in the content classroom promotes valid assessment. To assess both at once puts a heavy burden on the ELL student. Process and product

TABLE 11.2 Rubric for Evaluating a Student's Content Learning in a Unit on Egypt

Name: _____

Topic: _____

		Criteria			
	1	**2**	**3**	**4**	**Points**
Organization	No topic sentence, few supporting details, and no conclusion.	Missing either a topic sentence or conclusion. Details are scanty.	Topic sentence is present with a conclusion. More than three details present.	Topic sentence and conclusion are clearly stated. Many details support the topic.	4
Content Knowledge	Student does not have grasp of information; student cannot answer questions about the subject.	Student displays general content knowledge and demonstrates basic concepts.	Student displays specific content knowledge and basic concepts.	Student demonstrates full knowledge (more than required) of content.	3
Neatness	Work is illegible.	Work has three or four areas that are difficult to read because of illegible handwriting.	Work has comprehensible handwriting.	Work is neatly done. Handwriting is legible and clear.	4
				Total points:	11/12

are both important, but without separating the two, teachers may never get a clear picture of what a student is learning in the content classroom. The picture will only show what the student has not yet learned.

Inform Teaching and Improve Learning

Assessment that informs teaching begins with scrutiny of the teacher's mastery objectives. What is it that the students will know or be able to do at the end of the instructional period? By aligning assessment closely to the content, language, and learning strategy objectives in the unit, teachers will have a clear direction for instruction. In many cases, these assessment techniques do not take time away from teaching, but enhance it, and can be integrated into various stages of the lesson plan: activating prior knowledge, checking for understanding, observing, questioning, and using interactional learning strategies, slates, sort tasks, and signals.

Effective classroom-based assessment improves student learning. An example of an improved learning opportunity is the pyramid rubric used in Table 11.2. By creating a rubric and sharing it with learners, the teacher has provided a snapshot of what a good performance looks like. With this snapshot in hand, a student has a greater chance of achieving at a high level.

Other learning opportunities are presented to students when teachers:

* support learners' practice sessions before oral presentations.
* provide multiple opportunities for learners to achieve desired outcomes (reteach and retest).
* teach learners how to support one another in revising and editing writing.
* teach the use of graphic organizers as organizing tools for research and writing.
* provide scaffolding for all forms of assessment.

Scaffolding is one way of reducing the language demands of the content classroom by providing contextual supports for meaning. But scaffolding can also be used to provide language support for content assessments. Manipulatives, graphic organizers, and visuals are examples of support structures. Examples of scaffolded assessment include the following (O'Malley & Valdez Pierce, 1996):

* *Exhibits or projects* that involve students in comprehending, organizing, and presenting content information
* *Visual displays* that enable students to comprehend vocabulary and content in order to complete graphic organizers, diagrams, or semantic maps
* *Organized lists* through which students present concepts or terms they have organized, sorted, or sequenced in some way
* *Tables or graphs* that demonstrate student organization, interpretation, and comprehension of data
* *Short answers* that ask students to focus on specific content area concepts

All of these examples control the language load on ELLs while allowing them to report on the extent of their content learning. The examples in Table 11.3 show common classroom tasks and the ways that teachers can scaffold those tasks depending on the proficiency levels of the learner.

Use Multiple Sources of Information

The best strategy for assessing ELLs is to use a varied approach to collecting information from multiple sources during classroom instruction. Although tests (even multiple-choice tests) can provide useful information, this information is necessarily narrow. One-shot testing cannot inform teachers as to the breadth and complexity of student understanding. Rich assessment uses multiple measures of learner success, including assessment in the student's primary language if that is feasible.

Writing portfolio assessment is an example of assessment that is informed through multiple sources of information. It provides opportunities for teachers and students to evaluate multiple writing pieces over a period of time. Students create writing in various genres and revisit selected pieces at later dates, self-assessing, rewriting, and perfecting with the help of teacher and peer conferencing. Writing portfolios may include writing in the L1 for students in the beginning stages of English learning. Gradually, as language proficiency increases, students add English vocabulary words and simple grammatical structures. The portfolio provides an excellent picture

TABLE 11.3 Scaffolding for Classroom Assessment

Assessment Task	Without Scaffolding	With Scaffolding
Make an oral presentation with note cards.	• Work individually to organize content. • Summarize on note cards. • Present to the class.	• Team two students. • Provide a graphic organizer to structure the presentation. • Divide the presentation in half. • Provide opportunity for oral practice with coaching before the final presentation.
Summarize a text reading.	• Read the chapter. • Write a summary.	• Provide hands-on activation experiences to uncover the concepts in the text. • Preview the pictures and graphics in the text. • Create questions from the bold print headers. • Make predictions about possible answers. • Provide a chapter outline. • Read the questions at the end of the chapter. • Team to read the chapter together. • Take notes on a T-list or semantic map.
Write a word problem.	• Create a word problem using your own numbers. • Provide a numerical equation. • Write the word problem story and question.	• Provide a cloze form of a word problem or a model problem. • Provide key sentence frames for the problem questions. • Provide a context for the problem. • Work with a buddy to create a problem. • Act out a word problem.
Write an essay describing the characters, plot summary, and setting of a narrative text.	• Provide an outline of the essay organization.	• After modeling, fill in the descriptions of plot, setting, and characters on a graphic organizer. • Complete the missing information on a cloze essay.
Define a concept.	• Write a paragraph describing the concept.	• Create a list of descriptors. • Label a picture that is provided.

Adapted from O'Malley & Valdez Pierce (1996).

of language development over time. Portfolios enable students to develop needed learning strategies as well as increase their writing competencies. Table 11.4 lists and describes some of the multiple categories of assessment techniques that are available to classroom teachers.

Use Familiar Instructional Techniques

One of the reasons why many ELLs may have difficulty with discrete skills tests, standardized tests, and summative evaluation in general is that the format of the assessment instrument is alien to their experiences in the classroom. Lack of experience with testing can lead to "test errors" or errors that result from the testing situation, rather than lack of knowledge of the content being tested. For example, students taking standardized tests make incorrect responses by writing too lightly on the bubble answer sheet or by skipping a row of answer bubbles. Classroom teachers often prepare students for standardized tests by providing learners with practice test experiences on marking answers, using time well, checking answers, and guessing strategies that are appropriate for the test.

Since ELLs may have limited experience in North American classrooms, their experience with test formats may also be limited. For these students, assessment that arises from familiar instructional techniques produces the most reliable, valid, and fair information about student achievement. In brief, we recommend that teachers assess what has been taught in the ways that it was taught.

Assessment techniques can be incorporated into every phase of the lesson. Indeed, checking comprehension throughout instruction assures teachers that all students are engaged

TABLE 11.4 Assessment Techniques for ELLs

Areas of Assessment	Student Tasks
Oral Language Assessment	• Point to the answer, picture, or object.
	• Draw a picture.
	• Use a signal to respond.
	• Write an answer on a slate.
	• Respond to one-word, yes/no, either/or questions.
	• Engage in buddy or group talk.
	• Paraphrase concepts.
	• Explain orally.
	• Present an oral report.
	• Respond with Numbered Heads Together, Think-Pair-Share, or other active learning strategies.
Reading Assessment	• Record concepts on a graphic organizer.
	• Record concepts on a T-list.
	• Listen and respond to a recorded book.
	• Engage in buddy reading.
	• Engage in reciprocal reading.
	• Read to the teacher.
	• Retell the story.
	• Engage in a teacher-guided collaborative dialogue.
	• Answer comprehension questions.
	• Complete a cloze passage.
Writing Assessment	• Record new learning in a journal.
	• Write to the teacher.
	• Engage in writing as a process.
	• Meet with the teacher for a writing conference.
	• Write from a graphic organizer.
	• Write in various genres: letter, poem, report, book review, slide presentation, compare/contrast essay, expository "how-to" essay, persuasive essay, literary analysis, etc.
	• Contribute regularly to a portfolio of writing that is evaluated by the student and the teacher.
Content Assessment	• Create a poster or mural.
	• Label a graphic organizer.
	• Role-play to show understanding.
	• Use pair or group reports.
	• Complete a cloze passage.
	• Complete a project.
	• Conduct research with oral interviews, the computer, or the library.
Other	• Self-assessment.
	• Portfolio assessment.
	• Skills and strategies checklists.

in the instructional conversation. Madelyn Hunter's description of **dipsticking** (described in Chapter 10) fits our criteria (Saphier & Gower, 1997). The metaphor of dipsticking comes from the act of checking the oil in your car. In dipsticking, teachers make a quick check of student comprehension. The attributes of dipsticking require that teachers check comprehension:

- of all of their students
- frequently
- on the same topic or concept
- throughout the lesson

Dipsticking can be accomplished in every phase of the lesson—from activation of prior knowledge to the summary at the end. Traditional classroom assessment involves teachers asking individual learners questions about what has been taught. This can be useful, but is very time-consuming, and can lead the teacher to think that everyone understands, when in truth only the few who volunteered to answer the questions "got it." To check the comprehension of all students, it is most efficient to use a variety of strategies and techniques in which many learners can respond at once. Some of the active learning strategies we have recommended in this book (shown in Table 10.3) can also be used to check student comprehension during instruction.

WHAT ARE THE CRITICAL FACTORS AFFECTING ASSESSMENT OF ELLS?

Summative versus Formative Assessment

Summative assessment is evaluation at the end of learning to determine whether learners have achieved goals. Standardized tests are an example of summative evaluation and are typically administered at the same time each year to compare learners with others in the same grade, as well as to compare the performance of schools, districts, and states. High-stakes standardized tests are used to determine, for example, whether learners may move on to the next grade or graduate from high school.

The No Child Left Behind Act (NCLB) of 2001 was enacted to improve the educational achievement of economically disadvantaged and minority children, including ELLs. It declared that schools would be held accountable for assisting all children to meet state standards, and it pressured states to include ELLs in large-scale assessment programs. States have responded by administering standardized tests to learners throughout the grade levels in math, language arts, and science.

The recent emphasis on large-scale assessment has had both positive and negative consequences for ELLs. Benefits from NCLB arise from the emphasis on raising standards for all students; schools are invested in the success of ELLs, who are challenged more than ever before to meet higher levels of academic achievement. On the other hand, major decisions regarding school funding, grade-level promotion, and graduation are often made on the basis of the standardized testing program. ELLs are at a disadvantage to show true achievement gains on these assessments because of problems with validity, fairness, and language load (Coltrane, 2002).

ELLs can be stigmatized by standardized summative testing. Basically, any test administered in English to a nonnative English speaker becomes a language test (Lachat, 2004). Limited language skills bring the reliability and validity of the test into question because of the possibility that the test may not be measuring what it was intended to measure. Some states, schools, and districts do not test ELLs until they have been in an instructional program for one to three years. Others require that ELLs be tested with everyone else, on the same instruments. In an urban district in California, the district sued the state over requirements of early testing of ELLs on standardized tests, which, the city argued, did not provide useful information on learners and could negatively affect them. At one point in the arguments, a district administrator challenged those involved with a math test in Chinese, and asked if the English speakers in the room felt that this test would show what they knew about math. This simple but dramatic demonstration made it clear to many that early use of such tests is not helpful or advisable.

Even if testing is delayed, standardized tests present problems for English language learners. A significant concern is the possibility that differing cultural values may adversely influence student responses. Hoover, Klingner, Baca, & Patton, (2008) identify six cultural and linguistic factors that directly impact the assessment of diverse learners:

1. *Language Function* Standardized assessments require academic language functions that increase with grade level and task complexity (*characterize, analyze, persuade*). Appropriate assessment begins with assessment of the learner's most proficient language, both for social and academic purposes.

2. *Acculturation* During the process of acculturation, behavioral side effects (anxiety, withdrawal, stress) will impact student learning and assessment outcomes.

3. *Conceptual Knowledge/Experiential Background* Past learning experiences related to the content assessment will affect a student's current knowledge and ability to learn new information.

4. *Higher Order Thinking Abilities* Thinking abilities such as comprehension, analysis, comparison, synthesis, and evaluation are relevant to standardized measurement. A failure to demonstrate any of these abilities due to insufficient prior learning or acculturation will affect assessment outcomes.

5. *Cultural Values and Norms* A culturally relevant assessment process integrates the variety of customs, life styles, values, and beliefs of the students. Positive evaluation of these differing customs avoids oversimplified generalizations.

6. *Teaching/Learning Styles* Student learning styles may be in conflict with the teacher's preferred modality. Awareness of the conflict helps to explain differences in student reasoning strategies and gives information on how the student learns best.

Accommodations in the standardized testing process are allowed in many states. An accommodation is a change either to a test or to a testing situation that increases an ELL's access to the content of the test while still preserving test validity (Rivera, 2006). Accommodations may include (but are not limited to):

- extended time periods for testing.
- use of a dictionary (bilingual, English to English, or customized for the particular test).
- separate setting with an ESOL teacher.
- translated or extended explanation of test directions.

Accommodations to the language load of the test can benefit ELLs taking standardized tests. The elimination of passive voice constructions, extraneous vocabulary, and lengthy compound/complex structures increases learner comprehension of the content question, affecting student response and improving test validity. When linguistically loaded questions are simplified, ELLs have been shown to increase their test scores (Abedi, 2002).

Other accommodations are being explored to increase the validity of standardized testing for ELLs; however, there is a limited research base on accommodations. Most research does not take important learner variables into account: level of language proficiency, language of instruction, literacy in the native language, and years of schooling. Each of these variables will determine appropriate test accommodations. Researchers are now suggesting that standardized testing "map accommodations to student need" in these critical areas (Rivera, Acosta, & Willner, 2008, p. 7).

Charlene Rivera, the Executive Director of George Washington University's Center for Equity and Excellence in Education (GW-CEEE), has researched state education department policies and practices to accommodate ELLs and found that, for the most part, state departments are inconsistent within and across states in regard to exemptions from testing, modifications of testing, and the use of alternative tests (Rivera et al., 2008). On the whole, state policies for testing accommodations for ELLs were influenced by the Elementary and Secondary Education Act (ESEA), which identified accommodations for disabled learners. Roughly a third of states still use guidelines for disabilities to provide accommodations for ELLs (Rivera et al., 2008). Rivera (2010, p. 1) suggests that:

States should consider the needs of ELLs in the new standards and assessment system. Policies must address how ELLs are defined, and address procedures for including and accommodating them in summative, benchmark, and classroom assessments. There is great need to clearly distinguish the linguistic needs of ELLs from cognitive, processing, or physical needs of students with disabilities. The delineation of policy at the state and consortium levels is important and should guide practice for the new assessment system which must be valid and reliable for all students including ELLs.

The Center for Research on Evaluation, Standards, and Student Testing (CRESST) recommends that policy makers and educators develop nationwide consistency with the following (Abedi, 2002):

- Modifying test questions to reduce unnecessary language complexity and thus narrow the performance gap between ELLs and native English students.
- Providing customized dictionaries (customized to the language of the test questions only) to offer an alternative to standard dictionaries.
- Monitoring and evaluating intended and unintended accommodations to determine effects on ELL achievement as well as native English student achievement.

A number of assessments have been used to determine the language proficiency of ELLs, including the Language Assessment Scales (LAS), the Woodcock-Muñoz, the Language Assessment Battery (LAB), and the California English Language Development Test (CELDT). Recently, as a response to NCLB, new standardized tests (e.g., the ACCESS Test for ELLs at http://www.wida.us/assessment/ACCESS.aspx) have been developed specifically to assist in appropriate placement of ELLs and to show ELL growth in language proficiency. Although designed to show levels of proficiency, they cannot take the place of ongoing assessment in the classroom.

Formative Assessment

Formative assessment takes place as learning is developing. It includes the multiple ways that teachers gather information about their students' learning throughout the instructional process and then use this information to evaluate their own teaching and their students' learning. Formative assessment is ongoing, occurs during instruction, and guides the teaching process. Much formative assessment is informal and occurs on the spot as the teacher observes students, converses, asks questions, conducts quick-writes, or engages in any number of classroom tasks that are not specifically graded according to a set of criteria (Echevarria, Vogt, & Short, 2004). Other forms of formative assessment are conducted as part of the instructional process, guided by standards and classroom objectives, graded and/or documented through the use of a checklist, anecdotal record, classroom quiz, or other data-collection technique. As such, formative, classroom-based assessment expands on the single test approach; assessment becomes part of teaching, and assessment tools closely resemble the instructional tools of the classroom.

Informal classroom-based assessment provides teachers with the information they need to determine if students comprehend the content and are achieving the objectives of the lesson. It is essential in helping teachers to adjust instruction, reteach, provide tutoring in special skills, or move on. Assessment, then, is not relegated only to the end of the lesson but is used during every phase of the lesson to ascertain prior knowledge, clear up misconceptions, and determine the level of understanding of the new concepts.

Cultural Issues in Testing

Annie Watts, the teacher we described in the chapter introduction, instinctively felt that her student Julio was making progress in reading in her classroom. But when she administered the district test, the results indicated that Julio did not comprehend the meaning of the reading passages well. Annie never considered that the questions Julio was asked to respond to were based on content that he had never been taught and that were not a part of his culture. Baseball and breakfast food are culturally associated with the specific North American culture. Julio enjoys and plays what he calls football, but that game is referred to as *soccer* in the United States. Finally, flowers that grow in the spring are not common in Julio's neighborhood or in the town in Central America where he was born.

Few diagnostic tools have been designed specifically for children who are exposed daily to two languages—one at school and the other at home (Valdes & Figueroa, 1994). In fact, "standardized" assessments presume a high degree of homogeneity of experiences among students. English language learners for the most part are not represented adequately by any existing norm samples (Ortiz, 2001). When differences exist between the experiences of the norm-referenced group and the children taking the test, bias can exist that renders the assessment less valid (Figueroa & Garcia, 1994; Ortiz, 2001).

Examples of test items requiring specific cultural knowledge have been illustrated by Mohan (1985, pp. 124–125) from widely used tests such as in the following examples.

An example from the Stanford Diagnostic Reading Test, Form X, Level 1, number 3:

1. Our flag contains one _____ for every state.
   (a) stripe   (b) star

From the Gates McGinitie Reading Test, Form 3M, number 1:

2. Sam won at marbles because he could _____ straighter than Bill.
   (a) show   (b) shoot
   (c) draw   (d) run

From the Comprehensive Test of Basic Skills, Form 4, Level 9, number 1:

3. Bill ran out on his front porch to watch the fire truck. He lives in _____
   (a) a big apartment.   (b) a city house.
   (c) a trailer.

Major testing corporations employ panels of experts to eliminate cultural bias from their standardized assessments, but state testing agencies are not always capable of this level of review. It would be preferable if the norm-referenced populations used for testing purposes included adequate numbers of language minority students. Assessment in two languages would also produce a more complete picture of an individual's global ability.

Certainly, Congress has spoken on this issue in the Improving America's Schools Act of 1994 that calls for assessing Limited English Proficient (LEP) students relative to state content standards, and "to the extent practicable in the language and form most likely to yield accurate and reliable information on what students know and can do, to determine mastery of skills in subjects other than English" (sec. 1111) (b) (3) (F) (i–iii) at http://www.ed.gov/legislation/ESEA/toc.html.

Cultural bias in testing is difficult for classroom teachers to recognize because culture is intrinsic to people who are raised in it. Like the air around us, we do not notice it until it is changed or taken away. And yet the results of bias in testing can have permanent effects on children. Tests such as the ones mentioned previously are used in schools to make important decisions about children's

- classroom placement.
- reading group placement.
- need for special education placement.
- placement in classes for the gifted.
- selection of remedial programs.
- selection of remedial learning materials.

Unless children have been specifically instructed in the rules of marbles or the symbolism of the stars and stripes on the American flag, it is inappropriate to test them on those cultural items under the premise of testing reading comprehension. Awareness of cultural bias and alertness to its presence in instruments used in our schools will help classroom teachers prevent some inappropriate placements of children.

Formative assessment can also be culturally biased. Teacher-made tests tend to reflect the cultures teachers live in and are familiar with. They may write sample items using idiomatic phrases or vocabulary that are not part of the classroom instruction. Consider the following word problem:

Tony mowed lawns one summer and was able to put away $5 a week for the month of June. If he followed this savings pattern over the course of the entire summer, how much money would he save?

In this problem, ELLs are presented with idiomatic phrases such as *put away* and *over the course of the entire summer* that may cause comprehension problems. Students from South American cultures might also be confused by the North American construct of *summer*. If we want to assess computation within a word problem framework, we must be aware of bias, idioms, and unknown vocabulary that can lead to comprehension failure.

Language versus Content

Language issues can easily color assessment of content learning in the classroom. When assessing learning of social studies concepts, for example, teachers may ask students to write summary paragraphs or essays. The grammatical errors in the writing, however, may have an effect on the teacher's reading of the concepts expressed in the essay. When creating math word problems, ELLs will have difficulty expressing their intent in the language of mathematics. Although learners may show that they understand the concepts of the problem, their language may give teachers the impression that they understand less than they actually do. The same type of problem may ensue in an oral discussion of literature. Learners' receptive skills may be much more advanced than their productive skills. Teachers' questions may be answered slowly, haltingly, and with inappropriate vocabulary and grammar, making it appear that students understand little about what they have read. Once again, poor language skills give the impression that the student does not understand the content concepts. Teachers have difficulty knowing whether the student lacks content knowledge or does not have the language skills to express that knowledge.

WHAT ARE EXAMPLES OF AUTHENTIC, PERFORMANCE-BASED CLASSROOM ASSESSMENT?

As we have seen, classroom-based assessment often involves some kind of "performance" in which a learner constructs a response—for example, responses to questions, story retelling, oral presentations, role-plays, writing pieces, captioned artwork, media products, and so on. Constructed-response assessments can improve educational achievement for ELLs by helping them to demonstrate learning and transfer learning from one application to another while developing mental habits, skills, and abilities that will aid them in lifelong learning (Valdez Pierce, 2002). We must also work to make this type of assessment valid by using rubrics, checklists, and other means to specify to learners what a good performance looks like and exactly how their performances will be evaluated.

Performance-based assessment is authentic when it is consistent with the kind of instruction used in the classroom involving knowledge and skills closely resembling those needed in the real world (Valdez Pierce, 2002). Authenticity in assessment involves "multiple forms of assessment that reflect student learning, achievement, motivation and attitudes on instructionally-relevant classroom activities" (O'Malley & Valdez Pierce, 1996, p. 4).

As previously noted, standardized testing frequently does not reflect classroom instructional techniques or the learning that has actually taken place within the classroom. Certainly, standardized tests do not give teachers information regarding student motivation or attitudes. We need day-to-day assessments to amass a more complete picture of learners to help guide future instructional planning.

Performance-Based Assessment (PBA)

Performance-based assessment generally falls into three types: *products, performances, and process-oriented* assessments (McTighe & Ferrara, 1998; Valdez Pierce, 2002). All three types can be used in the classroom with ELLs for different learning goals and for students at differing levels of language proficiency.

Table 11.5 provides examples of three types of performance-based assessments for use with ELLs. The table lists the types of assessments, their benefits, and the language levels at which these assessments are appropriate according to the 2006 TESOL proficiency levels (Level 1 Starting, Level 2 Emerging, Level 3 Developing, Level 4 Expanding, and Level 5 Bridging).

In our view of classroom assessment (which includes performance-based, authentic, ongoing, and constructive-response information gathering), the goal is not merely rote learning of content facts (although, of course, it includes some of this), but the development of the mental habits, skills, and knowledge that learners will need for lifelong learning of both language and content and their subsequent success in life. These include the ability to collect, comprehend, and analyze information, work collaboratively with others, solve problems, and perform complex, real-world tasks (Darling-Hammond, Ancess, & Falk, 1995). Three additional features of performance-based assessment help learners to achieve this goal: self-assessment, visible criteria, and rubrics.

TABLE 11.5 Performance-Based Assessments at Varying Language Proficiency Levels

Product Assessments	Benefits	Language Proficiency Levels: TESOL 2006
Illustrations	• Limited language load required for expression of content learning.	• Level 1 Starting • Level 2 Emerging
Projects	• Opportunity to display content learning outcomes in a team environment and with limited language requirements.	Levels 1–5 • Starting • Emerging • Developing • Expanding • Bridging
Poster Board Presentations	• Posters act as a scaffold for the oral language of the content presentation.	Levels 2–5 • Emerging • Developing • Expanding • Bridging
Dioramas	• Content learning display with a limited language load.	Levels 1–5 • Starting • Emerging • Developing • Expanding • Bridging
Lab Reports	• The format of the report acts as a scaffold for the description of a scientific process; opportunity to evaluate specific vocabulary learning.	Levels 3–5 • Developing • Expanding • Bridging
Portfolios	• Offer an opportunity to display long-term progress in content and language in multiple formats.	Levels 1–5 • Starting • Emerging • Developing • Expanding • Bridging
Graphic Organizers	• Limited language required for the content learning display.	Levels 1–5 • Starting • Emerging • Developing • Expanding • Bridging
Bio Poems	• Summarizing tool for social studies and/or language arts that is scaffolded through the use of a modeled format.	Levels 3–5 • Developing • Expanding • Bridging

TABLE 11.5 Performance-Based Assessments at Varying Language Proficiency Levels *(Continued)*

Product Assessments	Benefits	Language Proficiency Levels: TESOL 2006
Journals and Learning Logs	• An enduring sample of student language achievement, vocabulary acquisition, and a record of content learning.	Levels 1–5 • Starting • Emerging • Developing • Expanding • Bridging
Performance Assessments		
Role Plays	• Opportunity to assess oral language usage and content learning in a scaffolded role-play framework.	Levels 2–5 • Emerging • Developing • Expanding • Bridging
Oral Presentations	• Opportunity for oral language and content assessment supported with practice and notes.	Levels 3–5 • Developing • Expanding • Bridging
Interviews	• Opportunity to use practiced oral language structures (such as questions) multiple times while requiring comprehension of an unknown response.	Levels 2–5 • Emerging • Developing • Expanding • Bridging
Debates	• Opportunity for oral language and content assessment that is scaffolded with team support, notes, and prewritten questions.	Levels 4–5 • Expanding • Bridging
Group Discussions	• An informal oral language observation opportunity providing data on content learning.	Levels 2–5 • Emerging • Developing • Expanding • Bridging
Demonstrations	• Oral language and content assessment with realia, practice, and notes as scaffolds.	Levels 3–5 • Developing • Expanding • Bridging
Process-Oriented Assessments		
Self-assessments	• Opportunity to self-assess language, reading and writing skills, learning goals, and study skills.	Levels 1–5 • Starting • Emerging • Developing • Expanding • Bridging

(Continued)

TABLE 11.5 Performance-Based Assessments at Varying Language Proficiency Levels *(Continued)*

Product Assessments	Benefits	Language Proficiency Levels: TESOL 2006
Learning Logs	• Opportunity to self-assess logical thinking, writing, content learning, and vocabulary usage.	Levels 2–5 • Emerging • Developing • Expanding • Bridging
Think-Alouds	• Opportunity to self-assess in an aural-oral modality.	Levels 3–5 • Developing • Expanding • Bridging

Self-Assessment

Self-assessment that routinely accompanies instruction helps learners to process their own skill development and to take responsibility for their own learning, and guides them in the acquisition of the kinds of study skills, attitudes, and practices that will lead to greater learning achievement. For example, the checklist in Table 11.6 encourages students to assess their use of academic oral language. The assessment clearly conveys the kinds of oral language tasks that students will be able to accomplish at the end of the learning unit (in this case, a unit on the pyramids of Egypt). The self-assessment in Table 11.7 is a generic self-assessment for listening and speaking behaviors. Here, the teacher has indicated ways in which students can communicate better in the classroom.

Reading self-assessments can help learners know what good reading habits are and if they are using them. Even in primary grades, learners can rate themselves using a rubric like the one in Table 11.8. Study skills and learning goals can also be incorporated into self-assessment instruments, as shown in Table 11.9.

Visible Criteria

Performance-based assessment is enhanced when teachers share with students and parents the criteria they will use to evaluate learning. Visible criteria that are specific, communicated, and comprehensible to the learners improve the performance of ELLs (Valdez Pierce, 2002). Methods of sharing criteria range from showing examples of possible products to students (e.g., essays, lab reports, book reviews, poems, and essays) to the modeling of processes (e.g., lab skills, math computation, writing as a process, and oral reporting) to the use of rubrics that will eventually be used in evaluating learners' products and processes. Teacher modeling and sharing with good student models provide learners with clear targets for their own products and performances. Models make visible the achievement levels that we expect our students to attain.

TABLE 11.6 Self-Assessment: Content Unit on Egypt

Check (√) the box that describes your language.				
Task	**Not Well**	**Okay**	**Well**	**Very Well**
1. I can describe a pyramid.				
2. I can describe how pyramids were built in the past.				
3. I can understand my teacher talking about the pyramids of Egypt.				
4. I can understand a television program about pyramid building.				
5. I can give an oral report on pyramid building.				

TABLE 11.7 Self-Assessment: Listening and Speaking in the Classroom

Circle the word that tells how well you talk and listen in class.

When talking in class, I:

1.	Ask my classmates for help.	Never	Sometimes	Often
2.	Use my hands and face to add meaning and show feeling.	Never	Sometimes	Often
3.	Draw a picture to help explain something.	Never	Sometimes	Often
4.	Use a different way of saying something if I am not understood.	Never	Sometimes	Often
5.	Use a synonym when I can't think of a word.	Never	Sometimes	Often

TABLE 11.8 Self-Assessment: Good Reading Behaviors

Circle the face that shows how often you do these things.

What I do	Not Often	Sometimes	Usually
1. I read every day.	☹	😐	☺
2. I listen to my teacher read.	☹	😐	☺
3. I like to read.	☹	😐	☺
4. I read at home.	☹	😐	☺
5. I borrow books from the library every week.	☹	😐	☺

TABLE 11.9 Self-Assessment Checklist: Active Learning Behavior

Put a check (√) next to the active learning strategies you use.

	Not Often	Sometimes	Usually
1. I listen carefully to directions.			
2. I take notes from the blackboard.			
3. I study new vocabulary with my buddy.			
4. I ask for help if I don't understand something.			
5. I have a special place and time to study at home.			
6. I do my homework every night.			
7. I read every day.			
8. I check my written work for errors.			

Rubrics

As we have seen, **rubrics** are useful tools for both learners and teachers to evaluate products. Rubrics list the specific criteria used to evaluate a product or presentation and then indicate performance levels on a scoring scale that uses numbers, letters, or other descriptive labels. Teachers share rubrics with students prior to the learning experience and provide clear explanations and examples so that all learners will understand the criteria. Often, rubrics are accompanied by models of acceptable or outstanding products.

Rubrics can be designed for both teachers' and students' use. For learners, the rubric may be written in language that students can easily understand and that will guide them during the learning process. Often, learner rubrics are developed for specific projects such as the Pyramid Unit Rubric in Table 11.2. It is also very useful to develop learner rubrics for tasks and genres used frequently, such as process writing.

Rubrics designed for teacher use are often more complex and complete than those learners will use. Sometimes teachers on a grade-level team develop common rubrics for their use; other times rubrics are devised by grade levels, schools, or districts to evaluate specific student learning goals such as oral language, writing, or math problem solving. The Student Oral Language Observation Matrix (SOLOM) scale (Table 5.4, Chapter 5) is one example of a district-made rubric for teacher assessment of oral language.

Whether rubrics are developed for student or for teacher use, it is important that the criteria be precisely defined according to what a student should know or be able to do at the end of the learning experience. Qualities of the student's product or performance should be made specific so that students can assess their own learning and work to raise their achievement levels. Rubrics provide richer and more useful feedback to learners than a single letter or number grade, because they make it clear why learners scored as they did. Finally, rubrics ensure that assessment is fair and equitable because learners are made aware of what is being assessed and what performance is expected if they are to achieve at a high level.

Research supports the notion that rubrics lead to higher achievement gains in learners. Marzano (2000) reports on a study (Wilburn & Felps, 1983) that compared math achievement in middle school students using two assessment approaches: criterion-based rubrics and a norm-referenced, point-based approach. Average achievement gains were 14 percent higher for students who used rubrics than for those who did not. Particularly high gains were achieved by low-achieving students using rubrics as compared to higher achieving students. The average improvement was 24 percent higher than the average improvement of students assessed on the point-based approach. In addition, the rubric group showed more positive attitudes toward math, the content-area focus of this study.

Fuchs and Fuchs (1986) analyzed 21 different studies examining the use of rubrics. They found that when teachers used rubrics to make decisions about students, student achievement increased by 32 percent as compared with students whose teachers did not use rubrics. "Apparently, asking teachers to conceptualize the classroom progress of students by using rubrics encouraged teachers to clearly define the knowledge and skill strengths and weaknesses of their students and to act on them to promote student growth. Presumably, this perspective was passed on to students, who, in turn, improved their achievement" (Marzano, 2000, p. 63).

Table 11.10 is an example of a writing rubric devised for third-grade ELLs who are learning to write essays. Note that the criteria are clear; they include what the teacher has taught the students and how they are expected to perform.

Compare the elementary-level writing rubric in Table 11.10 to the secondary-level rubric in Table 11.11. Note that the teacher uses four levels of performance and provides more detail in describing the performances in Table 11.11. The four-column rubric in Table 11.11 displays a range of proficiencies that is wider than the three-part rubric in Table 11.10. Generally four-column rubrics are preferable to three-column rubrics in that they allow for descriptions of outstanding performances in all categories, providing goals to challenge even the most advanced learners in your class. In a four-column rubric, the third column, the proficient category, is the target for all students. This column describes the skills and knowledge that will be accomplished by learners who have mastered the lesson content.

The goal of the Likert-scale rubric in Table 11.12 is to assess student achievement on a range of study skills taught in conjunction with an elementary unit on the amphibian life cycle. The teacher gives students copies of the rubric at the start of the unit to clarify the learning goals they need to attain to achieve at a high level. The teacher must explain the terms clearly so that ELLs will be able to use the rubric appropriately. Learners then assess their own ability to use the desired study skills with a Likert scale. At the same time, the teacher can assess the students using a similar rubric.

The Amphibian Observation Rubric in Table 11.13 identifies the same goals as the rubric in Table 11.12, but from the point of view of the teacher. This rubric contains specific criteria

TABLE 11.10 Generic Essay Writing Rubric: Third-Grade Level

Your Writing Includes:	1	2	3
Parts of an Essay	No clear introduction, body, or conclusion. Theme is unclear.	Introduction, body, and conclusion are not easily identified.	Introduction, body, and conclusion are easily identified.
Paragraphs	You do not use paragraphs.	Your paragraphs are missing a topic sentence or only contain one or two details.	You include at least three paragraphs. Each paragraph has a topic sentence and about three details.
Ideas	You have no clearly developed ideas.	You have only one or two developed ideas.	You have at least three ideas that clearly develop your theme.
Words	Your vocabulary is limited and general.	You use mostly basic vocabulary but only a few descriptive words.	You use at least five interesting, descriptive words.
Sentences	You use little or no punctuation or capitalization, and unclear sentences.	Your sentences can be understood, but contain missing capitals, missing or incorrect punctuation, and some misspelled words.	Your sentences are neatly written and include capitalization, punctuation, and correct spelling.
Handwriting	Your handwriting is sometimes difficult to read because it is not neat or legible.	Your handwriting is legible.	Your handwriting is clear, neat, and legible.

TABLE 11.11 Generic Essay Writing Rubric: Secondary Level

	Novice	Apprentice	Practitioner	Expert
Purpose	• Writing lacks purpose. • Shows little understanding of concepts and assignment. • Does not state a main idea.	• Purpose is unclear. • Shows a minimal understanding of concepts and assignment. • Does not state the main idea. • Unrelated ideas are included.	• Purpose is evident. • Demonstrates a proficient understanding of concepts and assignment. • States the main idea. • Unrelated ideas may be included.	• Purpose is clear. • Establishes a thorough understanding of concepts and assignment. • States the main idea. • Remains on topic throughout.
Content Focus	• Topic is undeveloped. • Few to no details to support the topic.	• Topic is minimally developed. • Few details or examples support the topic.	• Topic is developed. • Details and examples are sufficient to support the topic.	• Topic is clearly and fully developed. • Contains extensive, relevant detail and examples to support the topic.
Organization	• Progression of ideas is difficult to impossible to follow. • Transitions are lacking. • An element of format (introduction, body, conclusion, beginning and ending sentences) is missing.	• Some organization is evident but progression of ideas has major inconsistencies. • Transitions are lacking or used incorrectly. • An element of format is missing or weak.	• Ideas are organized and progression of ideas is evident. • Transition words are used. • Complete format is evident.	• Ideas are ordered logically and are easy to follow. • Transitions are used throughout to aid coherence and unity. • All format elements are included.
Grammar, Usage, Mechanics	• Writing is filled with errors that impede communication.	• Writing has errors that at times begin to impede communication.	• Errors are evident but writing is fundamentally grammatical and communicative.	• Few, if any, errors occur.

TABLE 11.12 Self-Assessment Checklist: Learning Strategies for a Unit on Amphibians

- The aquarium contains a clump of frog eggs. Soon the eggs will grow into tadpoles and eventually grow into frogs.
- Observe the eggs every day and notice how the eggs change.
- Write or draw what you observe in your notebook.
- Think about how well you are doing this task.

	Never	Rarely	Sometimes	Usually	Always
1. I look carefully at the aquarium animals every day.					
2. I work with a friend to talk about what we see in the aquarium.					
3. I plan how I'm going to record my observations.					
4. I record my observations every day.					
5. I ask my teacher or a friend if I don't know the correct words to use in my notebook.					
6. I check my science notebook before I give it to my teacher.					

for each of the goals. Secondary school math content is assessed in the four-column rubric for a geometry lesson on quadrilaterals in Table 11.14.

The combination of self-assessment checklists, scales, and rubrics give students a clear picture of how to achieve at progressively higher levels. These tools also provide clarity for teachers, parents, and others in the school community about what is taught and assessed in the classroom.

TABLE 11.13 Rubric for Assessing Students' Learning Strategies in a Unit on Amphibians

Task	Poor	Fair	Proficient	Outstanding
1. Observe aquarium animals.	Observe once or twice.	Observe twice a week.	Observe almost every day.	Observe daily.
2. Talk with a friend about your observations.	Talk once or twice.	Talk twice a week.	Talk almost every day.	Talk daily.
3. Plan a record of your observations.	Write a few words about the animals in your learning log.	Write descriptive observations in your learning log.	Create an observation plan with sentence length descriptions.	Create an observation plan such as a daily diary with sentence length descriptions plus a chart or table.
4. Record your observations.	Record once or twice.	Record twice a week.	Record almost every day.	Record daily.
5. Ask a buddy, or the teacher for the meaning of new words.	Avoid using new words.	Take a guess at the meaning of new words.	Ask a buddy for the meaning of new words.	Use the dictionary to find the meaning of new words.
6. Edit your science notebook for neatness, spelling, complete sentences, clear meaning, and daily observations before giving it to the teacher.	Avoid editing the notebook.	Edit the notebook for neatness.	Edit the notebook for spelling and neatness.	Edit the notebook for spelling, neatness, and complete sentences.

TABLE 11.14 Polygon Rubric for Secondary Students to Self-Assess Math Learning

Polygons: Identification, Classification, and Computation of Quadrilaterals

	Awful	Awkward	Average	Awesome
Identify Geometric Quadrilaterals	• Identifies quadrilaterals by name with less than 60 percent accuracy.	• Identifies quadrilaterals by name with 60 percent accuracy.	• Identifies quadrilaterals by name with 80 percent accuracy.	• Identifies (or matches) 7 quadrilaterals by name with 100 percent accuracy.
Draw the Quadrilaterals	• Draws 7 quadrilaterals correctly. • They are not measured or marked. • Proportion is not correct in all drawings.	• Draws 7 quadrilaterals correctly. • Angles are measured incorrectly or marked incorrectly on some drawings. • Proportions are not correct in all quadrilaterals.	• Draws 7 quadrilaterals correctly. • Angles are measured and marked with few errors. • Proportions are correct.	• Draws 7 quadrilaterals correctly. • Angles are correctly measured and marked. • Proportions are correct.
Classify Quadrilaterals	• Can classify fewer than 7 quadrilaterals but cannot cite side and angle characteristics.	• Can classify fewer than 7 quadrilaterals by referencing either side or angle characteristics.	• Can classify 7 quadrilaterals by referencing side and angle characteristics.	• Can classify 7 quadrilaterals by referencing side and angle characteristics.
Compute the Perimeter of Quadrilaterals	• Computes perimeter with less than 60 percent accuracy with the help of a calculator.	• Can compute perimeter with 60 percent accuracy but may need a calculator.	• Can apply formulas to compute perimeter with 80 percent accuracy.	• Can independently and correctly compute perimeter with 100 percent accuracy.

HOW DO STANDARDS AFFECT CLASSROOM ASSESSMENT?

Standards have been developed in the United States in many content areas (math, science, social studies, etc.) and at national and state levels for each of the grades PreK–12. Currently, a state-led effort coordinated by the National Governors Association Center for Best Practices (NGA Center) and the Council of Chief State School Officers (CCSSO) is in progress to support the adoption of the Common Core State Standards in English Language Arts and Mathematics for Kindergarten through 12th grade. These "robust and relevant" standards were developed by teachers and school leaders to improve student chances of academic success in college and later careers. As of our publication date, 45 states have formally adopted the standards or are in the process of doing so.

In addition, Teachers of English to Speakers of Other Languages (TESOL) has developed two standards documents specifically for English language learners (1997, 2006). There is no shortage of standards documents available for students and teachers.

Teachers find standards helpful in identifying the specific content to be taught at a grade level within a school year. However, some districts and states have developed standards that are more helpful than others. Consider the following characteristics of good standards when evaluating your district/state/national standards (Lacina, Levine, & Sowa, 2006, pp. 37–39):

1. *Standards must be clear* for teachers, parents, and students to understand what they will teach and what they will learn. This means that content standards should be detailed and precise enough to guide a teacher's instructional program.
2. *Standards must be specific.* When written in a general and vague manner, they leave teachers wondering about their interpretation and provide a barrier to student learning. Asking ourselves if a standard can be measured is one test of standard specificity. Note: Many standards that are written broadly also use subcategories of performance indicators and/or rubrics to specify performances expected within each standard.

3. *Standards must be comprehensive* with adequate breadth and depth to enable students to understand the content area at every grade level.

4. *Standards must be manageable*, that is, not overwhelming for the teacher or impossible to implement within the course of a school year.

5. *Standards must be rigorous* for all students and set high expectations for them.

6. *Standards must be public* so that teachers, parents, and students are aware of what the target is and all can have a part in hitting it squarely.

7. *Standards must include a balance between skills and knowledge.*

8. *Standards must be cumulative* in that the skills and knowledge learned at one grade level are used to build increasingly more complex and abstract levels of skills and knowledge in the next grade level.

9. *Standards must be measurable* in order to be easily assessed.

When all of these characteristics are in place, teachers can use standards documents to guide instruction and create meaningful assessment. Table 11.15 is an example of a standard from the Sunshine State Standards of Florida (State of Florida, 1996) fourth grade to fifth grade science content area and addresses the topic, "Processes of Life."

The general learning arenas in Table 11.15 are made more specific in the Grade Level Expectations, where benchmarks are provided for each standard (see Table 11.16). The benchmarks are specific to number 5 in Standard 1: "Knows that similar cells form different kinds of structures" (SC.F.1.2.5).

From this progression of general standards to benchmarks to grade-level expectations, Shelly Marx, a fifth-grade science teacher in Florida, is able to construct a grade-level unit for her class, which includes both ELLs and proficient English-speaking students. The standards and benchmarks provide her with a level of specificity, clarity, and comprehensiveness, yet are manageable within the time frame available to teach the unit. The progression of knowledge from the fourth to the fifth grade reminded Shelly of what students had learned in previous years. However, Shelly could not take this learning for granted, particularly because many of her students were children of migrant farm workers who rotated in and out of the school according to the requirements of the citrus season.

Shelly developed a unit based upon her state's guidelines that she used when she assessed her students' learning. For example, when teaching the parts of plant and animal cells, Shelly determined which aspects of plant and animal cells she wanted students to know and understand. The science text provided her with some of this information and Shelly adapted the material, prioritizing the most important elements of cells and their functions, and creating science, language, and learning strategy objectives based upon this information.

Shelly determined that she would need multiple assessments for her cellular unit to accommodate the diversity of her classroom. Four of the students were beginning language learners from Mexico and Central America; other students were functioning bilinguals; a few were monolingual English speakers; and three were designated special education students. Several of these groups required differential assessments. Shelly planned that her assessments would include:

- frequent comprehension-checking throughout instruction.
- peer review and evaluation of final cell products.

TABLE 11.15 Florida Science Standard 1 for Grades 4 and 5

Processes of Life

Standard: The student:

1. describes patterns of structure and functions in living things. (SC.F.1.2)

2. knows that the human body is made of systems with structures and functions that are related.

3. knows how all animals depend on plants.

4. knows that living things are different but share similar structures.

5. knows that similar cells form different kinds of structures.

TABLE 11.16 Grade Level Expectations for Florida Science Standard 1

Grade Level	Expectations
Fourth grade student	1. knows that living things are composed of cells.
	2. knows that processes needed for life are carried out by cells.
Fifth grade student	1. uses magnifying tools to identify similar cells and different kinds of structures.
	2. knows the parts of plant and animal cells.
	3. understands how similar cells are organized to form structures (e.g., tissue, organs) in plants and animals.

- a summary paragraph of a nonfiction reading on cellular structure.
- a short quiz.
- a Venn diagram comparing plant and animal cells, and their structures.
- a "Cellular cookie" showing the structures created using candy and decorative frosting.

In order to ensure that all students in the class would accomplish the assessments successfully, Shelly provided multiple scaffolds throughout the lesson:

- sticky-note summaries in the text books
- class and individual Venn diagrams
- summaries in the science notebooks
- small supportive groupings with mixed L1 and L2 speakers
- use of the native language for clarification among groups
- individual vocabulary cards listing cellular structures and their functions
- classroom charts and handouts on which to take notes

After determining her assessments based upon state standards, Shelly fleshed out her objectives for the lesson (see Table 11.17).

As we have seen, standards and assessments were the starting point in Shelly's planning for her fifth-grade science class. Starting with standards and the assessment of those standards assured Shelly that all of her students would be working at rigorous, grade-level content learning. Her instructional practices were part of her assessment plan and included techniques that were familiar to the students. Her scaffolding and variety of instruction and assessment ensured that all students would have access to the learning and be assessed in a fair, reliable, and valid manner. Finally, Shelly used multiple sources of information for her assessment throughout the learning process rather than relying on a quiz or test at the end of the unit. Shelly's planning for teaching and assessment is itemized in Table 11.18.

TABLE 11.17 Shelly's Science Lesson Objectives

Type of Objective	Specific Objective
Content Objective	Students will describe the components and their functions for both plant and animal cells using a completed vocabulary card of cellular structures and functions.
Thinking/Study Skill Objective	Students will match the cell components with their functions on a chart.
Language Objective	Students will use the target vocabulary and signal words to compare the differences between plant and animal cells; and tell the functions of parts of the cell using passive voice verbs, a vocabulary card, and a class chart.

Source: Lacina et al. (TESOL, 2006, p. 19). Used with permission.

The Common Core State Standards in English Language Arts and Mathematical Practice are also written to progress from generalized "Anchor" standards to more specific grade-level standards and from there to student objectives. Consider this English Language Arts Anchor Standard (http://www.corestandards.org/the-standards/english-language-arts-standards) for Key Ideas and Details, K-Grade12:

- *Read closely to determine what the text says explicitly and to make logical inferences from it; cite specific textual evidence when writing or speaking to support conclusions drawn from the text.*

Compare the general Anchor Standard to these more specific standards at grade 3:

- *Ask and answer questions to demonstrate understanding of a text, referring explicitly to the text as the basis for the answers.*
- *Recount stories, including fables, folktales, and myths from diverse cultures; determine the central message, lesson, or moral and explain how it is conveyed through key details in the text.*
- *Describe characters in a story (e.g., their traits, motivations, or feelings) and explain how their actions contribute to the sequence of events.*

Or to the version at grade 5:

- *Quote accurately from a text when explaining what the text says explicitly and when drawing inferences from the text.*
- *Determine a theme of a story, drama, or poem from details in the text, including how characters in a story or drama respond to challenges or how the speaker in a poem reflects upon a topic; summarize the text.*
- *Compare and contrast two or more characters, settings, or events in a story or drama, drawing on specific details in the text (e.g., how characters interact).*

From these grade-level standards, teachers can consult the Common Core Curriculum Maps project located at http://www.commoncore.org/maps. Here, more specific student objectives relating to the standards are integrated into units of study to serve as exemplars for standards use. Some examples from grade 3, Unit 1 (Stories Worth Telling Again and Again, 2010 edition) include:

- *Tell stories from personal experiences and write narratives telling those stories.*
- *Revise and edit narratives with the help of peers and adults.*
- *Determine and analyze characters' traits and motivations in realistic fiction such as* The Stories Julian Tells.
- *Compare and contrast two "grandparent" books, specifically, the characters and message of the books.*
- *Determine the trickster, the fool, the problem, and the solution in various cultures' trickster tales.*

TABLE 11.18 Shelly's Assessment and Instruction Plans

1. Identify state content standards for the topic. Locate the appropriate benchmarks. Identify grade-level expectations for the prior grades leading up to the current grade level.

2. Determine content, language, and learning skill objectives for the grade-level expectations.

3. Determine a variety of assessment procedures that will adequately assess learning for all language proficiency levels in the class.

4. Identify appropriate scaffolding for assessments: interactional grouping and structures, pictorial and graphic supports.

5. Determine a variety of activities that will enable all students to reach the proficient level for each objective.

6. Determine methods of scaffolding instruction.

7. Clearly communicate objectives to all learners.

8. Communicate and demonstrate success to all learners in the form of rubrics, self-assessments, models, demonstrations, and/or completed products.

* *Research one of the trickster tale's cultures, as part of responding to class-generated questions.*
* *Create a class book or a multimedia presentation based on the culture research.*

In the grade 5 Unit 1 (Playing With Words, 2010 edition) curriculum map, the following student objectives are suggested:

* *Read classic and humorous stories and poems.*
* *Conduct research on people of interest, notably scientists.*
* *Create digital presentations.*
* *Write responses to a variety of literature and poetry.*
* *Participate in group discussions about poetic techniques and figurative language.*

Standards, whether state or national, are becoming more familiar to classroom teachers. If used appropriately, they will enable all students to achieve at higher levels. The challenge currently facing educators concerns professional development for teachers in the use of state and national standards. "Standards do not offer guidance on the process of their implementation; therefore, teachers themselves must translate the language of the standards into instructional practice. This requires that teachers have a thorough understanding of standards and standards-driven teaching and learning. However, most teachers do not feel well prepared to use standards in the classroom" (Menken, 2000, p. 17). Professional development in the use of standards "positively impacts teachers' ability to implement standards-based curriculum and, subsequently, improve student performance" (Menken, 2000, p. 17).

ELLs assessed according to the principles described here, illustrated in Shelly's classroom, and grounded in grade-appropriate standards-based instruction, will have the opportunity to display their content-learning strengths while acquiring the language they need to become fully functional in an English language classroom. Equitable, varied, and scaffolded assessment is the foundation of good instruction.

ASSESSMENT FOR ELLS IN AN RTI ORGANIZATIONAL MODEL

RTI was originally conceived as a form of assessing and rapidly applying interventions for young children who struggle with the basic skills of literacy. As a result, much of the research and information regarding this model applies to children in grades K to 2. Recently, RTI has evolved to also involve mathematics instruction, ELLs, and older learners, but there is little research to guide these programs at present. Because of this, much of what we say about assessment issues at Tier 2 levels applies to younger learners. The recommendations for Tier 1 assessment apply to both elementary and secondary learners.

Assessment is important in the education of ELLs because it determines their educational placement, their need for support services, their grade retention, their curriculum, and their expectations for success. Because of the importance of assessment, we advocate for assessments that are culturally sensitive to diverse students, their languages, and their cultures. However, any test that is standardized and administered strictly to identify which students fall above or below a certain cutoff point will be insensitive to the fine distinctions of culture, language, years of schooling, literacy opportunities in the L1, and the quality level of differentiated classroom instruction (Rivera, Moughamian, Lesaux, & Francis (2008). Because of this, ELLs may be disproportionately placed into special education, particularly in disability categories related to speech and language. ELLs who truly have special needs, on the other hand, may be overlooked because schools assume that their limitations are related to low-level language proficiency. These children may be delayed for special education placement for two or three years longer than their native English peers (McCardle, Mele-McCarthy, Cutting, Leos, & D'Emilio, 2005).

RTI assessment has two major functions: screening and progress monitoring. Screening is typically accomplished by administering a brief measure three times a year (early fall, winter, and late spring) designed to predict outcomes related to a state or district reading assessment. The outcomes of these tests are compared to a benchmark (cutoff point) and used to determine risk status for each student. Screening measures, ideally, "should be multifaceted, developmentally appropriate, and criterion referenced. In addition, they should meet psychometric standards and be reliable and valid" (Thomlinson & Santangelo, 2010, p. 17).

The screening instruments used for ELLs are the same as those used for native-English speakers. The idea that the same measures can be used with both populations has been criticized (Klingner & Edwards, 2006; Orosco & Klingner, 2010). For example, assessing phonological awareness in ELLs who may speak a language not containing English phonemes would inappropriately show that these students are unable to discriminate between sounds. In addition, sound placement differs across languages and letters may appear to be the same but have different sounds—such as Spanish and English vowels (Orosco & Klinger, 2010). Some researchers have also suggested that benchmarks and rates of progress may differ between bilingual and English-only learners (Linan-Thompson, Cirino, & Vaughn, 2007).

One continuing controversy in the assessment of language-diverse students pertains to standardization and norming issues of assessment devices (Hoover et al., 2008). Most general aptitude and ability assessments rely on a student's prior learning and cultural knowledge. When these experiences are vastly different, as they are for language learners, then elements of assessment bias can affect the reliability and validity of the results. The interpretations of the results, however, may be more distorted than the actual assessment bias. Baca and Clark (1992) found that assessment instruments were responsible for 25 percent of bias. But 75 percent was found in the process of the assessment or in the interpretation of the results. This study reminds us that those administering and interpreting assessments for diverse populations must be culturally and linguistically competent to do so.

The second function of RTI assessment is progress monitoring. Progress monitoring occurs at all tiers and provides detailed information about current student performance and growth (Thomlinson et al., 2010). **Curriculum-based measurement (CBM)** is typically used for progress monitoring in early elementary school. CBM uses standardized methodology rather than teacher-made testing procedures to assess student performance. When used appropriately, CBM is as reliable and valid as most standardized norm-referenced tests (Hammill & Bartel, 2004; Hoover et al., 2008). CBM involves using short, timed tests on a consistent and frequent basis. Examples are tests of oral fluency that involve having students read aloud from unpracticed passages or lists of words, alphabetic knowledge, and phonemic awareness measures. In math, CBMs include measures of number sense and computational fluency (Fisher & Frey, 2010).

Progress monitoring in Tier 1 enables a teacher to more clearly differentiate instruction for learners. In Tier 2, the primary function of progress monitoring is to determine the effectiveness of interventions. Tier 3 progress monitoring is highly individualized and more frequent than earlier tiers. Data from progress monitoring is compared to benchmarks and instructional decisions are made based upon the results.

In any discussion of assessment with culturally diverse students, it is important to note that multiple sources of assessment are needed to guide programming and intervention decisions. Varied assessment allows for a fuller picture of a child with sociolinguistic, cultural, schooling, and language differences. Varied measures are more likely to include academic skills related to content-area success. Whenever possible, it is helpful to use native language assessments to provide a more complete picture of a child's knowledge.

RTI TIER 1 SAMPLER

- Conduct a language screening at the start of the school year for all new students to determine if a language other than English is used in the child's home. If a second or third language is used with the child, conduct a language assessment to determine language dominance and proficiency, including literacy in the L1 and L2. Some suggested measures for language assessment include running records, Language Assessment Scales (LAS), and oral language samples.

- Determine the preferred learning style of the student from classroom-based observations, task analysis, and parent meetings. Look for patterns of behavior and document them with written notes or checklists.

- Determine the level of acculturation of students to prevent problems with emotional adjustments to the school and national culture. Use classroom-based assessments, student observations, and cross-cultural interviews with parents and family members.
- Determine a student's prior experience with formal, school-based learning and preferred academic subjects. Use a review of school records and parent and family interviews to gather this information.
- Use language samples and/or journaling to have students document classroom-based learning. The journals will show indications of literacy skills, thinking processes, and cultural differences between the classroom and the home culture. If students are unable to write in English, encourage writing in the native language and ask for help from home in the translations.
- Analyze student work samples to identify strengths and weaknesses, gaps in learning, and learning strategies. Use these work samples to assist in breaking down larger tasks into smaller parts and infusing these discrete parts with needed language and learning strategy instruction.
- Assess decoding of known vocabulary frequently using the cloze procedure from leveled texts, high-frequency word lists, and vocabulary rating charts.
- Check comprehension of all students frequently throughout the lesson using student responses that are observable. In the last five minutes of the class, summarize, or have students summarize learning based upon lesson objectives.
- Give students clear feedback on their performance. For language errors, use repetition and reformulation to model grammatical, academic language forms. For written products, provide models of excellence and select one or two areas of the writing for reworking.
- Identify normal expectations for behavior and learning in your classroom. Select a variety of teaching strategies to propel students toward normal expectations. Use weekly progress monitoring to determine student progress. Adjust the teaching situation as student performance requires.

RTI Tier 2 Sampler

- Consult the child-study or teacher-assistance team in the school to outline a process for gathering information related to cultural and linguistic factors that may affect academic achievement. Modify intervention techniques to conform to the student's cultural and linguistic background.
- Schedule exams of vision and hearing.
- Conduct formative assessments of ELLs to screen for reading problems and monitor progress in literacy. Assess phonological processing, alphabet knowledge, phonics, and word reading skills using authentic classroom materials. Combine these assessments with commercial, standardized curriculum-based measurements (CBMs) such as Dynamic Indicators of Basic Early Literacy Skills (DIBELS).
- Monitor progress on a weekly or biweekly basis.
- Modify basic literacy instruction based upon frequent progress monitoring. Increase and intensify the time for instruction in discrete skills such as phonological awareness, familiarity with the alphabet and the alphabetic principle, reading of single words, and knowledge of basic phonics rules.
- Identify and train school-based teams of teachers to identify students at risk, interpret standardized screenings, and determine the instructional adjustments needed for students to progress.
- Consider testing students in their L1 for a fuller, richer picture of their skill levels.
- Continue to monitor progress in content vocabulary, oral language, and language structure development in English. Use checklists for vocabulary and student self-assessment inventories. Record samples of oral language at intervals to determine progress in fluency and grammatical structure.

- If progress monitoring of language and literacy indicates slow or little growth, intensify instruction through increased time or individualized instruction. Structure the nature of the intervention to relate specifically to the skills that are delayed.
- Analyze data collected on an individual student by charting and graphing the data collected at frequent intervals. The graph that emerges should show a trend line rising upward to indicate student progress. Use these graphs to focus collaborative conversations among involved school personnel and to result in informed adjustments to curriculum and instruction.

Questions for Reflection

1. We have advocated for differentiated assessment techniques that are adjusted to the needs of the learner. By adapting assessments, we have argued that language learners can receive more equitable treatment in evaluating their content learning. What might the arguments be against this thinking? How would you explain your method of assessment to parents of monolingual students?

2. Many teachers have difficulty differentiating between the language of the student and the content learning expressed in that language. Others in the school community may not understand how a student can receive a grade of B on an assignment that contains ungrammatical elements. Can these assignments be proudly displayed on bulletin boards in school hallways? What responses would you give to critics of this grading system?

3. Assessments should be grounded in state, national, and content standards. Others would argue that assessments should be grounded in the strengths and needs of the students in the classroom. Prepare arguments for both of these positions.

Activities for Further Learning

1. Summative assessments can sometimes contain elements of cultural bias. Conduct an analysis of a summative assessment used in your state or school district. Determine the percentage of cultural bias in that assessment.

2. Using the listings of classroom instructional practices presented in this chapter, create an assessment that rates content learning separately from language learning.

3. Choose/create a lesson plan for content learning. Write a student rubric that can be used to assess student learning of that lesson.

4. Devise an observation checklist that teachers can use to evaluate the aural-oral skills of students while they are engaged in group work and discussion.

5. Compare the Core Content Standards in either English Language Arts or Mathematics to the standards of your current school district at one grade level. Do you agree that the Core Standards are "robust and relevant" at that grade level? What evidence can you show for your opinion?

6. Devise two self-assessment instruments that students at two different grade levels can use to self-assess one of these language areas (e.g., reading, writing, listening, or speaking).

7. Create an assessment plan using at least five different forms of assessment for a lesson or unit you have created or taught in the past.

8. Standards are often the starting point for good assessment. Look at the standards in your state for math, science, social studies, and language arts. Are the standards and benchmarks sufficiently specific to determine learning objectives and assessments? Choose a content area, select standards for that content at a specific grade level, and determine assessments and objectives for a diverse class of learners based upon those standards. Argue for or against the usefulness of your state standards.

Suggested Reading

August, D., & Hakuta, K. (1998). *Educating language-minority children*. Washington, DC: National Academy Press. This short volume summarizes a report entitled *Improving schooling for language-minority children: A research agenda* (1997). The chapter on student assessment itemizes the key findings of the research in that report.

Brown, J., & Hudson, T. (1998). The alternatives in language assessment. *TESOL Quarterly, 32*(4), 653–676. The authors examine three types of assessment useful for classroom purposes. They then describe how teachers can best select appropriate assessments for various objectives.

Carr, J., & Harris, D. (2001). *Succeeding with standards: Linking curriculum, assessment, and action planning*. Alexandria, VA: Association for Supervision and Curriculum Development. This book describes a comprehensive plan for aligning local curriculum to local, state, and national standards. Although not aimed specifically at ELLs, the authors are concerned with improving academic performance for all students.

Leung, C., & Lewkowicz, J. (2006). Expanding horizons and unresolved conundrums: Language testing and assessment. *TESOL Quarterly, 40*(1), 211–234. In an article scrutinizing the state of assessment in the TESOL profession, the authors discuss current concerns in standardized testing as well as key issues in classroom-based teacher assessment of second-language learners.

Short, D. (1993). Assessing integrated language and content instruction. *TESOL Quarterly, 27*(4), 627–656. This is a practical article that explores content instruction for ELLs and the various ways to assess their learning in classrooms PreK–12.

Teachers of English to Speakers of Other Languages, Inc. (2006). *PreK–12 English language proficiency standards.* Alexandria,

VA: TESOL. A resource for teachers seeking to align content standards with language learning standards. The volume includes standards for language arts, social studies, math, and science as well as the TESOL standards for social, intercultural, and instructional purposes within a PreK–12 school setting. Varying language proficiencies are included with appropriate performance indicators.

References

Abedi, J. (2002). Assessment and accommodations of English language: Issues, concerns, and recommendations. *Journal of School Improvement, 3*(1). http://www.icsac.org/jsi/.

Baca, L. M., & Clark, C. (1992). *EXITO: A dynamic team assessment approach for culturally diverse students.* Minneapolis, MN: CEC.

Coltrane, B. (2002). English language learners and high-stakes tests: An overview of the issues. *CAL Digest* EDO-FL-02-07. http://www.cal.org/resources/digest/ 0207coltrane.html.

Common Core Curriculum Maps: English Language Arts. (n.d.) http://commoncore.org/maps/index.php.

Common Core State Standards: English Language Arts Anchor Standards. (n.d.) http://www.corestandards.org/the-standards/english-language-arts-standards.

Darling-Hammond, L., Ancess, J., & Falk, B. (1995). *Authentic assessment in action: Studies of schools and students at work.* New York: Teachers College Press.

Echevarria, J., Vogt, M., & Short, D. J. (2004). *Making content comprehensive for English learners: The SIOP model* (2nd ed.). New York: Pearson.

Figueroa, R. A., & Garcia, E. (1994, Fall). Issues in testing students from culturally and linguistically diverse backgrounds. *Multicultural Education,* 10–19.

Fisher, D., & Frey, N. (2010). *Enhancing RTI: How to insure success with effective classroom instruction and intervention.* Alexandria, VA: ASCD.

Fuchs, L., & Fuchs, D. (1986). Effects of systematic formative evaluation: A meta-analysis. *Exceptional Children, 53*(3), 199–206.

Hammill, D. D., & Bartel, N. R. (2004). *Teaching students with learning and behavior problems.* Austin, TX: Pro-Ed.

Hoover, J. J., Klingner, J., Baca, L. M., & Patton, J. M. (2008). *Methods for teaching culturally and linguistically diverse exceptional learners.* Upper Saddle River, NJ: Pearson.

Klingner, J. K., & Edwards, P. (2006). Cultural considerations with response to intervention models. *Reading Research Quarterly, 41,* 108–117.

Lachat, M. A. (2004). *Standards-based instruction and assessment for English language learners.* Thousand Oaks, CA: Corwin Press.

Lacina, J., Levine, L. N., & Sowa, P. (2006). *Collaborative partnerships between ESL and classroom teachers: Helping English language learners succeed in preK–elementary schools.* Alexandria, VA: TESOL.

Linan-Thompson, S., Cirino, P. T., & Vaughn, S. (2007). Determining English language learners' response to intervention: Questions and some answers. *Learning Disability Quarterly, 30,* 185–195.

Marzano, R. (2000). *Transforming classroom grading.* Alexandria, VA: Association for Supervision and Curriculum Development.

McCardle, P., Mele-McCarthy, J., Cutting, L., Leos, K., & D'Emilio, T. (2005). Learning disabilities in English language learners—identifying the issues. *Learning Disabilities Research and Practice, 20*(1), 1–5.

McTighe, J., & Ferrara, S. (1998). *Assessing learning in the classroom.* Washington, DC: National Education Association.

Menken, K. (2000, December). Standards-based education reform and English language learners. In *Framing effective practice: Topics and issues in educating English language learners. A technical assistance synthesis by the National Clearinghouse for Bilingual Education.* (Task 4.3 Contract No. ED-00-00-0113). (pp. 13–19). http://www.ncbe.gwu.edu/files/rcd/BE024351/framing.pdf. Washington, DC: U.S. Department of Education.

Mohan, B. A. (1985). *Language and content.* Reading, MA: Addison-Wesley.

No Child Left Behind Act of 2001. 107th Congress of the United States of America. http://www.ed.gov/legislation/ESEA02/107-110.pdf.

O'Malley, J. M., & Valdez Pierce, L. (1996). *Authentic assessment for English language learners: Practical approaches for teachers.* Reading, MA: Addison-Wesley.

Orosco, M. J., & Klingner, J. (2010). One school's implementation of RTI with English language learners: "Referring into RTI." *Journal of Learning Disabilities, 43*(3), 269–288.

Ortiz, S. O. (2001). Assessment of cognitive abilities in Hispanic children. *Seminars in Speech and Language, 22*(1), 17–37.

Rivera, C. (2006). Using test accommodations to level the playing field for ELLs. Presentation at the LEP Partnership Meeting, Washington, DC, August 28–29, 2006. http://www.ncela.gwu.edu/spotlight/LEP/Presentations/Charlene_Rivera.pdf.

Rivera, C. (2010, April 28). *ESEA reauthorization: Standards and assessment. Testimony for the Senate Health, Education, Labor, and Pensions Committee.* Washington, DC: George Washington University Center for Equity and Excellence in Education (GW-CEEE).

Rivera, C., Acosta, B. A., & Willner, L. S. (2008). *Guide for refining state assessment policies for accommodating English language learners.* Arlington, VA: The George Washington University Center for Equity and Excellence in Education (GW-CEEE).

Rivera, M. O., Moughamian, A. C., Lesaux, N. K., & Francis, D. J. (2008). *Language and reading interventions for English language learners and English language learners with disabilities.* Portsmouth, NH: RMC Research Corporation, Center on Instruction.

Saphier, J., & Gower, R. (1997). *The skillful teacher: Building your teaching skills.* Carlisle, MA: Research for Better Teaching.

State of Florida, Department of State. (1996). *Science: PreK–12 sunshine state standards and instructional practices.* Tallahassee, FL: Author.

Student Oral Language Observation Matrix (SOLOM). San Jose Area Bilingual Consortium. http://www.cal.org/twi/evaltoolkit/appendix/solom.pdf.

Teachers of English to Speakers of Other Languages, Inc. (1997). *ESL standards for preK–12 students.* Alexandria, VA: Author.

Teachers of English to Speakers of Other Languages, Inc. (2001). *Scenarios for ESL standards-based assessment.* Alexandria, VA: Author.

Teachers of English to Speakers of Other Languages, Inc. (2006). *TESOL preK–12 English language proficiency standards in the core content areas.* Alexandria, VA: Author.

Thomlinson, C. A., & Santangelo, T. (2010). *Integrating differentiated instruction and response to intervention: From theory to practice. E-Book.* Alexandria, VA: ASCD.

Valdes, G., & Figueroa, R. A. (1994). *Bilingualism and testing: A special case of bias.* Norwood, NJ: Ablex.

Valdez Pierce, L. (2002). *Performance-based assessment: Promoting achievement for English language learners.* ERIC/CLL News Bulletin. http://www.cal.org/resources/archive/news/2002fall/performance.html.

Wilburn, K., & Felps, B. (1983). *Do pupil grading methods affect middle school students' achievement: A comparison of criterion-referenced versus norm-referenced evaluations.* Unpublished document. Jacksonville, FL: Wolfson, H. S. (ERIC Document Reproduction Service No. ED 229 451).

MyEducationLab™

Go to the Topic, Assessment, in the MyEducationLab (www.myeducationlab.com) for your course, where you can:

- Find learning outcomes for Assessment along with the national standards that connect to these outcomes.
- Complete Assignments and Activities that can help you more deeply understand the chapter content.
- Apply and practice your understanding of the core teaching skills identified in the chapter with the Building Teaching Skills and Dispositions learning units.
- Examine challenging situations and cases presented in the IRIS Center Resources.
- Check your comprehension on the content covered in the chapter by going to the Study Plan in the Book Resources for your text. Here you will be able to take a chapter quiz, receive feedback on your answers, and then access Review, Practice, and Enrichment activities to enhance your understanding of chapter content.
- **A+RISE** A+RISE® Standards2Strategy™ is an innovative and interactive online resource that offers new teachers in grades K-12 just in time, research-based instructional strategies that meet the linguistic needs of ELLs as they learn content, differentiate instruction for all grades and abilities, and are aligned to Common Core Language Arts standards (for the literacy strategies) and to English language proficiency standards in WIDA, Texas, California, and Florida.

CHAPTER 12

Putting It All Together Thematically: Developing Content-Based Thematic Units

Donna Norman's fourth-grade district curriculum includes the study of various regions of the United States. For the next three weeks, her class will explore the Southwest region. Donna teaches a mixed class of learners that includes six children who are learning English as a second language. Donna has met with her grade-level colleagues, Sally and Bob, to talk about ways to integrate the teaching of the history, geography, and peoples of the Southwest with the language arts skills that she emphasizes for all of her students. After looking at the district curriculum and assessing the needs and interests of the students, Donna, Sally, and Bob decide to teach a three-week integrated unit called "War and Peace in the Old Southwest."

Donna knows that this theme will appeal to her students. She also thinks that the theme is broad enough to include content objectives related to historic struggles between Native Americans and cattle ranchers; warfare over scarce resources; conflicts between warring Native American groups, hunting, and gathering populations; and challenges from the harsh environment.

In the past, Donna has motivated her students by engaging them in concrete experiences that help them to understand the big picture of the learning unit. But this unit has her stumped. Living in the Northeast, she has little access to Native American artifacts. Donna confers again with Sally and Bob, and they brainstorm ideas. Finally, they agree on a combination of simulation and story-reading to introduce the unit. The teachers arbitrarily divide each class into two groups, Navajos and Apaches, and provide cloth headbands labeled with the name of each tribe. Once the headbands are in place and the tribes identified, Donna explains to her class what will happen next:

"For the next three weeks we will learn about your people who lived in the American Southwest long ago. We will learn how your families functioned, how you found food, the animals you used, the crafts you produced, your religions, where you lived, who your enemies were, and some of the major struggles you had in your lives. Your job is to learn about your own tribe so that you will be able to explain it to others from outside the Southwest region. We will start today reading a story about one young boy who lived in the Southwest years ago and his relationship to a wild white horse."

How do you develop content-based thematic units?

· ·

- What is thematic instruction?
- Why teach thematically?
- How are thematic units structured?

- What about standards in a thematic unit?
- How is content curriculum organized in a thematic unit?
- How is language curriculum organized in a thematic unit?
- How are learning strategies incorporated into thematic instruction?

WHAT IS THEMATIC INSTRUCTION?

Thematic instruction for English language learners (ELLs) refers to an approach to teaching where an organizing principle, point of view, or theme is used as the "conceptual glue" integrating content area knowledge with language learning. The content/language learning is organized and sequenced around developmentally appropriate broad-based themes that may take several weeks to complete. Students have opportunities to learn concepts in depth, participate in a wide variety of activities that foster learning, and develop the academic language skills necessary to read and write about the new learning.

Thematic instruction comes from an educational tradition that structures curricula around activities reflecting the interests and experiences of the learners. Dewey (1916) expressed this philosophy, which focused on active participation of learners in activities related to life experiences; and Mohan (1986, p. 40) reiterated that "Doing is not an alternative for knowing: it is a way of knowing. And activity is not an alternative to talk: it is a context for talk." Activity-based communicative language learning grows out of Dewey's basic principles.

Although thematic instruction is not the only way to organize learning for ELLs, it is the most effective and efficient organization scheme that we have encountered. Because we know that our students have a limited time in the classroom, and yet are required to learn to the same high level as their classmates, it is necessary to organize instruction in such a way that vocabulary, concepts, grammar, and language skills are constantly reused and recycled. Thematic instruction makes this possible.

Thematic instruction can be structured in a variety of ways, depending on the age of the learners and the preferences of the teacher and the school. Theme units are traditionally determined by district curriculum and teacher choice, but may also be generated by student inquiry and interest. Integrated learning units and interdisciplinary instruction are examples of thematic instruction from the primary to the secondary school level. The term **thematic instruction** represents the continuum of instructional options from units to courses—all of them characterized by the integration of learning within the classroom.

Marina Sanchez has developed thematic units for her primary class that include several low to intermediate ELLs. One that she usually teaches in October centers on the characteristics of animals, but Marina calls it her "Monster" unit. She uses the children's excitement about Halloween and their natural curiosity about monsters to motivate them to learn the scientific characteristics and academic language that describe the various aspects of animals: their physical descriptions, habitat, diet, methods of obtaining food, sleep cycles, and other interesting information. Although the children begin the unit learning about mythical and strange monsters, they eventually begin to focus on the real animals that are interesting to them. The month-long unit takes the children through many different areas of learning. They begin with comics and mythological stories, and proceed to singing and marching in monster parades, reading library

A Monster Unit Is Powerfully Motivating to Young Elementary Students

books, exploring information on the computer, organizing information on graphic organizers, reporting on various animals, and finally, creating their own monster animals with pictures and oral reports describing their life habits.

Criteria for Thematic Instruction

Marina's unit incorporates the nine principles of Activity-Based Communicative teaching and learning. These principles overlap with instructional criteria that are thought to produce effective thematic instruction (Enright & McCloskey, 1988; Peregoy & Boyle, 2008).

1. *Active, Varied Engagement:*   Thematic instruction offers variety in many ways, in class groupings, in skill use, in topics and choices, in methods of learning, in task difficulty, in roles and responsibilities, and in presentations. There are many ways for children to learn about the themes, and each student can become expert in at least one of them. Marina's students read comics and myths, sang and marched, researched on the computer, completed graphic organizers, and reported on and drew pictures of their monsters. The goal is total engagement of all learners.

2. *Cultural Relevance and Student Interest:*   Thematic instruction is successful when teachers are able to match the instructional goals of the state or district curriculum to their own students' interests, lives, and cultures. As the unit progresses, students often take the lead in the direction of the inquiry as they suggest new questions to explore and use their own experiences to guide them. Those students who like to sing were delighted with Marina's monster parade. But others in her class were far more interested in exploring learning on the computer and in the library. All of her students related well to the mythological creatures described in their home cultures. For some of her students, creating drawings of their own imaginary monsters was the high point of the month.

3. *Collaboration:*   Collaboration enables ELLs to practice language in an academic context, develop a broad range of language functions, and increase academic vocabulary. Students work together with buddies, small groups, various teachers, and their families to negotiate their understanding of content and determine the meaning of the new language and concepts. For this unit, Marina expanded the instructional conversation of the classroom by using student pairs and small-group work projects. Marina's student groupings changed as activities evolved. Other adults in the school were consulted when questions needed to be answered. For example, the school librarian helped with the research; and the fifth-grade teacher, Ms. Leary, gave insights from her extensive knowledge of birds.

4. *Learning Strategies:*   Learning strategies expand student learning beyond the classroom and maximize learning potential. Marina used the computer frequently during this unit. Skills that the students had learned in the computer lab could be practiced in her classroom. Marina focused on search strategies for specific information for this unit. In addition, she used graphic organizers once again, a learning strategy that her students were becoming accustomed to throughout all of their learning.

5. *Comprehensible Input with Scaffolding:*   The teacher determines what forms of sheltering and scaffolding need to be used for each of the activities in the unit to ensure that all students are participating as fully as possible. The monster unit utilized many pictures of both real and imaginary animals. These spiked the students' interest and helped them understand the new terminology. Graphic organizers supported the writing assignments, and group work ensured that each student had multiple opportunities to speak and be spoken to.

6. *Activating Prior Knowledge and Building on Prior Experience:*   Students need to reflect upon what they already know about the topic in order to be ready to learn more. Marina Sanchez reminded her students of the unit they had studied the year before on toads and frogs. She also encouraged them to think about monster stories they knew from their own cultures. Some students recalled hearing the story of Bigfoot and described that mysterious creature. Others told about Nessie, the Loch Ness monster. Many of the children knew a great deal about dinosaurs. Far from blank slates, her students had their own experiences to bring to the topic.

7. *Integration of Content Learning with Language:*   As students proceed through the unit, their language skills develop, particularly in connection with the vocabulary and methodology required by the topic. Marina's students were learning the language and methodology

of zoologists. The vocabulary of the topic became increasingly accessible to them as they used it in a variety of activities and learning formats. Their final reports and presentations reflected this language growth in addition to the information they had learned about animals.

8. *Differentiation:*   Thematic units can accommodate differences in language, literacy, cognitive levels, dimensions of learning, learning styles, and interests because units extend over a period of time when content learning can be explored in a variety of different ways and on a range of language proficiency levels.

9. *Clear Goals, Feedback, and Purpose:*   Students are involved in purposeful activities for which there is an audience and a goal. Marina's students knew they had to learn about animal characteristics to be able to design their own monsters, report on them to the class, and display them during the Halloween season. Marina was also clear in her feedback to students by providing abundant modeling, both of processes and products, and using rubrics for oral presentations.

Marge Gianelli (1991) is a big fan of thematic instruction. As director of bilingual and ESL programs at Canutillo Independent School District near El Paso, Texas, she worked for over five years to develop content-based thematic units for grades K through 6. The school district was concerned about the fragmented nature of children's learning in their traditional classrooms. Students were confused about what they were learning, and reading scores were low. After the introduction of thematic instruction, the results have been "dramatic" (p. 13). Teachers enjoy teaching this way, learners are interested and involved, and reading has increased and improved. Gianelli attributes the success to, among other things, the in-depth involvement of students in a great deal of meaningful language within a supportive learning environment.

The teachers at the Canutillo School District proceeded to organize for thematic instruction in much the same way that Marina Sanchez did. They began by scouring their state and district curricula to determine possible themes. It is important that the themes have broad relationships to those topics typically required in the content curriculum of a grade level. Marina Sanchez knew that her third graders would be spending the year in science and social studies learning about plant and animal habitats from four regions of the world. She chose her monster theme to provide some of the language, skills, and knowledge her students would need for that content.

The next step in the process is to determine the specific content area topics to be studied. Most teachers do not have a district curriculum committee to do this for them. Instead, they ask their students to help plan the unit. Barbara Agor (2000), a middle school teacher in Rochester, New York, enlisted her students to help her plan a unit on the Middle Ages. Barbara began by overwhelming her students in the first days of the unit with what she calls the "book circle"— a circle of books all around the room, differentiated by reading proficiency and all dedicated to the Middle Ages. Barbara gave her students time to look through as many books as possible, about three minutes per book on the first day. Later, they went through these books a second time with colored sticky notes, marking important pages and pictures, writing questions, and focusing on topics. The sticky notes were used when Barbara helped the class create a graphic organizer of all the topics they wanted to study. The graphic helped them to group topics and create subtopics under major headings. Barbara also had a question wall where she wrote student questions as they popped up. The graphic organizer and the question wall acted as a road map for the rest of the unit.

From here, Barbara sequenced the activities, collected and adapted materials for differing language proficiencies, and created content and language objectives. For the next five weeks, her students learned about the Middle Ages (dates, places, lifestyles, problems) and they also learned how to ask questions, report, imagine, research, and present information about the Middle Ages, a combination of content and process, and skills and knowledge.

WHY TEACH THEMATICALLY?

"Everything is connected to everything else" (Sylvester, 1995, p. 140). Whether we study ecology or the neural networks of the human brain, we will find that connections are vital to the health and growth of the intellect and the planet. Brain research has shown us that learning results from the connections between neurons in our brains. As our neural networks grow and develop, we get smarter and are able to transfer our learning from one sphere of knowledge to the other. Thematic instruction enables students to see the connections between aspects of the curriculum and to make those connections in their brains.

Connections between neurons are supported by the growth of dendrites—spiny tree-like projections that help electrochemical impulses leap from one neuron to another. It is through active learning experiences that dendrites are produced. Wolfe (2001, p. 187) reminds us that "The person doing the work is the one growing the dendrites." In thematic instruction, the student is the one doing the work while the teacher facilitates learning. Thematic instruction emphasizes dynamic, experiential, inquiry-based learning over passive-listening classrooms. The idea of action here refers to mental action primarily, those activities involving choices, research, and problem solving. Students are involved in processes of constructing meaning and discovery. They seek to find answers rather than being told them. This kind of learning is advantageous for all learners. Thematic instruction "creates optimal content, language, and literacy learning opportunities for both native and non-native English speakers" (Peregoy & Boyle, 2008, p. 94).

Thematic instruction assists the brain in an innate effort to create patterns and thus give meaning to new information that would otherwise be dismissed and forgotten. New information is organized and associated with previously relevant information, connecting neural networks in the brain into connected patterns, and thus increasingly developing the ability to comprehend wider and more complex contexts. In the early grades, teachers are better able to see the connections, themes, and underlying principles than are the children because adults have a wider array of accumulated knowledge with which to make connections. But older learners can make these connections for themselves as they have had more time to accumulate sufficient data and to see patterns emerge. Interdisciplinary and cross-disciplinary models in middle and high schools create more relevance for learners, helping students to see how economics relates to geography, math to music, and ecology to politics (Jenkins, 1998).

The unique nature of thematic instruction also encourages memory enhancement. Consolidation of new information into long-term memory requires deep processing and/or multiple opportunities for recollection and use with the brain's executive functions. These repetitions reinforce the neuronal connections of the brain's axons, dendrites, and synapses. When neuronal connections are stimulated, dendrites are strengthened, and memory becomes more enduring (Willis, 2006). In thematic instruction, the brain perceives information repeated in multiple ways and in a variety of contexts. This process makes encoding of that information more efficient and more enduring. The result is consolidation of information:

> *Consolidation of information involves using the most effective strategies to first acquire information and then practice and rehearse it. The best-remembered information is learned through multiple and varied exposures followed by authentic use of the knowledge by processing it through the executive function centers* (Willis, 2006, p. 30).

Thematic units provide a learning experience that facilitates consolidation of information and long-term memory storage. Thematic learning also enhances the brain's ability to create patterns from new content information and to make connections between related content areas, such as the connections between science and math or the relationship between literature and history.

Many school districts have chosen to sequence curricula thematically because of the belief that learning is most likely to occur and be transferred from one situation to another when concepts and activities are interrelated in the classroom as they are outside the classroom (Richard-Amato, 2009). In addition, thematic instruction provides the context and concrete experiences necessary for many students, including ELLs, to learn abstract concepts. The collaborative nature of these experiences motivates and involves students while providing them with a purpose for learning. Indeed, Ritter (1999) reports a study that suggests the engagement rates of students were higher for thematic instruction than for single-subject lessons. Teacher observations and student self-perceptions confirmed that third and fourth graders in the study were more involved in learning when social studies, reading, and math were integrated than when they learned those subjects individually.

Language skills are placed at center stage throughout thematic instruction. Collaborative problem solving, project work, inquiry-based research, and sharing of information enable learners to use and hear both social and academic language. The social language skills for communicating and functioning within a small group are facilitated as the groups assign roles, make suggestions, praise, edit, and create together. The sharing of information between and within groupings requires the use of the academic language related to the content subject. Reading and writing skills develop as students are exposed to source material both within and outside the textbook. Writing skills also develop, as students are required to write about and present information that they have learned to others. Finally, the integration of these skills makes more effective use of classroom time than if the skills were taught individually in separate lessons. Thematic instruction is time efficient.

HOW ARE THEMATIC UNITS STRUCTURED?

> *It is clear that . . . we need to develop an organizing framework of language and thinking skills that apply across the curriculum. We need to go beyond techniques that help a student understand a particular lesson; we need to help the student to acquire the ability to develop this understanding independently. This calls for general language and thinking skills that can be transferred. The organizing framework must help the students to connect work in the language class and the content class.*

> BERNARD MOHAN, 1986, PP. 18–19.
> Used with permission.

All thematic units require structure—a skeleton upon which teachers can develop the content, language, and thinking objectives they wish their students to learn. The nature of that skeleton will differ from teacher to teacher, but there are some general principles that apply to the structuring of all thematic instruction. We will consider three:

- Concrete to Abstract Learning
- Low to High Cognitive and Language Levels
- Simple to Complex Content Structures

Concrete to Abstract

Thematic instruction is a process of organizing learning experiences along a continuum of increasing abstraction. Recent brain research emphasizes this approach, and our own experiences reinforce that thinking. There are at least three kinds of learning that help neural networks to form:

- concrete experience
- representational or symbolic learning
- abstract learning

This continuum of abstraction (shown in Figure 12.1) begins with practical, "hands-on" concrete experience. Experiential learning is most effective in producing long-lasting learning. In fact, the strongest links in the brain's neural networks develop as a result of concrete experience (Wolfe, 2001). When we think about our own learning, we realize that we did not develop our computer skills by reading books about computers, but rather by actually using one. Even though we have studied foreign languages in classrooms, our language skills began to grow and develop when we traveled to countries where those languages were spoken. We finally understood the usefulness of algebra when we had to comparison shop for mortgage rates, determine the rate of earnings or loss from our stock portfolios, or predict how long a car trip might take us.

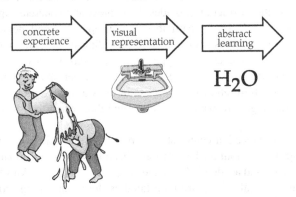

FIGURE 12.1 Learning Progresses from Concrete Experience and/or Visual Representation to Abstract Learning

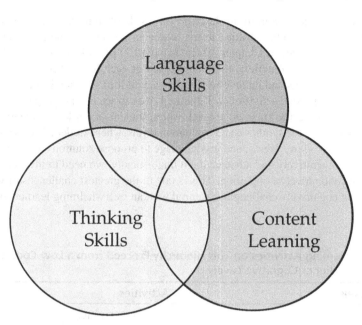

FIGURE 12.2 Thematic Units Integrate Three Kinds of Skill Development within Carefully Planned Lessons

Teachers of young children are aware of the importance of concrete experiences. Play is an important part of the kindergarten curriculum, and "hands-on" learning is crucial to primary education. Older learners also need concrete experiences to begin to develop an understanding of difficult abstract concepts.

Representational or symbolic learning is the next level of abstraction. Using pictures and graphics, teachers can help learners to understand new concepts. However, these tools are only as useful as the degree to which learners have had concrete experience with the concept. Showing a picture of a computer to a child who has never seen or used one may not lead to retention of that image or the word identifying it. Understanding a visual diagram of the water cycle is easier when children have had experiences seeing condensation on the side of a cold glass and monitoring rain clouds.

Abstract learning involves acquiring concepts through words and numbers. Reading about concepts and learning through reading is possible when "students have a strong neural network formed by concrete experiences and representations" (Wolfe, 2001, p. 138). Indeed, there are many concepts that require abstract learning. Abstract ideas such as *democracy, culture*, and *justice* can be understood by learners depending on their age, level of language development, number of examples provided by the teacher, prior knowledge, and amount of student involvement in related experiences (Wolfe, 2001).

The continuum from concrete to abstract reflects the kinds of language needed to process learning experiences. Concrete experiences require language for here-and-now, face-to-face dialogue. This language is simpler than the academic language required for abstract learning. The thinking skills required also increase in complexity as students move along the continuum from simple to complex, concrete to abstract. The interconnections between content, language, and thinking skills (Figure 12.2) provide a model for teachers of language-learning students. Thematic instruction allows us to sequence learning events in such a way as to introduce academic terminology within a meaningful context of a concrete experience and gradually increase the abstraction of the learning activities, the complexity of the language, and the difficulty of thinking skills required.

Low to High Cognitive and Language Levels

Bloom's Taxonomy (Bloom, Englehart, Furst, Hill, & Krathwohl, 1956) is a framework that can be used to structure thematic learning experiences from a low cognitive level to a high cognitive level. We introduced using the taxonomy in Chapter 10 as a resource for developing content and language objectives. Here, we suggest that the hierarchy can also be used as a framework for structuring learning experiences for thematic instruction.

Bloom designed the hierarchy to describe six levels of thinking, from the concrete and practical knowledge level to the abstract levels of analysis, synthesis, and evaluation. The cue words appended to the chart in Chapter 10 (in Table 10.2) provide suggestions for the learning activities and language functions that could occur at each level. Table 12.1 describes the taxonomy of thinking levels and includes examples of activities for each level.

From the few suggested activities on Table 12.1, we can see that language demands increase as the teacher moves from the knowledge level, where students are asked to identify vocabulary and recall information, to the synthesis and evaluation levels, where students are asked to persuade others of their point of view, debate, and use language to propose solutions to problems. In order to challenge ELLs cognitively and advance them linguistically, we need to involve them in tasks beyond the application level of cognition. This is one of the greatest challenges of working with ELLs—providing cognitively challenging material without overwhelming learners linguistically.

TABLE 12.1 Learning Activities on This Hierarchy Proceed from a Low Cognitive Level to Higher Cognitive Levels

Thinking Levels	Activities
Knowledge Remembering previously learned material	• name the state. • define photosynthesis. • label the parts of a flower. • list characteristics of Greek drama.
Comprehension Grasping the meaning	• Explain the life cycle of a butterfly. • Summarize the story of . . . • Identify the hero-heroine. • Explain how the digestive system works.
Application Generalize; use the material in new and concrete situations	• Illustrate the setting of the story. • Act out the fairy tale. • Sequence the life cycle of a frog. • Demonstrate the solution of a math problem on the chalkboard.
Analysis Break down material so that it is more easily understood	• Compare the two characters in . . . • Map the best route for your vacation trip. • Research the products of . . . • Infer the reason why the solution turned color.
Synthesis Compose; put material together to form a new whole	• Construct a dinosaur that could swim and eat meat. • Design a playground for our school. • Propose a campaign platform. • Design a contour map for an alien landing field.
Evaluation Judge the value of material for a given purpose	• Convince the class of the value of your product. • Persuade the group to end the story your way. • Decide which character is the most heroic. • Evaluate the benefits of immigration.

Source: Levine (1995).

Simple to Complex Content Structures

Bloom's Taxonomy gives teachers a framework for sequencing language and thinking skills, but is not explicit about the nature of the content-learning concepts that must be integrated into the unit of instruction. Mohan (1986) provides helpful suggestions regarding content integration (Table 12.2). Mohan advises previewing the content unit to get a general, overall sense of the knowledge structures within the content learning. By knowledge structures, we mean the informational structures used to convey the content information. If the content is dedicated to describing the attributes of a concept or an individual, we can say that the knowledge structure is *description.* If the topic lends itself to a recount of historical events, we may focus on *sequence.* Learning about the conflicts, decisions, or dilemmas of a situation is a *choice* structure. In most learning situations, these three structures can be based within a concrete situation or can be represented visually through pictures or graphics.

In the thematic unit that Donna Norman and her colleagues developed, she began by searching the school library and the book room for fiction stories about the Southwest. She found a copy of an illustrated book that told a poignant story of a Native American boy and a proud white horse. This text provided her with a concrete situation that would be appealing to her students and arouse their interest. The knowledge structures of the illustrated text can be viewed in terms of Mohan's framework (see Figure 12.3). Donna wanted to help her students *describe* the characters and setting of the story, specifically the little boy, the horse, and the southwestern region in which they lived. Donna helped students find this information through a series of before, during, and after activities that are part of her routine for reading-skill instruction.

Next, Donna helped the students to focus on the *sequence* of events in the story and the *choices* that the boy and the horse made as a result of those events. In this way, Donna helped her students to focus on a specific situation, understand the situation, and use their language skills to interpret meaning from that situation. From there, Donna began to focus on the more abstract content information that she wanted her students to learn: notions regarding the lifestyles of historic Native American groups; agrarian versus hunting economies; relationships between geography, food supply, and culture; and others. For this aspect of the unit, Donna used the general, theoretical knowledge structures of *concepts* and *classification, principles,* and *evaluation.*

Classification refers to how concepts and ideas are related to each other. In her unit, Donna focused on the agriculture of the regional tribes, the differences in family structure of Navajo and Apache, and their settlement and nomadic patterns, religion, and warfare. By comparing two tribes in this way, Donna's students came to understand some of the *principles* that govern all cultures. These principles include the cause-and-effect factors relating to agrarian and nomadic economies, the methods by which we study cultures, and the norms by which we evaluate their successes and failures. Finally, Donna helped her students to *evaluate* the lifestyles of the Native American tribes and determine why they made the choices they did.

Donna knew that her students would learn a great deal of language as they proceeded through this unit because she planned to choose language arts activities that reflected the structure of the content that she was teaching. She used Bloom's taxonomy to suggest activities that related to each of these knowledge structures. For example, for *description,* Donna used cue words from the knowledge and comprehension levels of Bloom. *Sequence* lent itself to the level

---

TABLE 12.2 Mohan Suggests Using These General Procedures for Organizing Information in Thematic Units

1. Preview the content to get an "overall sense" and determine specific, practical cases or examples that will illustrate the more abstract theoretical knowledge.

2. Choose a specific example that you can present as a picture story, demonstration, drama, experience, film, process, or narrative.

3. Present the general, theoretical knowledge in charts, tables, or other suitable forms such as reading passages. At times, enable students to gather and express this information themselves.

4. Use the particular case to illustrate general principles and use general principles to help the students interpret the particular case.

5. Use the knowledge structures of the particular case (description, sequence, choice) to develop corresponding thinking skills and language skills. Do the same for the knowledge structures of the general information (classification, principles, evaluation). Using graphic organizers, charts, or other visuals will help you to do this easily with ELLs.

Adapted from Mohan (1986, p. 34).

Specific, Practical Action Situation		General, Theoretical Background Knowledge	
Description	•a large white stallion	•Navajo food gathering •Apache hunting practices	**Concepts and Classification**
Sequence	•rode across the plains •hunted by horse thieves	•Navajo are agrarian •Apache are nomadic	**Principles**
Choice	•live in captivity or die	•compare Navajo and Apache lifestyles	**Evaluation**

FIGURE 12.3 A Unit on the Southwest Begins with a Concrete Situation Related to a Story and Proceeds to Include Theoretical Concepts Related to Geography, History, and Economics

of application. Analysis dealt with the *concepts* she presented and the *principles* she wanted her learners to determine for themselves. The last level of both the hierarchy and the knowledge framework is *evaluation*. This was the culmination of the unit as students evaluated their own learning as well as the cultures they had studied.

Once Donna had structured the content she wanted to teach along these general lines, she slotted activities into the unit in their proper sequence. Donna planned several activities before she began to teach, but usually selected others as she proceeded based upon the learning needs and interests of her students. It was also at this time that she differentiated each of the activities to accommodate the various language and literacy proficiencies in her classroom. For example, Donna used reciprocal reading often to help learners read for specific information in texts. She used graphic organizers to help categorize the information in preparation for writing. And she appealed to the families of a few students who had familiarity with the Southwest to share their knowledge with the class through structured student interviews and slide shows.

WHAT ABOUT STANDARDS IN A THEMATIC UNIT?

Reform movements in education in the United States have brought about a shift toward the development of rigorous standards aimed at helping all learners achieve at the highest levels. These **content standards** have provided teachers and curriculum writers with explicit information on what children at each grade level should know or be able to do. The standards are now being aligned with testing programs, curriculum frameworks, instructional materials, professional development efforts, and preservice education. They have become the foundation of much educational effort in the United States.

ELLs have not been eliminated from the standards movement. The Common Core State English Language Arts (ELA) standards are intended for all learners—both first- and second-language learners—and many teachers use these standards to guide their instruction. Common Core ELA standards are necessary but not sufficient for the many children learning English in public schools. Those learners have needs that extend beyond the scope of the Language Arts standards. As a result, Teachers of English for Speakers of Other Languages (TESOL) developed and published *ESL Standards for PreK–12 Students* (1997, p. 2). These original standards serve to:

- Articulate the English development needs of ESOL learners.
- Provide directions to educators on how to meet the needs of ESOL learners.
- Emphasize the central role of language in the attainment of other standards.

The ESL standards are organized around three main goals with three standards for each goal (TESOL, 2006, p. 9):

- Goal 1: To use English to communicate in social settings.
- Goal 2: To use English to achieve academically in all content areas.
- Goal 3: To use English in socially and culturally appropriate ways.

The standards for each goal reflect the varied uses of language. Standard 1 relates to the use of language for social or classroom interactional purposes. Standard 2 refers to the use of non-verbal communication and spoken and/or written language. Standard 3 targets the use of learning strategies to enhance language learning.

The second TESOL goal is the one that most teachers feel is in their domain of experience. Goal 2 includes the kinds of standards that teachers are familiar with, such as helping students to use language to process subject area information. Goals 1 and 3, however, are crucial to the success of Goal 2. If students are unable to use language in the social setting of the classroom, or use it in appropriate ways, learning of content will not occur. For this reason, we believe that teachers need to become aware of these standards and use them in planning for instruction.

The ESL standards can be incorporated into thematic instruction at the point where the teacher identifies the content-area standards and objectives for the unit. These standards will provide guidance in selecting appropriate language objectives for the unit. For example, when Donna Norman planned her unit on the American Southwest, she wanted students to work together in cooperative groups researching historical and cultural aspects of either the Navajo or Apache Indians. Donna realized that the language learners in the class needed help in using cooperative language forms in their small groups. She consulted Goal 2, Standard 1 for specific progress indicators that addressed the needs of her students. Donna selected the following (TESOL, 1997, p. 83):

- Use polite forms to negotiate and reach consensus.
- Negotiate cooperative roles and task assignments.
- Take turns when speaking in a group.

Once Donna had specified the behaviors she wanted her students to learn, she devised activities to help them practice these behaviors. For the first objective, Donna created a list of polite negotiating forms and listed them on a large chart that she hung in the classroom for easy reference. She modeled the forms with a small group of students, and then gave all the groups an easy task to complete while practicing the polite forms. Donna observed and recorded the results, praising those groups that used the polite forms most consistently. In later group sessions, Donna reminded her students to continue their practice and encouraged them from time to time.

For the second objective, Donna held a class discussion asking students to brainstorm ways to negotiate roles and assignments in their small groups. She posed *What if . . . ?* questions that represented some of the problems she thought might occur in her class:

- *What if one person doesn't want to accept the assignment?*
- *What if the same person always takes the same role?*
- *What if some students are not capable of handling assignments as well as others?*

The students were able to generate many solutions to these questions, and Donna collected them on a Group Work chart that hung in the classroom.

For the third objective, Donna used a cooperative learning structure called *Talking Chips* (Kagan, 1994). She asked each person in the group to place a "chip" such as a pen in a cup in the center of the table when they wanted to talk. The chip stayed in the cup and could not be used again until all students in the group had spoken. Donna felt this activity would encourage her language-learning students to speak during the group work while preventing other students from monopolizing the conversations.

In 2006, TESOL issued a second volume of standards, *PreK–12 English Language Proficiency Standards*. This second volume expands on the first by addressing the content learning needs of ELLs in four areas: language arts, mathematics, science, and social studies. These instructional arenas are further differentiated into five levels of language proficiency over twelve grade levels and into the four language skills of listening, speaking, reading, and writing.

The *PreK through 12 English Language Proficiency Standards* provide an excellent model for teachers to learn how to differentiate and scaffold for language learners in their classrooms.

For example, while studying atoms, cells, and molecules, learners at Level 1 might be asked to *identify, point to,* or *illustrate* cellular and atomic models while listening to a teacher's directions. In the same lesson, Level 4 students are asked to *reproduce, create,* or *build* cellular or atomic models based upon information gleaned from video tapes, CDs, videos, or lectures (TESOL, 2006, p. 84). All of these tasks challenge a student's listening skills.

In the speaking domain of social studies, a learner at Level 1 might be asked to *respond to questions with words or phrases* (TESOL, 2006, p. 86) while supported with illustrated historical scenes. A Level 4 student could be asked to *take a stance* or *state a position* using full sentence conditional language (TESOL, 2006, p. 86).

Because many classrooms now have ELLs at varying language proficiencies, ranging from very limited speakers to those at the transitional level, these examples illustrate how a teacher can provide for multiple learning opportunities on the same topic within the same classroom.

ORGANIZING CONTENT CURRICULUM IN A THEMATIC UNIT

Most teachers of content subjects take guidance from their state and/or district curricula and standards when planning instruction. This has become increasingly important due to federal- and state-mandated standardized testing required at certain grade levels, especially in the language arts, math, and science. We encourage teachers to attend to required content curricula and work to use it in ways that meet the needs of all learners, including ELLs. Content curricula provide another way to structure thematic learning.

Currently, the Common Core State Standards in the English Language Arts provide guidance for teachers when infusing ELA objectives into content-rich thematic units. The Common Core Curriculum Maps web site (http://commoncore.org/maps/index.php) is a useful tool for finding how to integrate ELA standards into thematic content units.

For Donna Norman's unit on the Navajo and Apache, an illustrated fiction book provided the initial introduction to the unit. This was followed by multiple nonfiction texts, which provided necessary information. Donna found the following focus standard from a fourth-grade unit to be appropriate for her class (http://commoncore.org/maps/index.php/maps/grade_4_unit_5/):

- Compare and contrast the treatment of similar themes and topics (e.g., opposition of good and evil) and patterns of events (e.g., the quest) in stories, myths, and traditional literature from different cultures.

Donna modified this standard to create ELA objectives for her class, confident that she was instructing her students to a nationally accepted standard.

Many teachers like to begin the planning phase of their lessons with a brainstorming process. Some teachers prefer to brainstorm ideas using a semantic web; it helps them to expand their thinking visually and in several directions. Brainstorming ideas come from the content curriculum, the language arts curriculum, literature resources, personal interests of the teacher, ideas from colleagues and, most importantly, ideas from the students themselves (see Figure 12.4).

Student brainstorming is an important part of the planning phase of a thematic instructional unit. Teachers who use thematic instruction believe that student choice empowers and involves students from the beginning of the unit. It is a powerful motivating force for learning. We ask students to give us ideas about what they think is important or interesting to learn about a particular topic. This web then becomes a road map that we and the students can follow for the rest of the unit. We like to use semantic webs on large pieces of chart paper when brainstorming ideas for a unit. We use various colored markers to identify the categories of ideas and then keep the charts posted as the unit progresses so that students can see which areas we have worked on and others that will come later.

Figure 12.5 shows an example of a brainstorming web that middle school students created for a unit on circulation. The teacher has written down all of the students' ideas and then chosen one of these categories to expand into a K-W-L chart (see Table 12.3). In the chart activity, students have the opportunity to rephrase their ideas as questions that ask more specifically what they want to know.

From the list of topics and questions generated by the teacher and students, it is then possible to start thinking about the content and language objectives for each phase of the unit. We have often used checklists of goals and objectives to ensure that we are focusing on all important areas and adhering to the content standards. In addition, writing objectives into our

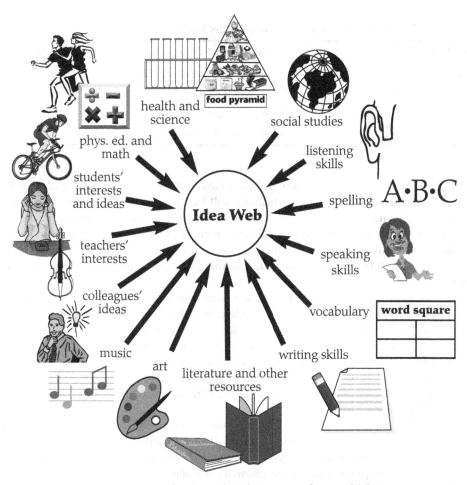

FIGURE 12.4 The Components of a Thematic Unit Can Come from Multiple Sources

daily plans helps us to be more explicit about what we want students to know and be able to do during that lesson, and how we will differentiate the content, language, process, and assessment to meet our learners' needs. This explicitness enables us to communicate that information to our students as well. Objectives that are explicitly embedded into thematic activities communicate to parents, colleagues, and administrators that our instructional units are based upon a set

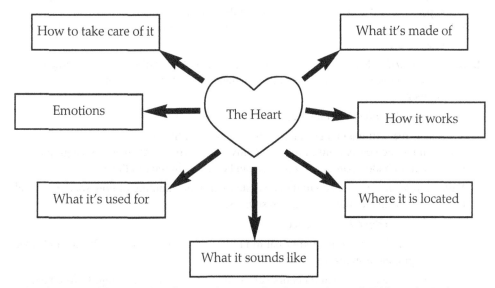

FIGURE 12.5 Middle School Students Brainstormed to Create a Semantic Web on the Topic of Circulation

TABLE 12.3 K-W-L Chart on the Functions of the Heart

What I *Know*	What I *Want to Know*	What I *Learned*
The heart has muscles and blood.	What are the parts of the heart?	
The heart pumps blood.	How does the heart pump blood?	
The heart keeps us alive.	Why does it stop pumping?	
	Where does the blood go?	

of standards that the school community has agreed upon. Objectives are meaningless, however, unless we can specify what successful learning will look like. How will students demonstrate that they have learned the big ideas of the content unit? How will they demonstrate ability to understand and communicate using the academic language of the topic? What kinds of products will they produce to demonstrate competency and success? Even at this "big picture" stage of planning, it is helpful to know what student learning will look like and to specify those products and tasks.

Learning activities necessary to produce successful products and teach essential skills should be determined next. As mentioned earlier, the Bloom cue words suggest a variety of activities that can be adapted to the needs of the learners. If we want ELLs to *report,* for example (comprehension level), we need to think about whether students need to become capable in oral or written reporting or both. We also need to determine ways to scaffold the reporting through student groupings, key sentence frames, and graphic organizers that assist organization of information. Finally, we need to provide an appropriate audience for the report and determine how we will assess it.

Donna Norman's unit on the American Southwest incorporated content objectives based upon the social studies standards from her state. The standards provided guidelines for her content, but Donna needed to create objectives for her class that were more specific. She included research objectives in preparation for the research paper the students would write the following year. She emphasized oral and written language objectives because of the ELLs in the class. Finally, she added objectives that stretched the thinking skills of the students and helped them to develop learning strategies. A sampling of Donna's content objectives includes:

1. *State Standard:* Students will demonstrate their understanding of major themes, ideas, and turning points in the history of the Southwest.

   Donna's Objectives included:

   - Read or listen to selected books and modified texts about the Navajo or Apache culture. Use highlighting with teacher support for finding specific information on the geography and peoples of the southwestern region in the 1800s.
   - List information about one tribe to include in an illustrated report supported by a note-taking chart.

2. *State Standard:* Students will demonstrate their understanding of the geography of the interdependent world of the Southwest—including the distribution of people, places, and environments.

   Donna's Objectives included:

   - Locate tribe settlement areas on a map of the United States.
   - Determine the yearly rainfall for the southwestern settlement areas from a graphic.
   - Research in buddy pairs the crops that can be grown in the Southwest.

3. *State Standard:* Students will demonstrate their understanding of how societies develop economic systems to allocate scarce resources.

   Donna's Objectives included:

   - Compare and contrast the traditional food gathering practices of the Navajo and Apache using a graphic organizer.

Assessment of a thematic unit occurs before, during, and after learning. Before beginning the unit, activating activities give teachers information on students' prior learning or misconceptions and learning gaps. While presenting and working on the unit, teachers observe and

TABLE 12.4 Unit Design for Thematic Instruction

Steps for Constructing Thematic Unit	Planning Guidelines
Step 1: Identify and Prioritize the Content Objectives.	1. Select grade-appropriate content standards to underlie the unit.
	2. Determine the key ideas, operating principles, major concepts, or themes that are essential to the unit.
	3. List the specific language skills, forms, and functions that students need to learn and communicate this content successfully.
	4. Choose a selection of learning strategies that students need to be successful with this content.
	5. Prioritize the knowledge and skills in the unit to ensure that all students will learn the most important elements.
Step 2: Determine What Student Success Will Look Like (Progress Indicators).	1. Describe (perhaps using a rubric) the skills and behaviors that students will demonstrate to show that they have been successful.
	2. Describe the products (perhaps using a rubric) that students will create to demonstrate mastery of the learning.
Step 3: Create Scaffolded Learning Activities and Locate a Variety of Materials and Resources at Differing Proficiency Levels.	1. Create a variety of differentiated activities for each learning objective.
	2. Collaborate with colleagues to locate materials and resources to facilitate student understanding at varying language proficiency levels.
	3. Determine which activities will best meet the needs of which learners.
Step 4: Assess Student Learning.	1. Before beginning the unit, activate student learning and determine what students already know about the topic.
	2. For each activity, observe, and record student strengths as well as areas where they need more instructional support. Select follow-up activities to meet needs and fill gaps revealed by assessment.
	3. Create a culminating activity that will provide an overall assessment of the important objectives of the entire unit.

record students' performance for each objective. The final assessment is usually a part of the final culminating activity of the unit. This approach provides the teacher with an assessment that informs teaching at each phase of the unit. A framework for constructing a thematic unit is suggested in Table 12.4.

ORGANIZING LANGUAGE CURRICULUM IN A THEMATIC UNIT

Each content subject is communicated in language that differs in its grammar and vocabulary, thus making different demands on the language learner. In addition to grammar and vocabulary, ELLs must master the core knowledge of facts and ideas (**declarative knowledge**) as well as the skills and operations related to the subject (**procedural knowledge**). In general, students must be able to have a basic ability to read about the content, construct meaning, understand and participate in classroom discussions, make inferences, cite examples of major constructs, and determine cause and effect relationships (August & Hakuta, 1998). These generalized similarities are critical for all content subjects.

There are major differences in the language skills needed for individual content subjects, however. This is probably most obvious for subjects such as math that have specific notational systems. But the language of science and social studies differs in more than vocabulary. The verb tenses, sentence structures, and grammatical forms of these subjects are distinct. The language of science is the language of description and process. Social studies texts use specific past tense forms (uncommon in oral language) and complex, embedded sentence structures.

Because of the language demands of each of the content subjects, it is important to provide instruction for learners that will help their language skills grow and develop. The human costs of not addressing the needs of ELLs are devastating. Although graduation rates for high school students have improved over the past decade (reaching 71.7% in 2008), Latino, African American, and Native American students still lag behind with graduations rates of 58 percent,

57 percent, and 54 percent respectively (Swanson, 2011). The reading gaps between Hispanic and non-Hispanic students in 2009 were 25 points in grade 4 and 24 points in grade 8. These scores equate to a two-year differential between student groups (Sparks, June 23, 2011). It is time to acknowledge that language is essential to the teaching and learning of every content subject and that every teacher is a language teacher.

We have already discussed how language skills and knowledge can be integrated into the content curriculum in a way that permits ELLs to understand and communicate about the content while also expanding the range of language and vocabulary at their command. Scaffolding is one way that teachers can accomplish this goal. The sequencing of the language is also critical to student learning. Just as content learning is sequenced from the specific to the general, the practical to the theoretical, language skills need to be sequenced from practical to theoretical discourse. This sequencing principle happens naturally as we plan language-learning activities that increase the distance from the speaker to the hearer (Mohan, 1986). For example, the language used for Show and Tell and informal conversations occurs in a "here and now" context with limited distance from the speaker to the hearer. Gestures and situational context add meaning to the language. Giving a report or narrating a story requires greater distance from the speaker to the hearer and tends toward a more abstract use of language. Writing an essay or a research report requires even greater generalization, abstract language, and distance from speaker to hearer. As the distance increases, language must be more precise as there is limited context to support meaning. Ideally, each phase of the thematic unit will lead ELLs into greater abstraction and require more specific academic language use.

HOW CAN LEARNING STRATEGIES BE INCORPORATED INTO THEMATIC INSTRUCTION?

Learning strategies are an important part of thematic unit preparation for all of our students. For ELLs, they are particularly important. ELLs need to use these strategies to help them compensate for their limited language proficiencies. Learning strategies (mentioned in Chapter 10) include generic strategies such as:

- organizing main ideas
- planning how to complete a learning task
- listening to information selectively
- self-checking aural and reading comprehension,
- planning when, where, what, and how to study
- using reference materials
- taking notes
- summarizing
- relating new learning to prior learning
- predicting and inferring meanings
- asking questions of teachers and peers
- working with others in a group

First, learning strategies are most effectively taught within an integrated framework of content and language learning rather than as separate or incidental learning experiences. Effective teachers create objectives for including explicit instruction of certain strategies into their thematic units. Since most students can profit from this kind of explicit skill instruction, all learners in the class will benefit.

Second, learning strategies must be taught explicitly to ELLs using the modified teaching tools that are successful with them. Teachers model, demonstrate, develop needed language, and provide structured practice and independent practice. They teach the strategies needed for understanding, remembering, and applying content learning. This means that teachers identify essential skills for the learning task, create an objective, name the skill, model its use, and provide abundant practice of the skill in a variety of situations. At a later date, when introducing tasks in which the skill could be used again, students can be asked to review their lists of learned strategies (these are in student notebooks or on large charts on the wall) and decide which skills are most useful in completing the task successfully.

Third, ELLs should be asked to reflect upon their learning and self-assess what they have learned, how well they have learned, and what strategies were most useful in helping them learn. Even very young students can engage in simplified forms of self-assessment. The internal reflection helps to cement the use of the skill and ensure that it will be carried over into similar learning experiences without explicit reference from the teacher. The kinds of questions that can be used for self-assessment include the following:

- *What have I learned today (this week, in this unit)?*
- *How can I use this learning in the future? How are this knowledge and these skills important in the world outside of school?*
- *In what areas am I making progress?*
- *What do I need to improve?*
- *What is my goal for tomorrow (next week, the next unit)?*
- *What did I enjoy the most today (this week, in this unit)?*

ELLs need to learn strategies that help them become better learners, such as:

- organizing main ideas
- planning how to complete a learning task
- listening to information selectively
- checking their own comprehension
- planning when, where, and what to study

Learners also need to know how to:

- use reference materials
- take notes
- summarize
- relate new learning to prior learning
- predict and infer meanings

During class, they need to be able to:

- ask questions of the teacher and their peers
- work with others in a group

We cannot assume ELLs have learned these essential strategies from prior educational experiences. If we want learners to use learning strategies to achieve, we have to plan for their use.

Rona Wilson begins each year with her seventh-grade students by concentrating on social learning strategies of questioning, encouraging, participating, and cooperating. She plans lessons in which she defines the social skill, models the skill, and then sets up situations that require her students to practice each of the skills. Rona supports the ELLs in her class by writing the language necessary to the skill on large charts that she hangs on the wall.

- For stating a personal opinion, she writes sentence frames on the board and encourages learners to practice specific comments: *In my opinion ..., It seems to me ..., Let's consider ..., My idea is ...*
- For disagreeing agreeably, sentence frames might include: *That may be true but consider ..., I have a different idea ..., I see the problem differently ...*

After a while, students no longer need the wall charts as they incorporate the language into their growing language systems.

There is probably nothing that we do in the classroom that is as important as challenging our students cognitively and teaching them to learn effectively and to think clearly. These are the skills that will enable all of our students to compete successfully in school and in the world. ELLs must be included in this essential skill learning as early as possible in their educational development.

A LAST WORD

Teaching thematically at first glance appears to be a challenging endeavor. It is at second glance as well. The level of teaching skills required to teach in this way are weighty, and we do not learn them in our first year of teaching. It is important, however, to begin to learn them early on.

The way that we learned was by reading, talking to colleagues, implementing and evaluating units, asking questions when we did not know the answers, and sharing the successes and challenges that came about as we experimented with our students.

Our first attempt at thematic teaching resulted in a file folder of notes, materials, graphic organizers, and student products. That unit was pulled out the next year and adapted to the new crop of students in the classroom. As years went by, we were able to share our materials with colleagues and expand our repertoire of units—improving them constantly. In this way, we implemented what we believe is a very valuable teaching practice with a minimum of repeated effort on our part.

We know that many teachers work in a school environment filled with expectations, and that adding this challenge to others may appear daunting. But imbedding the standards and goals that are expected into meaningful, purposeful, and interesting learning experiences will pay off powerfully for our students.

RTI TIER 1 SAMPLER

- Interview students to determine their interests, their activities outside school, their reading habits, and their television habits. Use this information to determine the basis of the thematic units you will teach during the school year. Be prepared to learn about the cultures of the ELL students in the class in order to include aspects of these in your units.
- Introduce the "big picture" of a thematic unit through a visual modality if possible. For example, use movie clips and computer videos or an informational television program to show an overview of the upcoming theme.
- Collect a variety of books on a wide range of literacy levels related to the unit. Be sure to include picture books and illustrated children's books along with nonfiction text with pictures. Allow students time to peruse the collection of books to further acquaint themselves with the overall ideas in the thematic unit. At this time, students may begin to ask questions about the material. Write these questions down for the entire class to see and hear.
- Explain the thematic unit orally and in writing. Indicate the culminating activity and how long the unit will take for the class to complete. Tell why learning the content information in the unit is important, and provide examples from your life and your students' lives to help them make connections with the content. For example, if the class will study a theme called *Cycles* incorporating life and weather cycles, help students relate to weather cycles in their community and life cycles within their own families.
- Begin the unit with an activity that will involve all learners in the class in a personal way. If students will be learning an historical topic, assign an identity to each student (*Abraham Lincoln, Ulysses S. Grant, Yankee soldier, Rebel soldier*, etc.) that they can assume throughout the unit. As time goes on, each student will learn more about his or her own identity and interact with others in the class as the historical figures might have done.
- Describe each day's content and language objectives. Provide an outline of the lesson or an outline of the content learning for the day. Use these outlines to help students summarize their learning.
- Avoid lecture as an input methodology. Use peer-assisted reading, computer-aided instruction, tape-recorded text reading, small-group or partner research, videos, newspapers and magazines, and multiple texts.
- Use a variety of grouping patterns throughout the lesson. Give students opportunities to work with small groups and partners on limited assignments.
- Use a semantic map to show the connections between the concepts and ideas that are explored throughout the unit. Provide students with copies of these maps. Add to the maps incrementally as the unit progresses.
- When assessing objectives throughout the unit, use a variety of assessment instruments. Provide opportunities for scaffolding of assessment for ELLs and others who have difficulty with the reading and writing requirements of the unit. Assess content separately from language.

RTI TIER 2 SAMPLER

- Throughout the unit, provide opportunity for small-group or individualized instruction with a culturally and linguistically knowledgeable professional. Use these teaching opportunities to preview the unit prior to introduction to the class, for incremental skills lessons, opportunities for language interaction, reteaching, and retesting.

- Set specific objectives for individualized instruction. Use class content and language objectives, and teach them in incremental steps while checking comprehension and skill usage throughout instruction.

- Select text and input materials from those available to the class. Modify materials to match language proficiency and interest levels of the learners. Scaffold materials with tape-recorded readings or computer assistance if necessary. Teach learning strategies related to textbook usage along with information about content.

- Make connections between content learning and the culture and language of ELLs in Tier 2 interventions. Teach vocabulary cognates, for example. Relate U.S. social studies to the world arena. Collect input from students and their families related to the theme of the unit.

- Use clear input strategies: Give directions in a step-by-step manner, with clear reference to the written version. Ask for student understanding of directions before proceeding. Provide models of all products and demonstrate all processes. When using texts, read aloud from important sections and ask students to highlight those sections or rewrite the ideas on a sticky note. Use all section headers in the text to create questions that identify the important elements of the reading. Use Teach the Text Backward strategies with the text. Preview major ideas of the unit with visuals, videos, or computer-assisted instruction.

- Embed academic language into all small-group instruction. Provide key sentence frames for language support. Create multiple opportunities for students to report, recall, summarize, and question. Pair students and assign them tasks that require the exchange of academic information. Teach the appropriate language needed for that task. Teach and reteach required and academic vocabulary frequently. Use student self-assessment of vocabulary. Use sort tasks, graphic organizers, and other visuals to provide more exposure to vocabulary terms.

- Provide opportunities for hands-on projects related to the theme. Integrate language skill learning into these projects by requiring students to use language forms and functions related to the tasks. For example, if two students are constructing a poster, teach them to report on the poster. Scaffold the reporting with a cloze report, note cards containing key sentence frames, and opportunities to practice prior to the actual reporting event.

- Continue checking for comprehension throughout instruction. Create many opportunities for students to provide correct answers. If students answer incorrectly, use pinpoint questioning to help them arrive at the correct answer. If students provide a correct answer, continue to question them further to extend that information to other aspects of the lesson. For example, if you ask a student *What are the three branches of government?*, follow up that correct answer with an open-ended question that allows the student to talk at length about what he or she knows, for example: *What can you tell me about the three branches of government?*

- Scaffold assessment instruments for students with low-language proficiency so that you will be able to determine what they know about the content of the unit.

- Collect data on multiple assessment instruments frequently during the Tier 2 intervention. Review the data with the school-based team to more closely align instruction to student need.

Questions for Reflection

1. Thematic units generally flow from concrete experience to visual representation, and finally, to abstract learning. Consider the reasons given for this progression in the chapter.
   - Do you agree that this progression is helpful for long-term student learning?
   - Do you find this progression to be prevalent in most classrooms that you have observed or been a part of? Why or why not?
   - Give examples of recent lessons you have seen or taught where this progression was utilized.

2. Thematic instruction in the elementary and middle school grades is similar to interdisciplinary instruction in high schools. In what ways are they the same and different? Are the benefits equal at both stages of learning?

3. This chapter suggests a variety of different organizational structures that can be used to coordinate a thematic unit. What about state and content standards? Are they useful tools for organizing content thematically? Why or why not?

Activities for Further Learning

1. Visit the Techtrekers web site (http://www.techtrekers.com/ Thematic.htm) and locate their "10 Key Reasons" for using thematic units. Working with a partner, prioritize these reasons from the most relevant for your situation to the least relevant. Next, identify reasons that are not included on the list and add them in order of priority. Write an explanation for the top three reasons on your list.

   • Why did you choose these three?
   • Why are they important?
   • Would these reasons compel your colleagues to begin to write their own thematic units?

2. Observe several lessons in classrooms with English language learners. Were there elements of these lessons that were concrete, visual, and abstract? What were the language requirements of learners for each of these lesson phases?

   • What did students have to listen to, say, read, or write during the concrete experience phase of the lesson?
   • What did students listen to, say, read, or write during the visual representation phase of the lesson?
   • What did students listen to, say, read, or write during the abstract learning phase of the lesson?
   • Did the language increase in grammatical complexity? Semantic complexity? Give examples.
   • Did the level of vocabulary become more specific? Give examples.

3. Review the two models described for the structure of a thematic unit: Bloom's taxonomy and Mohan's knowledge framework. Compare and contrast the two models for the following:

   • progression from concrete to visual to abstract
   • progression of language from contextualized to decontextualized
   • progression of thinking skills from simple to complex

   Which model appeals to you? Why? What problems do you anticipate in using either of these models?

4. Choose a thematic unit from among those available on the Internet or from the Common Core Curriculum Maps (http://commoncore.org/maps/index.php). Categorize the objectives, activities, and language usage in the unit according to Bloom's and Mohan's models. In what ways could you improve or modify the unit?

5. Using the same thematic unit, indicate additional methods for scaffolding the learning for ELLs at a lower level of language proficiency.

6. Create a graphic organizer that structures language and content topics for a thematic unit based on language arts and social studies. Identify the grade level.

7. Create a graphic organizer that structures language and content topics for a thematic unit based on integrated math and science objectives. Identify the grade level.

8. Review the learning strategies listed in this chapter.

   • Which of these strategies do you habitually use when attending this class?
   • Which strategies do you use when working with colleagues?
   • Which strategies are most useful for students at the grade level you teach?
   • Which strategies have you taught? Which ones have you never taught?

9. Create a thematic unit. Choose one grade level and a general theme or organizing principle that will integrate content from social studies, science, math, and language arts. Use national, state, or district standards as a guide. Be sure to include scaffolding for language learners and lessons targeted to their various language needs. Determine how you will assess your students.

Suggested Reading

Enright, D. S., & McCloskey, M. L. (1988). *Integrating English: Developing English language and literacy in the multicultural classroom.* Reading, MA: Addison-Wesley. This book has an extensive chapter on the development of thematic units. There are also two units provided in the back of the book in specific detail and at different grade levels.

Freeman, Y. S., & Freeman, D. E. (1998). *ESL/EFL teaching: Principles for success.* Portsmouth, NH: Heinemann. The Freemans relate the theory behind thematic teaching and learning, describe whole-to-part teaching, learner-centered education, and meaningful, purposeful, and social literacy learning. Includes a section on thematic unit organization and offers lesson plans to show how thematic planning is accomplished.

Freeman, Y. S., Freeman, D. E., & Mercuri, S. (2002). *Closing the achievement gap: How to reach limited-formal-schooling and long-term English learners.* Portsmouth, NH: Heinemann. This more recent book contains an entire chapter dedicated to thematic units.

Morales-Jones, C. A. (2002). Curriculum design and day-to-day ESOL instruction. In H. Zainuddin, N. Yahya, C. A. Morales-Jones, & E. N. Ariza, *Fundamentals of teaching English to speakers of other languages in K–12 mainstream classrooms* (pp. 136–170). Dubuque, IA: Kendall-Hunt. Chapter 13 provides a thorough discussion of interdisciplinary content-based thematic instruction and illustrates a variety of ways to develop these units.

Richard-Amato, P. (2009). *Making it happen: Interaction in the second language classroom from theory to practice* (4th ed.). New York: Longman. There is a short discussion of theme cycles and a more extensive section on thematic curriculum. Four large webs are provided that show how content is related in thematic curricula in Kindergarten through third grade.

References

Agor, B. (2000). Understanding our past: The middle ages. In S. Irujo (Ed.), *Integrating the ESL standards into classroom practice: Grades 6–8* (pp. 1–27). Alexandria, VA: TESOL.

August, D., & Hakuta, K. (Eds.). (1998). *Educating language-minority children.* Washington, DC: National Academy Press.

Bloom, B., Englehart, M., Furst, E., Hill, W., & Krathwohl, D. (Eds.). (1956). *Taxonomy of educational objectives: The classification of educational goals. Handbook I: Cognitive domain.* New York: David McKay.

Common Core Curriculum Maps: English Language Arts. http://commoncore.org/maps/index.php.

Common Core State Standards: English Language Arts Standards. (2010). http://www.corestandards.org/the-standards/english-language-arts-standards.

Dewey, J. (1916). *Democracy and education.* New York: Macmillan.

Enright, D. S., & McCloskey, M. L. (1988). *Integrating English: Developing English language and literacy in the multilingual classroom.* Reading, MA: Addison-Wesley.

Gianelli, M. (1991). Thematic units: Creating an environment for learning. *TESOL Journal, 1*(1), 13–15.

Jenkins, E. (1998). *Teaching with the brain in mind.* Alexandria, VA: Association of Supervision and Curriculum Development.

Kagan, S. (1994). *Cooperative learning.* San Clemente, CA: Kagan Cooperative Learning.

Levine, L. N. (1995). Outline of topics and skills covered in teaching ESL K–12. In *English as a second language teacher resource handbook: A practical guide for K–12 ESL programs* (2nd printing) (pp. 61–83). Thousand Oaks, CA: Corwin Press.

Mohan, B. (1986). *Language and content.* Reading, MA: Addison-Wesley.

Peregoy, S., & Boyle, O. (2008). *Reading, writing, and learning in ESL: A resource book for K–12 teachers* (5th ed.). New York: Longman.

Richard-Amato, P. (2009). *Making it happen: Interaction in the second language classroom from theory to practice* (4th ed.). New York: Longman.

Ritter, N. (1999). *Teaching interdisciplinary thematic units in language arts.* Bloomington, IN: ERIC Clearinghouse on Reading English and Communication. (ERIC Identifier No. ED436003).

Sparks, S. (2011, June 23). *Study finds gaps remain large for Hispanic students.* http://www.edweek.org/ew/articles/2011/06/23/36hispanic.h30.html?tkn=LQXFupllPvXDBxWxw9CSBjL8ahV9z1NnDDZN&cmp=clp-sb-ascd.

Swanson, C. B. (2011, June 9). Nation turns a corner. *Education Week.*

Sylvester, R. (1995). *A celebration of neurons: An educator's guide to the human brain.* Alexandria, VA: Association for Supervision and Curriculum Development.

Teachers of English to Speakers of Other Languages, Inc. (1997). *ESL standards for pre-K–12 students.* Alexandria, VA: Author.

Teachers of English to Speakers of Other Languages, Inc. (2006). *PreK–12 English language proficiency standards.* Alexandria, VA: Author.

Willis, J. (2006). *Research-based strategies to ignite student learning.* Alexandria, VA: Association for Supervision and Curriculum Development.

Wolfe, P. (2001). *Brain matters: Translating research into classroom practice.* Alexandria, VA: Association for Supervision and Curriculum Development.

MyEducationLab™

Go to the Topic, Content Area Learning, in the MyEducationLab (www.myeducationlab.com) for your course, where you can:

- Find learning outcomes for Content Area Learning along with the national standards that connect to these outcomes.
- Complete Assignments and Activities that can help you more deeply understand the chapter content.
- Apply and practice your understanding of the core teaching skills identified in the chapter with the Building Teaching Skills and Dispositions learning units.
- Examine challenging situations and cases presented in the IRIS Center Resources.
- Check your comprehension on the content covered in the chapter by going to the Study Plan in the Book Resources for your text. Here you will be able to take a chapter quiz, receive feedback on your answers, and then access Review, Practice, and Enrichment activities to enhance your understanding of chapter content.
- **A+RISE** A+RISE® Standards2Strategy™ is an innovative and interactive online resource that offers new teachers in grades K-12 just in time, research-based instructional strategies that meet the linguistic needs of ELLs as they learn content, differentiate instruction for all grades and abilities, and are aligned to Common Core Language Arts standards (for the literacy strategies) and to English language proficiency standards in WIDA, Texas, California, and Florida."

GLOSSARY

3-2-1 summary: A summarizing structure in which students list three important elements, then two important elements, then the one most critical piece of information in response to the teacher's questions. The cognitive challenge increases as students complete the tasks. The report of three elements is a recall task. Two elements is generally at the comprehension level. The final element is at the analysis level of Bloom's Taxonomy.

ABC summary: A summarizing technique for content learning. Students are required to summarize all that they have learned by structuring information alphabetically. Thus, in a lesson on reptiles and mammals, students might begin "Alligators are reptiles. Bears are mammals . . ." and so on.

Academic Word List (AWL): Compiled by Averil Coxhead, this is a list of 570 word families used commonly across a variety of academic areas. The first 2000 most frequent words are excluded from the list.

Academic words: Words used commonly in academic oral and written language that are not generally developed from informal conversation—they are usually learned in school and are required in general academic usage or refer to technical terms from the sciences, social studies, and so on.

Acculturation: The process by which an individual adds the characteristics, values, and beliefs of a new culture while still retaining the characteristics, values, and beliefs of a native or home culture; the ability to be bicultural, to take part in and understand the dominant culture without giving up the traditions and values of the home culture.

Acquisition: Developing ability in a language by using it in natural communicative situations.

Activator: Any endeavor that helps bring to mind students' current or prior knowledge.

Active engagement: A principle of language teaching and learning in which learners play enjoyable, engaging, and active roles in the learning experience.

Activity-based communicative teaching and learning (The ABC Model): The research-based model of teaching upon which this book is based, including nine principles of teaching and learning.

Activity-based teaching and learning: One of the two dimensions of the ABC Model, which focuses on what learners bring with them to the classroom and the active role they play in the language acquisition process.

Affective filter: A cognitive screen that is raised or lowered depending on the motivation and self-esteem of the learner. A low filter allows the learner to interact easily with native speakers and receive increasingly larger amounts of comprehensible input.

Alphabetic language system: A language system in which one symbol generally represents one sound, for example, Latin, Vietnamese, English, most European languages, and many African languages.

Analytical learner: This type of learner prefers individual work and sequential learning.

Anticipation guide: A pre–post reading activity in which a reader responds to the content of a reading before reading, then compares the answers with the text after reading.

Assimilation: To trade one culture for another, usually exchanging a native or home culture for the dominant culture.

BICS (Basic Interpersonal Communication Skills): Language that occurs within a context-embedded social environment.

Bilingual education: A program model in which two languages are used within a classroom for the purpose of instruction by both the teacher and the students. Bilingual education takes many forms in the United States, including transitional, developmental, or two-way bilingual education.

Bio poem: A writing support structure that provides partially completed sentences in a poem format. Students insert their individual characteristics in the blank slots of the poem.

Bottom-up approaches: Approaches to reading in which the focus is placed on developing the building blocks of reading in sequence, which may include the ability to hear sounds, decoding skills, vocabulary and word study skills, fluency, and comprehension.

CALLA (Cognitive Academic Language Learning Approach): An instructional approach that integrates academic language development with content-area instruction and learning strategies.

CALP (Cognitive Academic Language Proficiency): The coded, reduced language of a textbook or a test.

Carousel brainstorming: An activator requiring small groups of students to respond in writing to prompts written on large sheets of poster paper that are taped on the walls of the room.

Choral reading: A reading strategy in which students each have their own copies of a text and all read together. Often the teacher or a student stands in front of the class to lead the oral reading.

Clarity: Teacher language has clarity when it is easy to hear, comprehensible, and specific; avoids idiomatic expressions, jargon, and slang; and utilizes repetition, gestures, and word stress.

Clock buddies: An activity in which learners write the names of partners next to each number on a clock face; the partners provide pre-assigned pairs for various pairwork tasks in later activities.

Cloze: A reading task in which every fifth word (or so) is deleted. The structure of the text remains intact while teachers eliminate random words, target vocabulary, or nonessential vocabulary. Cloze can be used as a frame for writing or as an assessment of content learning.

Cognitively demanding: Cognitively demanding communication tasks require cognitive involvement on the part of the ELL for acquiring meaning.

Cognitively undemanding: Cognitively undemanding communication tasks are automatized or mastered by the learner and require little mental challenge for meaning to be communicated.

Collaborative dialogue: This teacher-led strategy promotes learning of academic language through oral conversations with students. The teacher scaffolds production of the academic language with questioning, wait time, modeling of vocabulary and language structures, negotiation of meaning, and opportunities to summarize learning.

Collocation: The frequent use of certain words together and/or in a certain order.

Communicative competence: The ability to use language to achieve a communicative purpose.

Communicative teaching and learning: One of the two dimensions of the ABC Model, which focuses on the importance of authentic, comprehensible communication in the learning of language.

Comprehensible input: Language directed to the learner that is understood by the learner.

Conga line: An activity in which pairs stand in two parallel lines facing their partners. One of the lines rotates at short intervals to provide different partners for vocabulary study.

Content standards: Statements that clearly state what students should know or be -able to do in any specific content area. They include the knowledge, skills, and understanding that schools need to teach students in order for those students to reach a predetermined level of competency.

Content-based ESL: The goal of this program is achievement in both content and language. Instruction is led by a qualified ESL teacher. In some cases, a qualified ESL teacher co-teaches with a qualified content teacher.

Context-embedded: Context-embedded communication tasks or activities are made more comprehensible for ELLs because they include background information, pictures, graphic information, or other context surrounding the communication act.

Context-reduced: Context-reduced language is decontextualized and abstract, with few if any context clues to support spoken or written words to help make the language comprehensible.

Cooperative learning: A specific kind of group work in which learners collaborate for the purpose of content learning, language learning, and social-skills building.

Corners: An activator (or summarizer) in which students choose one of four corners designated by different choices relating to an opinion, a decision, or a preference. Students move to their chosen corner and talk to other students there about why they have made their choice.

Corpus: A large collection of written or transcribed oral language used for linguistic analysis.

Cultural dissonance: An uncomfortable sense of discord, confusion, conflict, and anxiety that occurs when deeply held values come into conflict with other, differing values; unwelcome changes in cultural dynamics that are unexpected and not understandable.

Cultural mediator: Translator of culture; guide to the patterns and norms of behavior within a culture.

Cultural relevance: One of the principles of the ABC Model, in which classrooms respect and incorporate the cultures of learners in the classroom while helping them to understand the new culture of the community, the school, and the classroom.

Culturally responsive instruction: A pattern of instruction that recognizes and utilizes students' language and culture, acknowledges students' differences and commonalities; instruction based on student experiences and strengths; instruction designed to promote equity and sociocultural consciousness.

Culture: The values, traditions, social and political relationships, and world view shared by a group of people bound together by a combination of factors that can include a common history, geographic location, language, social class, and/or religion.

Curriculum-based measurements (CBMs): Used for progress monitoring in many states, CBMs can be either standardized or criterion referenced. CBMs employ standardized methodology, focus on long-term instructional goals, and are evidence based.

Declarative knowledge: The facts and ideas that make up the knowledge load of a content unit.

Developmental bilingual: The goal of this organizational model is to develop some proficiency in the native language and full proficiency in English. Instruction is begun in the native language in elementary school. English instruction is gradually increased as a part of the school day until students are fully mainstreamed in English-only classrooms.

Differentiated instruction: Teachers vary their instructional practices, both processes and procedures, to accommodate the needs of varied learners.

Differentiation: In this principle of the ABC Model, learning activities accommodate different language, literacy, and cognitive levels and incorporate many dimensions of learning: different learning styles, intelligences, and preferences.

Dipsticking: A form of checking for understanding in which all students are checked, frequently, on the same topic throughout the lesson.

Discourse: Verbal expression in speech or writing.

Display questions: Questions asked even though the answer is well known to the questioner, typical of "school" questions.

Draw a picture/diagram: A lesson summarizer that requires students to present their learning in a picture or diagram format.

Dual language: A program model of bilingual education that uses two or more languages in content areas.

Early exit transition: A program model using the native language in early elementary school and swiftly transitioning to English-only instruction.

Early fluency: The third of four literacy levels. Learners begin to use multiple clues to make meaning from text and are able to understand the main ideas of texts as well as their emotional impact.

Early literacy: The second of four literacy levels. Learners at this level understand that books have messages that do not change and that there are certain conventions regarding how print is presented.

Emergent literacy: The first of four literacy levels. Learners at this level understand that print can carry meaningful messages, but are still learning to encode, decode, and understand these messages.

English as a second language (ESL): A field of study dedicated to teaching English as an additional language; often taught in an English language setting.

English language development (ELD): Courses or classes dedicated to teaching English as an additional language.

English language learners (ELL): Students at the beginning to advanced level of acquiring English who are identified as needing special instruction in English.

English language proficiency test: A test specifically designed to assess language development of ELLs, often used to assess learners' and schools' progress toward meeting standards.

English to speakers of other languages (ESOL): A course in which the content is the study of English for speakers of other languages. This acronym is sometimes used in place of English as a Second Language (ESL) or English as a Foreign Language (EFL).

ESL pull-out: A type of program model in which ELLs are taken out of their classrooms for specialized English language instruction. This model is most often used at the elementary level or in districts where there is a low incidence of ELLs.

ESL push-in: A type of program model in which a second-language specialist (ESL or ELD teacher) comes into classrooms to team-teach or turn-teach with the mainstream classroom teacher for the benefit of the ELLs in the classroom.

Explanatory devices: Any teaching aids that support student comprehension of the content learning.

Feature analysis: A strategy in which learners use a matrix to explore how terms and concepts are related to one another and to make distinctions between them.

Field independent: A learning style in which learners perceive discrete items as separate from the organized field.

Field sensitive: A learning style in which learners tend to perceive the organization of the field as a whole rather than its parts.

Fluency: At this fourth literacy level, learners are becoming mature readers. They make sense of longer and more complex texts approaching or at the level of their native-speaking peers; they use a variety of strategies flexibly to accomplish their reading purposes.

Form: The internal grammatical structure of words, the grammatical structure.

Formative assessment: Classroom-based assessment consisting of the multiple and various ways that teachers gather information about their students' learning throughout the instructional process.

Fossilization: Grammatical errors that persist and remain impervious to change.

Function: The purpose for which language is used, for example, to report information or to request permission.

General Service List: A list of about 2000 words, compiled by West (1953) that includes the most frequent and serviceable words in English.

Global learner: A learner who has a preference for learning that focuses on the whole rather than the parts.

Graphic organizers: Pictures, designs, or diagrams with graphical elements used by teachers and learners as visual clues to meaning to outline text and to illustrate principles within a text.

Graphophonemic aspects of language: The connection between sound patterns of words and word parts with spelling patterns.

Guided reading: In this reading approach, teachers work with small groups with similar reading processes using progressively leveled readers. Teachers select and introduce new books, teach reading skills and strategies, and support children as they read the text to themselves.

Holistic measures of reading: Reading assessments that give an overall view of a learners' ability. They may have sub-scores for specific skills.

I have/Who has?: A vocabulary study activity in which learners each have a card with a definition and a non-matching term. A student reads a definition aloud and the person who has the matching term answers, then reads the next description.

Informal reading inventories: An individually administered reading assessment in which learners read aloud and teachers use evaluation codes and questions to evaluate the reading. It is designed to help teachers determine students' reading instructional needs (see Reading inventory).

Inside-outside circles: A cooperative learning structure that requires students to form two circles, with one circle inside the other and students in both circles facing each other. Pairs answer teacher questions, solve problems, or review for a test. One circle rotates to provide new partners.

Instructional conversation: Developing learners' language and thinking through assisted performance, which may include modeling, feeding back, contingency managing, directing, questioning, explaining, and task structuring.

Intensive reading: Students are directed to read a duplicated text several times, each time for a different purpose, each time marking their discoveries in the text in different ways (underlining, highlighting, annotating, etc.).

Interaction: Student-to-student communication regarding content learning or language learning.

Interference: The transference of elements of one language to another at various levels including phonological (letters and sounds), grammatical (structures and word order), lexical (words and word meaning), and orthographical (writing system).

Jigsaw: A cooperative learning technique in which a text or content information is divided among a small group of learners. Each learner becomes an "expert" in one part of the learning experience and then teaches that part to other learners in the group.

Key sentence frames: Model sentences containing grammatical structures to be learned. Students use these models to create their own sentences.

K-W-L chart: A chart containing three columns labeled "What I Know," "What I Want to Know," and "What I Learned." The chart is used both to activate and to summarize content information.

Language content: Instruction in language content includes instruction in language forms, functions, discourse structures, and content and academic vocabulary.

Language experience approach: After a discussion of a shared or recalled experience, students dictate a narrative as the teacher writes it on a chart, projected computer screen, or transparency. Teacher and students revise and edit the text together and use it for learning about reading.

Language skill: Listening, speaking, reading, and writing are the four language skills.

Language transfer: A communication strategy for learning language by using rules from the native language to understand and speak the new language.

Late exit transitional: The goal of this organizational model is to develop some proficiency in the native language and full proficiency in English. Instruction is begun in the native language in elementary school. English instruction is gradually increased as a part of the school day until students are fully mainstreamed in English-only classrooms.

Learner dictionary: A dictionary created specifically for second-language learners, containing clear definitions and extra features such as illustrative sentences and information about the grammatical features and uses associated with words.

Learning logs: Notebooks in which students write brief summaries of content learning on a frequent or daily basis.

Learning strategies: Cognitive tools used by learners to enhance their learning and develop their language competence. These strategies can be observable behaviors, steps, or techniques, or nonobservable thoughts or mental practices, such as visualization or positive thinking.

Learning: Developing conscious knowledge of language elements to increase language proficiency.

Lexical aspects of language: Aspects related to words and meaning.

Lexicon: The vocabulary of the language.

Limited English proficient (LEP): A term used by the U.S. government to designate English language learners. Most ESL/ELD professionals prefer not to use this term because of its negative connotations.

Line-ups: An instructional strategy in which learners stand in two lines facing each other and respond to their partners based on a teacher's questioning. The line-up order can be determined by criteria such as alphabetical order or birth month or date.

Linguistic competence: The ability of a speaker to control pronunciation, morphology, syntax, and social uses of a language.

Literacy: When students learn to construct and convey meaning from their own written texts and the texts of others. It includes all four modes of language: reading, writing, listening, and speaking.

Logographic language: A system in which one symbol represents the meaning of a concept, individual word, or part of a word. Arabic numerals and mathematical symbols are examples of logographic symbols. Chinese and Japanese (Kanji) are examples of logographic languages.

Maintenance bilingual: The goal of this organizational model is to develop some proficiency in the native language and full proficiency in English. Instruction is begun in the native language in elementary school. English instruction is gradually increased as a part of the school day until students are fully mainstreamed in English-only classrooms.

Minimal pairs: Pairs of words that differ in only one speech sound such as *fin* and *thin*.

Miscue analysis: An examination of learner reading errors or substitutions as the basis for determining learner strengths and weaknesses in reading.

Modeling: Explicitly showing students how to perform processes or create products that are the result of classroom instruction.

Monitor: An internal grammatical editor that is called into play as students learn the formal structure and requirements of a language.

Morpheme: A word or part of a word that conveys a grammatical or lexical meaning (such as the *-ed* ending that turns a present tense verb into the past tense).

Morphology: The linguistic system dealing with meaningful units of language and how they are combined to form words (e.g., want, wanted, wanting, unwanted).

Multiple intelligences: A framework for teaching/learning based upon eight different kinds of learning aptitudes and preferences.

Numbered heads together: A cooperative learning strategy in which students in small groups each receive a number. Teachers then ask a question of the class. Students in each group put their heads together to confirm the correct answer. The teacher then spins a dial, tosses dice, or pulls a number card to find a student with that number to answer the question.

One-question quiz: A summarizer in which the teacher asks a summarizing question and students respond in written form.

Overgeneralization: A communication strategy in which ELLs perceive patterns of language usage, generate a rule from many examples heard in the environment, and apply the rule in a speaker–listener conversation where the rule is not usually used (e.g., "He goed outside").

Performance-based assessment: A form of assessment involving a "performance" in which the learner constructs a response—for example, responses to questions, storytelling, oral presentations, role-plays, writing pieces, captioned artwork, media products, and so on. Performance-based assessment generally falls into three types: products, performances, and process-oriented assessments.

Personal dictionary: A dictionary developed by a learner with personal words, along with definitions, descriptions, pictures, examples, translations, and/or non-examples.

Phonemes: The smallest unit of speech sounds that can make a difference in meaning (such as the vowel sounds in *pin/pen*).

Phonemic awareness: A critical precursor to a child's ability to read. It is defined as the understanding that spoken language is composed of a series of discrete sounds that may be broken down, combined, and manipulated in a variety of ways.

Phonics: A method of teaching elementary reading and spelling based on the phonetic interpretation of ordinary spelling.

Phonology: Rules governing the sound system of English, including sound-symbol relationships, intonational variations, stress, pitch, and juncture.

Picture walk: A strategy to help activate ELLs' prior knowledge and set the stage for reading. The teacher "reads" the pages of a picture book without reading the words; pointing out, and having students point out pictures of key characters, aspects of the setting, events, and/or ideas; and having them ask questions and make guesses about the content of the book.

Point of view: A reading comprehension technique in which students take on the role of characters in a fiction or nonfiction text, and work to understand the motivation behind the actions of characters from a story.

Portable words: A term used by Kinsella (2011) to describe words that are useful for access to academic learning in a variety of disciplines.

Portfolio assessment: A form of assessment that uses multiple pieces of writing, encourages reflection and self-assessment on the part of the student, and provides for increasing development of skills over a long period of time.

Positive transference: Learners use aspects of their first language to help them develop skills in a second language, e.g., writing, speaking, and reading.

Pragmatics: The conversational rules guiding the use of language in a social situation. These rules change as a variety of social factors change: context, age, purpose, etc.

Prior knowledge: One of the principles of the ABC Model, in which teachers help learners use their prior knowledge of language, content, and the world to develop new language and increase learning.

Problem-based learning: A teaching/learning structure which provides meaningful learning for students by basing the curriculum on solving real-life problems facing the community and the world.

Procedural knowledge: The skills and operations consistent with a content area, for example, reading for comprehension and solving a word problem.

Process grade: An assessment of process learning such as essay writing or delivering an oral report.

Product grade: An assessment of the amount of content knowledge learning displayed by the learner.

Progress indicator: Description of observable behaviors that indicate students are showing progress in meeting a learning standard.

Project learning: One form of content learning that embeds the content into a multistep task that is engaging to learners.

Prompting: During teacher-guided collaborative dialogues, the teacher asks questions that require the student to restate using academic language.

Pull-out: An organizational model of instruction in which the ESL teacher instructs students in a classroom separate from the mainstream class.

Push-in: An organizational model of instruction in which the ESL teacher instructs students within the mainstream classroom, either in a separate group or integrated within the mainstream class.

Question-Answer-Relationships (QAR): Students learn to ask different types of questions and to locate answers in a text. Teachers model, teach, and help learners practice the four levels of questions of QAR: "right there" questions, "think and search" questions, "author and you" questions, and "on your own" questions.

RAFT: A type of role-play. The teacher creates a scenario about the content being studied, defining the Role, Audience, Form, and Time of the scenario.

Read, retell, summarize: An activity in which teachers dictate a list of key words in a passage to learners. In pairs, learners read the passage, and then summarize the passage using the key words as a prompt.

Reading inventory: A form of holistic assessment of reading. The inventory is administered individually, using progressively more difficult texts. Teachers assess oral reading fluency and then ask targeted questions to determine reading comprehension.

Recasting: During teacher-guided collaborative dialogues, the teacher repeats a student utterance and supplies or models the academic vocabulary.

Reciprocal teaching/reading: A reading strategy in which teachers model and explain four types of questioning strategies: summarizing, clarifying, question-generating, and predicting. Then learners read passages to one another, taking turns in the "teacher" role, asking their partners the four kinds of questions about the reading.

Reformulation: During teacher-guided collaborative dialogues, the teacher restates a student utterance using academic language forms, functions, and vocabulary.

Register: In linguistics, a register is a subset of a language used for a particular purpose or in a particular social setting. Register is dependent on the context of language use, the topic, the relationship of speaker and hearer, and the channel of communication.

Reliability: Occurs when there is consistency and dependability in assessment results that occur over a period of time and when scored by different raters.

Repetition: During teacher-guided collaborative dialogues, the teacher repeats and may expand a student utterance.

Response cards: These are cards, signals, or other items such as pictures held up by learners simultaneously in response to teacher prompts.

Response to Intervention (RTI): A tiered organizational model that ensures early intervention for students experiencing problems in learning as indicated by ongoing assessment and data collection.

Robust vocabulary instruction: A term used by Beck, McKeown, and Kucan (2002) to describe instruction that creates an environment that celebrates and values words, teaches vocabulary deeply and directly, then posts the targeted words and uses them with learners in a variety of ways.

Role-plays: These learning activities are dramatic skits scripted by the teacher or by the students and often based upon content learning concepts or situations.

Rubric: A scoring scale using numbers or letters that identify specific criteria for evaluating a product or presentation, often at several levels of performance.

Running record: An informal reading assessment tool in which teachers ask learners to read texts at appropriate levels and use a coding system to record what learners read, including repetitions, corrections, mispronunciations, and so on. Teachers also ask for a retelling to assess comprehension. The resulting data is then analyzed to determine a number of subscores in learners' reading used for diagnostic teaching.

Scaffolding: Assistance and contextual support provided by teachers, parents, and knowledgeable peers to help learners comprehend and achieve at higher levels.

Scaffolds: Various types of support provided to learners, including language adaptations, contextual cues such as graphics, visuals, and interactive peer activities that add support to the language and content learning.

Schema: A cognitive framework or concept that helps organize and interpret information. Schema developed in one language may be transferred to another language.

Second language learners: Students learning English as an additional language.

Self-assessment: A form of assessment that helps learners to process their own skill development, take responsibility for their own learning, and acquire the kinds of study skills, attitudes, and practices that will lead to greater learning achievement.

Semantic feature analysis: The use of a matrix with target words on the vertical axis and possible features or attributes on the horizontal axis on which learners determine relevant meaning relationships.

Semantic gradient: A vocabulary activity in which words are arranged in order on a specified scale: e.g., greater-lesser, longer-shorter, older-younger, etc.

Semantic mapping: Sometimes called "spider mapping," this is a graphic display of a cluster of words that are related in meaning. Words are arranged like the spokes of a wheel around a central concept.

Semantic sets: Sets of words with a common superordinate, for example, names of fruits, months of the year, or types of trees. Research has shown that it can be more difficult to learn related words like these in lists than words that are meaningfully related in context.

Semantics: The scientific study of meaning in language.

Sentence machine: An activity in which students stand in a line and answer questions asked by class members in complete sentences, with each person supplying a word of the sentence in sequence.

Service learning: A form of instruction that gives learners the chance to apply the content of their studies to real problems in their communities. Academic objectives are integral to service learning.

Shared reading: Teachers and learners read together using enlarged texts (such as big books, charts, or projected texts), which all learners can easily see. Teachers use a pointer to direct students to look at the text being read as they engage learners in experiencing reading. Teachers and students use the text in many ways to explore and learn about language.

Shared writing: Teachers use the shared writing strategy to model writing, and to encourage a rich academic conversation as they guide learners through the writing process using text generated by the learners.

Shared-to-guided reading: In this bridging strategy, designed for ELLs, teachers first "walk" learners through the text, using picture cues to develop vocabulary. Then teachers set the scene, read and reread the text aloud, and help students recall and discuss the content. Students read the book independently or with partners and follow up on reading with recall, skill development, and expressive responses to the literature.

Sheltered Instruction Observational Protocol (SIOP): An observational form and a model of instruction for teaching language learners about content and language.

Sheltered instruction: An approach for teaching content to English language learners in strategic ways that make the subject matter concepts comprehensible while promoting the students' English language development.

Signal words: Words that show a text's organizational structure. Sets of signal words are used for different types of texts, for example, chronological sequence (*first, second, next, last . . .*), comparison/contrast (*but, on the other hand, although . . .*), or description (*above, outside of, appears to be . . .*).

Signaling: See prompting.

Signals: Student responses to teacher questions that are nonverbal codes—they may use hands or other objects to show responses.

Silent period: A period of time in which language learners resist speaking the target language while listening to, learning from, and analyzing comprehensible input.

Simplification: A communication strategy in which ELLs avoid speaking about complex topics, using full grammatical utterances, or using word forms that they do not yet know.

Simulation: Dramatic activity, more structured than a role-play, that is an imitation of some real thing, state of affairs, or process. The teacher structures the learning concretely for the students and often encourages them to develop a script.

Slates: Individual writing boards used for practice and assessment of student comprehension during a lesson.

Sociolinguistic aspects of language: Aspects of language related to social and cultural contexts; for example, the way one's speech changes with people of different status in a society or in different social settings.

Sort tasks: Students choose categories and sort vocabulary to further their comprehension and recall of the words.

Specially Designed Academic Instruction in English (SDAIE): A model for sheltered instruction designed to promote cognitively challenging content and language learning.

SQ3R (Survey, Question, Read, Recite, Review): A reading comprehension strategy technique that includes strategies for before, during, and after reading. The "S" asks students to survey the text they are about to read (e.g., preview headings, illustrations, and boldface terms.) Then students create questions (the "Q") they expect will be answered in the text. The 3 "Rs" stand for "read," "recite" (stop to reflect and/or take notes on what they have read, checking their comprehension), and "review" (summarize and revisit what they've learned from the reading).

Standardized reading achievement test: An objective test that is given and scored in a uniform manner. Standardized tests are carefully constructed and items are selected after trials for appropriateness and difficulty. Standardized reading achievement (or performance) tests are not developed with ELLs in mind.

Stir the class: A classroom-based assessment technique in which learners walk slowly around the room, gather in groups in response to a teacher's signal, carry out a conversation task, and then, at another signal from the teacher, prepare to discuss or respond in a new group.

Structured English immersion: English-only classrooms in which ELLs are taught by qualified ESL teachers who may have a receptive knowledge of the students' native languages.

Summarizer: An activity at the end of a learning period to help students and teacher assess and organize the day's learning.

Summative assessment: The process of evaluating the learning of students at a point in time. Formal summative assessment is administered in order to evaluate programs, curriculum, and/or district or state education performance. Summative assessment may be accomplished by district-wide standardized testing.

Syllabic language: A language system, such as Japanese or Korean, in which one symbol represents a syllable, or consonant-vowel combination.

Syntactic aspects of language: Aspects of language related to language patterns and grammar.

Syntax: The study of the rules by which words or other elements of sentence structure are combined to form grammatical sentences.

Teach the Text Backward: A technique for increasing comprehension of textbook reading that begins with hands-on activities and follows with group discussion and perusal of the questions at the end of the chapter. Only then, do students prepare to read the text. Teach the Text Backward progresses from the concrete to the conceptual, from the known to the unknown, and from simple concepts to more difficult ones.

Text: Written language that serves as input in a content lesson. Text may be from a textbook, a teacher-prepared handout, or a computer program. Text may or may not be accompanied by visuals.

Thematic instruction: Sequenced learning activities revolving around many aspects of a central topic or theme, offering students opportunities to visit the learning objectives of the unit through a variety of activities using many modes of learning.

Think-aloud strategy: A strategy in which the teacher states thought processes and steps in a learning sequence out loud, helping learners to acquire them.

Think-pair-share (TPS): An interactional routine in which students think about a response to a teacher's question, pair themselves with another student to discuss their responses, and finally share their responses with another group or the full class.

Thumbs up/Thumbs down: A way for students to signal their answers by turning their thumbs up (true) or down (false).

Ticket to leave: A structure in which students are asked summary questions that they must answer correctly, orally or in writing, before leaving class.

Tier 1 words: The basic words that are reasonably easy to teach, usually because there is some kind of physical referent (clock, baby, happy, and walk.)

Tier 2 words: High-frequency words used by proficient, mature speakers that are found and used across many content areas.

Tier 3 words: Lower-frequency specialized words that are specific to one content area.

Top-down approaches: Approaches to reading that focus on getting meaning from text, and teach skills in the context of meaning.

Total physical response (TPR): A language teaching method in which learners perform actions in response to a series of oral commands. It is based upon the research indicating that language can be learned through kinesthetic responses to auditory commands.

Transfer: A communication strategy in which learners apply aspects of a language they know to a new language. They use native language rules and concepts to understand and speak the new language. In addition, generic literacy concepts and skills are also thought to transfer from the L1 to the L2. Transfer can be positive, helping learners with the new language, or negative, interfering with learning the new language.

Translation dictionary: A specialized dictionary used to translate words or phrases from one language to another.

Two-way bilingual: The goal of this program model is that students from an English-only background and students from another language background will each become proficient in the other language as well as their own. Programs are typically started in early elementary school and continued throughout the school years.

Two-way immersion: See two-way bilingual.

Validity: Occurs when assessment instruments measure what they were designed to measure.

Visual thesaurus: An interactive dictionary and thesaurus that provides semantic webs of words that include meaning and branches to related words.

Vocabulary profile: An online tool (Cobb 2011; Heatley & Nation 2004) that analyzes vocabulary in a text to determine words in a variety of categories, including frequency and Academic Word List.

Wait time: The teacher waits approximately 3 to 5 seconds after asking a comprehension question before calling on a student. A longer-than-usual wait time increases the quality and quantity of student responses.

WebQuest: An inquiry-oriented lesson format in which most or all the information that learners work with comes from the Web. The teacher provides the links necessary to complete the quest so students can focus on the materials rather than spending time looking for them. One version of the WebQuest has five parts: Introduction, Task, Process, Evaluation, and Conclusion.

Word cloud: Visual arrays of words in a text that give greater prominence to words that appear more frequently in the source.

Word family: A group of words that have a common base word, with various prefixes and suffixes added.

Word frequency: The number of occurrences of words in corpora. Words that occur more frequently are highly useful to second language learners.

Word sort: An activity in which learners sort a set of words according to preset or self-chosen categories.

Word square: A vocabulary learning technique in which a note card is divided into four quadrants. The target word is placed in one of the quadrants. The other three quadrants require students to create a definition, write a native language equivalent, find a synonym or antonym, write a dictionary definition, locate the part of speech, draw a picture, or copy a sentence from the text.

Word wall: An organized (often alphabetical) collection of important words that are displayed in large visible letters on a wall, bulletin board, or other display surface in a classroom.

WordSift: An online tool that analyzes source texts to produce a word cloud, semantic maps of selected words, and a selection of pictures that may help in explaining/ understanding the word.

Wordsplash: A selection of vocabulary words that are splashed across a sheet of chart paper or on an overhead transparency. The content topic is centered on the paper. Students are asked to make predictions about how the words are related to the content concept by generating sentences.

The Wordsplash is usually used prior to instruction or prior to reading the content information.

Writers' workshop: A process approach to writing that allows students to write in class frequently, choosing their own topics, evaluating their writing, and growing as writers.

Writing portfolio assessment: A form of assessment that uses multiple pieces of writing, encourages reflection and self-assessment of the part of the student, and provides for increasing development of skills over a long period of time.

Writing process: This approach to teaching writing uses step-by-step phases that guide a learner through the selection of a topic, understanding the purpose of the writing, collecting and organizing ideas, drafting, editing, revising, and "publication" of a finished work.

Zone of proximal development (ZPD): A concept developed by Lev Vygotsky (1962), through which he described the place where learning and development meet as the ideal focus of classroom instruction. In the ZPD, teachers (and peers) can enable learners to achieve learning just beyond their current developmental level.

INDEX

ABC model. *See* Activity-based communicative teaching and learning model
ABC summary, 316
About Me worksheet, 70
Abstract learning, 300–301
Academic language, 29, 98. *See also* Cognitive Academic Language Learning Approach; Cognitive Academic Language Proficiency
  learning, 87–89
Academic proficiency assessment, 267
Academic Word List (AWL), 147, 316
Academic words, 316
Acculturation, 42, 48, 274, 316
Achebe, Lydia, 3
Acquisition, 24, 316. *See also* Language acquisition
Acquisition-learning hypothesis, 24–25
Activator, 250, 316
Active engagement, 2–3, 35, 297, 316
Activities
  challenging, 45
  expansion and application, 119
  joint productive, 45
  learning, 308
  pair-share, 4
  physical, 22–23
Activity-based communicative teaching and learning model (ABC model), 1–14
  prior knowledge and, 319
  summary, 316
  writing and, 211–212
Activity-based teaching and learning, 1–2, 316
  principles, 2–5, 13
Advance organizers, 132
Affective filter, 25, 316
After-school programs, 49
Age, 30–31
  appropriate content, 9–10, 196–197
  literacy development and, 194–199
Agor, Barbara, 250, 252, 298
Airport play, 137, 138
Alphabetic language system, 184–185, 316
Amphibian Observation Rubric, 282, 284
Analysis
  feature, 188–189, 318
  miscue, 200, 319
  semantic feature, 159, 160, 188–189, 320
  text, 148
  thinking level, 240, 302
Analytical learner, 64, 316
Angelou, Maya, 3
Anoka-Hennepin Independent School District, 49
Anticipation guide, 185–186, 316
Application, 74
  expansion activities and, 119
  thinking level, 240, 302
Argumentation, 255–256
Arnow, Sheila, 58–59
Arrival/survival stage, 48
Assessment, 11–13, 272. *See also* Classroom-based assessment; Reading assessment; Self-assessment; *specific types and techniques*
  beyond lesson phase, 258–259
  careful and continuous, 196
  content, 272
  content learning and, 139–140
  cultural issues and, 275–276
  DI and, 69
  ELP, 267
  factors affecting, 273–277
  fair, reliable, and valid, 267–268
  fluency, 200
  formative, 258, 275, 318

into lesson phase, 258
through lesson phase, 259
listening, 139–140
literacy development, 199–201
of oral language development, 108–110, 139–140, 272
performance-based, 267, 277–280, 319
portfolio, 270, 319, 322
process-oriented, 277
RTI model, 289–290
SIOP, 75
standards affecting, 285–289
summative, 258, 273–275, 321
types and techniques, 266–267, 272
of vocabulary development, 162–164
writing, 225–229, 272
Assimilation, 42, 316
Ausubel, David, 246
AWL. *See* Academic Word List

Background. *See also* Prior knowledge
  building, 74, 219
  language, 184–185
Basic Interpersonal Communication Skills (BICS), 29, 316
Beck, I. L., 147, 150
Bela, Diana, 207
Beyond lesson phase, 238, 254–259
Bias
  cultural, 275–276
  negative, 29–30
BICS. *See* Basic Interpersonal Communication Skills
Bigelow, M., 26
Bigler, Liz, 9
Bilingual, 266
  classroom, 9
  developmental, 67, 317
  education, 316
  maintenance, 319
  two-way, 67, 322
Billows, F., 255, 256
Bingo, 137
Bio poem, 278, 316
Bloom, B., 239–240, 243, 301–302
Bode, P., 41
Bottom-up approaches, 171–173, 316
Boyle, O. F., 76
Bridging stage, 94, 96–97
Brisken, Anita, 59
Brown, H. D., 32
Brown, K., 235
Bruner, J., 103, 181
Buddies
  clock, 144, 316
  learning, 106–107
Bulletin board, 59–60
Bunch, G. C., 225
Burke, Jim, 147

Calkins, Lucy, 226
CALLA. *See* Cognitive Academic Language Learning Approach
CALP. *See* Cognitive Academic Language Proficiency
Carle, Eric, 150
Carousel brainstorming, 78, 249, 316
Carousel reports, 78
CBM. *See* Curriculum-based measurements
CCSSO. *See* Council of Chief State School Officers
Center for Research on Education Diversity and Excellence (CREDE), 44–45
Chalkboard (whiteboard), 59
  personal, 253–254
Chants, 132–134

Checklist, 226
  editing, 227
  grammar, 228
  self-assessment, 284
Choice independent reading, 186
Chomsky, Noam, 20, 24–26
Choral reading, 188, 316
Clarity (clarification), 198, 236, 250–251,
     285, 316
  of feedback, 11–13, 35
  of goals, 11–13, 35
  of teacher, 97–100
Classification, 303
Classroom, 9
  community building in, 61
  furniture in, 58–59, 61
  instructional organization, 67–81
  language development in, 32
  organization of, 28, 44–45, 58–61
  participation, 198
  private space, 61
  public area, 59–61
  routine, 137
  socialization style of, 43–44
Classroom-based assessment, 266
  fundamental principles of, 267–273
  informal, 275
  scaffolding for, 271
Classroom environment, 27, 34, 35
  preparing, 57–58
  social, 61–66
Clipboards, 110
Clock buddies, 144, 316
Close confusers, 129
Cloze, 316
Cloze procedure, 164
Cobb, Thomas, 147–148
Cognition. See Thinking
Cognitive Academic Language Learning
     Approach (CALLA), 72–73, 316
Cognitive Academic Language Proficiency
     (CALP), 29, 88, 316
Cognitive empathy, 99–100
Cognitively demanding, 68, 316
Cognitively undemanding, 68, 316
Cohen, E. G., 225
Cohen, G. L., 29, 41
Collaboration, 4, 35, 61, 297
  with community, 51
Collaborative dialogue, 103, 234, 316
Collaborative reading strategy (CRS), 26
Collier, V. P., 96
Collocation, 145, 316
Common Core Anchor Standards,
     244, 256, 257, 288
Common Core Curriculum Maps, 288
Common Core Standards in Math, 126,
     127, 129
Common Core State Standards in
     English Language, 115
Communication, 29, 50, 316. See also
     Clarity (clarification)
  of high expectations, 41
  strategies, 33
Communicative competence, 316
Communicative teaching and learning, 1–2, 317.
     See also Activity-based communicative teaching
     and learning model
  principles, 5–14
Community
  building, 61
  collaboration with, 51
  support, 49, 51
Compleat Lexical Tutor, 147–148
Comprehensible input, 25, 74, 317
  with scaffolding, 6–7, 35, 297
Comprehension

oral language, 8
  reading, 145, 197
  SOLOM, 109
  thinking level, 240, 302
  written language, 8
Comprehensive Test of Basic Skills, 276
Concepts, 100, 303
Conceptual glue, 296
Conceptual knowledge, 274
Concrete experience, 300–301
Conga line, 161, 317
Content
  age-appropriate, 9–10, 196–197
  appropriate, 235
  assessment, 272
  based writing, 212
  curriculum in thematic unit, 306–309
  DI and, 69
  goals, 10
  high, 28–29
  information, 245
  input, 250–251
  language, 241, 318
  language versus, 277
  objectives defined, 239–240
  simple to complex structures, 303–304
  standards, 304, 317
Content-based ESL, 66, 317
Content-based thematic units, 295
Content learning, 10, 115–132, 297–298.
     See also specific subjects
  assessment and, 139–140
  integrated, 9–11, 35, 234
  logs, 215–216
Context, 163
  cultural, 42
  embedded, 29, 68, 317
  guessing from, 150
  reduced, 29, 68, 317
Contextualization, 45
Contextualized language, 22
Conversation, 1, 255
  instructional, 45, 104–105, 190, 318
  topic in response to child, 23
Cooperative learning, 26, 62, 75–78, 317
  basic principles, 76–77
  literacy and, 197
  structures, 78
Coping, 48
Corners, 248, 317
Corpus, 317
Corrective feedback, 237
Correspondence, 255
Council of Chief State School Officers
     (CCSSO), 285
Coxhead, Averil, 147
CREDE. See Center for Research on
     Education Diversity and Excellence
Criterion-referenced assessment, 267
CRS. See Collaborative reading strategy
Cultural bias, 275–276
Cultural context, 42, 71–72
Cultural differences, 30–31, 89–90
Cultural dissonance, 42, 317
Cultural illiteracy, 43–44
Cultural information, 57
Culturally responsive instruction, 41, 317
  features of, 41–45
  practices, 42–43
  RTI model and, 52–53
Cultural mediator, 41, 43–45, 317
Cultural organizers, 43
Cultural relevance, 3, 35, 199, 297, 317
Cultural values, 274
Culture, 41, 317
  shock, 31–32, 48
Cummins, J., 67–68, 88, 235

Curriculum-based measurements (CBM), 290, 317
Cycle chart, 116, 117

"Dear Teacher" letter, 244
Debates, 279
Decision making, 51
    new word flow chart, 153
Declarative knowledge, 309, 317
Demonstration, 129, 279
    of meaning, 163
    scientific, 131
Developing stage, 93, 96–97
Developmental bilingual, 317
Dewey, John, 11, 296
DI. *See* Differentiated instruction
Dialogues, 122
    collaborative, 103, 234, 316
DIBELS. *See* Dynamic Indicators of Basic Early Literacy Skills
Dictation, 138–139
Dictionary
    learner, 318
    personal, 7, 162, 319
    translation, 322
Differentiated instruction (DI), 68–70, 317
Differentiation, 5, 35, 298, 317
Dioramas, 278
Dipsticking, 252–253, 258, 273, 317
Direct instruction, 151–152
Directions, giving, 100
Direct performance assessment, 267
Disabilities, 274
Discourse, 29, 317
Display questions, 90, 317
Distance, 255
Drafting, 218, 219–220
Drama, 255–256
Draw picture/diagram, 219, 257–258, 317. *See also* Graphs and charts
    for math, 127
    for vocabulary development, 154–156
Dual language, 67, 266, 317
Duink, Lenore, 4
Dynamic Indicators of Basic Early Literacy Skills (DIBELS), 200

Early exit transition, 67, 317
Early fluency, 180, 317
    reading material for, 187–188
    strategies for developing, 181–182
Early literacy, 180, 200, 317
    reading material for, 187
    strategies for developing, 181–182
Echevarría, J., 71–72
Editing, 218
    checklist, 227
    revising, 218, 219–220
EFL. *See* English as foreign language
ELD. *See* English language development
Elementary and Secondary Education Act (ESEA), 274
El Naggar, Nadia, 169–170
ELL. *See* English language learners
ELP. *See* English language proficiency
Emergent literacy, 180, 317
    reading material for, 187
    strategies for developing, 181–182
Emerging stage, 93, 95–96
Emotions, 24
Encourage, Question, Suggest (EQS), 218
Engagement, active, 2–3, 35, 297, 316
English (L2), 9, 175
English as foreign language (EFL), 317
English as second language (ESL), 10, 24, 317
    content-based, 66, 317
    pull-out, 266, 317

push-in, 266, 317
    standards, preK-12, 304–305
English language development (ELD), 10, 44, 67, 268–269, 317
English language learners (ELL), 10–11, 19, 317
    comfort of, 57
    literacy development, 174–179, 183
    literacy development with older, 194–199
    literacy tools, 181–194
    needs, 175–176
    writing development, 210–211
English language proficiency (ELP)
    assessment, 267
    performance-based assessment at varying levels of, 278–280
    standards for grades PK-12, 11, 12, 305–306
    tests, 199, 317
English to speakers of other languages (ESOL), 317
EQS. *See* Encourage, Question, Suggest
Error correction, 31
ESEA. *See* Elementary and Secondary Education Act
ESL. *See* English as second language
ESL Standards for PreK-12 Students, 304–305
ESOL. *See* English to speakers of other languages
Evaluation, 303
    CALLA phase, 72–73
    program, 266
    thinking level, 240, 302
Examples and nonexamples, 163
Expanding stage, 93–94, 96–97
Expansion
    application activities and, 119
    CALLA phase, 72–73
Experiments, 131
Explanatory devices, 99, 250, 318
Exposition, 255–256
Expressing opinion, 198

Fairness, 267–268
Family
    involvement, 3, 45–48
    school-, partnership, 48–49, 50–51
    teacher connection to, 45–48
    words, 322
Feature analysis, 188–189, 318
Feedback, 101, 298
    clear, appropriate, 11–13, 35
    corrective, 237
Field independent, 64, 318
Field sensitive, 64, 318
Fillmore, L. W., 87
Fitzgerald, J., 175
Fitzsimmons, S., 196
Florida Science Standard, 286
Fluency, 107–108, 180, 318. *See also* Early fluency
    assessment, 200
    reading material for, 187–188
    SOLOM, 109
    strategies for developing, 181–182
Folse, Keith, 149–150
Form, 242, 318
Formal operations, 22
Formative assessment, 258, 275, 318
Fossilization, 318
Fraction sequencing, 126
Fuchs, D., 282
Fuchs, L., 282
Function, 242, 318
    language, 245, 274
    words, 60
Furniture arrangements, 58–59, 61

Garcia, J., 29
Gates McGinitie Reading Test, 276
Gebril, Kamal, 4

General Service List, 146–147, 318
Gestures, 137
Gianelli, Marge, 298
Gibbons, P., 88
Gill, Kathy, 233
Global learner, 64, 318
Goals, 10, 59, 298
 clear, appropriate, 11–13, 35
 writing, 226–227
Goodman, K., 172
Grade Level Expectations, 286, 287
Gradual Release of Responsibility model, 183
Graduation rates, 309–310
Grammar
 checklist, 228
 SOLOM, 109
 universal, 20
Graphic organizers, 100, 116, 117, 189–190,
 207, 217, 278, 318
Graphics, 7
Graphophonemic, aspects of language,
 176–177, 318
Graphs and charts, 270. *See also specific types*
 for science, 131
Groups
 discussion among, 279
 project, 62, 63
Grouping, 62–63
 heterogeneous, 235
 varied, 128
Guided practice, 251–254, 259
Guided reading, 169–170, 190, 318

Hadaway, N. L., 216
Hands-on learning, 301
Harklau, L., 234
Harris, Bill, 61
Hart, B., 108
Heath, S. B., 90
Higher education, 88
Higher order thinking, 274
Holistic measures of reading, 200, 318
Holt, J., 20
Home language (L1), 9, 175
Home-school connections, 178, 190
How Children Fail (Holt), 20
Hunter, Bob, 102
Hunter, Madelyn, 252, 273

IEP. *See* Individualized education plan
"If I Were ..." game, 138
Igoa, C., 32, 61
I have/Who has?, 160–161, 318
Illustrations, 278
Independent practice, 254–256, 259
Indirect performance assessment, 267
Individual accountability, 76–77
Individualism, 64
Individualized education plan (IEP), 34
Informal reading inventories, 200, 318
Information
 basic, 57
 consolidation of, 299
 content, 245
 cultural, 57
 gathering, 57
 multiple sources of, 270–271
 in thematic unit, organizing, 303
 transmitting, 103
Inform teaching, 270
Initiation, response, feedback (IRF), 101
Input, 250–251. *See also* Comprehensible input
 hypothesis, 25
 language, 21, 28
Inside-outside circles, 318
Instructional conversation, 45, 104–105, 190, 318
Instructional organization, 67–81

Instructional programs, 66–67
Instructional techniques, 124, 130–132, 271–272
Integrated approaches, 172–173
 to literacy, 179
 to reading, 172–173
Integrated learning, 24
 content, 9–11, 35, 234
 lesson planning for, 237–238
 principles, 1–14
Integrated teaching principles, 1–14
Intensive reading, 190, 318
Interaction, 318
 between learners, 251
 opportunities, 74
 simultaneous, 76–77
Interactional structures, 105–108
Interactionist position, 26–27
Interdependence, positive, 76–77
Interference, 318
 errors, 211
Interpersonal project, 80
Interviews, 279
Into lesson phase, 238, 239–249, 258
Intrapersonal project, 80
IRF. *See* Initiation, response, feedback
Izumi, S., 26

Jigsaw, 76, 77, 318
 reading, 190
 strategy, 251
Joint productive activity, 45
Journals, 279
 interactive, 214–215
 literary, 216

Kagan, S., 76
Karl, L., 80
Kessler, S., 12
Key sentence frames, 252, 318
Kinesthetic learners, 65
Kinesthetic project, 79
King, Lynn, 40
Kinsella, Kate, 147, 198, 242, 243
Klingner, J. K., 26
Knowledge, thinking level, 240, 302
Krashen, S. D., 6–7, 24–26, 91, 175
Kropp, R., 80
Kucan, L., 147, 150
K-W-L chart, 247–248, 306, 308, 318

L1. *See* Home language
L2. *See* English
Lab reports, 278
Language. *See also* Academic language;
 English; Home language; Oral language;
 specific tests and programs
 alphabetic system of, 184–185, 316
 arts, 115–118
 backgrounds, 184–185
 comprehension of written, 8
 content, 241, 318
 content *versus,* 277
 contextualized, 22
 culturally diverse patterns of, 89–90
 curriculum in thematic unit, 309–310
 dual, 67, 266, 317
 experience approach, 191, 318
 function, 245, 274
 goals, 10
 graphophonemic aspects of, 176–177, 318
 input, 21, 28, 250–251
 levels, 91
 levels, TESOL, 91
 lexical aspects of, 176, 318
 load, 28–29
 logographic, 184, 319
 nature of first environment, 22–24

objectives, 239, 240–244
second, learner, 320
skill, 241, 318
social, 29, 98
sociolinguistic aspects of, 178, 321
syllabic, 184, 321
syntactic aspects of, 178, 321
teaching, 1
transfer, 33, 175, 318
unclear, 99
veritable bath, 22
Language acquisition
device, 20
emotions and, 24
environment, 27
factors affecting, 28–32
first, 19, 20–21
language learning *versus,* 24–26
natural aspect of, 19–20
during play, 22
within social environment, 23
strategies, 33
topics for, 23
universal aspect of, 19
Language development, 1, 2, 45
in classroom, 32
stages, 93–94
Language learning, 1, 87
academic, 87–89
language acquisition *versus,* 24–26
Language/literacy matrix, 179–180
Late exit transitional, 318
Lawrence, Mike, 86
Le, Mary, 56
Learner. *See also* English language learners
accommodating, 184–185
analytical, 64, 316
dictionary, 318
global, 64, 318
interaction, 251
kinesthetic, 65
second language, 320
strengths, 196
visual, 65
Learning, 24, 318. *See also* Activity-based
communicative teaching and learning
model; Activity-based teaching and
learning; Communicative teaching and
learning; Content learning; Cooperative
learning; Integrated learning; Language
learning; *specific models and approaches
to learning*
abstract, 300–301
acquisition-, hypothesis, 24–25
activities, 308
buddies, 106–107
experiences, 64
hands-on, 301
at home, 51
improve, 270
log, 279, 280
logs, 257, 318
opportunities, 270
oral language, 87
problem-based, 79, 319
project, 79–81, 270, 319
service, 256, 320
social, 87
stating reasons for, 100
supports, 245–246
symbolic, 300
vocabulary, 249–250
Learning strategies, 4–5, 33, 35, 65, 74,
297, 318. *See also specific strategies*
active, 258
objectives, 239, 244–245
thematic unit and, 310–311

Learning styles, 274
characteristics of, 65
matching, 63–66
teaching suggestions for, 66
Leki, I., 212, 225
LEP. *See* Limited English proficient
Lesson delivery, 74
Lesson planning
characteristics of successful, 234–237
for integrated learning, 237–238
RTI and, 259–261
three-part format, 237–259
Lexical aspects of language, 176, 318
Lexicon, 29, 318
Limited English proficient (LEP), 276, 318
Lindholm-Leary, K. J., 234
Line-ups, 78, 319
Linguistic competence, 102–103, 319
Listen and choose, 137–138
Listening, 136–137
assessment, 139–140
for understanding, 137–139
Literacy, 170, 171, 319. *See also*
Early literacy; Emergent literacy
cooperative learning and, 197
early, 317
integrated approach, 179
matrix, 179–180
tools for ELLs, 181–194
transfer from L1 to L2, 175
Literacy development, 2–3, 178–179
assessment, 199–201
ELLs, 174–179, 183
with older ELLs, 194–199
RTI model, 201–202
strategies, 183, 229–230
Literary journals, 216
Logical/sequential project, 80
Logographic language, 184, 319
Lotan, R. A., 225

Macaulay, David, 4
Mailbox, 213
Maintenance bilingual, 319
Manipulatives, 126–127
Marzano, R. J., 147, 282
Material supports, 245
Mathematics, 122–123
Common Core Standards in, 126, 127, 129
demonstrations, 129
draw picture/diagram, 127
factors affecting achievement, 123–124
function words, 60
groupings, 128
instructional techniques for, 124
journal, 214–215
manipulatives, use of, 126–127
oral language for success in, 124
prior experience, 125
question isolation and signal words, 127
repetition, 129
role-plays, 128
rubric using ELP standards, 12
self-assessment, 285
standards, 124
visuals in, 128–129
Matluck, Marie, 6
Mayer, R. E., 238
McKeown, M. G., 147, 150
Merchant, P., 236, 248
Message boards, 213
Mind pictures, 6
Mini-lessons, 226
Minimal pairs, 319
Miscue analysis, 200, 319
Modeling, 250, 319. *See also specific types of models*
Mohan, B., 255–256, 276, 296, 300, 303

Monitor, 26, 319
 hypothesis, 26
Monolingual classroom, 9
Monster units, 296
Morpheme, 29, 319
Morphology, 29, 319
Motivation, 41
Multi-lingual, 266
Multiple intelligences, 319
My Painted House, My Friendly Chicken, and Me (Angelou), 3

Narrative, 255–256
National Council of Teachers of Mathematics (NCTM), 122–123
National Research Council (NRC), 130
Native speakers (NS), 26
Natural approach, 24
Naturalist project, 80
Natural order hypothesis, 25
NCLB. *See* No Child Left Behind Act
NCTM. *See* National Council of Teachers of Mathematics
Needs, 22, 175–176
Negative bias, 29–30
Negotiation of meaning, 26
Neighborhood environments, 49
New word decision-making flow chart, 153
Nieto, S., 41
No Child Left Behind Act (NCLB), 172, 273
Nonsense Word Fluency (NWF), 200
Norman, Donna, 295, 303–309
Norm-referenced assessment, 267
Note-taking, 139
NRC. *See* National Research Council
NS. *See* Native speakers
Numbered heads together, 75, 77, 78, 319
NWF. *See* Nonsense Word Fluency

Olmedo, I. M., 121–122
One-question quiz, 253, 319
Open-ended questions, 96, 103, 237
Oral history, 120–122
Oral language
 comprehension, 8
 learning conditions for, 87
 for math success, 124
 reporting, 125–126
 textbooks and, 118–120
Oral language development, 86, 90–91, 178–179
 approaches to, 132–136
 assessment, 108–110, 139–140, 272
 content learning and, 115–132
 scaffolding, 102–108
 stages, 91–97
 teacher tools for, 97–108
Oral presentation, 279
Organized lists, 270
Organizers
 advance, 132
 cultural, 43
 graphic, 100, 116, 117, 189–190, 207, 217, 278, 318
Overgeneralization, 33, 319
Overload, 150
Ownership, 198–199

Paired verbal fluency (P-V-F), 107–108
Pair-share activity, 4. *See also* Think-pair-share; Timed-pair-share
Palinscar, A. S., 193
Paraphrase passport, 108
Paraphrasing, 198
Parental involvement, 3, 45–48
Parenting, 50
Parent-teacher conference, 46–47
Participation

classroom, 198
 equal, 76–77
Peregoy, S. F., 76
Performance-based assessment, 277–280, 319
 direct and indirect, 267
Performances, 277
Personal dictionary, 7, 162, 319
Personal needs, 22
Persuasive essay, 228
Phonemes, 28, 319
Phonemic awareness, 177, 185, 319
Phonics, 177, 185, 319
 adapting, 182–185
Phonology, 28, 319
Physical activity, 22–23
Pickering, D. J., 147
Picture, 163. *See also* Draw picture/diagram
 books, 197
 mind, 6
 sequencing, 138
 walk, 191, 319
Place value chart, 128
Poetry, 132–134
 bio, 278, 316
Point of view, 191, 319
Portable words, 319
Portfolio, 278
Portfolio assessment, 319
 writing, 270, 322
Positive transference, 210, 319
Poster board presentations, 278
Practice phase, 72–74
Pragmatics, 29, 319
Predicting, 198
Preparation
 CALLA phase, 72
 SIOP, 74
Preproduction, 91–92, 136
Presentation
 CALLA phase, 72
 formats, 62
 oral, 279
 poster board, 278
Pre-writing, 217–218
Prior knowledge, 7–9, 35, 273, 297, 319
 activating, 246–249, 258
 from experience, 125
Private space, 61
Problem-based learning, 79, 319
Problem-solving strategies, 33, 125, 127
Procedural knowledge, 309, 319
Process. *See also* Writing process
 DI and, 69
 grade, 268–270, 319
Process-oriented assessment, 277
Product, 277
 DI and, 69
 grade, 268–270, 319
Program evaluation, 266
Program models, 66
Progress indicator, 319
Project, 79–80, 278
 group, 62, 63
 learning, 79–81, 270, 319
Prompting, 104, 319
Pronunciation, SOLOM, 109
Provisioning, 57
Public area, 59–61
Publication, 255
Publishing, 218
Pull-out, 66, 319
 ESL, 266, 317
Purpose, 298
Push-in, 266, 320
 ESL, 266, 317
P-V-F. *See* Paired verbal fluency
Pyramid (Macaulay), 4

Questions, 4, 218, 321
  display, 90, 317
  isolation, 127
  one-, quiz, 253, 319
  open-ended, 96, 103, 237
  patterns, 100–101
  teacher, 103
Question-answer-relationship (QAR),
  191–192, 320

Raca, Julia, 10
RAFT. *See* Role, Audience, Form, Time
Raps, 132–134
Read, retell, summarize, 159–160, 320
Reader's theater, 118
Reading, 26. *See also* Literacy
  aloud, 115, 192–193
  bottom-up approach, 172–173
  choice independent, 186
  choral, 188, 316
  comprehension, 145, 197
  development, 182–194
  guided, 169–170, 190, 318
  holistic measures of, 200, 318
  informal inventories, 200, 318
  integrated approaches, 172–173
  intensive, 190, 318
  inventory, 320
  jigsaw, 190
  L1 *versus* L2, 175
  reciprocal, 193, 320
  self-assessment while, 164
  shared, 193, 320
  shared-to-guided, 193–194, 320
  skills test, 200–201
  standardized test, 199, 321
  top-down approach, 171–172
Reading assessment, 272
  publisher-made, 201
  teacher-made, 202
Reading First Program, 172–173
Reading material, 197
  choosing/adapting, 186–188
  types of, 221, 224
Recasting, 88–89, 104, 320
Reciprocal teaching/reading, 193, 320
Reflection, 255
Reformulation, 89, 104, 320
Register, 29, 88, 320
Relevant Common Core Anchor Standards,
  115, 118
Reliability, 266, 268, 320
Repetition, 104, 129, 320
Response
  cards, 253, 320
  to child, 23
  patterns, 100–101
  student, 103
  tailoring, 236
  TPR, 92, 136, 321
Response to Intervention (RTI), 5, 13–14,
  81–82, 110–111, 140–141, 320. *See also*
  Tier 1; Tier 2; Tier 3
  assessment and, 289–290
  characteristics of, 33–34
  culturally and linguistically appropriate, 71–72
  culturally responsive instruction and, 52–53
  lesson planning and, 259–261
  literacy development, 201–202
  thematic instruction and, 312–313
  vocabulary teaching and, 165
  writing and, 229–230
Revising, 218, 219–220
Rhythmic project, 80
Richmond, Dana, 236
Risley, T. R., 108
Ritter, N., 299

Rivera, Charlene, 274
Robust vocabulary instruction, 320
Role, Audience, Form, Time (RAFT),
  134–135, 320
Role-play, 134–135, 279, 320
  in math, 128
Round robin, 78
Roundtable, 78
RTI. *See* Response to Intervention
Rubric, 139, 140, 227, 268, 269, 281–282, 284, 285, 320
  generic essay, 283
  mathematics, using ELP standards, 12
  persuasive essay, 228
Running record, 200, 320

Sanchez, Marina, 296, 298
Sanders, Shelly, 114
Sarcasm, 97
Sayers, D., 235
Scaffolding, 8, 103, 104, 181, 245, 251, 255, 270, 320
  for classroom assessment, 271
  comprehensible input with, 6–7, 35, 297
  oral language development, 102–108
  writing process and, 216–224
Scaffolds, 320
Scavenger hunt, 1
Schema, 2, 210, 254, 320
School-family partnership, 48–49, 50–51
Schooling, previous, 57
Science, 104, 129
  factors affecting achievement in, 130
  Florida Standards for, 286, 287
  instructional techniques, 130–132
SDAIE. *See* Specially Designed Academic
  Instruction in English
Second language learners, 320
Self-assessment, 110, 202, 272, 279, 280, 281, 311, 320
  checklist, 284
  math, 285
  while reading, 164
  writing, 227
Self-rating scale, 164
Semantics, 29, 320
  feature analysis, 159, 160, 188–189, 320
  gradient, 126, 320
  mapping, 154–156, 246–247, 320
  sets, 150, 320
  web, 307
Sentence, 208
  key frames, 252, 318
  machine, 161–162, 320
Service learning, 256, 320
Shared reading, 193, 320
Shared-to-guided reading, 193–194, 320
Shared writing, 218–220, 320
Sheltered instruction (SI), 66, 73–75, 321
Sheltered instruction observational protocol
  (SIOP), 74–75, 321
Short, D., 196
Short answers, 270
Show and Tell, 256
SI. *See* Sheltered instruction
SIFE. *See* Students with Interrupted Formal Education
Signaling, 321
Signals, 321
Signal words, 163, 219, 220, 321
  in math, 127
Silent period, 25, 321
Simplification, 33, 321
Simulation, 135–136, 321
SIOP. *See* Sheltered instruction observational protocol
Slates, 321
Snow, C. E., 87
Social contracts, 43
Social differences, 30–31
Social environment, 23, 61–66
Social integration, 61–62

Socialization, 43–44, 62
Social language, 29, 98
Social learning, 87
Social studies, 118–122, 226, 241
Social support, 245
Sociolinguistic aspects of language, 178, 321
SOLOM. *See* Student Oral Language
    Observation Matrix
Songs, 132–134
Sorenson, Jane, 120
Sort tasks, 132, 321
Sound-symbol transfer, 184–185, 196
Special education, 71
Specially Designed Academic Instruction in
    English (SDAIE), 66, 74, 321
Spelling, 227
Spider mapping, 246–247, 320
SQ3R. *See* Survey, Question, Read, Recite, Review
Stalzer, Jim, 7
Stand and deliver, 78
Standards. *See also specific standards*
    affecting assessment, 285–289
    content, 304, 317
    ELP, preK-12, 11, 12, 305–306
    ESL, preK-12, 304–305
    for Mathematics Practice, 124
    TESOL Proficiency, 226
    in thematic units, 304–306
Standardized reading achievement test, 199, 321
Standardized testing, 266. *See also specific tests*
    accommodations in, 274–275
    cultural issues and, 275–276
Standards-based curriculum, 289
Stanford Diagnostic Reading Test, 276
Starting stage, 92, 93, 94
Stereotype, 41
Stir the class, 108, 321
Storytelling, 115–117
Structured English immersion, 66, 321
Students
    getting to know, 69–70, 195
    interest, 297
    response, 103
    sticking with, 101–102
Student Oral Language Observation
    Matrix (SOLOM), 109, 282
Students with Interrupted Formal
    Education (SIFE), 195
    writing and, 224–225
Summarizer, 321
Summary phase, 256–258, 259
Summative assessment, 258, 273–275, 321
Support
    community, 49, 51
    learning, 245–246
    material, 245
    social, 245
Supported practice, 236
Survey, Question, Read, Recite, Review
    (SQ3R), 4, 321
Syllabic language, 184, 321
Symbolic learning, 300
Syntactic aspects of language, 178, 321
Syntax, 29, 321
Synthesis, thinking level, 240, 302

Talking chips, 108
Talking Chips, 305
Teacher
    clarity of, 97–100
    as cultural mediator, 43–45
    family connection to, 45–48
    made reading assessment, 202
    oral language development tools for, 97–108
    parent-, conference, 46–47
    question, 103
    role of, 88–89

Teacher-centered transition model, 26
Teacher-directed instruction, 234–235
Teacher-facilitated negotiation of
    meaning, 103–104
Teachers of English to Speakers of Other
    Languages International Association
    (TESOL), 11, 285, 304
    language levels, 91
    Proficiency Standards, 226
Teaching. *See also* Activity-based communicative
    teaching and learning model; Activity-based
    teaching and learning; Communicative
    teaching and learning
    inform, 270
    integrated, 1–14
    language, 1
    learning style suggestions, 66
    reciprocal, 193, 320
    RTI and vocabulary, 165
    writing, 212
Teach the Text Backward, 119, 120, 321
Teambuilding, 77
Terrel, T. D., 24–26, 91
TESOL. *See* Teachers of English to Speakers of
    Other Languages International Association
Text, 321. *See also* Reading material;
    Teach the Text Backward
    analysis using VP, 148
Textbooks, 118–120
Thematic instruction, 296, 298–300,
    311–312, 321
    criteria for, 297–298
    RTI and, 312–313
    unit design, 309
Thematic unit
    content-based, 295
    content curriculum in, 306–309
    language curriculum in, 309–310
    learning strategies and, 310–311
    organizing information in, 303
    standards in, 304–306
    structured, 300
Think-aloud strategy, 193–194, 280, 321
    for math, 124–125
Thinking, 30–31
    Bloom's taxonomy of, 239–240, 243, 301–302
    concepts, 100
    higher order, 274
Think-pair-share (TPS), 107–108, 321
Thomas, W. P., 96
Three-tier model, 13–14. *See also specific tiers*
3-2-1 summary, 257, 316
Through lesson phase, 238, 249–254, 259
Thumbs up/Thumbs down, 253, 321
Ticket to leave, 257, 321
Tier 1
    instruction, 13–14, 34, 36, 52, 71, 81, 110,
        140–141, 165, 201, 229, 259–260,
        290–291, 312
    words, 147, 321
Tier 2
    instruction, 13–14, 34, 36, 53, 71, 82, 110, 141,
        165, 202, 230, 260–261, 291–292, 313
    words, 147, 321
Tier 3
    instruction, 13–14, 71
    words, 147, 321
Timed-pair-share, 77
Top-down approaches, 171–172, 321
Total Physical Response (TPR), 92, 136, 321
TPS. *See* Think-pair-share
Transfer, 33, 175, 322
    sound-symbol, 184–185, 196
Translation dictionary, 322
Tuning out, 136–137
Two-way bilingual, 67, 322
Two-way immersion, 67, 322

Unclear language, 99
Universal grammar, 20

Valdés, G., 225
Validity, 266, 268, 322
Vaughn, S, 26
Venn diagram, 219
Verbal/linguistic project, 80
Veritable language bath, 22
The Very Hungry Caterpillar (Carle), 150
Visible criteria, 280
Visual displays, 270
Visual learners, 65
Visual memory, 63
Visual project, 80
Visuals
    in math, 128–129
    in science, 131
Visual thesaurus, 322
Vocabulary
    assessment of development, 154–156, 162–164
    building, 145–146
    choosing what to teach, 146–149
    direct instruction, 151–152
    effective instruction, 150–151
    independent progress, 152–154
    ineffective instruction, 149–150
    interactive strategies, 154–162
    learning, 249–250
    listen and choose, 137–138
    new word decision-making flow chart, 153
    robust instruction, 320
    RTI model, 165
    SOLOM, 109
Vocabulary Profile (VP), 148, 163–164, 322
Vogt, M., 71–72
Volunteering, 50
Vygotsky, L., 6, 73, 102–103, 105

Wait time, 6, 102, 322
Walton, G. M., 41
Watts, Annie, 265, 275
WebQuest, 136, 322
Wein, Betty, 252
"Why Mei Still Cannot Read and What
    Can Be Done," 194
WIDA. *See* World-Class Instructional
    Design and Assessment
Willett, J., 43–44
Wilson, Rona, 311
Wolfe, P., 80, 299

Wong, Nancy, 252, 256
Words, 147, 200, 316. *See also*
    Signal words
    academic, 316
    choice, 227
    cloud, 322
    decision-making flow chart, 153
    family, 322
    frequency, 147, 164, 322
    function, 60
    portable, 319
    sort, 157, 158, 322
    square, 4–5, 157, 322
    tier 1, 147, 321
    tier 2, 147, 321
    tier 3, 147, 321
    wall, 159, 322
WordSift, 148, 149, 322
WordSplash, 157, 158, 248, 322
Workplace, 88
World-Class Instructional Design and
    Assessment (WIDA), 11, 12
    Consortium, 226
Writers' workshop, 322
Writing
    ABC and, 211–212
    aspects of, 211
    assessment, 225–229, 272
    challenges of teaching, 212
    content-based, 212
    ELL development of, 210–211
    environment, 212–213
    goals, 226–227
    interactive, 213–216
    portfolio assessment, 270, 322
    pre-, 217–218
    process, 322
    RTI and, 229–230
    running record of pieces, 229
    self-assessment, 227
    shared, 218–220, 320
    SIFE and, 224–225
    strategies, 207–209
    types and features, 221–222
Writing process, 216–218
    scaffolding and, 216–224

Young, L., 236, 248
Young, T. A., 216

Zone of proximal development (ZPD), 103, 322

PHOTO CREDITS